LONGMAN LINGUISTICS LIBRARY

Greek: A History of the Language and its Speakers

LONGMAN LINGUISTICS LIBRARY

General editors:

R. H. ROBINS, *University of London*

GEOFFREY HORROCKS, *University of Cambridge*

DAVID DENISON, *University of Manchester*

For a complete list of books in the series see pages v and vi

Greek: A History of the Language and its Speakers

GEOFFREY HORROCKS

LONGMAN

LONDON AND NEW YORK

Pearson Education Limited
Edinburgh Gate
Harlow, Essex CM20 2JE
England

and Associated Companies throughout the world

Published in the United States of America
by Pearson Education Inc., New York

© Addison Wesley Longman Limited 1997

First published 1997
Second impression 1999

ISBN 0 582 30709–0 Paper
ISBN 0 582 03191–5 Cased
British Library Cataloguing-in-Publication Data

A catalogue record for this book is
available from the British Library

Library of Congress Cataloging-in-Publication Data

Horrocks, Geoffrey C.
　　Greek: a history of the language and its speakers / Geoffrey Horrocks.
　　　　p.　cm.—(Longman linguistics library)
　　Includes bibliographical references (p.) and index.
　　ISBN 0–582–30709–0.—ISBN 0–582–03191–5
　　1. Greek language—History.　2. Greek language, Medieval and late—
History.　3. Greek language, Modern—History.　4. Greece—
Civilization.　I. Title.　II. Series.
PA227.H76　1997
480′.9—dc20

96–38590
CIP

Set by 35 in 10/12pt Times
Printed in Malaysia (VVP)

General editors:

R. H. ROBINS,
University of London

GEOFFREY HORROCKS,
University of Cambridge

DAVID DENISON,
University of Manchester

A Short History of Linguistics
Fourth Edition
R. H. ROBINS

Introduction to Text Linguistics
ROBERT DE BEAUGRANDE and
WOLFGANG ULRICH DRESSLER

Psycholinguistics
Language, Mind, and World
DANNY D. STEINBERG

Principles of Pragmatics
GEOFFREY LEECH

Generative Grammar
GEOFFREY HORROCKS

The English Verb
Second Edition
F. R. PALMER

A History of American English
J. L. DILLARD

English Historical Syntax
Verbal Constructions
DAVID DENISON

Pidgin and Creole Languages
SUZANNE ROMAINE

A History of English Phonology
CHARLES JONES

Generative and Non-linear Phonology
JACQUES DURAND

Modality and the English Modals
Second Edition
F. R. PALMER

Dialects of English
Studies in Grammatical Variation
Edited by PETER TRUDGILL and
J. K. CHAMBERS

Introduction to Bilingualism
CHARLOTTE HOFFMANN

Verb and Noun Number in English:
A Functional Explanation
WALLIS REID

Linguistic Theory
The Discourse of Fundamental Works
ROBERT DE BEAUGRANDE

General Linguistics
An Introductory Survey
Fourth Edition
R. H. ROBINS

Historical Linguistics
Problems and Perspectives
Edited by C. JONES

A History of Linguistics Vol. I
The Eastern Traditions of Linguistics
Edited by GIULIO LEPSCHY

A History of Linguistics Vol. II
Classical and Medieval Linguistics
Edited by GIULIO LEPSCHY

Aspect in the English Verb
Process and Result in Language
YISHAI TOBIN

The Meaning of Syntax
A Study in the Adjectives of English
CONNOR FERRIS

Greek: A History of the Language and
its Speakers
GEOFFREY HORROCKS

Latin American Spanish
JOHN M. LIPSKI

A Linguistic History of Italian
MARTIN MAIDEN

Modern Arabic
CLIVE HOLES

Frontiers of Phonology:
Atoms, Structures, Derivations
Edited by JACQUES DURAND and
FRANCIS KATAMBA

An Introduction to the Celtic
Languages
PAUL RUSSELL

Causatives and Causation
A Universal-Typological Perspective
JAE JUNG SONG

Grammar and Grammarians in the
Early Middle Ages
VIVIEN LAW

The New Comparative Syntax
LILIANE HAEGEMAN (ed.)

The Structure and History of
Japanese
LONE TAKEUCHI

To come:

Volume V
The Twentieth Century

For Sophie

Contents

Preface

The writing of this book has taken five years, and had I realized at the outset the scale of the task I was undertaking, I am not sure I would have had the courage to begin. The history of Greek starts with the Mycenaean documents dating from the second half of the second millennium BC, and many scholars have found sufficient interest and material in every period between then and the present day to build their careers on the study of issues which here have often had to be treated in a single subsection.

Obviously no one writer can be an expert on everything, and I am deeply conscious of my reliance on the publications of those who have devoted themselves to the detailed study of specific topics and periods. It is a pleasure, therefore, to record my particular debt to the works of Roddy Beaton, C. Brixhe, Robert Browning, C. D. Buck, John Chadwick, P. Chantraine, Anna Davies, F. T. Gignac, A. N. Jannaris, E. M. and M. J. Jeffreys, Peter Mackridge, A. Meillet, A. Mirambel, L. R. Palmer, H. Tonnet, and M. Triandafyllídis. Without the outstanding contributions of these scholars, it would have been impossible to acquire the conceptual grip necessary to deal with nearly 3,500 years of language history. I would also like to thank David Holton, Torsten Meissner, and Bobby Robins, each of whom read through earlier drafts of various sections of the material in this book, and saved me from all-too-many errors of fact, judgement and omission.

Because the work covers such a long period, it deals with issues that have traditionally concerned classicists, Byzantinists, and neo-Hellenists, as well as historical linguists. I have tried to make it accessible to all these groups by avoiding excessive use of technical jargon (though no serious discussion can dispense with it altogether), and by transcribing, glossing, and translating every Greek text. Since the orthography of Greek has remained conservative, the transcriptions (inevitably often based on more or less controversial reconstructions of pronunciation) in fact serve a useful purpose, but I remain conscious that different aspects of the presentation will be irritating to different subsets of potential readers; I ask for forbearance in the interests of those with different academic backgrounds.

The book, however, is not a teach-yourself manual, and I have had to assume some minimal familiarity with Greek in order to say anything at all. Bobby Robins recently pointed out to me that, even today, discussion of Greek is almost automatically assumed to concern the ancient language in the absence of indications to the contrary. Following the Robins dictum, I have therefore taken ancient Greek to be the 'unmarked' option, though I hope that this will not prove to be an insuperable obstacle to those who bring different perspectives to the material presented here.

I should say at the outset that the work has been a labour of love, founded in a profound admiration for the achievements of Greeks and speakers of Greek throughout their long and turbulent history, and in a long-term fascination for their language in all its forms. It will perhaps surprise those who know me exclusively as a classicist, as a theoretical syntactician, as a historical linguist, or as someone with a growing interest in medieval and modern Greek, to discover that I am in fact all of these things simultaneously. Indeed, had I not been, this book could not have been written. Despite the traditional emphasis on antiquity, the history of Greek does not end with the classical period, or even with the Hellenistic Koine, and my purpose has been to stress the continuity of linguistic development, on through the Roman imperial, Byzantine, and Ottoman periods, down to the present day.

Most histories of (ancient) Greek focus on Mycenaean and the official and literary dialects of the classical period, with the Koine treated almost as an afterthought. In the context of the history of Greek as a whole, however, the ancient Attic dialect, and the Koine that evolved out of its wider use in the Greek-speaking world, are of paramount importance. The emphasis here, therefore, is necessarily placed on the rise of Attic, the development and spread of the Koine, and the role and development of this 'common Greek' in the Roman and Byzantine periods. Though there are now some excellent treatments of the development of modern Greek from this source within the context of the 'language question' (i.e. the problems arising from the historical split between conservative written forms of Greek and the spoken forms that evolved more naturally), it is still the case that the Byzantine period in particular remains for many a closed book. I hope very much that the present work will do something to help prise it open.

That said, I believe very strongly that attempts to confine the history of Greek to the study of the 'vernacular', motivated in large part by a desire to be seen to be on the 'right side' in the highly politicized language debate of the nineteenth and twentieth centuries, result in distortion, and guarantee that only half the story is told. Now that that debate has been effectively settled, it is possible to acknowledge that standard modern Greek has in fact incorporated many elements from the learned written tradition, and that it continues to do so. It seemed to me, therefore, that the history of written Greek, and of the cultural circumstances that led the Greek-speaking intelligentsia, from Roman times until surprisingly recently, to employ archaizing written styles, had to be included, and I make no apologies for doing so. The two traditions interacted at all times, and a projection into the past of the artificially polarized positions adopted by theorists of both persuasions in the first 150 years of Greek independence does not do justice to the complexity of the issues involved.

Anyone attempting to write the history of a language has to choose from among three options: dealing with its 'external' history, presenting its 'internal' history, or attempting to do both. For me, the choice was easy, even if the implementation of that decision proved, in the event, to be rather more difficult. Some years ago, a friend (who, it should be said, was a theoretical linguist with no background in

Greek) made her first visit to Athens, and on her return confessed herself disappointed to find that it did not resemble Rome with its wealth of architectural and artistic treasures. Since ancient Greece and modern Greece now occupy much the same geographical space, her natural assumption was that the one had simply emerged out of the other, and that the Greeks had somehow carelessly mislaid their medieval and Renaissance heritage. I suspect that there is little general awareness of the fact that Greek was the dominant language of the whole Roman empire in the east, or that Constantinople (Istanbul) was the epicentre of Greek/Byzantine culture for well over 1,000 years, during most of which Athens was little more than a village in an imperial backwater. Nor, despite general awareness of contemporary Greco-Turkish hostility, are non-specialists usually conscious of the devastating impact on the Greek-speaking world of the crusades and the Turkish conquests of the Middle Ages, or of the fact that for nearly 400 years there was no Greek state at all. Despite the obvious risks, this is therefore a history of the Greek language and its speakers, and the treatment of internal linguistic developments is carefully interwoven into a study of the changing cultural, political, and military circumstances of those who used it. Indeed, it seemed to me that much of what happened linguistically makes sense only when placed in its wider historical context.

It remains to thank John Chadwick, who, many years ago, first aroused my interest in the history of Greek, and whose inventive work remains a source of inspiration. I should also like to record my thanks to Professor N. M. Panayiotákis and the staff of the Greek Institute in Venice for their generous hospitality and for the opportunity to do some valuable research in the middle of a frantic term. Above all, however, I must take this opportunity to thank my wife Gill, and my daughters Amy and Sophie, for their endless support and mainly cheerful, though sometimes necessarily stoic, tolerance of my irritable and distracted state during much of the time I spent putting this book together. Last, and by no means least, I should also like to express my gratitude to everyone at Addison Wesley Longman involved in the production of this book, not only for their unfailing patience and courtesy but also for their quiet and efficient professionalism in dealing with a very complex and difficult typescript; and to Juliet Bending for her help with the proofs.

So, all too well aware of my limitations in many of the fields in which I have had to venture, I offer this book to those who will read it, in the hope that they will come to share at least some of my fascination with this remarkable language.

Geoffrey Horrocks
Cambridge
February 1997

Publisher's acknowledgements

The Publishers are grateful to the following for permission to reproduce copyright material:

The Cambridge Philological Society for the map of The Ancient Greek Dialects from J. M. Hall 'The role of language in Greek ethnicities'. Proceedings of the Cambridge Philological Society 41: 83–100 (1995); and Weidenfeld and Nicolson Limited for the Linguistic Map of the Byzantine Empire *c.* 560 from C. Mango: *Byzantium, the Empire of the New Rome* (1980) pp. 14–15.

The Greek Alphabet

Although the Mycenaean civilization (dating from the second half of the second millennium BC) had a syllabic script for the writing of Greek, the art of writing disappeared with the collapse of that civilization *c.* 1200 BC, and the first examples of the new alphabetic writing (involving inscriptions on pottery) come to light only from the second half of the eighth century BC onwards, with letter forms and spelling conventions displaying considerable regional variation for several centuries thereafter (the Latin alphabet, for example, derives ultimately from that employed by Euboean colonists in Italy).

It seems that these local Greek alphabets were initially developed during the latter part of the ninth century BC on the basis of a brilliant adaptation of the Phoenician script which, like those used for other Semitic languages, did not note vowel sounds. By redeploying letters that denoted consonant sounds irrelevant to Greek the vowels could now be written systematically, thus producing the first 'true' alphabet. During the fourth century BC the version of the alphabet developed in Ionia (the western coast of Asia Minor and the adjacent islands), having first been adopted in Athens in 403/2 BC, gradually assumed the status of a standard throughout the Greek-speaking world, a status which it has retained ever since. It will be useful at the outset to present this alphabet for reference purposes, along with the customary reconstructed pronunciation of the Athenian dialect of the fifth/ fourth centuries BC (cf. Sturtevant (1933), Allen (1987a)) and the standard modern pronunciation. Digraphs and diacritics are appended.

Greek letter (name)	Ancient pronunciation (5/4C BC)	Modern pronunciation
Aα (alpha)[1]	[a, aː]	[a]
Bβ (beta)	[b]	[v]
Γγ (gamma)	[g]	[ɣ, j]
Δδ (delta)	[d]	[ð]
Eε (epsilon)	[e]	[e]
Zζ (zeta)	[zd]	[z]
Hη (eta)	[ɛː]	[i]
Θθ (theta)	[tʰ]	[θ]
Iι (iota)	[i, iː]	[i, j]
Kκ (kappa)	[k]	[k]

$\Lambda\lambda$	(lambda)	[l]	[l]
$M\mu$	(mu)	[m]	[m]
$N\nu$	(nu)	[n]	[n]
$\Xi\xi$	(xi)	[ks]	[ks]
Oo	(omikron)	[o]	[o]
$\Pi\pi$	(pi)	[p]	[p]
$P\rho$	(rho)	[r]	[r]
$\Sigma\sigma/s$ (sigma)[2]		[s]	[s]
$T\tau$	(tau)	[t]	[t]
$Y\upsilon$	(upsilon)	[y, yː]	[i]
$\Phi\phi$	(phi)	[pʰ]	[f]
$X\chi$	(chi)	[kʰ]	[x, ç]
$\Psi\psi$	(psi)	[ps]	[ps]
$\Omega\omega$	(omega)	[oː]	[o]

1   The distinction between capital and lower-case letters is not ancient; the former are now conventionally employed in printed texts of ancient authors both for the initial letter of proper names and for the initial letter of the first word of a passage of direct speech (but not to mark the first word of each new sentence). The modern conventions are as for English.

2   σ is used at the beginning or in the middle of words, s is used word-finally.

Digraphs	Ancient pronunciation (5/4C BC)	Modern pronunciation
$\alpha\iota$	[ai]	[e]
$\alpha\upsilon$	[au]	[af, av]
$\epsilon\iota$	[eː]	[i]
$\epsilon\upsilon$	[eu]	[ef, ev]
$o\iota$	[oi]	[i]
$o\upsilon$	[uː]	[u]
α (with ι subscript)[1]	[aːi]	[a]
η (with ι subscript)	[ɛːi]	[i]
ω (with ι subscript)	[oːi]	[o]
$\gamma\gamma$	[ŋg]	[(ŋ)g]
$\gamma\kappa$	[ŋk]	[(ŋ)g]
$\gamma\chi$	[ŋkʰ]	[ŋx]
$\mu\pi$	[mp]	[(m)b]
$\nu\tau$	[nt]	[(n)d]

1   Iota in these 'long' diphthongs is standardly written subscript in modern texts of ancient authors, but was originally written on the line in antiquity. This residual graphic retention after loss in actual pronunciation was due to later 'archaizing/puristic' tendencies.

Diacritics[1]	Ancient pronunciation (5/4C BC)	Modern pronunciation
' (smooth breathing)	[null]	[null]
' (rough breathing)	[h]	[null]
' (acute accent)	[rise (+ fall on following syllable)]	[stress]
' (grave accent)	[absence of rise]	[stress]
^ (circumflex accent)	[rise-fall]	[stress]

1   These were retained in the writing of Modern Greek (despite their redundancy in the case of the breathings and their equivalence in the case of the accents), until the orthographic reform of 1982, which introduced the 'monotonic' system whereby the breathings were abandoned and accented vowels were consistently marked by means of the acute accent alone.

Ancient Greek: from Mycenae to the Roman Empire

Chapter 1

Ancient Greek and its dialects

1.1 Introduction

The Mycenaean civilization in Greece, so called after the Bronze Age palace of Mycenae near Argos in the Peloponnese, dates from the second half of the second millennium BC, and is now seen as the product of the impact of the brilliant 'Minoan' culture of Crete (named after the legendary king Minos) on the civilization of the mainland sometime towards the end of the sixteenth century BC. Mycenaean Greece had a highly developed command economy, the detailed administration of which was recorded on clay tablets by officials installed in palaces which controlled their surrounding regions. The destruction of these palaces by fire (*c.* 1200 BC in mainland Greece) led to the accidental baking and preservation of collections of tablets at Pylos on the western coast of the Peloponnese, Mycenae and Tiryns in the Argolid, and Thebes in Boeotia.

The original language of Minoan Crete remains unknown, but the script used to write it is called 'Linear A', since this was the earlier of the two linear syllabaries discovered to have been in use at the palace of Knossos in Crete by the British archaeologist Sir Arthur Evans. In the period when the Mycenaean civilization of the mainland was still developing under Minoan influence, this script was apparently adapted as 'Linear B', presumably to facilitate the writing of the Mycenaean language which, thanks to Michael Ventris's brilliant decipherment in the early 1950s, we now know to have been Greek (see Chadwick (1967) for an account of the decipherment, Ventris and Chadwick (1973), Chadwick (1976a), Hooker (1980), and Morpurgo Davies and Duhoux (1985) for surveys of the script, language and content of the tablets, together with relevant bibliography). Interestingly, the administrative documents which come from the period of the final destruction of the palace at Knossos (now believed to be *c.* 1250–1200 BC, see Olivier (1993)) are also written in Linear B, and not in Minoan Linear A as might have been expected. This points to a Mycenaean takeover of the territory of their erstwhile mentors, probably following an earlier destruction of the principal Minoan sites in the fifteenth century BC.

'Mycenaean' has thus emerged as the earliest dialect of Greek, which now boasts the longest recorded history of any European language (from the thirteenth century BC to the present day). Unfortunately, writing disappeared with the collapse of the Mycenaean civilization, and the Greek world entered a 'Dark Age'. But during the late ninth or early eighth century, writing was reintroduced in the form of an adaptation of the Phoenician alphabet, in which redundant consonant signs were redeployed for the first time to represent vowel sounds The earliest surviving alphabetic inscriptions can be dated to the latter part of the eighth century, and the volume of epigraphic material increases steadily thereafter, with large collections of inscriptions on stone and bronze available from most parts of the Greek world after 400 BC. It was at this time that the Ionic version of the alphabet was standardized, and the modern version used in this book derives ultimately from that source (see THE GREEK ALPHABET, page xix, for details of classical and modern pronunciation).

A sample Linear B document from Pylos (PY Ta722) is given below in the conventional transcription of the Linear B syllabary, followed by the probable phonetic interpretation (based on our knowledge of later Greek, supplemented by internal and comparative reconstruction), which vividly reveals the inadequacies of the script. An item-for-item gloss is given beneath, together with a free translation:

(1) Ta-ra-nu   a-ja-me-no   e-re-pa-te-jo   a-to-ro-qo   i-qo-qe
    po-ru-po-de-qe po-ni-ke-qe   FOOTSTOOL 1

   [tʰrâːnus aiaːménos elepʰanteíoːi   antʰróːkʷoːi híkkʷoːi   -kʷe
   stool(nom.) inlaid(nom.) of-ivory(dat.-instr.) man(dat.-instr.) horse(dat.-instr.) -and

   polupódei   -kʷe pʰoiníːkei   -kʷe]
   'manyfoot', i.e. octopus(dat.-instr.) -and   griffin/palm tree(dat.-instr.) -and

   'One footstool inlaid with a man and a horse and an octopus and a griffin/palm tree in ivory'

[FOOTSTOOL transcribes an ideogram; the ancient 'pitch' accent marked in the transcription was in reality a contonation involving either a monosyllabic rise-fall on a single long vowel or diphthong (marked ^), or a rise (marked ´) on one syllable followed by a fall (unmarked) on the next; in certain circumstances, not exemplified here, the rise was neutralized in some way (marked ˋ). See Allen (1973, 1987a) for details].

In the course of nearly three and a half thousand years since this tablet was written, Greek has obviously undergone many changes, but speakers of the modern language might still recognize in (1) extremely ancient correspondents of a number of contemporary words:

(2) θρανίο [θra'nio] 'desk/form'
   ελεφάντινος [ele'fa(n)dinos] 'made of ivory'
   άνθρωπος ['anθropos] 'man'
   ίππος ['ipos] 'horse' (when talking of 'horse power')
   πολύποδας [po'lipoδas] 'polypod, polyp'
   φοίνικας ['finikas] 'phoenix/palm tree'

Just as surprisingly, perhaps, the Athenian dialect equivalents of these modern Greek words were already spelled in very much the same way at the end of the fifth century BC (especially if we discount morphological changes), though they were pronounced rather differently at that time:

(3) θρανίον [tʰraːníon]
   ἐλεφάντινος [elepʰántinos]
   ἄνθρωπος [ántʰroːpos]
   ἵππος [híppos]
   πολύπους [polýpuːs]
   φοῖνιξ [pʰoíniːks]

This very simple example, based on just six vocabulary items, can serve as a token illustration of the essential continuity of Greek. But the data in (2) and (3) also demonstrate how a highly conservative orthography, which represents the (reconstructed) pronunciation of the fifth/fourth centuries BC quite accurately, but is clearly much less appropriate for the modern language, effectively conceals the sometimes major sound changes of the last 23 centuries.

The series of changes involved and the reasons for this orthographic conservatism will be explained in the chapters that follow. Here we should simply note that the overwhelming prestige of Athens and its literature in the classical period of the fifth and fourth centuries BC had a remarkable 'fossilizing' effect on the form of written Greek throughout the subsequent history of the language, not merely orthographically, but in every other respect. The resulting problem of 'diglossia' (cf. Ferguson (1959) for a classic account) has therefore dominated the history of the language from around the first century BC almost to the present day, with the spoken language, particularly of the uneducated, evolving in a 'natural' way, and the orthography, grammar and lexicon of the learned written language changing very slowly or, in certain styles, hardly at all.

This enduring emphasis on the supposed 'perfection' of the written word in its classical form has allowed the fact of sound change to be very largely ignored, and Greeks throughout their history have simply read the texts of earlier periods using whatever the current pronunciation of the language happened to be. It has also fostered and perpetuated the view among those who had mastered the archaizing written language that change in spoken Greek represented a form of linguistic decay that should not be reflected in writing.

The historical linguist, working exclusively with written documents, is therefore faced with severe difficulties in trying to detect and date the changes that took place in spoken Greek. Concrete evidence is often available only in the form of orthographic errors and grammatical or lexical departures from classical usage in texts which, whether by accident or design, exhibit some degree of compromise with the contemporary spoken language. Considerations of authorial intention and capability, as well as of generic conventions, are therefore paramount, and only when we have answered the question of how far a particular author was attempting, or indeed capable of, a 'classicizing' style can we turn to issues concerning the incidence and chronology of change. An archaizing writer of the later Middle Ages, for example, would continue to use classical φοῖνιξ (though by then pronounced ['finiks]) long after modern φοίνικας ['finikas] had become standard in both spoken and subliterary written styles. Thus despite the unbroken continuity and the massive volume of documentary material from the time of the first alphabetic inscriptions down to the present day, many uncertainties still remain concerning the dating of, and motivation for, a considerable number of key linguistic developments.

Many histories of the Greek language treat the archaizing written language as an artificial construct devoid of interest for the historical linguist, a 'dead' language which persistently stifled creativity because of its ever greater remoteness from the realities of spoken Greek (cf. Browning (1983)). This point of view accurately reflects the sympathies of most linguists with respect to the great language debate of the nineteenth and twentieth centuries in Greece between the merits of the traditional written language and the natural spoken language as a basis for the development of a modern national standard (cf. Section III), but it involves an anachronistic projection of near-contemporary issues into ancient and medieval worlds with rather different perceptions and preoccupations.

Furthermore, since those who learned to write in these traditional ways also spoke Greek in a contemporary way, interference between written and spoken varieties among the educated was an inevitable fact which the historian of Greek cannot, and should not, ignore. Ideology apart, there is no good reason to assign a uniquely privileged position to the development of the spoken language of the illiterate. Instead, efforts should be made to understand the reasons for the persistence of diglossia, and to evaluate its profound impact on the development of the Greek language over the last 2,000 years. It is, after all, emphatically not the case that contemporary standard modern Greek represents the 'pure' product of the evolution of the spoken language in communities unsullied by the deleterious effects of literacy in a dead and semi-foreign language.

This book will therefore look at the language in all its varieties, and in the context of the changing social and historical circumstances of its speakers/writers. In this way, it is possible not only to explain, summarize and exemplify the principal facts of change, but also to render comprehensible a long-term language situation that has often been dismissed as the product of reprehensible folly and slavish imitation on the part of those fortunate enough to have enjoyed the benefits of a 'proper' education.

Given that the principal purpose of this book is to present the development of Greek in a broad historical context, the first step towards that objective is to examine the array of Greek dialects in the period up to the fifth century BC. Against this background we can then seek to account for the emergence of the Attic dialect of the region of Athens (Attica) as the preeminent form of Greek in the fourth century. This prestigious dialect was the principal foundation for the so-called Hellenistic Koine (κοινή, ancient [koinέː], modern [ḱiˈni], = 'common (dialect)'), which was carried throughout the East by the conquests of Alexander the Great in the latter half of the fourth century BC, and subsequently formed the basis for the development of the dialects of medieval and modern Greek.

1.2 The prehistory and early development of Greek

If a group of travellers had set out from Athens in the early fifth century BC and made their way westwards in the direction of Megara they would, as they left the region of Attica (cf. Map 1 for this and subsequent 'trips'), have encountered forms of speech strikingly different from the Attic dialect of Athens and its environs. Megarian was a member of the 'Peloponnesian Doric' subgroup of dialects, spoken in fact not only in the Peloponnese (with the major exception of the remote central region of Arcadia), but also on the islands of the southern Aegean (e.g. Melos, Crete, Thera, Cos, and Rhodes), and in many of the Greek cities of Magna Graecia ('Great Greece', the heavily colonized regions of Southern Italy) and Sicily. These dialects, along with those of North West Greece, together formed the 'West Greek' family (so called from the general geographical distribution of the majority of its members).

If on the other hand our travellers had made their way northwards from Athens into Boeotia, they would again have heard dialects very different from that of Attica, but this time also distinct from those of the West Greek family, including the specifically North West Greek varieties spoken immediately to the west of Boeotia. Continuing northwards, however, they would have perceived a clear relationship between Boeotian and the dialects of Thessaly. But if they had instead boarded a ship in the Piraeus and made their way eastwards, island-hopping across the central and northern Aegean to the central regions of the coast of Asia Minor, they would have encountered a continuum of very closely related forms of speech, the Ionic dialects, with at least the western variants (on the island of Euboea) displaying a close affinity with the Attic of their point of departure.

The Ancient Greeks, like speakers of any other language, were sensitive to such dialectal differences, and had divided themselves into three principal 'tribes': Ionians (comprising speakers of Attic and the Ionic dialects); Dorians (speakers of the North West Greek and Peloponnesian Doric dialects); and Aeolians (speakers of Boeotian and Thessalian, together with speakers of the dialects of Lesbos and the adjacent territory on the northern Aegean coast of Asia Minor). Within these broad groupings, however, many local differences existed, and since the Greek world in this period was politically fragmented, with each major city forming, together with its surrounding territory, an autonomous state, it was usual for local dialects to enjoy 'official' status as written languages and to be employed, in a slightly elevated or refined form, to record both public and private business. Nonetheless, in areas where larger political units began to emerge, as first with the major Ionian cities of Asia Minor, a 'regional' written standard, transcending the most obvious local peculiarities, quickly began to emerge. As we shall see (Chapter 3), it was precisely the emergence of such a larger political unit in the fifth century BC which lay behind the initial development of Attic as an administrative language outside Attica.

Greek is therefore one of the few ancient languages for which we have a reasonably detailed picture of the overall dialect situation. Modern research has, overall, confirmed the validity of the ancient dialect divisions, though it is usual now to recognize a fourth dialect group comprising Arcadian (spoken in the central Peloponnese) and Cypriot, and further to divide Ionic into Western, Central and Eastern varieties, treating Attic as a closely related but distinct member of a superordinate Attic-Ionic group. Attic-Ionic and Arcado-Cypriot are collectively known as 'East Greek', just as Peloponnesian Doric and North West Greek

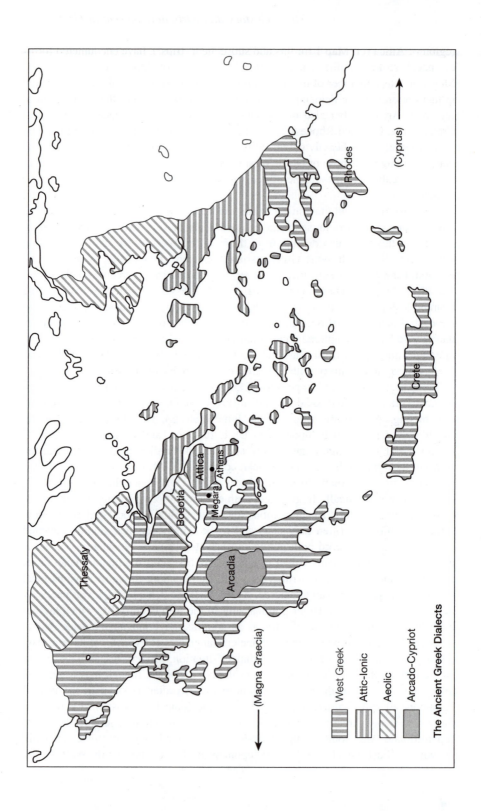

The Ancient Greek Dialects

West Greek
Attic-Ionic
Aeolic
Arcado-Cypriot

Thessaly

Boeotia

Attica
Megara · Athens

Arcadia

(Magna Graecia)

Rhodes

Crete

(Cyprus)

together constitute 'West Greek', the labels reflecting their general distribution in the period when they are first documented. Aeolic is now widely seen as fundamentally of West Greek type, but to have undergone an early period of independent development before undergoing renewed West Greek influence on the mainland and East Greek influence in Lesbos and neighbouring territory (García-Ramón (1975); see below for a more detailed account).

Work on Ancient Greek dialectology has tended to fall into two broad types. The first stresses the importance of the compilation of comprehensive descriptions and analyses of the evidence provided by the surviving documents in all its chronological, spatial, and social diversity, as an essential prerequisite for a successful classification of the dialects and a proper understanding of their historical development (see, for example, the reviews of recent work in Brixhe (1985, 1988)). Since most traditional handbooks (e.g. Buck (1928/1955)) have based their descriptions on phenomena attested in relatively small corpora of inscriptions, a great deal has been achieved in recent years to improve our knowledge of the make-up and diversity of the different dialects.

The other approach has emphasized the way in which different sets of selected isoglosses (i.e. points of agreement between dialects at a given point in time) can be interpreted as having arisen through linguistic innovations that took place at different times in the past. Such a relative chronology can then serve as a basis for reconstructing the prehistory of Greek (see, for example, Risch (1955), Chadwick (1956), García-Ramón (1975)). To be successful, such an approach requires a very careful evaluation of the reasons for the emergence of any given isogloss.

Thus isoglosses may in principle result from the fact that the dialects which share them have descended directly from a 'common ancestor' which had the features in question. In other words, we may interpret synchronic agreements as evidence for an earlier unity, so that Attic-Ionic, for example, becomes not only the name of a group of historical dialects sharing certain characteristics but also the name of their putative prehistoric ancestor. By dating the emergence of different groups of isoglosses to different periods, a dialect 'family tree' can be constructed. Consider, for example, the diagram in (4) (which is presented here simply to illustrate the point at hand and is not intended to be in any way definitive):

(4)

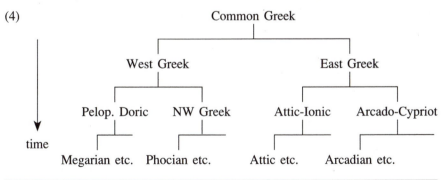

Map 1   adapted from J. M. Hall (1995) 'The role of language in Greek ethnicities'. *Proceedings of the Cambridge Philological Society* 41, 83–100

Here the isoglosses linking Megarian etc. (i.e. the Peloponnesian Doric dialects) are assumed to have been inherited from a prehistoric 'Peloponnesian Doric' dialect. The features linking this group with the North West Greek group are then assumed to have been inherited in an earlier period from a prehistoric 'West Greek' dialect. And the characteristics shared by both West Greek and East Greek dialects are assumed to have derived earlier still from an undifferentiated 'Common Greek' (distinguished in turn by a set of characteristically 'Greek' innovations from Proto-Indo-European).

This kind of model, central to traditional studies of Greek dialectology and deriving from standard methodological assumptions of nineteenth-century work on Indo-European comparison, is obviously based on the view that periods of common development are followed by later divergence initiated by innovation on the part of subgroups within a previously uniform parent. Only shared innovations resulting from a period of common development prior to such splits are therefore relevant to the construction of the tree diagram.

It is obvious, however, that isoglosses of this kind have to be distinguished from those that arise through convergence caused by the 'accidental' contact in subsequent periods of dialects which are, genetically speaking, remote from one another, since the latter are of no value in the determination of the structure of a family tree like that in (4). Equally clearly, other isoglosses may be due simply to 'accidental' independent innovation, and so again lack evidential value for the family tree. Finally, other isoglosses still may represent archaic residues of the supposed common source of all the dialects. These are likely to be scattered rather randomly among its descendants (the conservative varieties displaying more of these than the innovative ones), and so again lack significance for the grouping of the dialects into 'subfamilies'. The obvious consequence, given that isoglosses do not come with labels and dates attached, is that scholars often disagree about the significance of any particular point of agreement with respect to the reconstruction of prehistory.

Furthermore, since convergence cannot simply be ignored in considering the prehistoric development of a language, it is obvious that any family-tree account must in any case be 'corrected' in the light of a more realistic model which does not simply assume the existence of clean and permanent splits (clearly implausible in the case of Greek, evolving within the confines of the Balkan peninsula) but which allows for 'mixed' dialects, partial divergences, and periods of parallel development promoted by contact.

The application of 'modern' dialectological methodology has led, through the seminal works of Porzig (1954) and Risch (1955), to a radical reappraisal of the prehistory of Greek. None the less, the detailed reconstruction of the developments behind the geographical arrangement of dialects seen in the fifth century BC remains an issue of controversy. Since the issues involved are not strictly relevant to the major theme of this book, what follows is simply an attempt at a 'consensus view', based on key works of the last 40 or so years, among which we may note the following:

(5) (a) General surveys: Chadwick (1956, 1963, 1976b); Porzig (1954); Risch
        (1955, 1979); Wyatt (1970).
    (b) The position and interpretation of Mycenaean: Cowgill (1966); Morpurgo
        Davies and Duhoux (1985); Risch (1966); Ruijgh (1961, 1967, 1991).
    (c) The origins and development of the West Greek dialects: Chadwick (1976c);
        Bartonek (1972); Méndez-Dosuna (1985); Risch (1986).
    (d) The emergence and development of Aeolic: García-Ramón (1975); Ruijgh
        (1978a); Blümel (1982).

The spread of Peloponnesian Doric westwards to Italy and Sicily and eastwards
across the Aegean, the presence of Aeolic speakers in Lesbos, the close relationship
between Arcadian and geographically remote Cypriot, and the existence of an Ionic
dialect continuum across the central Aegean extending into central and southern
regions of the Asia Minor littoral can all be explained by reference to the extensive colonization movements from the Greek mainland which began during the
so-called Greek 'Dark Age' following the collapse of the Mycenaean civilization
and continued down to the sixth century BC.

Some difficult issues, however, remain, especially the question of how far back
in time the familiar dialect divisions go, and, if things were indeed radically different in the Dark Age and beyond, what pattern of dialect distribution preceded
them. A major obstacle to the development of clear-cut answers to these questions is the relative dearth of alphabetic material from before the sixth century BC
and the complete absence of documentary evidence from the period between the
earliest alphabetic inscriptions (eighth century BC) and the time of the latest Linear
B tablets.

The traditional solution to the problem of the distribution of the Greek dialects was provided by means of a theory of three successive 'waves' of invaders
(Kretschmer (1896, 1909)); according to this, Greek was supposed to have developed as a separate branch of the Indo-European family somewhere outside the
Balkan peninsula and to have split into dialects prior to the settlement of the Greek
mainland. First the ancestors of the Ionians (*c.* 2000 BC), then the 'Achaeans'
(*c.* 1700 BC, this group comprising the ancestors of the Aeolians and Arcado-
Cypriots, who were thought to represent the northern and southern branches respectively of an originally unitary dialect group), and finally the Dorians (*c.* 1200
BC) allegedly swept into Greece in turn, with each invasion leading to displace-
ments of the established population. In this way the overthrow of the Mycenaeans
and the isolated position of Arcadian in historical times could be explained as the
result of a massive influx of Dorians into the Peloponnese which left only a small
pocket of the earlier population in the remote central mountains.

This approach, however, has now been shown to entail quite serious archaeological and linguistic difficulties. First, it soon became clear that there was little
evidence in the archaeological record for the influx of Dorians that the theory
required. Secondly, it was noted that all Greek dialects had adopted place names
and borrowed other vocabulary from the pre-Greek languages of the Aegean basin,

but that many of the words concerned had undergone dialectally diagnostic sound changes. The borrowed word for 'sea', for example, has the following forms:

(6) (a) Attic/Boeotian θάλαττα [tʰálatta]
    (b) Other dialects θάλασσα [tʰálassa]

both of which reveal dialectally standard products of the palatalization of an original dental or velar by a following semi-vowel (normally *[j], see Allen (1957) for further details). Consider the example in (7):

(7) (a) Original *φυλάκ-jω [pʰulák̑-joː] 'I guard'
    (cf. Attic φύλαξ [pʰýlak-s], genitive φύλακ-ος [pʰýlak-os] 'a guard', showing the root-final velar)
    (b) Attic/Boeotian φυλάττω [pʰylátto:/pʰulátto:]
    (c) Other dialects φυλάσσω [pʰulásso:]

The fact that loanwords undergo developments identical to those undergone by 'native' vocabulary (even though we cannot, of course, discover the exact form in which such words were first borrowed) strongly suggested that the division of Greek into the historical dialects attested in literature and alphabetic inscriptions had taken place only after all the speakers of prehistoric Greek had become established in the Aegean area.

Furthermore, just as the old questions of Greek dialectology began to be re-examined, the language of the Linear B tablets was successfully deciphered by Michael Ventris, thus adding an important new dimension to the problem by revealing a form of Greek many centuries older than anything hitherto attested. It very quickly became apparent that, although the tablets from Knossos and Pylos came from sites quite remote from one another, the Mycenaean dialect employed was in general remarkably uniform, presumably reflecting a 'standard' written language which differed in some respects from ordinary spoken varieties of the period. It is, however, a dialect which is already clearly of East Greek type, displaying, for example, the characteristic innovatory 'assibilation' of original [t] before [i] (i.e. [ti] > [tˢi] > [si]) in a variety of contexts including the original primary (non-past) 3pl. suffix [-nti], which is preserved intact in West Greek:

(8) (a) (i) Mycenaean e-ko-si [ékʰonsi] 'they have'
        (ii) Arcadian ἔχο-νσι [ékʰonsi] Attic-Ionic ἔχου-σι [ékʰuːsi][†]
    (b) West Greek ἔχο-ντι [ékʰonti]

[†] The group [-ns-] has here been simplified, and the preceding vowel lengthened in 'compensation' to maintain the original 'heavy' syllable quantity. The ancient pitch accent was associated with a predominantly syllable-timed rhythm, reflected directly in poetry, which required fixed metrical sequences of light and heavy syllables, the latter being 'closed' (by a consonant or length), the former 'open' (i.e. not so closed). See Allen (1973) for a full discussion of the issues.

Furthermore, Mycenaean was apparently in use in large parts of central and southern Greece where either West Greek (the Peloponnese and Crete) or Aeolic (Boeotia) were spoken in later times.

Clearly, then, dialects ancestral to West Greek/Aeolic must have co-existed with Mycenaean and other East Greek varieties in the Mycenaean period, and the collapse of the Mycenaean civilization must have entailed considerable population movement if we are to explain successfully the changes of dialect involved in several areas of the mainland. One obvious possibility is that Mycenaean central and southern Greece were 'East Greek'-speaking (note that, on this view, the traditional terminology is no longer appropriate for the earlier period, and some writers have therefore substituted 'South' or 'South-East' Greek), while non-Mycenaean northern, and more specifically north-western, Greece was 'West Greek' in speech (again, some writers have substituted 'North' or 'North-West' Greek). West Greek speakers from the north might then have moved into the power vacuum as the Mycenaean civilization failed, leaving pockets of East Greek speakers in the Attic peninsula and the mountains of Arcadia (with many others emigrating to the Aegean islands and Asia Minor).

This remains the standard view, but in the continued absence of convincing archaeological evidence for a large-scale Dorian invasion, Chadwick (1976c) has suggested that many West Greek speakers were already living in the south as a 'working class' to serve the Mycenaean aristocracy. If correct, this would mean that the former underclass simply took control in areas where it had always lived. In support, Chadwick noted that some variation of usage in the tablets had already been interpreted as evidence for the existence of two Mycenaean dialects (Risch (1966), Nagy (1968), Woodard (1986)). But where Risch argued that 'special' Mycenaean reflected the spoken East Greek of the lower classes and constituted the source of historical Arcadian and Cypriot ('normal' Mycenaean having died out with the overthrow of the Mycenaean artistocracy), Chadwick argued that certain features of this 'special' variety in fact correspond to West Greek and so proposed that the Mycenaean lower classes were in fact speakers of West Greek.

But the whole theory of dialect variation in the Linear B tablets has now been seriously challenged (cf. Reinl (1994) and Thompson (1995)). If well-founded, this new scepticism undermines both Risch and Chadwick to the extent that the 'lower-class' language which they postulate (whether of East- or West-Greek type) would no longer be attested even sporadically in the documentary record. It does not of itself rule out either theory, of course, since we should not necessarily expect *any* non-prestigious spoken variety to infiltrate official documents composed by a scribal élite, but the absence of Dorian names is striking, given that the non-Greek names of indigenous peoples appear in some numbers.

Whatever the truth of the matter, much of the dialect diversity of the Classical age is now widely taken to be of post-Mycenaean origin. The old assumption of successive waves of invaders has been abandoned in favour of the view that the 'Greeks' came to Greece in a single, though possibly gradual, population movement around the end of the third millennium BC, and that Greek *in toto* is the product of the contact between the Indo-European dialect(s) of the incoming population and the language(s) of the indigenous populations.

The division into East- and West-Greek varieties had clearly taken place by the late Bronze Age, as the dialect of the Linear B tablets shows, perhaps as a simple function of geographical and political separation, perhaps under different substrate influences. Much necessarily remains uncertain about this remote period, but when we turn to the later historical dialects it is clear that Arcadian remains the closest to a direct descendant of the weakly differentiated 'East Greek' varieties assumed to have been spoken in southern Greece. The closely related Cypriot must represent the later development of the East Greek dialect of early Bronze Age colonists, and it is surely significant that Cypriot is the only dialect of the classical period still written with a syllabary (apparently representing an independent development of the Linear A system). The North West Greek dialects are correspondingly taken to represent the more or less direct descendants of the weakly differentiated 'West Greek' dialects of the Bronze Age.

Other cases, however, are more complex. The Ionic dialects, for example, including here Attic, share typical East Greek innovations with Arcado-Cypriot (e.g. assibilation of original [t]), and so must in origin represent co-descendants of the East Greek group in the Bronze Age. They have, however, undergone a number of characteristic innovations to the exclusion of Arcado-Cypriot, many of which are demonstrably post-Mycenaean, including the shift of original [aː] to [ɛː] (complete in Ionic, more restricted in Attic), so that Attic-Ionic μήτηρ [mɛ́ːtɛːr] 'mother', for example, corresponds to μάτηρ [máːtɛːr] elsewhere, including Mycenaean (cf. the place name ma-to-(ro)-pu-ro [maːtrópulos]). Many therefore now regard Attic-Ionic as a dialect group that acquired a strongly independent identity only after *c.* 1000 BC, probably in an area comprising eastern Attica and, following colonization, the western and central Aegean basin.

Interestingly, Attic-Ionic also shares a number of innovations with Peloponnesian Doric to the exclusion of both Arcado-Cypriot and North West Greek. The preposition ἐν [en], for example, was used originally both locatively with the dative (= 'in') and allatively with the accusative (= 'into'), an archaism preserved in both Arcadian and North West Greek. In Attic-Ionic and Peloponnesian Doric, however, a final [-s] was added when the preposition was used allatively, giving originally ἐνς [ens] but subsequently forms such as ἐς [es] and εἰς [eːs] through simplification of the cluster and 'compensatory' lengthening (cf. the note appended to (8) above; ἐς [es] and εἰς [eːs] were originally preconsonantal and prevocalic contextual variants, with different dialects then making different choices). Thus both East Greek and West Greek seem to have divided in the early post-Mycenaean period into conservative and innovative members, i.e. Arcado-Cypriot (conservative) vs. Attic-Ionic (innovative) on the one hand, and North West Greek (conservative) vs. Peloponnesian Doric (innovative) on the other. Beginning with Risch (1955), this has been interpreted as evidence for a significant period of parallel development on the part of the innovative dialects, perhaps originating in southern Boeotia and northern parts of Attica as Dorians, making their way to the Peloponnese, passed through and/or settled in formerly East Greek-speaking lands. These innovations cut across the earlier and more general East–West division, thus making Attic-Ionic and Peloponnesian Doric 'mixed' varieties. Subsequently, however, particularly with the advent of colonization, the two groups must be assumed to have gone their separate ways.

The Aeolic dialects are also now commonly regarded as being largely post-Mycenaean developments (García-Ramón (1975), critically reviewed by Ruijgh (1978a)), originally only weakly differentiated from West Greek in the Bronze Age. One possibility is that Aeolic formed a kind of bridge between southern 'East' Greek and northern 'West' Greek at that time, since there is evidence that proto-Aeolic had already incorporated a number of East Greek features (e.g. 1pl. verb inflection -μεν [-men] in place of West Greek -μες [-mes]) into its otherwise broadly West Greek make-up. Many distinctively Aeolic features, however, can be shown to be innovations dating from the early post-Mycenaean era. A crucial example is the uniform development of labial reflexes of the labio-velar series [kʷ, gʷ, kʷʰ], inherited (with some modification) from Proto-Indo-European and still preserved in Mycenaean. All non-Aeolic dialects, in contrast, show dental reflexes before front vowels (via palatalization): thus Boeotian πέτταρες [péttares] 'four', contrasts with Attic τέτταρες [téttares], while Mycenaean qe-to-ro- [kʷetro-] (attested only in compounds) still shows the initial [kʷ].

Since the dialect of eastern Thessaly best preserves these Aeolic innovations, this area is the most likely locus for the initial development of the dialect. It must, however, have been quite widely diffused at one time, even though, in the historical period, Thessalian and Boeotian are already geographically separated by North West Greek, and the dialects of western Thessaly and Boeotia both show clear signs of West Greek convergence and geographical retreat. In Boeotia, for example, we begin to find the substitution of the typically West Greek velar suffix -ξα- [ksa] for 'true' Boeotian -ττα- [tta] in the aorist (past perfective) of verbs with an original dental stem; e.g. ἐκομιξάμεθα [ekomiksámetʰa] for ἐκομιττάμεθα [ekomittámetʰa] < *[e-komid-sa-metʰa] 'we carried away', (the extension of the velar being based on the existence of presents in -ζω [-zdoː] from both dental (*[-d+joː]) and velar (*[-g+joː]) stems, with subsequent paradigmatic confusion).

Within this overall approach, Lesbian represents the dialect of colonists from Thessaly who made their way across the Aegean around 1000 BC and whose speech subsequently underwent a period of development under the influence of neighbouring Ionic, producing yet another mixed variety, but this time with a heavily East Greek component. Particularly significant in this connection is the Lesbian infinitive of athematic verbs (i.e. those in which inflectional endings are added directly to the root without the 'thematic' or stem-forming vowel [e/o]; contrast ἔσ-μεν [éz-men] 'we are', with πείθ-ο-μεν [peítʰ-o-men] 'we persuade'). This has the suffix -μεναι [-menai], which seems to combine the original West Greek/Aeolic -μεν [-men] with the East Greek -ναι [-nai].

1.3   Attic

This brief and selective overview is intended to do no more than supply the background against which to present the later history of Greek. Many scholars would certainly wish to challenge aspects of the account which has been presented here, particularly by insisting on a greater degree of dialect differentiation in the Bronze Age than has been allowed for. Obviously, no view is wholly unproblematical, since all are necessarily based on partial knowledge and on particular selections and interpretations of isoglosses.

We have, however, left open the question of Attic and its 'aberrant' relationship with Ionic. This dialect certainly shares most of its characteristic innovations with Ionic, as noted, but, significantly, it also has important innovations in common with Boeotian. We may note, for example, the history of palatalization, which seems in its early phases to have followed Ionic (both dialects having, e.g., τόσος [tósos] 'so much', against Boeotian τόττος [tóttos], all from *[tot-jos]), but subsequently to have fallen into line with Boeotian (Ionic having, e.g., φυλάσσω [pʰylássoː] 'I guard', against Attic/Boeotian φυλάττω [pʰyláttoː]/[pʰuláttoː], all from *[pʰuláḵ-joː], cf. (7) above). The most likely explanation is that western Attica, separated by high mountains from the eastern areas, came under Boeotian influence in the post-Mycenaean period some time after Ionic, which included at least eastern Attica in its developmental domain, had begun to evolve as a distinct variety. The subsequent political unification of Attica would then have produced the 'mixed' dialect of the classical period, a dialect of broadly Ionic type, but with a number of strikingly discordant features *vis-à-vis* the Ionic norm.

An evolved form of Attic was soon to play the dominant role in the subsequent development of Greek, a history from which all other ancient dialects eventually disappeared virtually without trace. This story will be taken up in detail in Chapter 3, but first we must consider the role of the ancient dialects in literature, and in particular the emergence of specifically literary dialects, since this issue lies at the heart of the 'problem' of diglossia which has characterized Greek for most of its history.

Chapter 2

Classical Greek: official and literary 'standards'

2.1 Introduction

Though there were certainly differences based on class, age and gender within the dialect of any given city, there is little to suggest that there was any significant difference in prestige between the geographically defined varieties of spoken Greek down into the classical period. Indeed, there was no basis for such differentiation in the absence of a unified Greek state and the cultural pre-eminence typically associated with the dialect of a dominant class within a larger political structure transcending the boundaries of individual cities.

Much the same situation obtains for the 'official' versions of local dialects known to us from inscriptions, though, as noted in Chapter 1, the Ionian cities of Asia Minor seem to have adopted a single official standard from early times. The first dialects to acquire a Panhellenic status were in fact those employed in early Greek literature during the seventh, sixth and fifth centuries BC. Though our texts have suffered from editorial 'correction' and copyists' error over the centuries, enough remains clear to enable us to conclude, on the basis of comparison with inscriptional material, that the earliest examples of work in any particular genre are typically composed in stylized versions of the dialects of the regions where those who first gave that genre its definitive form lived and worked.

The prestige attaching to 'classic' works soon led to what seems, from a modern point of view, a rather surprising development. Although we have no 'Lesbian' lyric other than from Lesbos before the Hellenistic period (beginning in the late fourth century BC), and the earliest elegiac and iambic poetry comes exclusively from Ionia, most other genres attracted authors from across the Greek-speaking world, and such works were routinely composed in the traditionally associated literary dialects even if the authors concerned came from areas in which a different variety was spoken. This genre-conditioning of dialect is a striking feature of the earliest Greek literature and is not only a sign of respect for tradition but also a natural consequence of the ready availability within a particular written dialect of established and refined literary conventions and verbal 'tools of the trade'.

2.2 The language of Homer and its influence

To understand this situation, we must first examine the language of the earliest surviving Greek literature, that of the 'Homeric' epic poems the *Iliad* and the

17

Odyssey (the true author(s) are unknown, but it is convenient to retain the name of Homer). The dialect of the texts that have been transmitted to us is essentially an archaic eastern Ionic but with an admixture of Aeolic, and a number of conspicuous archaisms not characteristic of any one historical dialect or region (see Palmer (1962), Horrocks (1980, 1987, forthcoming)).

This artificiality is standardly explained by arguing that the Greek epic tradition was an oral one (see Parry (1928a, 1928b, 1930, 1932) for the original hypothesis, which has since spawned a massive bibliography), with its origins almost certainly going back into the Bronze Age (cf. Horrocks (1980)), and its final development, culminating in the *Iliad* and *Odyssey*, taking place in Ionia during the eighth century BC. Dialect mixture and archaism are typical of oral poetry, and the reason has to do with the 'formulaic' character of oral diction which normally develops, within the framework of a fixed metre, as an aid to composition and memory. Homeric formulas, for example, fill well-defined 'slots' within dactylic hexameters, which consist of six feet composed of patterned heavy (-) and light (˘) syllables forming either dactyls (- ˘˘, truncated in the sixth foot - ˘), or spondees (- -); the fourth foot is typically, and the fifth foot overwhelmingly, dactylic:

(1) | - ˘̱ | - ˘̱ | - ˘̱ | - ˘̱ | - ˘̱ | - ̱ |

Recurrent formulas are regularly developed into complex and adaptable systems, which give the poet a variety of metrically different ways of saying the same or similar things (cf. Hainsworth (1968)). Ultimately the feasibility of composition, memorization and performance depends on networks of formulaic and semi-formulaic options, and facility in composition and performance would quickly break down if such systems were casually destroyed by the routine replacement of archaic or 'borrowed' forms with new or 'native' formations with different metrical values (cf. Horrocks (1980), and see Horrocks (1987, forthcoming) for arguments that Homer's Aeolicisms were borrowed from a parallel tradition rather than representing the residue of an earlier Aeolic 'phase' of the tradition). The propensity of oral traditions to retain archaic and 'foreign' dialect forms long after the introduction of more modern equivalents with identical functions needs no further explanation.

Although such an artificial language could never have been the spoken dialect of any region, it should be emphasized that the fundamentals of epic grammar and diction were subject to regular modernization, broadly in line with the contemporary spoken Greek of the localities where epic bards were working, albeit with archaic and 'foreign' dialectal retentions at each stage. Thus, in the case of the Homeric poems, it is the eastern Ionic dialects of the eighth century BC that provide the latest 'layer' of linguistic fabric into which other, more traditional elements are woven. Only when the tradition shifted from a 'creative' to a 'recitative' phase, a change standardly associated with the advent of writing during the late eighth/early seventh centuries, did the form and content of the Homeric poems come to be seen not as something inevitably to be adapted with the passage of time but rather as a definitive 'text' for recitation and as a linguistic model for any future (now literate) composition. The first Greek literary dialect was thus created, and its impact was to be immense and lasting.

The prestige that attached to the Homeric poems in antiquity cannot be overestimated. They were felt to embody the essence of Greek culture and quickly formed the cornerstone of traditional education throughout the Greek world. It was therefore entirely appropriate, though accidental, that their dialect was not that of a particular region but a 'poetic' variety which, while clearly related to contemporary Ionic, transcended the parochialism of local and even official varieties through the elevating effects of archaism and 'high-flown' formulaic phraseology and the distancing effect of Aeolic loanwords and grammatical formatives. These linguistic qualities of the first, universally admired, masterpieces of Greek literature naturally determined the Greek view of what was linguistically appropriate within the higher levels of poetic discourse for many centuries to come (see, for example, Aristotle *Rhetoric* 1404 b, *Poetics* 1458 a–b).

The exploitation of mixed dialects in a single text (i.e. generalized local dialect alongside traditional 'poetic' features derived from a tradition) quickly became characteristic of other types of poetry as these began to emerge during the course of the seventh century BC. This is not to say that early Greek poetry is unoriginal. On the contrary, the development of innovatory genres and new literary dialects is a major characteristic of the period down to the fifth century BC. All of these, however, display in some degree the same 'stylized' quality which derived from a universal and profound appreciation of the epic and which served as an expression of authorial determination to impart a universal 'feel' in works aimed increasingly at a Panhellenic audience.

A good example is provided by choral lyric poetry, which had its roots in both Aeolic- and Doric-speaking areas (with features of the latter type predominating in the work that has come down to us). Initially, it seems that such poetry was commissioned for local occasions and normally employed something very close to the appropriate local dialect as its base. Thus Alcman, for example, who was probably himself an Ionian but worked in Dorian Sparta during the seventh century BC, naturally used a variety of Laconian (the dialect of the region of Laconia, where Sparta is situated). This is, however, already tempered in our texts with 'foreign' features of apparently Lesbian origin. It is not impossible, however, that at least some of these were introduced by Alexandrian editors in the Hellenistic period as 'corrections' based on a conception of Doric derived from the dialect of neighbouring Cyrene which happened, unlike the majority of West Greek dialects, to share relevant innovations with Lesbian (see Page (1951), Risch (1954)).

As time went on, however, choral lyric came to be associated with the celebration of major Panhellenic festivals such as the games at Olympia, Delphi and the Isthmus of Corinth (e.g. the victory odes of Pindar, born in the last quarter of the sixth century in Boeotian Thebes). With the advent of a wider audience and more weighty subject matter, the language of choral lyric developed quickly into a conventionalized 'Doric', which, rather in the manner of Homer's 'Ionic', vaguely suggested its regional origins but simultaneously transcended them. By the end of the sixth century BC the language of choral lyric, all of whose major practitioners were by then of non-Dorian origin, had evolved into a standardized amalgam in which a foundation of regionally non-specific Doricism was combined, in keeping with its non-Ionian roots, with a set of traditional Aeolicisms (assuming that we can trust the tradition) and predominantly non-Ionic or de-Ionicized epicisms.

Although choral lyric as such began to fall out of favour during the second half of the fifth century BC, it continued to play an important part in the developing Athenian drama, where the 'chorus' retained an integral role. Such was the power of tradition that a conventional set of Doric features, abstracted from earlier practice, was still employed to impart the necessary 'colouring' to the otherwise Attic-based (though not contemporary Attic) language of the choral lyrics of the tragedies of Aeschylus, Sophocles, and Euripides. The relatively 'naturalistic' spoken dialogue, however, was composed not in lyric metres but in lines comprising six iambi (˘-), with spondaic and other variants permitted in certain positions. The basic metrical pattern is given in (2):

(2) | ˘- | ˘- | ˘- | ˘- | ˘- | ˘- |

But even this was written in a generally archaizing Attic which regularly replaced 'low-status' Atticisms with unusual neologisms (e.g. ἀπότιμος [apóti:mos] 'dishonoured/unworthy' for ἄτιμος [áti:mos]; ὅμαιμος [hómaimos] 'brother', lit. 'same blood', for ἀδελφός [adelpʰós], etc.) and other elements taken from literary Ionic, comprising now not only poetry (the epic, together with later elegiac, iambic and trochaic poetry which had developed under epic influence) but also prose writing (on which see 2.3 below). While some of these elements doubtless imparted a more dignified poetic quality to the language, the use of other, very ordinary, grammatical and lexical features of Ionic seems to reflect the more general influence of Ionian literature on the evolution of a literary form of Attic in this period. In combination with these more recent elements, there is also a characteristically 'tragic' vocabulary drawn partly from Homer but also from Dorian dramatic traditions that perhaps originated in the great cities of Magna Graecia.

Amongst the non-Homeric Ionicisms we may note features such as:

(3) (a) the routine avoidance of parochial Attic phonology such as the -ττ- [tt] in words like θάλαττα [tʰálatta] 'sea' (Ionic and Panhellenic θάλασσα [tʰálassa] is always preferred).

(b) the replacement of typically Attic morphology, such as the use of 3pl. imperatives formed by the addition of -σαν [-san] to the 3sg. in -τω [-to:] rather than with the original suffix -(ό)ντων [(ó)nto:n], e.g. ἴτωσαν [íto:-san] beside Attic ἰόντων [i-ónto:n] 'let them go'.

(c) selected vocabulary (the normal Attic is given in brackets): ἱστορῶ [historô:] 'I enquire' (ἐρωτῶ [ero:tô:]); ἀγρεύω [agreúo:] 'I hunt' (θηρεύω [tʰɛːreúo:]); φερνή [pʰernɛ́:] 'dowry' (προῖξ [proîks]); νεοχμός [neokʰmós] 'new'/'novel' (νεός [neós]).

Typical archaic/epic features selected deliberately to elevate the diction include (ordinary Attic equivalents again in brackets):

(4) (a) paradigms such as perfect ὄπωπα [ópoːpa] 'I have seen' (ἑόρακα [heóraːka]), gen. sg. δορός/δουρός/δούρατος [dorós/duːrós/dúːratos] 'spear' (δόρατος [dóratos]).

  (b) epic vocabulary such as ἔχθος [ékʰtʰos] 'hatred' (ἔχθρα [ékʰtʰraː]); εἷμα [hêːma] 'cloak' (ἱμάτιον [hiːmátion]); ἱππότης [hippóteːs] 'horseman/knight' (ἱππεύς [hippeús]); πόσις [pósis] 'husband' (ἀνήρ [anéːr]); δάμαρ [dámar] 'wife' (γυνή [gynéː]); μολεῖν [moléːn] 'to go' (ἐλθεῖν [eltʰêːn]); λεύσσειν [leússeːn] 'to see' (ὁρᾶν [horâːn]).

Finally we may note vocabulary items that seem to come from the literature of the western Greek world of Sicily and southern Italy (cf. Björck (1950)):

(5) δαρός [daːrós] 'long'; ὀπαδός [opaːdós] 'attendant'; κυναγός [kynaːgós] 'hunter', lit. 'hound-leader'; ναός [naːós] 'temple'; λαός [laːós] 'people'.

These all contain original long -*a*- [aː] in contexts where, if they have the words at all, both Attic and Ionic had converted [aː] to [ɛː] prehistorically. Furthermore, the standard Attic forms for the last two items listed are νεώς [neóːs] and λεώς [leóːs], derived by 'quantitative metathesis' ([ɛː] > [e] and [o] > [oː]) from the expected νηός [nɛːós] (attested in Homer and Ionic historiography) and ληός [lɛːós] (not Homeric, where λαός [laːós] is always used, but attested in some manuscripts of the historian Herodotus).

This determined avoidance of Attic parochialism and the striving for an 'international' style linked to prestigious literary traditions served to distance the language of tragedy from that of everyday discourse in a way conditioned by precedent and felt to be essential for any dialect with literary pretensions. As with the other literary dialects discussed above, this kind of Ionicized Attic in turn evolved into a Panhellenic common language, but in this case its use was no longer strictly genre-conditioned. Instead Attic eventually emerged as *the* common literary language for the Greek world, effectively replacing all other dialects (apart from periodic artificial revivals in certain poetic genres). Obviously the linguistic experimentation of the Athenian dramatists paved the way for this later development, but the final triumph of Attic as not only a literary but also an official 'common language' for the whole Greek world depended ultimately on the development of Attic prose writing and above all on the political circumstances of the fifth and fourth centuries BC. These issues will be discussed in detail in the chapters that follow, but first we must consider the origins and growth of prose writing in Ionia, which played the central role in the evolution of a belletristic Attic prose style.

2.3 Official and literary Ionic

Much early literature is in verse because fixed rhythms and formulaic phraseology are invaluable aids to composition and memorization in predominantly oral cultures. But by the sixth century BC Ionia was at the centre of the development of Greek commercial life and more generally of the first flowering of 'classical'

Greek civilization. As such it offered a highly congenial, prosperous and increasingly literate social context for the revolutionary deployment of Greek prose for intellectual pursuits such as scientific and philosophical speculation and historiography that went far beyond the mere recording of official and personal business.

Although some early Ionian philosophers, perhaps *faute de mieux*, attempted to expound their doctrines in the already established Ionic literary mode (epic-style hexameters), the novel character of the material which many scholars wished to present did not lend itself readily to expression in a medium which had, after all, evolved in very different circumstances and for a very different purpose. Since prose was already widely used for official business, it could perhaps be adapted to fulfil more ambitious functions.

As noted above, from the earliest times official Ionic inscriptions from the twelve major cities of Asia Minor reveal a 'standard' written dialect, one clearly distinct from local spoken varieties (Herodotus I. 142 speaks of four main dialect groups), and a crucial indicator of the existence of an Ionian civilization that had already transcended the limits of the traditional city state. Unsurprisingly, then, the dialect employed in early prose work is also of a generalized Ionic character overall, parallel, as far as we can tell, to that of official documents in its major characteristics. Unfortunately, we cannot be sure just how well our texts represent original usage, since once again they have passed through the hands of later editors and copyists who have 'restored' on *a priori* grounds what they took to be 'correct' Ionic.

It is significant, however, that literary Ionic fails to correspond to the usage of official inscriptions of the period in at least one major respect: while the interrogative adverbs of official Asiatic Ionic begin with π-, as elsewhere in Greek, including the Homeric poems and most of the Ionic elegiac and iambic poetry of the seventh and sixth centuries, these same words begin with κ- in Ionic scientific and literary prose (with only a few inscriptional examples attested from far-flung colonies in the western Mediterranean). This reflects two different treatments of the original initial labio-velar *[kʷ-]:

(6) Official Ionic   Literary Ionic
 πῶς [pɔ̂ːs]   'how?'   κῶς [kɔ̂ːs]
 πότε [póte]   'when?'   κότε [kóte]
 ποῦ [pûː]   'where?'   κοῦ [kûː]
 πόθεν [pótʰen]   'where from?'   κόθεν [kótʰen]

It seems, then, that the dialect of literary prose must have had its ultimate origins in a region whose peculiarities of speech had been suppressed not only in Ionic poetry (for the most part) but also in the development of official Ionic, and that the literary standard was therefore somewhat closer to local speech, or at least to one variety of it, than the official standard. The effect of this difference was to introduce, perhaps deliberately, a distinctive 'marker' of scientific/technical prose writing. Unlike in poetry, there were as yet no prestigious traditions to take account of, and so no basis for 'deferential' archaism or dialect borrowing. Clarity and directness were paramount in the newly emerging intellectual disciplines.

The prestige of Ionian achievement soon led to this new literary language becoming the model for prose writers outside Ionia, above all for historians and scientists who readily exploited a vocabulary and expository style that had been developed specifically for the treatment of their respective disciplines. Thus the historians Antiochus of (Dorian) Syracuse and Hellanicus of (Aeolic) Lesbos both used the Ionic literary standard in the last quarter of the fifth century BC, as did Hippocrates from (Dorian) Cos when compiling his medical treatises (assuming that at least some of the writings collected in the Hippocratic corpus may be attributed to an individual author of that name). Perhaps the most famous Ionic prose author, however, is Herodotus, who was born in the early fifth century BC in the once Dorian and then only recently Ionicized city of Halicarnassus (modern Bodrum) at the south-western tip of Asia Minor, and who wrote a monumental history of the Greco-Persian conflicts of the sixth and fifth centuries.

In Athens we have already seen that the local dialect was acceptable in tragic dialogue only in a form which incorporated 'hallmarked' material derived from earlier poetic traditions. Athenian prose writers were similarly influenced by the linguistic usage of their Ionian predecessors, despite the fact that Athens had acquired an empire during the course of the fifth century and was building a formidable reputation of its own as a centre of education and culture. We can therefore trace significant differences between the official Attic of the period and the literary Attic of, for example, Thucydides, who wrote his famous history of the war between Athens and Sparta in the latter part of the fifth century BC. The rise of this Ionicized Attic prose as both a literary and an official language must now be considered.

Chapter 3

The rise of Attic

3.1 Attic as a literary standard

By the time of Herodotus' history Ionia had long lost its independence to Persia. Athens, however, as a leading city of the Ionian tribe, had not only supported an unsuccessful Ionian revolt, but also played a leading role in defending Greece proper against the consequential Persian aggression of the early fifth century BC. The city emerged from these confrontations as a major maritime power, with most of the islands of the Aegean and a number of important cities around its coasts falling under Athenian domination. By the mid-fifth century Athens was an imperial city which could rival Dorian Sparta, the established military power, for the leadership of Greece, a rivalry which extended also into the political sphere, since Athens was the foremost democratic city of the age, while Sparta retained a more traditional oligarchic form of government.

At the same time, and partly in consequence of its new pre-eminence in other spheres, Athens was rapidly becoming a major centre of learning, attracting leading intellectuals (the so-called 'sophists', peripatetic teachers of various skills and theories who provided higher education for the well-to-do) from all parts of the Greek world, and beginning the development of its own cultural and educational institutions. Most importantly, in this atmosphere of growing national pride, the Athenians developed a literature in a version of their own dialect, particularly in the fields of tragedy, comedy, history, oratory and philosophy.

The core of the language of Athenian tragedy, as noted in Chapter 2, is essentially Attic, despite the overlay of traditional and Ionic 'distancing' features. But the ordinary (i.e. non-parodic) language of comedy, familiar from the plays of Aristophanes, is, as far as we can tell, quite close to the educated colloquial of the period. Similarly, rhetoric, one of the most notable 'inventions' of the fifth-century Greek enlightenment, and the key instrument of democratic political life, achieved its definitive form in the dialect of Athens. Many sophists laid great emphasis on the importance of effective speaking as a means of managing one's affairs and manipulating circumstances to one's advantage, and found many willing customers for their educational services in a society which gave free rein to the exploitation of such skills. Notable names in this connection include Protagoras, from Abdera in Thrace, Gorgias of Leontini in Sicily, and Thrasymachus from Chalcedon on the Asian side of the Bosporus. The evolution of a specifically Attic prose style is certainly due in part to the influence of these mainly Ionic-speaking visitors, an influence which manifests itself both in the style and organization of argument and in the use of language, particularly through the introduction of Ionic technical terminology and the semantic extension of existing vocabulary.

Unsurprisingly, then, the historian Thucydides, who was born around 460 BC and exiled in 424 BC for his failure as a general during the 'Peloponnesian' war between Athens and Sparta (431–404 BC), wrote his account of that conflict in a rather old-fashioned Attic, which, as noted, suppressed the most characteristically Attic features in favour of Ionic equivalents. His style was perhaps typical of the sophist-trained generation of pre-war days in that nothing in the work (which includes 'speeches' put in the mouths of key figures at critical moments) suggests the direct influence of the highly specific codification of rhetorical practice initiated by Gorgias from 427 BC onwards. This latter involved what is, to a modern sensibility, a rather unnatural striving for impact through antithesis, formal parallelism, and the routine exploitation of auxiliary rhythmical and phonetic 'special effects'. Thucydides' narrative, in contrast, is quite straightforward, and even the speeches, though often broadly antithetical in their articulation of material, display none of the precise matching and equalization of clauses espoused by Gorgias, but instead aim for a deliberate variety of phrasing and syntax. What is perhaps most characteristic of Thucydides' speeches is the extreme compression of both thought and diction, which often leads to highly complex structures that demand the most careful reading. This style is therefore in equally marked contrast to the doctrines of Thrasymachus, who advocated logical ordering and clarity of expression as the primary virtues of a good rhetorical style.

In all probability, then, the reputation of Gorgias as the 'founding father' of Attic prose is exaggerated. It seems more likely that he developed and refined tendencies that were already in train, as seen perhaps in Thucydides' speeches, and attempted to formulate the results as rules of composition. His excessive mannerism, however, though doubtless initially highly effective in what was still a very new domain, fell rapidly out of favour, and it is the work of Thrasymachus that had the more lasting influence. This shift can perhaps be traced in the work of the orator Antiphon (executed in 411 BC), whose early speeches are markedly antithetical, with some use of clausal equalization and associated phonetic contrivances, but who later adopted a more expansive sentence structure with fewer Ionic or 'poetic' characteristics (which often amount to the same thing, since much of what was current in early Ionic prose had come to be felt as poetic because of the continued use of the same words and expressions in archaizing poetry). It is in any case worth noting that there is a clear contrast between Antiphon's rhetorical exercises and his genuine forensic oratory, which makes a much more straightforward appeal, as appropriate to its 'real-world' context. Lysias (born around the middle of the fifth century) also wrote speeches for the Athenian middle class, and again did so in a relatively ordinary Attic with few blatant rhetorical 'tricks'; a 'colloquial' directness and simplicity of diction apparently gave a better impression of honesty in a court of law.

Perhaps the most important figure in this field, however, is the rhetorical theoretician Isocrates (436–338 BC) who, though a pupil of Gorgias in his youth, owed a great deal more to Thrasymachus in his development of a technically refined (though to some modern tastes rather bland) prose style, most particularly in his emphasis on precision of diction, the avoidance of 'poetic', i.e. often Ionic, expression, the paramount importance of transparency of sentence structure within the context of a complex 'periodic' style, and the need for a restrained approach to the rhythmical reinforcement of the message. The later influence of Isocratean rhetoric on the great Roman statesman and man of letters Cicero, and through him on the subsequent evolution of prose writing in Europe, cannot be overestimated.

We should not, however, leave the subject of rhetoric without first observing that a broadly 'rhetorical' style comes to characterize other genres besides oratory. The case of Thucydides' history has already been mentioned, but no one can read a play of Euripides or Aristophanes without becoming aware of the impact of a rhetorical education on the construction of dramatic dialogue, particularly in set-piece confrontations. It is quite clear that early rhetoric had the most profound effect, not only in the context of the Athenian Assembly and the law courts but much more generally through the education system, on the vocabulary and thinking of the educated classes, and ultimately on the lexicon and stylistic conventions of literary and even official varieties of the Attic dialect.

Alongside the development of rhetoric we see in Athens in the late fifth century the growth of moral philosophy. This was directly associated with the general intellectual ferment of the period and particularly with the pressing need for a fundamental examination of basic ethical and political issues in the context of the freedoms and responsibilities afforded by democratic government. Some philosophers, among whom Socrates stands out as one who claimed to have nothing to teach but only questions to ask, favoured a dialectic method over exposition; and a new literary genre, the philosophical dialogue, eventually emerged, with Socrates' pupil Plato (427–348/7 BC) its greatest exponent.

Plato came from a highly cultured background and was steeped in the traditions of Greek poetry. Despite his general distrust of poetry (as perpetuating a distortion of reality), it is striking that when his subject matter becomes more abstract and his purpose more overtly didactic, as in the famous 'mythical' passages of the *Republic*, the style and vocabulary begin to exhibit marked similarities with those of Attic tragedy. In the more 'natural' parts of his dialogues, however, we seem to be dealing, as in Aristophanes (always allowing for differences of genre and intent), with an artful approximation to the ordinary conversational style of the educated classes.

With the development of literature in a purely Athenian context during the late fifth and early fourth centuries BC we see the gradual emancipation of Attic prose from the direct influence of Ionic precedent, though it should be emphasized that certain lexical and grammatical features of Ionic prose had by then become permanent fixtures and a hallmark of the 'high' style. The influence and prestige of this variety were enormous, so that, by the time of Plato, Attic prose is the only prose literature of which we have any surviving record. This clearly demonstrates that Attic literature had by then come to dominate Greek culture, and that the Attic dialect, as the international language of intellectual endeavour (even, it should be noted, in the field of historiography, where Ionic had earlier reigned supreme), already served as a model for the whole Greek-speaking world. In an earlier age Thucydides had felt obliged to 'tone down' his Attic; but now the fourth-century historian Theopompus, who came from the Ionian island of Khios, had little choice but to write in the established literary Attic of his period. The role of Classical Attic as the model for literary composition was assured, and its influence was to last for the next 2,000 years.

3.2 'Great Attic' as an administrative language

This state of affairs is all the more remarkable when one reflects that at the beginning of the fifth century, Attic was the local dialect of a still backward and isolated region, highly archaic and conservative in its grammatical structure, with its literary potential wholly undeveloped. In the sharpest contrast, eastern Ionic, as the dialect group of a burgeoning 'frontier' region with a mixed colonial population, had long been dynamically innovative. It had, furthermore, already been used in a developed form in poetry, and was at that time in the process of being forged into a sophisticated instrument of scientific and historical exegesis. In the course of its development Ionic had lost many grammatical archaisms that Attic still retained, and these sometimes quite radical simplifications had naturally found their way into Ionic literary productions. We may note, for example, the disappearance of the following categories and forms:

(1) (a) the dual number.
    (b) morphological irregularities, such as:
        (i) ἴσμεν [íz-men], ἴστε [ís-te], ἴσασι [ís-aːsi], the plural forms of οἶδα [oîd-a] 'I know' – replaced by the predictable οἴδαμεν [oíd-amen], οἴδατε [oíd-ate], οἴδασι [oíd-asi].
        (ii) ἔθεμεν [é-tʰe-men], ἔθετε [é-tʰe-te], ἔθεσαν [é-tʰe-san], the plural of past perfective (aorist) ἔθηκα [é-tʰεːk-a] 'I put' (and other plurals of the aorist of athematic verbs with root alternation) – levelled to the singular to give ἐθήκαμεν [e-tʰέːk-amen], ἐθήκατε [e-tʰέːk-ate], ἔθηκαν [é-tʰεːk-an].

Given this background, it should not be surprising that the earliest literary manifestations of Attic, such as tragedy and Thucydides' history, not only rejected the most characteristically 'local' and unliterary phonological features, such as the use of -ττ- [tt] and -ρρ- [rr] in words like γλῶττα [glôːtta] 'tongue' and θάρρος [tʰárros] 'boldness', in favour of the more 'international' and prestigious Ionic forms with -σσ- [ss] and -ρσ- [rs], but also began to adopt Ionic grammatical characteristics by e.g. restricting the use of the dual and incorporating 3pl. aorist forms such as those in (1)(b):

(2) (a) 3pl. παρῆκαν [par-hêːk-an] 'they let go/passed over' (Thucydides IV.38.1).
    (b) 3pl. ἀνῆκαν [an-hêːk-an] 'they sent forth/let go' (Euripides *Bacchae* 448).

Despite the dramatic transformation in Athens' fortunes during the course of the
fifth century, and the advent of a greater willingness to use local Attic forms in
certain kinds of literary composition, Ionic prestige continued to shape the development of Attic as a literary language. And before long many Ionic characteristics
which had first appeared in literary texts also began to appear in official Athenian
inscriptions. To illustrate the point, we may note examples such as the following
(see López-Eire (1986, 1993) for a full discussion):

(3) the verb ἐπαινῶ [epainôː] 'praise' takes the dative in the earliest Attic inscriptions, exactly as in Homer:

ἐπαινέσαι τοῖς   Σιγειεῦσιν
[epainésai toîs   sigeːeûsin]
to-praise   the(dat.) Sigeans(dat.)

(IG I³ 17, 6: 451/50 BC)

In Herodotus's Ionic, however, we find the accusative used for the object, as with
'regular' transitive verbs, and this Ionic construction is regularly preferred in Athenian literature:

(4) πάντας ὑμέας ἐπαινέω
[pántas hyméas epainéoː]
all(acc.) you(acc.) I-praise

(Sophocles *Ajax* 1381)

By the end of the fifth century this usage also begins to compete with the traditional
one even in official documents, and eventually supplants it:

(5) (a) ἐπαινέσαι τοῖς   Νεαπολίταις
[epainésai toîs   neapolítais]
to-praise   the(dat.) Neapolitans(dat.)

(IG I² 101 7: 410/9 BC)

(b) ἐπαινέσαι Θρασύβōλον
[epainésai tʰrasýbuːlon]
to-praise   Thrasyboulos(acc.)

(IG I² 102 6: 410/9 BC)

As already noted, the extension of the root-form of the singular to the plural in the
aorists of athematic verbs with 1sg. present in -μι [-mi] occurs first in Ionic prose
(e.g. Herodotus III.128.4) and passes from there into Athenian literature (cf. (2)
above). It also begins to appear in official Attic inscriptions in the early part of the
fourth century (e.g. IG II² 1412 23: 385/4 BC). We might also note that Ionic literature employs the conjunctions ὡς ἄν [hoːs án] or ὅπως [hópoːs] + subjunctive
in purpose clauses ('in order that'), while traditional Attic in early 'conservative'
inscriptions uses ὅπως ἄν [hópoːs án]. However, ὡς ἄν [hoːs án] and bare ὅπως
[hópoːs] appear already in Thucydides' history (cf. VI.91 for the former, I.126 for
the latter), and then start to turn up in Attic inscriptions from the later fifth century
onwards (e.g. IG I³ 156 2: 440–25 BC for ὡς ἄν [hoːs án], IG I² 226 40: 343–2
BC for ὅπως [hópoːs]).

The overall picture that emerges is of an unequal struggle between a traditional 'conservative' Attic and a more 'modern', Ionicized Attic, already well-established in literature and educated discourse, which finally supplants its rival even in administrative documents. Other diagnostic features of this modern style include:

(6) (a) a liking for periphrases consisting of a noun + the verb ποιοῦμαι [poiû:mai] 'I make': e.g. ἐπιμέλειαν ποιοῦμαι [epiméle:an poiû:mai], lit. 'I make care (for)' in place of the verb ἐπιμελοῦμαι [epimelû:mai] 'I take care of', first in Ionian prose (e.g. Herodotus VI.105.2), then in Attic literature (e.g. Thucydides VII.56.1) and finally in Attic inscriptions (e.g. IG II² 659 10: 287 BC).

   (b) 'short' dative plurals in -οις/-αις [-ois/-ais] in place of -οισι/-αισι [-oisi/ -aisi]. (This is a development internal to Attic based on the generalization of the short forms already standardized in the article at the beginning of the fifth century.)

   (c) σύν [sún] for ξύν [ksún] 'with'.

Interestingly, in IG I³ 40 (a treaty of 446 BC between Athens and the city of Chalcis on the island of Euboea) the traditional forms of (6)(b) and (c) are used in the formal oath to be sworn by the Athenians and the Chalcidians, but the modern ones appear in the additional clauses proposed by individual Athenians, a distribution which highlights perfectly the contrast between the traditional official and educated spoken/written styles of the period.

Unsurprisingly, it is the more modern forms which eventually find their way into the Attic-based Koine, which was the natural continuation of this evolved and Ionicized form of official Attic, often called 'Great Attic' since the pioneering work of Thumb (1901, 1906). No longer the written dialect of Athens alone, it was used for all official written communication within the Athenian empire, and its subsequent use spread still wider, doubtless aided by the prestige of literary Attic as the embodiment of 'classical' Greek culture. Thus even after Athens had been defeated by the Spartans in 404 BC, the importance of its written administrative language remained intact, and its use for official purposes in territories outside Attica continued and even expanded, particularly with the revival of Athens in the fourth century and the formation of a second Athenian Alliance in 377 BC. It is no accident that a document recording the decision of a federation of all Greek cities (except Sparta) not to assist the semi-autonomous rulers of the territories of Western Asia Minor (the 'satraps') in their revolt against the Persian king (IG IV 556: 362/1 BC) should be composed in Great Attic: we may note, for example, forms like innovative 3pl. οἴδασιν [oídasin] 'they know', in place of traditional Attic ἴσασιν [ísa:sin]. If literary Attic in its developed form represented a Panhellenic 'high style' for belletristic purposes, Great Attic represented the ordinary written style of business and administration among the middle and upper classes. It was, we may assume, quite close to the ordinary spoken language of educated Athenians but rather different from both the dialect of the urban masses and the formal speech of aristocratic circles, as well as from the conservative varieties of rural Attica; it was, in other words, a form of language sufficiently prestigious for export as an official medium, but not one over-adorned with pretentious stylistic markers. A fragment of Aristophanes (552/706 K–A) perhaps draws attention to this everyday/educated level of Attic usage:

(7) διάλεκτον ἔχοντα μέσην τῆς πόλεως οὔτ᾽ ἀστείαν ὑποθηλυτέραν οὔτ᾽
      ἀνελεύθερον ὑπαγροικοτέραν.

[diálekton ékʰonta   mésɛːn têːs póleoːs úːt   astéːaːn
speech   having(mas. acc. sg.) middle   of-the city   neither urban

hypotʰɛːlytéraːn úːt aneleútʰeron hypagroikotéraːn]
rather-effeminate   nor rude   rather-subrustic

'(a man) with the middle-of-the-road speech of the city, neither the rather effeminate urban variety [*i.e. associated with the aristocracy*] nor the crude rather countrified one.'

This process of Attic-Ionic convergence can be seen from another perspective in Ionic documents of the fifth and fourth centuries BC, in which Attic forms and phrases, first introduced through Athenian administrative and legal documents, begin to infiltrate steadily. Only the most characteristic 'markers' of Ionic are resolutely adhered to, such as the use of -η [ɛː] after ι/ε/ρ [i/e/r], where Attic had retained the original long -α [aː], e.g. συμμαχίη [symmakʰíɛː] 'alliance' not συμμαχία [symmakʰíaː]. There is interesting confirmation of the widespread prestige of Great Attic in the fourth century BC in the fact that the incorporation of Attic characteristics applies not only to the inscriptions of original Ionic-speaking communities but also to those of foreign territories such as Caria (in south-west Asia Minor), where the ruling class had earlier adopted the Greek of the Ionian cities as its official language (cf. Brixhe (1987, 1993b)). In SIG 167 (367–54 BC), for example, which comprises three decrees of the Carian city of Mylasa, we still find a strongly Ionic foundation, but many Attic features already intrude (e.g. ἀτέλεια [atéleːa] 'freedom from taxation' for ἀτελίη [ateliːɛː]; οὐσίη [uːsíɛː] 'property' for ἐουσίη [euːsíɛː], though retaining the Ionic ending in -η [-ɛː]; genitive singulars of masculine 1st declension nouns in -ου [-uː] as well as Ionic -εω [-eoː], etc.).

It is typical of this infiltration process that it seems first to have affected 'small' grammatical words, where the process would have been largely subconscious, or to have involved the use of technical terminology in a legal or other institutional context in which earlier Athenian jurisdiction and continuing influence would have introduced and standardized the Attic forms.

Similar observations can be made about dialect inscriptions from other areas during the course of the fourth century, as the impact of Great Attic becomes steadily more visible through the encroachment of interference phenomena. We may note, for example, the use of Athenian legal terminology, albeit in dialect guise, such as ὑπόδικον [upódikon] 'liable to trial/forfeit' in IG XII 2 1, a monetary agreement in Lesbian between the city of Mytilene and Ionic-speaking Phocaea dating from the first half of the fourth century, or the appearance of typically Attic phraseology such as τῶν περὶ Πύρρωνα δαμιοργῶν [tôːn perì púrrhoːna daːmiorgôːn] 'the demiurgi (officials) under Pyrrhon', complete with Attic περί [perí] for local πάρ [pár], in an Elean inscription of 335 BC (Schwyzer 424). As the dominant position of Athens, politically and culturally, became increasingly apparent, more and more educated people became familiar with written Attic, official and literary, and this growing familiarity translated itself steadily into direct influence on the formal expression of official business in dialect inscriptions from all parts of the Greek-speaking world.

The particularly rapid convergence between Attic and Ionic at the official level must have been complemented by the fact that most of the subject peoples of the Athenian empire in the fifth century BC were Ionic speakers who had to deal routinely with Attic-speaking Athenian officials and with Athenian administrative documents composed in Attic. It was, furthermore, Athenian practice to send out colonies ('cleruchies') to imperial territories, where speakers of Attic and Ionic mixed freely. Conversely, many Ionic speakers inevitably had to come to Athens on business, and some took up residence there alongside other 'aliens' who had been drawn to what was emerging as the principal commercial and educational centre of the Greek world. The consequential changes in the city vernacular during the fifth century naturally prompted complaints from elderly conservatives about the degenerate state of the contemporary language (The Old Oligarch/(Xenophon) *Athenaion Politeia* 2. 7: cf. Cassio (1981)).

It should not, then, be surprising, given the close relationship between Attic and Ionic and the early onset of convergence set in train by Athenian administration, that Ionic should be the first of the classical dialects to disappear from the written record before the spread of Great Attic (Ionic is effectively defunct as an official dialect by *c.* 300 BC). We should not, however, forget that this expanded Attic had itself incorporated far-reaching Ionic influences in its own developmental phase, and that this was the form of Attic that was shortly to evolve into the Hellenistic Koine.

Chapter 4

Greek in the Hellenistic world

4.1 Introduction

During the latter half of the fourth century BC the kingdom of Macedonia became the controlling power in mainland Greece, and then, through the spectacular conquests of Alexander III ('the Great', 356–323 BC), acquired control of the whole of the eastern Mediterranean, including Asia Minor, Syria and Egypt, and finally extended its rule throughout the former Persian empire to the borders of India. Great new cities were founded in the conquered territories, most notably Alexandria in Egypt, Pergamum in Asia Minor, and Antioch in Syria, and Greek culture and language were spread as far as the plains of the Punjab.

Curiously there was no consensus in antiquity as to whether the Macedonians were themselves of Greek origin or not, with Herodotus perhaps in favour of the proposition (I.56, VIII.43) and Thucydides against (IV.124–7). But as the growing power of Macedonia under Philip II began to threaten the autonomy of the Greek city states in the fourth century BC, the argument became intensely politicized, and those who advocated a strong military response to the growing threat, such as the Athenian orator Demosthenes, were in no doubt that they were 'barbarians' (i.e. non-Greek-speakers, cf. *Olynthiacs* III 24). There is in fact evidence to suggest that Macedonian was not readily understood by most Greeks (e.g. Plutarch, *Alexander* 51 4), and this fact alone would distinguish it from the Greek dialects that were discussed earlier, since we never hear otherwise of Greeks being unable to understand one another. We should not, however, discount the possibility that what is being described in such sources as 'Macedonian' is in fact the language of Paeonian, Illyrian or Epirote subjects of the Macedonian king.

For what it is worth, the few fragments we have of what is alleged to be the Macedonian language suggest that it was either a highly aberrant Greek dialect or an Indo-European dialect very closely related to Greek, perhaps representing the speech of a group who had become detached from the majority of the invaders who, further south, eventually became speakers of Greek during the first half of the second millennium BC (cf. Chapter 1). It had, for example, apparently failed to undergo certain otherwise 'common' Greek sound changes, such as the de-voicing of the voiced aspirated series of plosives standardly reconstructed for Indo-European, but to have de-aspirated them instead. We therefore find Macedonian names such as $Bερ(ε)νίκη$ [ber(e)níkɛː] instead of $Φερενίκη$ [pʰereníkɛː] 'Bringer-of-victory', where the first element derives from the Indo-European root *bher-, 'bear/carry'.

For further discussion see Kalléris (1954/1976), Katičič (1976), Crossland (1982), and Sakellaríou (1983).

Whatever the truth of the matter, the Macedonian dialect/language clearly lacked the prestige necessary to serve as the linguistic and cultural concomitant to Macedonian imperial ambition. But Attic, as the dialect of the culturally dominant city of classical Greece, already widely in use outside its region of origin as a literary and administrative language, obviously suited the purpose. It was therefore natural that the Macedonian kings, in search of a 'civilization' to underpin their growing power, should have established the study of Classical Greek literature, much of it in literary Attic, as a central plank of their education system and adopted Great Attic as their own official language. Though this formally took place during the reign of Philip II (360/59–336 BC), the introduction of Greek civilization from the south had begun during the late fifth century BC, when the Athenian tragic poet Euripides, along with other famous artists of the period, had spent time at the court of king Archelaus. This Atticization of the Macedonian aristocracy was to be the crucial factor in the future history of Greek, since, continued Athenian cultural prestige notwithstanding, the emergence of Great Attic as a true national language (the Koine) would surely have been long delayed, or even prevented altogether, without the substitution of the military and political power of Macedonia for the declining influence of Athens.

Alexander's conquests ushered in the Hellenistic age, which is conventionally dated from his death in 323 BC to the battle of Actium in 31 BC, in which the forces of Mark Antony and Cleopatra VII, the last Greco-Macedonian monarch of Egypt, were defeated by Octavian, soon to be the first acknowledged Roman emperor with the title Augustus. It should be noted, however, that Roman involvement in the Greek world had begun much earlier (see the introduction to Chapter 5), and that a clear dividing line between the later Hellenistic and Roman periods cannot be drawn.

In the early Hellenistic period the conquered territories were divided into a number of hereditary monarchies, though a few well-established kingdoms in Asia Minor managed to retain their autonomy, notably Bithynia and Pontus on the southern shores of the Black Sea, and Cappadocia in central Anatolia. The major dynasties included the Antigonids of Macedonia, the Ptolemies of Egypt and the Seleucids of Syria and Persia. Since the Macedonian aristocracy had long been Atticized, the study of classical literature remained central to the Hellenistic education system, and the Koine or 'common' written language of the Hellenistic world, employed from the outset as an official language by the new Macedonian rulers of the East, was simply the product of the natural evolution of Great Attic within its extended new environment.

4.2   The Koine as an extension of Great Attic

Since it has been argued (Frösén (1974)) that the Koine was a creole that grew out of a putative Attic 'pidgin' used in the Athenian empire in the fifth century BC, it is important to stress that, quite apart from the inherent implausibility of such a pidgin in the Attic-Ionic context, where the dialects were not only mutually comprehensible but very closely related, all the empirical evidence points to its being essentially the established language of commerce, diplomacy, and officialdom, a variety distinct even from the Attic vernacular of the Athenian lower classes let alone the kind of pidgin put in the mouth of a Scythian archer by Aristophanes in the *Thesmophoriazousae* (cf. Brixhe (1990), Brixhe and Hodot (1993), López-Eire (1986, 1993)).

Thus the language of the decrees of the Macedonian kings is in practice indistinguishable from the 'evolved' Great Attic/Koine already familiar from the official inscriptions of a number of Greek cities outside Athens in the same period (see, for example, SIG 286, a treaty between Olbia, on the north coast of the Black Sea, and its mother city Miletus in Ionia, dated *c*. 330 BC). This is quite clear from an example such as the decree in (1) below (Nachmanson HGI 52), in which, after his victory over the Persians at the river Granicus in 334 BC, Alexander makes arrangements for the residents of Naulochum (the old port of the Ionian city of Priene in Asia Minor). The stone is fragmentary, though modern editors have supplied likely restorations for at least some of the lacunae:

(1) βασιλέως Ἀλ[εξάνδ]ρου. τῶν ἐν Ναυλόχῳ κ[ατοικούν]των ὅσοι μέν εἰσι
[Πριηνεῖ]ς αὐτο[νό]μους εἶναι [καὶ ἐλευθ]έρους, ἔχ[οντ]ας τήν τ[ε γῆν
κ]αὶ τὰς οἰκίας τὰς ἐν τ[ῇ π]όλει πά[σας] καὶ τὴν χώραν· ὅ[σο]ι [δὲ μὴ]
Πριηνε[ῖς, οἰκ]εῖ[ν ἐν κώμαις], αἷς ἂν δέω[νται αὐτοί]· . . . χώραν [γ]ινώσκω
ἐμὴν εἶναι. τοὺς δὲ κατοικοῦντας ἐν ταῖς κώμαις ταύταις φέρειν τοὺς φόρους·
τῆς δὲ συντάξεως ἀφίημι τὴμ Πριηνέωμ πόλιν, καὶ τὴμ φρου[ρὰ]ν . . .

[basiléoːs aleksándruː. tôːn   en naulókʰoːi katoikúːntoːn hósoi
of-king   Alexander.   of-those in Naulochum living   as-many-as

mén   eːsi prieːnêːs autonómuːs êːnai kaì eleutʰéruːs, ékʰontas téːn
on-the-one-hand are Prienians   autonomous to-be and free,   having   the

te gêːn kaì tàːs oikíaːs tàːs en têːi póleː páːsaːs kaì tèːŋ kʰóːraːn;
both land and the houses   those in the city all   and the country-estate;

hósoi   dè mèː prieːnêːs, oikêːn eŋ kóːmais, haîs àn déoːntai
as-many-as but not Prienians, to-live in villages, which ever they-request

autoí; . . .   kʰóːraːn giːnóːskoː emèːn êːnai. tùːs dè katoikûːntas en taîs
themselves; . . . estate   I-determine mine   to-be. those but living   in the

kóːmais taútais pʰéreːn tùːs pʰóruːs; têːs   dè syntákseoːs apʰíeːmi tèːm
villages these   to-pay   the tribute; from-the but contribution I-release the

prieːnéoːm   pólin, kaì tèːm pʰruːràːn . . .]
of-the Prienians city, and the garrison

'(Decree) of king Alexander. (I command that) all of those living in Naulochum who are Prienian citizens shall be autonomous and free, retaining both their land and all the houses in the city and their country estates; but all those who are not Prienian citizens shall live in whatever villages they themselves request; . . . I decree to be my own estate.

(I also command that) those living in these villages shall pay tribute; but I exempt the city of the Prienians from the contribution, and the garrison . . .'

The only clear marker of the Koine here is the use of γινώσκω [giːnóːskoː] for classical Attic γιγνώσκω [gignóːskoː], an originally Ionic form that had passed into the everyday/official written language of the Greek world but not into the more literary registers of Attic. Indeed, the documents of Macedonian officialdom are often hard to distinguish linguistically from those of contemporary Athens, displaying such characteristically Attic features as:

(2) (a) the change of *[aː] > [ɛː] except after ι/ε/ρ [i/e/r] (the change applies across the board in Ionic).

   (b) regular contraction of εα/εο [ea/eo] > η/ου [ɛː/uː] (often uncontracted in Ionic).

   (c) the conditional conjunction ἐάν/ἄν [eáːn/áːn] 'if' (Ionic has ἤν [ɛ́ːn]).

   (d) the gen. sg. of masc. a-stem (1st declension) nouns in -ου [uː] (Ionic has -εω [eoː]).

   (e) the gen. sg. of i-stem and eu-stem nouns in -εως [-eoːs] and -έως [-eóːs] respectively (cf. βασιλέως [basiléːs] above: Ionic often has -ιος [-ios] and -έος [-éos]).

   (f) the participle of the verb 'to be' is ὤν [óːn] (Ionic has ἐών [eóːn]).

   (g) the use of ἤνεγκα [ɛ́ːneŋka] as aorist of φέρω [pʰéroː] 'I carry' (Ionic has ἤνεικα [ɛ́ːneːka]).

   (h) the use of μείζων [méːzdoːn] 'bigger', κοινός [koinós] 'common', ἐκεῖνος [ekêːnos] 'that' (Ionic has μέζων [mézdoːn], ξυνός [ksunós], κεῖνος [kêːnos]).

Nonetheless, a number of 'local' Attic features are either missing, or of highly restricted occurrence in the administrative Attic used outside Athens/Attica, and Macedonian Attic is no exception. Thus in addition to the use of γινώσκω [giːnóːskoː] 'I know/judge', and γίνομαι [gíːnomai] 'I become', with the simplification of Attic -γν- [-gn-] mentioned above, we may also note:

(3) (a) preference for -σσ-/-ρσ- [ss/rs] over -ττ-/-ρρ- [tt/rr].

   (b) avoidance of contraction is common where it would produce an anomalous paradigm: e.g. ὀστέον [ostéon] 'bone' is preferred to ὀστοῦν [ostûːn], to maintain conformity with the regular paradigm of 2nd declension neuters in -ον [-on].

   (c) much regularization of once irregular verbs, by which the stem of the sg. is carried over to the pl.: e.g. οἴδαμεν [oídamen], etc. for ἴσμεν [ízmen] 'we know', after οἶδα [oîda] 'I know'; ἐδώκαμεν [edóːkamen], etc. for ἔδομεν [édomen] 'we gave', after ἔδωκα [édoːka] 'I gave', etc. (cf. 3.2).

   (d) more limited use of the optative mood (very widely employed not only to express wishes but also in a range of subordinate clauses in 'past-time' contexts in classical Attic).

Such traits, mainly of Ionic origin, represent simplifications or regularizations of their traditional Attic counterparts, and having passed into Great Attic during the course of the fifth and fourth centuries BC continued straightforwardly into the Koine. Even Athenian Attic assimilated some of these into its literary registers, and they eventually also began to appear, at first sporadically, in official Athenian documents as the prestige of Great Attic/Koine began to outstrip that of the local form of the dialect (cf. Chapter 3).

There is, however, one feature of the Koine which calls for special comment. A particular subset of words which had undergone first the Attic-Ionic shift of *[aː] > [ɛː] and then the Attic change of quantitative metathesis had produced an anomalous paradigm (the so-called 'Attic' declension); thus where most dialects had λαός [laːós] 'people', and ναός [naːós] 'temple', normal Attic had λεώς [leóːs] 'people', and νεώς [neóːs]. But Great Attic in part, and the Koine quite regularly, employ the former in preference to the 'genuine' Attic variants except when the words appear as the first element of compounds and no declensional difficulties arise. The reason once again is the desire to avoid morphological irregularity (regular 2nd declension masculine nouns end in -ος [os]). But while it is doubtless true that this represents the 'natural' selection of the 'majority' Greek forms against the 'parochial' Attic(-Ionic) ones, it does seem strange, given the general dialectal make-up of Great Attic/Koine, that the Ionic forms ληός [lɛːós], etc. were not adopted instead.

We should note here that a number of other words with original [aː] also find their way into the Koine without there being any parallel morphological justification. Examples include ὀπαδός [opaːdós] 'attendant', still used in Modern Greek, and various compounds involving the root of the verb ἄγω [ágoː] 'lead', such as ποδαγός/ὁδαγός [podaːgós]/[hodaːgós] 'guide', though these latter were employed alongside the corresponding 'Attic' forms with -η- [ɛː]. It is surely not accidental in this connection that the Attic tragedians also routinely employed the 'common' Greek forms of these particular words with [aː], and that some of them also appear later in Athenian comedy and prose (cf. Chapter 3). The conclusion seems inescapable that this set of items containing [aː], originally characteristic of a particular variety of literary Attic, and perhaps first borrowed from an earlier dramatic tradition of Dorian Sicily, had begun to find their way into ordinary speech and even official documents during the later fifth century BC (just like many of the Ionic-inspired simplifications in (3)), and that these had passed into Great Attic/Koine as being the 'Attic' forms that not only corresponded to majority dialect practice but in crucial cases avoided a parochial morphological anomaly. It is important to note that the Koine cannot have incorporated these words directly from West Greek or Aeolic sources, despite standard views to the contrary, since there is simply no reason why dialects which otherwise made no substantive contribution to the formation of the Koine should have been plundered for just this otherwise random set of words.

4.3 The impact and status of the Koine

What has been said so far has concentrated on the Koine as a written standard. It was, however, also increasingly spoken throughout the Greek world, first by the upper and middle classes as a common language of business and social interaction, and then more generally. The uniformity of the written Koine in its higher registers across a vast geographical area almost certainly implies a corresponding homogeneity in the speech of the Greek élite as far as lexicon, syntax and morphology are concerned, though we may safely assume that there were regional differences in pronunciation.

Within 'old' Greece this expansion of the Koine took place at the expense of the ancient dialects, written and spoken, while in the new Hellenistic kingdoms the Koine was from the first the only written standard, and the spoken language of the Greco-Macedonian aristocracy. It was soon learned widely by non-native speakers (though not always perfectly), and it inevitably shaped the development of spoken Greek among the colonists who went out from many different parts of Greece to populate the newly founded cities. It is essential, then, to see the Koine not only as the standard written and spoken language of the upper classes (periodically subject to influences from belletristic classical Attic), but also more abstractly as a superordinate variety standing at the pinnacle of a pyramid comprising an array of lower-register varieties, spoken and occasionally written, which, in rather different ways in the old and the new Greek worlds, evolved under its influence and thereafter derived their identity through their subordinate relationship to it (cf. Consani (1991, 1993)).

4.4 The fate of the ancient Greek dialects

4.4.1 Introduction

The Hellenistic monarchs controlled the international affairs of the Greek world and between them imposed centralized government on most of the old cities and their colonies. In 'old' Greece, therefore, an inevitable consequence of the routine conduct of business in the Koine, backed up by an education system based on the reading of 'classical' authors, was a steady decline in the status of the local dialects, which eventually became purely spoken varieties, characteristic of the uneducated population of remote areas, before finally dying out in late antiquity.

During the transitional period, however, even the middle and upper classes still spoke their local dialects at home, and also continued to write them for a time when dealing with local affairs. But the prevailing diglossia is manifested in the ever-growing Koine interference in dialect inscriptions of the era (cf. Bubenik (1989) for a recent study of the top-down 'Koineization' of the dialects). By Roman imperial times, written dialect had been largely abandoned, apart from 'revivals' (most notably in Laconia, cf. Bourguet (1927), and Lesbos, cf. Cassio (1986), Hodot (1990)) representing temporary elevations of spoken patois, perhaps under the stimulus of Roman imperial policy (essentially 'divide and rule').

4.4.2 Koineization: the case of Boeotian

The general situation is well illustrated by the collection of Boeotian manumission decrees dating from the third and second centuries BC. These grant freedom to slaves in return for a payment, the act of manumission often taking the form of a dedication or sale to the divinity of a local shrine who then serves as guarantor. As might be expected in the light of what has been said above, some of these documents are in dialect (as befits documents of purely local significance), some are in the Koine (as the 'standard' administrative language), and some are in a mixture of the two; unfortunately it is still very difficult to reconstruct the detailed socio-linguistics of this complex situation, and what is desperately needed, both for Boeotia and elsewhere, is a detailed analysis of the inscriptional corpora in the light of modern socio-historical studies (See now Vottéro (1996)).

A good example of the dialectally mixed category of inscription is provided by IG VII 3352 from Chaeronea:

(4) ... Διουκλεῖς κὴ Κωτίλα ἀντίθεντι τὰν Ϝιδίαν θρεπτάν, ἧ ὄνιουμα Ζωπουρίνα, ἱαρ[ὰν] τεῖ Σεράπει, παραμείνασαν αὐτεῖς ἇς κα ζῶνθι ἀνενκλείτως, τὰν ἀνάθεσιν ποιούμενει διὰ τῶ σ[ο]υνεδρίω κατὰ τὸν νόμον.

[... diuklê:s kè: ko:tíla: antíthenti tà:n widía:n threptán, hê: ónjuma
       Diocles   and Cotila   dedicate   the   their-own slave,   to-whom name

zo:purí:na:, hiarà:n tê: serápe:, paramé:na:san   autê:s   hâ:s ka:
Zopurina,   holy   to-the Serapis, remaining(acc. fem. sg.) with-them until ever

zô:nthi anenklé:to:s, tà:n anáthesin pojú:mene: dià   tô: sunhedrío:
they-live without-reproach, the offering   making(nom. pl.) through the council

katà   tòn nómon.]
according-to the law

'Diocles and Cotila dedicate their slave, whose name is Zopurina, to the safe keeping of Serapis, provided that she has remained in service with them blamelessly for as long as they live; they make this dedication through the council according to the law.'

A few words about the orthography of Boeotian inscriptions are in order at this point, since this contrasts sharply with Attic practice. The old Attic orthography had naturally been based on the speech of the Athenian aristocracy, and this remained the case after the adoption of the Ionic alphabet at the end of the fifth century BC (cf. Teodorsson (1974)). Subsequently the existence of a 'classic' literature (regarded as a Panhellenic possession), together with the widespread use of Attic outside Attica as a written language (for both creative writing and official business), resulted in an early conservative standardization of the orthography, so that even when sound change began to affect upper-class Athenian speech, the spelling conventions of what had become the written standard remained fixed according to classical precedent; it was clearly impossible, and in the case of classic texts undesirable, for the orthography to be adapted locally to reflect the pronunciation of all who used it.

By contrast, Boeotian, in the absence of any prestigious literary tradition or 'national' status, seems to have regularly adapted its orthography in line with sound change, both before and especially after the introduction of the Ionic alphabet (Morpurgo Davies (1993)). Accordingly, certain sound changes in Boeotian, some of which probably also characterized the lower registers of local Attic at roughly the same time (see Chapter 6 for details), are directly represented in official as well as private Boeotian inscriptions.

Particularly striking in (4) above are the monophthongization of /ai/ to /ɛː/, written -η- (e.g. in κή [kɛ́ː] 'and'), and the associated, chain-effect, raising of original /ɛː/ to /eː/, written -ει- (e.g. in Διουκλεῖς [diukléːs]). These are both features in which Boeotian seems to 'anticipate' developments in Attic and the Koine, though it may well be that the apparent time-lag has been exaggerated by the camouflaging effects of the standardized Attic orthography. Other typical Boeotian characteristics include:

(5) (a) the preservation of /w/, e.g. in Ϝιδίαν [widían].
   (b) the apocopation of prepositions/preverbs (as in ἀν-τίθε-ντι [an-títʰe-nti], where Attic would have ἀνα- [ana-]).
   (c) the preservation of original [t] in the 3pl.-suffix in the same form (where East Greek assibilated to [s]), and its occasional aspiration to [-tʰi] (e.g. in ζῶνθι [zôːntʰi] 'they live' (subjunctive)).
   (d) the use of the West Greek modal particle κα [kaː] (where East Greek uses ἄν [án]).
   (e) the monophthongization of original /oi/ to /eː/, as in masc. dat. pl. αὐτεῖς [autêːs].

The spelling change in (5)(e) began in the early second century BC and perhaps represents the completion of a series of shifts [-oi-] > [-øi-] > [-øː-] > [-eː-]. The letter υ is used to represent the penultimate stage in earlier Boeotian inscriptions.

Alongside these, however, there are also a number of Koine forms:

(6) (a) non-apocopated preverbs and prepositions are also used (e.g. in παρα-μείνασαν [para-méːnaːsan] and κατὰ τὸν νόμον [katà tòn nómon]).
   (b) original initial [zd-], written ζ-, had evolved to [z-] in the Koine but to [d-] in Boeotian; the Koine form appears in ζῶνθι [zôːntʰi].
   (c) the original form of the participle ποιούμενει [pojúːmeneː] was ποιε-όμενοι [poje-ómenoi]. In Boeotian antevocalic [e] was raised to [i] and then sometimes lost, giving ποι(ι)όμεν-υ/-ει [poj(i)ómen-øː/-eː], while in Attic/Koine [e] and [o] contracted to give [uː]; ποιούμενει [pojúːmeneː] is a conflation, involving a Boeotian pronunciation of the Koine form.

In general, it is easy to imagine how a higher education system involving the study of Attic authors combined with an ever greater use of the Koine for ordinary business transactions and administration to lead to the progressive adoption of Attic-style detail even in dialect writing and speech among the educated classes. Eventually the borderline between a version of Boeotian heavily influenced by the Koine and a local version of the Koine with residual Boeotian features and a local pronunciation was crossed; and a similar pattern of development can be traced throughout the areas of old dialect speech.

For the first time the notion of 'Greek', which hitherto had unified the dialects only as an abstraction, acquired a more or less concrete instantiation (cf. Morpurgo

Davies (1987)), and the local spoken dialects and their written variants came stead-ily to be subsumed under this unifying standard. True dialect writing thus dis-appeared, partly through erosion, but ultimately as a conscious choice in the face of the international prestige of the Koine and the diminished status of the local varieties. At the same time genuine dialect speech (as opposed to dialect-influenced Koine) became increasingly restricted to the illiterate population of country dis-tricts, and even there eventually succumbed, in varying degrees, to the irresist-ible influence of the common tongue. But the emergence of a standard should not blind us to the protracted existence of variably Koineized spoken varieties, and it is clear that many of the (rural) spoken dialects of modern Greek, in so far as these still survive as distinct variants beneath the 'umbrella' of standard modern Greek, descend ultimately from regional forms of the Koine that first emerged during the Hellenistic and Roman periods.

4.4.3 Doric Koines; Tsakonian

Some particularly strong dialect 'survivals' are worthy of mention at this point. In most Doric inscriptions we find evidence of Attic influence by the late fourth cen-tury BC, but there gradually evolved more standardized Doric varieties, stripped of major local peculiarities and with a non-haphazard (i.e. consciously selected) Attic/Koine admixture, which prevailed in official use in the last three centuries BC, and which can be viewed as temporary Dorian rivals to the Attic-based Koine of the period.

The first such Doric koine, based on the power of the island of Rhodes as the principal emporium of the eastern Mediterranean and major trading partner of Ptolemaic Egypt, was employed for a time in official documents throughout the southern Aegean islands in which Doric dialects were traditionally spoken. The second Doric koine was associated with the political activity of the Achaean league (*c.* 280–146 BC), a federation of Peloponnesian townships south of the Gulf of Corinth, which had been formed initially to resist the power of Macedonia but even-tually found itself appealing for Macedonian help against the Spartans. A similar situation prevailed in north-western Greece, where we find a parallel adaptation and standardization based on the North West Greek dialects, again with a controlled Attic/Koine mixture. The use of this written variety was again closely associated with the political power of a federation, this time the Aetolian league (*c.* 290–146 BC), whose purpose was also to achieve a degree of political independence from Macedonia, but which found itself fighting the Achaeans after they had enlisted Macedonian aid against Sparta.

These West Greek written standards are clear testimony to the exceptional under-lying tenacity of Doric speech and Dorian identity in the face of the spread of the Attic-based Koine. Indeed, we hear of dialect speakers well into the Christian era, particularly in Rhodes (Suetonius *Tiberius* 56) and the less accessible parts of the Peloponnese (Strabo 8. 1. 2, Dio Chrysostom *Orations* 1. 54, Pausanias 4. 27. 11). Though progressively Koineized as time went on, clear Doric substrate features, particularly lexical items and toponyms preserving the original -$\bar{a}$- [aː] in contexts where Attic/Koine has -η- [ɛː] (modern [i]), persist in the modern Greek dialects of a number of areas of traditional Doric speech (see Kapsoménos (1958: 26–31)).

The most striking example, however, is that of Tsakonian, spoken (though now exclusively in conjunction with standard modern Greek) in villages on the north-eastern slopes of Mount Parnon in the Peloponnese. Despite having undergone very considerable influence from the Koine and its later local descendants, this dialect has retained an unusually large number of features of ancient Laconian type (cf. Bourguet (1927), Pernot (1934), Kostákis (1951, 1980), Kapsoménos (1958), Kharalambópoulos (1980)), and we can perhaps see here a unique survival of the kind of intermediate phase that all other local dialects went through in antiquity before finally losing their identity to the Koine.

4.5 The Koine in the Hellenistic kingdoms

The establishment of Greek civilization in vast new territories demanded a high-prestige vehicle for its expression, a role which only Great Attic/Koine and its 'classical' literary counterpart could perform. This combination fulfilled an important unifying function, particularly for the Greco-Macedonian élite, by cementing in place the idea of a common Greek culture based on a common intellectual heritage expressed in a common Greek language. Furthermore, in territories without a Greek past, the top-down imposition of the Koine by the ruling dynasties and their aristocratic courts very quickly began to shape the development of new forms of Greek among the dialectally heterogeneous immigrant masses from old Greece, most of whom came from areas where dialects other than Attic and Ionic were spoken. Their native speech, uprooted by the simple fact of emigration, had no status in the new communities, and the result was a fairly rapid process of homogenization in which army service, where the Koine was the sole language of command, played a vital role. Thus written documents showing traces of the old dialects are exclusively early (e.g. Egyptian papyri of the fourth century BC, such as UPZ I 1), and it seems that the common language was widely adopted not only as a written but also as a spoken medium by the immigrant population during the course of the third century BC, though in the latter case almost certainly alongside native varieties for at least a time. Lines 87–95 in Theocritus' poem number XV, for example, strongly imply that a form of Doric was still used by the Dorian immigrants of Alexandria in the third century (see Ruijgh (1984) for an assessment of Theocritus's Doric).

Already spoken by the Greco-Macedonian élite and increasingly by the immigrant population as a whole, the Koine soon came to be used (with varying levels of competence) by sectors of the indigenous populations too, especially, but by no means exclusively, in the Hellenized cities. A knowledge of Greek was essential for employment in the army or the civil service, and doing any kind of business with Greek speakers presupposed at least a minimal command of the language. In this regard, we are fortunate that ancient papyri from Egypt (see below) provide us with a wide cross-section of text-types reflecting both formal and informal styles of composition by both Greeks/Macedonians and native Egyptians. While some are clearly the work of barely literate authors of non-Greek origin, the majority of the informal documents composed by and for Egyptians in Greek, despite the fact that they come from areas outside the capital, in fact display a surprisingly competent knowledge of the language, suggesting that Hellenization, including exposure to traditional education at a basic level, had progressed quickly and efficiently. Thus even those who have difficulties with the orthography, reflecting the widening gulf between classical spelling and contemporary speech in later periods, regularly control morphology, syntax and lexicon with some facility, and the differences between official and more informal private documents do not generally stem from imperfect knowledge, but simply reflect differences of stylistic level that are paralleled in other areas.

Thus Great Attic/Koine quickly shaped the development of a broad spectrum of subordinate spoken and written varieties. As the only official variety of Greek, it was the only form of the language worth learning, and all local vernaculars, whether reflecting regional dialects still spoken by incoming soldiers and tradesmen, or the product of interference between the Koine and native languages, were increasingly perceived as no more than substandard variants of the superordinate Koine. And once the Koine had become firmly established in the new territories, it naturally began to develop independently of the local Attic of Attica, which, in accordance with the loss of political power under Macedonian hegemony, and eventually even of cultural prestige in the face of the rise of the major new centres of learning such as Alexandria and Pergamum, itself came eventually to accept the 'common' forms involved.

4.6   The Koine as an official language

4.6.1   Introduction

While it is true that the education system encouraged classicizing tendencies in even official documents when these were designed to impress upon the world the achievements of an imperial dynasty or dealt with issues of national or international importance, the vast majority of official documents deal with more routine matters, and display a clear pattern of linguistic evolution in their own right, involving a continuous compromise between natural developments in the educated spoken language and a certain conservativism of usage characterized by traditional 'markers' of the official style, and permitting formulaic variants determined by 'genre' (e.g. imperial edicts, public proclamations, reports of official inquiries, judicial proceedings and petitions, contracts and tenders, official correspondence, etc.). Good examples of the official/business Greek of the Hellenistic period are provided by the collections of inscriptions from the great cities of Asia Minor, specifically: Magnesia (Kern (1900), Nachmanson (1903), Thieme (1906)); Priene (Hiller von Gärtringen (1906), Dienstbach (1910), Stein (1915)); Pergamum (Schweizer (1898)); and Miletus (Scherer (1934)). There is also Dittenberger's *Orientis Graeci Inscriptiones Selectae* (1903), while for Egypt we have a wealth of Ptolemaic, and later

Roman imperial, papyri (Grenfell, Hunt *et al.*, 60 volumes (1898–1994); a representative selection of the public documents is conveniently compiled in Hunt and Edgar (1934)).

Since the upper classes spoke a conservative variety of the Koine and the classical orthography remained unchanged, the spelling of these documents is much less revealing of phonological developments than that of the more heterogeneous private documents (cf. 4.11 and Chapter 6). Nonetheless, the beginnings of a gap between (classical) Attic and the official Koine in terms of grammar and lexicon can still be discerned from as early as the end of the third century BC, and this gap widens steadily as we pass into the later Hellenistic and Roman periods.

4.6.2 Macedonian Koine: the development of infinitival constructions

We may consider first the extracts in (7) from two letters of the Macedonian king Philip V, dated 219 and 214 BC respectively, to the city of Lárisa in Thessaly, and included in the text of a decree of that city (IG IX.ii.517):

(7) (a) ἐνεφάνιζόν μοι ὅτι καὶ ἡ ὑμετέρα πόλις . . . προσδεῖται πλεόνων οἰκητῶν·
  . . . ἐπὶ τοῦ παρόντος κρίνω ψηφίσασθαι ὑμᾶς ὅπως τοῖς κατοικοῦσιν
  παρ' ὑμῖν Θεσσαλῶν . . . δοθῆι πολιτεία.

  (b) πυνθάνομαι τοὺς πολιτογραφηθέντας κατὰ τὴν παρ' ἐμοῦ ἐπιστολὴν
  . . . ἐκκεκολάφθαι· εἴπερ οὖν ἐγεγόνει τοῦτο, ἠστοχήκεισαν οἱ
  συνβουλεύσαντες ὑμῖν . . . τοῦ συμφέροντος τῆι πατρίδι . . . ὅτι γὰρ
  πάντων κάλλιστόν ἐστιν . . . τήν τε πόλιν ἰσχύειν . . . , νομίζω μὲν οὐδ'
  ὑμῶν οὐθένα ἂν ἀντειπεῖν . . . πλ[ὴ]ν ἔτι δὲ καὶ νῦν παρακαλῶ ὑμᾶς
  ἀφιλοτίμως προσελθεῖν [πρὸς τὸ] πρᾶγμα καὶ τοὺς μὲν κεκριμένους
  . . . ἀποκαταστῆσαι εἰςς τὴν πολιτείαν, εἰ δέ [τινες] . . . μὴ ἄξιοί εἰσιν,
  περὶ τούτων τὴν ὑπέρθεσιν ποιήσασθαι . . . · τοῖς μέντον κατηγορεῖν
  τούτων μέλλουσιν προείπατε ὅπως μὴ φανῶσιν διὰ φιλοτιμίαν τοῦτο
  ποιοῦντες.

> [The transcription is an attempted reconstruction of the standard educated pronunciation of the period; full details of the phonological developments involved are given in Chapter 6].

[(a) enepʰánizón moi hóti kaì heː hymetéraː pólis . . . prozdîːtai pleónoːn
      they-revealed to-me that also the your   city . . . needs   more
oikeːtóːn; . . . epì tûː paróntos kríːnoː pseːpʰísastʰai hymâːs hópoːs toîs
inhabitants; . . . for the present I-judge vote(inf.)   you   that   to-the
katoikûːsin par   hymîːn tʰessalôːn . . . dotʰêː   politéːa.
living   among you   Thessalians   be-given(subjunctive) citizenship.

'They revealed to me that your city too needs more inhabitants; for the present I decree that you vote that citizenship be granted to those of the Thessalians living among you.'

(b) pyntʰánomai tùːs poliːtograpʰeːtʰéntas   katà   tèːm par emûː

I-discover   the   having-been-enrolled-as-citizens according-to the   from me

epistolèːn . . . ekkekolápʰtʰai; íːper   ûːn egegóniː tûːto, eːstokʰéːkiːsan

letter . . .   to-have-been-erased; if-indeed then had-happened this,   had-missed

hoi symbuːleúsantes hymîn . . . tûː sympʰérontos têː   patrídi . . . hóti gàr

the having-advised   you   the best-interests   for-the country . . . That for

pántoːn kállistón estin . . . téːn te pólin iskʰýiːn . . . , nomízoː mèn

of-all   best   is . . . (for) the both city to-be-strong . . . , I-think   on-the-one-hand

uːd   hymôn uːtʰéna àn   antiːpîːn . . . plèːn éti dè kaì nŷːn parakalôː

not-even of-you anyone   would deny . . .   So   still and even now I-call-upon

hymâːs apʰilotíːmoːs proseltʰîːn pròs tò prâːgma kaì tùːs mèn

you   without-ambition to-approach to   the matter   and the on-the-one-hand

kekriménuːs . . . apokatastêːsai iːs tèːm politéːan, iː dé tines . . . mèː áksioí

selected . . .   to-reinstate   to the   citizenship, if but any . . .   not   worthy

iːsin, perì   túːtoːn tèːn hypértʰesin pojéːsastʰai . . . ; toîs   ménton

are,   concerning these   the   postponement make . . . ;   to-those however

kateːgorîːn túːtoːn mélluːsin proíːpate hópoːs mèː pʰanôːsin   dià

to-condemn   these   intending tell   that   not   they-be-revealed for

pʰilotiːmíaːn tûːto pojûːntes.]

personal-ambition this   doing.

'I discover that those who had been enrolled as citizens in accordance with my letter have been erased from the register. If indeed this is the case, those who advised you failed to promote the best interests of your country. For I do not think any one of you would deny that it is best of all for the city to be strong. So I persist even now in calling upon you to approach the matter without personal ambition and to restore their citizenship to those who had been selected, while postponing judgement on those who are unworthy; warn those about to condemn these people, however, not to be found to be acting in this way for reasons of personal ambition.'

A number of 'post-classical' features are already in evidence here. The following are perhaps most worthy of comment:

(8) (a) the use of a prepositional phrase in place of a possessive adjective or the genitive of a personal pronoun, as in τὴν παρ' ἐμοῦ ἐπιστολήν [tèːm par emûː epistoléːn], lit. 'the from me letter', at the beginning of (7)(b); although the original source sense is still appropriate here, expressions of this kind lie behind the later 'simple possessive' use that is highly characteristic of the official Koine.

(b) The use of οὐθείς [uːtʰíːs] 'no one' in (7)(b) in place of classical οὐδείς [uːdíːs], the latter representing the product of the prehistoric compounding of οὐδὲ and εἷς [uːdè + hêːs] 'not-even + one': [uːdè hêːs] > [uːde(h)éːs] > [uːdéːs] > [uːdíːs]. The innovative form here originates with the semantic weakening and fresh composition that affected the fifth century Athenian revival of this same phrase in the emphatic sense 'not one': [uːdè hêːs] >

[uːd hêːs] > [uːt hêːs] > [uːtʰéːs] > [uːtʰíːs]. This replaces the classical form in Athenian inscriptions after 378 BC as a marker of 'Athenian' Attic, whence it passed for a time into Great Attic/Koine texts in recognition of the continuing prestige of Athens. Thereafter, Athenian Attic lost ground with the growth of the importance of the new Hellenistic cities and the classical form superseded it as the written standard in the Koine. After *c.* 60 BC this form was also reintroduced into Athenian inscriptions, in conformity with the now standard practice of the Koine.

(c) The verb πολιτογραφῶ [poliːtographôː] 'I enrol as a citizen', and the noun ὑπέρθεσις [hypértʰesis] 'postponement' are not attested classically; indeed the phrase ὑπέρθεσιν ποιεῖσθαι [hypértʰesin pojiːstʰai] is expressly criticized by the later Atticist Julius Polydeuces (Pollux) as a Koine cliché (9. 137). Evidently official business quickly spawned a jargon of its own.

(d) the occasional replacement of the classical accusative and participle construction after 'factive' verbs of knowledge and perception (i.e. those whose complements necessarily express facts, e.g. lit. *I know [him being in trouble]* = 'I know that he is in trouble') with the more common accusative and infinitive construction, as in the first sentence of (7)(b), though the latter is itself already under pressure from alternative markers of complementation.

Indeed, from the point of view of the later history of Greek, the most important issue here concerns the spread of complement structures containing finite verbs. In (7)(a), for example, the verb 'vote' is followed by a clause introduced by ὅπως [hópoːs] 'that', lit. 'how', + subjunctive. In classical Greek this construction was used to introduce a 'final' (purpose) clause, though the same conjunction could also be used with a future indicative after verbs of 'planning/organizing the future' (e.g. 'see to it [that/how X will happen]'). Though we might, by a simple extension, have expected the latter option after a verb such as 'vote', the classical language in fact used an infinitive, either alone ('vote [to X]') or with an accusative subject if this was distinct from the subject of the main verb ('vote [(for) X to do Y]').

A striking feature of the official Koine (and *a fortiori* of lower level compositions) is the decline in the use of such accusative + infinitive constructions, which were employed classically both to complement verbs of 'saying' etc. (still used, for example, in the first sentence of (7)(b)) and, as in the example under discussion, to express intended future outcomes after potential 'control' verbs (i.e. those whose subjects or objects may 'control' the interpretation of the unexpressed subject of an infinitival complement: e.g. *I intend to leave* means 'I intend that I leave', etc.). In the former type the alternative classical construction of ὅτι [hóti] 'that', + indicative eventually superseded the infinitival option, while in the latter type, as here, it was the 'final' construction that predominated.

This should be seen primarily as an internal simplification by which one type of subordinate complement clause (the accusative and infinitive construction) was gradually replaced in its two different functions by distinct, but already existing, constructions that were semantically more transparent. As a result, all subjects could be nominative, and the verbs of all subordinate clauses with an expressed subject could be finite, the choice between indicative and subjunctive being determined by the 'type' of main verb involved.

Infinitives remained standard, none the less, in cases involving true control relations (i.e. in which main and subordinate subjects were semantically identical, and no subject was expressed overtly in the subordinate clause). There was, however, a gradual advance even here of clauses with subjunctive verbs, beginning in late antiquity and continuing through the Middle Ages, with the result that in standard modern Greek the infinitive has disappeared altogether. The tracing of this process will be a major theme of the chapters that follow (cf. Joseph (1983) for a survey of the data and issues).

We might also note in passing the rather restricted use of participles in comparison with classical literary Attic. There the participle might well be described as the instrument of subordination *par excellence*, with virtually every type of clausal adjunct and even certain types of complement permitting, or in some cases requiring, a participial realization. Even the longest sentences therefore regularly contain relatively few finite verb forms in comparison their English translations. While there was no resistance to subordination as such in the official Koine, the use of participles in this function was considerably reduced in favour of clauses containing finite verbs introduced by conjunctions. Thus for the most part the participles in (7) are used with the article to form substantives (e.g. lit. *the having X-ed* = 'those who had X-ed', etc.), while participles with a subordinating function tend to be confined to 'circumstantial' function (though there are no examples in this particular extract). This could again be seen as a simplification of the grammar in favour of structures which avoided the frequently rather complex long-distance agreement requirements of participial adjuncts. Wider use of explicit conjunctions also promoted precision and clarity of expression in legal, technical and official documents.

4.6.3 The articular infinitive

There was, however, one particular non-finite alternative to classical participial syntax which combined much of the flexibility of the latter with the formal precision of finite alternatives, but also crucially avoided complex agreement patterns. This was the substantivized infinitive functioning as a gerund (lit. *the to-do X* = 'doing X'), typically governed by a preposition to impart a determinate sense to the expression, but also used alone in the genitive to express purpose (a usage perhaps derived from an adnominal origin, e.g. lit. *intention/plan/desire [of-the to-do X]*). This latter construction, in line with the weakening of the sense of the original final conjunctions in subjunctive clauses, was then employed simply as a 'strengthened' infinitive, used loosely as an exegetical adjunct or even as a complement after control-type verbs in rivalry with the ὅπως [hópoːs] + subjunctive construction.

In sharp contrast with the fate of the accusative and infinitive as a complement structure, the nominalized infinitival quickly became a stock feature of the Koine and, though based on a classical construction, soon acquired a frequency and range of usage that went well beyond the practice of classical prose writers. By way of illustration, consider the following extract from a letter of King Attalus II of Pergamum (Dittenberger (1903), no. 315 IV S.486), dated 159 BC and addressed to Attis, a priest of Cybele at Pessinus:

(9) Μηνόδωρος, ὃν ἀπεστάλκεις, τήν τε παρὰ σοῦ ἐπιστολὴν ἀπέδωκέμ μοι, οὖσαν ἐκτενῆ καὶ φιλικήν, καὶ αὐτὸς ὑπὲρ ὧν ἔφησεν ἔχειν τὰς ἐντολὰς διὰ πλεόνων ἀπελογίσατο. ἀποδεξάμενος οὖν τὴν παρὰ σοῦ αἵρεσιν διὰ τὸ θεωρεῖν ἐμ παντὶ καιρῶι σε πρόθυμον ὄντα πρὸς τὰ ἡμέτερα πράγματα καὶ αὐτὸς τούτωι ἅπερ ἐνόμιζον ἀναγκαῖον εἰδέναι σε κεκοινολογημένος εἴρηκα ἀναγγέλλειν.

[meːnódoːros, hòn apestálkiːs, téːn te   parà sûː epistolèːn apédoːkém moi,
Menodoros,   whom you-had-sent, the   both from you letter   gave   to-me,

ûːsan ektenêː kaì pʰilikéːn, kaì autòs hypèr   hôːn épʰeːsen ékʰiːn tàs
being long   and friendly,   and himself concerning what he said   to-have the

entolàs dià   pleːónoːn apelogísato.   apodeksámenos ûːn tèːn parà sûː
orders   through more-things he-gave-an-account. Having-accepted   then the   from you

haíresin dià   tò tʰeorîːn em pantì kairôːi se prótʰyːmon ónta pròs   tà
purpose   because-of the to-consider on every occasion you well-disposed being towards the

heːmétera práːgmata kaì autòs túːtoːi   háper enómizon anaŋkaîon
our   affairs   and myself to-this-man what I-thought (it) necessary

iːdénai   se kekoinologeːménos íːreːka   anaŋgéliːn.]
to-know (for) you having-discussed   I-have-told to-announce

'Menodoros, whom you sent, gave your long and friendly letter to me, and himself gave an account at length of the matters about which he said he had instructions. I accepted your proposal because I consider you to be well-disposed towards our affairs on all occasions, and I myself then discussed with him what I thought it necessary for you to know and told him to announce this to you.'

The key feature here is the long infinitival structure in the last sentence introduced by the preposition διά [diá] 'because of'. A writer of classical Greek would probably have used the participle θεωρῶν [tʰeoːrôːn] 'considering', agreeing with the subject of the sentence and preceded by the particle ὡς [hoːs] 'as', to show that a reason was being given. Here this has been replaced by a substantivized infinitive, which avoids the need for agreement, and conveniently retains the complement structure that the corresponding participle would have required. This construction became a favourite form of subordinate adverbial clause in the Hellenistic chancelleries, and was frequently used, by reason of its inherent compactness and precision, in preference even to finite alternatives. Its capacity to turn a complex proposition into an inflectable nominal expression was indispensable not only in legal/administrative contexts but also in abstract philosophical discourse (on which see 4.7), and its popularity persisted well into the Middle Ages.

4.7   Language and literature in the Hellenistic world: the place of the Koine as a literary dialect

4.7.1   Introduction

Some scholars deny the existence of a 'literary' Koine, and reserve the term for the continuum of non-literary varieties of Greek ranging from 'higher' written forms (attested in public and private documents of various kinds) to 'lower', spoken forms (used e.g. by traders and soldiers and, because freed from the normalizing effects of literacy, more prone to the influence of foreign languages and regional substrates). However, many prose authors of both Hellenistic and Roman imperial times, with the historian Polybius (*c.* 200–120 BC) and the essayist and biographer Plutarch (*c.* AD 46–120) among the best known examples, used a literary language distinct from the 'classical' Attic of Athenian authors of the fifth and fourth centuries BC which might fairly be regarded as an artistically 'developed' version of the Koine employed by the Hellenistic/Roman bureaucracies. Whether we choose to see this as a diluted variety of classical Attic or refer to it rather as a 'literary' version of the Koine is no more than a terminological issue.

4.7.2   Historiography: Polybius

To illustrate, we may take the example of the historian Polybius, who came from Megalopolis in Arcadia, a prominent member city of the Achaean league. When the Romans under the younger Scipio broke the power of Macedonia at the battle of Pydna in 169 BC (see 5.1), a number of prominent Achaeans, including Polybius, were taken to Rome. Initially a prisoner, Polybius soon became a friend of Scipio's, and wrote an account of Rome's imperial expansion in the conviction that this was to prove decisive for the future history of the world. His grammatical usage loosely follows that of the classical historians, with the optative, for example, still employed in ways which would already be unusual in contemporary official documents. Nevertheless its occurrence is clearly limited in comparison with classical practice, and we can see here the emergence of a distinction between classical Attic (studied in school) and even belletristic forms of the contemporary Koine. Typically the latter are characterized by a conservative compromise which preserves certain classical features as a mark of the literary style, but employs them in a more limited way that obliquely reflects their diminished status in contemporary speech and in writing of a more practical nature.

Such mild classicism apart, however, Polybius is very much a man of his times, both in his choice of vocabulary, which manifests a liking for the innovative abstract nominal formations characteristic of Hellenistic technical writing (see immediately below), and in his overall style, which exhibits the verbosity of the Hellenistic chancellery, most particularly in the complex sentence constructions which make characteristically heavy use of nominalized infinitives.

A number of other non-classical features are typical of the general evolution of the language at this time:

(10) (a) Extensive use of deictic pronouns to control discourse structure and to link complex sentences (cf. 4.7.7 on Menander and 4.7.8 on the Septuagint).

   (b) Some blurring of the formal distinction between the comparative and superlative degrees (with the article + comparative sometimes substituting for the latter).

   (c) A more restricted use of the dative case and a corresponding increase in prepositional phrase replacements, particularly in adverbial functions (temporal, comitative, causal and instrumental).

   (d) A more restricted use of certain participles, most particularly the future.

These traits all reflect developments in the contemporary spoken and written languages of educated discourse, and *a fortiori* in lower-level spoken varieties too, where they had already gone further. They are highly significant for the evolution of the language in later times, and we shall have occasion to mention them in other contexts below.

Alongside Polybius's many lexical and grammatical innovations, however, we also find words which from the point of view of classical Attic prose were 'old Ionic' or 'poetic', i.e. associated with poetry of an archaizing type such as tragedy, but which in reality had remained in current use in many spoken idioms outside Athens and now made their first appearance in prose writing. Many survive in modern Greek (albeit with modifications in their phonetic and sometimes their morphological form). Examples include:

(11) ἀσυλία [asylíaː] 'inviolability'
    δόλιος [dólios] 'crafty/deceitful'
    ζόφος [zópʰos] 'darkness'
    λαίλαψ [laílaps] 'storm/hurricane'
    ψαύω [psaúoː] 'touch'

4.7.3 The Koine as the language of 'technical' prose

Apart from its use in historiography, the written Koine, having evolved as an administrative language by combining an expanding technical vocabulary with a formal precision of style, proved to be a particularly good vehicle for philosophy, science and scholarship across a whole range of technical subjects. The great philosophical systems of Cynicism, Stoicism and Epicureanism all have their roots in the Hellenistic age, and the founding of the great library at Alexandria promoted editorial work on the manuscripts of ancient Greek authors and led to study of earlier forms of Greek, including its ancient dialects and the 'sources' and meanings of rare and unusual words in classical texts. Significant progress was also made in astronomy, geography, medicine and mechanics, much of this built on the brilliant mathematical foundations provided by figures such as Euclid (late fourth/early third centuries BC, origins unknown) and Archimedes (287–212 BC, from Dorian Syracuse in Sicily). An extensive scientific and philosophical vocabulary of some range and precision was already available from the earlier Ionic-Attic tradition, and this furnished the precedents of word-formation necessary for the coining of new terms for new concepts and technical innovations. It is not perhaps widely appreciated that much of the technical, scientific and abstract vocabulary of modern European languages in fact goes back ultimately (often via Latin calques) to the lexical inventiveness of the Hellenistic philosophers, mathematicians and scientists who used the Koine in their ground-breaking work.

4.7.4   Reaction against the Koine (1): Hellenistic poetry

But a universal prose language devoid of local roots and specifically adapted for administrative and scholarly purposes proved to be lacking in literary vitality and emotional resonance. In the context of a growing scholarly interest in the ancient literary dialects, the Hellenistic poets, among whom the third century BC contemporaries Callimachus, Apollonius and Theocritus are the greatest, rejected the Koine, and turned to the dialects and genres of early Greek literature in search of the 'character' that the Koine could not provide. This concrete expression of the artistic links between the old and the new Greek worlds reflects the beginnings of the problem of the 'burden of the past' created by a canonized corpus of classical literature, and resulted, for example, in Hellenistic epic in the language of Homer, Hellenistic epigrams in the language of early Ionian poetry, and even Hellenistic imitations of the Lesbian poets Sappho and Alcaeus, though always with subtle variations of phraseology and imaginative innovations in content and approach as well as in lexicon and style.

A striking example of Alexandrian inventiveness is provided by Theocritus, who *inter alia* elevated the traditional singing of shepherds into the literary genre of pastoral poetry through the juxtaposition of epic metre with rustic subject matter, and employed for the purpose a Doric dialect (recall the tenacity of Doric in many rural areas) which was based partly on literary precedent but which also reflected, albeit in the oblique fashion of the literary dialects of the classical period, aspects of contemporary spoken varieties (including perhaps that of the Doric-speaking community of Alexandria, drawn largely from the old city of Cyrene to the West, cf. Ruijgh (1984)).

This approach was possible because such literature was written by and for an urban élite which, largely excluded from political activity, had turned instead to the great libraries and the study of the roots of their culture. Creative writing soon became immensely learned and allusive, with its practitioners seeking novelty and strangeness in hitherto underexplored subject matter, in arcane mythology and in the examination of personal relationships. But perhaps most importantly from our point of view, the careful editing and preservation of classical texts, in prose as well as verse, raised for the first time serious questions to do with the determination of linguistic 'correctness' in the context of an awareness of earlier linguistic diversity and subsequent language change, and thus prompted serious consideration of issues of grammar and lexicography from a non-philosophical and non-rhetorical point of view (see Matthews (1994) for a recent survey). The essentially retrospective approach of the tradition of prescriptive grammar, with rules based on the usage of the 'best' authors of earlier 'classical' periods, derives ultimately from the philological work of this era, and the resultant prioritizing of traditional forms of the written language was soon to have enormous consequences for the history of the Greek language (see 5.4).

4.7.5 Reaction against the Koine (2): Asianism and Atticism

The role of rhetoric also changed in post-classical times. Although a well-crafted appeal to the autocratic rulers of the Hellenistic world might still make an impact on the course of events, few were in a position to take advantage of such opportunities, and the cultivation of eloquence became primarily an educational objective. The relevant techniques were learned and practised in the classroom through the study of classical Attic models as part of the process of familiarizing the élite with the tradition that gave the Hellenistic world its cultural cohesion.

During the course of the third century BC, however, there was a reaction against the symmetrical periods and easy intelligibility of the Isocratean style, motivated in part by a desire for something fresh in the face of the uniformity engendered by an increasingly rigid approach to the teaching of composition and the strict conventions of official discourse. As with poetry, so with rhetoric, this reaction took the form of a creative revival of the past, and the Asianic school (so called because it began in Asia Minor) was characterized by the abandonment of the traditional period and a return to Gorgianic precepts (cf. Chapter 3), involving the emotive accumulation of vocabulary and rapid successions of short antithetical clauses with a heavy emphasis on metaphor, word play, 'poetic' vocabulary, and contrived rhythmic and phonetic effects. Asianism blossomed, and influenced other forms of literary composition and eventually even official writing, with the long inscription of Antiochus I of Commagene (Dittenberger (1903), *Orientis Graeci Inscriptiones* I. 383) standing as a major example in the latter category of the 'lofty' pretensions of the Asianic style.

The inevitable counter-reaction to the often overwrought vacuousness of much Asianically inspired composition set in during the first century BC in the form of a return to the classical models that Asianism had supplanted. This new Atticist movement was dedicated to the re-establishment of the practice, and above all the language, of the 'best' writers of classical Attic, and its impact was to be both profound and lasting, not only in the field of rhetoric but in all literary composition thereafter. Where earlier historians like Polybius had settled for a practical compromise between the classical Attic of the writers studied and the usage of the contemporary Koine, the ideologues and devotees of revivalist Atticism modelled their style and usage directly on that of the authors of ancient Athens. This crucial development in the history of written Greek marks the beginning of the diglossia that plagued attempts to develop a standard form of modern Greek in the nineteenth and twentieth centuries (cf. Chapters 5 and 17).

4.7.6 'Popular' literature: romances

The Hellenistic world was not, however, exclusively a locus of scientific enquiry, scholarship, and élitist literary experimentation. Other, more popular, literary forms also flourished, most notably the prose romance. Its two stock themes are travelling adventures, usually with a fabulous dimension, and the passion of love, and the appearance of a new genre binding these two thematic elements together was in many ways a natural reaction to the times. Just as the new philosophical systems of Stoicism and Epicureanism emerged as ways of coping intellectually with individual powerlessness in a world where the scope for political action lay exclusively in the hands of autocrats, so the romance, by focusing on foreign/imaginary lands and idealized images of constancy in the face of the arbitrariness of fate, emerged as a response to the need for escapism and as a reflection of the renewed importance of personal loyalty.

Though substantial fragments of a number of Hellenistic romances, most notably the *Ninus Romance* (dating probably from the second century BC), are now known to us thanks to the relatively recent discovery of ancient papyri, preserved in the desert sand by the dry Egyptian climate, the best-known examples (Chariton's *Chaireas and Callirhoe*, Heliodorus' *Aethiopica*, Longus' *Daphnis and Chloe*, and Xenophon of Ephesus' *Ephesiaca*) belong to the period of the Roman empire. There is, however, a clear linguistic distinction between Chariton's polished literary Koine and the increasingly elaborate artificiality of the language of the other romances, and on the basis of this evidence it seems that, 'popular' content notwithstanding, they were designed primarily for the entertainment of an educated audience, familiar with the classical language and equipped with a rhetorical higher education (see Chapter 5 for a full account of the impact of Atticism on the Greek literature of the Roman empire).

4.7.7 Drama: the 'new' Attic comedy

A great deal of other, previously unknown, material of a broadly 'popular' character, and composed in a more natural form of language, has also become known from papyrus discoveries. The importance of the non-literary documents will be discussed below (Chapter 6). Of particular interest in the present context are Athenian New Comedy and the fragments of a kind of urban music-hall tradition based on the traditional mime, a dramatic portrayal of some aspect of daily life, associated originally with the Greek west, and first developed into a distinct literary form in the fifth century BC by Sophron of Syracuse. These will be considered briefly in turn.

In the wake of Alexander's conquests the city of Athens, remote from the new economic and commercial centres, soon lost its pre-eminence. Political decisions were now taken by a Macedonian governor, and, with the abandonment of the democratic practice of public payment for attendance at the assembly and law courts, social divisions increased dramatically. The drift of power to the east also diminished the opportunities for enterprise and the acquisition of capital, and what wealth remained was increasingly invested in land and property as the best guarantee of steady value. The rentier class therefore came to control the residual public life of the city, and the social and political ties that had bound the classical polis together were replaced by a culture of individualism. Thus whereas the Old

Comedy of Aristophanes had been intensely political, and targeted at prominent individuals, the New Comedy of Menander (*c.* 342/1–291/290 BC) focused on the 'dramas' of middle-class family life, revealing little of the external chaos of the times, and we move from a world of political satire to a form of situation comedy.

Menander's language reflects the contemporary development of spoken Greek in Attica, with the style carefully adapted to the age, social status and gender of speakers (a feature much admired in antiquity, cf. Quintilian 10. 1. 69 and 71). But the fact that he could not be regarded as a reliable example of 'pure' (i.e. classical) Attic was damaging to the preservation of his plays once the Atticist revival came to dominate attitudes to language, and our knowledge of them therefore depends exclusively on papyrus discoveries. A comparison with the (non-parodic) dialogue of Aristophanes provides a good measure of the extent of the changes over two centuries, and what we find is a 'local' form of Attic that reveals the contemporary state of the spoken language in Attica as a variety which is rather more conservative than the 'international' Attic/Koine of the Hellenistic world at large.

Features of Menander's language (ultimately, mainly of Ionic origin, cf. Chapter 3) that reflect the contemporary development of the Koine include:

[The phonetic transcriptions in what follows are an attempt to reconstruct the likely conservative/upper-class pronunciation of Attic in Attica in the late fourth century, cf. Teodorsson (1974, 1978) for details, and see Chapter 6.]

(12) (a) Absence of the dual number (used routinely in Aristophanes).
   (b) The parallel use of οὐδείς [uːdíːs] and οὐθείς [uːtʰíːs] 'no one', perhaps reflecting the use of both as spoken forms in the period (cf. 4.6.2, (8)(b)).
   (c) A tendency for declensionally anomalous nouns to be replaced with regular synonyms, e.g. 2nd declension neuter πρόβατον [próbaton] 'sheep' for irregular 3rd declension οἶς [oîs], etc.
   (d) The routine use of regularized (sub)paradigms of many irregular verbs in -μι [-mi], a sporadic feature already apparent in fifth-century literary works under the impact of Ionic, but now standard: e.g. ἔθηκαν [étʰeːkan] 'they put (aorist)' for ἔθεσαν [étʰesan], δεικνύω [diːknýoː] 'I show' for δείκνυμι [díːknyː-mi], etc.
   (e) The replacement of the old Attic γίγνομαι [gígnomai] 'I become', γιγνώσκω [gignóːskoː] 'I (get to) know' with forms beginning γιν- [giːn-].
   (f) The beginnings of the breakdown of the functional distinction between the aorist (past perfective) and perfect (originally expressing the present relevance of a past action, especially a resultant state).

On the other hand, many features reveal a slightly 'retarded' process of development in comparison with contemporary Koine:

(13) (a) The optative disappeared quickly in non-literary registers, except in its 'core' meaning of expressing a wish, because its classical use in subordinate clauses in past-time contexts was often semantically opaque, as in

reported speech, or already subject to replacement by subjunctives, as in final clauses; various modal auxiliaries were also available to take on the sense of possibility which, in conjunction with the particle ἄν [án], it conveyed in main clauses. Menander, however, still employs the optative quite regularly in all its traditional functions, though overlaps with the subjunctive are more common than in classical Attic.

(b) Where the Koine fully regularized the paradigm of οἶδα [oîda] 'I know', Menander has 2nd sg. οἶσθας [oîstʰas] rather than οἶδας [oîdas] for original οἶσθα [oîstʰa]; this semi-regularizing 2nd sg. -ς [-s] is also added to ἦσθα [êːstʰa] 'you were', where the Koine increasingly favoured the fully regularized ἦς [êːs].

(c) In classical Attic the middle and passive voices were morphologically distinguished only in the aorist and the future. In the Koine, the endings of the aorist middle (-(σ)άμην [-(s)ámeːn], -όμην [-ómeːn], etc.) were increasingly replaced by those of the aorist passive (-(θ)ην [-(tʰ)eːn], etc.), but the original forms are routinely retained by Menander (e.g. ἐγενόμην [egenómeːn] 'I became', ἀπεκρινάμην [apekrinámeːn] 'I answered').

As an example of Menander's style we may consider the following extract from the *Dyscolus* (370–82), involving an interchange between Sostratos (a wealthy young man in love), Gorgias (a young peasant farmer), and Daos (Gorgias' slave):

(14) So: ἕτοιμος πάντα πειθαρχεῖν· ἄγε.   370
Go: τί κακοπαθεῖν σαυτὸν βιάζῃ;
Da: βούλομαι
ὡς πλεῖστον ἡμᾶς ἐργάσασθαι τήμερον,
τοῦτόν τε τὴν ὀσφῦν ἀπορρήξανθ' ἅμα
παύσασθ' ἐνοχλοῦνθ' ἡμῖν προσιόντα τ' ἐνθάδε.
So: ἔκφερε δίκελλαν.   375
Da: τὴν παρ' ἐμοῦ λαβὼν ἴθι.
τὴν αἱμασιὰν ἐποικοδομήσω γὰρ τέως
ἐγώ· ποιητέον δὲ καὶ τοῦτ' ἐστί.
So: δός.
ἀπέσωσας.
Da: ὑπάγω, τρόφιμ'· ἐκεῖ διώκετε.
So: οὕτως ἔχω γάρ· ἀποθανεῖν ἤδη με δεῖ
ἢ ζῆν ἔχοντα τὴν κόρην.   380
Go: εἴπερ λέγεις
ἃ φρονεῖς, ἐπιτύχοις.

[*So*: hétoimos pánta   piːtʰarkʰîːn; áge. / *Go*: tí   kakopatʰîːn sautòn
      Ready   in-all-things to-obey;   come-on.   Why to-suffer   yourself

biázdeː? / *Da*: búːlomai hoːs plîːston heːmâːs ergásastʰai téːmeron, tûːtón
you-force?   I-wish   as   most   us   to-work   today,   him

te tèːn ospʰŷːn aporréːksantʰ háma   paúsastʰ enokʰlûːntʰ heːmîːn
and the back   having-sprained at-the-same-time to-stop   pestering   us

prosiónta t   ent^{h}áde. / *So*: ékp^{h}ere díkellan. / *Da*: tè:n par emû:
coming   and here.   Bring-out mattock   The from me

labò:n   ít^{h}i. tè:n haimasjàn epoikodomé:so: gàr téo:s   egó:; poe:téon
having-taken go. The dry-stone wall I-shall-build-up   for meanwhile I;   to-be-done

dè kaì tû:t estí. / *So*: dós. apéso:sas. / *Da*: hypágo:, tróp^{h}im; ekî:
and also this is.   Give. You-saved.   I-go,   master;   there

dió:kete. / *So*: hú:to:s ék^{h}o: gár. apot^{h}anî:n é:de: me dî: è: zdê:n
follow.   Thus   I-am for. To-die   now   me it-is necessary or to-live

ék^{h}onta tè:n kóre:n. / *Go*: í:per   légi:s hà p^{h}ronî:s, epitýk^{h}ois.]
having the girl.   If-indeed you-say what you-mean, may-you-succeed.

'*So*: I'm ready to do all I'm told. Come on.   *Go*: Why force yourself to suffer?   *Da*: [*aside*] I want us to do as much work as possible today and for him to sprain his back while he's at it so he stops coming here and pestering us.   *So*: Bring out a mattock.   *Da*: Take mine and go ahead. Meanwhile I'll build up the dry-stone wall. That needs doing too.   *So*: Hand it over. You've saved my life... *Da*: I'm off, young master. Follow me on there.   *So*: ... for this is my position. I must now die in the attempt or win the girl and live.   *Go*: If you mean what you say, good luck to you.'

Note the heavy use of personal and demonstrative pronouns, in conformity with the naturally deictic/vivid character of dialogue, and the comparative rarity and frequently odd placement of the 'second position' connective and discourse particles so typical of elaborated classical Attic (cf. γάρ [gár] as fourth word in l. 376, emphasizing the preceding verb). While we may safely assume that tone of voice and context could do much in a dramatic interchange to supply the information provided explicitly by particles in a more discursive style, it is surely no accident that the later history of Greek in its lower-level spoken and written forms provides eloquent testimony to the decline of these elements.

Other features of the colloquial style include the frequent elision of final -αι [-ai] (cf. παύσασθ(αι) [paúsast^h(ai)] in l. 374), the use of prepositional phrases to express possession in place of possessive adjectives or the genitives of personal pronouns (cf. τὴν παρ' ἐμοῦ [té:n par emû:] l. 375, cf. 4.6.2, (8)(a)), and the use of ὑπάγω [hypágo:] and διώκω [dió:ko:] to mean simply 'go' and 'follow' rather than 'advance/withdraw slowly' and 'pursue'. This use of the former is already attested in Aristophanes (cf. *Birds* 1017), and is the source of Modern Greek πάω ['pao] 'go'; the use of 'expressive' words in 'simple' meanings is, of course, typical of colloquial speech.

The local Attic character of the language is also well illustrated by the use of τήμερον [té:meron] in l. 372 rather than σήμερον [sé:meron] 'today'; -ττ- [-tt-] is also routinely preferred to -σσ- [-ss-] in words such as τέτταρα [téttara] 'four', where the penultimate a-vowel is also local Attic, the Koine normally employing Ionic τέσσερα [téssera].

Turning now to the later Hellenistic period and the mime, one particular adaptation of the genre is now familiar from the work of the third-century poet Herodas, who, in characteristic Alexandrian fashion, combined its low-life subject matter with the dialect (Ionic) and metre ('limping' iambics, i.e. with a final spondee) of Hipponax, a vitriolic poet of the sixth century BC. But there seems to have been a great diversity of such mimetic presentations, reflecting a wide variety of folk-loric traditions and involving both songs and spoken pieces, prose and verse, mono-logue and scenic performance.

A good example is provided by the fragments of a farce (D. L. Page, *Literary Papyri* (1950: no. 76)), written in vaguely rhythmical prose with verse interludes, which are contained in a papyrus of the second century AD, but which perhaps belongs in origin to a somewhat earlier period (the original editors, Grenfell and Hunt, placed it in the second/first century BC (1903: 41 ff.)). It appears to be a parody of Euripides' play *Iphigenia in Tauris* in which a Greek girl, Charition, is living against her will among Indians. Her friends eventually succeed in rescuing her after various ludicrous complications, the whole being punctuated (somewhat incomprehensibly) by the persistent farting of a clown. The language is of a ver-nacular character and is characterized by the presence of a number of decidedly 'modern-looking' features, including:

(15) (a) The use of θέλω ['tʰelo] 'I want', with a 'bare' subjunctive complement when the subject of the complement clause is distinct from that of the main clause (ll. 21–2), alongside the classical infinitival construction when like subjects are involved (l. 57). As noted for the official Koine, this development (with or, as here, without a conjunction) marks the begin-ning of the replacement of the infinitive as a complement to 'control' verbs like 'want/expect', initially involving cases where a distinct (accus-ative) subject had to be specified.

(b) The use of λοιπόν [ly'pon] (l. 59) as a sentence connective meaning 'so/well then' (literally and originally 'as for the rest') in very much the modern Greek way.

[There is evidence that a number of major sound changes had gone through in the speech of the majority of Greek speakers by *c.* 150 BC, and these are reflected in the phonetic transcription here and in subsequent sections: these include loss of distinctive vowel length, the related shift from a pitch to a stress accent, the monophthongiza-tion of all diphthongs with [-i] as their second component, and the development of a fricative articulation [ɸʷ/βʷ], later [f/v], for the second element of diphthongs ori-ginally ending in [-u]; double consonants tend to be simplified, and voiced plosives are beginning to develop fricative articulations. See Chapter 6 for a full summary.]

4.7.8 Jewish literature: the Septuagint

This Greek translation of the Old Testament, made in the third–second centuries BC, constitutes one of our most important examples of surviving 'vernacular' lit-erature of the period. By the third century the majority of the Jews of Ptolemaic Egypt (perhaps as many as one million, cf. Philo *In Flacc.* 43) had Greek as their mother tongue, and it was judged essential that they should have a translation of their holy scriptures if knowledge of them was not to be confined to an increasingly narrow circle. The work was supposedly entrusted to a team of 72 scholars summoned from Jerusalem and is accordingly known as the Septuagint (*septuaginta* is Latin for '70').

Given the nature of the material, the translation in general reflects neither the Greek literary tradition nor the preoccupations of the rhetoricians. It was once thought that the considerable differences between the Greek of the Septuagint and the literary Greek of the mainstream tradition were due to Semitic substrate and translation effects, but while it is undeniable that, as a close translation of a sacred text, it embodies Hebraisms (especially where the obscurity or formulaic language of the original led to literalness), the analysis of the language of contemporary documents from Egypt has demonstrated conclusively that its general grammatical and lexical make-up is that of the ordinary, everyday written Greek of the times. It therefore constitutes an important source of information for the development of the language in the Hellenistic period, with the translation of the Pentateuch, for example, reflecting a very natural contemporary Koine (Thackeray (1909: 13)). Certain other books, however, display a mechanical literalness (e.g. Lamentations), while others exemplify a spread ranging from near-vernacular (e.g. Tobit, from the Apocrypha) to consciously 'literary' (e.g. Esther, with 4 Maccabees being positively Atticizing).

The following extracts from the Second Book of Kings (18. 17–21) provide a good example of the 'normal' Koine style:

(16) 17. καὶ ἀπέστειλεν βασιλεὺς Ἀσσυρίων ... τὸν Ῥαψάκην ... πρὸς τὸν βασιλέα Ἐζεκίαν ἐν δυνάμει βαρείᾳ ἐπὶ Ἰερουσαλήμ ... 18. καὶ ἐβόησαν πρὸς Ἐζεκίαν, καὶ ἦλθον πρὸς αὐτὸν Ἐλιακείμ ... καὶ Σόμνας ... 19. καὶ εἶπεν πρὸς αὐτοὺς Ῥαψάκης, Εἴπατε δὴ πρὸς Ἐζεκίαν, τάδε λέγει ὁ βασιλεὺς ὁ μέγας βασιλεὺς τῶν Ἀσσυρίων, "Τί ἡ πεποίθησις αὕτη ἣν πέποιθας;" 20. εἶπας ... "Βουλὴ καὶ δύναμις εἰς πόλεμον·" νῦν οὖν τίνι πεποιθὼς ἠθέτησας ἐν ἐμοί; 21. νῦν ἰδοὺ πέποιθας σαυτῷ ἐπὶ τὴν ῥάβδον τὴν καλαμίνην τὴν τεθλασμένην ταύτην, ἐπ᾿ Αἴγυπτον· ὃς ἂν στηριχθῇ ἀνὴρ ἐπ᾿ αὐτήν, καὶ εἰσελεύσεται εἰς τὴν χεῖρα αὐτοῦ καὶ τρήσει αὐτήν· οὕτως Φαραὼ βασιλεὺς Αἰγύπτου πᾶσιν τοῖς πεποιθόσιν ἐπ᾿ αὐτόν.

[17. ke a'pestilen basi'leɸʷs asy'rion ... ton r̩a'psakęn ... pros ton

    And sent   king   of-Assyrians ... the Rab-shakeh ... to   the

basi'lea heze'kian en dy'nami ba'rẹa e'pi jerusa'lẹm ... 18. k(e)

  king   Hezekiah   in force   heavy against Jerusalem   And

e'boẹsan pros heze'kian, k(e) 'ẹltʰon pros aɸʷ'ton elia'kim ... ke

  they-shouted to Hezekiah, and came   to   him   Eliakim ...   and

'somnas ... 19. ke 'ipen pros aɸʷ'tus r̩a'psakẹs: ''ipate dẹ   pros

Shebna ...   And said to   them   Rab-shakeh 'Tell   indeed to

heze'kian, 'tade   'leji o basi'leɸʷs o 'meɣas basi'leɸʷs asy'rion,

Hezekiah, these-things says the king   the great   king   of-Assyrians:

"ti hẹ pe'pøtʰẹsis 'haɸʷtẹ hẹn 'pepøtʰas?" 20. 'ipas ... , "bu'lẹ ke

"what the confidence   this   which you-trust?"   You-said ...   "counsel and

'dynamis is 'polemon;" nyn un 'tini   pepø'tʰos e̦'tʰete̦sas   en e'mø?
strength   for war;"   now then in-whom trusting   you-refused-assent in me?

21. nyn i'du 'pepotʰas saɸʷ'to   e'pi te̦n 'r̥abdon te̦n kala'mine̦n te̦n
     Now look you-trust   for-yourself on   the staff   the of-reed   the

tetʰlaz'mene̦n 'taɸʷte̦n, ep 'ejypton; hos an ste̦ri'kʰtʰe̦ a'ne̦r ep aɸʷ'te̦n, ke
bruised   this,   on Egypt;   who ever leans   man on it,   and

ise'leɸʷsete is te̦n 'kʰira aɸʷ'tu ke tre̦si   aɸʷ'te̦n; 'hutos pʰara'o
it-will-enter   into the hand of-him and it-will-pierce it;   thus Pharaoh

basi'leɸʷs e'jyptu 'pasin tøs pepø'tʰosin ep aɸʷ'ton.']
king   of-Egypt for-all the trusting   on him.'

'17. And the king of Assyria sent . . . Rab-shakeh . . . to king Hezekiah with a heavy
force against Jerusalem . . .   18. And they shouted to Hezekiah, and Eliakim . . . and
Shebna . . . came to him (Rab-shakeh).   19. And Rab-shakeh said to them: "Tell
Hezekiah (that) the king the great king of Assyria speaks thus, 'What is this confidence
in which you trust?'   20. You say . . . , 'Counsel and strength for war'; in whom then
do you place your trust in refusing to accede to my will?   21. Look, you trust now
on your own behalf in this staff of bruised reed, in Egypt; if any man leans on it, it
will enter his hand and pierce it through; such is Pharaoh king of Egypt for all those
who place their trust in him."'

Since a comprehensive treatment of phonological developments in the Koine is
provided in Chapter 6, the following observations are confined to points of grammar and lexicon. The simple paratactic style is at once apparent; although this certainly reflects the organization of the original, it is also characteristic in some
degree of all mid- to low-level writing in the Koine, and in fact constitutes a feature
of unsophisticated language throughout the history of Greek. The only probable
Semitism here (i.e. feature of Hebrew wholly alien to Greek) is the 'redundant' use
of καί [ke] 'and', to introduce the main clause of the second sentence in para. 21
(cf. also the discussion of New Testament Greek in Chapter 5).

Compared with classical Greek, there is again a marked increase in the use of
pronouns in positions where the literary language would permit, indeed almost
require, an ellipsis, the sense being the obvious one in context. We may note again
the penultimate sentence of 21, which contains the possessive αὐτοῦ [aɸʷ'tu],
referring as a bound variable to any man who leans on the staff, and the direct
object αὐτήν [aɸʷ'te̦n], referring to such a man's hand, introduced as the object of
a preceding verb. Already apparent in Menander (cf. 4.7.7, discussion of (14)), this
becomes the normal usage of colloquial Greek henceforth.

Also noteworthy is the decline in the range of the dative (cf. Polybius' usage at
even the highest levels, 4.7.2, (10)(c)), a development most apparent here in the use
of prepositional phrase replacements after verbs of 'saying', 'trusting' and 'dis-
obeying'. Note in this connection that a particular feature of the ordinary Koine in
this and the immediately following period is the widespread use of ἐν [en] + dative
as a semantically 'empty' means of strengthening the flagging dative in a variety
of functions (e.g. comitative in para. 17, simple verbal complement to ἠθέτησας
[e̦'tʰete̦sas] in para. 20). Despite this rearguard action, however, the accusative is

already advancing as the primary prepositional case at the expense of the dative: cf. verbs of 'saying' and 'shouting' with πρός [pros] + accusative in paras. 18 and 19, and πέποιθα ἐπί ['pepyt^ha e'pi] and στηρίζομαι ἐπί [stẹ'rizome e'pi] + accusative in para. 21.

4.8 Clitic pronouns and the shift towards VS word order

We should also note in this last extract the dramatic increase in the frequency of verb–subject order compared with classical Greek, a feature which is again typical of the ordinary Koine in general. The reasons for this shift are complex, but seem to have been connected with the problems presented by clitic pronouns (cf. Horrocks (1990) for a full discussion).

Originally these typically collocated with sentence connectives in second position in a sentence (cf. Wackernagel (1892), a proposal which has since spawned a vast descriptive and theoretical literature):

(17) ἐν <u>δέ</u> <u>οἱ</u> ἐλάσσονι χρόνῳ . . . ἡ γυνὴ αὕτη τίκτει . . .

(Herodotus 6. 63. 2)

[en dé hoi   elássoni khrónoːi . . . (h)εː gynèː (h)aúteː tíkteː . . .]

in   and for-him less   time . . .   the   woman this   gives-birth-to . . .

'and in less time this woman bears for him . . .'

The frequently wide separation of such pronouns from their natural governors soon led, however, to a tendency for them to appear instead immediately after the relevant head in a syntactic phrase:

(18) πυρετοὶ δέ <u>παρηκολούθουν</u> <u>μοι</u> συνεχεῖς   (Demosthenes 54. 11)

[pyretoì dè parεːkolúːt^huːn moi synek^hêːs]

fevers   and followed   me   continuous

'and continual fevers hounded me'

But as we move into the Hellenistic period, the tension between these two options began to be resolved by placing the verb initially before clitic pronouns in second position, thus combining the traditional distribution of the latter, as in (17), with the semantically transparent head–complement order seen in (18). The result was an increasingly standard V(erb)–clitic–S(ubject)–O(bject) order, with VSO then becoming routine even in the absence of a motivating clitic, as in (16).

This distribution was typically disrupted when some clausal element, including a subject, was preposed as an emphatic/contrastive 'focus', or when some sentential 'operator' (e.g. expressing negation, interrogation, or modality over the clause as a whole) occupied the initial slot. In these cases we find instead the order F(ocus)/ Op(erator)–clitic–V, i.e. with V as near to initial position as possible, but still adjacent to its dependent pronoun; all other constituents follow.

Verb-final thus ceased to be a 'natural' order in popular Greek, and typically arose only when an object was preposed for emphasis. Furthermore, the dual distribution of clitics (i.e. V–cl in most cases, cl–V in the presence of initial F/Op) continued into medieval Greek, and even into some modern dialects (e.g. Cypriot). In standard modern Greek, however, the order clitic–verb has now been generalized except in the case of imperatives and gerunds (cf. 6.5.1 and 11.4).

As an example of both types together, consider the following sentence from an early Ptolemaic will (P. Eleph. 2. ii. 10–11, 284 BC):

(19) ἐὰν δέ τι ἐξαπορῶνται ... Διονύσιος ἢ Καλλίστα ζῶντες, <u>τρεφέτωσαν</u>
<u>αὐτοὺς</u> οἱ υἱεῖς πάντες ...

[eà:n dé ti   eksaporô:ntai ...   dionýsios è̩ kallísta zô:ntes,
if   but anything are-in-need-of (subjunctive) ... Dionysios   or Kallista living,

trepʰéto:san a(u)tù:s hoi hyjê:s pántes]
let-support   them   the sons   all

'If Dionysios or Kallista should be in need during their lifetimes, their sons collectively shall support them.'

In the subordinate clause there is a conditional conjunction in initial position, controlling the subjunctive mood of the following verb; the clitic pronoun therefore appears second and the verb follows immediately, with subject and other elements in its train. In the main clause, however, the 3rd person anaphoric pronoun, functioning effectively as a clitic (i.e. these do not occur sentence-initially, cf. Dover (1960)), follows the verb in initial position, with the subject once again coming last.

4.9 Analogical pressures on the strong aorist paradigm

Returning to (16), we may note finally the beginnings of the levelling of the distinction between the irregular 'strong' aorist paradigm (with 1/2/3 sg. forms ending in -ον [-on], -ες [-es], -ε [-e]) and the regular 'weak' aorists (with 1/2/3 sg. forms in -(σ)α [-(s)a], (σ)ας [-(s)as], (σ)ε [-(s)e]). Thus alongside 'classical' ἦλθον ['eltʰ-on] (in para. 18) we find εἶπας ['ip-as] (in para. 20), in which the classical εἶπες ['ip-es] has been replaced by a form with the weak suffix.

For certain verbs (including εἶπον ['ipon]) this paradigm shift was already characteristic of classical Ionic. It affected the Attic equivalents only in part, but passed into the Ionicized Koine, and with time spread to become an increasingly common feature of its middle-to-low registers; the final product of this interference will be considered in 5.8 and again in 11.8.6.

4.10 The spoken Koine: regional diversity

4.10.1 Introduction

The examination of the linguistic usage of 'vernacular' literature leads the way to a general consideration of the lower registers of the Koine, in particular of the written evidence available for reconstructing aspects of its structure and history as a 'popular' spoken language.

The issue of regional variety in 'old' Greece has already been considered above in connection with Boeotian/Koine and Doric/Koine interference (4.4.2, 4.4.3). Outside the territories in which it had been long established, however, Greek in the early third century BC was essentially the native language of the educated élite of the new urban centres and of the relatively impoverished colonists who had gone out to populate them. It was not the native language of the Hellenistic world as a whole, and only in Asia Minor did Greek eventually, after many centuries, come anywhere close to eliminating the indigenous languages as a universal medium of communication (cf. 8.2). Nonetheless many people of non-Greek origin acquired a knowledge of Greek as a second language, and any who looked for employment in government service had to have a good command of the language, both spoken and written. Thus although the Greco-Macedonian élite remained determinedly monolingual for the most part, many low-ranking local officials of native origin became fully competent in Greek, in part as a result of a rigorous training to judge from the very high grammatical and orthographic standards of even very ordinary 'official' papyrus documents from Egypt.

Again, though the upper classes kept themselves to themselves, intermarriage and routine daily contact between Greeks and non-Greeks in the lower strata of society inevitably promoted bilingualism, and it is above all in private documents composed by the (more or less) literate members of this sector of the population that the interference phenomena of daily speech are best reflected and evidence of regional variety within the lingua franca of ordinary Greeks, Egyptians, Arabs, Syrians, Jews, and Persians can most clearly be discerned.

We should recall, however, that the category of 'private' documents is a broad one, and we should not expect that they will all be equally revealing of interference or 'substandard' phenomena, or that statistical analyses of different usages will necessarily be informative; some composers of private documents were highly educated, and others could always hire the services of a professional scribe who was fully literate and well trained in the conventions of the relevant document-type. Nonetheless, where the Koine was superimposed on indigenous languages other than Greek, we do find good evidence for diatopic variation in many lower-level documents (cf. Bubenik (1989: ch. 5), Consani (1993)), and we may take as illustrative examples the Koine of Egypt and Asia Minor.

4.10.2 Egypt

As with many alleged 'Semitic' phenomena in the Septuagint (and the New Testament, see 5.10.2), a large number of features once thought to be 'Egyptian' have now been shown, both through their recurrence in contemporary Greek elsewhere and their continuation in medieval and modern Greek, to belong to the true internal history of the language. As an example, Coptic (the final form of the old Egyptian language prior to its demise) regularly used voiced allophones of its plosives after nasal consonants, and this is also attested in Greek documents from Egypt, rarely at first, but with growing frequency as we move into the Roman period: e.g. $\pi\alpha\theta\epsilon\hat{\iota}\nu$ δι [patʰîn di], with δι for τι [ti] 'to suffer something'. But there is evidence for voicing in this context from elsewhere (most strikingly in Pamphylia, because of its very early attestation there in the fourth century BC), and voicing is now the rule in standard modern Greek. In such cases, we must be dealing with sporadic 'phonetic' spellings reflecting a current pronunciation even among monoglot Greek speakers, and not only in Egypt but in many other areas of the Greek-speaking world.

In the case of Egypt, however, the work of Mayser-Schmoll (1970), Gignac (1976, 1981), and Teodorsson (1977) has provided a solid philological base for the identification of markers of Egyptian Greek, at least some of which are due to the impact of Coptic. Most bilingual regionalisms, of course, tell us more about the substrate language than about Greek, and these have no real significance for the subsequent development of the language as a whole, even if they sometimes coincide with general patterns of evolution in the language.

Concentrating here on phonology, which is arguably the most important area of differentiation in 'standard' languages, the following characteristics of Egyptian Koine emerge most clearly (cf. Consani (1993), and see the relevant sections of Teodorsson (1977) and, for the Roman period, Gignac (1976), where full documentation is provided):

(20) (a) (i)   The graphic interchange of aspirated and voiced plosives with their voiceless counterparts. The voiceless/aspirated overlaps are contextually conditioned in the main (after [s], before another aspirate, and in the context of liquids and nasals) and reflect an internal development of Egyptian Greek that is paralleled in part in some ancient dialects; the cases that fall outside the usual patterns are perhaps due to the fact that only one Coptic dialect (Bohairic, spoken in the Delta area) had aspirated stop phonemes.

(ii)   With respect to the unconditioned voiced/voiceless interchanges, we should note that the number of spelling mistakes involving the labials is fewer than those for the dentals and velars. Since Coptic lacked contrasts in its plosive system based on voice but did have a phonologically significant opposition between the voiceless labial plosive /p/ and the voiced fricative /β/, the explanation seems straightforward; errors decrease in number in the articulatory area where a voicing opposition existed in the 'native' language (cf. Worrell (1934, Till (1961), Vergote (1973)).

(b)   Spelling interchange between σ and ζ, also reflects the absence of a phonemic contrast between /s/ and /z/ in Coptic.

(c)   The common graphic interchange of o/ω and ου implies some confusion of /o/ and /u/ in the speech of some writers; this is also probably a Coptic substrate effect since the contrast between /o/ and /u/ was neutralized after [m] and [n], and frequently in final position when the vowel was unstressed.

(d) Similarly interchanges between α and ε/αι, α and ο/ω, and ο/ω and ε/αι
in unaccented (i.e. by now unstressed) syllables imply the assimilation of
the low/mid unstressed vowels [a], [e] and [o] to the /ə/ of Coptic.

Certain other features, however, seem to be internal developments of Egyptian
Greek itself. We may note, for example, the sporadic omission of the liquids [l]
and [r] in the context of occlusives, and the frequent interchange of αι and α in
Ptolemaic papyri, implying a period of lower than usual articulation for the former
(i.e. as [æ] rather than [e], with consequential αι/α, as well as the more usual
αι/ε interchanges).

The weakness of word-final [n] is also often reflected directly by its omission
in spelling, but this particular feature seems to have been widespread in 'popular'
Greek quite generally to judge from the evidence, say, of Attic inscriptions (cf.
Teodorsson (1974, 1978)). We may compare here the modern Greek situation
in which, certain dialects such as Cypriot apart, final [n] survives in only a handful of words, and under specific contextual conditions (cf. 11.2, example (3)). The
more general weakness of syllable-final nasals before plosives, however, as evidenced by frequent omission and hypercorrect insertion, though occasionally paralleled in Asia Minor Koine and classical dialects (cf. Teodorsson (1978: 89), Brixhe
(1987: 33)), seems to have been specially characteristic of Egyptian Greek from
Ptolemaic times onwards. Both medially and word-finally this process sometimes
involved not simply the loss of the nasal, with or without nasalization of the preceding vowel, but a complete assimilation to the following consonant: cf. spellings
like προσήνεκκεν [prosé:nekken] 's/he brought', for προσήνεγκεν [prosé:neŋken],
third century BC.

On the other hand evidence for the retention of the medial nasal and for its
voicing effect on a following voiceless plosive increases steadily in the Roman
period, as noted above, and this seems to have been the general situation elsewhere,
to judge from the evidence of modern Greek.

4.10.3 Asia Minor

Turning briefly to Asia Minor, the pioneering work of Brixhe (1987) has provided
important new insights and a comprehensive bibliography (cf. also Consani (1993)).
Here the coastal regions had undergone early Hellenization, as noted, but the indigenous populations of the interior were, unlike in Egypt, extremely heterogeneous
both ethnically and linguistically, with Phrygian and Pisidian in particular surviving alongside Greek into the Christian era. The impact of the Koine was therefore
variable according to region, but certain recurrent features represent part of the
general development of the language. We may note, for example, the steady increase in instances of aphaeresis (loss of initial unaccented vowels) and syncope,
the co-occurrence of standard αυ/ευ [af/ef] and substandard α/ε spellings (the latter
reflecting allegro pronunciations) in words such as α(ὐ)τόν [a(f)'ton] 'him', and the
synizesis of [i] and [e] in the context of a following vowel (e.g. [-ia]/[-ea] > [-ja],
with accent shift to the final vowel if the [i] or [e] was originally stressed).

On the other hand, evidence for the weakness of word-final nasals, otherwise widely attested, is notably sparse in this region, and it is interesting to observe that the systematic retention of final [-n] was characteristic of Cypriot Koine (cf. Consani (1986, 1990)), and that this remains a feature of the contemporary dialect. It is also a marked feature of the modern dialects of Khios and the Dodecanese, and was also typical of those Greek dialects (Cappadocian, Bithynian and Pontic) formerly spoken in Asia Minor up until the exchange of populations with Turkey in 1923 (see Section III). Here, then, there seems to be evidence for a specifically 'eastern' Koine spoken in Asia Minor, Cyprus and other adjacent islands (cf. Thumb (1901: ch. 5, 1906), Dawkins (1916: 213–4)). Other features shared by some or all of these modern dialects, at least until recently, include the continued use of the article as a relative (Cyprus, Rhodes, Cos, Cappadocia; an old Asiatic Ionic characteristic, common in Homer and Herodotus, and also shared by ancient Lesbian), the continued use of possessive adjectives (Khios, Cappadocia, Pontus; replaced elsewhere by prepositional expressions, now defunct, or the genitive of personal pronouns), and a pool of common vocabulary items and/or special senses of otherwise familiar words.

Other features, however, seem once again to be plausibly attributable to local substrate effects. For example, though the contextually conditioned closure of unaccented [e] > [i] and [o] > [u] is familiar from some ancient dialects, the regularity of these changes and their general restriction to unstressed final syllables in the Asia Minor Koine might well reflect the parallel properties of the /e/~/i/ and /o/~/u/ neutralizations of Phrygian. Such vowel raising remained, incidentally, a characteristic of many varieties of modern Cappadocian, Bithynian and Pontic, in which, unlike in the northern dialects of modern Greek (cf. 11.5, 14.2.5), it was again largely confined to post-tonic, particularly final, syllables.

Similarly, the frequent graphic interchange of voiceless and aspirated plosives, though again partially paralleled elsewhere, seems to have a randomness right across Asia Minor (examples from Mysia, Lydia, Caria, Phrygia, Lycia, Pisidia, Pamphylia, Galatia, Lycaonia) that points to the general absence of such a contrast in the relevant native languages. And finally we may note that both the frequency of prothetic vowels and the not uncommon omission of σ [s, z] before τ, θ [t, tʰ] and μ [m] in Phrygia (simplifications otherwise unattested in Greek) must likewise reflect characteristics of the phonology of the local language.

Such 'local' features could also be compiled for the Koine of Palestine and Syria (cf. Bubenik (1989: 4.6, 5.2), where Aramaic (including Syriac) continued in use until after the Arab conquest of the seventh century AD. Unfortunately relatively little work has been done on the inscriptions of this region, and most effort has been concentrated on the supposed Semitisms of the Septuagint and the New Testament. But enough has been said to illustrate the point that the Koine was, in its more popular registers, far from being a 'uniform' language; its considerable heterogeneity, both in old Greece and in the new kingdoms, is already clearly apparent from documents of the later Hellenistic period, with local differences deriving from both ancient dialectal/foreign-language substrate effects and language-internal developments within particular regions.

4.11 Private inscriptions and papyri: some major trends

4.11.1 *Introduction: datives; future periphrases; the nom./acc. plural of consonant-stems*

We have already seen that literary texts written in a language subject to the influence of literary and grammatical tradition reveal relatively little of the development of spoken Greek, and that even more 'popular' productions, though reflecting certain grammatical and lexical changes more directly, show almost nothing by way of phonological change because written in the standard orthography.

By contrast, even though all who had learned to write had, by the very nature of the exercise, come into contact with the grammatical/literary tradition, the private documents of the less well-educated sometimes provide vital additional insights, through their numerous spelling mistakes and relatively unselfconscious grammatical structures, into changes at all linguistic levels in the everyday language of the majority of the Greek-speaking population.

We may begin with the following extract from a papyrus letter written by one Apollonios to his elder brother ('father' in the piece is a conventional form of address to a man older than oneself), dated *c.* 152 BC (P. Par. 47/UPZ 70):

(21) Ἀπολλώνιος Πτολεμαίωι τῶι πατρὶ χαίρειν. ὀμνύο τὸν Σάραπιν, ἰ μὴ μικρόν
τι ἐντρέπομαι, οὐκ ἄν με ἶδες τὸ πόρσωπόν μου πόποτε, ὅτι ψεύδηι πάντα
καὶ οἱ παρά σε θεοὶ ὁμοίως, ὅτι ἐνβέβληκαν ὑμᾶς εἰς ὕλην μεγάλην καὶ οὗ
δυνάμεθα ἀποθανεῖν κἂν ἴδης ὅτι μέλλομεν σωθῆναι, τότε βαπτιζώμεθα.
γίνωσκε ὅτι πιράσεται ὁ δραπέτης μὴ ἀφῖναι ἡμᾶς ἐπὶ τῶν τόπων
ἶναι· ... οὐκ ἔστι ἀνακύψαι με πόποτε ἐν τῇ Τρικομίαι ὑπὸ τῆς αἰσχύνης,
ἰ καὶ αὐτοὺς δεδώκαμεν ...
πρὸς τοὺς τὴν ἀλήθειαν λέγοντες.

[apoˈlonios ptoleˈmæo to paˈtri   ˈkʰærin. omˈnyo   to(n) ˈsarapin, i mę̞
Apollonios   to-Ptolemy   the father (I-bid) to-rejoice. I-swear (by) the   Serapis,   if not

miˈkron di   enˈdrepomæ, uk an   me ˈides   to ˈporsoˈpom mu
little   something I-feel-shame,   not would me you-have-seen the face   of-me

ˈpopote, ˈhoti   ˈpseβʷdi ˈpanda kæ hø paˈra se tʰeˈø hoˈmøos, ˈhoti
ever,   because you-lie   always and the with   you gods likewise,   because

emˈbeβlę̞kan hiˈmas is   ˈhylę̞n meˈɣalę̞ kæ hu   dyˈnametʰa apotʰaˈnin
they-had-cast us   into matter great   and where we-may   to-die

kan ˈidę̞s   ˈhoti ˈmelomen soˈtʰę̞næ, ˈtote βaptiˈzometʰa. ˈjinoske ˈhoti
and-if you see that   we-shall   to-be-saved, then   we-are-sunk.   Know   that

piˈrasetæ ho draˈpetę̞s mę̞ aˈpʰinæ hiˈmas eˈpi ton ˈdopon ˈinæ ... uk
will-try   the runaway   not to-let   us   on   the places   to-be ... Not

ˈesti   anaˈkypsæ me ˈpopote en di trikoˈmia hyˈpo   tę̞s æˈskʰynę̞s,
it-is-possible to-lift-the head me ever   in the Trikomia because-of the shame,

i kæ   haɸʷˈtus deˈdokamen ...   pros tus tę̞n aˈlę̞tʰean ˈleɣondes.]
if indeed selves   we-have-given ... (A reply) to   those the truth   saying

'Apollonios to Ptolemaios his father [*i.e. older brother*] greeting. I swear by Serapis that if I did not have a little compunction you would never have seen my face again, because you lie all the time and your gods likewise, because they dropped us [*the letter reads* you, *but this is an error*] into a grand business in which we may well die and if ever you see [*in a vision*] that we are about to be saved we are sunk at once. Know that the 'runaway' [*a term of abuse for an enemy*] will try to stop us being in the place . . . It is impossible for me to hold up my head in Trikomia ever again for shame that we have given ourselves away . . .
A reply to the purveyors of truth.'

Particularly striking here is the author's reluctance to use the dative outside the formulaic greeting at the beginning. Thus in the main clause of the conditional sentence that follows we would perhaps have expected a so-called 'ethic' dative expressing oblique involvement, but instead we find the accusative μϵ [me]. The often 'goal-orientated' sense of the indirect object (cf. 'give to/send to', etc.), together with the use of two accusatives after verbs such as 'teach', encouraged overlaps between the dative and the accusative, and a tendency to replace datives with accusatives quickly spread to other uses too, most particularly in the case of clitic pronouns, as here. The development later extended to full noun phrases (cf. 6.5.3, 6.5.4 for this, and related overlaps involving the genitive).

As further evidence of the decline of the dative we should note that the accus-ative σϵ [se] in the prepositional possessive οἱ παρά σϵ θϵοί [hø pa'ra se tʰe'ø], lit. 'the beside you gods', is in fact an authorial correction for dative σοι [sø]; only after the preposition ἐν [en] 'in' does Apollonios feel comfortable with the dative case, and we have already noted above how this particular preposition came to be used as a virtually meaningless support for the declining dative in a variety of adverbial functions.

Similar remarks apply to the use of accusative μϵ [me] after οὐκ ἔστι [uk 'esti] 'it is impossible', where the classical language would ordinarily have employed a dative; this could be interpreted as a shift to an accusative and infinitive construc-tion (*it is impossible for-me [to X] > it is impossible [{for} me to X]*), but the general trend was away from such structures.

Other features of interest here include the avoidance of the future passive in favour of a periphrasis with μέλλω ['melo] + aorist passive infinitive, μέλλομϵν σωθῆναι ['melome(n) so'tʰɛnæ] 'we-are-about to-be-saved'; such periphrases gradu-ally spread throughout the future system with the passage of time, particularly after sound change had effectively destroyed the distinction between the aorist subjunct-ive and the future indicative in the active paradigm of many verbs (cf. 5.3, (2) and (3)). The use of the classical optative (in conjunction with the particle ἄν [an]) in the 'root' sense of possibility has similarly been replaced by the use of modal aux-iliaries, both personal (δυνάμϵθα [dy'nametʰa] = 'we may' rather than 'we are able', and in the sense 'it is possible that we . . .' rather than 'we are allowed to . . .') and impersonal (ἔστι ['esti] 'it is possible'), both in conjunction with infinitival complements.

Finally, we should note the use of the 3rd declension nominative in -ϵς [-es] for the accusative in -ας [-as] in the participle λέγοντϵς ['leɣondes] at the very end of the document (in fact on the reverse). This is also paralleled in some dialect inscriptions, and seems to be associated with the shift from a pitch to a stress accent (on which see immediately below). In some areas, including Egypt where the substrate had a strong stress accent and marked vowel weakening in unstressed syllables, the effect was to produce a degree of neutralization between the low and mid short vowels (cf. (20)(d) above), particularly in final syllables, and especially when these were the maximum two syllables away from the stressed vowel, as in λέγοντες ['leɣondes], etc. The resulting obscure vowel sound apparently sounded more like an allophone of /e/ than anything else, and was written accordingly. The long-term effect, however, was to undermine the distinction between the nominative and the accusative plural, first by extension throughout the 3rd (consonant-stem) declension, and then also in the 1st (a-stem) declension, as a result of further changes to be discussed below. In modern Greek, masculine and feminine nouns of the 3rd declension have very largely assimilated to the 1st declension, and all have nominative and accusative plurals in [-es].

4.11.2 *Phonological developments*

Full details of the phonological development of the Koine in Egypt and elsewhere in the Hellenistic and Roman periods are provided in Chapter 6. The major points to be discussed here are therefore mainly methodological.

First, we should note that many private letters written at much later times than (21) employ a more 'correct' orthography, and that level of education is at least as important a factor as date in determining the extent to which spelling reflects sound change directly. Here, for example, there is a frequent substitution of ι for ει (cf. ἰ [i] for εἰ 'if', ἴδες ['ides] for εἴδες 'you saw' and several other examples), which clearly demonstrates the raising of at least some allophones (especially in preconsonantal and word-final positions) of 'classical' /e(ː)/ (written ει) to [i], and correlates with what we see both in earlier official Boeotian inscriptions and more sporadically in low-level Attic documents from the fifth century onwards (cf. Teodorsson (1974: 175–8, 251, 254 ff.)). The change was completed in the later Roman period and the resultant merger is a feature of modern Greek.

Similarly, the regular confusion of o and ω (cf. ὀμνύο [om'nyo] for ὀμνύω, βαπτιζώμεθα [βapti'zometʰa] for βαπτιζόμεθα, etc.) shows that vowel-length oppositions had already disappeared, a change that is directly correlated with the shift from the classical pitch accent to an accent characterized primarily by greater loudness.

There are many indirect signs of this shift even in classical dialect inscriptions. Here we should simply note that the phonological contrast between the acute accent (rise on the accented vowel, fall on the following syllable) and the circumflex accent (rise–fall on the accented long vowel) could not be sustained when there ceased to be inherently long vowels (and diphthongs) capable of bearing the accentual contonation alone. On the assumption that the equalization of vowel length resulted in a neutralization in favour of the acute accent, and that the rise in pitch had always been associated secondarily with at least some increase in amplitude, the final result would have been a single type of word-accent characterized by both a rise in pitch and an increase in volume, but with the latter now placed in sharper focus by the loss of contrastiveness in the former. In due course, and doubtless with the help of substrate languages with primary stress accents such as Coptic, the rise in pitch came to be interpreted increasingly as a secondary concomitant of greater loudness.

On the other hand, though 'classical' /oi/ eventually merged with /y/, οι and υ are never confused in (21), implying that for this speaker at least the former still represented an intermediate stage in the development from [oi], namely [ø]. On the other hand, the word for 'us' (normally ἡμᾶς) is spelled ὑμᾶς, the word for 'you'. Since this is a not uncommon error in the papyri of the period, it seems that in certain circumstances (e.g. in initial pretonic syllables, particularly where a labial context would encourage dissimilation of a rounded front vowel) and/or in certain words of high frequency (e.g. personal pronouns) changes had already gone through that otherwise took effect rather later. Thus despite the absence of confusion between υ and η elsewhere, it seems that in these words at least both letters represented the same sound, namely [i], and that the two pronouns were therefore homophonous. This naturally led to the eventual replacement of the classical forms (see 6.5.4 and 11.7.8(e)).

Apparently, then, [ẹ] and [y] had shifted to [i] under certain conditions, but the fact that contemporary /ẹ/, (written η, the product of the raising of 'classical' /ɛː/ to fill the 'gap' created by the partial merger of original /eː/ with /i(ː)/), had not itself yet raised to merge with /i/ across the board (as in modern Greek) is strongly implied by the absence of interchanges between η and ει/ι. The parallel absence of interchanges between υ and ει/ι similarly shows that /y/, represented by υ, had not yet generally lost its lip-rounding (again cf. modern Greek for confirmation of this development), despite the isolated use of υ to represent [i] in ὑμεῖς. Similarly, the absence of ε/αι confusion implies a transitional value [æ] for the latter, intermediate between classical [ai] and its final realization as [e] (cf. 4.10.2 on Egyptian Koine).

Notice that the attempt to interpret the evidence of the spellings has been based on both graphic interchanges (or the lack of them) internal to the document and the general picture that can be built up by a comparison with other documentary evidence, both contemporary and from other periods, and drawn not only from the same region but also from elsewhere. The whole exercise is subject to overall interpretation in the light of the final outcomes known from modern Greek and its dialects. In this way, 'odd' mistakes and purely local developments can be distinguished fairly reliably from phenomena of genuine significance for the history of the language.

Many of the changes first attested in the private documents of the moderately educated eventually begin to make a sporadic appearance in official documents too. But if they do appear in such texts, there is often a very considerable time-lag in matters of grammar and lexicon, and as far as spelling is concerned we should never forget that the aim of all who composed official texts throughout the history of Greek was to use the classical orthography correctly. It is important also to recognize that the same sets of changes may have gone through at slightly different times in different areas, or even at different times in the same area, with the variation being determined by factors such as social class (the aristocracy being generally very conservative, the urban masses more innovative, and the majority of the literate population occupying a middle position).

Nor should we forget that in Athenian Attic innovation seems to have begun from the bottom up, while in the new Greek territories, such as Egypt, it seems to have been the emergent middle-register norm, continuing the old Attic-based language of business and administration, that crucially shaped both the originally mixed dialectal speech of the lower classes and the second-language Greek of the native populations. We should not, then, be surprised to discover that evidence for a given set of changes in Egyptian or in other varieties of the Hellenistic Koine is generally later than that for Athenian Attic/Koine.

4.11.3 Other morphological developments: the partial merger of the 1st and 3rd declensions

A fuller account of the relevant changes in this domain will be presented in Chapter 11, once the further developments of the Roman and Byzantine eras have been examined. Here, to effect the transition to the later period, we may add just one final example of a private document, an inscription on a statue base from Magnesia on the Meander (Kern (1900: 145)), dating from the first century BC:

(22) *Σοφῆιαν θυγατέρα τὴν Λευκίου Σοφῆιου, γυναῖκαν δὲ Λευκίου Οὐαλερίου Λευκίου υἱοῦ Φλάκκου τοῦ ἀνθυπάτου.*

[soph'ean thyga'tera tẹn luː'kiu soph'ẹu, jy'nekan de luː'kiu wale'riu
Sophea   daughter   the of-Lucius Sopheus, wife   and of-Lucius Valerius
luː'kiu hy'u 'flaku tu anth'y'patu.]
of-Lucius son Flaccus the proconsul

'Sophea, daughter of Lucius Sopheus, and wife of Lucius Valerius Flaccus, son of Lucius, the proconsul.'

The kingdom of Pergamum, which included the city of Magnesia, had been bequeathed to the Roman state by king Attalus III in 134 BC, probably to avoid a social revolution. The document is testimony to Roman pragmatism in adopting the established language of their new province of Asia not only for official but also for private purposes (see also Chapter 5).

The really important point here is the addition of final -ν [-n] to the accusative singular γυναῖκα-ν [jy'neka-n] 'wife'. The accusative singular marker in all declensions in which the final element of the stem was vocalic was -ν [-n]: -αν [-an], -ον [-on], -ιν [-in], -υν [-yn]. In the consonant stems, however, the classical ending was -α [-a], the prehistoric product of a syllabic *[ŋ] conditioned by the consonantal context. It was, of course, only a matter of time before an analogical -ν [-n] was added to the consonant-stem accusative ending, and sporadic examples duly appear in classical Cypriot, Thessalian and Elean inscriptions (Buck (1955: 89), in the later inscriptions of many other dialects, and in the Ptolemaic papyri from the third century BC onwards (Mayser-Schmoll I². 1. 172). There are also occasional examples in some manuscripts of the Septuagint (where they may, of course, be due to later copyists).

The example here is one of the earliest inscriptional examples in the Koine, and is testimony to the steady spread of the phenomenon from local and substandard varieties of spoken Greek into somewhat higher written registers. It is of crucial importance for the later history of Greek because it marks the beginning of the destruction of the distinction between the old consonant-stems and the a-stems of the 1st declension. Eventually new nominatives in -α [-a] (feminine) and -ας [-as] (masculine) were built to these accusatives in -αν [-an], and the whole class of masculine/feminine nouns was finally absorbed into the a-stem paradigm (as in standard modern Greek). The process, however, took many centuries to approach completion, because of the normative influence of the literary and official written languages. Indeed, some modern dialects still retain examples of the old consonant-stem genitive singular suffix -ος [-os], while written forms such as Ελλάς [e'las] 'Greece', genitive Ελλάδος [e'laðos], also persist, e.g. on the T-shirts of national sports teams and in the names of banks, alongside the more colloquial Ελλάδα [e'laða], genitive Ελλάδας [e'laðas].

4.12   Conclusion

It should be clear from this selective survey of the development of the Koine in the Hellenistic period that many changes characteristic of modern Greek were already beginning to take effect in the more popular spoken and written varieties of the language in the last centuries of the pre-Christian era. These are best reflected in the private documents of the less well-educated, but grammatical and lexical innovations also have some impact on popular literary styles, and even official writing, though the influence of the classical language increases steadily as we move towards higher-level official and self-consciously belletristic styles.

To a great extent this pattern of development continues throughout the Roman and Byzantine periods, with the important difference that the Koine ceases for a time to be a genuinely literary language under the impact of the Atticist movement. Henceforth high-level literary productions (i.e. those that fall into the genres of the classical tradition) aim more consistently at an Attic or Atticizing style, while the language of the official Koine and more popular forms of literature (e.g. novel genres such as chronicles and hagiography) continues to compromise, in varying degrees according to the genre/level of the text in question, between its own conservative practice and the usage of the contemporary spoken language. These issues are taken up and developed in Chapters 5 and 6.

Chapter 5

Greek in the Roman Empire

5.1 Roman domination

The Seleucids lost control of Alexander's far-eastern conquests, Persia and Bactria, during the mid-third century. But the heartlands of Hellenistic civilization, in Greece and Macedonia, in Asia Minor, in the middle East (Syria and Palestine), and in North Africa (Egypt and Cyrenaica) progressively fell first under the influence and then under the direct control of Rome during the course of the second and first centuries BC, as Republican Rome began its dramatic period of imperial expansion.

Southern Italy and Sicily were already largely in Roman hands by the end of the third century, the latter as a direct result of Rome's first war with Carthage (264–241 BC). But the Romans' deadly struggle with the Carthaginians was far from resolved; by 215 BC the Carthaginians under Hannibal had attained an apparently dominant position, and in Greece the squabbling Aetolian and Achaean leagues, the latter in alliance with Philip V of Macedon, had quickly sought to close ranks when brought face to face with the dire implications of an imminent resolution to this conflict. Philip, however, made a treaty with Hannibal, and the Romans replied swiftly by concluding their own treaty with the Aetolians and waging war on Macedonia. Although the Romans proclaimed 'Greek freedom' (i.e. from Macedonia) as their motive, the consequence of their military successes was a tightening of the constraints on the freedom of action left to the cities of the Greek mainland. Roman victory thus left the Aetolians, who had aided their Roman allies against Philip, seriously disgruntled.

At this time Antiochus III, the Seleucid monarch of Syria, was seeking to extend his own control over the cities of the Asia Minor seaboard, and the Aetolians therefore rashly invited him to 'liberate Greece' and settle their grievances with Rome. In the ensuing war (192–188 BC) the Romans won another decisive victory, with the result not only that Aetolian power was further diminished in Greece but also that the Seleucids were effectively banished from Asia Minor west of the Taurus mountains. This left the friendly Attalid kings of Pergamum, who had already established their independence from the Seleucids in the first half of the third century BC, as the dominant power in Asia Minor.

Though Philip had fought as a Roman ally against Antiochus, he too received little in return, and his successor Perseus tried to recover Macedonian influence in Greece. The Romans promptly initiated a third Macedonian war (171–168 BC) in which Perseus was subjected to a crushing defeat. After a short period organized as four 'independent' tribute-paying republics, Macedonia was made into a Roman province in 149 BC. Shortly afterwards the continued intransigence of the Achaean League led in 146 BC to the destruction of Corinth, the dissolution of the League and the final subjection of the Greek city-states to the direct control of the Roman governor of Macedonia.

A little later, in 133 BC, Attalus III, king of Pergamum, fearing revolution, bequeathed his kingdom to the Romans, and this fabulously rich territory was henceforth administered as the new province of Asia. Alarmed by this seemingly irresistible spread of Roman power, Mithridates VI, king of Pontus, sought, soon after his accession to the throne in *c.* 120 BC, to consolidate his position by seizing control of the neighbouring, and previously independent, kingdoms of Bithynia and Cappadocia. Though Mithridates was eventually driven out of his Asian 'empire', Nicomedes IV of Bithynia decided to follow Attalus's example, and to leave his kingdom too to the protection of Roman government (74 BC). His concern was understandable, since in 88 BC Mithridates had sought to take advantage of Roman preoccupations in Italy (a rebellion of Italian states) by invading Macedonia and Greece, where a number of states supported his cause. Though Mithridates was also forced out of Europe by Sulla, his final defeat took place only in 66 BC. The victorious general Pompey then organized Bithynia and Pontus together into another new province (63 BC), and at the same time converted the much-reduced Seleucid kingdom, long racked by internal disunity and economic decline, into the province of Syria.

Now only Ptolemaic Egypt remained formally independent of Rome, but though the country's last monarch, Cleopatra VII, sought to preserve and even revive her empire through her association first with Julius Caesar and then with Mark Antony, Egypt too was finally annexed when in 31 BC Antony's Romano-Egyptian fleet was defeated at Actium off north-west Greece by his enemy and arch rival Octavian (soon to be known as Augustus, the first emperor of Imperial Rome).

5.2 The fate of Greek

Though these conquered and inherited territories were administered as Roman provinces, Greek remained routinely in use alongside Latin, knowledge of which remained rather limited among the Greek-speaking population despite its imposition in the legal profession and the army, and the obvious need for bilingualism in the bureaucracy. As the vehicle of the widely admired ancient Hellenic civilization and the long-established official language and universal *lingua franca* of the East, Greek was simply too prestigious and too well entrenched for any more far-reaching programme of Latinization to seem either desirable or practicable (see e.g. Cicero *Pro Archia* 23), and the Romans were by and large content to come to terms with the status quo.

Indeed, it became a matter of routine for the Roman élite, in recognition of the status of Greek as the primary cultural and international language of the age, both to learn a 'practical' Koine and to acquire at least a reading knowledge of literary Attic (cf. Kaimio (1979), Biville (1993)). The extent to which Greek was appropriated is tellingly revealed by the biographer Suetonius, who has the emperor Claudius remark in surprise at a 'barbarian's' command of both Latin and Greek (*Claudius* 42. 2): 'you know both our languages' (*utroque sermone nostro*). Even the Atticist/Asianist controversy (cf. 4.7.5 and see below) was reflected directly in the theory and practice of Roman orators (cf., for example, Cicero *Orator* 226, *Brutus* 325), and one of the leading ideologues of the early Atticist movement, Dionysius of Halicarnassus, came to Rome in 30 BC and taught there for the next 22 years. We may also compare the case of Plutarch, who was able to lecture in Rome between *c.* AD 75 and 90 in his own language, and never felt it necessary to master Latin, while the whole of Quintilian's *Institutio Oratoria* provides eloquent testimony to the pervasiveness of Greek language and culture among the Roman aristocracy.

The combined effect, unsurprisingly, of Roman administration of the east, the partial politico-economic assimilation of the Greek aristocracy, and the cultural Hellenization of its Roman counterpart was a great deal of reciprocal lexical borrowing/calquing (cf. Quintilian I. 5. 58) and a certain amount of phonological and grammatical convergence between Greek and Latin in their higher registers, particularly literary and official Latin (cf. Coleman (1976)) and official Greek (the Latinisms of the latter having a limited 'trickle-down' effect in more popular registers, cf. García Domingo (1979)).

5.3   The impact of bilingualism

The most that can be attempted here is a brief examination of a number of apparently parallel developments in the two languages that took place in the period up to the fourth/fifth centuries AD. The Greek influence on Latin, as noted, became increasingly pervasive as the latter took on the role of a world language. The Latin influence on Greek, by contrast, was more restricted. Interaction with the Roman administration and exposure to Roman institutions quickly led to the standard use of borrowed/calqued vocabulary items and phraseology, and their spread in the language was supported by the long-term presence of Latin-speaking officials, traders and soldiers, whose native Latin may eventually have assimilated certain Hellenisms and whose acquired Greek, with its Latin substrate effects, may in turn have come to influence native practice.

In general, such developments involved extensions of usage based on loan translation effects and/or the natural selection and subsequent evolution in parallel of constructional options which were already available in both languages. Much direct grammatical influence, however, was limited to the official Koine, and reflected the cumulative impact on bureaucratic Greek of the large-scale translation of administrative documents composed originally in Latin; such features (including, for example, a liking for verb-final word order and the general use of the accusative and infinitive construction) were often rather alien to the natural direction of development in Greek, and so tended not to affect its subsequent evolution significantly.

We may begin, uncontroversially, with the administrative, military, commercial and other vocabulary that was borrowed directly into spoken and 'business' Greek, but rarely if ever used in the literary language, in the period up to the end of the fifth century AD (cf. Viscidi (1944), Zilliacus (1935)). Typical examples include:

(1) (a) Names of the months.
   Ἰανουάριος [janu'arios] – *Ianuarius* 'January', etc.
 (b) Officials, legal/administrative terms, etc.
   δικτάτωρ [ðik'tator] – *dictator*
   κολωνία [kolo'nia] – *colonia* 'colony' (city with privileges)
   λίμιτον ['limiton] – *limes* 'boundary'
   μαγίστωρ/μάγιστρος [ma'jistor/'majistros] – *magister*
   πραίτωρ/πραιτώριον ['pretor/pre'torion] – *praetor/praetorium*
 (c) Military terms
   ἀκτουάριος [aktu'arios] – *actuarius* 'paymaster'
   ἅρμα/ἁρμάριον ['arma/ar'marion] – *arma/armarium* 'arms/ armoury'
   βιγλεύω/βίγλα [vi'ɣlevo/'viɣla] – *vig(i)lo* 'keep watch'
   κεντυρίων/κεντυρία [kendy'rion/kendy'ria] – *centurio/centuria* 'centurion/ century'
   κόρτη ['korti] – *co(h)ors* 'cohort'
   κουστωδία [kusto'ðia] – *custodia* 'military guard'
   λεγεών [leji'on] – *legio* 'legion'
   οὐετρανός [wetra'nos] – *vet(e)ranus* 'veteran'
 (d) Money, finance, etc.
   ἀσσάριον [as'arion] – *assarium* (a coin)
   δηνάριον [ði'narion] – *denarius* (a coin)
   ἰνδικτίων [indik'tion] – *indictio* '15-year cycle for fiscal purposes'
   κῆνσος ['kinsos] – *census* 'tax'

Where possible syntactic convergence is concerned, however, things become more controversial, and even where influence is likely, the crucial question of its direction is often uncertain; in many cases we may simply be dealing with shared developments based on a pre-existing structural similarity or parallel developmental trend.

To take a simple example of the highly complex interactions that may be at work, we may consider the case of αὐτός [af'tos]. The pre-articular, demonstrative use of αὐτός [af'tos] is standard in modern Greek (cf. αυτό το βιβλίο [af'to to vi'vlio], lit. 'this the book', etc.), and sporadic examples can already be found in the papyri of the Roman period. But in the classical language αὐτός [af'tos] before the definite article meant only 'self' (in the intensifying sense, e.g. *the general himself*, etc.), while after the article it meant '(the) same'. In the absence of any co-occurring nominal, the oblique cases were also used as 'weak' (effectively enclitic) anaphoric pronouns.

Modern Greek, however, has two sets of pronouns derived from this element; independent 'strong' forms, related to the demonstrative use of αὐτός [af'tos], and clitic forms, with concomitant loss of the first syllable, derived from the weak pronominal αὐτόν [af'ton], etc.

The shift of meaning from 'the same' to 'this' can readily be explained in terms of overlapping discourse functions, since 'the same X' can be used to refer back anaphorically to some previously mentioned entity in much the same way as the true demonstrative 'this X'; it is then simply a matter of extending the discourse-internal use of 'the same' to parallel the genuinely exophoric (deictic) use of the demonstrative. Once this true deictic use was established, αὐτός [af'tos] began to appear in the pre-articular position of other demonstratives: e.g. τῷ αὐτῷ χρόνῳ [to af'to 'xrono] '(in) the same year/(in) this year' > αὐτῷ τῷ χρόνῳ [af'to to 'xrono] '(in) this the year'. And once established as a demonstrative, αὐτός [af'tos] quickly acquired the related use as a 'strong' anaphoric pronoun.

In the same period, however, i.e. from around the end of the second century AD, Latin *ipse* (or in its more 'vulgar' form *ipsus*), meaning 'self', came to be used in combination with other demonstratives (e.g. *hic ipse* 'this self', *iste/ille ipse* 'that self', cf. Italian *stesso* < *iste ipse*) in the sense of 'the same', replacing the original form *idem*. A little later, *ipse* also came to be used alone as a demonstrative/anaphoric pronoun (cf. Italian *esso*) in competition with *iste/ille*; examples are common in texts from around AD 400.

Clearly, the Greek and Latin developments are very similar. But was the development of *hic ipse* as a replacement for *idem* modelled on the classical Greek construction ὁ αὐτός [o af'tos]? We might equally well ask whether the anaphoric/demonstrative use of ὁ αὐτός [o af'tos] was connected with the comparable use of *idem* and its replacements; or whether the development of a demonstrative ('strong' pronominal) use of hitherto 'weak' αὐτόν [af'ton], etc. derived not only from partial identification with the newly demonstrative αὐτός [af'tos] but also from the fact that Latin demonstratives (*hic/ille/iste*) doubled as anaphoric pronouns; or indeed whether the demonstrative/anaphoric use of the hitherto intensive *ipse* was acquired through association with the new demonstrative/'strong' anaphoric uses of the intensive αὐτός [af'tos]. These questions cannot be satisfactorily answered at the present time, and we may simply observe here that (a) the changes are semantically 'natural' and so could in principle be independent, but that (b) the very close parallelism of development in the same period is at least highly suggestive.

To complete this survey of possible areas of convergence in the popular spoken registers of Greek and Latin it may be useful to append a few further parallels, this time involving the development of the verb system:

(2) The extension of finite (subjunctive) clauses introduced by final conjunctions, especially ἵνα ['ina], at the expense of infinitival structures: this was possibly connected with the historically wider range of uses of Latin *ut*, e.g. in final and consecutive clauses, indirect commands, and various 'future-referring' complement and adjunct structures.

Since this process began in the Hellenistic period (cf. 4.4.1), however, the most we can say is that contact with Latin may have reinforced and/or accelerated the trend. Thus in classical Greek the present and future indicative were distinguished from the present and aorist subjunctive respectively, by distinctions of vowel quality and vowel length that were subsequently lost (quite widely by the middle of the second century BC, cf. 6.2 and 11.8.6(a)): e.g. παύ-εις [paú-eːs] 'you stop', παύ-ῃς [paú-ɛːis] 'you may stop', both > ['paβ\u02b7is]; παύ-σ-ομεν [paú-s-omen] 'we shall stop', παύ-σ-ωμεν [paú-s-oːmen] 'we may stop', both > ['paφ\u02b7somen]. The damaging effects of sound change therefore led to a growing need to 'mark' sub-junctives as such, and ἵνα ['ina] began to develop language-internally as an 'empty' mood marker, first in subordinate, but eventually also in main clauses that required a modal verb form (a process that was finally completed in the Middle Ages).

Similar observations apply both to the progressive loss of distinctive middle morphology (outside the future and aorist paradigms, middle and passive forms were always identical, and some middle verbs already employed passive suffixes in the aorist even in classical Greek), and to the disappearance of the optative mood, which was steadily replaced, according to its function, by subjunctives (e.g. in past-time final clauses), indicatives (e.g. in past-time indirect speech after ὅτι ['oti] 'that'), or modal periphrases (e.g. in speculative future conditionals, and generally in the potential sense of what 'could happen'). These processes can also be traced back to developments in classical and Hellenistic Greek, and were largely motiv-ated by a desire for greater semantic transparency (the optative contributing very little that was clearly definable in the majority of its uses outside the basic sense of expressing a wish). Thus the fact that Latin has only one set of medio-passive endings (e.g. *uertor* = 'I turn (myself) round/I am turned round', etc.) and a single subjunctive mood that fulfilled the combined functions of the Greek subjunctive and optative (in part) seems once again to have been no more than an external reinforcement for an internally motivated evolution.

(3) The formal renewal of the future by means of periphrases involving a modal verb + infinitive (at first replacing the future passive, but later more generally, following the changes in the vowel system discussed in (2)). Initially ὀφείλω [o'pʰilo] 'I owe/ought', and μέλλω ['melo] 'I intend/am about to', were more common, but later ἔχω ['ekʰo] 'I have/am able/must', and θέλω ['tʰelo] 'I wish', became the preferred variants. This allowed the marking of aspect in the future for the first time, by providing a choice between the aorist (perfective) and present (imperfective) infinitives. Although this was not reflected in Latin, where time reference always took precedence over aspect, the general pattern of development may be connected with the parallel replacement of the future in Vulgar Latin by infinitival periphrases with *debeo* 'I owe', *uolo* 'I wish', and above all *habeo* 'I have/am able/must': cf. French *donner-ai/donner-as* < *donare habeo/donare habes*.

Although Balkan Romance forms its futures with *uolo* 'wish', rather than *habeo,* we should note that the Romanian forms are not attested until relatively recently, by which time periphrases with θέλω ['θelo] 'wish', had also replaced those with ἔχω ['exo] in Greek. This may therefore represent one of the convergent features of the famous Balkan 'Sprachbund' (see 8.6). In earlier periods, however, when the Roman/Byzantine empire still extended over much of the eastern Mediterranean, there is no reason to expect Greek in general to have anticipated specifically Balkan developments of the later Middle Ages.

Thus even though the use of periphrases to replace the future passive began in Hellenistic times, the subsequent parallelism of development in late antiquity is particularly striking, and probably reflects a mutual reinforcement of already partly convergent constructional innovations. We may also note the parallel use of the past tenses of ἔχω ['ekʰo]/*habeo* (and the other future auxiliaries) + infinitive to supply a 'conditional' (or future-in-the-past) to express 'unreal' or 'hypothetical' consequences in the sense of 'would/would have'.

(4) The falling together of perfect and aorist, functionally and then formally (cf. 6.5.2), may have been influenced by the dual use of the Latin perfect as a past perfective and a present stative. The renewal of the 'true' (stative) perfect by periphrases with ἔχω ['ekʰo] 'have' and εἰμί [i'mi] 'be' + perfect (or function-ally equivalent aorist) passive participle, the former in an active sense, the latter in a passive one, may also reflect the influence of the parallel (Vulgar) Latin constructions: cf. *hoc habeo factum* 'this I-have in-a-having-been-done-state' = 'I have done this'; *hoc factum est* 'this in-a-having-been-done-state is' = 'this is done'.

We should note, however, that this functional merger of aorist and perfect had also begun in Hellenistic times (cf. 4.7.7). Furthermore, the passive construction with εἰμί [i'mi] 'be' was already an option in classical Greek, alongside an active equiva-lent (i.e. with a perfect or aorist active participle). Originally used primarily to form active and passive 'modal' perfects (subjunctive and optative) and the morpholo-gically difficult 3pl. perfect indicative passive (where the final consonant of a verb stem could not readily be combined with the suffix -νται [-ntai]), the periphrastic constructions gradually spread through the paradigm in the popular Koine, pre-sumably because of their semantic transparency and the fact that the paradigms of the verb 'to be' and the relevant participles had in any case to be mastered independently.

But as the use of the inflected participles of the 3rd declension (i.e. present/ future/aorist active, and aorist passive) began to wither away, in part because of their morphological complexity (cf. 6.5.3), the periphrasis with the perfect passive participle, which deployed a combination of 'regular' 2nd and 1st declension end-ings, -μένος (masc.)/-μένη (fem.)/-μένον (neut.) [-'menos/-'meni/-'menon], emerged as the major survivor in popular Greek of the medieval period. (The use of the past tense of 'be' with an aorist active participle, originally fully inflected in -σας (masc.)/-σασα (fem.)/-σαν (neut.) [-sas/-sasa/-san], but later reduced to the invari-ant -σαντα [-sanda] and then remodelled on the pattern of the indeclinable pres-ent participle in -οντα [-onda], is also well attested as a pluperfect substitute (cf. 11.8.3).) There is, then, little reason to see here any particular impact of the Latin perfect in general or of the Latin perfect passive periphrasis in particular, other than as providing a general external stimulus to the Greek trends already under way.

The situation is rather different, however, in the case of ἔχω ['ekʰo] + perfect passive participle used in an active, transitive sense. This is a wholly unclassical construction, which begins to appear in the more polished 'literary' registers of the Koine in the Roman period (e.g. in the writings of the historian Diodorus Siculus or the biographer and essayist Plutarch). It is not used by the Atticists (cf. 5.5 and

5.6), and it does not appear in low-level literary or subliterary texts. Furthermore, with the advent of a more stringent Atticist approach in the second century AD, it quickly disappeared even from stylistically middle-brow compositions, and eventually reappears in popular varieties of Greek only after the 'Latin' conquest of much of the Byzantine empire after the capture of Constantinople by the Fourth Crusade in 1204 (see Chapter 7 and 11.8.3). This construction is therefore a very strong candidate for classification as a 'Latinism' in the Koine, though not one which made much impact at the time, even if it was later reintroduced with more lasting effect, following the collapse of the Byzantine state.

Looking at all these developments together, therefore, it seems that those which had a long-term impact represent no more than the carrying through of changes which had already begun in the classical or early post-classical language. Although many can be paralleled in imperial Vulgar Latin, it is probably safe to conclude that the majority are simply a by-product of the transition of both (Attic) Greek and Latin from the status of local dialects to world languages, with the well-known drift towards greater grammatical analyticity that such a role almost invariably entails, at least in more popular registers. Given that the changes in question are for the most part structurally and semantically 'natural', and that the two languages were members of the same 'family', with many partial structural correspondences, a certain parallelism of evolution under similar external conditions was only to be expected. Against this background, the fact of extensive Greek/Latin bilingualism in the six centuries prior to the collapse of the Roman empire in the west can have been only a contributory factor in the promotion of convergence.

5.4   *Romanitas* and *Hellenismós*

The pervasive influence of Greek language and culture remained highly problematical for many Romans throughout the imperial period. Conversely, despite the political and economic advantages of Roman rule, many Greeks felt a profound sense of alienation; continuity with the past was correspondingly highlighted, and Roman literature and education largely ignored. Thus, even though some material aspects of Roman culture did begin to make an impact, the overall outcome of Greco-Roman cohabitation, even after several centuries, could hardly be called harmonious.

The reasons are not hard to find. For the Romans 'civilization' was defined primarily in terms of long-standing customs (urban life, the rule of law, ethical ideals, etc.) which were never regarded as exclusive property. Rather, the Roman aristocracy felt proud, having adopted these values and mores, to have imposed them upon subject peoples and 'Romanized' them. Since Roman identity so conceived was not underwritten by ethnic origin or a common native language, the incorporation of outsiders was seen as a demonstration of Rome's success in its civilizing mission.

But although this view worked well enough for the 'barbarian' west, the incorporation of the Hellenistic world presented difficulties. The Greeks had not only reached a high level of 'civilization' without Roman help, but had also contributed to the development of the very customs and practices of which the Romans were so proud. This bred a respect for the Greeks which the Romans did not feel for other subject peoples. But when the vast and superior cultural resources of 'alien' Hellenism began to make a wider impact on Roman life, the changes seemed to many to threaten their Roman identity. This led to a more selective approach to Greek culture based on a sharp distinction between the Greeks of old, who were believed to have had 'true' civilization, and the Greeks of the contemporary world, who were increasingly seen as frivolous and insincere, and so just as much in need of the firm hand of Roman rule as western provincials, albeit for different reasons.

By contrast, the Greeks themselves had always had an exclusive definition of their own identity, built upon notions of common religion, common descent from mythical ancestors and the use of a common language. Thus 'barbarians', including Romans, could never become Greek, however far their adopted Hellenism went, while the participation of Greeks in the economic and social advantages of the empire in no way undermined their Greekness. Nonetheless, the Roman view of the Greeks as a people with a great past readily reinforced the Greeks' own increasing obsession with former glories. Nostalgia therefore became an increasingly central characteristic of the Greek world view in the early Empire, though it should be stressed that this reverence for the past was not wholly divorced from contemporary considerations, since, as we shall see in 5.5, (qualified) Roman respect for earlier Greek achievement offered enterprising Greeks of the second and third centuries AD an important resource to exploit in jockeying for support and patronage (cf. Woolf (1994)).

5.5 Atticism and the Second Sophistic

As we have already seen, the role of rhetoric had changed considerably in postclassical times, since neither the Hellenistic monarchies nor the Roman Empire provided a context in which public speeches by individuals could be expected to have a major impact in the wider world of politics and international affairs.

Nevertheless, the demand in aristocratic circles for a rhetorical education remained consistently high in the Roman period, and the *rhetors* (or 'sophists'), i.e. public speakers offering rhetorical training, enjoyed a correspondingly high social status. The reasons are not hard to find. Administration and civic life still demanded rhetorical skills, since formal speeches, often with some political content, were routinely given on major public occasions. A successful performance could lead directly to imperial patronage and the channelling of resources towards a particular city or project, while a reputation for eloquence could readily lead to significant personal advancement. Eulogies of the emperor naturally constituted an important genre, but speeches were also given to commemorate visits by imperial officials, appointments to imperial consulships, the construction of monumental buildings and, after the adoption of Christianity by Constantine I (reigned AD 306–37), the dedication of major churches.

Although there had been some cultural nationalism (marked in particular by an efflorescence of rhetoric) as early as the late Republic, it is perhaps from the reign of Augustus (27 BC–AD 14) onwards that we see the beginnings of a true revival in Greek self-confidence, based at least in part on Roman willingness to allow the major Greek cities to retain a degree of autonomy within which a continuing Hellenic identity could foster the illusion of the survival of past glories. During the second century AD, however, a series of positively Philhellenic emperors (Hadrian, Antoninus Pius and Marcus Aurelius) ushered in a period of economic resurgence distinguished by monumental building, civic benefactions, and increasing Greek membership of the equestrian and senatorial orders. The Greeks were quick to appreciate that linking their past to the Roman present offered a fast route to money and privilege, and the second century marks the beginning of a period of flamboyant Hellenism known as the 'Second Sophistic' (the term was coined by the Athenian sophist Philostratus in the early third century AD, the 'First Sophistic' having occurred in the fifth century BC, cf. Chapter 3). A wealthy aristocracy was now only too pleased to pay distinguished sophists to teach its sons, while citizen bodies, increasingly culturally aware, looked forward to regular entertainments by renowned speakers in the newly built *odeia*. Against this background, the leading sophists evolved into an intellectual and social élite, offering ostentatious displays of competitive disputation and enjoying high-ranking connections and popular adulation on a scale reserved today for rock stars and Hollywood heroes.

While those looking for a higher education had had, since the time of Plato and Isocrates, a choice between rhetoric and philosophy, the greater accessibility and sheer entertainment value of the former now led to the temporary eclipse of the latter. The sophists soon became the primary symbol of the resilience of the Greek urban aristocracy, and the central component of a literary and cultural renaissance founded in nostalgia for a lost but glorious past. Indeed, Christianity notwithstanding, the long-term influence of these guardians of the Hellenic heritage, whose knowledge and learning seemed to allow them to commune directly with the ancient classics, was so profound that they effectively determined the linguistic and literary mind-set of the Greek élite for the next 1,800 years.

It is against this background that the phenomenon of 'Atticism' must be assessed. The perception of the written Koine as a 'technical' or 'bureaucratic' language had always militated against its unadorned use as a vehicle for 'higher' purposes (cf. 4.7.4, 4.7.5), and the Hellenistic education system therefore required the study and imitation of classical authors. But an initial preference for the Isocratean 'periodic' style was soon replaced, with the advent of the Asianic reaction in the third century BC, by a striving for a quirky Gorgianic restlessness that quickly became fashionable and never ceased to attract adherents. This movement enjoyed something of a revival in Nero's time (reigned AD 54–68), and again in the second century in the age of Hadrian (reigned AD 117–38).

As already noted, the 'Atticist' response, which set in during the first century BC, was dedicated to re-establishing the style and ultimately the language of the 'best' Attic writers. Though both Asianism and Atticism can be seen as the product of dissatisfaction among writers of literary prose with the perceived sterility of the

Koine, the eventual triumph and long-term success of Atticism can ultimately be attributed to the fact that it found its natural milieu in the context of the antiquarianism of the Second Sophistic. The precious link with the classical past could, it seemed, best be secured by addressing the ancient masters in their own Attic dialect, thereby obtaining their tacit endorsement for the products of the present. While the written Koine could be accepted as the language of business, the expression of the highest forms of Greek culture demanded better, and only Attic, the embodiment of the 'purest' form of the language, could serve as its vehicle (cf. Aelius Aristides *Panathenaic Oration* 322–30).

This development had the further advantage that it 'solved' the problem of the widening gap between the language of the classical texts studied in school and the different varieties of contemporary Greek. Educated Greeks soon came to feel that their contemporary language fundamentally *was* Attic, if only it had not been allowed to decline through vulgarity and ignorance, and an ability to use the classical language (rather like the use of 'BBC English' until very recently) came to be regarded as a conspicuous and exclusive badge of class membership. The resultant dichotomy between an unchanging Attic ideal and the Koine in all its heterogeneity quickly established a formal state of diglossia that became steadily more problematical with the passage of time, and which was not to be finally abandoned until the late twentieth century (see Section III).

It should be stressed, however, that the notion of a clear-cut dichotomy, though ideologically vital, was in reality largely theoretical. In the first place, there was no consensus as to which 'classical' authors could legitimately be appealed to, nor was there any overall consistency of usage in even the subset of authors who were generally acknowledged as suitable models. Thus few, if any, writers were in practice able to sustain a consistent 'Attic' style, and many simply fell back on the expedient of decorating a grammatically antiqued Koine (key 'rules' were learned at school, see 5.6. below) with vocabulary and phraseology randomly excerpted to meet the needs of the moment. Self-doubt and confusion were rife, and what had begun as a mildly 'classical' corrective to Asianic excess soon evolved into an increasingly problematical obstacle to clear and confident self-expression (cf. Schmid (1887–97) for detailed statistics about the usage of particular authors, and Anderson (1994: ch. 4) for an up-to-date bibliography and a general survey of the issues).

At the same time the highest registers of the written and spoken Koine, employed by people who had been educated to think of Attic as the 'correct' form of the language, inevitably absorbed an increasing number of Attic traits with the passage of time. The educated/standard Koine thus found itself uneasily poised between the cultural imperative of unchanging Attic perfection and the practical need for a 'working' written language that recognized and represented (at least some of) the changes in spoken Greek. In the Roman imperial and Byzantine periods, therefore, the official language of administration at the highest levels became somewhat more detached from even educated spoken Greek than had previously been the case.

Since the all-important distinction between classical Attic and the Koine was far from absolute, even the most learned devotees of Atticism routinely left themselves open to attack for their 'solecisms' (cf. Fabricius (1962: 20)), and Atticism might best be thought of not as a well-defined body of doctrine but as a state of mind inculcated by the education system and reinforced by the practice and prejudices of the aristocracy. Well-known practitioners of 'puristic' Attic revivalism in the period of the Second Sophistic include: the orators Aelius Aristides (*c.* AD 129–*c.* 189) and Herodes Atticus (AD 101–77, the multi-millionaire benefactor of Roman Athens); the writer of 'philosophical' medleys Claudius Aelianus (Aelian: *c.* AD 172–*c.* 235); the historians Flavius Arrianus (Arrian: *c.* AD 95–175) and Appian (second century AD); the sophists' biographer Philostratus (born *c.* AD 160/170); the antiquarian/geographer Pausanias (second century AD); and the romance writers Achilles Tatius (*c.* second century AD) and Longus (*c.* late second/ early third century AD).

From a modern perspective, however, Lucian, born in Syrian Commagene *c.* AD 120, and a native speaker of Syriac who 'learned his Greek at school' (*Bis Accusatus* 27), is perhaps one of the more successful practitioners. By adopting a relatively relaxed attitude to classical precedent, he managed to impart an unusual degree of 'vitality' to a language already 'dead' for some five centuries, while his attitude (amused scepticism) and subject matter (essays, treatises and dialogues on a wide range of issues of intellectual interest) are more immediately congenial than those of many other contemporary writers.

Yet as early as the first century AD the essayist and biographer Plutarch (*c.* AD 46–120) was complaining about the banality of thought and clichéd verbiage that the doctrine of Atticism was tending to produce in its less talented practitioners (*Moralia* 42 DE); and even Lucian himself, despite having begun his career as a successful, if rapidly disillusioned, orator, repeatedly satirizes the excesses of Atticist pedantry (*Lexiphanes*, *Pseudologista*, *Pseudosophista*). Plutarch, however, was among the last exponents of the Hellenistic tradition, exemplified by writers such as Polybius (cf. 4.7.2) and the historian/geographer Strabo (*c.* 64 BC–AD 19), a tradition which was increasingly out of tune with the mood of the times. Despite the fact that Atticism tended to smother natural invention by encouraging a preoccupation with linguistic form and institutionalizing a state of mind that equated a surface dressing of 'hallmarked' items with learning and good taste, the hold of the movement was such that those who failed to display the expected knowledge of approved grammar and diction forfeited all prospect of serious consideration by their peers. Only writers of scientific prose, such as the Pergamene physician Galen (AD 129–99), were in a position to reject its demands in the interests of clarity.

Following the excesses of the second century, however, a more realistic Atticism, well exemplified by the historian Cassius Dio (Cocceianus) (*c.* AD 155–235), eventually began to prevail. This shift in part reflects the diminution of scholarly activity in the midst of very real political and economic difficulties (the period enjoyed no fewer than 23 emperors, or would-be emperors, between AD 238 and AD 284 (see Chapter 4)), but the gradual recognition of the practical unattainability of the Attic ideal led to the near-universal acceptance of certain non-classical constructions alongside strictly Attic usage, and to the development of a generally 'Atticizing' style, in which Attic grammatical and lexical elements were combined with certain well-established features of the higher-level Koine (cf. Fabricius (1962)). This standard prose language was used by virtually all literary writers, whose styles now differed principally in the degree to which they incorporated specifically Attic markers into their writing. This literary standard remained, subject to greater or lesser degrees of Atticizing, the basis for belletristic writing throughout late antiquity and the Middle Ages down into the modern period (cf. 8.4.2, Chapter 9), its relationship with spoken Greek becoming ever more tenuous.

A more practical, non-Atticizing Koine was, however, retained for everyday purposes in the Chancery, although even this 'simple' administrative style, despite making concessions to change in the interests of communicative efficiency, became increasingly conservative, irrespective of sporadic Atticist infiltration, through the rigorous training of clerical officials (and indeed all who learned to read and write at a basic level) in the conventions of traditional 'business Greek'.

But one particular version of basic written Greek eventually evolved, under the influence of the unpretentious language of the New Testament (cf. 5.10.2), into a rival 'middle-brow' literary language that permitted aspects of contemporary speech to be directly represented, and which was widely employed in biographies and works of reference aimed at the edification of a wider audience (cf. 8.5.5, 8.5.6, 10.2, 10.3). But the spoken language itself was not to become a primary basis for the development of a written form of Greek until the later Middle Ages, and even then was subject to strict genre-conditioned restrictions on its use (cf. 8.4.3–8.4.6, and Chapter 11).

In the following sections a sample of varieties of Greek from the Roman period (ranging from the first to the fifth centuries AD) will be presented and discussed, beginning with the Atticizing style of belles lettres, and passing on to official and (semi-)literary versions of the Koine. The evidence for spoken Greek provided by the private documents of the less educated is considered in Chapter 6.

5.6　Atticist grammars and lexica: Aelius Aristides

Those who wanted to write the best Attic clearly needed help. And since no one had spoken the prescribed model Attic for centuries, grammatical handbooks and lexica became indispensable for the would-be author. Important hallmarks of correct Attic usage included the following:

[The transcription of the Attic variants is intended to reflect the pronunciation of the Atticizing élite in the second century AD; that of the corresponding Koine forms the contemporary, moderately educated norm.]

(5) (a) -ττ- [tt] and -ρρ- [-rr-] for -σσ- [ss] and -ρσ- [-rs-] in the relevant words, e.g. θάλαττα ['tʰalatta] 'sea' and θάρρος ['tʰarros] 'courage'.
   (b) ξύν [ksyn] for simplified σύν [syn] 'with'.
   (c) the formation of abstract nominals with the neuter article τό [to] and an adjective in agreement.
   (d) regular use of the dual number (long-dead in the Koine).

(e) extensive use of the dative in all its traditonal functions (often to excess, and sometimes wrongly, in an attempt to demonstrate one's 'education').

(f) use of the 'contracted' forms of nouns in which the root/stem originally ended in a vowel and the inflectional ending began with a vowel; the Koine (following Ionic) generally preferred the uncontracted variants: e.g. ὀστοῦν [o'stuːn] not ὀστέον [o'steon] 'bone', etc.

(g) retention of the Attic declension of λεώς/νεώς [le'oːs/ne'oːs] in place of λαός/ναός [la'os/na'os] 'people/temple'.

(h) γίγνομαι ['jiɣnomai] 'I become', γιγνώσκω [ji'ɣnoːskoː] 'I get to know', for simplified γίνομαι ['jinomai], γινώσκω [ji'nosko].

(i) the use of the synthetic perfect rather than periphrases with the perfect middle/passive participle and the verb 'to be' in the subjunctive, optative and 3pl. middle/passive; so λέλυνται ['lelyntai] rather than λελυμένοι εἰσί [lely'meny i'si] 'they have been set free'.

(j) extensive use of middle verb forms, both where the Koine had replaced anomalous middles with regular actives or passives, and also gratuitously as a mark of 'learning'.

(k) use of the optative in its full range of classical functions, sometimes also erroneously, again in an effort to emphasize the writer's 'knowledge'.

(l) the use of monolectic perfect forms with a 'stative/present' rather than a 'simple past' meaning (perfect and aorist were already falling together in the Koine as past tenses).

In the same sort of way lexicographers established a 'correct' (i.e. classically attested) vocabulary. The most important of such lexica is the *Selection (Ecloga) of Attic Verbs and Nouns*, from the work *The Atticist* by Phrynichus (later second century AD). Adopting Plato, the orators Aeschines, Isocrates and Lysias, and the tragedians Aeschylus, Sophocles and Euripides as his principal (if far from homogeneous) models, he then excoriated selected later authors for their failure to write the Attic of the fifth and fourth centuries BC as employed by his chosen masters.

   Phrynichus' dictionary entries usually take the form of simple injunctions as to what to say and what to avoid, thus indirectly providing valuable information (under the heading of what is to be avoided) about the ordinary usage of the period. For example:

(6) ἀκμήν ἀντὶ τοῦ ἔτι. Ξενοφῶντα λέγουσιν ἅπαξ αὐτῷ κεχρῆσθαι. σὺ δὲ φυλάττου χρῆσθαι, λέγε δὲ ἔτι.   *Ecloga* 100

[ak'meːn   an'ti   tuː 'eti. kseno'pʰoːnta 'leɣuːsin 'hápaks au'toːi
akmen (='still') instead-of the *eti*.   Xenophon   they-say   once   it

ke'kʰreːstʰai. sy de pʰy'lattou 'kʰreːsthai, 'leje de 'eti]
to-have-used. You but avoid   to-use,   say   and *eti*.

'*Akmen* for *eti*. They say Xenophon used it once. But you avoid using it and say *eti*.'

In almost every case it is of course the stigmatized form (if any) that has survived in modern Greek; thus the modern word for 'still/yet' is ακόμη/ακόμα [aˈkomi/aˈkoma], derived from ἀκμήν [akˈmeːn], apparently under the influence of Italian *ancora*.

All in all, the Atticist lexicographers' often contradictory and sometimes mistaken advice only contributed to the difficulties faced by the would-be writer. Koineisms, analogical hyper-Atticisms and straight grammatical mistakes occur in even the most carefully contrived compositions, a natural product of attempts to employ a form of the language which was, by definition, imperfectly controlled and understood.

We may conclude this section with a brief extract from a work of Aelius Aristides, addressed, as one might expect of a true Atticist, to Plato himself, in order to illustrate the 'hard-core' Atticizing style:

(7) οὐ γὰρ τόν γε τοῦ παντὸς ἐσφαλμένον ὡς ἀνέλοι σοφώτατον ἀνθρώπων πιστεῦσαι θεμιτὸν περὶ τοῦ θεοῦ. τέχνην δέ, ὡς ἔοικεν, ἔφασκεν οὐκ ἀσκεῖν, ἀληθῆ λέγων. ᾧ γοῦν συνεγένετο Ἀναξαγόρᾳ, οὐ τἀκείνου τιμήσας φαίνεται. ἓν μὲν δὴ τοῦτο μαρτυρεῖ Σωκράτης, οὐκ αἰσχρὸν εἶναι τὸ μὴ τέχνην κεκτῆσθαι, εἴπερ περὶ αὐτοῦ λέγων οὐκ ᾐσχύνετο.

To Plato: In Defence of Oratory, 78–9 (25 D).

[uː ɣar ton je   tuː panˈtos espʰalˈmenon hoːs anˈ(h)eloi
(it is) not for   the   at-any-rate of-the everything failed   that   he-ordained

soˈpʰoːtaton anˈtʰroːpoːn pisˈtewsai tʰemiˈton peˈri   tuː tʰeˈuː. ˈtekʰneːn
wisest   of-men   to-believe right   concerning the god.   Art

de, hoːs ˈeoiken, ˈepʰasken uːk asˈkiːn, aleːˈtʰeː ˈleɣoːn. hoːi   ɣuːn
but, as   it-seems, he-used-to-say not to-practise, true-things saying.   Whereas at-all-events

syneˈjeneto   anaksaˈɣoraːi, uː taːˈkiːnuː   tiːˈmeːsaːs   ˈpʰainetai. hen
he-associated-with Anaxagoras,   not the-things-of-him having-honoured he-is-revealed. One

men   deː   ˈtuːto martyˈriː soːˈkrateːs, uk aiˈskʰron ˈiːnai to meː
on-the-one-hand indeed this   bears-witness Socrates,   not disgraceful to-be   the not

ˈtekʰneːn keˈkteːstʰai, ˈiper   peˈri   hawˈtuː ˈleɣoːn uːk iːˈskʰyneto.]
art   to-have-acquired, if-indeed concerning himself speaking not he-was ashamed.

'For it is impious to believe of the god that he proclaimed one who had failed in everything (to be) the wisest of men. But Socrates, it seems, was telling the truth when he used to say that he was master of no craft. So though he did study with Anaxagoras, he clearly did not respect his teachings. To this one fact, then, Socrates does bear witness, that it is no disgrace not to have mastered a craft, if indeed he was not ashamed to talk about himself.'

Note in particular the rather 'unnatural' word order in the first sentence, where the predicate, comprising θεμιτόν [tʰemiˈton], 'right (according to divine law)', and its infinitival complement appear together as the final constituent rather than immediately after the negative οὐ [uː], and where θεμιτόν [tʰemiˈton] itself (the head of the predicate expression) is placed in penultimate position in its phrase, splitting the infinitive from its prepositional phrase dependent. This tendency to place the verb next-to-last, thereby creating a discontinuity between the elements of its complement structure (hyperbaton), was a classical stylistic option and one which became highly characteristic of Atticist writing, even infiltrating the higher levels of the Koine (cf. 5.7). In some writers (e.g. Eusebius, the author of a fourth-century history of the early Christian church), it is so habitual as to become something of an irritation.

There is also an 'error' in the use of the optative ἀνέλοι [an'(h)eloi] 'he ordained', in the indirect statement dependent on πιστεῦσαι ὡς [pi'stewsai hoːs] 'believe that'. Strictly, the optative may be used in subordinate clauses of this type when the verb that introduces the indirect statement is in a past tense; it should not be employed simply when what is said or believed occurred in the past, as here. 'Mistakes' of this kind are so common that it is more constructive to look at the Atticist programme less as an attempt to recreate the language of the past, and more as a commitment to forge a contemporary written style which, while employing the grammatical and lexical resources of the past, also allowed these to be developed in unclassical ways, the primary objective being to distance the literary language from the Koine. Attic might then be seen as a learned, and learnèd, 'living' language rather than strictly as a 'dead' one, and we should not then be surprised, given the relative freedom from constricting associations with the contemporary vernacular, to see evidence of purely internal developments that conflict with, or at least display a freedom of usage that goes well beyond, the 'rules' of the classical language. We may compare the language of the epic, or the literary revivals of classical dialects in Hellenistic times, for similar processes of internal evolution in the literary dialects of earlier periods.

This use of Atticized Greek as a semi-living language by the educated classes is highly problematical for most modern scholars, and the whole issue has in any case been distorted by the anachronistic interpretation of the phenomenon in the terms of the language controversy of the nineteenth and twentieth centuries (the struggle between those who advocated a classicizing written language and those who sought a national language based on the vernacular, cf. Section III). We should never forget that, however unnatural this situation may seem to us, the Greek élite was content to employ a classicizing written style, without complaint, right up until the modern period and the belated impact of the European Enlightenment on a Greek world under Ottoman domination. Neither late antiquity nor the Middle Ages provided a socio-political environment in which the empowering of the masses through access to literature and knowledge could ever become an issue; the primary consideration throughout was for the educated minority to maintain its Greco-Roman identity through cultural and linguistic continuity with the classical (and later Christian) tradition, an objective that eventually came to be equated with national survival in the dark days of Turkish oppression.

5.7 The official Koine in the Roman Republican period

Macedonia became a Roman province in 149 BC, and not long afterwards the Achaean league was crushed and the city of Corinth razed to the ground. Within the Greek cities, however, pro-Roman parties had begun to emerge much earlier, and civil discord between traditionalists and Roman apologists became common. Against a background of land shortage and indebtedness, the situation was readily exploited by the shrewd Roman oligarchy, and Roman willingness to use the Koine as an official language of diplomacy and administration is well illustrated by the following extracts from a translation of a decree of the Senate, dated 170 BC, concerning the city of Thisbae in Boeotia. This decree, incidentally, is contemporaneous with the manumission decree in Boeotian dialect discussed in 4.4.2 (text (4)), and so provides a nice example of the relative status of local dialects and the Koine in the period.

(8) . . .

περὶ ὧν Θισ[β]εῖς λόγους ἐποιήσαντο· περὶ τῶν καθ'αὑ[τ]οὺς πραγμάτων,
οἵτινες ἐν τῆι φιλίαι τῆι ἡμετέραι ἐνέμειναν, ὅπως αὐτοῖς δοθῶσιν [ο]ἷς τὰ
καθ' αὑτοὺς πράγματα ἐξηγήσωνται, περὶ τούτου τοῦ πράγματος οὕτως
ἔδοξεν· ὅπως Κόιντος Μαίνιος στρατηγὸς τῶν ἐκ τῆς συνκλήτου [π]έντε
ἀποτάξῃ, οἳ ἂν αὐτῶι ἐκ τῶν δημοσίων πρα[γμ]άτων καὶ τῆς ἰδίας πίστεως
φαίνωνται. ἔδοξε.

. . .

οἵτινες εἰς ἄλλας πόλεις ἀπήλθοσαν καὶ οὐχὶ πρὸς τὸν παρ' ἡμῶν στρατηγὸν
παρεγένοντο, ὅπως μὴ εἰς τάξιν καταπορεύωνται, περὶ τούτου τοῦ πράγματος
πρὸς Αὖλον ['Ο]στίλιον ὕπατον γράμματα ἀποστεῖλαι ἔδοξεν, ὅπως περὶ
τούτου τῆι διανοίαι προσέχῃι, καθὼς ἂν αὐτῶι ἐκ τῶν δημοσίων πραγμάτων
καὶ τῆς ἰδίας πίστεως φαίνηται. ἔδοξεν.

. . .   *SIG* II. 646

[The following transcription assumes a conservative pronunciation, as appropriate for an official document.]

[perì hôːn   tʰizbîːs lóguːs epojéːsanto; perì tôːn katʰ hautùːs
About which-things Thisbians words   made;   about   the   by   themselves

pragmátoːn, hoítines en tîː pʰilíaːi tîː heːmetéraːi enémiːnan, hópoːs autoîs
affairs,   whoever in the friendship the ours   remained,   that   to-them

dotʰôːsin   hoîs   tà katʰ hautùːs prágmata ekseːgéːsoːntai, perì
be-given (the things) by-which the by   themselves affairs   they-may-conduct, about

túːtuː tûː prágmatos húːtoːs édoksen;   hópoːs 'kʷintos 'mainios strateːgòs
this   the matter   thus   it-was-resolved; that   Quintus Maenius governor

tôːn ek têːs syŋkléːtuː pénte apotáksiː,   hoì àn autôːi ek tôːn
of-the from the Senate   five   should-delegate, who ever to-him from the

deːmosíoːn pragmátoːn kaì têːs idíaːs písteoːs pʰaínoːntai.   édokse.
public   affairs   and the private faith   should-seem-good. Resolved.

hoítines iːs állaːs póliːs apéːltʰosan kaì uːkʰì pròs tòn par heːmôːn
Whoever to other   cities   departed   and not   to   the from us

strateːgòn paregénonto,   hópoːs mèː iːs táksin kataporeúoːntai, perì
governor   presented-themselves, that   not to rank   they-should-return, concerning

túːtuː tûː prágmatos pròs 'aulon ho'stilion hýpaton grámmata apostîːlai
this   the matter   to   Aulus Hostilius consul letters   to-send

édoksen,   hópoːs perì túːtuː tîː   dianoíaːi prosékʰiː, katʰòːs àn autôːi
it-was-resolved, that about this to-the intention he-pay-heed, just-as ever to-him

ek tôːn deːmosíoːn pragmátoːn kaì têːs idíaːs písteoːs pʰaíneːtai.
from the public   affairs   and the private faith should-seem good.

édoksen.]
Resolved.

'Concerning those matters about which the citizens of Thisbae made representations. Concerning their own affairs: the following decision was taken concerning the proposal that those who remained true to our friendship should be given the facilities to conduct their own affairs; that our praetor/governor Quintus Maenius should delegate five members of the senate who seemed to him suitable (arbiters) in the light of their public actions and individual good faith. Resolved.

Concerning the (Thisbians') proposal that those who left for other cities and did not present themselves to our praetor/governor should not return to their station, it was resolved to send a letter to the consul Aulus Hostilius to the effect that he should pay heed to our intentions in whatever way seemed most appropriate in the light of their public actions and individual good faith. Resolved.'

The rather pompous formulaic style of officialdom is at once apparent, and a number of other familiar features of the official Koine also recur, including the liking for prepositional possessives and the tendency for clauses with modal verb forms introduced by 'final' conjunctions to replace future-referring accusative and infinitive structures (e.g. routinely after ἔδοξε [édokse] 'it was resolved', whenever a subject is expressed in the dependent clause). We should also note the regular use of subjunctives, even in a past time context, at the expense of the classical optative, a mood increasingly associated exclusively with the literary language.

A further feature worthy of comment is the use of the subjunctive in a relative clause to express purpose, as in the first passage (οἷς ... ἐξηγήσωνται [hoîs ... ekseːgéːsoːntai] 'by which ... they may conduct'). This is characteristic of Latin (the 'native' construction requiring the future indicative), and may be an example of 'translation' Greek (cf. the liking for verb-final word order), but we should also recall that changes in popular pronunciation, especially the loss of vowel-length distinctions, were already undermining the distinction between the aorist subjunctive (3pl. middle ending -σωνται, classical pronunciation [-soːntai]) and the future indicative (3pl. middle ending -σονται, classical pronunciation [-sontai]).

5.8   Past tense morphology

A final noteworthy development in (8) involves the suffix of 3pl. aorist ἤλθο-σαν [éːltʰo-san] 'they went', in the second extract. The interaction in the Koine between the regular weak aorists in -(σ)α [-(s)a] and the irregular strong aorists in -ον [-on] has already been discussed in 4.9. On this basis, we might have expected a 3pl. ἤλθ-αν [êːltʰ-an] to replace classical ἤλθ-ον [êːltʰ-on], and this is indeed well attested (becoming in due course the preferred form). But in the higher Koine many strong aorists resisted such assimilation to the weak paradigm for a considerable period. Thus even early replacements such as εἶπα [î:pa] for εἶπον [î:pon] 'I said', and ἤνεγκα [é:neŋka] for ἤνεγκον [é:neŋkon] 'I brought', are used only as variants for the corresponding strong forms.

It was, however, a particular mark of the official Koine in this period to allow the substitution of the regular weak suffix -σαν [-san] for the original -ν [-n] in the 3pl. of the strong aorist, as here. This simply continued an analogical extension which had already affected many 3pl. aorists and imperfects in the irregular -μι [-mi] paradigm (cf. Attic/Koine ἔ-θε-σαν [étʰe-san] 'they put' for original ἔθε-ν [etʰe-n], ἐ-τίθε-σαν [etítʰe-san] 'they used to put' for original ἐτίθε-ν [etítʰe-n], etc.). It now began to affect 3pl. strong aorists and imperfects more widely (the imperfect shared the endings of the strong aorist, the two paradigms being distinguished by root allomorphy or suppletion), since the innovation distinguished 1sg. from 3pl. both of which originally ended in -ον [-on]. Early examples are found in late dialect inscriptions as well as in the Ptolemaic papyri and the Septuagint.

Eventually, however, the strong aorist/imperfect paradigm, including this innovative 3pl. form, succumbed to the model of the weak aorists, but as often happens in cases of paradigm interference, the final product in the Byzantine period shows that the process was in fact a two-way one. What eventually emerged was a common set of 'past tense' endings with elements taken from both paradigms:

(9) 1/2/3sg.: -(σ)α/-(σ)ες/-(σ)ε
                [-(s)a/-(s)es/-(s)e]
     1/2/3pl.: -(σ)αμεν/-(σ)ετε, -(σ)ατε/-(σ)αν
                [-(s)amen/-(s)ete, -(s)ate/-(s)an]

Here the a-vowel comes from the weak aorists and the e-vowel from the strong aorists/imperfects (3sg. -ε [-e] being common to both); the s-element naturally appears in just those forms (the majority of weak aorists) which had displayed it in the classical language.

5.9 Official writing of the Roman imperial period

To complete this brief sketch of the Koine in Roman times we may turn briefly to the imperial period proper, and to the following letter addressed by the emperor Hadrian in AD 119 to the Egyptian prefect Rammius (BGU 140). Originally composed in Latin, it was translated into Greek and put on public display in accordance with the emperor's wishes:

[The transcription is again supposed to represent an educated pronunciation of the period.]

(10) ἐπί[σ]ταμαι, Ῥάμμιέ μου, τ[ο]ύτους [ο]ὓς οἱ γονεῖς αὐτῶν τῷ τῆς
      στρατείας ἀνείλαντο χρόνῳ τὴν πρὸς τὰ πατρικὰ [ὑ]π[ά]ρχοντα πρόσοδον
      κεκωλῦσθαι, κ[αὶ τ]οῦτο οὐκ ἐδόκει σκληρὸν ε[ἶ]ναι [τοὐ]ναντίον αὐτῶν
      τῆς στρατιω[τι]κῆς [διδα]χῆς πεποιηκότων. ἥδιστα δὲ αὐτὸς προείεμαι
      τὰς ἀφορμὰς δι’ ὧν τὸ αὐστηρότερον ὑπὸ τῶν πρὸ ἐμοῦ αὐτοκρατόρων

σταθὲν φιλανρωπότερ[ο]ν ἑρμηνεύω. ὅνπερ τοιγαροῦν τ[ρόπ]ον οὔκ εἰσιν
νόμιμοι κληρο[νόμ]οι τῶν ἑαυτῶν πατέρων οἱ τῷ [τ]ῆς στρατείας χρόνῳ
ἀναλημφθέντες, ὅμως κατοχὴ[ν] ὑπαρχόντων ἐξ ἐκείνου τοῦ μέ[ρ]ους τοῦ
διατάγματος οὗ καὶ τοῖς πρὸς [γ]ένους συνγενέσι δίδοται αἰτεῖσθαι δύνασθαι
καὶ αὐτοὺς κρε[ίν]ω.

[e'pistame,	'ṛami'e mu,	'tutus hus	hy	ɣo'nis	aφ'ton to		tis
I-know,	Rammius my,	these	whom	the parents	of-them	in-the of-the	

stra'teas	a'nilando		'kʰrono	ten	pros ta	patri'ka	hy'parkʰonda
military-service	they-acknowledged	time (from)	the	to	the paternal	property	

'prosodon keko'lystʰe,		ke	'tuto uk	e'doki	skle'ron	'ine,	tunan'dion
succession	to-have-been-prevented,	and	this	not	seemed	hard	to-be,	the-opposite

aφ'ton	tes	stratioti'kes	dida'kʰes	pepye'koton.	'hedista	de	aφ'tos
these-people	of-the military	discipline	having-done.		Most-gladly	but	myself

pro'hieme	tas apʰor'mas	di		hon to	aφste'roteron	hy'po tom	pro
I-put-forward	the principles	through	which	the rather-strictly	by	the	before

e'mu aφtokra'toron	sta'tʰen		pʰilantʰro'poteron	herme'neβo.	'homper
me emperors	established(thing)	more-humanely	I-interpret.	In-what

tyɣa'run	'tropon	'uk isin	'nomimy	klero'nomy ton	heaφ'tom	pa'teron hy
therefore	way	not are	lawful	heirs	of-the of-themselves fathers	the

to	tes	stra'teas		'kʰrono	analem'(p)ftʰentes,	'homos	kato'kʰen
in-the of-the	military-service	time	acknowledged,		nevertheless	possession

hypar'kʰondon	eks e'kinu tu	'merus tu	ðja'taɣmatos hu	ke tys	proz
of-property	from that	the part	of-the edict	where also	to-the by

'jenus synge'nesi	'didote	e'tistʰe	'dynastʰe ke	aφ'tus	'krino.
birth kinsmen	it-is-given	to-claim	to-be-able	also these	I-judge.

'I know, my dear Rammius, that persons who were acknowledged to be legitimate by
their parents in the time of their military service have been prevented from succeeding
to their fathers' property, and this did not seem harsh in so far as they had acted
contrary to military discipline [*i.e. soldiers were forbidden to marry and their children
were therefore illegitimate*]. But I myself very gladly put forward the principle by
which I interpret more humanely the rather strict rule established by the emperors
before me. Therefore, although those acknowledged as legitimate in the time of their
fathers' military service are not their fathers' lawful heirs, I decree that they too are
able to claim possession of the property through the clause of the edict in which this
right is granted also to kinsmen by birth.'

The impact of the Atticist revival is apparent here in the avoidance of prepositional possessives, in the penultimate position of the verb ἀνείλαντο [a'nilando]
within the relative clause of the first sentence, splitting up the temporal expression
('hyperbaton': cf. 5.6), and in the use of a simple dative of time (e.g. τῷ ... χρόνῳ
[to ... 'kʰrono]; recall that prepositions were earlier standard in support of the
increasingly 'weak' dative case (cf. the phrase ἐμ παντὶ καιρῶι [em pantì kairô:i]
in example (9) in 4.6.3)).

The routine use of accusative and infinitive constructions, where at least some finite clause replacements might have been expected on the basis of earlier official practice is perhaps to be explained in the same way, though the impact of the Latin original (presumably itself composed in a style closer to the 'classical' than to the 'vulgar' language, where this construction was standard) should not be discounted. In this connection we may also note the predilection for placing verbs in clause-final position, a feature clearly contrary to the general drift in the development of spoken Greek (cf. 4.8). The cumulative impact of such interference phenomena undoubtedly had some effect on educated written usage even among native speakers, at least for as long as the two languages remained in close contact.

5.10 'Colloquial' literature

5.10.1 Epictetus

Epictetus (c. AD 60–140) was a slave from Hierapolis (modern Pamukkale, 'Cotton Castle', famous for its spectacular calcified spring) in Phrygia in Asia Minor. He owed his freedom to his master, a court official by the name of Epaphroditus, and having had the opportunity to hear the Stoic philosopher Musonius, himself taught in Rome before gathering a circle of students at Nicopolis in Epirus. Although he apparently wrote nothing himself, his 'discourses', in a plain and forceful language, have been 'preserved' for us by his admirer Arrian (c. AD 95–175), the author of the famous account of Alexander's expedition. The language of these homely presentations of aspects of Stoic philosophy is probably the closest thing we have, with due allowance for the philosophical terminology and a certain abstractness of style engendered by the subject matter, to a representation of the educated spoken language of the second century AD.

The following brief extract (II.6, 3–4) is typical:

[The pronunciation is intended to reflect that of normal spoken discourse among the educated classes at the time.]

(11) καλὸν δὲ καὶ τὸ εἰδέναι τὴν αὐτοῦ παρασκευὴν καὶ δύναμιν, ἵν᾽ ἐν οἷς μὴ παρασκεύασαι, ἡσυχίαν ἄγῃς μηδ᾽ ἀγανάκτῃς εἴ τινες ἄλλοι πλεῖον σου ἔχουσιν ἐν ἐκείνοις. καὶ γὰρ σὺ ἐν συλλογισμοῖς πλεῖον ἀξιώσεις σεαυτὸν ἔχειν, κἂν ἀγανακτῶσιν ἐπὶ τούτῳ, παραμυθήσῃ αὐτούς· 'ἐγὼ ἔμαθον, ὑμεῖς δὲ οὔ.'

[ka'lon	de	ke	to	i'dene	tin	haɸ'tu	paraske'βęn	ke	'dynamin,	hin	en
Good		and	also	the	to-know	the	of-self	preparation	and power,		so-that in

hys	mę	para'skeβase,	hęsy'kʰian	'ajis	męd	aɣa'naktis	'i
which-things	not	you-are-prepared,	stillness		you-may-conduct	and-not be-angry	if

tines	'aly	'plion su		'ekʰusin en e'kinys.	ke	ɣar sy en sylojiz'mys
some	others	more	than-you have	in these.	And for	you in arguments

'plion aksi'osis	seaɸ'ton 'ekʰin,	kan	aɣana'ktosin epi 'tuto,
more	you-will-expect yourself	to-have,	and-if they-are-angry at this,

paramy'tʰęsi	aɸ'tus;	'e'ɣo	'ematʰon,	hy'mis de 'u.']
you-will-console	them;	'I	have-studied,	you	but not.'

'Knowledge of one's own preparation and resources is a good thing too, so that in matters for which you have not prepared yourself you may be at peace, and not get angry if others have the advantage over you in these. For you in turn will expect yourself to have the advantage in philosophical reasoning, and if they get angry at this, you will console them: "I have studied, but you have not." '

5.10.2 The New Testament

There are clear parallels between Epictetus' style and diction and the language of parts of the New Testament. In general, this is not, any more than that of the Septuagint (4.7.8), a special variety of Greek used by the Jews of the Near East, as once was commonly thought, but a reasonably close reflection of a range of everyday Greek styles in the early centuries AD.

But even though the New Testament was composed in the main by men without a higher education, and so is largely devoid of Atticistic traits, it was nonetheless written in an area where Aramaic was the first language of the majority, and some books at least are probably translations from Aramaic originals. Furthermore, some knowledge of the Septuagint must be supposed for the mainly Jewish authors/translators involved. We therefore find evidence of substrate and translation effects, as well as sporadic Septuagintisms, particularly in traditional passages, such as the two hymns in Luke 1, 46–55 and 68–71.

The identification and classification of relevant examples has long been, and still remains, a matter of controversy. By way of illustration, we might list the following phenomena from the gospel according to St Mark (cf. Maloney (1981), Blass-Debrunner (1984: 273 ff.), Bubenik (1989: 65–7) for detailed discussion):

(12) (a) καί [ke] 'and', beginning a new paragraph.
      (b) καί [ke] 'and', introducing the apodosis of conditional clauses.
      (c) noun–genitive–adjective order, instead of the usual prehead position for the adjective.
      (d) use of modifying genitive NPs where ordinarily Greek would use an adjective.
      (e) use of positive adjectives with the value of comparatives.
      (f) εἷς [is] 'one' (masculine), or ἄνθρωπος ['antʰropos] 'man', used as an indefinite pronoun (instead of τις [tis] 'someone').
      (g) use of redundant resumptive pronouns in relative clauses introduced by an appropriately inflected relative pronoun.
      (h) (nominative) topic, with 'weak' resumptive pronoun (αὐτόν [aɸ'ton] 'him', etc.).

Most of these can be paralleled in the Septuagint, and most could equally well reflect contemporary Hebrew or Aramaic (with (b) and (d) perhaps most likely to reflect some direct influence from the contemporary vernacular). But many can also be paralleled in low-level Koine documents from Egypt (e.g. (a), (b), (f) – at least for εἷς [is], and (h)), and so presumably reflect either more general tendencies of colloquial Greek which were reinforced by Jewish bilingualism in Palestine, or accidental correspondencies between Coptic and Hebrew/Aramaic.

The identification of substrate/translation effects is likely to remain problematical, however, since it must be based on clear evidence that the construction in question is alien to the natural development of Greek. This is a less straightforward matter than might at first appear to be the case. Taking the example of nominative topic + 'weak' resumptive pronoun (12)(h), we should note that this type of dislocated structure is also typical of early legal and gnomic texts in many Indo-European languages, but that classical Greek here demands a 'strong' demonstrative pronoun (e.g. ἐκεῖνος [ekênos] 'that (one)'). On the face of it examples such as St Mark, 4.25: ὃς γὰρ ἔχει, δοθήσεται αὐτῷ [(h)os ɣar 'ekʰi, do'tʰesete aɸ'to], lit. 'who for has, it-shall-be-given to-him', would appear to violate this rule. But the same is true of related examples from Egypt, e.g. P. Merton 23 (second century AD), P. Fay. 127 (second/third century AD), and BGU 385 (second/third century AD), where loosely constructed nominative topics are typical of the breakdown of formal agreement patterns seen also in the case of adjunct participles (cf. 6.5.3). There is also sporadic evidence from this period that stressed αὐτός was already in use as a demonstrative, exactly as in modern Greek, e.g.:

(13) ὑπὲρ αὐτοῦ τοῦ πράγματος   BGU 1655.42 (169 AD)

[i'per aɸ'tu tu 'praɣmatos]

on   this   the matter

'concerning this matter'

There is, then, no obstacle in principle to taking the use of αὐτός [af'tos] in 'popular' Koine texts as reflecting this development, so that, where necessary, the relevant forms could be stressed and used as 'strong' pronouns equivalent to demonstratives. There is, therefore, no compelling reason to treat (12)(h) as a Semitism, despite the obvious parallels in Hebrew/Aramaic.

Though not every putative Semitism can be explained away in such terms, the language of the New Testament in general reflects quite closely the natural development of the language in the early centuries AD, always allowing for stylistic variation determined by the level of education of the author. Thus Hebrews and James are in some respects quite 'classical' (though far from Atticist), while Luke, Acts and the Pauline epistles are written on a higher level than Matthew, Mark and John (Luke, for example, sometimes implicitly 'corrects' the corresponding passage in Mark, cf. Browning (1983: 49)). John and Revelation (Apocalypse), however, are almost wholly uninfluenced by the archaizing conventions of the literary and/or official traditions, and the author of the latter in particular has been seen by some as revelling in his imperfect command of Greek and deliberately adopting an 'anti-cultural' style (cf. Robertson (1919: 135), Moulton (1929: 33)).

The generally 'popular' quality of the language overall is perhaps most clearly demonstrated by a comparison of standard New Testament usage with the injunctions of Phrynichus (cf. 5.6), who was of course commenting on the kinds of 'mistake', i.e. non-classical elements of living Greek, typically made by pupils in literary composition. One example will serve to illustrate the point. Compare *Ecloga* 10:

[It is assumed that Phrynichus would have employed a highly conservative pronunciation.]

(14) <u>εὐχαριστεῖν</u> οὐδεὶς τῶν δοκίμων εἶπεν, ἀλλὰ <u>χάριν</u> <u>εἰδέναι</u>

['ewkʰaris'tiːn'   ud'iːs toːn do'kimoːn 'iːpen, al'la ''kʰarin iː'denai']

eukharistein ('thank') no-one of-the approved   said,   but   *kharin   eidenai*

'None of our approved models said *eukharistein* but *kharin eidenai*.'

with John, 11.41:

(15) *Πάτερ, εὐχαριστῶ σοι*

['pater, eɸkʰari'sto sy]

Father, I-thank   you

The following extract from the beginning of St John's gospel provides a nice example of the 'simple' Koine style within the spectrum of New Testament writing:

[A pronunciation typical of the majority of the basically literate is assumed in the transcription.]

(16) 1. *ἐν ἀρχῇ ἦν ὁ λόγος, καὶ ὁ λόγος ἦν πρὸς τὸν θεόν, καὶ θεὸς ἦν ὁ λόγος.*
2. *οὗτος ἦν ἐν ἀρχῇ πρὸς τὸν θεόν.* 3. *πάντα δι' αὐτοῦ ἐγένετο, καὶ χωρὶς αὐτοῦ ἐγένετο οὐδὲ ἕν ὃ γέγονεν.* 4. *ἐν αὐτῷ ζωὴ ἦν, καὶ ἡ ζωὴ ἦν τὸ φῶς τῶν ἀνθρώπων·* 5. *καὶ τὸ φῶς ἐν τῇ σκοτίᾳ φαίνει, καὶ ἡ σκοτία αὐτὸ οὐ κατέλαβεν.* 6. *ἐγένετο ἄνθρωπος, ἀπεσταλμένος παρὰ θεοῦ, ὄνομα αὐτῷ Ἰωάννης.* 7. *οὗτος ἦλθεν εἰς μαρτυρίαν, ἵνα μαρτυρήσῃ περὶ τοῦ φωτός, ἵνα πάντες πιστεύσωσιν δι' αὐτοῦ.* 8. *οὐκ ἦν ἐκεῖνος τὸ φῶς, ἀλλ' ἵνα μαρτυρήσῃ περὶ τοῦ φωτός.* 9. *ἦν τὸ φῶς τὸ ἀληθινόν, ὃ φωτίζει πάντα ἄνθρωπον, ἐρχόμενον εἰς τὸν κόσμον.*

[1. en ar'kʰi   in   o   'loɣos, ke o   'loɣos im bros to(n) tʰe'o(n), ke tʰe'os

In beginning was the word   and the word   was by   the   god,   and god

in o 'loɣos. 2. 'utos in en ar'kʰi   pros to(n) tʰe'o(n). 3. 'panda di

was the word.   This was in beginning by   the   god.   All-things through

aɸ'tu e'jeneto, ke kʰo'ris aɸ'tu e'jeneto ude   'en   o   'jeɣonen. 4. en

him   happened, and without him   happened not-even one-thing that happened.   In

aɸ'to zo'i in, ke i   zo'i in to pʰos ton an'tʰropon; 5. ke to pʰos en di

him   life   was, and the life   was the light of-the men;   and the light in the

sko'tia 'pʰeni, ke i   sko'ti(a) a(ɸ)'to u ka'telaβen.   6. e'jeneto

darkness shines, and the darkness it   not put-out/understood.   Came-into being

'antʰropos, apestal'menos pa'ra tʰe'u, 'ono'ma (aɸ)to jo'anis. 7. 'utos 'iltʰen

man,   sent   from   god,   name   to-him John.   This   came

is marty'rian 'ina marty'risi pe'ri tu pʰo'tos, 'ina 'pandes pi'steɸsosin

to witness   that he-witness about the light,   that all-men   may-believe

di   aɸ'tu. 8. uk in e'kinos to pʰos, al 'ina marty'risi pe'ri tu pʰo'tos.

through him.   Not was that-man the light, but that he-witness about the light.

9. in to pʰos to alitʰi'non, o   pʰo'tizi 'pand(a) 'antʰropon,

Was the light the true,   which illuminates every   man,

er'kʰomeno(n) is   ton 'gozmo(n).

coming   into the world.

'In the beginning was the Word, and the Word was with God, and the Word was God. The same was in the beginning with God. All things were made by him; and without him was not anything made that was made. In him was life; and the life was the light of men. And the light shineth in darkness; and the darkness comprehended it not. There was a man sent from God, whose name was John. The same came for a witness, to bear witness of the Light, that all men through him might believe. He was not that Light, but was sent to bear witness of that Light. That was the true Light, which lighteth every man that cometh into the world.'

Apart from the obvious simplicity of construction, involving routine coordination of clauses with finite verbs, we may note the simple but effective rhetorical device of repeating a key noun phrase from one sentence as the initial 'topic/subject' of the next. This typical feature of the simple Koine falls into line with the use of the subjunctive in the final clause after a past-time main verb in 7. (the classical optative having long been a mark of the archaizing literary style). Note too, in contrast with the lowest levels of the Koine as discussed in Chapter 6, that the correct use of the dative in its core functions (e.g. indirect object, locative after prepositions, etc.), and the appropriate use of correctly inflected participles (e.g. in 9) are still routine. It cannot be overemphasized that, despite obvious departures from classical usage, this is in fact good, basic Koine Greek of its time.

One developing feature of this variety is the use of subjunctive clauses introduced by ἵνα ['ina], as in 8. Though the sense of this particular example is not altogether certain (perhaps 'he should/must bear witness'), it is clear that this 'conjunction', like its successor να [na] in modern Greek, could already be used with a main verb to express permission/obligation, and that it had accordingly been downgraded in certain contexts to the status of a mood-marker, thus becoming available in main as well as subordinate clauses. There are clear examples of such usage in the Septuagint and elsewhere in the New Testament, and there are also instances in the Egyptian papyri, though these are comparatively rare.

5.11 Later Christian literature: stylistic levels

5.11.1 *The Apostolic Fathers*

The Christian writers of the earliest period (the so-called Apostolic Fathers) generally followed the model of the New Testament and continued to write in a simple Koine style, partly as a mark of their contempt for pagan grammarians and rhetoricians, but partly also from a conviction that the message would be better received by the masses if it were presented in a language that they understood and which crucially lacked the taint of snobbery conveyed by the archaizing literary norm. Thus the New Testament Apocrypha and many of the early saints' lives are composed in a language that displays a fairly consistent lack of regard for the 'purist' tradition and follows the practice of the unelaborated day-to-day written Koine of the time.

We may consider, for example, the following extract from *The Shepherd* (I, 1–2), a mid second-century work comprising a series of revelations made to an individual by the name of Hermas:

(17) ὁ θρέψας με πέπρακέν με Ῥόδῃ τινὶ εἰς Ῥώμην. μετὰ πολλὰ ἔτη ταύτην
ἀνεγνωρισάμην καὶ ἠρξάμην αὐτὴν ἀγαπᾶν ὡς ἀδελφήν. μετὰ χρόνον τινὰ
λουομένην εἰς τὴν ποταμὸν Τίβεριν εἶδον καὶ ἐπέδωκα αὐτῇ τὴν χεῖρα καὶ
ἐξήγαγον αὐτὴν ἐκ τοῦ ποταμοῦ. ταύτης οὖν ἰδὼν τὸ κάλλος διελογιζόμην
ἐν τῇ καρδίᾳ μου λέγων· Μακάριος ἤμην, εἰ τοιαύτην γυναῖκα εἶχον καὶ
τῷ κάλλει καὶ τῷ τρόπῳ. μόνον τοῦτο ἐβουλευσάμην, ἕτερον δὲ οὐδὲ ἕν.

o   'tʰrepsaz   me 'pepra'ke(m) me 'rodi   tini   is 'romi(n). me'ta
The having-nurtured me sold   me to-Rhoda a-certain in Rome.   After

po'la 'eti 'taftin   aneɣnori'samin ke ir'ksamin a(f)tin aɣa'pan os
many years this (woman) I-recognized   and I-began   her   to-love as

adel'pʰi(n). me'ta 'kʰronon dina   luo'menin is tim bota'mon 'tiverin
sister.   After time   some (her) washing   in the river   Tiber

'idon k(e) e'pedo'ka (af)ti tiŋ 'kʰira k(e) e'ksiɣaɣon a(f)tin ek   tu
I-saw and I-gave   to-her the hand and pulled   her   out-of the

pota'mu. 'taftis   un i'don to 'kalos ðjeloji'zomin en di kar'dja
river.   Of this (woman) then seeing the beauty I-began-to-reflect in the heart

mu 'leɣon: 'ma'karjos 'imin,   i ty'afti(n) jy'neka 'ikʰon ke to   'kali
of-me saying: 'Happy   I-would-be, if such   woman I-had both in-the beauty

ke to 'tropo.' 'mono(n) 'tuto evulef'samin, 'eteron de u'de   'en.]
and the character.' Only   this I-resolved,   other (thing) and not (even) one.

'The man who brought me up sold me to a certain Rhoda in Rome. After many years I recognized her qualities, and began to love her as a sister. After a while I saw her washing in the River Tiber, and gave her my hand and pulled her out of the river. Then when I saw her beauty I began to reflect in my heart saying: "I would be happy if I had a wife of such beauty and character." I resolved on this alone, and nothing else.'

We may note once again that this is a 'good' Koine style of the period, involving *inter alia* a full range of inflected participles, the correct use of the dative in its core functions, aorist middle forms (often replaced by the aorist passive in less accomplished writing), and a willingness to vary word order for stylistic effect (e.g. the preposing of the participial complement clause dependent on εἶδον ['idon] 'I saw', leaving the main verb in final position).

Other standard features of the basic Koine at this time include:

(18) (a) The use of the accusative with εἰς [is] in locative function in place of classical ἐν + dative (a feature already well established as an option in the New Testament and the papyri); only the 'extended' usage ἐν τῇ καρδίᾳ [en di kar'ðja] 'in the heart', shows the classical construction.

   (b) The perfect πέπρακεν ['peprake(n)] 'he sold', used as a simple alternative to the aorist (cf. 6.5.2 for an extended discussion of this development).

(c) The use of the imperfect in the protasis and apodosis of a 'remote' future conditional in place of the classical optative (combined with $\check{a}\nu$ [an] in the apodosis). The development of modal syntax is considered in detail in 9.4, cf. also Horrocks (1995).

(d) The beginning of the transfer of the verb 'to be' from the irregular -$\mu\iota$ [-mi] paradigm to the regular middle paradigm in -$\mu\alpha\iota$ [-me], This seems to have begun, as here, with the recharacterization of the 1sg. imperfect $\mathring{\eta}\nu$ [in] as $\mathring{\eta}\mu\eta\nu$ ['imin], a form which is already well attested in the Ptolemaic papyri, and served to distinguish the 1sg. from the homophonous 3sg.; Phrynichus (130) naturally stigmatizes it. From this base a largely middle paradigm was gradually built up in more popular registers of the Koine through the later Roman and early Byzantine periods, the major exception being the forms of the 3sg./3pl. present indicative, which derive from the use of the accented preposition $\check{\epsilon}\nu\iota$ ['eni], first used synonymously with the compound $\check{\epsilon}\nu$-$\epsilon\sigma\tau\iota$ ['en-esti] 'there is/are', but later as a simple replacement for classical $\dot{\epsilon}\sigma\tau\acute{\iota}$ [es'ti]/$\epsilon\dot{\iota}\sigma\acute{\iota}$ [i'si] 'is/are'. The form was eventually adapted to the rest of the paradigm, with first the suffix (-$\nu\alpha\iota$ [-ne]) then the stem ($\epsilon\dot{\iota}$- [i-]) recharacterized on the model of 1sg./2sg. $\epsilon\dot{\iota}\mu\alpha\iota$ ['ime]/$\epsilon\dot{\iota}\sigma\alpha\iota$ ['ise]. We thus obtain the following paradigm for the early/middle Byzantine period (cf. Section II, 11.8.5 (34)(a) for details):

Present: $\epsilon\dot{\iota}$-$\mu\alpha\iota$ ['ime]/$\epsilon\dot{\iota}$-$\sigma\alpha\iota$ ['ise]/$\check{\epsilon}\nu\iota$ ['eni]

  $\epsilon\dot{\iota}$-$\mu\epsilon\theta\alpha$ ['imeθa]/$\epsilon\dot{\iota}$-$\sigma\theta\epsilon$ ['isθe]/$\check{\epsilon}\nu\iota$ ['eni]

Past: $\mathring{\eta}$-$\mu\eta\nu$ ['imin]/$\mathring{\eta}$-σo ['iso]/$\mathring{\eta}$-τo ['ito]

  $\mathring{\eta}$-$\mu\epsilon\theta\alpha$ ['imeθa]/$\mathring{\eta}$-$\sigma\alpha\sigma\theta\epsilon$ ['isasθe]/$\mathring{\eta}\tau\alpha\nu$ ['itan]

[2pl. has borrowed the aorist middle ending, and 3pl. has been recharacterized with -τ- [-t-] on the basis of the 3sg.; many earlier forms remained in use alongside these, however, especially 2sg./pl. $\mathring{\eta}s$ [is]/$\mathring{\eta}\tau\epsilon$ ['ite] and 3pl. $\mathring{\eta}\sigma\alpha\nu$ ['isan]].

5.11.2 *The impact of Atticism*

This use of the 'common' style worked well for as long as Christianity was primarily a religion of the poor and underprivileged. But as it began to make an impression on the educated classes, there arose a need to preach and develop doctrine in a more 'acceptable' form of language. Christian discourse was therefore increasingly 'elevated' from the 'vulgar' level of the New Testament, and, from the beginning of the third century onwards, intellectual apologists such as Clement of Alexandria (second/third century AD), Origen (184–254), and Eusebius (*c.* AD 260–340) began to expound Christian history and doctrine in a language and style adapted from the pagan Greek historical, rhetorical and philosophical traditions that blended the new religious terminology into a variably Atticized 'scholarly' Koine.

This trend was soon consolidated by political developments. By the early fourth century AD profound changes were taking place in the administration of the Roman empire. The inland site of Rome was becoming more impractical as Italy became increasingly vulnerable to barbarian incursions. Since the Balkans and Asia Minor were already the main sources of recruitment to the Roman army, it was natural that when the emperor Constantine I (ruled 306–37 AD) decided to found a 'New Rome', he should select a site in the eastern part of his empire. His choice was the apparently impregnable site of ancient Byzantium, perched on the end of a peninsula and surrounded on three sides by the sea of Marmara, the straits of the Bosporus and the deep river estuary of the Golden Horn. Constantine, who was himself a formal convert to Christianity on his death-bed, had earlier instituted a policy of religious tolerance, and Constantinople (*Κωνσταντινούπολις* [konstandi'nupolis]) was founded on 11 May AD 330 as a Christian city which incorporated three great churches, the Holy Wisdom (*Ἁγία Σοφία* [a'jia so'fia]), the Holy Peace (*Ἁγία Εἰρήνη* [a'jia i'rini]) and the Holy Apostles (*Ἅγιοι Ἀπόστολοι* ['aji a'postoli]), within its grand design.

By the end of the century imperial patronage had secured for Christianity a position as the official religion of the Roman state, and many of the great church fathers of the fourth century, such as St Basil ('the Great', *c.* AD 329–79), St Gregory of Nazianzus (*c.* AD 330–*c.* AD 389), St Gregory of Nyssa (*c.* AD 335– *c.* AD 394), and John Chrysostom (*c.* AD 347–407) were naturally members of the upper classes who had received a higher education. They in turn instinctively turned their backs on the lowly origins of their faith and wrote in the language of their class, though the prestige of the scriptures was indirectly maintained in the form of 'quotations' of key terms and passages. The incorporation of Christianity into the Roman establishment and the new religious impetus behind the classicizing tradition created an archaizing 'ecclesiastical' Greek that quickly permeated the upper strata of Roman society and guaranteed the perpetuation of the diglossia initiated by the first Atticists nearly 500 years before. Though a more basic style of Christian writing continued in the form of saints' biographies and chronicles, the opportunity provided by the new status of Christianity for the development of a high-prestige written language based on contemporary spoken Greek was thus effectively lost.

5.11.3 Callinicus and Theodoret

We may, by way of illustration, take the work of two fairly minor Christian authors of the fifth century AD (the data in what follows are taken from Hult (1990)). At one end of the spectrum, in the *Life of Hypatius* by the monk Callinicus, we find a high concentration of relatively 'low' features, consistently avoided by those adopting a self-consciously classicizing style. Many of these can be seen in ordinary administrative documents from the Hellenistic period onwards, and include:

(19) (a) The widespread use of the pleonastic genitive article *τοῦ* [tu] to strengthen infinitive complements after adjectives, verbs of commanding, and verbs of promising.

(b) The use of *τοῦ* [tu] + infinitive in a final sense (where the classical construction involves a future participle or, more regularly, *ἵνα* ['ina] '(in order) that', + subjunctive or optative, according to whether the tense of the main verb is non-past or past.

(c) The frequent use of ἀπό [a'po], lit. 'from', to mark the agent in passive constructions (where the classical language has ὑπό [y'po], παρά [pa'ra], and various other prepositional options, or, with the perfect passive, a simple dative).

(d) The use of 'final' ἵνα ['ina] to introduce consecutive clauses (where the classical language has ὡς/ὥστε ['oste] '(so) that', + infinitive), and conversely, the use of 'consecutive' ὡς/ὥστε ['oste] + infinitive to introduce a final clause.

(e) The use of 'final' ἵνα ['ina] after verbs of 'commanding' (where the classical language has a simple infinitive).

(f) Parataxis involving finite (subjunctive) verb forms rather than an infinitive complement after verbs of 'wishing' (though sometimes also with ἵνα ['ina]).

(g) The use of the present indicative of ἔχω ['exo], lit. 'have', with an aorist (perfective) infinitive in place of the classical synthetic future.

Other non-classical features of Callinicus' style, however, also occur in more middle-brow writing, and even crop up occasionally in the work of those who strive hardest for puristic effect. These might be thought of as 'established' Koineisms derived from the higher, i.e. official and scientific/technical, registers of the written language, which were clearly also acceptable in unpretentious 'literary' composition:

(20) (a) The use of ὅτι ['oti] 'that' after verbs of 'thinking' (the classical usage is regularly an accusative and infinitive), and verbs of perception (where in classical Greek we have an accusative and participle).

(b) The use of quoted speech rather than a subordinate clause after verbs of 'saying'.

(c) A liking for the 'impersonal' passive 'it is said [that X]', etc. (where the classical language more usually has 's/he is said [to X]', etc.).

(d) The use of articular infinitives governed by a 'goal-denoting' preposition to express purpose, and more generally of 'prepositional' infinitives functioning in the manner of gerunds.

In general, then, we have the impression of a fairly natural written Koine into which only certain well-established elements from the higher registers of the official language have intruded. By contrast, the *History of the Monks in Syria* by Theodoret (born in Antioch in the late fourth century AD), who clearly received an excellent education, is replete with Atticizing traits such as the use of the dual and the avoidance of normal contemporary vocabulary (e.g. ἀρχιερεύς [arçie'refs], lit. 'chief-priest', is employed for the regular ἐπίσκοπος [e'piskopos], lit. 'overseer', the ultimate source of our word 'bishop'). Typical syntactic markers of the 'high' Attic style, which are unusual in the Koine and wholly absent from Callinicus include:

(21) (a) The use of future participles, or ὡς (ἄν)/ὅπως ἄν [os (an)/'opos an] 'so that', with the subjunctive in final constructions (alongside the more neutral ἵνα ['ina]); ὅπως ἄν ['opos an] was particularly characteristic of official Attic in the fifth century BC, after which time it dropped out of favour.

(b) The use of ὑπό [y'po] with the dative (rather marginal in classical Attic, but so much the better from an Atticist perspective), πρός [pros] with the genitive, or a simple dative to mark the agent of a passive construction, alongside the neutral ὑπό [y'po] + genitive; the popularity of the moribund dative, whether after prepositions or alone, was a specially clear Atticist trait.

(c) Overuse of the indicative beside the more regular infinitive in consecutive clauses with ὥστε ['oste] '(so) that'.

(d) A general effort to preserve the synthetic future in all its forms.

There are, however, certain other Attic features in Theodoret's style that also recur in middle-register writing. These may be seen as 'unmarked' elements of the less elaborated literary style of the period, i.e. as Atticisms which were used relatively unselfconsciously rather than as part of a deliberate demonstration of learning. They may be seen as complementing the 'neutral' Koineisms of (20):

(22) (a) The infinitive in indirect commands, especially the use of an active infinitive in a context where no agent is specified – 's/he ordered [to send messengers]', etc.

(b) The use of the irregular verb φημί [fi'mi] 'say' with an accusative and infinitive beside the regular λέγω ['leɣo] with ὅτι ['oti] 'that', + finite verb.

(c) The 'personal' passive construction 's/he is said [to X]', for the more popular 'it is said [that X]', etc.

(d) The use of the optative in past tense contexts in both final clauses and in indirect speech (replaced by the subjunctive and the indicative respectively in less elevated literary work).

Overall, therefore, we gain the impression of a clear preference for constructions that were either under pressure in, or had already disappeared from, the ordinary spoken language, whether pure antiques or Attic traits that had become embedded as conservative elements in the higher registers of the Koine.

We thus have to deal with a scale of registers running from (a) more or less strict Atticism, through (b) a blend of Attic with 'high-level' written Koineisms, down to (c) an amalgam of 'standard' written Koineisms with ordinary contemporary speech; only those with minimal education wrote in a style (d) that was virtually free of such written Koineisms altogether (see Chapter 6 for exemplification). It seems, then, that all educated writers strove, in accordance with the relevant generic conventions, for a style that was in some degree distanced from the spoken vernacular, with a more or less clear division emerging between (a) and (b) on the one hand (Attic ⟷ high-level official/technical Koine) and (c) and (d) on the other (basic/administrative Koine ⟷ vernacular). In other words, while a blend of (a) and (b) was quite normal (with attempts at (a) alone reserved only for the most ambitious forms of literary composition), a combination of (a)/(b) with either (c) or (d) was relatively 'unnatural', and generally the mark of an over-ambitious stylist with an inadequate educational background.

This state of affairs is entirely to be expected, since learning to write necessarily meant learning, however imperfectly, one or more of the standard forms of written Greek. Only in the later Middle Ages did the vernacular begin to make a serious impact on literary composition, and then only in selected genres and/or under circumstances of political fragmentation and foreign rule (see 8.4.4–8.4.6 and Chapter 12). We should not, however, imagine that choice of style was simply a function of social class. Certain forms of Christian writing, such as martyrdoms and biographies, were traditionally more 'popular' in character than those with a classical/Hellenistic heritage, since their authors' primary purpose was to reach as wide an audience as possible. Our earliest examples include the anonymous *Martyrdom of Polycarp* (probably second century AD) and Athanasius of Alexandria's *Life of St Anthony* (fourth century AD). But there is no reason to doubt that many such authors, like Athanasius, were in fact very well educated indeed (cf. 8.5.6, 10.3).

The Christianization of the empire also brought with it the need for the chronological harmonization of the contemporary world and its classical past with the Hebrew world of the Old Testament, and so brought into being the important new genre of the universal chronicle. By the fifth century AD such chronicles were a major source of reference for Christians of all classes, and their compilers, while again aiming for a wide audience, assumed that it would at least overlap with readers of 'literary' histories of the traditional kind (cf. Jeffreys, Croke and Scott (1990)). But while histories required the high style, the more practical function of world chronicles demanded the use of the routine written language of the day, based on the normal language of administration (cf. 8.5.5, 10.2).

But before examining further the transition of the (eastern) Roman empire from the sophisticated urban civilization of antiquity to the medieval world of Orthodox Byzantium, it remains to complete Section I of this book by considering the evidence for the development of the Koine as a spoken language in the Roman period.

Chapter 6

Spoken Koine in the Roman period

6.1 Introduction

A great deal of valuable information about the evolution of 'normal' Greek in the Roman period is provided by the private documents of the not-very-well-educated, both inscriptions and, in the case of Egypt, papyri. The extracts from private papyrus letters given below give a fair sample of the relevant phenomena. But before looking at these in detail, a general survey of the phonological developments of the Hellenistic and Roman imperial periods will help to set the scene.

6.2 Summary of the principal developments in the vowel system

Before elaborating the details of the attested graphic interchanges and their implications, it will be useful to summarize the principal developments by means of conventional vowel diagrams, and to list the spelling options employed in substandard works for the representation of particular sounds in particular periods.

The process can be seen as a radical simplification and reduction of the classical system of long vowels and diphthongs, with the effect that, once distinctions of vowel length were lost, the former long- and short-vowel systems fell naturally together into a simple six-vowel triangle distinct from the modern Greek system only in the continued presence of /y/.

To a very large extent the changes involved can be explained in terms of a series of 'chain-effects', as proposed, for example, by Ruipérez (1956) and Allen (1987), and motivated by the principle of maximizing the differentiation of the realization of phonemes within the available articulatory space (cf. Martinet (1955)). Teodorsson has provided detailed studies of Attic for the late classical (1974) and Hellenistic (1978) periods, and also of Ptolemaic Koine (1977), while the Roman and early Byzantine papyri have been analysed by Gignac (1976). We may compare Ruijgh (1978b) for a 'conservative' critique of Teodorsson's (1974) methodology and rather 'radical' results.

The emergence in Attic, perhaps during the late ninth century BC, of a new long vowel /aː/, as the product of cluster simplification and compensatory lengthening (e.g. nom. sg. *$\pi\alpha\nu\tau$-s [pants] 'all', > *$\pi\alpha\nu$-s [pans] > $\pi\hat{\alpha}s$ [paːs]), seems to have had the effect of rephonologizing the reflexes of the original long a-vowel inherited from Indo-European, which fell in the articulatory range of /æː/. The 'lower' allophones of this latter, occurring after [i, e, r], merged with the new long a-vowel, while its remaining 'higher' allophones were 'pushed' up the front axis of the vowel triangle to merge with those of original /ɛː/ (for convenience, the resulting long a-vowel will be represented /aː/ henceforth):

(1)

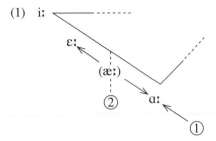

Shortly afterwards, probably in the eighth or early seventh century BC, the original diphthongs /ei/ and /ou/ were monophthongized to produce new mid-high vowels /eː/ and /oː/. Since the system already contained the inherited mid vowels /ɛː/ and /ɔː/, the result was overcrowding, particularly on the back axis, and the consequence was a raising of /oː/ towards /uː/, a movement which in turn 'dragged' original /ɔː/ towards the position of /oː/ and 'pushed' original /uː/ around to the front axis to become /yː/:

(2)

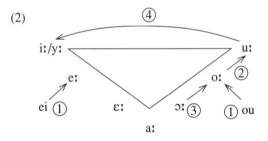

This is essentially the classical long-vowel system as described, for example, in Allen (1987a), where ι = /iː/, ει = /eː/, η = /ɛː/, α = /aː/, ω = /oː/, ου = /uː/, υ = /yː/.

Subsequently, the relative infrequency of original /iː/ and the overcrowding following the advent of /eː/ had the combined effect of pulling /eː/ (ει) towards /iː/ (affecting first the preconsonantal and word-final allophones, but then applying generally), with which it eventually merged. This seems in turn to have pulled original /ɛː/ (η) towards the position abandoned by /eː/, which then exercised a monophthongizing effect on /ai/ (αι) to create a new phoneme /æː/, later /ɛː/, to fill this further vacant slot:

(3)

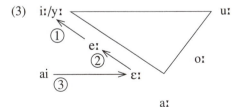

This still somewhat 'crowded' front axis then underwent further simplification, through a second raising of /eː/ (η) to /iː/, and a corresponding upward drift of /ɛː/ (αι) towards the vacated position. In broadly the same period, the distinction between long and short vowels was also lost (in conjunction with the shift from a primary pitch to a primary stress accent), so that the changes represented in (4):

(4)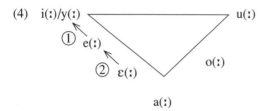

led to a system that easily merged with the existing short-vowel system in (5) (which had changed only in the fronting of original /u/ to /y/, in line with the corresponding development in the long-vowel system):

(5)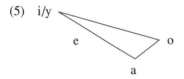

This gave the new six-vowel system in (6):

(6)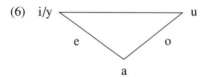

The picture is complicated slightly by the development of the remaining diphthongs. Already in the classical period /yi/ (υι) had begun to merge with /yː/, at least in popular registers, and this then fell together with /y/, as noted. Similarly, /oi/ (οι) had shifted, via /øi/, to /œi/ or /øi/, which in turn then monophthongized to /œ(ː)/ or /ø(ː)/, and finally raised to /y/. Eventually /y/ (υ, οι, υι) lost its lip-rounding to merge once again with /i/, though the completion of this last shift belongs to the middle Byzantine period.

Of the long diphthongs, /aːi/ (αι/ᾳ) and /oːi/ (ωι/ῳ) simply lost their final element and merged with the corresponding long vowels, which then fell together with the corresponding short vowels, as we have seen. In at least popular registers, however, the diphthong /ɛːi/ (ηι/ῃ) seems to have partly fallen together with /eː/ (normally written ει, cf. the spelling of the 2sg. middle ending with either -ηι/ῃ or -ει) from the middle of the fifth century BC; it then underwent the same development as /eː/, eventually merging with /i/.

The diphthongs ending in [u], namely /au/ (αυ), /eu/ (ευ) and /ɛːu/ (ηυ), adopted an ever-closer articulation of the final element, a process that eventually led, via the development of [w̥]/[w] > [ɸʷ]/[βʷ] > [ɸ]/[β], to a pronunciation [af/v], [ef/v], [if/v], with voicing triggered by a following voiced segment.

For most of these developments, the crucial issue of chronology still remains to be established. This will be considered first for Athenian Attic, and then for Egyptian Koine (with some additional observations about the Koine in general).

6.3 Some illustrative examples

6.3.1 Athenian Attic

In 4.4.2 above it was noted that orthographic changes in official Boeotian inscriptions are regularly taken to indicate that this dialect underwent many of the changes listed above at a very early date in comparison with, say, Attic. We thus find ι used for ει already in the fifth century BC (implying /eː/ > /iː/), and, from the early fourth century, η used for αι and ει for η (implying /ai/ > /ɛː/ following the shift of original /ɛː/ > /eː/, with later substitution of ι suggesting further raising of the latter to /i(ː)/). By the mid-third century the use of υ for οι similarly suggests that /oi/ had already been monophthongized to /ø(ː)/, while the occasional second-century use of ει for οι implies an early loss of lip rounding (i.e. [ø] > [e̞]).

These developments have been placed in an interesting new light by Teodorsson (1974). Using an impressive range of inscriptional and secondary evidence to draw a distinction between the conservative pronunciation of the aristocracy and the more popular pronunciation of the majority (as evidenced in the spelling mistakes of private documents and the casual observations of contemporary writers), it is argued that 'vernacular' Attic, far from being slow off the mark in comparison with Boeotian, had in fact already undergone many of the changes listed above by the end of the fourth century BC. The onset of these 'progressive' developments is associated directly with the new role of Athens as an imperial capital and major emporium, and particularly with the 'extreme' democratic form of government which gave unusual prominence and prestige, at least temporarily, to more popular forms of the dialect.

Much inevitably hinges on the interpretation of the significance of what remains a fairly small number of documents exhibiting the relevant errors, and the overall picture depends on the extent to which we can be sure that the mistakes in question were committed by local native speakers rather than by resident aliens, including non-native speakers of Greek, who may have had difficulty with the subtleties of the Attic dialect (cf. Ruijgh (1978b)).

But even if Teodorsson has somewhat over-interpreted particular phenomena in his corpus, he is right to emphasize the importance of distinguishing different levels within the Attic of the period, and it is helpful to be able to see the Boeotian facts as forming part of a more general pattern of development in the fifth and fourth centuries BC rather than as revealing an isolated and otherwise unexplained 'pioneer'.

By the mid-fourth century a clear distinction may be drawn between a conservative system retained by the aristocracy and an innovative system representing the speech of the majority of the moderately educated (which is further distinguished from the truly 'vulgar' Attic of the urban poor, a variety that was in some respects still more innovative).

Teodorsson's reconstruction (1978: 94–6) of the conservative system is given in (7), where /--C,V,# = 'in the context of a following consonant, vowel, or word-boundary':

(7) (a) **phoneme**   **spelling**

/iː/	ι, ει/--C or #
/i/	ι
/yː/	υ, υι
/y/	υ, υι
/eː/	ει/--V, η, ηι(η)
/e/	ε
/aː/	α
/a/	α
/oː/	ω
/o/	ο
/uː/	ου
/u/	ου

(b) **diphthongs**   **spelling**

/aːi/	αι (ᾳ)
/ai/	αι
/au/	αυ
/eu/	ευ
/eːu/	ηυ
/oːi/	ωι (ῳ)
/oi/	οι

Subsequently, he finds evidence only for the loss of the final [i]-element from the relevant long diphthongs in the period between *c.* 150 and *c.* 50 BC. The eventual elimination of vowel-length distinctions and the associated shift from a primary pitch to a primary stress accent (on which see below) thus belong to the Roman imperial period.

By contrast the majority system was already highly advanced by *c.* 350 BC (Teodorsson (1974: 286–99)):

(8) (a) phoneme | spelling

phoneme	spelling
/i/	ι, ει/--C or #, η, ηι (ῃ), υ, υι
/y/ (? /ø/)	οι
/ẹ/	ε, ει/--V
/ɛ/	αι
/a/	α, αι (ᾳ)
/ɔ/	ωι (ῳ)
/o/	ο, ω
/u/	ου

(b) 'diphthongs' | spelling

'diphthongs'	spelling
/iw/	ηυ
/ew/	ευ
/aw/	αυ

Here distinctive vowel length had already been lost, the primary stress accent was already in place, and monophthongization was complete, including the onset of the frication of the final [u]-element of the relevant diphthongs. There is also evidence of the shift of [i] > [j]/--V (i.e. of synizesis), particularly in the suffix -ια [-ia/-ja]. Most strikingly, the loss of lip-rounding in /y/ (υ) also seems to have been largely completed, though the product of the monophthongization of /oi/ (οι) seems not yet to have been affected by this process; perhaps, then, this latter should more accurately be represented as /ø/, in order to explain its continued distinctiveness at this time.

From 330 BC onwards, however, the prestige of the innovative system seems to have declined under the growing importance of oligarchic groups under Macedonian hegemony. Thus the only further change in the period up to *c*. 50 BC involves the merger of the mid vowels on the front, and perhaps also the back axis, while the more conservative variety became steadily more prevalent among the educated population.

6.3.2 Egyptian Koine

It is of the greatest importance to note that the Koine was based on a conservative variety of Attic, continuing the spoken and official written Attic (Great Attic) used widely in the Greek world from the fourth century BC onwards. The Macedonians thus made a decisive contribution to the preservation of 'Old Attic' phonology for several centuries, so that the evolution of the Koine follows the general pattern of development seen in popular Athenian Attic, but is retarded by comparison, with some of the changes that are already in place by the fourth century BC in (non-conservative) Athenian Attic occurring only in the late Hellenistic or even Roman imperial periods.

In Egypt specifically, it seems that the royal court in Alexandria maintained a conservative pronunciation throughout the Ptolemaic period, but that the majority of the educated population quickly developed its own standard from this foundation. At the lowest levels, however, this rapidly evolving Koine-base was inevitably influenced both by the native dialects of Greek immigrants (though only in the earlier period) and by the Coptic substrate of the native population (cf. 4.5, 4.10.2).

The 'standard' (i.e. non-aristocratic, non-vulgar) pronunciation of the educated majority in the mid-third century BC can be represented as follows (Teodorsson (1977: 251–6)):

(9) (a) phoneme   spelling

/iː/	ι, ει/--C or #, ηι (η)
/i/	ι
/yː/	υ
/y/	υ
/eː/	ει/--V, η
/e/	ε
/aː/	α
/a/	α
/oː/	ω
/o/	ο
/uː/	ου
/u/	ου

(b) diphthongs   spelling

/yi/	υι
/eu/	ευ
/eːu/	ηυ
/aːi/	αι (ᾳ)
/ai/	αι
/au/	αυ
/oːi/	ωι (ῳ)
/oi/	οι

This is essentially the same as the conservative version of Athenian Attic set up for the mid-fourth century BC, except that the diphthong /yi/ (υι) has not been monophthongized to /yː/ (presumably a feature of Great Attic as opposed to its Athenian analogue), and the old diphthong /ɛːi/ (ηι, η), which in conservative Athenian Attic simply lost its final element and merged with /ɛː/, the two together then raising to /eː/, has here merged with the product of the early monophthongization of original /ei/ (ει), namely /eː/, and so, along with the latter, has raised instead to /iː/; we may again note in this connection the conflict between -ηι/η and -ει as the spelling for the 2sg. middle ending in Athenian Attic, the former representing a conservative, the latter a modernizing trait, apparently followed in the Koine.

By the mid-second century, however, the majority system had itself undergone important changes, most notably monophthongization, the loss of distinctive vowel length, and the shift to a primary stress accent:

(10) (a) phoneme   spelling

phoneme	spelling
/i/	ι, ει/--C or #, ηι (η)
/y/	υ
/ẹ/	ει/--V, η
/ø/	οι
/e/	ε, αι
/a/	α, αι (ᾳ)
/o/	ο, ω, ωι (ῳ)
/u/	ου

(b) 'diphthongs'   spelling

'diphthongs'	spelling
/yi/	υι
/iw/	ηυ
/ew/	ευ
/aw/	αυ

The change of /ø/ (οι) > /y/ seems to have affected the majority pronunciation by the middle of the first century BC, though the lip-rounded pronunciation of υ/οι remained standard for many centuries to come. In the later Roman and early Byzantine periods the positional allophones of /ẹ/ (ει/--V, η) progressively merged with those of /i/, while the frication of the [u]-element of the relevant diphthongs progressed through [ɸʷ/βʷ] to [ɸ/β], and probably, by early Byzantine times, to [f/v] ([f]/--[−voice], [v]/--[+voice]). The result is essentially the modern Greek system, apart from the final merger of /y/ (υ, οι) with /i/:

(11) (a) phoneme   spelling

phoneme	spelling
/i/	ι, ει, η, ηι (η)
/y/	υ, υι, οι
/e/	ε, αι
/a/	α, αι (ᾳ)
/o/	ο, ω, ωι (ῳ)
/u/	ου

(b) 'diphthongs'   spelling

/if, iv/	ηυ
/ef, ev/	ευ
/af, av/	αυ

The written evidence for the chronology of these developments, as attested in the papyri, can be summarized briefly as follows:

(12) The general graphic interchange of ε and αι, of υ and οι, and of ι, ει and η (/ɛːi/ having probably merged with /eː/ by the beginning of the fourth century BC), provides good evidence for the final merger, through a combination of systematic monophthongization and the loss of distinctive vowel length, of the classical /e/ and /ai/ to /e/, of /y(ː)/ and /oi/ to /y/, and of /i(ː)/ and original /eː/ to /i/. These developments began in the Koine in the third and second centuries BC, but considerably earlier in many of the old Greek dialects.

(13) (i) Interchange of η and ι/ει is attested from late Ptolemaic times onwards, but, despite more frequent occurrence with the passage of time, never quite becomes general in the Roman period.

Many of the earlier examples involve the substitution of η for ει in a prevocalic context, and so provide evidence that the older value of ει, namely [ẹ], was retained there for a time: i.e. original /ɛː/, written η, raised to /ẹ/ when original /eː/, written ει, merged with /i/ other than prevocalically during the third century BC, thus making both η and ει available to render /ẹ/ before vowels.

(ii) A specially close articulation of /ẹ/ seems to have been employed, however, both prevocalically and before liquids, nasals and /s/, so that alternations of η with ει/ι are particularly frequent in all these contexts, cf. Teodorsson (1977: 252). (There is parallel evidence for the raising effect of these same environments on allophones of /e/, producing ε/αι interchanges with η and interchanges of all three graphs with ι/ει, cf. Gignac (1986: 330).)

(iii) In the Roman period many other examples of the interchange of η with ει/ι occur in unaccented syllables or unstressed 'minor' words, where a clear distinction between a close [ẹ] and [i] is relatively difficult to sustain; others still seem to have been conditioned by a dental environment (tongue-tip articulations perhaps encouraging a closer articulation of a neighbouring [ẹ]), or by a variety of non-phonetic considerations (e.g. the general falling together of aorist and perfect in the popular Koine led to confusion between aorist ἧκα ['hẹka] and perfect εἷκα ['hika], from ἵημι ['hiẹmi] 'send'; the resultant perfect/aorist is sometimes therefore misspelled ἷκα ['hika]).

(iv) But given the absence in even the most uneducated productions of routine interchanges of η with ει/ι on the scale of those between ει and ι or αι and ε, it would probably be premature to assume the full merger of /ẹ/ and /i/ before the early Byzantine period.

(14) Similar observations apply to the interchanges of υ with ει/ι and of υ with η (where the latter represents [i]), except that these are far less common, thus strongly implying that /y/ did not merge with /i/ for the majority in the Roman period, and that any partial overlap was due to specific phonetic environments (e.g. dissimilation in a labial context) and/or substrate effects (Coptic having no /y/ phoneme). The final falling together of these phonemes in educated speech probably took place as late as the ninth/tenth century AD.

(15) (i) The progressive narrowing of the articulation of the second element of the original diphthongs /au, eu/, beginning in the third century BC and leading, via [aw, ew], to audible friction, i.e. [aɸʷ/βʷ, eɸʷ/βʷ], is first attested in the spellings α(υ)ου/ε(υ)ου, which seem to reflect the consonantal character of the second element. By the Roman period, after the loss of simultaneous lip rounding, we seem to be dealing simply with a pronunciation [aɸ/aβ, eɸ/eβ], or perhaps even [af/av, ef/ev] as in modern Greek; spellings with β (which by this time represented /β/ or /v/, see below), become increasingly common in late Roman and early Byzantine documents.

   (ii) We should also note spellings in which the second element has been dropped altogether, a 'popular' characteristic reflecting allegro pronunciations and affecting unstressed pronouns in particular, e.g. ἀτόν [a'to(n)] for αὐτόν [af'to(n)] 'him', etc. These occur sporadically in 'vulgar' Attic texts from late classical times and begin in the Ptolemaic papyri from the mid-third century BC onwards.

(16) The frequent omission of prevocalic /i/ is standardly taken to mark a popular and/or allegro pronunciation [j] in that position (cf. Mayser-Schmoll (1970: 126–7), Teodorsson (1977: 237, 1978: 82)). Such synizesis was naturally associated with a shift in the position of the accent when /i/ had originally been the accented vowel: e.g. [-'ia] > [-'ja], etc.

(17) (i) The change from a primary pitch accent to a primary stress accent was directly associated with the loss of vowel length distinctions, and was widespread by the middle of the second century BC; it is occasionally associated in writing with the omission of unstressed vowels and/or with some confusion of vowel quality.

      Evidence for such a shift is also provided by certain late dialect inscriptions (see, for example, Chadwick (1993) on Thessalian).

   (ii) As noted earlier, the loss of long vowels and diphthongs destroyed the environment for the occurrence of the circumflex accent (= rise–fall on a single 'long' syllable), and so neutralized the contrast between circumflex and acute (= rise + fall over two successive syllables). This in turn highlighted the increase in volume that was originally associated secondarily with the rise in pitch, a development which was aided regionally by substrate effects (e.g. Coptic had a strong stress accent) and which led eventually to the perception that increased amplitude was the primary marker of word accent.

6.4   The development of the consonant system

The most important changes of the Hellenistic and Roman periods are listed below (see Gignac (1976) for a detailed survey of the evidence):

(18) In the consonant system the voiceless plosives /p, t, k/ remained unchanged, except that voiced allophones were increasingly regularized after nasals: hence μπ, ντ, γκ = [mb, nd, ŋg].

(19) (i)   The shift of the voiced plosives /b, d, g/ to voiced fricatives /β, ð, ɣ/ was complete for the majority of literate speakers by the fourth century AD (cf. Gignac (1976: 64)), the only exception being the allophones after nasals, where a plosive pronunciation was retained. This process apparently began with the velar /g/, and had perhaps been carried through by the second century BC (cf. Teodorsson (1977: 254)). The new /ɣ/ phoneme seems to have had the allophones [j] before the high front vowels [e, i], [g] after a nasal, and [ɣ] elsewhere.

(ii)   Frication then affected the labial /b/ (β = /β/) by the first century AD, again except after nasals), and finally the dental /d/ (the pronunciation [ð] occurring first before [j], i.e. prevocalic /i/, from the first century AD, then before /i/ generally from the third century, and eventually in all positions, other than after nasals, from the fourth century onwards).

(20) (i)   Neither Teodorsson (1977) nor Gignac (1976) finds any compelling evidence for the corresponding shift of the voiceless aspirates /pʰ, tʰ, kʰ/ to fricatives /f, θ, x/ in Egypt in the Hellenistic, Roman imperial or early Byzantine periods. Whether this reflects a conservative peculiarity of Egyptian Greek under the influence of Coptic (at least the Bohairic dialect had /pʰ, tʰ, kʰ/, and special symbols distinct from φ and χ were introduced to represent /f/ and /x/ in those dialects which had these phonemes), or reflects a more general state of affairs in the Koine, is difficult to determine.

(ii)   There is, however, direct evidence that /tʰ/ > /θ/ in Laconian in the fifth century BC (cf. spellings such as σιός, presumably = [θiós] 'god/goddess', in Athenian attempts to represent Laconian pronunciation, and the use of the same spellings by the Spartans themselves after the adoption of the Ionic alphabet in the fourth century; it seems that this eventually developed to /s/, perhaps quite early, since many Tsakonian words show /s/ where the rest of modern Greek has /θ/).

(iii)   There is also possible evidence for a fricative pronunciation of /kʰ/ (second century BC) and /pʰ/ (second century AD) in the Asia Minor Koine (Schweizer (1898: 109–15)).

(iv)   Similarly, Threatte (1980: 470) agrees with Meisterhans (1900: 78) in finding evidence for the change of /pʰ/ > /f/ in spellings such as Ἐφφρονίς ([ef(f)ro'nis], IG 2².11507: for Εὔφρονίς [efpʰro'nis]) and Ἐφραῖος ([efʰ(f)reos], IG 2².5310: for Εὔφραῖος [ef'pʰreos]) in less literate Attic inscriptions of the early second century AD.

(v)   Thus, though the evidence is frankly meagre, it would perhaps be reasonable to assume that frication in the Koine began in various areas outside Egypt during the Hellenistic period and that it had been widely, though by no means universally, carried through by the end of the fourth century AD.

(vi)   The change presumably involved an initial assimilatory shift from [pʰ, tʰ, kʰ] to [pf, tθ, kx], followed by loss of the plosive element. To judge from the examples given in the preceding paragraph, a likely starting place for this loss was in the position after a voiceless fricative. One such context arose with the frication of the second element of the former diphthongs αυ and ευ, where the difficult sequences [f-pf], [f-tθ], [f-kx] would be highly prone to simplification ([f-pf, f-tθ, f-kx] > [f-f, f-θ, f-x]).

(vii)   A similar reduction would presumably apply to these elements after the fricative /s/ ([s-pf, s-tθ, s-kx] > [s-f, s-θ, s-x]), and also when they occurred in combination, involving initially the second and then the first member of the pair ([pf-tθ, kx-tθ] > [pf-θ, kx-θ] > [f-θ, x-θ]), cf. Bubenik (1983: 104–8).

(viii)   From here the shift to a fricative pronunciation in all contexts was only a matter of time, though doubtless this was initiated and carried through at different times in different areas (with Egypt retaining a conservative system because of the local substrate).

(21)   Assimilation affected original /zd/ (written ζ) to produce [zz], with subsequent simplification to [z], first word-initially and then across the board; this created a new phoneme /z/, since the occurrence of [z] (as an allophone of /s/) was no longer exclusively conditioned by a following voiced consonant.

(22)   The simplification of double consonants generally, beginning from the third century BC onwards, is indicated by the apparently arbitrary use of double graphs in the private documents of the less well-educated in most areas.

(23)   The phoneme /h/, occurring only word-initially (and in composition), was progressively lost during the period of the Koine, beginning with more popular varieties in Hellenistic times (so-called 'psilosis' was already a feature of many Ionic dialects), but eventually affecting even the pronunciation of the most educated speakers by the late Roman/Byzantine period.

(24)   Throughout the Hellenistic and Roman periods there is widespread evidence for the articulatory weakness of both final [n] and final [s], especially before a following plosive. This takes the form of omission and/or assimilation (the latter, however, involving only nasals, sometimes also in medial positions), though there is no clearly definable contextual delimitation to these processes.

Only final [n] eventually came close to disappearing in the later Middle Ages, with just a small number of resilient exceptions surviving into standard modern Greek (though now under precise phonetic conditions).

6.5 Some Egyptian texts

With this background, we may examine some extracts from a number of papyrus letters dating from the early second to the late fourth century AD. The phonetic transcriptions are intended to indicate a pronunciation typical of the popular Koine of the relevant period, and specifically Egyptian phenomena (cf. 4.10.2) are suppressed if they have no direct bearing on the subsequent development of Greek.

6.5.1 Letter 1: clitic pronouns and word order; control verbs with ἵνα ['ina]-complements

The first piece (P. Fay. 114, AD 100) is written by a discharged veteran to his son:

(25) Λούκιος Βελλῆνος Γέμελλος Σαβίνωι τῶι οἰείωι χαίρειν. εὖ οὖν πυήσας
κομισάμενός μου τὴν ἐπιστολὴν πέμσις μυ Πίνδαρον εἰς τὴν πόλιν τὸν
πεδιοφύλακα τῆς Διονυσιάδος, ἐπὶ ἐρώτησέ με Ἑρμόναξ εἶνα αὐτὸν λάβῃ
εἰς Κερκεσοῦχα καταμαθῖν τὸν ἐλαιῶνα αὐτοῦ, ἐπὶ πυκνός ἐστιν καὶ θέλι
ἐξ αὐτὸν ἐκκόψαι φυτά, εἶνα ἐνπίρως κοπῇ τὰ μέλλοντα ἐκκόπτεσθαι . . .

['lukios be'lẹnos 'gemelos sa'bino   to y'jo 'kʰerin.   ev   un   py'isas
    Lucius   Bellenus   Gemellus   to-Sabinus the son   greetings. well then doing

komi'same'noz mu   tin episto'li(n) 'pem(p)siz my   'pindaron is tim 'bolin
    having-received   of-me the letter   you-will-send to-me Pindaros   to the city

tom bedio'pʰylaka tiz   ðjony'sjados, e'pi e'roti'se me er'monaks 'in(a)
    the   field-guard   of-the Dionysias,   since asked   me   Hermonax   that

a(f)ton 'lavi   is kerke'sukʰa katama'tʰi(n) ton ele'on(a) a(f)'tu, e'pi py'knos
    him   he-take to Kerkesoucha to-examine   the   olive-grove of-him, since dense

estin ke 'tʰeli   eks af'ton e'kopse pʰy'ta, 'ina em'biros ko'pi   ta
    it-is   and he-wants from it   to-cut-out plants, so-that skilfully   may-be-cut the

'melonda e'koptestʰe . . .]
    going   to-be-cut-out . . .

'Lucius Bellenus Gemellus to his son Sabinus greetings. On receipt of my letter you will kindly send me Pindarus the field-guard from Dionysias to the city, as Hermonax has asked me for permission to take him to Kerkesoucha to examine his olive grove, as it is dense and he wants to cut down some trees from it, so that those to be cut down may be cut skilfully . . .'

Many of the major phonological developments listed above are well illustrated here. We may note for example:

(26) (a) interchange of ει/ι: οἰείωι (υἰῶι) [y'jo] 'son', εἶνα (ἵνα) ['ina] '(so) that',
πέμσις (πέμψεις) ['pem(p)sis] 'you will send', ἐπί (ἐπεί) [e'pi] 'since',
καταμαθῖν (καταμαθεῖν) [katama'tʰin] 'to examine', θέλι (θέλει) ['tʰeli]
'wants', ἐνπίρος (ἐμπείρως) [em'biros] 'skilfully'.
(b) interchange of οι/υ: οἰείωι (υἰῶι) [y'jo] 'son', πυήσας (ποιήσας) [py'isas]
'having done', μυ (μοι) [my] 'to me'.

(c) confusion of long/short vowels: ἐνπίρος (ἐμπείρως) [em'biros] 'skilfully'. Ἐξ αὐτὸν (ἐξ αὐτῶν) [eks af'ton] 'from them' is a possible further example, if this pronoun is indeed genitive plural; the sense, however, is better if we take it as an accusative singular, αὐτόν [af'ton], and assume that the preposition takes a non-classical accusative in place of the genitive (a development already under way with the largely synonymous ἀπό [a'po] 'from').

Other features worthy of note include:

(27) (a) The avoidance of verb-final order except in the formulaic address (cf. 4.8), with subjects typically following an initial verb, especially in subordinate clauses. Clitic pronouns normally appear immediately after the verbs that govern them, except where there is another sentence-initial element (e.g. conjunction, interrogative, negative, focus). After ἵνα ['ina], for example, the pronoun retains second position in the clause and the verb follows: cf. εἵνα αὐτόν λάβῃ ['in(a) a(f)ton 'lavi] 'that he may take him'. This dual pattern continues into (vernacular) medieval Greek and survives in certain modern dialects, though standard modern Greek has generalized preverbal clitic position.

(b) The use of a subjunctive clause introduced by the 'final' conjunction ἵνα ['ina] in place of an infinitival construction after ἐρώτησε [e'rotise] 'asked'. Since this is in principle a control structure (*he asked to take . . .*), we might have expected the infinitive to survive, but the inclusion of an object pronoun (με [me] 'me') introduces a potential ambiguity (*he asked me to take . . .* , = 'that he take' or 'that I take'?) and the finite construction with overt agreement morphology on the verb is therefore preferred. We may assume that structures of this type represent the first step towards the generalization of subjunctive clauses even where co-referential subjects are involved in main and subordinate clauses (cf. Modern Greek θέλω να πάω ['θelo na 'pao], lit. 'I-want that I-go', etc.). Infinitives otherwise survive strongly, both as complements (e.g. ἐκκόψαι [e'kopse] 'to cut off' after θέλι ['tʰeli] 'wants'), and as adjuncts (e.g. καταμαθῖν [katama'tʰin] 'to examine', used to express a purpose clause).

(c) Participles are still used freely to express background circumstances (e.g. κομισάμενος [komi'samenos] 'having received') and in nominalized structures (e.g. τὰ μέλλοντα ἐκκόπτεσθαι [ta 'melonda e'koptestʰe] 'the (ones) about to be cut down'). Note, however, that the future passive participle has again been replaced by a periphrastic construction with a future auxiliary and a passive infinitive (cf. 4.11.1).

(d) The origins of the 3rd person clitic pronouns of modern Greek can be seen in structures such as εἵνα αὐτόν λάβῃ ['in(a) a(f)ton 'lavi] 'that he may take him', where the weak form of the pronoun follows a word ending with [-a], with resultant elision of the final vowel. Resegmentation as ['ina ton] then produces the basis for a paradigm τον/την/το [ton/tin/to] 'him/her/it', etc. Cf. τὸν ἐλεῶνα αὐτοῦ [ton ele'on(a) a(f)'tu].

6.5.2   Letter 2: 'short' 2nd declension forms; the merger of aorist and perfect

Our second letter (P. Oxy. 1155) dates from AD 104, and reveals a number of additional phenomena characteristic of vernacular Greek in the early second century:

(28) Θωνᾶς Ἀπίονι τῷ φιλτά[τῳ] πλῖ[στ]α χ(αίρειν). γινώσκιν σε [θε]λω ἔτι
εὐθὺς ἐπιβέβηκα ἰς Ἀλεξάνδρηαν, εὐθέως ἐμέλκε ἐμοὶ περὶ τοῦ πράγαματος
οὗ με ἠρώτηκες. εὗρον τὸν ἄνθροπον καλῶς πράσοντα τὰ μεγάλα. ἀσπάζου
πάντες τοὺς φίλους. αὐτὸ τὸ πρόγραμα τοῦ ἡγεμόνος ἔπενψα σοι ἵνα ἐπίγοις
πρὸς τί σοί 'στι . . .
ἀπόδος ἰς τὸ Ἰσῖν Ἀπίωνι παστοφόρῳ.

[tʰo'nas a'pioni to pʰil'tato 'plista 'kʰerin. ji'noskin se 'tʰelo əti ef'tʰys
Thonas   to-Apion the dearest   most   greeting. To-know   you I-want that directly

epi'vevika is ale'ksandria(n), ef'tʰeos   e'meḷk(e)   emy pe'ri tu
I-have-gone to Alexandria,   immediately it-has-concerned to-me about the

'praɣəmatos u   me i'rotikes. 'evron ton 'a(n)tʰropo(n) ka'los 'prasonda
matter   which me you-asked. I-found the   man   well   doing

   ta me'ɣala. a'spazu 'pandəs tus 'pʰilus. af'to to 'proɣrama tu
(for) the great.   Greet   all   the friends. Itself the written-order of-the

ije'monos 'epempsa sy   'ina e'pijys   pros 'ti   sy   sti . . .
governor   I-sent   to-you that you-might-hasten to   what for-you is . . .

a'podos is to i'sin a'pioni pasto'pʰoro.]
give   to the Isieum to-Apion priest (who carries the image of the god Isis)

'Thonas to his dearest Apion very many greetings. I want you to know that I have gone [*or* went] directly to Alexandria, I (have) immediately addressed the matter you asked me to. I found the man doing well in the main. Greet all our friends. I (have) sent you the governor's actual written order so that you might deal promptly with what concerns you . . . Give this to Apion the priest at the temple of Isis.'

Over and above the now familiar graphic interchanges, we should note that the use of iota subscript here, as in other papyri, is simply a modern editorial device. Iota in the 'long diphthongs' was written adscript for as long as it was pronounced, and it is therefore frequently omitted in papyri from the middle of the second century BC onwards. Its graphic restoration from the end of the second century AD is testimony to the impact of Atticism and the renewed emphasis on 'correct' usage (cf. 5.5, 5.6).

Other points of phonological significance include:

(29) (a) Evidence of vowel weakening in unaccented syllables (a concomitant of
        the shift from pitch to stress) is provided by the spelling ἔτι [əti] (for ὅτι
        [oti]) 'that', and by the accusative plural πάντες ['pandəs] (for πάντας
        ['pandəs]) 'all'. The latter phenomenon, as already noted, lies behind the
        levelling of nominative and accusative plural endings in the 3rd and,
        eventually, 1st declensions (cf. 4.11.1, 4.11.3).

(b) The accentual shift also lies behind the simplification of double consonants, syllable quantity, determined in part by whether or not a syllable was
'closed', having ceased to be a significant factor in the determination of
rhythm: cf. πράσοντα ['prasonda] (for πράσσοντα ['prasonda]) 'doing',
and πρόγραμα ['proɣrama] (for πρόγραμμα ['proɣrama]) 'affair'.

(c) (i)   The form Ἰσῖν [i'sin], for Ἰσιεῖον [i'sion] 'temple of Isis', provides
a nice example of a development which began as early as the third
century BC and involved the apparent loss of the o-vowel in certain
categories of 2nd declension noun, namely personal names in -ιος
[-ios] and neuters in -ιον [-ion] or -ίον [-'ion].

(ii) This neuter suffix was particularly productive in the Koine as a
diminutive formant, not only because of its 'affective' quality but
also because it provided morphologically regular alternatives to 3rd
declension nouns with more 'difficult' declensional patterns involving stem allomorphy: e.g. παῖς [pes], gen. παιδός [pe'ðos] 'child',
replaced by παιδίον [pe'ðion], gen. παιδίου [pe'ðiu], etc. This general type, without the o-vowel, has become a major neuter subclass
of modern Greek.

(iii) In the specific example above, it seems that the -ειον [-'ion] suffix,
characteristic of the names of 'establishments', has been assimilated
to the diminutive pattern.

The change in (c) could have been a by-product of the shift from a pitch accent,
involving the weakening and eventual loss of an unstressed vowel (e.g. [-(')io-] >
[-(')iə-] > [-(')ij-] > [-(')i-]), but we would rather have expected the more regular
change of prevocalic [i] to [j], as elsewhere (cf. (4)(e) above); this latter occurs, for
example, in the genitive singular of neuter diminutives, so that παιδίου [pe'ðiu] >
παιδιοῦ [pe'ðju], etc., the standard formation in modern Greek, but with examples
from the first century AD onwards. The loss of [o] must therefore be assumed
to antedate the synizesis of antevocalic [i], an assumption for which there is no
compelling evidence; the apocopation is in any case suspiciously selective in its
impact.

   It might therefore seem better to assume that the influx of Romans into the East,
and more particularly the influx of Roman names, led to the borrowing of the Latin
vocative suffix of the relevant 2nd declension nouns in -*ius*, namely -*i,* and that new
nominative/accusative forms were built to this innovation, perhaps under the influence of parallel Latin forms such as *Claudis* for *Claudius*, etc. Unfortunately the
earliest Greek examples date from the third century BC, which precludes a Latin
source, and this approach in any case leaves the parallel development of the neuters
unexplained.

   Perhaps, then, we are simply dealing in origin with hypocoristic forms of masculine names and neuter diminutives used as names (cf. Jannaris (1897): 113, 293):
e.g. Ἀντώνιος [an'donios] > Ἀντώνις [an'donis], 'pet' names in -ιον [-ion] > -ιν
[-i(n)], etc. The change could then have spread to 2nd declension neuter diminutives generally, and finally embraced other neuters in [-ion] and [-'ion]. In the

masculine paradigm, however, in the absence of major classes of nouns in -ιος [-ios] other than personal names, the spread was limited to adjectives (sometimes used as nouns) with this suffix, e.g. the Latin loan -άριος [-'arios], and its occurrence is therefore more sporadic and the change correspondingly restricted.

Returning to (28), the major grammatical issue is the merger of the aorist and the perfect. Note first of all the form ἠρώτηκες [i'rotikes] 'you (have) asked', where the 'past tense' 2sg. suffix -ες [-es] has replaced the classical -ας [-as]. The set of common 'past tense' endings (cf. 4.9, 5.8) in fact came to be used increasingly in the perfect paradigm too (though with perfect -κ- [-k-] in place of aorist -σ- [-s-] where relevant), a formal development promoted by the diminution of the functional distinction between perfect and aorist revealed by the increasing use in the Koine of the perfect as a simple past tense. In (28), for example, it is clear that, while some perfect forms may be interpreted as true perfects, e.g. ἐπιβέβηκα [epi'vevika] 'I have gone', ἐμέλκε [e'melke] 'it has concerned' (with syncopation of unstressed [i] and augment for reduplication, cf. (μ)εμέληκε [(m)e'melike]), neither of these actually demands a perfect reading. On the other hand, the form already cited in the preceding paragraph, ἠρώτηκες [i'rotikes], seems clearly to have an aoristic value here (= 'you asked'), while the aorist ἔπεμψα ['epempsa] 'I sent', seems equally clearly to require a perfect interpretation in the context (= 'I have sent').

The merger perhaps in part reflects the influence of Latin, where the so-called perfect forms performed both functions, but its origins can be seen already in the usage of authors such as Menander, and it reflects a natural tendency seen also in Romance. The basis for the development can be explained as follows.

The perfect involves the postulation of a 'viewing point' from which a given 'event', having previously taken place, is seen to be already completed. This is the essence of perfect aspect, which entails the notion of some continued relevance for the earlier event at the later viewing point (often, but not necessarily, involving a resultant state: cf. τέθνηκα [teth'neka] 'I have died/I am dead').

The viewing point may then be located in time. In the case of a past perfect (pluperfect), the event is earlier than a viewing point which is itself in the past with respect to the time of utterance. In the case of a future perfect the event is earlier than a viewing point which is in the future with respect to the time of utterance. In the case of the present perfect, of course, there can be no present viewing point distinct from the time of utterance (the present is the present), and the event is simply earlier than 'now'. In each case, therefore, the time reference of an aspectually perfect tense form is determined by the location not of the viewed event but of the viewing point with respect to the time of utterance.

But the importance of the formal expression of this retrospective 'viewing' of an earlier event is easily downgraded: cf. the virtual equivalence, when uttered by someone who wants to start cooking, of *'have you got the chops out of the freezer?'* and *'did you get the chops out of the freezer?'* In this way the simple past may come to be seen as an alternative to the perfect (with present relevance inferred), an overlap from which a more general equivalence may then develop.

We should note, however, that the process of formal interference was, as often, bidirectional, and that perfect 3pl. -ασι [-asi] came to rival -αν [-an] as a past tense suffix in both aorist and imperfect paradigms (e.g. ἐπ-ήλθ-ασι [ep-'ilt^h-asi] 'they came', BGU 275.5, AD 215). The survival of this particular perfect formant was favoured by the existence of the formally parallel 3pl. present ending -ουσι [-usi], and it is in fact still retained in many of the modern dialects of the South-eastern subgroup (Cypriot and some Dodecanesian varieties).

The merger was also supported by a set of further morphological considerations. Past tenses were characterized in classical Greek by the addition of the 'augment', ordinarily the syllable ἐ- [e-], to the beginning of the relevant verb form: e.g. 1sg. aorist ἔ-λυ-σα [é-ly:-sa], from λύ-ω [lý:-o:] 'I set free'. Perfects, by contrast, were characterized by 'reduplication', involving the addition of a syllable, typically Cε- [Ce-], to the beginning of the relevant form (where C = the initial consonant of the verb root): e.g. 1sg. perfect λέ-λυ-κα [lé-ly-ka] 'I have set free'. But where a verb began with a vowel, the augment regularly took the form of a lengthening of that vowel, and the reduplication was identical (e.g. aorist ἥμαρτ-ον [hé:mart-on], perfect ἡμάρτ-ηκα [he:márt-ε:-ka], from ἁμαρτ-άνω [hamart-án-o:] 'I err'). Similarly, if a verb began with a consonant cluster (other than stop + liquid) it was usual for the augment ἐ- [e-] to serve also as the reduplication: e.g. aorist ἔ-γνω-ν [é-gno:-n], perfect ἔ-γνω-κα [é-gno:-ka], from γι-γνώ-σκω [gi-gnó:-sko:] 'I ascertain'.

In the Koine, however, once the functional merger of the aorist and perfect began in earnest, reduplication ceased to have any clear independent significance, and the already established partial equivalence of augment and reduplication spread quickly even to verbs beginning with a single consonant. For a time, therefore, alongside increasingly common augmented 'perfects' such as ἐ-πλήρω-κα [e-'pliro-ka] 'I filled/have filled' (for classical πε-πλήρω-κα [pe-'pliro-ka]: P. Oxy. 2729.21, fourth century AD), we find both perfect forms with no reduplication (e.g. πτόκεν ['ptoken] 'I fell/have fallen', for classical πέπτωκε(ν) ['peptoke(n)]: P. Mich. 235.3, AD 41), and aorists with reduplication in place of the augment (e.g. πεπλήρωσα [pe'plirosa] 'I filled', for the classical ἐπλήρωσα [e'plirosa]: P. Oxy. 1489.5, third century AD).

Ultimately, however, augmented perfects came to be seen as simply alternative forms of the aorist, and a number of modern Greek spoken dialects (e.g. some Peloponnesian varieties, including Tsakonian in part, together with the so-called Old Athenian group, cf. Kondosópoulos (1981: xv)) eventually generalized the forms ending in (vowel +) -κα [ka] at the expense of standard -σα [-sa].

Finally, we should note that the functional merger of perfect and aorist inevitably led to a formal renewal of the true perfect. For the most part this involved the extension of a periphrasis that had already been in use in classical Greek, namely εἰμί [i'mi] 'I am', emphasizing a current state, in combination with either a perfect or an aorist participle (active or passive) expressing the past event. This is well attested in the papyri, especially where modal (subjunctive/optative) perfects are required. In the Byzantine period only the stative construction with the perfect passive participle survives strongly, essentially because of its morphological regularity (cf. 6.5.3 and 11.8.2).

6.5.3 Letter 3: the decline of 3rd declension participles

Our third letter (BGU 846) also dates from the second century AD and is addressed by a contrite young man to his long-suffering mother, who has apparently washed her hands of him:

(30) Ἀντώνις Λόγγος Νειλοῦτι [τ]ῇ μητρὶ π[λ]ῖστα χαίρειν. καὶ διὰ παντὸ[ς]
εὔχομαί σαι ὑγειαίνειν. τὸ προσκύνημά σου [ποι]ῶ κατ᾽ αἰκάστην ἡμαίραν
παρὰ τῷ κυρίῳ [Σερ]άπειδει. γεινώσκειν σαι θέλω ὅτι οὐχ [ἤλπ]ιζον ὅτι
ἀναβένις εἰς τὴν μητρόπολιν. χ[ά]ρειν τοῦτο οὐδ᾽ ἐγὼ εἰσῆθα εἰς τὴν πόλιν.
αἰδ[υ]σοπο[ύ]μην δὲ ἐλθεῖν εἰς Καρανίδαν ὅτι σαπρῶς παιριπατῶ. αἴγραψά
σοι ὅτι γυμνός εἰμει. παρακα[λ]ῶ σαι, μήτηρ, διαλάγητί μοι. λοιπὸν οἶδα
τί [ἐγὼ] αἱμαυτῷ παρέσχημαι. παιπαίδδευμαι καθ᾽ ὃν δῖ τρόπον. οἶδα ὅτι
ἡμάρτηκα. ἤκουσα παρὰ το[ῦ . . .] υμου τὸν εὑρόντα σαι ἐν τῷ Ἀρσαινοείτῃ
καὶ ἀκαιρέως πάντα σοι διήγηται. οὐκ οἶδες ὅτι θέλω πηρὸς γενέσται εἴ
γνοῦναι ὅπως ἀνθρόπῳ [ἔ]τι ὀφείλω ὀβολόν; . . .
Νειλοῦτι μητρεί ἀπ᾽ Ἀντωνίω Λόγγου υειοῦ.

[an'donis 'loŋgos ni'luti ti mi'tri 'plista   'kʰeri(n). ke ðja   pan'dos
Antonius Longus to-Nilous the mother very-much greeting. And through everything
'efkʰo'me se y'jeni(n). to pros'kyni'ma su   py'o kat e'kastin i'mera(n)
I-pray   you to-be-well. The supplication of-you I-make on each   day
pa'ra to ky'rio se'rapidi. ji'noski(n) se 'tʰelo 'oti ukʰ 'ilpizon   'oti
before the lord Serapis.   To-know   you I-wish that not I-was-expecting that
ana'venis is ti(m) mi'tropoli(n). 'kʰarin   'tuto ud e'ɣo is'i(l)tʰa is tim
you-go-up to the metropolis.   Because-of this nor I   went   to the
'bolin. edyso'pumin de el'tʰin is kara'nidan 'oti   sa'pros peripa'to.
city. I-was-ashamed and to-go to Karanis   because filthily I-go-about.
'eɣra'psa sy   'oti jim'nos imi. paraka'lo se, 'metir, ðja'laji'ti my. li'pon
I-wrote   to-you that naked I-am. I-call-upon you, mother, be-reconciled to-me. Well,
'yda ti   e'ɣo ema(f)'to pa'reskʰime. pe'pedevme   katʰ
I-know what I   for-myself have-provided. I-have-been-taught-a-lesson according-to
on 'di   'tropo(n). 'yda 'oti i'martika. 'ekusa pa'ra tu . . . ton
which is-necessary way.   I-know that I-have-sinned. I-heard from the . . . the
ev'ronda se en do arsino'iti ke ake'reos 'panda sy ðj'ejite.   uk
having-found you in the Arsinoite-nome and straight everything to-you has-been-told. Not
'ydes   'oti 'tʰelo pi'ros je'neste i 'ɣnune 'opos an'tʰropo 'eti o'pʰilo
you-know that I-wish crippled to-become than to-know that   to-a-man still I-owe
ovo'lo(n)?
obol?
ni'luti mi'tri ap ando'niu 'loŋgu y'ju.]
To-Nilous mother from Antonius Longus son.

'Antonius Longus to Nilous his mother very many greetings. I pray always that you are well. I also make supplication for you before the lord Serapis every day. I want you to know that I was not expecting you to be going up to the metropolis [*Arsinoe, the capital of the Fayum nome*]. Therefore I did not go to the city either. I was ashamed to come to Karanis [*a village in the Fayum where Nilous lives*] because I walk around in filth. I wrote to you that I am naked. I beg you, mother, be reconciled to me. When all is said and done, I know what I have brought upon myself. I have learned the necessary lesson. I know that I have sinned. I heard from . . . who found you in the Arsinoite nome, and you have been told everything just as it is. Do you not know that I would rather be crippled than realize I still owe a man an obol [*a small coin*]? . . .

To Nilous his mother from her son Antonius Longus.'

A number of further phonological developments are well illustrated here:

(31) (a) Interchange of $\alpha\iota$ and ϵ is routine and shows that classical /ai/ has now merged with /e/; cf. $\sigma\alpha\iota$ [se] for $\sigma\epsilon$ 'you', $\alpha\iota\kappa\acute{\alpha}\sigma\tau\eta\nu$ [e'kastin] for $\dot{\epsilon}\kappa\acute{\alpha}\sigma\tau\eta\nu$ 'each', $\mathring{\eta}\mu\alpha\acute{\iota}\rho\alpha\nu$ [i'mera(n)] for $\mathring{\eta}\mu\acute{\epsilon}\rho\alpha\nu$, $\dot{\alpha}\nu\alpha\beta\acute{\epsilon}\nu\iota\varsigma$ [ana'venis] for $\dot{\alpha}\nu\alpha\beta\alpha\acute{\iota}\nu\epsilon\iota\varsigma$, etc.

   (b) The erratic, frequently hypercorrect, marking of assimilatory aspiration in word-final consonants before words which in earlier Koine (and in educated usage probably still) began with /h/ shows that, for this writer at least, the sound was no longer real; cf. $\kappa\alpha\tau$' $\alpha\iota\kappa\acute{\alpha}\sigma\tau\eta\nu$ [kat e'kastin] for $\kappa\alpha\theta$' $\dot{\epsilon}\kappa\acute{\alpha}\sigma\tau\eta\nu$ [kat^h he'kasten], $o\mathring{\upsilon}\chi$ $\mathring{\eta}\lambda\pi\iota\zeta o\nu$ [uk^h 'ilpizo(n)] for $o\mathring{\upsilon}\kappa$ $\mathring{\eta}\lambda\pi\iota\zeta o\nu$ [uk 'elpizon].

   (c) Note the apparent confusion of genitive and dative in the final line: $\mathring{A}\nu\tau\omega\nu\acute{\iota}\omega$ (?dat.) $\Lambda\acute{o}\nu\gamma o\upsilon$ (gen.) [ando'niu 'loŋgu]. The spelling reflects the raising of unstressed final [o] to [u] in popular speech, surely a contributory factor in the loss of the dative. Thus the unstressed 2nd declension (o-stem) ending [-u] is used indiscriminately both as a true genitive and as a dative by this writer, and the iotas could therefore legitimately be removed from $\tau\hat{\omega}$ $\kappa\upsilon\rho\acute{\iota}\omega$, which might perhaps be more accurately transcribed [tu ky'riu]; recall that the addition or omission of iota subscript is simply a matter of modern editorial choice.

In view of the evidence here and elsewhere of the progressive desystematization of the dative case (cf. 4.11.1), we should note that the phrase:

(32) $\tau\grave{o}$ $\pi\rho o\sigma\kappa\acute{\upsilon}\nu\eta\mu\acute{\alpha}$ $\sigma o\upsilon$ $\pi o\iota\hat{\omega}$

[to pros'kyni'ma su   py'o]

the supplication   of-you I-make

could be interpreted as involving the transfer of the genitive clitic pronoun from the government domain of the noun (= possessive) to that of the verb, thus making the genitive here do the work of an indirect object (= beneficiary). We may compare examples like P. Flor. 127, $\lambda\alpha\mu\beta\acute{\alpha}\nu\epsilon\iota\varsigma$ $\mu o\upsilon$ $\tau\grave{\alpha}$ $\gamma\rho\acute{\alpha}\mu\mu\alpha\tau\alpha$ [lam'banis mu ta 'ɣramata] 'you-receive of-me the letters', where the attraction of the possessive to the classic 'second position' for enclitics encourages comparison/overlap with the 'ethic' dative. This is precisely the sort of situation in which dative–genitive functional

overlap was first actively promoted, and it is striking that substitution of the genitive for the dative occurs quite widely in the clitic pronoun system (beginning in
the first century BC) before it spreads to full noun phrases in the early centuries AD
(cf. also 6.5.4).

Further points of grammatical interest include:

(33) (a) Retention of the accusative and infinitive only in formulaic phrases:
εὔχομαί σαι ὑγειαίνειν ['efkʰo'me se y'jenin] 'I pray (for) you to be
well'; γεινώσκειν σαι θέλω [ji'noskin se 'tʰelo] 'I want you to know'.
Thus the verbs ἤλπιζον ['ilpizon] and οἶδα ['yda], for example, take
finite clauses introduced by ὅτι ['oti] 'that'.

(b) The spread of prepositional expressions at the expense of the dative: e.g
κατ᾽ αἰκάστην ἡμαίραν [kat e'kastin i'mera(n)] '(on) every day', in place
of the simple dative of 'time when'. The classical use of this preposition
in temporal expressions is distributive, 'day by day', and the use here is
an easy extension.

(c) The spread of the accusative as the 'default' prepositional case: e.g. χάριν
τοῦτο ['kʰarin 'tuto] 'because of this', in place of classical τούτου χάριν
['tutu 'kʰarin] 'for the sake of this', with a dependent genitive pronoun
and postnominal position for what was originally an adverbial use of an
accusative noun.

(d) (i) The apparent breakdown of agreement in participial syntax: παρὰ
το[ῦ . . .]. υμου [tu . . . ymu] (gen.) τὸν εὑρόντα σαι [ton e'vronda
se] (acc.), lit. 'from the . . . the (one) having-found you'. This seems
to reflect a growing sense of the accusative as the default oblique case
(seen also in its spread after prepositions). The genitive, for example,
is used when semantically motivated, i.e. to express possession (and
other forms of adnominal dependence) and increasingly as a dative
substitute to mark secondary involvement with the verbal action; but
the purely 'formal' agreement involved in cases like this is less carefully observed, and accusative participles begin to appear in a variety
of looser, appositive structures.

(ii) In a similar fashion the nominative starts to appear as the unmarked
case for loosely constructed 'topics', cf. BGU 385, second/third century AD: ὁ ἐνιγὼν σοι τὴν ἐπιστολήν, δὸς αὐτῷ ἄλλην . . . [o
eni(ŋ)'go(n) sy tin episto'li(n), dos af'to 'ali(n) . . .], lit. 'the (one)
bringing you the letter (nom.), give to-him (dat.) another . . .'.

This kind of grammatical imprecision is almost certainly connected with more general pressure on the complex morphology of the participle system. Eventually, in
popular varieties of late antique and early medieval Greek an indeclinable participle in -οντα [-onda], ultimately formed from the imperfective stem alone, was
used virtually as an adverb (as if one could say *s/he left running(-ly)*, etc.), with its
interpretation progressively restricted, in the absence of the agreement morphology
necessary to link it to specific noun phrases, to that of a subject-orientated gerund
expressing manner or circumstantial background.

This reduction of the participial system was motivated in part by the ambiguity inherent in the various subordinating functions of participles, but more importantly by the morphological complexity of most of the relevant classical paradigms. Consider, for example, the imperfective active participle of λύω ['lyo] 'I set free':

(34) masc. λύ-ων ['ly-on]; fem. λύ-ουσ-α ['ly-us-a]; neut. λῦ-ον ['ly-on]

where the feminine form belongs to the 1st declension and the masculine and neuter forms to the 3rd declension, and the latter exhibit further stem allomorphy, e.g. gen. sg. λύ-οντ-ος ['ly-ond-os], dat. pl. λύ-ου-σι ['ly-ou-si]. When the masculine and feminine consonant-stem nouns of the 3rd declension began to be shifted to the more regular 1st declension (the a-stem paradigm, cf. 4.11.3, 11.8.2), the fate of the increasingly isolated 3rd/1st declension participles (i.e. the majority, including present, future, aorist and perfect active, and aorist passive) was effectively sealed, though they survived in learned literary works throughout the later history of the language, and for a time also in formal educated discourse more generally.

A reasonably plausible account of this process can be reconstructed on the basis of sporadically attested forms and usages in the Roman and early Byzantine papyri. Evidence of paradigm levelling, for example, is quite common from around the first century AD onwards, typically involving the substitution of masculine forms for feminine, and the use of the accusative masculine singular in -οντα [-onda] for the neuter nominative/accusative singular in -ον [-on]. Since the borrowed ending of the neuter singular was usually homophonous with that of the neuter plural (e.g. both end in -οντα [-onda] in the case of participles), the result was a tendency towards the formal and functional identification of the neuter singular with the neuter plural in the nominative/accusative. The old plural (or new singular) forms predominate in this dual function, though there are also parallel examples, at least for a time, of the old (unrecharacterized) singulars doubling as plurals.

Such nominative/accusative 3rd declension neuters (both original singulars and new singular/plurals) then began to be used to represent any case function of the singular or plural. This must reflect uncertainty about which set of oblique endings (singular or plural) to use to complete the paradigms of nominative/accusative neuter forms that were neutral with respect to number. As an example we may take SB 9251.2, second/third century AD: πρὸ μὲν πᾶν [pro men pan], lit. 'before on-the-one-hand everything', with an (old) accusative singular, in place of the formulaic πρὸ μὲν πάντων/παντός [pro men 'pandon/pan'dos], with the genitive plural or the genitive singular.

Given that neuter plural adjectives in -α [-a] had been used adverbially from classical times, the uncertainty and attendant loss of morphological distinctiveness in the neuter adjectival paradigms must have helped promote the interpretation of neuter participles in -οντα [-onda] as essentially adverb-like modifiers, with no need for agreement morphology. This assumption, once it began to take root widely, led to the progressive elimination even from the masculine/feminine paradigm of inflected forms other than the masculine accusative singular -οντα [-onda], which, being homophonous with the neuter singular/plural, was identified with it formally and functionally.

In the long transitional period, however, we find increasing numbers of examples involving violations of concord, and a growing preference for the accusative as an all-purpose oblique case, both in the singular, because of the favoured -οντα [-onda] suffix, and in the plural, where nominative and accusative were in any case tending to fall together formally, cf. 4.11.1, 6.5.2, thus applying pressure in turn on the still distinct nominative singular in -ων [-on]. The level of success in reproducing the classical forms depends very much on the level of education of the author. A nice example is provided by P. Merton 91.6, AD 316: ἡμεῖν ... εὖ βιοῦντες [i'min ... ev vi'undes], lit. 'for us (dat.) ... well living (nom./acc. pl.)', where the participle shows agreement in number and gender, but not in case (the irregular βιοῦσι [vi'usi], involving a dying case within an independently dying paradigm, being beyond the writer's control).

6.5.4 Letter 4: the decline of the dative; personal pronouns

Our final extract (P. Oxy. 1683) dates from the final years of the fourth century AD, and is addressed by one Probus to his 'sister' Manatine:

(35) τῇ κυρίᾳ μου ἀδ[ελ]φῇ Μανατίνῃ Πρῶβ[ο]ς ἀδελφῷ χαίριν. πρὼ [μ]ὲν
πάντων εὔχωμαι τῷ κυρίῳ θεῷ περὶ τῆς σῆς ὠλοκληρίας ὅπως ὑιένοντα
σοὶ καὶ εὐθυμοῦντι ἀπωλάβῃς τὰ παρ' ἐμοῦ γράμματα. [γι]γνώσκιν σε
θέλω, κυρία μου ἀδελφή, ἄπελθε πρὸς Πετρώνιν τὼν ἐνγυησάμενόν μου·
δέξε ἀ[π' α]ὐτοῦ ἐκ τοῦ μισθοῦ μου ἔναν ὕμιση ... οἶδες γ[ὰ]ρ καὶ σὺ ὅτι
[ο]ὐδὲν ἔχωμεν μάρτυρων ε[ἰ] μὴ ὁ θε[ό]ς καὶ σὺ καὶ ἡ γυνή μου. ἀπώδως
οὖν αὐτὰ τῇ γυναικίν μου. μὴ λυπήσις οὖν ἐμέναν· δὸς οὖν αὐτά, ἐπιδὲ
χρίαν αὐτὰ ὁ υἱός μου. σημίου δὲ χάριν, ὥπου ἡπάντηκά σου ἰ[ς] τὸ
Κησάριον καὶ εἴρηκά σου ὥτι δὸς ἐμοὶ κέρμα ἀπὼ τῶν ἔχις με ἵνα ἀγωράσω
ἐματῷ ἔναν λέβιτων ..., καὶ εἶπές με ὥτι ... ἄρων τὰ ἀπ' ἐσοῦ καὶ ἄρτι
δέ σε δ[ίδ]ω ...

[ti   ky'ria mu   aðel'fi mana'tini 'provos aðel'fo(s) 'çerin. pro
to-the lady of-me sister   Manatine   Probus   brother   greeting. Before

men   'pandon 'efxome to   ky'rio θe'o pe'ri   tis sis olokli'rias
on-the-one-hand everything I-pray to-the lord god concerning the your health

'opos y'jenonda sy ke efθi'mundi   apo'lavis ta par e'mu 'γramata.
that being-well you and being-in-good spirits you-receive the from me letter.

ji(γ)'noski(n) se 'θelo, ky'ria mu   aðel'fi, 'apelθe pros pe'tronin ton
To-know   you I-want, lady of-me sister,   go   to   Petronius the (one)

eŋgyi'sameno(n) mu. 'ðekse ap af'tu ek   tu mis'θu mu   'enan
having-guaranteed of-me. Receive from him out-of the wages of-me one   (and)

'imisi ...   'γðes γar ke sy 'oti u'ðen   'exome(n) 'martyro(n) i mi
half (talents). ... You-know for also you that nothing/not we-have   witness   if not

o θe'os kai sy ke i jy'ni mu. a'poðos un a(f)'ta ti   jyne'kim mu.
the god and you and the wife of-me. Hand-over then them to-the wife of-me.

mi ly'pisis un e'menan. ðos un a(f)'ta, epi'ði 'xrian   a(f)'ta o
(Do) not vex   then me.   Give then them,   since   need   (of) them   the

y'joz mu <'eçi>. si'miu ðe 'xari(n),   'opu i'pandi'ka su is to ki'sario(n)
son   of-me (has).   Of-proof and for-the-sake, when I-met   you in the Caesareum

ke 'iri'ka su 'oti ðos e'my 'kerma a'po ton   'eçiz   me 'in(a)
and I-told   you that 'give me   coin   from the (ones) you-have (for) me that

ayo'raso ema'to   'ena(n) 'leviton . . . , ke 'ipez   me 'oti . . . 'aron t(a)
I-may-buy for-myself a   pot . . .',   and you-said me that '. . . take   the (ones)

ap e'su ke 'arti ðe   se 'ðiðo . . .]
from you   and soon   on-the-other-hand you I-give . . .'

'To my lady sister Manatine Probus her brother greeting. Above all I pray to the lord god concerning your well-being that you receive my letter in good health and in good spirits. I want you to know, my lady sister, (that you must) go to Petronius my guarantor. Get from him out of my pay one and a half (talents) . . . . For you too know that we have no witness but god and you and my wife. So hand them over to my wife. Do not then cause me distress. Give them to her, therefore, since my son needs them. As proof, when I met you in the Caesareum and said to you "give me one of the coins that you keep for me so I can buy myself a pot . . .", (and) you said . . . "take your own and I will give it to you later . . .".'

The general drift is more or less apparent, though the author is not well educated and lacks the gift of clear exposition; in particular, the intended significance of the absence of other witnesses and the import of the 'proof' are rather difficult to determine.

The participle ὑιένοντα [y'jenonda] 'in good health', employed as an indeclinable subject-orientated adjunct in place of the nominative feminine singular ὑγιαίνουσα [(h)y'jenousa], is exactly what we might have expected in the light of the discussion above, and it presumably corresponds to the author's normal usage. He has, however, done some work on his consonant-stem paradigms, and can also manage the masculine singular dative form εὐθυμοῦντι [efθi'mundi] 'in good spirits', apparently in agreement with nominative [sy], misspelled as dative σοι, a wonderful example of a purely 'graphic' agreement!

Behind all the uncertainty and confusion, however, important indications of the contemporary state of colloquial spoken Greek can be discerned, in particular concerning the fate of the dative. Note, for example, the substitution of genitive and accusative pronouns: cf. ἠπάντηκά σου [i'pandi'ka sou], lit. 'I met to you', εἴρηκά σου ['irika su] 'I said to you', with genitive for dative, alongside ἔχις με ['eçiz me] 'you have (for) me', εἶπές με ['ipez me] 'you said (to) me', σε δίδω [se 'ðiðo] 'I give (to) you', with accusative for dative. Datives are still used, however, in δός ἐμοί [ðos e'my] 'give to me', and ἀγοράσω ἐματῷ [ayo'raso ema'to] 'I buy for myself' (note, incidentally, the reduced form of the pronoun ἐμ-αυτῷ [em-af'to], lit. 'me-self'), though the apparent dative ἀδελφῷ [aðel'fo(s)], used in apposition to nominative Πρῶβος ['provos], is probably an example of ω [o] for o [o], with an editorial iota subscript and final -ς [s] omitted (as not infrequently in low-level papyri).

For comparable uncertainty about the dative in this period we may compare P. Oxy. 1300, from the fifth century AD:

(36) προσαγορεῦσαί σε . . . καὶ τοῦ ἀδελφοῦ Θέωνι καὶ τῇ κυρίᾳ μου ἀδελφῇ . . . καὶ τῶν γλυκητάτον μου ἀδελφίον Ἡραεὶν καὶ Νόννᾳ . . . καὶ Φοιβάμων . . .

[prosaɣo'refse se . . . ke tu aðel'fu 'θeoni ke ti ky'ria mu aðel'fi . . . ke to(n) ɣlyki'tatom mu aðel'fio(n) ira'in kai n'ona . . . ke fy'vamo(n) . . .]

'to-send-greetings (to) you (acc.), . . . and to-the brother (gen.) Theon (dat.), . . . and to-the lady of-me sister (dat.) . . . and (to) the sweetest of-me little-sibling (acc.) Herais (acc.) and Nonna (dat.) . . . and Phoebammon (no ending) . . .'

Of the two 3rd declension consonant-stem forms Θέωνι has a dative ending, but the other, Φοιβάμων [fy'vamon] (a nice blend of Greek and Egyptian), is apparently treated as indeclinable. In the 2nd declension (cf. ἀδελφοῦ/ἀδελφίον [aðel'fu/aðel'fion]) both genitive and accusative mark the recipient of the greeting, while in the 3rd declension i-stems it is the accusative which fulfils this function (cf. Ἡραείν [ira'in]; this was originally a dental-stem with accusative -ίδα [-'iða], which has been assimilated to the i-stems because of the identical nominative forms in -ίς [-'is]). Only in the 1st declension does a separate dative seem to be in semi-regular use (cf. τῇ κυρίᾳ μου ἀδελφῇ [ti ky'ria mu aðel'fi]), though we should not forget the weakness of final -ν [-n], and the frequent homophony of dative and accusative forms (the usual provisos concerning accentuation and subscript iotas apply). All these functionally equivalent case forms (which are at best only partially differentiated formally) are freely combined in structures involving apposition and coordination, according to the author's idiosyncratic preferences and/or knowledge of 'correct' orthography.

We are clearly very close here to the demise of the dative in popular Egyptian Greek, and equally close to a time when either genitive or accusative forms will be automatically substituted.

Other important features in (35) include:

(37) (a) The use of οὐδέν [u'ðen] apparently as a simple negative, exactly as in modern Greek (having suffered aphaeresis to δεν [ðen], cf. 11.2, 11.3).

(b) The shift of masculine 3rd declension nouns to the 2nd declension (a temporary expedient for dealing with a dying declensional class, but popular for a time): cf. acc. sg. μάρτυρων ['martyro(n)] for μάρτυρα ['martyra].

(c) (i) The development of new 'strong' forms of personal pronouns (cf. ἐμέναν [e'menan] 'me', involving the addition first of a characterizing accusative -ν [-n] to the classical ἐμέ [e'me], and then of the typical 3rd declension accusative suffix -α [-a], perhaps on the analogy of elements like τινά [tina] 'someone', ἕνα ['ena] 'one/a(n)', a form itself finally recharacterized by the addition of a further final -ν [-n]).

(ii) The 2nd person pronoun σύ [sy] also acquired an initial ἐ- [e-], by analogy with 1st person nom./acc. ἐγω/ἐμένα(ν) [e'ɣo/e'mena(n)], to give ἐσύ/ἐσενα(ν) [e'sy/e'sena(n)], and new plural forms were then built to the singulars to solve the problem of the homophony of classical ἡμεῖς/ὑμεῖς [i'mis/i'mis] 'we/you', namely ἐμ-εῖς/ἐσ-εῖς [e'mis/e'sis].

(iii) The earliest examples of the fully extended accusative form of the 1st person singular pronoun date from the fourth century AD. The corresponding forms of the 2nd person singular pronoun apparently belong to the Byzantine period proper, though a version of the new 2nd plural forms is attested in P. Ross. Georg. iii, 10 (fourth/fifth century AD): acc./gen./dat. ἡσᾶς, ἡσῶν, ἡσῖν [i'sas/i'son/i'sin] (cf. 11.7.8(e)).

(d) The use of εἰς [is] with the accusative (ἰς τὸ Κησάριον [is to ki'sarion]) in place of ἐν [en] with the problematic dative to express location as well as goal (examples occur from Ptolemaic times onwards); another example of the accusative as the default prepositional case.

(e) The use of the article, almost always in oblique cases, as a relative pronoun (ἀπὸ τῶν ἔχις [a'po ton 'eçis] 'from what you have'). The classical forms ὅς/ἥ/ὅ [os/i/o] lacked bulk, and were prone to loss when preceding or following words that ended or began with a vowel. The use of the forms of the article, which began with a 'protective' plosive apart from masc./fem. nom. sg./pl., started in Hellenistic times (where it was perhaps in part a continuation of earlier Ionic practice), and became increasingly common with the passage of time (cf. 11.7.8(c)).

(f) The transfer of δίδωμι to the regular paradigm in -ω [-o], δίδω ['ðiðo]. Eventually all the verbs in -μι [-mi] were assimilated to the regular paradigm, though many older forms persist into the Byzantine period, even in more 'popular' texts, presumably because of their great frequency (cf. 11.8.5(a)).

6.6 Conclusion

The evidence of these low-level Roman papyri has been discussed in considerable detail, because the period was instrumental in the transition from ancient to modern Greek, with many of the most characteristic phonological differences between the classical and contemporary languages already in place by late antiquity, and the first stages of many of the more important grammatical changes well reflected in popular spoken and written varieties. With a clear understanding of the beginnings of this transition, we are now ready to consider the subsequent history of the language in the Middle Ages and beyond.

Byzantium: from Constantine I to Mehmet the Conqueror

Chapter 7

Historical prelude

7.1 The later Roman empire

After the stability of the first and second centuries AD, the 50 years after the fall of the Severan dynasty, from 235 to the accession of Diocletian in 284, was a critical period for the empire, with constant warfare against the Persians in the east and Germanic tribes to the north and west leading to an enhanced role for the military, economic difficulties, and a rapid turnover of emperors, each provincial army putting up, and as quickly murdering, its own pretenders (see Brown (1971), Cameron (1993)).

The result was a reduction in the importance of the old imperial capital as emperors increasingly based themselves in strategically important provincial centres. Decentralization also created a context in which local cultures (and local languages such as Coptic and Syriac) could thrive, and in which Christianity, still very much a minority and provincial religion, could begin to develop solid institutional structures.

Between the accession of Diocletian in 284 and the death of Constantine I in 337, the political and military situation stabilized and administrative reforms were put in place which formed the basis of the system of government until the 'end' of the Roman empire (Rome itself fell to a Gothic pretender in 476, though in the east we have to wait for the Arab conquests of the seventh century for a clear break with classical antiquity). In particular, Diocletian sought to bring the army under central control by consolidating its financial and administrative privileges and instituting a more reliable means of raising revenue so as to guarantee the supply of resources needed to defend the empire's security. He also reorganized provincial government by separating civil and military commands and reducing the size of the provinces themselves (thereby increasing their overall number, but reducing the power of individual governors).

Diocletian did not, however, succeed in reversing the long-term decline of Rome. In an attempt to end the political instability that had plagued the third century, he set up the 'tetrarchic' system by which power was to be shared between two senior emperors, or Augusti, each aided by a junior emperor, or Caesar, who would succeed him. This consolidated the tendency towards decentralization by dividing the empire informally into eastern and western spheres of influence, and led to the emergence of a number of new regional 'capitals'. Diocletian himself had his main residence at Nicomedia (Izmit) in Bithynia, his Caesar Galerius was based in Thessaloniki, while the other Caesar, Constantius, had his base in Augusta

Treverorum (Trier) close to the Rhine frontier. Emperors now spent a great deal of time travelling between such centres, and this in turn fostered new building and urban development, the foundation of Constantinople on the site of Byzantium by Constantine I being the most important example.

When Diocletian and his fellow Augustus Maximian abdicated on 1 May 305, Galerius succeeded in the east, Constantius in the west, as planned. But after Constantius died in York in the following year, his son Constantine was proclaimed Augustus by his father's troops. Maximian quickly returned from retirement, and the tetrarchic arrangements for the succession broke down. Constantine first sought to consolidate his position through an alliance with Maximian, but by 310 Maximian's son, Maxentius, had seized Rome, and Maximian himself had turned on both of them. Maximian, however, committed suicide when Constantine took up arms against him, and two years later, in 312, Maxentius was defeated at the battle of the Milvian Bridge outside Rome.

Things had become similarly confused in the east, where Licinius had been appointed Augustus at the Conference of Carnuntum in 308, despite the fact that Diocletian's immediate successor, Galerius, was still alive. When Galerius died in 311, his nephew Maximin seized Asia Minor from Licinius, and it was only in 313 that Licinius finally defeated his rival and emerged as sole Augustus of the East. Constantine and Licinius then concluded an alliance which continued, despite an inconclusive clash in 316, until the decisive campaign of 324 in which Licinius was defeated at Chrysopolis. Constantine then became the sole ruler of the Roman world until his death in 337.

In general, Constantine sought to consolidate Diocletian's military, provincial and administrative arrangements, but where previous emperors had tried period-ically to stifle Christianity by persecution, Constantine committed himself to its protection; and so began the process of integration which led to a crucial develop-mental period in which acceptance of Christianity became increasingly routine in even the highest levels of society, specifically Christian forms of art and literature were developed within the context of the cultural mainstream, and the first defini-tions of 'correct doctrine', or orthodoxy, were attempted. Constantine himself, in an important precedent for establishing the role of the emperor in the affairs of the church, presided over the first ecumenical council at Nicaea (Iznik) in 325, which had been called to pronounce on Arianism (the doctrine of Arius, a Syrian monk who had become presbyter of Alexandria, which denied Christ's full divinity and was duly declared a heresy).

When Constantine founded his 'New Rome' on the site of the old Greek city of Byzantium in May AD 330, therefore, it was not merely as a centre of Roman culture and Latinity in the east but also as a capital city associated from the outset with the Christian faith. In due course it provided the physical and spiritual 'centre' for the medieval Byzantine state.

Though at various times after Constantine's death several Augusti again ruled simultaneously, the traditional urban life of antiquity, with its largely money-based economy, continued more or less intact, and the empire remained at least formally undivided until the death of Theodosius I in 395. Thereafter, his sons Arcadius and

Honorius shared the Roman world between them, the former taking the east, the latter the west (with its capital now at Ravenna), in what was to prove to be a permanent division.

By this time 'barbarian' Germanic tribes, including the Franks and Alamanni in the west and the Visigoths and Ostrogoths in the east, had begun to occupy the richer lands adjoining the Mediterranean. The migration of the east German peoples from lands between the Danube and the Don was motivated chiefly by changing economic conditions, but the arrival of the Huns, a nomadic tribe from the steppes of central Asia, may have been a contributory factor. In their journey south and west the Goths defeated a Roman army at Adrianople (Edirne) in 378, and having been partly forced, partly bribed out of the Balkans by Theodosius, moved on into Italy, where they eventually sacked Rome in 410.

In this period, the recruitment of barbarian auxiliaries and even the appointment of barbarian generals had become routine, in order to avoid the trouble of conscription. The policy also proved (temporarily) profitable, to the extent that the treasury could exact taxes in lieu. But the resumption of political rivalry in both east and west after the death of Theodosius allowed ambitious barbarian generals, backed by their mercenary recruits, to exploit the situation for their own ends, and by the end of the fourth century even the regular army was in disarray.

Though the situation was eventually stabilized in the east, after the government in Constantinople firmly turned its back on barbarian troops and generals, the position in the west continued to deteriorate. In the face of political instability, economic weakness and institutional fragmentation, forces stationed in the provinces were withdrawn and Roman territory was progressively settled by Goths (Italy and Spain), Franks (France) and Vandals (North Africa). The end of Roman government finally came, according to the conventional dating, with the overthrow of the young Romulus Augustulus by his Gothic Master of the Soldiers, Odoacer, in 476.

Latin survived, however, as the language of administration, culture and everyday communication (as witnessed by the Romance languages), while many Roman traditions and institutions continued in modified forms. But there were to be no more Roman emperors in the west, and though Rome continued to be the seat of the senior bishop of the Christian church, the eastern Roman empire, with its capital at Constantinople, now stood alone.

7.2 The age of transition: Ioustinianós and the Arab conquests

After the formal division of the empire in 395, east and west grew steadily apart, and while the west declined, the eastern empire enjoyed considerable prosperity from the late-fourth to the early-sixth centuries, initiating major building programmes and seeing its cities grow substantially in size and population, (cf. Mango (1980), Whiting (1981)). The decision to abandon the recruitment of barbarians was a major factor in re-establishing effective government and military efficiency. Unlike in the west, where central control was weak and powerful provincial families had been allowed unrestrained extension of their wealth through land acquisition, the east retained a more resilient economic system based on the continuity of a free peasantry alongside the estates that emerged with the rise of the provincial aristocracy. Peasants paid taxes and were available for recruitment to the army, and this guaranteed the financial and military resources necessary to resist, or buy off, barbarian invaders.

With the reserves built up through the fiscal reforms of Anastásios I (ruled 491–518), the emperor Ioustinianós I (Justinian, reigned 527–65, a native speaker of Latin from an Illyrian peasant family) embarked on an ambitious campaign of reconquest in the west (see Moorhead (1994)). Having concluded a treaty with the Persians in 522 to safeguard the eastern frontier, he first sent his general Belisários to recover the Vandal kingdom in North Africa. Following his success there, Belisários was transferred to Italy, where, aided by the Armenian general Narsés, the eventual submission of the Ostrogoths was secured in 550. A third force was then dispatched to Spain in 552, and the south-east corner of the peninsula recovered, perhaps to provide a defensive barrier for Africa.

These military successes followed a major codification and reform of Roman law carried out by Ioustinianós's legal adviser Tribonianós, and coincided with a cultural revival and a great expansion of trade based on silk production (precious silkworm eggs having been smuggled out of the east). In the same period the great churches of San Vitale and Sant' Apollinare in Classe were built in the new western capital of Ravenna, while at Constantinople the vast new Hagía Sophía, which still stands, was constructed to replace Constantine's original church that had been destroyed by fire in the aftermath of an anti-government uprising in January 532.

This riot, named after the chant (νίκα ['nika] 'win!') employed by the Hippodrome factions (the Blues and Greens) involved in its instigation, seems to have been motivated by resentment of domestic repression and the high levels of taxation needed to fund the wars. After a day at the games, this crystallized into demands for the release of prisoners and the dismissal of unpopular officials, up to and including the emperor himself. The successful containment of the riot (some tens of thousands were massacred) gave Ioustinianós the pretext and the authority to assert his role as God's vicegerent on earth. This useful validating role was then assumed by all later Christian Roman emperors, and the Roman/Byzantine state now began to define itself increasingly in religious terms.

In his new capacity as God's agent, Ioustinianós felt a duty to define and impose Orthodox belief, though in this he was less successful. The Platonic Academy in Athens was closed in 529, and the teaching of pagan philosophy restricted to Christian institutions (philosophy thus becoming a 'historical' subject rather than a living body of rival doctrine). Then, having tried unsuccessfully to suppress the heresy of Monophysitism, which saw Christ as a God who had ceased to be also a man (and rather inconveniently included the emperor's wife Theodóra among its adherents), Ioustinianós sought to reconcile the Monophysites by making concessions, but succeeded only in antagonizing the western church, which was implacably hostile to the doctrine. He also alienated many of his own bishops from Egypt and Syria, where the doctrine enjoyed overwhelming support.

Ioustinianós's military successes also proved to be short-lived. The cost of re-asserting universal Roman rule was more than the empire could bear, and it was ill-equipped to deal with fresh assaults. The Lombards (another Germanic tribe) were therefore able to occupy all of north and central Italy before the end of the sixth century, and prosperity was seriously undermined by earthquakes and plague epidemics, which led to the collapse of many urban centres and to a serious reduc-tion in the quality of life in the cities that survived.

The situation became critical when the Balkans, already threatened by nomadic Turkic peoples in Ioustinianós's time, came under pressure from an alliance of Avars (nomads of Tartar origin) and Slavs (who had moved south from the river valleys of central Europe). By the 580s these groups had penetrated the Pelopon-nese, leaving only a few coastal towns in Byzantine control. Soon after, at the beginning of the seventh century, came the Persian invasions of Syria, Armenia, Asia Minor and Egypt. This devastating period marks the first clear break with classical antiquity in the east, and still worse was to come. In 626, while the emperor Herákleios (a capable soldier and administrator of Armenian descent, who reigned 610–41) was away on campaign against the Persians, an army of Persians, Avars and Slavs besieged Constantinople itself, though the capital held out thanks to its land walls and its control of the sea. This proved to be a turning point, and thereafter Herákleios succeeded in recovering the empire's losses in Asia Minor and Syria, and finally won a decisive victory at Nineveh in 627, which led to the collapse of the Persian empire. In 630 he was able to enter Jerusalem in triumph.

But success was again short-lived. The power vacuum was filled almost imme-diately by the recently Islamicized Arabs, who now embarked on a campaign of aggressive expansion. Persia, in disarray after Herákleios's triumph, fell in 636, and the Romans themselves came under attack immediately afterwards; Jerusalem fell again in 638, and remained under Islamic control until the first crusade at the end of the eleventh century. In 640 the Arabs advanced into Egypt, and then pressed on throughout north Africa, so that this territory too was lost permanently to the empire. On several occasions in the late seventh and early eighth centuries Con-stantinople was again besieged, though the emperor Léon III (a Syrian from Germanicea, reigned 716–40) began the long fight back by raising the second Arab siege of the capital in 717–18 and defeating an Arab army in 740.

The Arab advance by land was, however, halted in Asia Minor, the last great recruiting ground for the Roman/Byzantine army, and though raids continued for some 300 years, it was to be the Turks, not the Arabs, who finally deprived the empire of its last great territorial possession. Nevertheless, Byzantium had suf-fered a stupendous blow; Syria, Palestine and Egypt were among its richest prov-inces, and Egypt was a major supplier of grain to the capital. Henceforth the reproachful ghost of universal empire hung over the residual Byzantine state, incul-cating a state of mind to which the retrospective quality of mature Byzantine culture has often been attributed (cf. Mango (1980: 4–5)).

The successful resistance to the Arabs in Asia Minor was achieved because of the imposition of martial law and the fact that its provinces had earlier been divided by Herákleios into administrative/military districts known as 'themes', each under the command of a governor/general who reported directly to the emperor. This reform gave pre-eminence to the military as a career path, and circumscribed the power of the landed aristocracy by consolidating the position of the villages as the units of taxation and recruitment. Many soldiers had already been given lands in the themes so as to provide a standing army, but this period saw massive new population movements as different ethnic groups were relocated to meet fresh military contingencies.

As a result of this system of economic and military organization, Byzantine society, already isolated by the Slav settlements in Greece and the Balkans, was set on a radically different course from that of western Europe, so that feudalization began only in the tenth century, and a fully formalized system of feudal relations, as developed in the west, was never established because of the revival of urban life and a trading economy (see 7.3, 7.4 below). This separation of east and west was reinforced on the linguistic front. Knowledge of Greek in the west had already declined by the end of the fourth century. Similarly in the east, though Latin had originally been used in court circles in Constantinople, it was Greek which had always been employed for practical administrative purposes, and throughout the Roman imperial and Byzantine periods Greek remained the only language of higher education, the principal language of culture, and the sole vernacular *lingua franca* of the multi-ethnic empire, acquired as a first language by many, and as a second language by many more. The position of Latin as the language of the Roman 'establishment' therefore became increasingly precarious, though in the army, the legal profession, and imperial ceremonial it continued to enjoy prestige as the 'true' language of the Romans, and remained in use, albeit in an increasingly formulaic way, until the end of the sixth century.

But Greek had begun to supplant Latin in even its residual functions by the first half of the fifth century, when the key office of praetorian prefect, virtually that of deputy emperor, had been filled by a Greek-speaking Egyptian. A century later, Ioustinianós's praetorian prefect, Ioánnes the Cappadocian, reduced the use of Latin in the eastern prefecture still further in recognition of the linguistic realities, and his successor in that post was not familiar with Latin at all. Similarly, though Ioustinianós's codification of the law was carried out in the traditional legal language, the great bulk of the 'novels' (i.e. supplements to, or replacements of earlier legislation) were already composed in Greek, and a Greek version of the *Institutes* had already been published in 534.

Thus even though the influx of Italian refugees during the wars of reconquest· temporarily enhanced the Latin-speaking element in the capital, the Latin speakers were simply one of many minorities in the essentially Greek-speaking capital of an empire dominated by Greek culture and Orthodox Christianity. By the end of the sixth century it was already difficult to find anyone who could translate Latin, and thereafter the growing independence of Byzantium, and the need to devote all available resources to the struggle for survival, guaranteed its final demise.

7.3   The middle Byzantine period: iconoclasm, renaissance, and decline

The 'dark age' that lasted from the seventh century to the middle of the ninth was dominated by a religious crisis which jeopardized the very survival of Byzantine culture. In this desperate period, many had come to believe that the military disasters of the seventh century were divine punishment for a failure of religious observance, and in 730 the emperor Léon III, acting in accordance with his duty to purify the faith of his subjects, decreed that the icons be removed from churches. These images of Christ and the saints had acquired a central place in popular religious practice during the fifth and sixth centuries as providing a channel of communication through which, in response to prayer, intercession might be obtained and miracles worked. But many felt that they were being misused as objects of worship in their own right, and that view was apparently confirmed by the fact that the victorious Arabs had banned the use of figural images.

When Germanós the ecumenical Patriarch (the senior bishop and leader of the Orthodox Church) declined to comply with Léon's edict, he was summarily replaced, and the destruction of icons and persecution of dissenters began. The emperor's orthodoxy was swiftly rewarded by a dramatic improvement in Byzantine fortunes, which continued into the reign of his son Konstantínos V (ruled 741–75). Though iconoclasm was suppressed in 787 in a period of relative military security, it was reintroduced in 814 after fresh reverses in the Balkans, including the defeat and execution of the emperor Nikephóros I in 811 by Krum, the formidable Khan of the Bulgars (yet another Turkic tribe threatening the northern frontier; though eventually absorbed linguistically by their Slavic subjects, the name was retained), and the policy was permanently abandoned only in 843, at the beginning of what was to prove to be Byzantium's golden age. The pattern of enforced iconoclasm in the face of disaster followed by restoration of the images as circumstances improved suggests that the policy enjoyed little popular support, and was no more than stoically tolerated as a necessary expedient in times of crisis.

The eventual stabilization of the military situation had already engendered something of an intellectual revival under Theóphilos (reigned 829–42), the last of the iconoclast emperors, but the advent of the 'Macedonian' dynasty, marked by the succession, amid intrigue and murder, of Basíleios I (reigned 867–86), an illiterate peasant of Armenian descent from the Macedonian theme in Thrace, marks a crucial turning point in Byzantine fortunes. His son Léon VI (ruled 886–912) was known as 'the wise' because of his legal reforms, while his grandson Konstantínos VII Porphyrogénnetos (reigned 913–59, though until 944 under the shadow of a powerful regent) was a scholar who played a vital role in the 'Macedonian Renaissance' as patron of intellectual and creative activity in the capital.

In the same period Romanós I Lakapenós (another Armenian peasant, who became admiral of the fleet and ruled on Konstantínos's behalf 920–44), succeeded in neutralizing a renewed threat from the Bulgars under Symeón, while his general Ioánnes Kerkouás pressed on with the reconquest of territory from the Arabs.

Thereafter, through marriages with the powerful generals Nikephóros II Phokás (ruled 963–9, a member of one of the great Armenian military families of Asia Minor) and Ioánnes I Tzimiskés (ruled 969–76, an Armenian aristocrat from Tshemeshgadzak in Mesopotamia), who effectively usurped the throne by posing as guardians of the rightful heirs, the dynasty retained a tenuous grip on power, and Byzantium embarked on a fresh series of successful military campaigns. Nikephóros Phokás ('the white death of the Saracens') recovered Crete from the Arabs in 961, took Aleppo in Syria in 963, drove the Arabs out of Cyprus in 965, and in 969 regained Antioch itself. He had, however, rashly invited the Rus (Vikings from Sweden who had planted colonies along the Russian rivers) to invade Bulgaria as 'allies', and it was left to Ioánnes Tzimiskés, his wife's lover and his murderer, to drive them out of the Balkans. Tzimiskés then led a series of brilliant campaigns in the east, destroying the forces of the Emir of Mosul and the Egyptian Caliph, and restoring the Mediterranean coastline from Caesarea to Antioch, and many of the inland cities (though not Jerusalem) to Byzantine rule.

He was succeeded by Basíleios II (reigned 976–1025), the true heir of the Macedonian dynasty, who, having put down rebellions by relatives of his two pre-decessors, embarked on the destruction of the Bulgar state in a fifteen-year campaign which earned him the nickname 'Boulgaroktónos' (Bulgar-slayer). He also supervised the annexation of Georgia, and crucially sought to constrain the growing power of the landowning aristocracy, who were buying out the small farmers on whom the military and economic structure of the provinces depended. This problem of increasing prosperity had first been noted by Romanós Lakapenós, and was now addressed by new legislation to protect the interests of the peasants.

In this period of cultural self-confidence, a booming monetary economy and consistent military success, Byzantium had begun to turn its attentions northwards, to the Balkans and central Europe, and to the lands north of the Black Sea. Between the mid-ninth and mid-eleventh centuries Byzantine culture, spearheaded by Christian missions that brought with them religion, law, art and literature, was spread as far as the Baltic, leaving the legacy of the Cyrillic alphabet (an adaptation of the Greek alphabet designed by Byzantine monks for the writing of Slavic languages) and of Orthodox Christianity in much of this territory to the present day.

The mid-eleventh century also saw the resumption of scholarly study under the patronage of Konstantínos IX Monomákhos (reigned 1042–55), and the emergence of figures such as the philosopher, historian and statesman Mikhaél Psellós (1018–78 or –1096) and a group of contemporary scholars that included Ioánnes Mavrópous (teacher of Psellós, later bishop of Euchaita in Pontus), Ioánnes Xiphilinós (also trained by Mavrópous, later head of the law school and Patriarch of Constantinople), and Ioánnes Italós (a philosopher from southern Italy who studied with Psellós, but was later obliged to recant his 'heretical' ideas).

But underlying problems had long been building up. Of the two original patriarchates that had remained outside Arab control during the seventh and eighth centuries (i.e. Rome and Constantinople), it was the eastern capital which had come to enjoy the dominant position because of its unbroken association with the sole surviving Roman emperor. But the beginnings of a revival in the west soon led, with the crowning of the Frank Charlemagne as emperor in the west by the Pope in 800, to a rival bid for universal religious authority. The efficacy of the Patriarchate's ecclesiastical diplomacy in Moravia and Bulgaria during the ninth century, where Rome and Constantinople were fielding rival missions, only heightened the tension, and in 858 the appointment as Patriarch of the layman Phótios (one of the greatest scholars of the Middle Ages) scandalized the Pope and led to a temporary schism between the eastern and western churches.

The dispute also had a doctrinal dimension, the central issue being the interpolation by the western church of the word *filioque* ('and from the Son') into the statement in the Nicene creed that the Holy Spirit proceeds from the Father. Originally adopted in sixth-century Spain as a defence against Arianism, this addition spread through the Frankish empire and became a central plank of Charlemagne's 'anti-Greek' polemic, now actively promoted by missionaries from Rome among the Slavs and Bulgars. The Byzantines were greatly offended by this heretical doctrine of 'double procession', which in their view made a hopeless muddle of Trinitarian theology as established by the great ecumenical councils.

Though the crowning of Charlemagne as emperor 'in the west' caused equal offence, it carried little significance for the Byzantines, and the schism of 858 was quickly repaired. Even when the German king Otto I was crowned emperor 'of the Romans' in 963, his presumption could still be dismissed with contempt by Nikephóros Phokás. But by the mid-eleventh century western Christendom was beginning to pose a genuine threat to the authority of Constantinople, and when Latin Christians began to make pilgrimages to the Holy Land via the eastern capital they were treated with growing suspicion. Politico-religious conflict thus came to be a dominant factor in Byzantine affairs, and the final schism between the eastern and western churches in 1054, prompted by a clash between the Patriarch Mikhaél Keroullários and the Pope's legate, Cardinal Humbert, was no more than a reflection of the growing gulf in culture and ideology.

To add to these difficulties, governmental complacency had begun to set in following the death of Basíleios II in 1025. The military aristocracy, grown rich from warfare, was now using its wealth to buy out the peasantry, thus undermining the ability of the central administration to control its land and people. But where earlier emperors had sought to stem the tide by legislation, their eleventh-century successors did nothing, and the resultant subversion of the theme system was soon to prove disastrous.

The new landed gentry increasingly objected to living under what was effectively martial law imposed from Constantinople, and the most powerful families sought to establish a more independent relationship with the distant capital. The successful integrated autocracy of the middle Byzantine period thus gradually gave way to a more fragmented social system based on the local wealth of a semi-detached hereditary aristocracy, a trend which also initiated the development of a semi-feudalized society in rural areas. It was in this period that the use of surnames first became routine, as individuals sought to advertise their affinities with the great provincial families (e.g. Phokás, Komnenós, Doúkas, Palaiológos), some of which were soon to emerge as imperial dynasties.

This fatal weakening of the empire's cohesion, and its consequential incapacity to martial the resources necessary to defend itself, were all too soon made apparent. Though attacks by the Russians and the Petcheneks (another Turkic tribe) in the middle years of the eleventh century were successfully staved off, the invasion of the Byzantine provinces in southern Italy and Sicily by the Normans, culminating in the capture of Bari in 1071, quickly resulted in the loss of Byzantine control. Soon afterwards, the Normans crossed the Adriatic, seized Dyrrákhion (now Dürres in Albania) on the mainland, and advanced through Macedonia and Thessaly, seemingly with the intention of seizing the capital itself.

Meanwhile in the east, the Seljuks, chiefs of a confederation of Islamicized Turkish tribes that had taken over the Arab Caliphate in Baghdad, began to infiltrate Asia Minor, and in the fatal year of 1071 the Byzantine army was subjected to a crushing defeat at Manzikert (Malazgirt, north of lake Van in what is now eastern Turkey). So weak and overstretched had control of the empire's former heartlands become that no serious further resistance could be offered. Within a decade much of Asia Minor had been occupied, and the Turks had advanced as far as Nicaea. The new Sultanate of 'Rum' (Rome) was now permanently established on former imperial territory, with only a few residual strongholds remaining under the nominal control of the emperor.

Faced with a hostile and suspicious west and threatened by powerful enemies on all sides, the survival of what remained of the Byzantine state, so recently at the pinnacle of its wealth and influence, began to seem very doubtful indeed.

7.4 The late Byzantine period: stabilization, defeat, and fall

By the late-eleventh century Byzantium was obliged to turn for help to Venice, then still very much in thrall to Byzantine culture, but also, thanks to its shrewd exploitation of Byzantine weakness, on the brink of achieving military and economic domination of the Mediterranean (see Angold (1984)).

The middle Byzantine period was still characterized by the suspicion and dour self-reliance that had originated in the dark ages of the seventh and eighth centuries. This led to a lack of enterprise, which, in combination with renewed military crisis, left the Byzantines vulnerable to predatory outsiders. Venetian merchants had been settled in Constantinople since the tenth century, but when the Venetians recaptured the key port of Dyrrákhion, they demanded in return exemption from customs dues throughout the empire and grants of land for quays and warehouses in Constantinople. Other Italian cities quickly followed this lead, and the growing foreign domination of the Byzantine economy eventually led to its destruction.

For a time, however, the emperor Aléxios I Komnenós (reigned 1081–1118) was able to restore something of Byzantium's former authority. This was achieved partly through skilful diplomacy (by playing Venice off against the Normans in the west, engineering the destruction of the Petcheneks through the manipulation of another nomadic tribe, the Cumans, and recruiting Turkish 'allies' in Asia Minor), and partly through resolute military campaigning, in the face of repeated setbacks, against the Normans in the Balkans, the sole imperial territory in which the administration still worked effectively, and the only remaining source of imperial revenue. These external successes were largely facilitated by internal military and administrative reforms through which Aléxios exacted obligations from the hereditary landowners to supply troops, and instituted a revamped provincial administration which collected taxes and rounded up peasants for military service with the ruthlessness of an occupying army.

This remarkable military aristocrat was the founder of a dynasty which ruled until 1185 and gave the empire a century of desperately needed stability. The urban renewal which had begun during the late ninth century was therefore able to continue throughout the tenth and eleventh centuries, reaching a peak in the early twelfth. This was naturally accompanied by the growth of an urban bourgeoisie, a class which was instrumental in the promotion of a more lively intellectual climate, especially in the capital, and which, by the time of the Komnenoí, had grown accustomed to a comfortable lifestyle. Despite all the difficulties, therefore, the Komnenian period witnessed a renewed surge of interest in cultural and literary pursuits and the beginnings of a distinctively 'modern' outlook on the part of the Constantinopolitan intelligentsia.

Thus despite Aléxios's part in the suppression of philosophical 'heresy', as embodied in the Platonic and Neoplatonic research of Ioánnes Italós, other, less dangerous forms of scholarship and creative writing were allowed to flourish. Important figures of this period include: Aléxios's daughter, Anna Komnené (1083–c. 1153, who composed a history of her father's reign universally recognized as a masterpiece of Byzantine literature); Theódoros Pródromos (c. 1100–65, court poet of Aléxios's wife Eiréne Doúkaina, and of her son and grandson, Ioánnes II and Manouél I Komnenós); Ioánnes Tzétzes (c. 1110–c. 1180, a classical scholar of prodigious learning and energy); Eustáthios (c. 1115–c. 1195, a scholar, rhetorician and theologian, who served as bishop of Thessaloniki); and the brothers Mikhaél (c. 1138–c. 1222) and Nikétas (c. 1150–1215) Khoniátes (the former a pupil of Eustáthios who became bishop of Athens, the latter a distinguished statesman and one of the most important Byzantine historians).

In 1095, with the return of effective rule in the Balkans, Aléxios was ready to embark on the reconquest of Asia Minor; the main Seljuk empire in the middle east was beginning to break up, and the time seemed ripe to take advantage of the crisis. But his plans had to be shelved indefinitely when news reached Constantinople of the imminent arrival of hordes of westerners. After the Arab conquests Christian pilgrimage to the Holy Land had been allowed to continue, but this amicable arrangement came to an end with the arrival of the Seljuks in Jerusalem in 1077. Aléxios had repeatedly asked the west for help in recapturing Byzantine territory from the Seljuks, but was quite unprepared for the arrival of a mass crusade, backed by the Pope, with leaders from most of the states of western Europe.

Since the Normans were prominent among the leaders of the crusade, there could be no doubt that Byzantium faced a terrible threat, but Aléxios managed to force an oath of allegiance from the army outside the walls of his city, together with a promise to restore any recaptured territory to the empire. The collapse of Seljuk power in the middle east gave the crusaders their opportunity; Antioch fell in 1098, and in the following year Jerusalem was retaken. Unsurprisingly, these conquests were not handed over as promised, but instead became 'Frankish' (i.e. western/Latin) principalities, and when the Muslims were reunited under the Arab rulers of Mosul, their recovery of lost territory proceeded rapidly; Edessa and Damascus were taken in 1144 and 1154, and Jerusalem fell to Salah ad-Din (Saladin) in 1187. Prior to these counterstrikes, however, the empire enjoyed some successes of its own. In the course of a campaign in Asia Minor and Syria, Aléxios's son Ioánnes II (reigned 1118–43) forced the Latin ruler of Antioch to surrender and swear allegiance to him, while in 1159 his successor Manouél I (ruled 1143–80) compelled the king of Jerusalem to recognize Byzantine sovereignty over the Latin east as a whole.

At this point Manouél sought to extend a diplomatic olive branch, but his efforts were rebuffed by the western emperor Frederick Barbarossa, who dismissed him contemptuously as 'king of the Greeks'. Nevertheless, Manouél maintained a broadly conciliatory attitude towards the west, despite having had the increasingly lawless Venetian merchants arrested in 1171 as a threat to national security, and this approach eventually engendered a wave of anti-Latin feeling which led, soon after his death, to the massacre of Pisan and Genoese merchants in the capital in 1182. The Italian cities were now thirsting for revenge, and their opportunity was not long in coming.

An initially successful campaign against the Seljuks had turned to disaster with the crushing defeat of Manouél's army at Myrioképhalon in Asia Minor in 1176. Soon after, the different national groups in the Balkans began to break away into the independent states of Serbia and Bulgaria, and the Papacy was able once again to extend its influence in the region. Finally, an alliance between Hungary and Serbia led to an attack on the Balkan cities in 1183, and the Normans swept through Greece in 1185, destroying Thessaloniki on their way. What was left of the Byzantine state now virtually ceased to function; whole territories passed into the hands of powerful local families and the sad remainder was ground down by punitive taxation. In 1194 the German emperor Henry IV succeeded to the Norman kingdom of Sicily and demanded territory and tribute from Byzantium. This could no longer be raised by taxation and the tombs of the emperors in the Holy Apostles had to be stripped to raise the money. The end could not be far away.

In the east the crusades had greatly intensified ill feeling towards the Latins, and the greed of the Italian merchants had steadily sapped the empire's wealth, provoking still greater hostility and violence as people began to understand the full extent of Byzantine impotence. In the west, however, many argued that the Byzantines had deliberately sabotaged the crusades, and that their refusal to join the Roman church justified western intervention in the interests of their own salvation (not to mention the commercial interests of the invaders).

An unexpected opportunity soon presented itself after Pope Innocent III called for a fresh crusade to the Holy Land and Enrico Dandolo, doge of Venice, had agreed to provide the necessary ships and finance in return for the lion's share of any booty. At this critical juncture Aléxios Angelos, a pretender to the Byzantine throne, asked for western assistance in return for a large cash payment, and in 1203 the fourth crusade diverted to Constantinople to install him. The new emperor, however, faced with implacable public hostility towards the crusaders, sought to regain popular support by distancing himself from his backers. But without the crusaders' protection he was overthrown and murdered by Aléxios Moúrtzouphlos, who then set himself the task of destroying the foreign invaders. Though their position was increasingly desperate, with supplies running alarmingly low during the winter of 1204, the crusaders stuck to their task, and after a failed assault on 9 April 1204, finally secured a tenuous foothold within the city on 13 April. At this point Byzantine morale failed and the crusaders found that the city was theirs by default. They sacked it ruthlessly, and 1,000 years of accumulated treasure, including the most precious Christian relics, was stripped away, while the lands of the empire were partitioned among the 'victors'.

That the Christian capital of the east, which had survived all manner of barbarian and Islamic assaults for the best part of 1,000 years, should have been sacked by a Christian army from western Europe left a permanent legacy of irredeemable bitterness and distrust. The Venetians were the principal beneficiaries, gaining nearly half of Constantinople (including Hagía Sophía) together with most of the Greek islands and ports, including the Ionian islands, Euboea and Crete. Other Frankish lords carved up the rest of Greece, Thrace, and north-west Asia Minor, with Baldwin of Flanders installed as emperor overall. The Crusaders built castles throughout their new domain (many are still to be seen today) and formed a new feudal overlay above their Greek subjects.

Byzantium was not, however, totally obliterated. Governments-in-exile were formed, based on the local power of individual families, in Trebizond on the southeastern shore of the Black Sea, in Epirus in north-western Greece, and at Nicaea in north-west Asia Minor. Trebizond survived longest, falling to the Turks only in 1461, but was too far removed from the mainstream of events to have much influence on their course. The rivalry between Epirus and Nicaea was resolved by the defeat of the Epirote ruler by the Bulgarians, and though the territory retained its independence until formally incorporated into Serbia in 1337, only Nicaea remained in a position to claim the inheritance of the Byzantine empire.

The Latin empire had already suffered a defeat at the hands of the Bulgarians in 1205, and Thessaloniki was taken by the Epirotes in 1224. With the Latins apparently no longer able to maintain effective self-defence, the empire in Nicaea, already conducting itself as the legal government of Byzantium, finally sent its forces to enter Constantinople in 1261, and Mikhaél VIII Palaiológos, a general who had seized power at Nicaea three years before, was duly crowned emperor in Hagía Sophía.

But in reality his 'empire' was now a pathetic remnant. All national groups apart from the Greeks had fallen away, while the greater part of former Byzantine territory still remained in 'Frankish', Arab, or Turkish hands. Some land, however, was successfully recovered, most notably the south-east of the Morea (as the Franks called the Peloponnese) with its fortified townships of Mystrás and Monembasía, from which the reconquest of much of the rest of the Peloponnese was able to proceed. Mystrás in particular came to enjoy considerable prosperity, serving as the capital of the 'despotate' of the Morea, with its rulers drawn from families close to the throne, including a junior branch of the imperial family itself.

Though the recovery was inevitably only partial, the new geographical compactness gave political and cultural cohesion to the Palaiologan period, which produced one final Byzantine renaissance before the inevitable fall. The period also produced scholars central to the survival of classical Greek texts such as Máximos Planoúdes (*c.* 1255–1305) and Demétrios Triklínios (fourteenth century). But the material decline was all too apparent; Constantinople in particular was now far too big for its population and large areas of the city reverted to open countryside, while the Imperial Palace, having fallen into irreparable disrepair, was replaced by a much smaller and more affordable palace in the Blakhernai district, beside the city's land walls.

For the first 20 years of his reign Mikhaél Palaiológos was obliged to maintain an army to cover the western approaches in case the long-threatened Latin retaliation materialized. This left his eastern frontier dangerously undermanned, and when the Mongol invasions of the mid-thirteenth century brought confusion to the Seljuk states of Asia Minor, the emergence from among them of the aggressive Osmanli (Ottoman) dynasty presented a new threat against which the impoverished Byzantine state could mount no effective response. Nicaea fell in 1329, and by the 1350s Gallipoli on the European side of the Bosporus was also under the Sultan's control.

By this time the Byzantine coinage had been replaced by the Venetian ducat, and the 'empire of the Romans' was little more than a petty kingdom fought over by a succession of pretenders who were the vassals of the Italians or the Ottoman Sultan. As in the dark days of the eighth and ninth centuries, this political and economic crisis once again went hand-in-hand with a religious controversy. Monks on Mount Athos (the Holy Mountain) in Khalkidiké had developed a method of silent prayer called *hesykhía* (ἡσυχία [isi'çia] 'silence') based on the teaching of an eleventh-century mystic, and its practitioners soon came to be known as Hesychasts. Though approved by a Church Council in 1351, it became a central issue in the civil war between the general Ioánnes Kantakouzenós, who espoused the Hesychast cause, and the legitimate regent Ioánnes V Palaiológos (reigned 1341–91), who was supported by the mass of the populace and backed 'orthodox' religious practice. This view was also endorsed by the Patriarchs, who preached that all would eventually turn out well if only the Byzantines held to their true faith.

But Byzantium had not sought alliances with the other Balkan powers, including the expanding Serbian empire which now controlled most of Macedonia. These lands were picked off one by one by the Turks in the late fourteenth century, Macedonia in 1371, Serbia in 1389, and Bulgaria in 1393. Constantinople itself was blockaded in 1397 and saved only by the fact that the Mongols under Timur Lenk (Tamburlaine) attacked the Turks' eastern front and drew the besieging army away.

As Ottoman forces progressively overran eastern Europe, leaving only the capital and the despotate of the Morea in Byzantine hands, the hated west remained the sole possible source of help, and desperate appeals were duly made, including a personal tour of western capitals by Manouél II Palaiológos (ruled 1391–1425) in 1399. But the enduring schism between the eastern and western churches proved to be an insuperable problem. Proclamation of union on the basis of accepting the *filioque* clause in the creed was the price demanded for western aid, and this Byzantium could not pay in the face of resolute popular feeling against it.

The respite from the final act of Turkish aggression lasted for some 50 years and during this period several more attempts were made to achieve church union and so draw in the west. A draft agreement was eventually reached in 1438 by the emperor Ioánnes VIII Palaiológos, who had led a delegation to the Council of Ferrara-Florence, but he was still unable to impose the terms on his defiant subjects, whose distrust of the 'Franks' persisted unabated. The promised relief army was in any case destroyed by the Turks at Varna in 1444, and no further help was then forthcoming.

Byzantium therefore had to meet the final attack alone, though with the courageous assistance of the remaining Italian residents of the city. The Ottoman Sultan, Mehmet II ('the Conqueror'), prepared his forces meticulously and the siege began on 6 April 1453. Huge cannon blasted holes in the land walls, but the defenders, only some 7,000 in number, consistently managed to fill the breaches with rubble. A crucial moment came when the Sultan opened a second front by bringing his ships into the Golden Horn overland on a primitive railway, so bypassing the defensive mole across the entrance to this waterway and threatening the harbour walls directly.

By the last week in May the defenders could offer little further resistance and huge crowds gathered in Hagía Sophía on 28 May, despite their previous boycott in the face of the attempted imposition of church union. That same night the final assault was launched, and the Turks eventually broke through a small gate near the Blakhernai palace just before sunrise on 29 May. The last Roman emperor, Konstantínos XI Palaiológos, died in the fighting along with some 4,000 others. Approximately 50,000 more were taken prisoner and, in accordance with Islamic custom, three days of looting were permitted.

From this time until the proclamation of the independent Greek kingdom in the nineteenth century there was no Greek state, and the vast majority of ordinary Greeks were obliged to struggle for survival in a context of oppression and near-total ignorance of the artistic, cultural and technological developments that soon began to reshape the west.

Chapter 8

Greek in the Byzantine empire: the major issues

8.1 Introduction

The Byzantine state survived for over 1,000 years, and during that time underwent many ethnographic and territorial upheavals. It is perhaps most useful to begin with an account of the position of Greek in the early period, at the time of Ioustinianós's reconquests (cf. Mango (1980: 13–31)). Important changes in Byzantine national identity began to set in during the middle period, together with a changed perception of the role of Greek (see 8.3). These eventually came to be articulated in the form of diametrically opposed literary movements and a reappraisal of the potential of 'popular' Greek during the eleventh-/twelfth-century revival ushered in by the Komnenian dynasty after the loss of Asia Minor (see 8.4, and cf. Beaton (1989: 7–18)).

8.2 Greek and other languages in the early Byzantine period

In Ioustinianós's time Latin and Greek served as the primary cultural and sole official languages of the Roman empire, and in the cities would have served adequately for purposes of communication, written and spoken, at all levels. Linguistically, the empire was divided by a line running above Thrace, Macedonia, and Epirus, and down across the Mediterranean to divide north Africa at the western end of Cyrenaica: north and west of this line Latin was the common language; elsewhere Greek fulfilled this function. Each was spoken competently in its respective part of the empire by all educated people and by the majority of city-dwellers, even if neither Latin nor Greek was their native language. Before the fall of the west, many people had at least a working knowledge of the 'other' language as well, though this was already becoming rarer by the sixth century. The rural majority, of course, remained largely uneducated, and many who came from areas where other languages were learned natively would have known neither Greek nor Latin well, if at all.

Constantinople itself had been a cosmopolitan city from its foundation, and now included communities of Jews, Goths, Huns, Thracians, Syrians, Egyptians, Illyrians, and Italians. The last two groups still spoke Latin among themselves, but Greek had always been the first language of the majority in the city and was already in practice the official language of the state; all who aspired to high office were obliged to know and use it.

Map 2 adapted from C. Mango (1980) *Byzantium, the empire of the New Rome*, London, 14–15

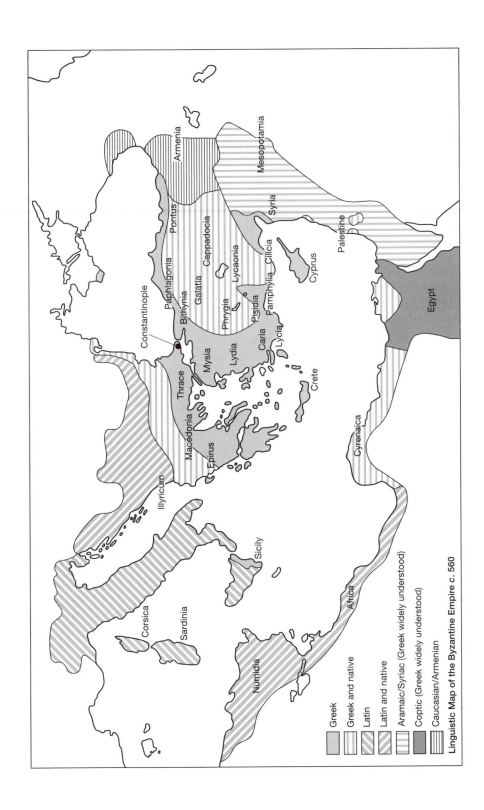

Linguistic Map of the Byzantine Empire c. 560

Greek

Greek and native

Latin

Latin and native

Aramaic/Syriac (Greek widely understood)

Coptic (Greek widely understood)

Caucasian/Armenian

Constantinople

Thrace
Macedonia
Epirus
Illyricum

Paphlagonia
Bithynia
Mysia
Lydia
Phrygia
Galatia
Cappadocia
Lycaonia
Pisidia
Pamphylia
Caria
Lycia
Cilicia

Pontus
Armenia
Mesopotamia
Syria
Palestine
Cyprus
Egypt

Crete
Cyrenaica
Africa
Sicily
Sardinia
Corsica
Numidia

The coastal areas of Asia Minor had been culturally and linguistically Hellenized (and then Romanized) for nearly a millennium and a half. Though the Anatolian plateau had come under the influence of this dominant culture only after Alexander's conquests, the descendants of indigenous peoples, as well as immigrant groups (Celts, Goths, Jews, and Persians), were also fairly well Hellenized by the sixth century, as evidenced by the thousands of public and private inscriptions in Greek from all areas in Hellenistic and Roman times, and by the survival of pockets of Greek in villages right across Asia Minor until the nineteenth or early twentieth centuries. By contrast, epigraphic evidence for the native languages of Asia Minor becomes quite meagre by the later Hellenistic period and dies out in early Christian times (cf. Neumann (1980)). Some of these languages presumably continued as spoken patois for a considerable time, but the evidence for the dominant position of Greek by the early Byzantine period is overwhelming.

To the east of Cappadocia lay the provinces of Armenia, which had been acquired in the fourth century AD and served as a buffer against Persia. Here Armenian had been developed as a literary language from the fifth century onwards, initially for the purpose of providing translations of Christian texts composed in Greek and Syriac, and this, in conjunction with Monophysite belief, had fostered a strong sense of national identity. Though many Armenians migrated into Asia Minor and as far as Thrace and Macedonia, the majority in Armenia itself proved consistently resistant to cultural and linguistic imperialism.

To the south of the Armenian provinces lay the western tip of Mesopotamia, where Syriac, the *lingua franca* of the Persian empire, remained the dominant language as part of the legacy of the Parthian occupation from the mid-second century BC to the mid-second century AD. Syriac and other Aramaic dialects also extended southwards through Syria and Palestine as far as the borders of Egypt, and from the fourth century onwards Syriac had also become an important religious and literary language in line with the growing importance of local cultures in the east.

Despite intensive colonization in the Macedonian period, and the continuous operation of a Greek-speaking administration, Greek in Syria and western Mesopotamia was still primarily confined to the major cities, where the upper classes at least were bilingual. The urban centres of the Phoenician coast (Byblos, Beirut, Sidon, Tyre), however, were more heavily Hellenized, and bilingualism in Greek and Phoenician had gradually given way there to the use of Greek alone, at least as a written language. To the south too, where Palestine enjoyed great prosperity because of pilgrimage to the holy places, Greek was widely known among the native population at all levels of society (cf. Rosén (1980)).

In Egypt, Greek was naturally the dominant language of Alexandria and the other Hellenistic foundations. Administrative documents intended for the population as a whole, however, were standardly published in both Greek and Coptic, and it seems certain that a great many Greeks and Egyptians remained virtually monolingual. But though the urban upper classes kept themselves to themselves (and intermarriage was expressly forbidden in certain cities), social interaction between ordinary Greeks and native Egyptians was more routine, and this, along with the widespread employment of Egyptians as local administrators, promoted bilingualism, as evidenced by the vast numbers of papyri written in Greek by Egyptians. Official documents in particular are routinely composed in an excellent Koine, and it is only in examples of private correspondence that any real variations in competence are revealed (cf. Teodorsson (1977: 11–24), Lüddeckens (1980: 248–60)).

Coptic, however, had always enjoyed high status among the native Egyptians because of its long written tradition and its association with the old religion. This prestige was enhanced from the end of the third century BC onwards, when a 'native reaction' to Ptolemaic rule began. From *c.* AD 300 Coptic became a major vehicle for Egyptian Christianity in a period when the local church, again committed to Monophysite doctrine, had begun to dissociate itself from the orthodoxy of the capital, and Greek was often presented as the language of an alien hierarchy.

The western provinces of north Africa had all been thoroughly Romanized in classical times, though Phoenician (residually in Carthage) and Berber (in country areas) remained in use alongside 'official' Latin. Across the Mediterranean, Latin naturally remained the principal language of Italy, and served as the official language in the new capital of Ravenna, though Greek survived strongly in the south of Italy and in eastern Sicily. The Balkans, however, were overrun by successive groups of invaders, and the native population was in great distress. By the early seventh century only major coastal cities such as Thessaloniki, Athens, and Corinth had been able to resist the barbarian influx intact, and many people sought refuge on offshore islands or simply emigrated. One can only assume, from the fact of the survival of Greek and the eventual elimination of Slavic dialects from the southern part of the Balkan peninsula, that a majority there continued to speak the language at this time.

8.3 The prestige of Greek: Byzantine identity in the middle period

If we follow Mango (1980: 23), and take the approximate population of the eastern empire in the mid-sixth century to have been around 30 million (8 million in Egypt, 9 million in the middle east, 10 million in Asia Minor, and 3 million in the Balkans), then Greek would probably have been a true first language for only about one-third of that population, the majority of these in Greece (including Macedonia and Thrace) and Asia Minor.

This can be explained partly by traditional Greek exclusiveness, which inhibited the Greco-Macedonian aristocracies of the Hellenistic age from pursuing an active policy of Hellenization, and partly as a result of the retention of a sense of national consciousness on the part of major ethnic groups such as Egyptians, Syrians and Armenians throughout the Roman period. But the fact that a great deal of 'popular' Christian literature (e.g. martyrdoms and saints' lives) was composed in a non-classicizing form of Greek in the late antique and early Byzantine periods (see 8.5.6) clearly implies a more extensive knowledge of the language. This was the inevitable product of long-term Roman/Byzantine administration, primary education, routine employment in the bureaucracy, and intermarriage.

Nevertheless, in the early Byzantine period, the development of a specifically 'Greek' national consciousness had scarcely begun. The élite, once so conscious of the cultural and ethnic differences between itself and its Roman rulers, had been steadily recruited into the higher levels of Roman society, where its pervasive influence transformed the old Roman ruling class and facilitated the creation of a genuinely Greco-Roman civilization. But in the course of this blending process the Greek-speaking upper classes had also been transformed. As the traditionally dominant group in the east, they had been able to retain a unique position of prestige and influence, and had once again come to dominate much of the political and economic life of the eastern provinces. They thus gradually became 'Romans' not merely in law but also in sentiment, as the principal beneficiaries of an administration which, with the passage of time, they could increasingly view as being under their own, rather than alien, control.

This growing identification of the Greek-speaking aristocracy with the interests of the Roman state undermined the development of any specifically Greek sense of 'apartness'. By the sixth century, Greek, as we have seen, was not only the native language of 'Greeks', but also the universal spoken, cultural and official language of the upper classes in four-fifths of what then remained of the Roman empire. Unlike Coptic, Syriac or Armenian, therefore, it could never be seen simply, or even primarily, as the defining characteristic of a particular national group. Indeed, since the Byzantines, irrespective of ethnic background, quite reasonably referred to themselves as 'Romans', the contemporary form of their language also came to be known as 'Roman', a name routinely used for spoken Greek until the nineteenth century, and sometimes still employed today ($\rho\omega\mu\alpha\ddot{\iota}\kappa\alpha$ [ro'meika]).

But Byzantine isolation during the seventh and eighth centuries led to greater cultural and religious divergence between east and west, and this began the long process of political and ecclesiastical alienation that was to culminate in the disaster of 1204. By the beginning of the middle period, 200 years of autonomous development had led to a growing awareness that contemporary 'Romania' was something quite different from the Frankish 'Holy Roman Empire'. The scholar–emperor Konstantínos VII Porphyrogénnetos (reigned 913–59), for example, notes in the introduction to his work *On the Themes* (Pertusi (1952)) that his predecessors in the time of Herákleios 'had been Hellenized and discarded the language of their fathers, the Roman tongue'. Konstantínos's assertion is true to the extent that this period indeed marks the final abandonment of Latin in even its residual functions. But it also reveals that among the Byzantine aristocracy in the tenth century a specifically 'east Roman' identity had been constructed by reference to a putative cultural and linguistic Hellenization process that had distinguished the ruling class in that part of the empire from the Romans of the west some 300 years before.

This marks an important shift towards the identification of eastern Romanness with the specifically Greek elements of the Byzantine cultural heritage, and it became a major preoccupation of the Byzantine élite to preserve and contribute to what was perceived as a continuous tradition incorporating ancient Greek, Hellenistic, Hellenized Roman and Orthodox Christian components.

8.4 'Greek' identity in the later empire: linguistic implications

8.4.1 National reappraisal

The end of the middle Byzantine period is often associated with the loss of eastern and central Anatolia to the Seljuks, and of Sicily and southern Italy to the Normans (e.g. Kazhdan and Franklin (1984: 14)). Thereafter, educated Byzantines were obliged to rethink their role in the world, and the following period, while certainly encompassing the 'decline and fall' of Byzantium, also laid the foundations for an emergent 'modern Greek' civilization (Beaton (1989: 7)).

The immediate effect of these disastrous territorial losses was the reduction of the Byzantine state to an area comprising Greece, the Balkans, and the coasts of Asia Minor, where the vast majority of the population, at all levels of society, were native speakers of Greek (Bryer (1981: 97)). Something very close to a Greek nation state therefore emerged accidentally out of the once multi-ethnic and multi-lingual Byzantine empire, and a new self-perception, founded in a community united by the use of spoken Greek, manifested itself *inter alia* in the growing anti-Latin feeling in Constantinople. This view gained steadily in strength with the passage of time, and successfully outlived the final fall of Byzantium, providing the basis for the eventual emergence of a modern Greek state.

In the Komnenian period (1081–1180), however, tension between this new outlook and the more traditional world view led to a number of important cultural innovations, including a renewal of interest in long-neglected fields such as romantic fiction and satire, and the appearance of a new genre of comic 'begging' poetry. This shift from the more 'profound' intellectual studies of the eleventh century to the more 'entertaining' fictional writing of the twelfth has plausibly been associated with the re-emergence of an urban bourgeosie which, for the first time since late antiquity, created an audience for secular literature that went beyond a small professional coterie (Mango (1980: 237)).

8.4.2 Byzantine belles lettres and the Atticist revival

This literary revival also had its linguistic analogue. Hitherto, written Greek in Byzantium had formed a continuum ranging from an updated literary Koine to plainer official and academic varieties. During the middle Byzantine period, these remained a powerful symbol of cultural prestige, and subsequently of national identity, and great efforts were made to sustain their 'living' use. But even the most literary of Byzantine writers did not think of themselves as actually writing classical Attic (cf. Renauld (1920), Dawkins (1953: 256), Ševčenko (1981)). Their contemporary styles derived ultimately from that of the prose writers of late antiquity who, after the excesses of second century Atticism, had combined selected features of Attic and the higher Koine into a more relaxed standard. After the dark age of the seventh and eighth centuries, this style returned into favour and, in the absence of a wider reading public in the early Middle Ages, began to influence other forms of composition which had traditionally employed a more popular register (see 8.5

below). Collections of martyrologies and saints' lives, for example, were transposed 'upwards' by the civil servant and monk Symeón Metaphrástes ('Translator', second half of the tenth century), and even chronicles came to be written in a more learned style.

After the military disasters at the end of the eleventh century, however, a new Atticist revival pushed the gap between spoken and literary Greek to unprecedented extremes. Rather like its ancient predecessor, this new Atticism represents, in a context in which Byzantium was set against both the Turkish/Islamic east and the Latin/Catholic west, a defiant reassertion of 'Greek' identity validated in the achievements of the past.

It should be noted, however, that those who strove for a high 'classical' style saw themselves as contributing to a continuous tradition, and felt free to model their usage as much on the practice of the writers of the Second Sophistic, or, once the revival was under way, on that of their immediate predecessors, as on that of classical writers *sensu stricto*. The complex intertextuality of the work of this period has often been underestimated, because of the misconception that all postclassical and medieval writers remained in a fixed linguistic relationship with models taken exclusively from the 'golden age' of Athens.

The 'high' Atticism of the great histories of Anna Komnené (dealing with the reign of her father Aléxios I, 1081–1118) or Nikétas Khoniátes (recounting the period from 1118 up to the capture of Constantinople by the fourth crusade in 1204) should be seen as part of an attempt to stake out a new vision of the future by retreating from an ideology of universal empire that was increasingly at odds with reality, and rethinking the troubled present in terms of a remote but authoritative 'ancient Greek' past. It cannot be overemphasized that such writers did not 'revive' the literary language and genres of ancient Greece in an attitude of mindless servility; their linguistic attitude was motivated by considerations of national self-definition, and their usage involved a creative blending and extension of the materials at their disposal (cf. 9.5).

It is, however, undeniable that much Byzantine literary prose, with its recherché vocabulary, over-elaborated word order and excesses of literary quotation, today conveys an impression of verbose and clichéd opacity. But we should not forget that élite Byzantine tastes and expectations were very different from ours; in particular, rhetorical elaboration was greatly enjoyed, and 'overt' originality (as opposed to inventive redeployment) was less highly valued in a cultural context in which the authority of the tradition remained paramount. Commonplace accusations of 'pastiche' and failure to write 'correctly' in the Attic of the fifth century BC (see, for example, Mango (1980: ch. 13)) are largely beside the point. All Greek literary dialects, beginning with that of the Homeric epic, evolved 'artificially' in the hands of later generations of practitioners, since we are dealing in each case not with slavish attempts to copy, but with the creative revival of learned forms of the language in new cultural contexts. Byzantine writers similarly composed creatively in a contemporary version of the traditional language of prose writing, and the new Atticists of the Komnenian and Palaiologan periods did no more than take these well-established procedures towards their logical conclusion.

We may not always like the product, but we should not criticize them for failure to achieve what had never been aimed for.

Nor should we forget that an anti-realist stylization of diction and content along generic lines was also characteristic of much ancient Greek writing. The apparent 'timelessness' of much Byzantine literary prose (often presented as at least an implied failing, cf. Mango (1980: 241)) merely reflects the fact that authors employed a learned art-language in the same tradition, following the established conventions of a 'transcendental' medium whose role in the present demanded formal continuity with the practice of the past.

8.4.3 *The first experiments with the vernacular*

The need for new ways of interpreting the world is often first appreciated in the context of crises which expose the limitations of traditional thinking. It is therefore no accident that a literary experiment of the greatest significance should have taken place during the twelfth century, when the Byzantines, shaken by the loss of Asia Minor, began at last to reconstruct their identity and role in the world.

Even the 'learned' romances of the Komnenian period, though written in a traditional form of archaizing Greek and looking back to antiquity for their inspiration, also built on the model provided by the 'popular' heroic tale of *Digenés Akrítes* (see 12.2.1 and cf. Beaton (1989: chs. 3 and 4), Ricks (1990), Beaton and Ricks (1993)). This work seems to have been composed originally in a language very much closer to contemporary speech, and is now widely seen as marking the beginnings of a genre of 'vernacular' epic-romantic poetry, designed to entertain a troubled world with its celebration of the exploits of 'Roman' heroes against the Arabs on the old Euphrates frontier.

Beaton suggests (1989: 46–7) that the original author may have been a moderately educated refugee, working in the capital some time after the battle of Manzikert (1071), who wished to preserve selected oral heroic poetry from his Anatolian homeland through compilation and reworking into a thematically linked 'literary' collection (cf. Ricks (1990)). An example of the ballad-style source material used is provided by the surviving *Song of Armoúres*, and we should note in particular the shared use of the unrhymed fifteen-syllable 'political' verse (on which see 12.1.3). This previously oral/popular genre was 'validated' through the superimposition of thematic and structural conventions taken from the middle-brow hagiographic tradition, and the incorporation of selected material familiar from the secular novels of Greco-Roman antiquity (the renewed interest in which is simultaneously reflected in the learned romances).

The language of the 'vernacular' version of the poem (E), preserved in a manuscript in the Escorial in Madrid, is certainly consistent with such a view, showing *inter alia* such 'oral' features as formulaic repetition, metrically motivated morphological heterogeneity, a preference for parataxis, avoidance of hiatus through elision and synizesis, and a general dislike of enjambement (the running-over of sense units across line boundaries). But other, more archaizing elements of grammar and diction, clearly drawn from the written tradition and exploited most notably in religious contexts (cf. Ricks (1990: 24)), suggest that these traditional materials were consciously worked up to create the first, still rudimentary, 'literary' language to be based primarily on the stylized vernacular of oral poetry. Such integration as took place between its oral and written components was presumably facilitated by the fact that many archaisms preserved in the oral tradition overlapped with the archaizing practices of written Greek (especially the ecclesiastical language, widely familiar because of church attendance).

This revolutionary use of vernacular poetry as the major source for a written epic offered a potentially radical alternative to high Atticism as a means of expressing a contemporary 'Greek' identity, but it was only in the later Palaiologan period that a more developed version of this 'mixed' language, involving a more homogenized blending of its popular and learned/archaic components, became the standard language for the composition of fictional literature (cf. 8.4.5, 12.3.1, and 12.3.4).

There was, however, a brief period of alternative experimentation with the vernacular prior to the capture of Constantinople in 1204, revealed in the four comic begging poems (*Poems of Poor Pródromos*) often attributed to the court poet Theódoros Pródromos (Eideneier (1991), Alexíou (1994)), and in a composition entitled *Verses Written while Held Imprisoned* by the chronicler and imperial civil servant Mikhaél Glykás. Though the first playfully exploits the spoken language of Constantinople at various levels and the second that of proverbial sayings and popular wisdom, both still rely heavily on the parallel use of middle registers of the written language (cf. 12.2.2). Evidently a written language based directly on spoken Greek could not yet be accepted as a medium for 'serious' literature, and the experimental writers in the capital aimed deliberately for a mixed style. Though there is no reason to doubt that the conversational Greek of the upper classes was much closer to the spoken norm than the artificial formal language of the court (cf. Dawkins (1953: 258)), the unadorned 'literary' use of a written version of spoken Greek could only have seemed an amusing distraction to an élite whose education led them instinctively to require validation by reference to ancient tradition, and for whom the capacity to read and write the forms of Greek supplied by that tradition (the only written forms hitherto available) remained fundamental to their sense of who they were.

An appreciation of the literary potential of the vernacular was therefore slow to develop. The crucial readjustment was initiated by the catastrophe of 1204, and promoted thereafter by the influx of western ideas and practices, and, for much of the former empire, western rulers and settlers. But any limited progress towards the evolution of a standard written form of modern spoken Greek was quickly halted by the Turkish domination of the bulk of Greek-speaking territory, including the former capital, and by the political and linguistic fragmentation of the lands which still remained, for a time at least, under western control (see Chapters 14 and 15).

8.4.4 The vernacular literature of the fourteenth and fifteenth centuries

Though 'serious' literature continued to require the use of more traditional media within the residual Byzantine territories, the widespread western use of the modern

Romance languages for writing, including the writing of romances, was clearly influential in the revival of the corresponding Greek idiom for the fictional literature which was once again in demand in the capital and elsewhere during the fourteenth and fifteenth centuries (cf. 8.4.5 and 12.3). Other 'vernacular' work of this period includes political allegories ostensibly dealing with animals, birds, fruit, and fish, the last two of which are, for the first time, written in prose (Beck (1971: 173–9)).

Another early consequence of western rule was an extension of the vernacular style to compositions with near-contemporary historical content. These are the *Chronicle of the Tocco*, celebrating the exploits of the ruling dynasty in Epirus, and the *Chronicle of the Morea*, an early-fourteenth century account of the capture of Constantinople and of the subsequent deeds of the de Villehardouin family in the Peloponnese (cf. 12.3.3). The latter is the work of an anti-Byzantine writer, probably of French immigrant stock, who cared little for the literary tradition and introduced elements of his own spoken Greek (presumably reflecting the Peloponnesian speech of the era) into the language of 'popular' poetry.

A further, long-term, consequence was the eventual emergence of distinctively 'dialectal' literature in major cultural centres such as Cyprus and Crete (cf. 12.4, and 14.2.4). There is no doubt that the spoken Greek of the Middle Ages, particularly among the lower social classes, was already well diversified regionally (cf. Chapter 11). But the decisive break with traditional cultural values occasioned by the advent of western governments brought such local varieties into prominence as written (official and literary) media in an unprecedented way, particularly in the two greatest of the Greek islands, both of which had already experienced serious disruption in the continuity of Byzantine rule even before 1204.

8.4.5 The romances

The earlier period of experimentation with spoken registers in the twelfth century had been brief, apparently dying out some 20 years before the capture of Constantinople in 1204 (Beaton (1989: 93)). When the vernacular reappears in work of the fourteenth and fifteenth centuries, including both original romances and tales translated from western originals, it is as an increasingly standardized 'art' language with little or no regional variation or local identity and a 'mixed' (contemporary/ learned) character overall. It is also clear from the array of variant readings in the surviving manuscripts that the verbal accuracy expected in the copying of classical or learned texts did not extend to work in the vernacular.

Of the original romances, only the tale of *Kallímakhos and Khrysorróe* can be attributed with any confidence to a known author, namely Andrónikos Palaiológos, nephew of the first Palaiologan emperor, Mikhaél VIII. The stories of *Kallímakhos and Khrysorróe*, *Bélthandros and Khrysántza*, and *Líbistros and Rodámne* can, however, all be dated to the period 1310–50. They display clear affinities not only with the earlier 'vernacular' work of the twelfth century but also with the learned romances of the same period (Beaton (1989: ch. 10)), and in all probability represent the work of a literary circle closely connected with the imperial court in Constantinople. *The Tale of Achilles* may well be earlier, serving as a 'transitional' text between *Digenés Akrítes* and the developed fourteenth-century romances, while *The Tale of Troy* is clearly later, drawing on an already well-established tradition (Beaton (1989: 105)).

By contrast, such evidence as we have suggests that the translations originated in the Latin-dominated lands. *The War of Troy* (from the *Roman de Troie* by Benoît de St Maure) is perhaps the earliest of these, dating to around 1350. It involves some reduction of the original, and also shows evidence of influence from a learned verse chronicle composed in twelfth-century Constantinople by Konstantínos Manassés (8.5.5). *Phlórios and Plátzia-Phlóre* (translated from a Tuscan version of the French *Fleur et Blanchefleur*) is usually assigned to the late-fourteenth/ early-fifteenth centuries, and the translator seems most probably to have lived in the French-occupied Peloponnese. Its relatively simple language and versification reflect a popular-vernacular style in some ways reminiscent of *The Chronicle of the Morea*, but the composition is more accomplished, and there is evidence of borrowing from the didactic poem *Spanéas* (a twelfth- or thirteenth-century transposition into the vernacular of an earlier Byzantine collection of moral precepts). *Impérios and Margaróna* is a précis rather than a translation of its apparent source (*Pierre de Provence et la Belle Maguelonne*), though the Greek text may well pre-date the earliest surviving French manuscript, dated 1453, and so be based on a version now lost. Both this tale and that of *Apollónios of Tyre* (translated from a fourteenth-century Italian prose text some time before 1450) enjoyed great popularity down into the early modern period, as evidenced by the publication in Venice of a new Greek translation of *Apollónios*, in rhyming couplets, *c.* 1525, and a rhymed version of *Impérios* in 1543. The Greek translation of Boccaccio's *Theseid* was also printed in Venice (in 1529), but the translation itself was most probably carried out in the late fifteenth/early sixteenth centuries in Venetian-ruled Crete. In language and style it shows clear evidence of influence from the earlier romances, and so directly links the fourteenth-/fifteenth-century tradition with the later dialect literature of the Cretan Renaissance (14.2.4).

The chief issue for historians of the Greek language is that of the origin and development of the mixed language of the romances (other than the isolated *The Old Knight*, which belongs to a different tradition). This is intimately connected with the question of why the romances display so many common themes and so much common diction, and why there are so many textual discrepancies among different versions of the same story. The various competing theories are surveyed by Beaton (1989: ch. 11), whose main conclusions are summarized here.

We may begin with the work of M. and E. Jeffreys, who have argued both individually (e.g. M. Jeffreys (1973, 1974, 1987), E. Jeffreys (1979, 1981)) and jointly (e.g. 1971, 1979, 1983, 1986) that the textual discrepancies are the product of partially oral transmission. According to this theory, the language, metre and formulaic diction of written vernacular poetry, though not its subject matter, were modelled on a centuries-old tradition of narrative verse which had naturally produced an amalgam of archaisms and more contemporary forms. Others have gone further, and argued that at least some of the poems are the direct products of such an oral tradition (e.g. Trypánis (1981: 535–43), or at least that the different manuscript readings reflect different performances of orally transmitted texts (e.g. Eideneier (1987), Smith (1987)).

By contrast, Spadaro (1966, 1975, 1976a, 1976b, 1977, 1978a, 1978b, 1981, 1987) has tried to explain the common features as the product of the straightforward plagiarism of phrases, lines, and motifs on the part of literate writers who lacked creative talent. Van Gemert and Bakker (1981), Bakker (1987) and Bakker and van Gemert (1988), however, have opted instead for an account in terms of scribal interpolation and contamination, the occurrence of which is well supported by the general character of the manuscript tradition, in particular by the conspicuous sharing of particular verbal characteristics by two or more poems in a single manuscript to the exclusion of other versions of the same poems.

But this last theory, though providing a plausible account of specific correspondences, is insufficiently general to explain the overall similarities of structure, theme, and diction, which must be due to other factors. But even though Spadaro's evidence for the general dependence of *Impérios* on *Phlórios* and of the various versions of the *Tale of Belisários* (a fictionalized 'history' of Ioustinianós's general warning against the dangers of envy) on *The Tale of Achilles* and perhaps also on *Impérios* is persuasive, his other comparative studies are less compelling, and the balance of evidence overall points in the direction of selective literary allusion rather than of plagiarism, involving in particular the incorporation of already 'traditional' Greek elements into the translated romances which would otherwise have lacked them (Beaton (1989: 167–72)).

Such traditional elements might, of course, be ultimately of oral origin, as proposed by the Jeffreys, even if they later became the subject of literary borrowing and interaction. But while we may accept that short 'heroic' ballads such as *The Lay of Armoúres* or the original components of the epic/romance of *Digenés Akrítes* belonged to a tradition that was long enough to have allowed the formation of a stock of themes and phraseology later incorporated into the written vernacular style, the oral-traditional hypothesis fails to take into account the evidence for purely literary connections between the original romances, composed in Constantinople, and related poetry of the twelfth century, both learned and vernacular.

Furthermore, although there are verbal and thematic resemblances between oral folk songs and the romances (cf. Kriarás (1955), Mégas (1956), and Steryélis (1967)), much of the 'oral' formulaic phraseology of the latter seems not to be compositionally functional, a fact which suggests that many parallels are the result of deliberate borrowings of oral-traditional material designed primarily to validate innovative work through association with the practice of a traditional authority. This is confirmed when we see that many other 'formulas' were in fact newly created using traditional literary resources (Bäuml (1984)), subsequently becoming established through the practice of widespread borrowing among the writers of the genre, a process clearly evidenced, for example, in the role of *Phlórios* as a 'source' for *Impérios*, or in the transposition of lines from the twelfth-century 'learned' chronicle of Manassés into *The War of Troy* (Beaton (1989: 172–6)).

To illustrate, we may take the example of the half-line μικροί τε καὶ μεγάλοι [mi'kri te ke me'ɣali] 'both small and great', which contains the archaic particle τε

[te] 'both' (cf. Eideneier (1982: 302)). Since this connective was already avoided by the writers of the New Testament gospels (apart from the relatively learned Luke), it can hardly have survived into the living vernacular of the early/middle Byzantine period on which medieval oral poetry was presumably based. Unsurprisingly, then, neither the word itself nor the phrase containing it occurs in *Armoúres* (which survives in fifteenth-century manuscripts) or in other ballad-style oral poetry (Beaton (1980: 209)). This is highly significant since, even though the bulk of material from this genre was first collected in the nineteenth and early-twentieth centuries, it clearly retains many structural and formulaic characteristics of a tradition which goes back at least to the twelfth century (M. Jeffreys (1974: 160), and see Section III, 14.3).

Such an approach to the language of the romances undercuts the notion on which the theories of Spadaro and the Jeffreys both rely, namely that the writers of the romances were wholly dependent, because of either creative deficiencies or residual orality, on a stock of ready-made material, and Beaton (1989: 177 ff.) therefore seeks to explain the common elements of the poems in a different way. Since the literate authors/translators of the romances, like all other writers in Greek at the time, felt the need for a 'traditional' validation of their work, they appealed simultaneously to Greek oral poetry, to the learned and vernacular literary compositions of the twelfth century, and to the contemporary fictional literature of the west. And since 'formulaic' oral poetry was the primary authority for the use of the vernacular, they developed formulas of their own, expressions often betrayed by their linguistic or metrical form, which were then borrowed and adapted in a process which represents the early stages of the creation of a partially genre-conditioned, but crucially modern, literary language.

But the status of such writing remained relatively low in the fourteenth and fifteenth centuries, and its transmission probably lay in the hands not of professional scribes but of people with a personal interest in its development, for whom copying may in any case have been part of the process of learning their craft (Eideneier (1982–3)). The variety of manuscript readings would then follow from the fact that such author–copyists had both the ability and the freedom from conventional scribal practice to adapt material to their own requirements, or to redeploy it, straightforwardly or parodically, in compositions of their own. A situation of this kind is demonstrable in the case of the later writers of Renaissance Crete (Beaton (1989: 179)), and would readily explain the range of facts dealt with by van Gemert and Bakker.

From this perspective, the mixed language of the romances reflects a very distant oral background, but is not itself primarily of oral origin. The initiative for using a written language based on the vernacular clearly came 'from above' in both the twelfth and the fourteenth centuries, and it represents a progressive innovation. But the earliest authors, members of the metropolitan élite who were trained only to write in various forms of archaic Greek and whose own speech was influenced by interference from the written language, clearly lacked any models of 'good' or 'consistent' vernacular usage, and were therefore obliged to forge a contemporary literary language out of the heterogeneous spoken and literary varieties familiar to them. The observed inconsistencies of usage are an automatic consequence of the character of the sources employed.

With the passage of time, however, the language of the romances becomes progressively more 'popular', as vernacular forms replace their learned counterparts in the context of the breakdown of political and educational institutions in the Greek-speaking world as a whole. But this evolutionary process was never completed in Byzantine lands, where, following the traumatic impact of the Turkish occupation, the survivors fell back on more traditional forms of written expression. In Venetian Crete, however, where the evolution of a modern written style continued until the island fell to the Turks in 1669, a mature literary vehicle was developed out of just such a blend of learned and spoken (now specifically dialectal) elements, cf. 14.2.4. But Crete alone could not provide a standard for the fragmented Greek world as a whole, and when partial Greek independence finally came in the nineteenth century, the debate about the form a modern standard language should take had to be resumed almost *ab initio* (cf. 15.4 and Chapter 17).

8.4.6 Other vernacular material

In the later Middle Ages the ability to read and write at a basic level began once again to extend down the social scale, and an élitist approach to literacy could not be maintained across-the-board in the face of the growing need for written communication and the demand for written information. From the beginning of the fourteenth century, therefore, we have the renewed appearance, both in Byzantine and Latin-dominated territories, of assorted low-level documentation, reference works (home cures, horoscopes and travel guides), homilies and sermons, all composed in a form of language that was very much closer to the spoken norms of the age (see Panayiotákis (1993)).

Much of this was naturally produced by those who simply did not know how to write in a more 'learned' fashion, but there are also texts written by members of the élite on practical matters, such as the three letters of Cardinal Bessaríon (1403–72), discussed in Lámbros (1908), which, apart from their elaborate introductions, contrast starkly with his Atticizing 'literary' letters (see Mohler (1942)). The volume of such material must once have been considerable, but its inherent banality militated against its survival in bulk, and the trend to wider literacy was in any case slowed by the advent of Turkish rule. It is, however, an important subsidiary source of information about the state of spoken Greek in the period.

8.5 'The Koine' in Byzantium

8.5.1 The inheritance from antiquity

As we have seen, 'the Koine' in late antiquity already represented a range of written and spoken styles. At the top of the spectrum was the classicized Koine used for literary composition and epistolography, which shaded into the official language of imperial and patriarchal administration and the more free-flowing style of academic and theological debate. All of these varieties retained an essentially ancient surface form, especially in morphology, but in different degrees incorporated elements of contemporary syntax and lexicon through interference with spoken Greek, many of which then became 'standard' through imitation and repeated use.

In the centre of the spectrum was the more routine language of day-to-day administration, which was syntactically simpler, and, in the interests of wider intelligibility, allowed a greater degree of compromise with spoken Greek. Alongside this variant was the 'literary' colloquial based on the practice of the New Testament and other early Christian writing. This was very much more lively and varied, and, at least in the early stages of its development, permitted a more direct interface with the spoken language.

Although the social and regional dialects of spoken Greek in late antiquity were also treated as varieties of the Koine in Section I, it is customary, as was done above, to refer to the spoken Greek of the Byzantine period, and to the written varieties eventually based on it, as 'the vernacular'. Henceforth, therefore, the term 'Koine' will be used to refer only to the forms of written Greek which were inherited from the ancient world and adapted in their Byzantine context. And since high-style literary composition, including its neo-Atticist offshoot, has already been discussed, it is the varieties of middle-range Byzantine writing that will be considered here.

8.5.2 Academic and ecclesiastical Greek

Alongside the 'literary' Koine of authors such as Mikhaél Psellós, we also have a less ambitious 'academic' style which continued the technical, philosophical and scientific Koine of late antiquity. This is well illustrated by the *Bibliotheca* of the ninth-century patriarch Phótios, certain sections of the private works of the emperor Konstantínos VII in the tenth century (see 8.5.4 and 10.4.1), the miscellaneous writings of the churchman Eustáthios from the twelfth century, and the scholarly work of Máximos Planoúdes and Theódoros Metokhités from the Palaiologan period. This practical style of the educated élite, employed for discussion of matters of a learned nature, shows a steady pattern of 'retarded compromise' with the evolution of educated varieties of spoken Greek.

The Church hierarchy also employed a plainer Koine for most purposes, since the more recherché classicizing of higher forms of secular writing was felt to be the mark of a literature associated with pagan antiquity. A distinctively ecclesiastical variant of scholarly Greek therefore evolved during the middle and late Byzantine periods, involving its own characteristic vocabulary, but lacking both the more 'elegant' (i.e. Attic and literary) features of secular belles lettres and the 'livelier' (i.e. vernacular) elements of more popular forms of written Greek. A good example is provided by the work of the fourteenth-century theologian Gregórios Palamás, Bishop of Thessaloniki and author of the work *Defence of the Holy Hesychasts* (Khréstou (1962, 1966, 1970)).

In the Turkish period the Greek intelligentsia became increasingly identified

with the Orthodox Church, which at that time offered the only institutional structures capable of sustaining scholarly activity. The language of ecclesiastical administration (see below) and the language of academic, now primarily theological,
discourse therefore developed hand-in-hand, until eventually the Greeks, first in
western and then in Ottoman territories, began to assume positions of influence and
responsibility in politics and commerce. Under the impact of the Renaissance (mainly
in the west) and of the European Enlightenment (more generally), the written language of the educated classes then began to evolve in line with the general revival
of secular learning. Many elements of contemporary educated spoken Greek were
absorbed, together with much new terminology calqued on the usage of western
languages, especially French, and by the latter part of the eighteenth century this
had led to the emergence of a common rhetorical style among Greek intellectuals
which formed the *de facto* basis for the first official language of the independent
Greek kingdom in the early nineteenth century (cf. Chapter 15).

8.5.3 Official and administrative Greek

The Egyptian papyri peter out in the eighth century in the wake of the Arab conquest, and inscriptions of all kinds become exceedingly rare after *c.* 600 (see 12.1.2
for the major exception). Our knowledge of administrative styles in the Middle
Ages therefore depends on the survival of manuscript copies of imperial and ecclesiastical decrees, diplomatic documents and official correspondence. Such archive
material begins to be preserved in ever greater quantity from the latter part of the
tenth century onwards (see, for example, the collections in Miklosich and Müller
(1860–90)), and is composed for the most part in a mildly updated version of the
'high' administrative Koine of late antiquity, providing eloquent testimony to the
ingrained conservatism of the Greek establishment (see 10.7).

During the period of western rule after 1204, however, and subsequently in the
Turkish period, Greek retained something of its status as a diplomatic language
in the eastern Mediterranean, and the style employed for such purposes by 'for-
eigners' and Greeks operating outside the sphere of the Constantinopolitan establishment was naturally rather closer to that of educated speech (cf. 15.1).

8.5.4 Practical writing in the middle period

Given the dearth of epigraphic material, we are obliged, in attempting to trace the
development of spoken Greek through the middle Byzantine period to rely heavily
on the 'literary' sources which, for traditional or generic reasons, permitted somewhat higher levels of compromise with change in the spoken language than the
varieties of the Koine considered so far.

In the purely secular domain we have a number of texts dealing with practical
rather than scholarly matters, and designed to inform rather than to entertain. These
typically employ a more basic style than that of strictly academic discourse, and,
especially when not intended for general publication, provide valuable insights
into the educated colloquial of their times. Notable in this connection are the

confidential works of the emperor Konstantínos VII Porphyrogénnetos (905–59), which originally circulated privately among the members of the imperial household. The *De Caeremoniis*, for example, is a guide to court ceremonial, while the *De Administrando Imperio*, composed in the form of an advisory memorandum to his son, Romanós II, includes secret information about foreign policy. In the introductions to both works, the emperor justifies, in a literary style, his deliberate avoidance thereafter of 'Atticized' writing in the interests of effective instruction (cf. 10.4.1). They remain, however, the works of a highly educated man, and range stylistically from a near-academic register, with influences from the language of imperial administration, to a more basic variant which owes much to the conventions of the chronographic tradition (see 8.5.5 below).

There are also military handbooks (the *Corpus Tacticorum*), and a late-eleventh-century piece entitled *Strategikón* ('generalship/strategy') by a man named Kekauménos, a landowner in northern Greece who belonged to a family of Armenian origin. He may or may not be the distinguished Byzantine general Katakálon Kekauménos, but he certainly based his manual of advice to his son on personal experience as a military commander and provincial governor. He professes not to have received a literary education (191), and writes accordingly in a simpler style overall than that of Konstantínos VII (see 10.4.2), revealing a written language poised between the constraints of ancient written precedent and modern spoken norms.

8.5.5 *Chronicles*

Perhaps the most important genre falling within the general category of middle-to-popular writing, however, is the world chronicle or chronography, in which secular and religious interests combine (cf. Croke (1990), Scott (1990), and see 10.2). Work of this kind had its origins in the Hellenistic period, when the clash of Greek, Egyptian, and Jewish traditions had first highlighted the need for the synchronization of different traditions and for the establishment of chronological priorities. Subsequent Christianization brought an increased sensitivity to such questions, centring on the origins of particular beliefs and principles of behaviour. But once the Christian Greco-Roman world, including its classical past and traditional mythology, had been 'successfully' synchronized with the Hebrew world of the Old Testament, the focus was transferred, towards the end of the third century, to the construction of an absolute chronology of 'events', from the creation, via the incarnation, to the present, and the development of a framework for the calculation of future events prophesied in scripture (above all the second coming and the end of the world). Many of the great Christian writers of the Roman imperial period (e.g. Clement, Origen, and Eusebius) played an important role in these enterprises, and by the sixth century a large body of relevant work had been compiled, which then served as source material for the eclectic chronographers of the subsequent era.

Chronicles and histories had fundamentally different purposes. Narrative history in the classical tradition, composed in an Atticizing style and carefully distinguishing 'history' from 'myth', dealt with designated periods in a spirit of enquiry, and was intended to provide knowledge and recreation for an educated élite. Chronicles on the other hand had universal scope, treated the creation and the wars of Ioustinanós alike as 'events' in time, and were intended to serve as works of reference for literate Christians of all ranks. In general they do little more than list occurrences by year, although religious and political polemic became an established component of the tradition.

This rather sharp distinction became somewhat blurred during the Iconoclastic period, when the writing of narrative history declined along with other scholarly activity, and traditionally 'popular' forms of writing were raised stylistically as the reading public became more or less restricted to an urban élite. Consequently, even as times improved, a rather high chronographic style prevailed, so that even Mikhaél Psellós was able to call his rather literary biographical memoirs of the emperors and empresses from 976 to 1078 a *Khronographía* (perhaps in part because it lacked the distanced formality of the Thucydidean tradition).

The early Byzantine chronicles reflect the emerging interpretation of history as the working out of God's plan for mankind, in which the emperor was seen as the instrument of divine will, and the empire as an earthly reflection of the divine kingdom (a Hellenistic conceit first adapted to the Christian/Roman context by Eusebius). There is no reason to think, as has sometimes been supposed, that they were chiefly composed by poorly educated provincial monks in an effort to present a Christian view of world history to the rural masses (cf. Beck (1965: 188–97), Mango (1980: 189–200) for some discussion of this important point). Though they may sometimes seem 'naive and uncritical' to a modern reader (Nicol (1991: 77)), many were in fact composed by high-ranking officials (some of whom later became monks), and they reflect, within a conceptual framework of considerable sophistication, the same preconceptions and preoccupations seen in contemporary histories (see, for example, the papers in Jeffreys, Croke and Scott (1990)). As practical works of reference, however, they employed, at least in the earlier periods, a style very close to that of day-to-day administration, with borrowings from the popular Christian tradition which supplied much of the source material.

The linguistic register of such work rose, however, as the literate population contracted, and the early chronographic style (as seen most clearly in the work of the sixth-century Syrian, Malálas) begins to merge with that of academic discourse from the tenth century onwards. Theophánes, writing in the early ninth century, is an important transitional figure in this development. In the later Byzantine period, therefore, we have the scholarly work of Ioánnes Zonarás, and the less impressive, though popular, verse chronicle entitled *Sýnopsis Istoriké* by the government official Konstantínos Manassés (also the author of a 'learned' verse romance). Both are in an elaborated middle-style Koine, in line with the conventions of the period, though Zonarás also reflects the more Atticizing style of some of his sources.

Subsequent chronographic work suffered a marked decline in quality, a process which can perhaps be explained by the particularly strong revival of 'literary' historiography in the Palaiologan period. Nonetheless, chronicles continued to be written even after the fall of Constantinople, and such works supplied the basic 'historical' reading matter for the bulk of the Greek people until the beginnings of the modern era. Their essentially medieval world view was severely limited by the superficiality of much of the ancient research on which the tradition was based, but they did help to foster the unquestioning piety that was promoted by the Church under the rigours of Turkish domination (Mango (1980: 199–200)).

8.5.6 Christian exegetical literature and hagiography

The precedent of the Septuagint and the New Testament, backed up by the works of the early Church fathers, offered a continuing validation for thematically related compositions in a basic Koine aimed at the still extensive reading public of late antiquity and the early Middle Ages.

Some of this 'popular' Christian work was strictly exegetical in character, and was often originally delivered in the form of sermons composed to explain the mysteries to the masses. Leading figures such as Cyril of Jerusalem and John Chrysostom played a central role in this enterprise, and collections of their works were circulated widely in a style which, while retaining a biblical feel, was de-signed to be widely accessible. An important example of work in this tradition from the Iconoclastic period is the *Ecclesiastical History and Mystical Contemplation* of St Germanós, patriarch of Constantinople from 715 to 730 (Meyendorff (1984)), which offers an allegorical account of the Orthodox liturgy that soon assumed near-definitive status. Its language remains very close to that of the scriptures, and indeed the author quotes widely from them, though it has been updated in a number of minor details and displays evidence of the author's considerable learning (see 10.3.2).

Hagiographic works (cf. 10.3.1) also continued to be composed in a basic Koine, and it should be noted that many were still being written by leading members of the Church hierarchy in the early Byzantine period. A major example is provided by the *Life of St John the Almsgiver*, patriarch of Alexandria, composed by his friend and fellow-Cypriot Leóntios, bishop of Neápolis (*c*. 590–*c*. 650). Other works were written by educated monks, including the collection of edifying tales in the *Leimón* (*Spiritual Meadow*) of Ioánnes Móskhos (*c*. 550–619), and the lives of the Palestinian saints by Kyrillos of Skythópolis (*c*. 524–*c*. 558). Once again, it should not be assumed that the use of a more popular form of Greek at this time reflects anything other than a desire to communicate widely. Móskhos, for example, travelled with Sophrónios, later patriarch of Jerusalem, before his death in Rome in 619, while many other 'monkish' writers in the genre were in fact employed in the Church administration or had enjoyed high-ranking civil-service careers before their retirement from the world.

During the middle Byzantine period, as noted (cf. 8.4.2), many lives were trans-posed into a higher-style Koine in order to bring them into line with the expectations of the now small and exclusively well-educated reading public in the cities. Thereafter, the Greek of this tradition tends to merge with that of the previously more elaborated ecclesiastical style to form a single spectrum (cf. the similar approx-imation of the chronographic and academic varieties in the same period).

The hagiographic tradition itself struggled on into the eleventh century, when a steep decline set in reflecting the greater sophistication of an age in which secular scholarship was reviving strongly. The exegetical tradition, however, underwent something of a revival from the latter half of the fifteenth century, when the first examples of homiletic in a truly modern vernacular style, composed by the clergy-man Nathanaél, or Neílos, Bértos, make their appearance in lands still ruled by western powers (Bértos lived in both Crete and Rhodes), where the successful use of contemporary Romance by Catholic priests had doubtless made a powerful im-pression on their Orthodox counterparts (see Panayiotákis (1993: 255–6), Schartau (1974: 11–85, 1976: 70–75)).

8.5.7   The Koine in the later empire: a new written standard

Taking a general view of the Koine in the later Middle Ages, it is perhaps best to think in terms of the steady evolution, from a variety of rather heterogeneous sources, of a single 'standard language' of educated discourse. This employed classical morphology overall, but had eliminated certain dead classical categories, and could be stylistically varied by the adoption or avoidance of particular sets of differential 'markers' (mainly lexical and phraseological). Increasingly, we see in such middle-register writing the crystallization of a common syntactic frame-work, defined more and more for such fundamental properties as word order by the norms of the modern language, but still requiring the mechanical addition and/or substitution of learned vocabulary items, and the use, in varying degrees, of tradi-tionally or generically established realizations of particular construction types.

In this connection, we should note especially the regular use of the dative to mark the indirect object and the instrument, the occasional appearance of optatives in hypothetical conditionals and other 'prospective' subordinate clauses, the use of the accusative and infinitive construction and of the articular infinitive after preposi-tions, and the retention of the full array of inflected participles. Only the highest 'literary' varieties deviate markedly from this norm through their more thorough-going adherence to classical diction and rules of syntax, and to that extent could be said to fall outside the boundaries of the late medieval Koine so defined.

From the Komnenian period onwards, therefore, between the innovative 'ex-tremes' of the Atticist revival and vernacular experimentation, this partially homogen-ized middle range of written Greek, drawing on both secular and religious traditions, continued to be used whenever communication was felt to be a priority (cf. Brown-ing (1978)). Many important writers of the period, including Theódoros Pródromos, Mikhaél Glykás, Konstantínos Manassés, and Ioánnes Tzétzes, used both high and middle styles (and in some cases also the vernacular) in their literary and scholarly output, the choice determined in part by their attitude and intended audience, in part by their subject matter (Beaton (1989: 12)).

The 'standard' character of this register is reflected directly in the continued practice of transposition, in which the transposer aimed for a minimally Atticized, but still clearly non-vernacular, variety which displayed mainly classical morpho-logy, but a simplified, if somewhat archaizing syntax, alongside a non-recherché, but still mainly traditional, vocabulary. At first the practice was applied only 'up-wards', to low-style works such as saints' lives, but in the Palaiologan period we also have examples of transposition 'down' from more classicizing forms of Greek, such as (probably) that of the moralizing poem *Spanéas*, and above all those of high-style histories, in which the transposers seem to have aimed for an educated idiom which has much in common with the language of the chronographic tradition in its later manifestations (see 10.5).

8.6   The Balkan *Sprachbund*; future formations

No discussion of Greek in the Middle Ages would be complete without mentioning the convergence phenomena exhibited by the languages of the Balkans whose origins go back to the Byzantine political and cultural domination of the region from the ninth century onwards.

Such convergence occurs naturally when bi- or multi-lingualism is widespread, and if that contact is prolonged, a set of characteristic 'areal' phenomena, irrespective of genetic relationships, may eventually emerge. The Balkans provide one of the most famous examples of this phenomenon, and the discipline of Balkan linguistics has been developed to try to address the problems raised (see e.g. Sandfeld (1930), Schaller (1975), Solta (1980), Joseph (1983)).

The languages involved in the Balkan *Sprachbund* are Greek, Albanian, Romanian, Serbian, Bulgarian, and Macedonian (i.e. the Slavic language closely related to Bulgarian which is spoken in the northern part of ancient Macedonia, formerly part of Yugoslavia, and now an independent republic). All are spoken in lands which were once administered by Constantinople or adjacent to former Byzantine territory, and their speakers were all under long-term Byzantine cultural influence, particularly that of the Orthodox Church. It is no accident that Croatian, despite its near identity with Serbian in most other respects, is excluded from the group, since the bulk of Croatia beyond southern Dalmatia (Ragusa/Dubrovnik) was never a Byzantine possession.

Sandfeld (1930) argued on the basis of the spatial extension of these features and their relative order of acquisition that Greek was the ultimate source of most of the innovations, though this conclusion has not commanded universal assent. The obvious setting for the beginning of the process is the middle Byzantine period, when relations with the re-emerging west were tentative and sometimes hostile, and the main thrust of Byzantine foreign policy and missionary activity was redirected northwards through the Balkans, towards the Black Sea and to Russia. As with many such cultural influences, it appears to have continued for many centuries, even after the collapse of Byzantine power and the fall of Constantinople to the Ottoman Turks.

Among the syntactic features typically discussed are two which exclude Greek and show that Sandfeld's thesis cannot be the whole story:

(1) (a) postposed definite articles (though with each language using an indigenous morpheme).
    (b) the numerals 11 to 19 formed to the pattern 'one-upon-ten', etc.

The first is a feature of Albanian, Bulgarian/Macedonian (the other Slavic languages lack an article), and Romanian. Its source remains disputed, though the suffixation of a definiteness marker to object nominals in Turkish is suggestive. The second unites the Slavic languages, Albanian and Romanian, but since the formation is shared by Russian outside the Balkan area (but not, for example, by extra-Balkan Romance) a Slavic source seems most likely.

There are, however, a number of other characteristics which strongly support the view that Greek played a central role in the convergence process. The most important of these is the tendency for infinitival complements to control verbs to be replaced by finite clauses with subjunctive verb forms. This had its origins in the Hellenistic Koine, as we have seen, and continued to spread thereafter (cf. Chapter 11 for the Byzantine developments), to the point where the infinitive now survives only vestigially in the perfect system. The phenomenon also spread through Macedonian and Bulgarian, but it peters out in areas more remote from Greek-speaking populations. The southern dialects of Albanian, for example, use the finite construction, but the northern dialects have kept their infinitives. Similarly, Serbian follows the areal pattern, but Croatian, like the rest of Slavonic outside the Balkans, continues to use infinitives. Romanian is interesting in that, though the spoken language also follows the areal pattern, the more conservative written form of the language retains the usual infinitival constructions of Romance.

It has been objected that non-Balkan Romance and much of Germanic also employ such finite complements with control verbs when the subjects of the main and subordinate clauses are referentially distinct. But the key innovation is the use of finite complements when the subjects are identical, and this is a peculiarly Balkan feature for the periods under investigation.

An important example of infinitival replacement is provided by the future. Beginning in the eleventh century, θέλω ['θelo] 'I wish' began to replace ἔχω ['exo], literally 'I have', as the standard future auxiliary with an infinitival complement. This periphrasis was used freely alongside νά [na] (< ἵνα ['ina] 'that') + subjunctive, which fulfilled both subjunctive and future functions in vernacular texts after the twelfth century. Somewhat later, however, θέ [θe] 'it will (be the case that)', probably representing a reduction of 3sg. θέλει ['θeli] used impersonally (still attested occasionally in sixteenth/seventeenth century Cretan literature), was used to strengthen νά [na] in its specifically future sense, and θὲ νά [θe 'na] is already standard, beside the older infinitival construction, in Cretan Renaissance literature (forms such as θενά [θe'na], θανά [θa'na], and even θελά [θe'la] are also attested dialectally and in folk songs). This was then simplified colloquially to θά [θa], the marker of futurity in standard modern Greek, but already established as one of the forms of the future in Cretan comedy (though not in more 'serious' genres), where it outnumbers examples of both θέλω ['θelo] + infinitive and θὲ νά ['θe na] + subjunctive (see Joseph (1990: chs 5 and 9), Holton (1993)).

A distinction between personal and impersonal uses of 'will' + νά [na] helped to distinguish the volitive from the future, and the impersonal form of the future marker directly reflected its semantic properties as a sentential operator (i.e. 'it will be the case that X', cf. the parallel μπορεί νά [bo'ri na] 'it may be the case that X', πρέπει νά ['prepi na] 'it must be the case that X'). The phonetic reduction to proclitic 'particle' status was a consequence of its now-diminished role as a tense-marker (cf. 11.3–4).

Significantly, while non-Balkan Romance and northern Albanian dialects form futures with 'have', just like post-classical and early medieval Greek and Latin, Romanian, the southern Albanian dialects, Macedonian and Bulgarian all form their futures with a reduced and uninflected auxiliary element derived from the verb 'wish', exactly like Greek in the later medieval and modern periods. (This is partly true also of Serbian, but with the difference that the auxiliary is inflected for person.) There is, therefore, good reason to believe that Greek was the source of this key Balkan characteristic, on both chronological and geographical grounds, since the emergence of such an uninflected clitic auxiliary in the later Middle Ages is unique to the Greek-speaking world and the European territories of the former Byzantine empire.

Chapter 9

Byzantine belles lettres

9.1 Introduction

Throughout the Byzantine era literary writers were imbued with a classicizing spirit, and were always eager to display their learning when circumstances permitted. This retrospection was fostered in the middle period by a developing pride in the continuity of their culture, which in turn promoted a sense of 'otherness' *vis-à-vis* 'barbarian' peoples and lent to the language of the writers, scholars, and saints in the unbroken chain linking the ancient to the medieval world a near-sacred authority. But as the empire went into decline at the end of the eleventh century, this literary language shifted still closer to its ancient Attic predecessor, as the Byzantines sought to build a new 'Greek' identity on the foundations of ancient Hellenism.

One consequence of this Atticist revival is that the language of the historian Prokópios, writing in the reign of Ioustinianós in the sixth century, can be hard to distinguish from that, say, of Mikhaél Kritóboulos, writing of the sack of Constantinople in the fifteenth. We should not forget, however, that most literary composition in the middle Byzantine period was less classical in style, or overlook the massive shift of outlook between late antiquity and the rather narrow piety of the early medieval period; the revival of thoroughgoing classicism began only with the advent of a more 'modern' (though, ironically, classically inspired) point of view among the Byzantine aristocracy in the eleventh century.

9.2 The early period: Prokópios (first half of the sixth century)

Prokópios was a staff officer to Ioustinianós's general Belisários, and his history of the wars of reconquest is a vivid eye-witness account modelled largely on Thucydides (speeches and all), but with many features of Herodotean style and vocabulary (see Haury (1905–13), Hunger (1978: I, 291–300), Cameron (1985)). He was also a fine practical linguist, and his account of the peoples of the empire and their enemies constitutes a uniquely important source for the history of the period.

The piece which follows comes from the *History*, and explains how the secret of silk production, a major source of future Byzantine prosperity, was first brought to Constantinople:

(1) Ὑπὸ τοῦτον τὸν χρόνον τῶν τινες μοναχῶν ἐξ Ἰνδῶν ἥκοντες, ... ἐς βασιλέα
γενόμενοι οὕτω δὴ τὰ ἀμφὶ τῇ μετάξῃ διοικήσεσθαι ὡμολόγουν, ὡς μηκέτι
Ῥωμαῖοι ἐκ Περσῶν τῶν σφίσι πολεμίων ἢ ἄλλου του ἔθνους τὸ ἐμπόλημα
τοῦτο ποιήσωνται ... ἐνδελεχέστατα δὲ διερευνωμένῳ τῷ βασιλεῖ καὶ
ἀναπυνθανομένῳ εἰ ὁ λόγος ἀληθής εἴη ἔφασκον οἱ μοναχοὶ σκώληκάς τινας
τῆς μετάξης δημιουργοὺς εἶναι ... ἀλλὰ τοὺς μὲν σκώληκας ἐνθάδε ζῶντας
διακομίζειν ἀμήχανα εἶναι ... εἶναι δὲ τῶν σκωλήκων τῶνδε τὸν γόνον
ᾠὰ ἑκάστου ἀνάριθμα ... ταῦτα εἰπόντας ὁ βασιλεὺς μεγάλοις τοὺς ἄνδρας
ἀγαθοῖς δωρήσασθαι ὁμολογήσας τῷ ἔργῳ πείθει ἐπιρρῶσαι τὸν λόγον. οἱ
δὲ ... τά τε ᾠὰ μετήνεγκαν ἐς Βυζάντιον, ἐς σκώληκάς τε ... μεταπεφυκέναι
διαπραξάμενοι τρέφουσί τε συκαμίνου φύλλοις, καὶ ἀπ' αὐτοῦ γίνεσθαι
μέταξαν τὸ λοιπὸν κατεστήσαντο ἐν Ῥωμαίων τῇ γῇ.   *History*, 8.17.1–7

[i'po   'tuton toŋ 'xronon 'ton dines mona'xon eks in'don 'ikondes, ... ez
 Around this   the time   of-the some   monks(gen.) from Indians having-come   to

vasi'lea je'nomeny 'uto ði   t(a)   am'fi ti me'taksi ðjy'kisesθe
 king   becoming   thus indeed the-things about the silk   to-administer(fut.)

omo'loɣun, os   mi'keti ro'mey ek per'son ton 'sfisi pole'mion i 'alu
 promised,   so-that no-longer Romans from Persians the to-them enemies   or other

tu   'eθnus to em'bolima 'tuto py'isonde ... endele'çestata ðe
 some race   the purchase   this   may-make ...   Most-persistently but

ðjerevno'meno to   vasi'li   ke anapynθano'meno i   o 'loɣos ali'θis
 examining(dat.) to-the emperor(dat.) and inquiring(dat.)   whether the story   true

'ii   'efaskon y mona'çy 'skoli'kas tinas tis   me'taksis ðimiur'ɣus
 was(opt.) said   the monks   worms   certain of-the silk   creators

'ine ... a'la tuz men   'skolikas en'θaðe 'zondas   ðjako'mizin
 to-be ... But the on-the-one-hand worms   here   living(acc.) to-convey

a'mixana 'ine ... 'ine ðe ton sko'likon 'tonde   ton 'ɣonon o'a e'kastu
 impossible to-be ... To-be but of-the worms   these(gen.) the offspring eggs of-each

a'nariθma ... tafta   i'pondas   o vasi'lefs me'ɣalys tus 'andras
 numberless ...   These-things having-said(acc.) the emperor with-great the men(acc.)

aɣa'θys ðo'risasθe omolo'jisas   to 'erɣo 'piθi   epir'rose tol
 benefits to-reward   having-promised(nom.) in-the deed persuades to-confirm the

'loɣon. y   ðe ... 'ta te o'a me'tineŋgan ez vy'zandion, es 'skoli'kas
 story.   They and   the both eggs brought   to Byzantium, into worms

te ... metapefy'kene djapra'ksameny, 'trefu'si te syka'minu 'fylys,   kj
 and ... to-transform   having-effected, ... they-nourish and of-mulberry with-leaves, and

ap af'tu 'jinesθe 'metaksan to   ly'pon kate'stisando en ro'meon ti ji.]
 from this to-happen silk   for-the future   they-established in of-Romans the land.

'Around this time some of the monks came from India [*in fact Sogdiana, where Nestorian
missionaries were active*] and, having presented themselves before the emperor, promised to manage the silk business so that the Romans need no longer purchase this com-
modity from their enemies the Persians, or from any other race ... When the emperor

interrogated them persistently and inquired whether their story was true, the monks replied that certain worms were the makers of silk . . . but that it was impossible to bring them there alive; . . . the offspring of these worms, however, were eggs produced by each in countless numbers . . . After they had spoken in this way the emperor promised to reward the men with great benefits and urged them to confirm their story in prac-tice . . . They then brought the eggs to Constantinople, and having effected their trans-formation into worms, fed them on mulberry leaves and thus established the production of silk in Roman lands for the future.'

Apart from the typically Herodotean word order in τῶν τινες μοναχῶν ['ton dines mona'xon] 'some of the monks', and similar phrases in which a pronoun is sand-wiched, the language is very largely based on the 1,000-year-old literary Greek of classical Athens, with even the Thucydidean ἐς [es] for εἰς [is] '(in)to'. The con-trast with contemporary papyrus letters which reflect the basic spoken language of the period could not be starker. Over and above the wholly classical lexicon and morphology, we may note here the frequent use of verb-final word order; the free use of participles and infinitives in all their classical functions, including the accus-ative and infinitive to mark the reported speech after ἔφασκον ['efaskon] 'they said'; the routine, non-emphatic preposing of possessive genitives; the appearance of a neuter plural adjective (ἀμήχανα [a'mixana] 'impossible') in impersonal con-structions, where logically the singular would be expected (a favourite Thucydidean trait); and the use of the optative εἴη ['ii] in the past-time context of the indirect question after ἀναπυνθανομένῳ [anapynθano'meno] 'inquiring'.

9.3 The middle period: Mikhaél Psellós (1018–78 or –96)

Psellós served the empire both as an administrative officer and as a minister, and was also appointed professor of philosophy in the imperial university, a post that was re-established at his instigation.

Among his voluminous writings the *Khronographía*, in which he recounts the history of his time in the form of vivid memoirs and character sketches, is perhaps the most famous (see Renauld (1926–8), Sewter (1966), Hunger (1978: I, 372–81), Wilson (1983: 156–66)). This work represents one of the high points of Byzantine prose writing, and the author's personal involvement in the events described im-parts an unusual vitality to the narrative. It is written in a moderately Atticized Koine rather than in the purer Attic style affected by later writers, and so contains many words and constructions of Hellenistic or Roman origin alongside the typ-ically tangled Byzantine word orders and complex noun phrases whose use was encouraged by the rhetorical bias of the higher education system.

Even though he generally retains the classical rules of morphology and syntax, including a particular liking for the dual, his work also displays evidence of devel-opment in the formation and use of other elements of classical Greek which had long been abandoned in the spoken language. The irregular verbs with 1sg. pres-ent indicative in -μι [mi], for example, still used in the Koine of the sixth and seventh centuries despite competition from 'regular' replacements in -ω [o], show a markedly simplified paradigm. Similarly, the perfect is often employed, in true

Koine fashion, as a substitute for the aorist, while the pluperfect, widely replaced in the Koine by periphrases with 'be' + aorist participle by the sixth century, usually lacks its classical augment. He also employs a number of characteristic Byzantinisms, such as the free use of the optative as a 'marked' variant of the subjunctive even in non-past contexts (much as 'may' and 'might' are now used almost interchangeably by many speakers of English; see also 10.4.1).

The following extract, describing the uprising against the emperor Mikhaél V Kalaphátes ('Caulker', his father's trade), gives a typical sample of Psellós's writing. Mikhaél had been adopted by the empress Zoé, the widow of his predecessor, but when, having come to the throne in 1041, he tried to have her shut away in a convent, the people deposed him:

(2) Ὥσπερ γάρ τινος ξύμπαντες κρείττονος μετεσχηκότες πνεύματος, οὐκ ἔτι ἐπὶ τῶν προτέρων ἑωρῶντο τῆς ψυχῆς καταστάσεων, ἀλλ' οἵ τε δρόμοι αὐτῶν μανικώτεροι καὶ χεῖρες ἐρρωμενέστεραι, καὶ τῶν ὀφθαλμῶν αἱ βολαὶ πυρώδεις τε καὶ ἐνθουσιῶσαι, οἵ τε τοῦ σώματος τόνοι ῥωμαλεώτεροι, μεταρρυθμίζεσθαι δὲ πρὸς τὸ εὐσχημονέστερον ἢ μετατίθεσθαι τῶν βουλευμάτων οὐδεὶς τῶν πάντων ἐβούλετό γε, ἢ τοῦ συμβουλεύοντος ἦν.
Δόξαν δὲ αὐτοῖς τὰ πρῶτα ἐπὶ τὸ γένος ἐκείνου χωρεῖν καὶ τοὺς σεμνοὺς ἐκείνων οἴκους καταστρέφειν καὶ ὑπερόγκους, ἔργου τε εἴχοντο, καὶ ὁμοῦ προσέβαλλον, καὶ τὸ ξύμπαν εἰς ἔδαφος κατερρήγνυτο, καὶ τῶν οἰκοδομημάτων τὰ μὲν ἐπικεκάλυπτο, τὰ δ' ἀνακεκάλυπτο· ἐπεκαλύπτοντο μὲν ὀροφαὶ εἰς γῆν πίπτουσαι, ἀνεκαλύπτοντο δὲ κρηπῖδες γῆθεν ἀναρρηγνύμεναι, ὥσπερ αὐτῶν τῆς γῆς τὸ ἄχθος ἀποφορτιζομένης καὶ ἀπορριπτούσης τοὺς θεμελίους.   *Khronographía*, 28–9

['osper 'ɣar tinos   'ksimbandes 'kritonos metesçi'kotes   'pnevmatos,
As-if   for   some(gen.) all-men(nom.) greater(gen.) having-shared(nom.) spirit(gen.),

uk 'eti e'pi tom bro'teron eo'rondo tis   psi'çis kata'staseon, al 'i te
not still in   the former   they-seemed of-the soul   states,   but the both

'ðromi a'ton mani'koteri ke 'çires erome'nestere, ke ton ofθal'mon e
runnings of-them more-frantic and hands stronger,   and of-the eyes   the

vo'le pi'roðis te   ke enθusi'ose, 'i te tu   'somatos 'toni
blows fiery   both and impassioned, the and of-the body   cords/sinews

romale'oteri, metariθ'mizesθe ðe pros   to efsçimo'nesteron i meta'tiθesθe
more-powerful, to-be-reformed and towards the more-dignified or to-change

tom   vulev'maton u'ðis tom 'bandon e'vule'to   je,   i tu
from-the plans   none of-the all   (would-have-)wished at-least, or of-the(-man)

simvu'levondos in.
advising   would-have-been.

'ðoksan   ðe af'tis ta 'prota e'pi to 'jenos e'kinu   xo'rin
It-having-seemed-good and to-them the first   against the family of-that(-man) to-go

ke tus sem'nus e'kinon 'ikus kata'strefin ke iper'oŋgus, 'erɣu te
and the grand   of-them houses to-overturn and over-sized,   task both

'ixondo,   ke o'mu   pros'evalon,   ke to 'ksimban is 'eðafos kate'riɣnito, ke
they-held-to, and together they-attacked,   and the all   to ground   was-torn-down, and

ton ikoðomi'maton ta-men   e'pike'kalipto, ta-ð   a'nake'kalipto;
of the houses   some (parts) became-covered, other (parts) became-uncovered;

epeka'liptondo men   oro'fe iz jin 'piptuse, aneka'liptondo
were-covered   on-the-one-hand roofs to earth falling,   were-uncovered

ðe   kri'piðes 'jiθen   anariɣ'nimene, 'osper af'ton tiz jis to
on-the-other-hand basements from-earth erupting,   as-if of-them the earth the

'axθos   apofortizo'menis ke apori'ptusis tus θeme'lius.]
burden(acc.) unloading   and casting-away   the foundations.]

'As if sharing in some greater inspiration, they seemed no longer to be in their former state of mind; their running was more frantic and their hands stronger, their glances fiery and impassioned, and their sinews more powerful. Not one of the whole mass of people (?would have) wished in any way to revert to more dignified behaviour or to depart from his intentions, nor would any have been on the side of a man who so advised them.

Having resolved first to march against the emperor's family and to tear down their grand and over-sized houses, they stuck to their task and made a general attack. Everything was razed to the ground, some parts of buildings becoming covered with debris, others exposed to the heavens; thus roofs falling to the ground were covered over, basements erupting from the earth were exposed, as if the soil were unloading the burden of them and casting away the foundations.'

Though most of the vocabulary here is familiar from classical Attic writers, the faithful 'copying' of the style of any one ancient model was evidently not the objective, as shown by the density of unusual vocabulary (e.g. in the first paragraph, the use of the passive ὁρῶμαι [o'rome] 'I am seen' in the sense 'seem'; ἐρρωμένος [ero'menos] 'healthy, vigorous'; ῥωμαλέος [roma'leos] 'strong of body'; μεταρρυθμίζομαι [metariθ'mizome] 'I reform/am reformed'), the co-presence of ξυν- [ksin-] and συν- [sin-] in different compounds, and the use of poetic phraseology as pure embellishment. Ὀφθαλμῶν βολαί [ofθal'mon vo'le], for example, lit. 'blows of the eyes', i.e. 'glances', occurs only in Homer and tragedy, while the word γῆθεν ['jiθen] 'from the ground' is exclusively tragic.

By contrast, a word such as ἀποφορτίζομαι [apofor'tizome] 'I unload' makes its first appearance in non-literary prose writers of the Hellenistic and Roman periods (in passages dealing, for example, with the 'unloading' of cargoes, or the contents of the stomach!), and was presumably an item of 'ordinary' vocabulary for Psellós. As noted, despite the deliberate striving for effect in particular phrases, there is no systematic effort to avoid the use of such words, whose routine appearance fully justifies Psellós's own description of the language of the *Khronographía* as the Koine.

The overall grammatical and stylistic impression, however, is broadly traditional, in that relatively few constructions are wholly unprecedented in ancient writers. Note in particular that Psellós follows the practice, going back at least to Herodotus, of using the imperfect as a 'vivid' or 'eyewitness' tense, its imperfective aspect involving readers directly, as it were, in the developing situation being replayed before them. But he also aims occasionally for special effects: note the deliberately 'interwoven' word order of the initial clause of the first paragraph; and the very odd construction at the end (assuming the text is sound), which combines the verb 'be' with the genitive of a substantivized participle, apparently in the sense 'be (on the side) of-the(-one) advising'.

A major feature of post-classical and medieval Greek, however, is the use of the imperfect in a modal sense, as apparently in the final sentence of the first paragraph (cf. Horrocks (1995) for a full treatment of this issue). Note that an interpretation of the imperfect ἦν [in] as a true past tense (i.e. 'was on the side of those who so advised') is precluded here by the sense of the preceding clause, which asserts that no one 'wished' (or, taking the imperfect ἐβούλετο [e'vuleto] as modal too, 'would have wished') to change his plans, so that the possibility of there being a party present that actually advised such a course of action is ruled out. This development requires careful explanation, and is considered separately in 9.4.

9.4 The modal imperfect

The past-tense forms of classical Greek doubled as 'hypotheticals' in counterfactual conditional protases. This can be explained on the basis that the occurrence of the supposed 'event' logically (rather than strictly temporally) 'precedes' the consequence expressed in the apodosis. Note that there is no necessary correlation with 'real' past time *vis-à-vis* the time of utterance, and that such hypothetical events are strictly atemporal (since they are not located in the real world). The imperfect could therefore be used with past or present force (the interpretation depending on context), even though the punctual aorist was excluded from present contexts (where progressiveness is presupposed).

But since this essentially atemporal modal use of the imperfect was in principle also compatible with future interpretations, the imperfect eventually came to be used in future-referring conditionals in place of the moribund optative (cf. the two readings of *if (ever) she came, . . .*). We therefore move into a situation in which imperfect indicatives in the protases of hypothetical conditionals could have past, present, or future time reference. This promoted a reinterpretation of the imperfect, in context, as a general marker of hypothetical/counterfactual modality, rather as if a clause such as *if she came* could mean not only 'if she were to come', but also 'if she were coming' and 'if she had come'. Thus when ἄν [an], the classical marker of hypothetical consequentiality in apodoses, began to disappear because of confusion with ἄν [an] 'if' (following loss of vowel length in the latter), it was the atemporal modal imperfect that replaced the optatives (future), imperfects and aorists (present/past) that had previously been used there in combination with it (as already often in the New Testament).

Consider the following sentence from Callinicus's *Life of Hypatius* (fifth/sixth century):

(3) εἰ γὰρ ἀνήγγειλας, παρεκαλοῦμεν καὶ ἡμεῖς   *Vita Hypatii* 98.4

[i gar an'iŋgilas,   pareka'lumen   ke i'mis]

if for you-called(aor.), we-were-comforting(impf.) also we

'For if you had appealed to us, we too would have comforted you.'

'Correct' classical usage would demand the use of the aorist + ἄν [an] in the apodosis in order to express the intended perfectiveness (and so indirectly the pastness) of the hypothetical consequence, but this option was no longer available to an author of the late antique period writing in more popular forms of the Koine.

There was, however, always a risk of ambiguity in the absence of an overt modality marker in the apodosis, and popular Greek therefore reintroduced a more overt system of marking hypothetical consequentiality by developing a 'conditional' periphrasis (= 'would X'), consisting of the imperfect of the future auxiliaries μέλλω ['melo], lit. 'intend/be about to', or ἔχω ['exo], lit. 'have/be able', + infinitive. These were then widely used in hypothetical apodoses, alongside bare modal imperfects, from late antiquity onwards (cf. 11.8.3).

This 'low' periphrastic option was not, of course, available to Psellós, who affected a more traditional style of writing which, if not always strictly classical, was at least validated by Koine writing of the Roman period. Since the modal imperfect remained in standard use throughout the Middle Ages (perhaps even in educated speech), the sentence from the extract above can quite reasonably be assumed to contain an example of such usage, as the sense demands.

9.5 The new Atticism: Anna Komnené (1083–c. 1153)

Anna Komnené was the eldest daughter of Aléxios I Komnenós and Eiréne Doúkaina. When her father died in 1118, she attempted unsuccessfully to prevent her younger brother Ioánnes II from coming to the throne, in the hope that her husband Nikephóros Bryénnios, the son of an earlier pretender, might succeed. She was then forced to retire to a convent, but maintained social contacts, not only founding a philosophical discussion group but compiling the material for her dramatic account of how her father saved the empire from its enemies in both the east (the Seljuks and Petcheneks) and the west (the Normans and the knights of the first crusade). Her unashamedly encomiastic narrative provides an invaluable insight into the contemporary medieval world in a language that is markedly more classical than that of Psellós, and replete with learned quotations and allusions (see Buckler (1929), Leib (1937–45), Sewter (1969), Hunger (1978: I, 400–9)).

The following extract describes the impact of the announcement of the Norman invasion led by Bohemond, son of Robert Guiscard, who had sailed from Bari to Avlona, south of Dyrrákhion (modern Dürres), in 1107:

(4) Ὁ δὲ βασιλεύς, ἔτι εἰς τὴν βασιλεύουσαν ἐνδιατρίβων, μεμαθηκὼς διὰ γραφῶν
τοῦ δουκὸς Δυρραχίου τὴν τοῦ Βαϊμούντου διαπεραίωσιν ἐπετάχυνε τὴν
ἐξέλευσιν. ἀνύστακτος γὰρ ὢν ὁ δοὺξ Δυρραχίου, μὴ διδοὺς τὸ παράπαν

ὕπνον τοῖς ὀφθαλμοῖς, ὁπηνίκα διέγνω διαπλωσάμενον τὸν Βαϊμοῦντον παρὰ
τὴν τοῦ Ἰλλυρικοῦ πεδιάδα καὶ τῆς νηὸς ἀποβεβηκότα καὶ αὐτόθι που
πηξάμενον χάρακα, Σκύθην μεταπεμψάμενος ὑπόπτερον δή, τὸ τοῦ λόγου,
πρὸς τὸν αὐτοκράτορα τὴν τούτου διαπεραίωσιν ἐδήλου. ὃς ἐπανιόντα
τὸν αὐτοκράτορα τοῦ κυνηγεσίου καταλαβών, δρομαῖος εἰσελθὼν καὶ
προσουδίσας τὴν κεφαλήν, τὴν τοῦ Βαϊμοῦντου διαπεραίωσιν τρανῶς ἐβόα.
ἅπαντες μὲν οὖν οἱ τότε παρόντες ἐπάγησαν, οὗπερ ἕκαστος ἔτυχε, καὶ
πρὸς μόνην τὴν τοῦ Βαϊμοῦντου κλῆσιν ἀποναρκήσαντες. ὁ δὲ αὐτοκράτωρ,
πλήρης θυμοῦ καὶ φρονήματος ὤν, λύων τὸν ἱμάντα τοῦ ὑποδήματος 'Πρὸς
ἄριστον,' ἔφη, 'το παρὸν τραπώμεθα· τὰ δέ γε κατὰ τὸν Βαϊμοῦντον αὖθις
κατασκεψόμεθα.'   *Alexiad* 12.9

[o ðe vasi'lefs, 'eti is tiɱ vasi'levusan enðja'trivon, memaθi'kos ðja
The but emperor,   still is in the   ruling (city)   staying,   having-learned through

ɣra'fon tu   ðu'kos ðira'çiu   tin du   vai'mundu ðjape'reosin epe'taçine
letters   of-the duke   of-Dyrrachium the of-the Bohemond   crossing   hastened

tin e'kselefsin. a'nistaktos ɣar on   o   ðuks ðira'çiu,   mi ði'ðus to
the departure.   Vigilant   for being the duke of-Dyrrachium, not giving the

pa'rapan 'ipnon tis   ofθal'mis, opi'nika   'ðjeɣno ðjaplo'samenon
altogether sleep to-the-eyes,   at-the-moment-when he-learned had-sailed-over(pple.)

toɱ vai'mundon pa'ra tin du   iliri'ku pe'ðjaða ke tiz   ni'os
the Bohemond(acc.) beside the of-the Illyricum plain   and from-the ship

apovevi'kota   ke af'toθi pu   pi'ksamenon 'xaraka, 'skiθin
had disembarked(pple.) and there   somewhere had-pitched(pple.) camp,   Scythian

metapem'psamenos i'popteron ði,   to   tu   'loɣu, pros ton
having-summoned   'winged'   indeed, (as) the(-thing) of-the saying, to   the

afto'kratora tin 'dutu   ðjape'reosin e'ðilu. os epani'onda ton
emperor   the of-this-man crossing   revealed. Who returning(acc.) the

afto'kratora tu   kinije'siu katala'von, ðro'meos isel'θon ke
emperor(acc.) from-the hunt   finding(nom.), at-a-run entering and

prosu'ðisas   tiɳ gefa'lin, tin du   vai'mundu ðjape'reosin tra'nos
bowing-to-the-ground the head,   the of-the Bohemond   crossing   clearly

e'voa. 'apandes men   un i 'tote   par'ondes e'pajisan,
he-shouted. All   on-the-one-hand then the at-that-time present   were-fixed,

'uper   'ekastos 'etiçe,   ke proz 'monin tu   vai'mundu
exactly-where each   happened (to be)/was, even at   mere   of-the Bohemond

'klisin aponar'kisandes. o   ðe afto'krator, 'pliris θi'mu ke fro'nimatos
calling having-become-stupid. The but emperor,   full   of-spirit and courage

on, 'lion ton i'manda tu   ipo'ðimatos 'pros 'ariston,' 'efi   'to
being, untying the strap of-the shoe,   'To lunch,'   he-said, '(for) the

pa'ron tra'pomeθa; ta   'ðe je   ka'ta   toɱ vai'mundon 'afθis
present let-us-turn;   the(-things) but by-contrast concerning the   Bohemond   later

kataske'psomeθa.']
we-shall-review."

'When the emperor, who was still in the imperial city, learned of Bohemond's cross-ing from the letters of the duke [*military commander*] of Dyrrákhion, he hastened his departure. For the duke had been vigilant, having altogether denied sleep to his eyes, and at the moment when he learned that Bohemond had sailed over beside the plain of Illyricum, disembarked, and set up camp thereabouts, he sent for a Scythian "with wings", as the saying goes, and informed the emperor of the man's crossing. The mes-senger found the emperor returning from his hunting party, and, entering at a run and bowing his head to the ground, shouted in a clear voice that Bohemond had crossed over. All those present at the time were rooted to the spot, exactly where they were, stupefied at even the mere mention of Bohemond. But the emperor, full of spirit and courage, untied the strap of his shoe and said, "For the present let us turn to our lunch; and as for Bohemond, we shall review the matter later."'

As often in Byzantine historiography, there is an Ionic colouring due to the influ-ence of Herodotus, and some of the words that appear 'poetic' from an Attic perspective occur in Ionic prose and later classicizing writers: thus both πεδιάς [pedi'as] and ὑπόπτερος [i'popteros], for example, are used by Herodotus, while the form of διαπλωσάμενον [ðjaplo'samenon] 'having sailed across', and the word προσουδίζω [prosu'ðizo] 'dash to the ground', are of Ionic origin.

There are also words of post-classical origin that belong to the mainstream Byzantine tradition (e.g. δούξ [ðuks] 'military governor'; ἐξέλευσις [e'kselefsis] 'departure'; διαπεραίωσις [ðjape'reosis] 'crossing'; ἀνύστακτος [a'nistaktos] 'vigil-ant'; ἀποναρκῶ (< -άω) [aponar'ko] 'be stupid'), and Anna clearly no more in-tended to 'copy' the style of the ancients than did Psellós; this was, after all, the 'living' literary language of educated Byzantines, and writers were free to exploit the full range of traditional resources in their compositions. Nevertheless, with due allowance given for the regular Byzantinisms, the overall effect is considerably more 'natural' than that of Psellós in its word order and avoidance of densely accumulated recherché vocabulary.

In matters of grammar, however, Anna is a purist at heart, showing an excellent control of classical morphology (though νηός [ni'os] 'of-ship', for Attic νεώς [ne'os] is perhaps a back-formation to dative νηί [ni'i] rather than a deliberate Homerism), and carefully employing such ancient syntactic rules as that requiring an accusat-ive and participle construction after verbs of knowledge and perception, cf. διέγνω διαπλωσάμενον τὸν Βαϊμοῦντον ['ðjeɣno ðjaplo'samenon ton vai'mundon], lit. 's/he-found-out having-crossed Bohemond'. In general, the attention to classical detail, and the avoidance of contorted word orders and overelaborated construc-tions, makes her Greek considerably easier to read than that of Psellós for those trained exclusively in the classical language.

We may note, however, the presumably 'accidental' use of εἰς [is] + accusative (originally = '(in)to') as a substitute for ἐν [en] + dative in the locative sense of 'in' (always asssuming that this is not a scribal error). There is also some functional confusion of future indicatives and aorist subjunctives. In the extract above, the subjunctive and the future indicative in Aléxios's dismissive remarks have been translated as such, but they could well have been intended to have equivalent force, since there are many other passages in which they are used side by side in contexts where the classical language would demand one to the exclusion of the other. This

functional overlap, based on the formal collapse caused by sound change and analogical levelling in late antiquity, was a major feature of medieval Greek in its
middle and popular registers too (cf. 11.8.3, 11.8.6 (a) for the details); and though
the two paradigms were kept formally distinct in the learned written language, contemporary perceptions of their functional equivalence, reinforced by the dual use
of *vá* [na]-constructions as both subjunctives and futures in the spoken language
(11.8.3), are often apparent in the writing of even the most learned of Byzantine
writers (with optatives also introduced as occasional 'learned' variants for both).

As with the Atticists of old, the temptation to parade learning, including the
incorporation of rare and unusual usages, can lead to effects which often seem
forced to those with a classical training. Nevertheless, the general impression, as
with Prokópios some 900 years earlier, is of a tastefully embellished 'classical'
style. There could hardly be a more graphic illustration of the centrality of the
ancient Greek literary tradition in high Byzantine culture at both the highest and
lowest points in the empire's fortunes.

But few had the educational background necessary to read, still less the talent
to write, such virtuoso compositions, and even if we allow that the formal spoken
language of the court also remained relatively classical, as suggested, for example,
by the conversation reported by the thirteenth-century historian and statesman
Geórgios Akropolítes (*History* ch. 39), or Filelfo's letter of 1451 describing the
seclusion of aristocratic Byzantine women (1478 edition, p. 183), more routine
forms of writing could scarcely avoid the more immediate influence of developments in the normal spoken language, and it is to these middle varieties that we
must now turn our attention in Chapter 10.

Middle styles in Byzantium

10.1 Introduction

The early Byzantine period was important for the production of chronicles and religious works in 'basic' forms of Greek that tolerated greater compromise with developments in the spoken language. After the disruption of the seventh and eighth centuries, however, a general stylistic elevation set in, facilitated by the collapse of literacy among the wider population, and thereafter the development of the middle range of written Greek involved a gradual coming together of the different forms of Koine composition inherited from antiquity, a process prompted by the essential unity of the political, academic, and theological establishments, and later by the re-emergence of an urban bourgeoisie. The later medieval Koine therefore continued the tradition of more elaborated Koine composition rather than that of earlier chronography and hagiography, though from the twelfth century onwards, the vacuum at the lower end of the spectrum was progressively filled by the revival of writing in the vernacular (see Chapter 12).

10.2 Chronicles in the early and middle periods

10.2.1 Malálas (c. 491–c. 578): generics

The chronicle by the Syrian Ioánnes Malálas, covering the 'period' from the creation to the reign of Ioustinianós, is the earliest surviving example of the genre, and graphically illustrates the impact on the typical Byzantine's interpretation of the past of the newly emerging conception of the Roman empire as a reflection on earth of the heavenly harmony embodied by Christ.

Unfortunately, only one surviving Greek manuscript covers the whole period of the original composition, and this is in part an abbreviation, presenting major textual difficulties, including a number of serious lacunas. The standard, but flawed text is still that of Dindorf (1831); Thurn's new edition, promised for the series *Corpus Fontium Historiae Byzantinae*, was still in preparation at the time of writing. See also Helms (1971–2), Jeffreys, Jeffreys and Scott (1986), and Jeffreys, Croke and Scott (1990) (especially ch. 8 on language, with contributions by A. James, M. Jeffreys, and E. and M. Jeffreys).

It is immediately clear from a comparison with contemporary papyri that, though Malálas's Greek is much closer to the spoken language than that of his contemporary Prokópios, it is still very much a written style. In particular, he employs technical terminology and bureaucratic clichés incessantly, and, in a period of transition from Latin to Greek governmental terminology, still uses the established Latin loanwords alongside their Greek replacements. In view of his 'administrative' perspective on history, it is now widely believed that he was employed in the middle-to-upper echelons of the imperial civil service in Antioch before moving to Constantinople, perhaps after the Persian sack of the Syrian capital in 540.

This 'basic' administrative style is characterized syntactically by familar markers such as parataxis and coordination in place of subordination; the use of ἵνα ['ina]-clauses alongside infinitives to complement control verbs, with the latter sometimes strengthened by ὥστε ['oste] 'so that', or pleonastic τοῦ [tu] (4.6.2–3, 6.5.1); confusion between final and consecutive clauses; the functional merger of perfect and aorist, involving many hybrid formations, and the use of 'be' + aorist participle to convey the sense of the 'true' perfect/pluperfect (cf. 6.5.2); and the virtual abandonment of the optative.

Particularly important, however, is the evidence for a shift in the use of inflected participles in middle-to-low registers of written Greek at this time. Malálas's sentences typically consist of a nucleus containing a single finite verb, surrounded by a set of loosely attached participial adjuncts: a standard pattern is 'having-W-ed, having-X-ed s/he-Yed, having-Z-ed', where the participles, typically nominative, may be strictly subject-orientated or contain subjects of their own, thus functioning as nominative absolutes. In the latter type, a genitive is sometimes substituted in the classical way, but this construction too is often extended to cases where agreement is possible. We seem therefore to have reached a situation in which, in the absence of regular agreement (other than with subjects), adjunct participles are syntactically dissociated from the main clause, with (modern) nominatives and (learned) genitives in free variation (cf. Weierholt (1963: 69–78)).

This usage is a characteristic hallmark not only of Malálas but of the chronographic style in general, and similar phenomena recur, for example, in the work of the well-educated Theophánes (see 10.2.2). We may therefore take it to be a mark not of ignorance but of the note-like style of administration, deemed appropriate also for the listing of events in chronography, in which case usage apparently reflected the more restricted participial syntax associated with the gradual breakdown of long-distance agreement in spoken Greek (6.5.3).

In nominal syntax, the dative is still routinely and correctly used in both grammatical and adverbial functions. There is, however, a general advance of the accusative against both the dative and the genitive as the primary prepositional case (cf. 6.5.4), and locative/allative 'confusion' between ἐν [en] + dative and εἰς [is] + accusative is common. Already familiar from antiquity, this derives from a natural indeterminacy in the interpretation of prepositional phrases with verbs expressing spatial transition, which may be seen as denoting either the location reached after movement ('come to be at', cf. *arrive at*) or the goal of the movement itself ('come to'). The dual use of the locative and allative prepositions in late antique and early medieval Greek follows directly, though εἰς [is] finally ousted its rival because of the independent decline of the dative.

We also find the legal(istic) expression ὁ αὐτός [o afˈtos], and its equivalent

ὁ ἴδιος [o 'iðios], lit. 'the same', endlessly repeated in discourse deictic function
(= 'the aforementioned'). This and other formulaic clichés reflect the formal pedantry characteristic of official and legal documents throughout history. Other markers
of the contemporary written Koine in its more basic form include: the preponder-
ance of strong aorists over their popular rivals (cf. 4.9, 5.8), and the use of regular
'perfect' active forms in place of irregular aorist actives, e.g. ἔγνωκα ['eɣnoka] for
ἔγνων ['eɣnon] 'I got to know', and strong aorist middles, earlier replaced by aorist passive formations in more popular styles, e.g. γέγονα ['jeɣona] for ἐγενόμην
[eje'nomin] 'I became'.

Malálas also makes regular use of the simple, classical forms of conditional and
temporal conjunctions rather than their popular counterparts. In antiquity the clitic
particle ἄν [an] '-ever', used to supplement the subjunctive in timeless and future-
referring conditional and temporal clauses (e.g. *if (ever)/when(ever) s/he comes*),
became formally attached to the preceding conjunction: cf. ἐ-άν [eáːn] < εἰ ἄν [eː
an] 'if ever'; ὅτ-αν [hótan] < ὅτε ἄν [hóte an] 'whenever', etc. In Hellenistic times,
however, the subjunctive was often replaced by the present indicative, with the
generic sense transferred to the 'compound' conjunction alone, and we soon start
to find imperfects used to denote indefiniteness in the past in a parallel way (replacing the classical optative): cf. ὅταν . . . ἐθεώρουν ['otan . . . etʰe'orun] 'whenever . . .
they-saw', Mark 3.11. Eventually a generic sense came to be seen as a matter of
purely contextual interpretation, with the imperfective aspect of the present or
imperfect indicative taken to indicate either repetition/indefiniteness or progressive-
ness/duration. At this point the compound conjunctions began to be used interchangeably with the simple forms, and with all tenses, finally superseding their
rivals in the spoken language because of their greater phonological 'bulk'.

In the case of free relative clauses, however, Malálas favours the popular Koine
construction of his time, in which the conjunction ἐάν [e'an] 'if' had gradually
begun to replace the increasingly anomalous free-standing use of generic ἄν [an] to
give ὃς ἐάν [os e'an] 'whoever'. This curious development depends not only on
confusion of ἐάν/ἄν [e'an/an] 'if', with generic ἄν [an], but also on conflation of
the functionally equivalent *if anyone knows*, and *whoever knows*, involving substitution of the relative pronoun into the conditional structure (in its usual initial
position). In this combination the conjunction was quickly reinterpreted as an indefiniteness marker.

The overall impression created by Malálas's style is one of simplicity, reflecting a desire for the straightforward communication of information in the written
language of everyday business as it had evolved under the influence of spoken
Greek. The following passage, which deals with the prelude to the Nika riot, provides a typical example of Malálas's use of the language, which, it is important to
re-emphasize, is in no sense 'vulgar', but closely reflects contemporary norms of
practical writing:

(1) Ἐν αὐτῷ δὲ τῷ χρόνῳ τῆς δεκάτης ἰνδικτιῶνος συνέβη ὑπό τινων ἀλαστόρων
δαιμόνων πρόφασιν γενέσθαι ταραχῆς ἐν Βυζαντίῳ, Εὐδαίμονος ἐπάρχου
πόλεως ὄντος καὶ ἔχοντος ἀτάκτους ἐν φρουρᾷ ἐξ ἀμφοτέρων τῶν μερῶν,

καὶ ἐξετάσαντος διάφορα πρόσωπα εὗρεν ἐξ αὐτῶν ὀνόματα ἑπτὰ αἰτίους
φόνων, καὶ ψηφισάμενος τῶν μὲν τεσσάρων καρατόμησιν, τῶν δὲ τριῶν
ἀνασκολοπισμόν. καὶ περιβωμισθέντων αὐτῶν ἀνὰ πᾶσαν τὴν πόλιν καὶ
περασάντων αὐτῶν, καὶ τῶν μὲν κρεμασθέντων, ἐξέπεσαν δύο τῶν ξύλων
ῥαγέντων, ἑνὸς μὲν Βενέτου, καὶ ἑτέρου Πρασίνου. καὶ ἑωρακὼς ὁ περιεστὼς
λαὸς τὸ συμβὰν εὐφήμησαν τὸν βασιλέα. ἀκηκοότες δὲ οἱ πλησίον τοῦ
ἁγίου Κόνωνος μοναχοὶ καὶ ἐξελθόντες, εὗρον ἐκ τῶν κρεμασθέντων δύο
ζῶντας κειμένους εἰς τὸ ἔδαφος. καὶ καταγαγόντες αὐτοὺς πλησίον θαλάσσης
καὶ ἐμβαλόντες ἐν πλοίῳ, ἔπεμψαν αὐτοὺς ἐν τῷ ἁγίῳ Λαυρεντίῳ ἐν ἀσύλοις
τόποις.   *Chronographía* XVIII, p. 473 of Dindorf's edition

[en af'to ðe to 'xrono tiz   ðe'katis indikti'onos syn'evi   y'po tinon
In this   and the year   of-the tenth   indiction   it-happened by   some

ala'storon ðe'monon 'profasin je'nesθe tara'çis em vyzan'dio, ev'ðemonos
avenging   demons (an) excuse   to-occur of-rioting in   Byzantium, Eudaímon(gen.)

e'parxu 'poleos 'ondos   ke 'exondos a'taktus em fru'ra eks amfo'teron
eparch   of-city   being(gen.) and having(gen.) criminals in   prison from both

dom me'ron, ke ekse'tasandos   'ðjafora 'prosopa 'evren eks af'ton
the   factions, and having-examined(gen.) various   people   he-found from them

o'nomata ep'ta e'tius 'fonon,   ke psifi'samenos   tom men
names   seven guilty of-murders, and having-decreed(nom.) of-the on-the-one-hand

de'saron kara'tomisin, ton   ðe   tri'on anaskolopiz'mon. ke
four   beheading,   of-the on-the-other-hand three   impaling.   And

perivomi'sθendon   a'ton a'na   'pasan dim 'bolin ke pera'sandon
having-been-led-around(gen.) them   through all   the   city   and having-crossed(gen.)

a'ton, ke tom-men grema'sθendon, eks'epesan 'ðyo   toŋ 'gzylon
them,   and some(gen.) having-been-hanged, fell-from   two(nom.) the   timbers

ra'jendon,   e'nos   men   ve'netu, k e'teru   pra'sinu. k   eora'kos
having-broken, one(gen.) on-the-one-hand Blue,   and other(gen.) Green.   And seeing

o peri'stos   la'os to sym'van e'fimisan   tom basi'lea. akiko'otes
the standing-around crowd the event   they-acclaimed the   emperor.   Having-heard(nom.)

ðe y pli'sion tu a'jiu 'kononos mona'çy ke eksel'θondes,   'evron
and the near   the St   Kónon   monks   and having-come-out(nom.), they-found

ek toŋ grema'sθendon 'ðyo 'zondas ki'menus is to 'eðafos.   ke
from the hanged   two   living   lying   on the ground(acc.). And

kataγa'γondes a'tus pli'sion θa'lasis ke emva'londes em 'blyo, 'epempsan
having-taken-down them beside   sea   and having-put-on   on boat,   they-sent

a'tus en do a'jio lavren'dio   en a'sylys   'topys.]
them in the St   Lauréntios(dat.) in   inviolable places(dat.).

'And in this year of the tenth indiction [*AD 531–2*] there happened to occur through
the agency of certain avenging demons a pretext for a riot in Byzantium. Eudaímon was
city prefect [*governor*] and holding criminals from both factions in custody. Having
examined various people, he found seven individuals from among them to be guilty of

murder, sentencing four of them to be beheaded and three to be impaled. After they had been paraded through the whole city and crossed over [*the Golden Horn*], and some had been hanged, two fell from the wooden scaffold as it broke, one a Blue, the other a Green. The people standing around saw the occurrence and acclaimed the emperor. But the monks near St Kónon's, hearing this and coming out, found two of those who had been hanged still alive lying on the ground. And bringing them down to the sea shore and putting them on a boat they sent them to St Lauréntios's to places of sanctuary.'

Dating at this time was by 'indictions', i.e. fifteen-year cycles originally introduced for taxation purposes, and Malálas retains the Latin term, even though shortly afterwards he uses the Greek ἔπαρχος ['eparxos] in place of the Latin *praefectus*. We may also note here the demonstrative use of αὐτός [af'tos] 'this', and χρόνος ['xronos] used in its modern sense of 'year' rather than 'time'.

The most striking feature, however, is Malálas's participial syntax. Eudaímon, for example, having initially served as the subject of a series of genitive absolute constructions, suddenly becomes the subject of a finite verb (εὗρεν ['evren]), whereupon the last participle (ψηφισάμενος [psifi'samenos]), which we might have expected to be a finite verb, appears in the nominative. We should also note the almost complete absence of the discourse particles and connectives so characteristic of the ancient language, and the regularity with which object and other pronouns are used in contexts where zero-anaphora would have been more usual in earlier periods.

10.2.2 Theophánes the Confessor (c. 760–818)

Theophánes was born during the Iconoclastic period into a wealthy metropolitan family with iconophile sentiments. After he was orphaned, the arch-iconoclast emperor Konstantínos V oversaw his education and upbringing, and he was briefly married, despite his inclination towards the cenobitic life, in order to circumvent the government's hostility to monasticism. When iconoclasm lost momentum with the death of Léon IV, he founded a monastery on the Asian shore of the Sea of Marmara, where he lived until 815 or 816. His refusal to sanction the destruction of images at the time of the revival of iconoclasm under Léon V led to his exile on Samothrace, where he died in 818. There is an engaging *Life* by the patriarch Methódios (died 847; see Spiridinov (1913)).

His chronicle begins with the accession of Diocletian (284) and ends with that of Léon V (813). The standard edition is that of de Boor (1883, 1963); see also Hunger (1978: I, 334–43), Turtledove (1982).

Writing now for a smaller, and well-educated audience, Theophánes reintroduces a range of themes and a level of detail not seen since the work of writers such as Eusebius in the third/fourth century, drawing also on techniques from ancient biography in his portrayal of leading characters. The result is something of a blend between history, biography, and chronography, and this important work marks the beginnings of the approximation of the formerly more 'popular' language of chronography with the more 'learned' language traditionally associated with the other two genres. Nonetheless, Theophánes's Greek still reflects many of the stylistic traits of the genre, a confirmation, in view of the author's educational background and the changing character of the audience, that he consciously employed an established set of chronographical conventions.

The following extract deals with the emperor Herákleios's triumphal return from his Persian campaigns:

(2) Τούτῳ τῷ ἔτει εἰρήνης γενομένης μεταξὺ Περσῶν καὶ Ῥωμαίων, ἀπέστειλεν
ὁ βασιλεὺς Θεόδωρον, τὸν ἑαυτοῦ ἀδελφόν, μετὰ γραμμάτων καὶ ἀνθρώπων
Σιρόου, τοῦ βασιλέως Περσῶν, ὅπως τοὺς ἐν Ἐδέσῃ καὶ Παλεστίνῃ καὶ
Ἱεροσολύμοις καὶ ταῖς λοιπαῖς πόλεσι τῶν Ῥωμαίων Πέρσας μετὰ εἰρήνης
ἀποστρέψωσιν ἐν Περσίδι, καὶ ἀβλαβῶς παρέλθωσι τὴν τῶν Ῥωμαίων
γῆν. ὁ δὲ βασιλεὺς ἐν ἓξ ἔτεσι καταπολεμήσας τὴν Περσίδα, τῷ ζ′ ἔτει
εἰρηνεύσας μετὰ χαρᾶς μεγάλης ἐπὶ Κωνσταντινούπολιν ὑπέστρεψε μυστικήν
τινα θεωρίαν ἐν τούτῳ πληρώσας. ἐν γὰρ ἓξ ἡμέραις πᾶσαν τὴν κτίσιν
δημιουργήσας ὁ θεὸς τὴν ἑβδόμην ἀναπαύσεως ἡμέραν ἐκάλεσεν· οὕτω καὶ
αὐτὸς ἐν τοῖς ἓξ χρόνοις πολλοὺς πόνους διανύσας τῷ ἑβδόμῳ ἔτει μετ'
εἰρήνης καὶ χαρᾶς ἐν τῇ πόλει ὑποστρέψας ἀνεπαύσατο.

   Khronographía AM 6119 (AD 627/8), pp. 327–8 of de Boor's edition

['tuto to 'eti i'rinis jeno'menis meta'ksy per'son ke ro'meon, ap'estilen
(In) this   the year, peace   coming-about between   Persians and Romans,   sent

o vasi'lefs   θe'oðoron,   ton eaf'tu   aðel'fon, me'ta ɣra'maton kj
the emperor(nom.) Theódoros(acc.), the of-himself brother,   with   letters   and

an'θropon si'rou,   tu vasi'leos per'son,   'opos tus   en e'ðesi ke pale'stini
men   of-Siróes, the king   of-Persians, so-that the(acc.) in Edessa and Palestine

ke jeroso'lymys ke tes ly'pes 'polesi ton   ro'meon 'persas   me'ta i'rinis
and Jerusalem   and the other   cities   of-the Romans Persians(acc.) with   peace

apo'strepsosin   em ber'siði,   kj avla'vos   par'elθosi   tin
they-may-return(subj.) in   Persia(dat.), and without-harm they-may-pass-through(subj.) the

don ro'meon jin. o   ðe vasi'lefs en eks 'etesi katapole'misas   tim
of-the Romans   land. The and emperor   in six   years   having-warred-down the

ber'siða, to ev'ðomo 'eti iri'nefsas   me'ta xa'ras me'ɣalis e'pi
Persia, (in) the seventh   year having-brought-to-peace with   joy   great   to

konstandi'nupolin y'pestrepse mysti'kin dina θeo'rian   pli'rosas.   eŋ ɣar
Constantinople   returned   mystic   some contemplation having-fulfilled. In   for

eks i'meres 'pasan diŋ 'ktisin ðimjur'jisas o   θe'os tin ev'ðomin ana'pafseos
six days   all   the creation having-made the God, the seventh   of-rest

i'meran e'kalesen; 'uto ke af'tos en dys eks 'xronys po'lus 'ponus
day   he-called; thus also himself in the six   years   many   labours

dja'nysas   to ev'ðomo 'eti met i'rinis ke xa'ras en di 'poli
having-completed (in) the seventh   year with peace   and joy   in the city

ypo'strepsas ane'pafsato.]
having-returned he-rested.

'In this year, with the advent of peace between the Persians and the Romans, the emperor sent his own brother Theódoros with letters and men of Siróes the Persian king, so that they might send home to Persia in peace the Persians in Edessa, Palestine, Jerusalem and the other cities of the Romans, and these might cross the land of the Romans unharmed. The emperor, having crushed Persia by war in six years, enforced a peace in the seventh and returned to Constantinople, performing a mystical celebration in this year. For God, having made all creation in six days, called the seventh day that of rest; so he too, having completed many labours in six years, rested, having returned to the city with peace and joy in the seventh.'

As expected, there are a number of more learned features of vocabulary and syntax here, partly deriving from the sources (which included non-excerpted versions of historical texts), partly reflecting Theophánes's education and that of his readership. The accusative and infinitive construction is used quite freely, for example, while verb-final order is not unusual, and even that literary favourite hyperbaton, typically involving the insertion of a verb in penultimate position between the component parts of its direct object, is occasionally encountered. In the passage above, the verbal and nominal morphology is also consistently 'classical'.

But though the concord of participial adjuncts in (2) conforms to the classical rules, Theophánes does sometimes employ the nominative absolute construction (e.g. κλιθὲν τὸ δένδρον προσεκύνησεν αὐτῷ [kli'θen to 'ðendron prose'kynisen a'to], lit. 'having-been-bent the tree (nom.), he worshipped it (dat.)', AM 5854, de Boor (1963: 49)), and the generic convention of accumulating subject-oriented participles around a single indicative verb is still very much in evidence in the passage above. We also have such non-classical usages as that of ἐν [en] + dative to mark both time 'during which' (instead of the bare genitive) and the 'goal' of a movement (in place of an allative preposition + accusative).

In general, then, Theophánes's chronicle still reflects many traditional chronographic characteristics, but its language is already moving in a more learned direction as the medieval Koine begins to assume its role as a written standard for the educated classes.

10.3 Hagiography and exegetical works

10.3.1 Ioánnes Móskhos (c. 550–619)

Móskhos was a monk in the monastery of St Theodósios near Jerusalem, but travelled with Sophrónios, later to become patriarch of Jerusalem, around Egypt, the middle East, and Cyprus, finally coming to Rome in 614, where he died. His *Spiritual Meadow*, a collection of engaging moral tales about the exploits of monks, hermits, and ordinary folk in the eastern Mediterranean, provides a vivid picture of the social conditions of the time. The modern critical edition being prepared by P. Pattenden is still eagerly awaited. In the meantime the text has to be read in Migne's *Patrologia Graeca* (87, part 3). See also Hesseling (1931), Baynes (1955), Beck (1959: 412–3).

The continued influence of the low-level literary tradition deriving from the Septuagint and New Testament is always apparent, but this work represents an important source for the development of the Greek language in the early Byzantine period because of the inclusion of passages of direct speech, which often display a more contemporary colloquial style. The following extract tells what happens after the author and Sophrónios, at a loose end in Alexandria, have made their way to a colonnade in the centre of the city and found a group of blind men:

(3) ἐλάλουν δὲ οἱ τυφλοὶ πρὸς ἀλλήλους καὶ λέγει ὁ εἷς τῷ ἄλλῳ· "Ὄντως σοι, πῶς γέγονας τυφλός;' καὶ ἀπεκρίθη λέγων· 'Ναύτης ἤμην νεώτερος· καὶ ἀπὸ Ἀφρικῆς ἐπλέομεν, καὶ ἐν τῷ πελάγει ὀφθαλμιάσας καὶ μὴ ἔχων πῶς περιοδευθῶ, τὰ λευκώματα ἔσχον ἐν τοῖς ὀφθαλμοῖς μου καὶ ἐτυφλώθην.' λέγει καὶ τῷ ἄλλῳ 'σὺ πῶς γέγονας τυφλός;' ἀπεκρίθη κἀκεῖνος 'ὑαλοψὸς ἤμην τὴν τέχνην καὶ ἐκ τοῦ πυρὸς ἐπίχυσιν ἔσχον οἱ δύο ὀφθαλμοὶ καὶ ἐτυφλώθην.' λέγουσιν ἄλλῳ κἀκεῖνοι 'σὺ πῶς γέγονας τυφλός;' ὁ δὲ ἀπεκρίθη 'ὄντως ἐγὼ λέγω ὑμῖν· ὅταν ἤμην νεώτερος, ἐμίσησα τὸν κάματον πάνυ· γέγονα δὲ καὶ ἄσωτος. οὐκ ἔχων οὖν πόθεν φάγω λοιπὸν ἔκλεπτον. ἐν μίᾳ οὖν τῶν ἡμερῶν μετὰ τὸ ποιῆσαί με πολλὰ κακὰ ἱστάμην οὖν ἐπὶ τὴν ἀγορὰν καὶ θεωρῶ νεκρὸν ἐξοδιζόμενον καλῶς φοροῦντα. ἀκολουθῶ οὖν ὀπίσω τοῦ ἐξοδίου ἵνα θεωρήσω ποῦ μέλλουσιν αὐτὸν θάπτειν... ἐγὼ δὲ... εἰσῆλθον εἰς τὸ μνημεῖον καὶ ἀπέδυσα αὐτὸν εἴτι ἐφόρει... καὶ ὡς ἀπέδυον αὐτὸν τὸ ὀθόνιον..., ἀνακάθηται ὁ νεκρὸς ἔμπροσθέν μου καὶ ἐκτείνας τὰς δύο χεῖρας αὐτοῦ ἐπ' ἐμὲ τοῖς δακτύλοις αὐτοῦ ἔξεσέν μου τὴν ὄψιν καὶ ἐξέβαλεν τοὺς δύο μου ὀφθαλμούς...'

Leimón 77, Migne p. 2930

[e'lalun   ð y ty'fly   pros a'lilus ke 'leji o is to   'alo, ''ondos
Were-talking and the blind(pl.) to   each-other and says the one to-the other, 'Truly

sy,   pos 'jeɣonas ty'flos?' kj ape'kriθi 'leɣon, ''naftis 'imin 'njoteros;
for-you, how you-became blind?'   And he-replied saying,   'Sailor I-was younger;

kj a'po afri'kis e'pleomen,   kj en do pe'laji ofθalm'jasas   ke mi
and off Africa we-were-sailing, and in the sea   having-got-eye-infection and not

'exon pos perjoðe'fθo, ta lef'komata 'esxon en dys ofθal'myz mu   kj
having how I-may-be cured, the cataracts   I-got in the eyes   of-me and

ety'floθin.' 'leji   ke to   'alo, 'sy pos jeɣonas   ty'flos?' ape'kriθi
I-was-blinded.' He-says and to-the other, 'You how you-became blind?'   Answered

ka'kinos   'leɣon, 'yalo'psos 'imin tin 'dexnin kj ek   tu py'ros e'piçysin
and-that(one) saying, 'Glass-maker I-was the trade and out-of the fire   splash

'esxon y 'ðyo ofθal'my kj ety'floθin.' 'leɣusin 'alo   ka'kini, 'sy pos
got   the two eyes   and I-was-blinded.' They-say to-other and-these, 'You how

'jeɣonas ty'flos?' o ðj ape'kriθi, ''ondos e'ɣo 'leɣo y'min; 'otan 'imin
you-became blind?' He and replied,   'Truly I   I-say to-you; when I-was

'njoteros, e'misisa toŋ 'gamaton 'pany; 'jeɣona ðe kj 'asotos.   uk
younger, I-hated the work   completely; I-became and even irredeemable. Not

'exon un 'poθen 'fa(ɣ)o, ly'pon 'eklepton. em 'mia un ton ime'ron
having then from-where I-may-eat, well I-used-to-steal. on one then of-the days

me'ta to py'ise me po'la ka'ka i'stamin un e'pi tin aɣo'ran ke
after the doing me many wicked (things) I-was-standing then at the market and

θeo'ro ne'kron eksodi'zomenon ka'los for'unda. akolu'θo un o'piso tu
I-see corpse being-taken for-burial finely wearing. I-follow then behind the

ekso'ðiu 'ina θeo'riso pu 'melusin a'ton 'θaptin . . . e'ɣo ðe . . . is'ilθon is
procession that I-may-see where they-will him bury . . . I and . . . entered into

to mni'mion kj ap'eðys a'ton 'iti e'fori . . . kj os a'peðyon
the tomb and I-stripped him whatever he-was wearing . . . And as I-was-stripping

a'ton t o'θonjon . . . , ana'kaθite o ne'kros 'embro'sθem mu kj
him the linen . . . , sits-up the corpse in-front of-me and

ek'tinas taz 'ðyo 'çiras a'tu ep e'me tyz ðak'tylys a'tu 'ekse'sem
stretching-out the two hands of-it against me with-the fingers of-it it-scratched

mu tin 'opsin kj eks'evalen tuz 'ðyo mu ofθal'mus . . .']
of-me the face and threw-out the two of-me eyes.'

'The blind men were talking among themselves and one said to another, "On your word, how did you go blind?" And he replied, "I was a sailor as a young man, and we were sailing off Africa when I caught an eye infection at sea, and having no means of finding a cure, I got cataracts in my eyes and went blind." He then asked the other, "How did you go blind?" And he replied, "I was a glassmaker by trade, and both my eyes got a splash from the fire and I was blinded." And then they asked the third, "How did you go blind?" And he replied, "I will tell you honestly. When I was a young man, I hated work completely; I actually became irredeemable. And since I had no way to get food – well, I used to steal. So, one day, after I had done many wicked things, I was standing by the market when I saw a body being taken for burial, very well-dressed. I then followed behind the funeral procession to see where they were going to bury him . . . Then I . . . went into the tomb and stripped him of everything he was wearing . . . And as I was taking off his underwear . . . , the corpse sat up in front of me and, reaching out for me with its two hands, it scratched my face with its fingers and pulled out my two eyes . . ."'

While there is nothing here which could be directly attributed to the influence of the high literary tradition, gross 'errors' of morphology and syntax, as seen in some of the personal correspondence from Egypt from the same period, are also absent. This is the simple narrative style of educated speakers of the period, which retained a number of features of the standard Koine that were almost certainly in decline in the popular speech of Móskhos's own time. Note, for example:

(4) (a) The normal use of the dative in its core grammatical (indirect object) and adverbial (instrumental) functions, even in the passages of dialogue.

    (b) The still essentially classical use of inflected participles in certain functions (e.g. circumstantial and temporal adjuncts, complements to verbs of perception), and the use of the articular infinitive after μετά [me'ta] as a temporal clause.

Other features, however, reflect the later evolution of the language of the popular Christian tradition under the impact of spoken Greek. We may note, for example:

(5) (a) The substitution of εἰ + τις ['itis]/εἰ + τι ['iti], lit. 'if anyone',/'if anything', for the earlier indefinite/generic relatives ὅστις ['ostis] 'whoever', and ὅσος ['osos] 'everyone who' (cf. again the functional parallelism of indefinite/ generic and conditional expressions in *whoever does X; if anyone does X*).

   (b) The absence of OV order, and the associated positioning of clitic pronouns in second position in their clauses, immediately after their governing verbs, which stand initially to provide the standard head-clitic order seen also in NPs with dependent possessive pronouns; the 'displacement' of such possessives into the sentential slot (cf. ἔξεσέν μου τὴν ὄψιν ['ekse'sem mu tin 'opsin] 'he-scratched of-me the face') again illustrates the basis for the replacement of the dative with the genitive, first in possessive-like indirect object functions, and then generally. But unlike in more vernacular papyri, this development has not yet affected the educated style used here.

   (c) The use of the infinitival future periphrasis with μέλλω ['melo] 'be about to'. Elsewhere Móskhos also uses the more popular periphrasis with ἔχω ['exo], and occasionally a 'progressive' periphrasis with the future of 'be' + present participle. But the regular expression of futurity, particularly in overtly future contexts, is the present indicative, already a marked possibility in classical Greek, and now strongly supported by the merger of the present indicative with the present subjunctive in the spoken language; aorist subjunctives are also widely used as futures, following the parallel merger of this paradigm with that of the future indicative (distinctive forms of which are now quite rare), cf. 11.8.3.

   (d) Middle forms of the verb 'be' (cf. ἤμην ['imin]), as often in papyri and earlier Christian texts (cf. 5.11.1, 11.8.5 (a)); note also the use of ὅταν ['otan] as a simple ('when') rather than a generic ('whenever') conjunction (10.2.1).

   (e) The avoidance of the aorist middle, cf. 'perfect' γέγονα ['jeɣona] for ἐγενόμην [eje'nomin] 'I became', aorist 'passive' ἀπεκρίθην [ape'kriθin] for ἀπεκρινάμην [apekri'namin] 'I replied'; even classical Greek had a number of 'deponent' aorist passives, but the beginning of widespread replacement goes back to Hellenistic and Roman imperial times, an aorist passive form being generally favoured, although, following the functional merger of aorist and perfect, an existing perfect active sometimes predominated.

10.3.2 St Germanós (c. 640–733)

Germanós's father was a relative of the emperor Herákleios, but having become implicated in the assassination of Herákleios's successor Kónstas, he was put to death by the latter's son, Konstantínos IV. Though allowed to keep his inheritance, Germanós was castrated because of his disastrous family connections, and then sought a career in the Church, eventually becoming patriarch of Constantinople in

715 just before the first iconoclastic crisis. When Léon III ordered the destruction of images in 725, Germanós refused, and in 730 he was deposed in favour of the iconoclast Anastásios.

He is best known for his commentary on the Orthodox liturgy (*Ecclesiastical history and mystical contemplation*), a radical and highly influential synthesis of Alexandrian and Antiochene interpretations belonging to the tradition of exegetical writing. It was aimed at the reading public at large, and composed in a traditional, but accessible, middle style, somewhere between the popular-biblical and more learned ecclesiastical registers (cf. 8.5.2, 8.5.6).

The standard text is that of Borgia (1912); see also Meyendorff (1984) for further background, bibliography, and translation. The following extract, in which the absence of the contemporary colloquial features seen in Móskhos is immediately apparent, explains the practice of praying towards the east:

(6) Τὸ κατὰ ἀνατολὰς εὔχεσθαι παραδεδομένον ἐστίν, ὡς καὶ τὰ λοιπὰ τῶν
ἁγίων ἀποστόλων· ἐστὶν οὕτως διὰ <τὸ> τὸν ἥλιον τὸν νοητὸν τῆς
δικαιοσύνης Χριστὸν τὸν Θεὸν ἡμῶν ἐπὶ γῆς φανῆναι ἐπὶ τοῖς μέρεσι τῆς
ἀνατολῆς τοῦ αἰσθητοῦ ἡλίου, κατὰ τὸν προφήτην τὸν λέγοντα, 'ἀνατολὴ
ὄνομα αὐτῷ', καὶ πάλιν, 'προσκυνήσατε τῷ Κυρίῳ πᾶσα ἡ γῆ, τῷ
ἐπιβεβηκότι ἐπὶ τὸν οὐρανὸν τοῦ οὐρανοῦ κατὰ ἀνατολάς', καὶ,
'προσκυνήσωμεν εἰς τόπον οὗ ἔστησαν οἱ πόδες αὐτοῦ', καὶ πάλιν, 'στήσονται
οἱ πόδες τοῦ Κυρίου ἐπὶ τὸ ὄρος τῶν ἐλαιῶν κατὰ ἀνατολήν.' ταῦτα φασὶν
οἱ προφῆται καὶ διὰ τὸ καραδοκεῖν ἡμᾶς πάλιν τὸν ἐν ἐδὲμ παράδεισον
τὸν κατὰ ἀνατολὴν ἀπολαμβάνειν καὶ, ὡς συνεχομένους, τὴν ἀνατολὴν τῆς
φωτοφανείας τῆς δευτέρας τοῦ Χριστοῦ καὶ τοῦ Θεοῦ ἡμῶν παρουσίας.

Ecclesiastical History and Mystical Contemplation 11

[to kat anato'las 'efçesθe paraðeðo'menon es'tin, os ke ta ly'pa
The towards east/risings to-pray handed-down is, as also the other(things)

ton a'jion apo'stolon; e'stin 'utos ðja to ton 'iljon ton noi'ton tiz
of-the holy apostles; it-is thus because-of the the sun the intelligible of-the

ðikeo'synis xris'ton ton θe'on i'mon e'pi jis fa'nine e'pi tyz 'meresi
justice Christ the God of-us on earth to-have-appeared at the places

tis anato'lis tu esθi'tu i'liu, ka'ta tom bro'fitin ton 'leɣonda,
of-the east/rising of-the perceptible sun, according-to the prophet the(one) saying,

'anato'li 'onom a'to,' ke 'palin, 'prosky'nisate to ky'rio 'pasa i ji,
'East/rising name to-him,' and again, 'worship(imp.) the Lord all the land,

to epivevi'koti e'pi ton ura'non t ura'nu kat anato'las,' ke,
the(one) having arrived to the heaven of-the heaven towards east/risings,' and,

'prosky'nisomen is 'topon u 'estisan y 'poðes a'tu,' ke 'palin, ''stisonde
'Let-us-worship in place where stood the feet of-him,' and again, 'Will-stand

y 'poðes tu ky'riu e'pi t 'oros ton ele'on kat anato'lin.'
the feet of-the Lord on the mountain of-the olives towards east/rising.'

'tafta fa'sin y pro'fite ke dja to karado'kin i'mas 'palin ton en
These(things) say the prophets also because-of the to-keenly-expect us again the in

e'dem par'aðison toŋ gat   anato'lin apolam'vanin ke, os synexo'menus, tin
Eden   paradise   the towards east/rising to-recover   and, as linked-together,   the

anato'lin tis   fotofa'nias tiz   ðef'teras tu   xris'tu ke tu   θe'u i'mon
east/rising of-the illumination of-the second   of-the Christ   and of-the God of-us

paru'sias.]
presence.

'Praying towards the east is handed down, like all the other practices of the holy
apostles. It is so because the intelligible sun of righteousness, Christ our God, appeared
on earth in the places where the perceptible sun rises, according to the prophet who
says, "East is his name," and again, "Worship the Lord all the earth, who came to
the heaven of heaven in the east," and, "Let us worship in the place where his feet
stood," and again, "The feet of the Lord shall stand upon the mount of olives in the
east." The prophets also say these things because we wait eagerly to receive again
the paradise in Eden that is in the east and, since they are bound together, the rising of
the dawn of the second coming of our Christ and God.'

Evidently a generally biblical style is the target, with εἰς [is] and ἐπί [e'pi] + accusative used locatively, genitive pronouns employed instead of the possessive adjectives of classical Greek, προσκυνῶ [prosky'no] 'I worship' used with the dative
rather than the classical accusative, etc. But a more learned background involving the influence of the elaborated Koine of ecclesiastical officialdom and theological debate is revealed in the continued use of verb-final orders, and the extended
hyperbaton and complex complementation of nominalized infinitivals used after
prepositions.

10.4   Paraenetic literature of the middle period

10.4.1   *Konstantínos VII Porphyrogénnetos (905–59)*

Konstantínos VII Porphyrogénnetos ('Born in the Purple') succeeded to the throne
at the age of seven, but had no power until 944 when the regent/emperor Romanós
I Lakapenós was deposed by his own sons, who resented his preference for
Konstantínos, the true heir of the Macedonian dynasty. The coup backfired, since
public opinion was strongly in favour of Konstantínos, and the perpetrators were
promptly exiled. He proved to be an effective emperor, whose reign saw the conversion of the Russian princess Olga of Kiev, and the safe defence of the northern
and eastern frontiers against the Bulgarians and Arabs.

During the regency, however, he had devoted himself to the study of the history
of Byzantine institutions, and promoted a renaissance of scholarship and creative
writing, including a continuation of Theophánes's chronicle and the compilation of
anthologies and encyclopaedias. He himself is now best known for his treatises,
composed in a straightforward style for didactic purposes, on the administration of
the empire, court ceremonial and the military districts ('themes') of the provinces
(see Reiske (1829–30), Vogt (1935–40), Jenkins and Moravcsik (1967), Pertusi

(1952), Toynbee (1973)). The prefaces to the works on administration and ceremonial contain conventional 'apologies' for the simple style employed thereafter. The following comes from chapter 1 of *De Administrando Imperio* ('on administering the empire'):

(7) 'And do not be at all surprised, my son, that I have used clear and well-worn diction and something approaching simple free-flowing prose for the presentation of my subject. For I have not endeavoured to make a display of fine writing or Atticized phraseology, swelling with the sublime and lofty, but rather I have striven to teach you the things of which I think you should not be ignorant through the medium of a routine, everyday expository style.'

This address to his son, Romanós, is composed in precisely the 'literary' style that he later avoids, and is a revealing statement of Byzantine attitudes. We must not, however, imagine that the emperor wrote the remainder in a version of the contemporary educated vernacular. Rather, he uses a range of middle styles that reflect both his privileged educational background and the heterogeneity of his source material. In his own original contributions, therefore, we have something approaching the contemporary language of scholarship, while excerpted and/or epitomized passages drawn from the imperial archives and from earlier chronicles reflect the relevant administrative and chronographic conventions.

Consider first the extract in (8), which is a good example of his more elaborated non-literary style:

(8) Ὅτι καὶ οἱ Ῥῶς διὰ σπουδῆς ἔχουσιν εἰρήνην ἔχειν μετὰ τῶν Πατζινακιτῶν. ἀγοράζουσι γὰρ ἐξ αὐτῶν βόας καὶ ἵππους καὶ πρόβατα . . . ἀλλ᾽ οὐδὲ πρὸς ὑπερορίους πολέμους ἀπέρχεσθαι δύνανται ὅλως οἱ Ῥῶς, εἰ μὴ μετὰ τῶν Πατζινακιτῶν εἰρηνεύοντες, διότι δύνανται (ἐν τῷ ἐκείνους τῶν οἰκείων ὑποχωρεῖν) αὐτοὶ ἐπερχόμενοι τὰ ἐκείνων ἀφανίζειν τε καὶ λυμαίνεσθαι. διὸ μᾶλλον ἀεὶ σπουδὴν οἱ Ῥῶς τίθενται (διά τε τὸ μὴ παραβλάπτεσθαι παρ᾽ αὐτῶν καὶ διὰ τὸ ἰσχυρὸν εἶναι τὸ τοιοῦτον ἔθνος) συμμαχίαν παρ᾽ αὐτῶν λαμβάνειν καὶ ἔχειν αὐτοὺς εἰς βοήθειαν, ὡς ἂν καὶ τῆς ἔχθρας αὐτῶν ἀπαλλάττωνται καὶ τῆς βοηθείας καταπολαύοιεν.   *DAI*, 2

['oti ke i ros   ðja-spu'ðis   'exusin   i'rinin 'eçin me'ta tom
That also the Russians zealous(lit. through zeal) are(lit. have) peace   to-keep with   the

batsinaki'ton. aɣo'razousi ɣar eks af'ton 'voas ke 'ipus ke 'provata . . . al
Petcheneks.   They-buy   for from them cattle and horses and sheep . . .   But

u'ðe   pros ipero'rius po'lemus a'perçesθe 'ðinande 'olos i ros,   i-mi
not-even for   cross-border wars   to-leave   can   at-all the Russians, unless

me'ta tom batsinaki'ton iri'nevondes, di'oti 'ðinande (en   do e'kinus
with the Petcheneks   being-at-peace, because they-are-able (during the them

ton   i'kion   ipoxo'rin) af'ti   eper'xomeni ta   e'kinon afa'nizin
from-the households to-be-away) these(men) attacking   the(things) of-them to-destroy

te ke li'menesθe. ði'o   'malon a'i   spu'ðin i   ros   'tiθende
both and to outrage.   Therefore more   always effort   the Russians put

(ðja   te   to   mi   para'vlaptesθe   par   af'ton   ke   ðja   to   isçi'ron   'ine   to

(because-of   both   the   not   to-be-harmed   by   them   and because-of the strong   to-be the

ti'uton   'eθnos)   sima'çian   par   af'ton   lam'vanin   ke   'eçin   a'tus   is   vo'iθian,

such   nation)   alliance   from them   to-take   and   to-have them   for help,

os-an   ke   tis   'exθras   a'ton   apa'latonde   ke   tiz   voi'θias

so-that   both   from-the hatred   of-them   they may-be-released(subjunc.)   and   the help

katapo'lavien.]

they-might-enjoy(opt.).

'(It is to be noted) that the Russians too are anxious to keep the peace with the Petcheneks. For they buy cattle, horses and sheep from them . . . Moreover, the Russians are altogether unable to set out for wars across their borders unless they are at peace with the Petcheneks, because (while they are away from their households) these people may attack, and destroy and vandalize their property. So the Russians make ever greater efforts (both to avoid being harmed by them and because this nation is strong) to retain their alliance with them and to have their support, so that they may both be freed from their hatred and enjoy the benefit of their help.'

This is well below the style of the introduction, but higher than that of passages which consist largely of lists of facts. Note the relatively sophisticated subordinating syntax and the presence of such learned markers as the use of ἔχω ['exo] 'have' + adverbial in the sense of 'be' + adjective, the long and complex nominalized infinitivals with accusative subjects, the use of verb-final order in subordinate clauses, and the use of ὡς ἄν [os an] as a final conjunction, followed by both subjunctive and optative in characteristically 'high' Byzantine fashion (cf. 9.3, 9.5).

To illustrate Konstantínos's most 'basic' style, we may take the following passage, which describes two of the cities of Dalmatia:

(9) Ὅτι τοῦ Ἀσπαλάθου κάστρον, ὅπερ 'παλάτιον μικρόν' ἑρμηνεύεται, ὁ βασιλεὺς Διοκλητιανός τοῦτο ἔκτισεν· εἶχεν δὲ αὐτὸ ὡς ἴδιον οἶκον, καὶ αὐλὴν οἰκοδομήσας ἔνδοθεν και παλάτια, ἐξ ὧν τὰ πλείονα κατελύθησαν. σώζεται δὲ μέχρι τοῦ νῦν ὀλίγα, ἐξ ὧν ἐστιν τὸ ἐπισκοπεῖον τοῦ κάστρου καὶ ὁ ναὸς τοῦ ἁγίου Δόμνου, ἐν ᾧ κατάκειται ὁ αὐτὸς ἅγιος Δόμνος, ὅπερ ἦν κοιτὼν τοῦ αὐτοῦ βασιλέως Διοκλητιανοῦ. Ὑποκάτω δὲ αὐτοῦ ὑπάρχουσιν εἰληματικαὶ καμάραι, αἵτινες ὑπῆρχαν φυλακαί, ἐν αἷς τοὺς παρ' αὐτοῦ βασανιζομένους ἁγίους ἐναπέκλειεν ἀπηνῶς . . .

Ὅτι τὸ κάστρον τὸ Τετραγγούριν νησίον ἐστὶν μικρὸν ἐν τῇ θαλάσσῃ, ἔχον δὲ τράχηλον ἕως τῆς γῆς στενώτατον δίκην γεφυρίου, ἐν ᾧ διέρχονται οἱ κατοικοῦντες εἰς τὸ αὐτὸ κάστρον. Τετραγγούριν δὲ καλεῖται διὰ τὸ εἶναι αὐτὸ μακρὸν δίκην ἀγγουρίου. ἐν δὲ τῷ αὐτῷ κάστρῳ ἀπόκειται ὁ ἅγιος μάρτυς Λαυρέντιος, ὁ ἀρχιδιάκων.   *DAI*, 29

['oti   tu   aspa'laθu   'kastron,   'oper   'pa'lation   mik'ron'   ermi'nevete,   o

That   of-the   Aspálathon   city,   which   'palace   small'   is-interpreted,   the

vasi'lefs   ðioklitia'nos   'tuto   'ektisen;   'içen   ðe   a'to   os   'iðion   'ikon,   ke

emperor   Diocletian   this   founded;   he-had and it   as   private   dwelling-place,   and

av'lin ikoðo'misas 'endoθen ke pa'latia, eks on   ta 'pliona
court   having-built   within   and palaces,   from which the more

kate'liθisan.   'sozete ðe 'mexri tu nin o'liɣa,   eks on   estin to
have-been-destroyed. Is-saved but until   the now few(things), from which there-is the

episko'pion tu   'kastru kj o na'os tu   a'jiu 'ðomnu, en o   ka'takite
bishop's-house of-the city   and the church of-the Saint Dóm(i)nos, in   which lies

o af'tos 'ajos 'ðomnos, 'oper in ki'ton   tu   af'tu vasi'leos ðioklitia'nu.
the same   Saint Dóm(i)nos, which was resting-place of-the same emperor   Diocletian.

ipo'kato ð a'tu i'parxusin ili'matike ka'mare, 'etines i'pirxon fila'ke,   en
Below   and this there-are   arched   vaults,   which   used-to-be prison-cells, in

es   tus par af'tu vasanizo'menus a'jius enap'eklien   api'nos . . .
which the by   him   being-tortured   saints   he-used-to-confine cruelly . . .

'oti to 'kastron to tetraŋ'gurin ni'sion es'tin mi'kron en di θal'asi, 'exon
That the city   the Tetrangoúrin island   is   small   in the sea,   having

ke 'traçilon 'eos   tiz jis ste'notaton 'ðikin jefi'riu, en o   'ðjerxonde i
also neck   as-far-as the land very-narrow like   bridge,   by which cross   the

kati'kundes is to af'to 'kastron. tetraŋ'gurin ðe ka'lite   ðja   to 'ine
inhabitants   to the same city.   Tetrangoúrin   and it-is-called because-of the to-be

af'to mak'ron 'ðikin aŋgu'riu. en ðe to af'to 'kastro a'pokite o 'ajos 'martis
it   long   like cucumber. In and the same city   lies   the holy martyr

lav'rendios, o   arçi'ðjakon.]
Lauréntios,   the archdeacon.

'(It is noted that) The city of Aspálathon [*Split*], which means "little palace", was founded by the emperor Diocletian. He had it as his private domus, building both a court and palaces inside it, most of which have been destroyed. But a few things are preserved to this day, among which are the city's bishop's residence and the church of St Domnus, which was the resting-place of the aforementioned Diocletian and in which the same St Domnus lies. Beneath are arching vaults, which used to be prison cells, in which he cruelly confined the saints who were being tortured by him . . .

(It is noted that) The city of Tetrangoúrin [*the idyllic Sveti Stefan in Montenegro*] is a small island in the sea, but with a very narrow neck reaching to the land like a bridge, over which the inhabitants cross to this city. It is called Tetrangoúrin because it is long like a cucumber [*angoúrion*]. In the same city lies the holy martyr Lauréntios, the archdeacon.'

A number of features here belong to the styles of record-keeping and/or chronography, most obviously the anaphoric use of ὁ αὐτός [o af'tos] 'the same'. Note too: the avoidance of complex subordination other than that involving relative clauses and participles, and the relatively 'loose' syntax of the latter (including elsewhere 'misused' genitive absolutes and syntactically unconnected nominatives); the use of ἐν [en] + dative to denote an instrument or, more concretely, a 'path' (an early replacement for the bare dative, common in the New Testament); the nominalized infinitives governed by prepositions, potentially with extended complementation; the comparative adjective with the definite article used as a superlative, cf. τὰ πλείονα [ta 'pliona], lit. 'the more', = 'the most'; the use of ὅσπερ ['osper], formerly 'who exactly', and ὅστις ['ostis], formerly 'whoever', as simple relatives to replace weak monosyllabic forms of the original paradigm; and last but not least, the routine use of initial ὅτι ['oti] 'that', ordinarily marking entries in a ledger or note-book, for each new item that Romanós is supposed to take account of – he inevitably turned out to be a hedonistic waster.

The widespread use of adverbs and adverbial case-forms as preposition sub-stitutes with the genitive (e.g. ὑποκάτω [ipo'kato] 'down-under', and elsewhere ἐπάνω [e'pano] 'up-on', κύκλῳ ['kiklo] 'in-circle (of)', i.e. 'around') reflects the beginnings of the disappearance of many of the classical prepositions from ordinary spoken Greek during the Middle Ages (cf. 11.7.1). In popular spoken Greek only εἰς (σε) [is (se)] 'at/on/in', ἀπό [a'po] 'from/by', για [ja] (< διά [ðja]) 'for/about', and μέ [me] (< μετά [me'ta]) 'with', eventually remained in general use, and many spatial and other functions came to be expressed by such adverbials. These retained the old genitive syntax when they governed a clitic pronoun, but were otherwise complemented by a prepositional phrase headed by one of the four 'survivors', e.g. πάνω στο (< εἰς το) βουνό ['pano sto vu'no] 'up(on) on-the mountain', etc.

With the examples (7)–(9) in mind, we can begin to appreciate the skill required to write 'appropriately' in a language that offered such a wide range of stylistic options. It is a tribute to the efficacy of the Byzantine education system that learned writers were able to compose more or less successfully, and consistently, at a number of different levels defined by different, but overlapping, parameters.

10.4.2 Kekauménos (eleventh century)

Kekauménos, like many landowners in northern Greece, belonged to a family that came originally from Armenia. The *Strategikón*, probably written in the decade after the battle of Manzikert (1071), provides guidance for his son on public and private conduct. The author's suspiciousness and deviousness provide a sad com-ment on the realities of life in an era when the empire, threatened on all fronts, was run as a military dictatorship, and people had to endure not only crippling taxation (50, 68) but the threat of being 'reported' if they dared to complain.

Since, as a provincial aristocrat, he did not receive a literary education (191), and since the work was in any case intended for distribution within his own fam-ily, much of the vocabulary and syntax of the *Strategikón* reflect contemporary usage quite directly. Δουλεύω [ðu'levo], for example, means 'serve/work (for)', not 'be a slave/subject to', and ὁμιλῶ [omi'lo] means 'speak' rather than 'associate with', while in syntax, the former final conjunction ἵνα ['ina] + subjunctive, is more widely used than hitherto to replace complement and adjunct infinitivals. The over-all impression is of an updated version of the kind of basic Koine writing seen in Móskhos. The standard edition of the sole manuscript is Wassiliewsky and Jernstedt (1896/1965); see also Moravcsik (1983: 350–2).

The following extract is fairly typical in style and content:

(10) Παραιτοῦ δὲ τὸ ὁμιλεῖν μετὰ ἀτάκτων καὶ πρόσεχε ὁπόταν μετὰ τῶν
συντρόφων σου ὁμιλεῖς ἢ μετὰ ἄλλου τινός. καὶ εἴπερ ἐμπέσῃ λόγος διὰ
τὸν βασιλέα ἢ τὴν δέσποιναν, τὸ σύνολον μηδὲ ἀποκριθῇς, ἀλλ᾽ ὑποχώρησον.
πολλοὺς γὰρ εἰς τοῦτο κινδυνεύσαντας εἶδον. λαλεῖ γὰρ ὁ ἄφρων ὡς παίζων,
εἶτα μετὰ πανουργίας καὶ στραφεὶς καταψεύσεταί σου ὡς σὺ ταῦτα εἶπες.
εἰ δὲ κἀκεῖνος ἐν ἁπλότητι ὡμίλησεν, ἄλλος τις πανοῦργος δραμὼν ἀναγγέλῃ
ταῦτα, καὶ εὐθυνθήσῃ διότι ἐκεῖσε παρευρέθης. καὶ τοῦ μὲν λέγοντος
καταφρονήσουσιν, τὴν δὲ αἰτίαν ἐπὶ σέ ἀναθήσουσι. πρόσεχε, τέκνον, τὰ
εὐκαταφρόνητά σοι δοκοῦντα· ταῦτα μεγάλων κινδύνων εἰσὶ πρόξενα.
πολλοὺς γὰρ εἶδον κινδυνεύσαντας ἐν τούτοις.   *Strategikón,* 6

[pare'tu ðe t omi'lin met a'takton   ke 'proseçe o'potan me'ta to(n)

Stop   and the to-speak with unruly(people) and beware   when   with   the

sin'drofo(n) su   omi'lis i met 'alu ti'nos. kj   'iper em'besi 'loɣos ðja

friends   of-you you-speak or with other some.   And if   crops-up talk   about

tom vasi'lea i ti(n) 'ðespinan, to 'sinolon mið   apokri'θis, al

the   emperor or the   mistress,   the altogether not-even reply(imp.),   but

ipo'xorison. po'lus ɣar is   'tuto kinði'nefsandas   'iðon.   la'li   ɣar o

withdraw.   Many   for in/by this   having-got-into-danger I-have-seen. Speaks for   the

'afron os   'pezon, 'ita me'ta panur'jias ke   stra'fis   kata'psefse'te

fool   as-if playing, then with   cunning   actually having-turned he-will-tell-lies-against

su os 'si 'tafta   'ipes. i ðe ka'kinos   en a'plotiti o'milisen, 'alos

you that you these-things said.   If and even-that(man) in simplicity spoke,   other

tis pa'nurɣos ðra'mon anaŋ'geli   'tafta,   kj efθin'θisi

some villain   having-run will-tell(subj.) these-things, and you-will-be-blamed(fut./subj.)

ði'oti e'kise pare'vreθis. ke tu men   'leɣondos

because there   you-were-found. And the on-the-one-hand speaking(person)

katafro'nisusin, tin ðe   e'tian epi 'se ana'θisusi.

they-will-despise(fut.), the on-the-other-hand blame to   you they-will-attribute(fut.).

'proseçe, 'teknon, ta   efkata'froni'ta si   ðo'kunda; 'tafta me'ɣalon

Beware,   child,   the(things) easily-dismissed to-you seeming;   these of-great

kin'ðinon isi 'proksena. po'lus ɣar 'iðon   kinði'nefsandas   en

dangers   are causing.   Many   for I-have-seen having-got-into-danger in/by

'dutis.]

these-things.

'Stop talking to ruffians, and be careful even when it is your friends you are talking
to, or anyone else. And if a conversation starts up about the emperor and our mistress,
do not reply at all and walk away, because I have seen many people fall into danger
this way. For the senseless man speaks as if in jest, then just turns round in his cunning
and pretends it was you who spoke. And even if he spoke honestly, some other villain
will run and tell, and you will be blamed because you were there. And though it is the
speaker they will despise, it is you they will pin the blame on. My son, be careful of
things which seem insignificant to you; great dangers follow from them. Many are
those I have seen fall into danger like this.'

Features of the basic written Greek of the period include: the use of both future indicatives and aorist subjunctives with a future sense; the overlap of ἐν [en] + dative and εἰς [is] + accusative in both spatial and instrumental/manner functions; the related use of once allative adverbs in a locative sense (ἐκεῖσε [e'kise] = 'there', not 'to there'); the generic use of ὁπόταν [o'potan] 'when(ever)', with a present indicative rather than a subjunctive; the use of παραιτοῦμαι [pare'tume] to mean 'stop', rather than 'avert (by entreaty)', and of διά [(ð)ja] + accusative to mean 'about', rather than 'because of'.

Note, however, that the morphology remains classically 'correct' throughout, that 'popular' future periphrases are not favoured, and that once again datives are still used routinely to mark the indirect object with no obvious genitive/accusative overlaps. Kekauménos may not have had a literary education, but he clearly wrote, and probably still spoke, a contemporary Koine that was far from 'vulgar'. For the true vernacular in this period, we have to look elsewhere (see Chapters 11 and 12).

10.5   The metaphrases of the Palaiologan period

Although the middle-register works of Konstantínos VII provide some of the best-known evidence for the 'normal' written Greek of educated Byzantines, there are other examples of stylistically related writing from the last centuries of Byzantium, involving the transposition into a more reader-friendly register of works by Nikétas Khoniátes, Geórgios Pakhyméres, Nikephóros Blemmýdes (*Andrías*), and part of Anna Komnené's *Alexiad* (from the middle of book XI to the end of XIII). The number of manuscripts overall points to the return of a wider reading public in the thirteenth and fourteenth centuries, who, though well educated by the standards of the time, still could not easily cope with the high style of the neo-Atticists.

Some of these metaphrases have been studied in detail in recent years (see especially Van Dieten (1979) on Nikétas Khoniátes, and Hunger (1981) on the *Alexiad*), and a clearer understanding of this register and its development is now emerging. Despite limited stylistic variation, it represents a fairly simple variant of the emerging written standard that had inherited its principal features from the tradition of educated practical writing represented in texts such as Theophánes's chronicle, Konstantínos VII's private works, Manassés's *Sýnopsis Istoriké*, and much of the technical writing of the later Byzantine period (for which see 10.6).

The example below is taken from the *Alexiad*, where the emperor is wrestling with the problems caused by the arrival of the First Crusade. His ally Raymond of Provence (Count of St Gilles) had contracted a fatal illness and sent for his nephew Guillaume-Jordan (Count of Cerdagne) to succeed him. But while the emperor Aléxios I tries to win Guillaume over to his side, the news breaks that Tancred, nephew of Robert Guiscard, has occupied Antioch and other cities of the region in contravention of the Normans' oath of allegiance. Aléxios therefore writes to the commander of the Norman force, Robert's son Bohemond, to express his displeasure. The original text is given first, followed by the metaphrase:

(11) (a) τούτου τοίνυν τὴν τελευτὴν μεμαθηκὼς ὁ αὐτοκράτωρ εὐθὺς πρὸς
τὸν δοῦκα Κύπρου διὰ γραμμάτων ἐδήλωσεν, ἵνα Νικήταν τὸν

Χιλίντζην μετὰ χρημάτων ἱκανῶν πρὸς τὸν Γελίελμον ἐκπέμψῃ ἐφ᾽
ᾧ ὑποποιήσασθαί τε αὐτὸν καὶ παρασκευάσαι ὀμωμοκέναι πρὸς
τὸν αὐτοκράτορα πίστιν βεβαίαν φυλάξαι εἰς αὐτὸν καὶ ὁποίαν ὁ
ἀποβεβιωκὼς θεῖος αὐτοῦ Ἰσαγγέλης μέχρι τέλους ἐτήρησεν.

εἶτα μεμαθηκὼς ὁ αὐτοκράτωρ καὶ τὴν τῆς Λαοδικείας παρὰ τοῦ
Ταγγρὲ κατάσχεσιν πρὸς τὸν Βαϊμοῦντον γράμματα ἐκτίθεται οὑτωσὶ
περιέχοντα· 'τὰ ὅρκια οἶδας καὶ τὰς ἐπαγγελίας, ἃς οὐκ αὐτὸς μόνος
ἀλλὰ καὶ ἅπαντες πρὸς τὴν βασιλείαν Ῥωμαίων ἐποιήσαντο. νῦν δὲ
αὐτὸς πρῶτος παρασπονδήσας τὴν Ἀντιόχειαν κατέσχες καὶ ἄλλ᾽ ἄττα
φρούρια ὑποποιησάμενος καὶ αὐτὴν δὴ τὴν Λαοδίκειαν. ἀπόστηθι τοίνυν
τῆς πόλεως Ἀντιοχείας καὶ τῶν ἄλλων ἁπάντων, δίκαιόν τε πρᾶγμα
ποιῶν, καὶ μὴ θέλε πολέμους ἄλλους καὶ μάχας κατὰ σαυτοῦ ἐρεθίζειν.'
Alexiad XI, 8–9

['tutu   'tinin tin delef'tin memaθi'kos,   o afto'krator ef'θis
Of-this(man) then   the end   having-learned(perf.), the emperor   immediately

pros ton 'ðuka 'kipru ðja   γra'maton e'ðilosen, 'ina ni'kitan ton
to   the duke of-Cyprus through letters   revealed,   so-that Nikétas the

xa'lindzin me'ta xri'maton ika'non pros ton je'lielmon ek'pempsi
Khalíndzes with   money   sufficient to   the Guillaume   he-may-send

ef-o   ipopi'isas'θe   te   a'ton ke paraske'vase
with-the-intention to-win-over-by-intrigue both him   and to-induce

omomo'kene pros ton aft'kratora 'pistin ve'vean fi'lakse is   af'ton,
to-swear(perf.) to   the emperor   faith   firm   to-keep towards him,

ke o'pian o apovevjo'kos 'θios a'tu isaŋ'gelis 'mexri 'telus e'tirisen.
even such-as the having-died   uncle of-him St Gilles until   end   kept.

    'ita memaθi'kos   o afto'krator ke tin tis   laoði'kias pa'ra tu
    Then having-learned(perf.) the emperor   also the of-the Laodicea   by   the

taŋ'gre ka'tasçesin pros ton vai'mundon 'γramata ek'tiθete uto'si
Tancred seizing   to   the Bohemond   letter   he-set-out thus

peri'exonda: 'ta 'orkia 'iðas   ke tas epaŋge'lias, as   uk af'tos
containing: 'The oaths you-know and the promises,   which not self

'monos, a'la ke 'apandes pros tin vasi'lian ro'meon epi'isando. nin ðe
alone, but also all   to   the empire   of-Romans made.   Now but

af'tos 'protos paraspon'ðisas tin andi'oçjan ka'tesçes   ke 'al ata
self first   having-broken-faith the Antioch   you-have-seized both other some

'fruria   ipopii'samenos   ke af'tin ði   tin lao'ðikjan. a'postiθi
fortified-towns having-gained-by-intrigue and itself indeed the Laodicea.   Withdraw

'tinin tis   'poleos andio'çias ke ton 'alon a'pandon, 'ðike'on di
therefore from-the city   Antioch   and the others all,   right   some

'praγma pi'on, ke 'mi 'θele po'lemus 'alus ke 'maxas ka'ta saf'tu
deed   doing, and not wish wars   other and battles against yourself

ere'θizin.']
to-provoke.'

'Accordingly, when the emperor learned of his [*St Gilles's*] death, he at once informed the Duke of Cyprus by letter, in order that he might send Nikétas Khalíntzes to Guillaume with plenty of money in an effort both to win him over and to induce him to swear to the emperor to maintain a sure allegiance towards him of the sort that his dead uncle St Gilles had observed until his death.

Subsequently, the emperor learned of the occupation of Laodicea by Tancred and set out a letter to Bohemond with the following contents: "You are aware of the oaths and promises which not only you yourself but everyone made to the empire of the Romans. Now you are the first to break your word, occupying Antioch and deviously winning over certain other fortified towns, including Laodicea itself. Act justly then, withdraw from the city of Antioch and all the other places, and do not keep seeking to provoke further wars and battles against yourself."'

(b) μαθὼν δὲ τὸν τοῦ Ἰσαγγέλη θάνατον, ὁ βασιλεὺς γράφει πρὸς τὸν δοῦκα τῆς Κύπρου ἵνα ἐκπέμψῃ τὸν Νικήταν τὸν Χαλίτζην μετὰ χρημάτων πρὸς Γελίελμον, ὡς ἂν οἰκονομήσῃ αὐτὸν καὶ ὀμόσῃ ἵνα φυλάττῃ τὴν πρὸς τὸν βασιλέα πίστιν αὐτοῦ ἀμετάθετον, καθὼς καὶ ὁ θεῖος αὐτοῦ ἐφύλαξεν.

ὡς δὲ ἔμαθεν ὁ βασιλεὺς ὅτι καὶ ὁ Ταγγρὲ τὴν Λαοδίκειαν ἐκράτησε, γράφει πρὸς τὸν Βαϊμοῦντον ταῦτα· 'γινώσκεις τοὺς ὅρκους καὶ τὰς ἐπαγγελίας ἃς οὐ σὺ μόνος, ἀλλὰ πάντες οἱ κόμητες πρὸς τὴν βασιλείαν ἐποίησαν. σὺ δὲ πρῶτον ἄρτι ἐπίορκος γεγονώς, ἐκράτησας τὴν Ἀντιόχειαν καὶ ἕτερα κάστρα καὶ αὐτὴν τὴν Λαοδίκειαν. ἔξελθε τοίνυν ἀπὸ τῆς πόλεως τῆς Ἀντιοχείας καὶ ἀπὸ τῶν ἄλλων ἁπάντων δι᾽ αὐτὸ τὸ δίκαιον, καὶ μηδὲν θελήσῃς κατὰ σοῦ πολέμους καὶ μάχας διεγεῖραι.'

Metaphrase 41–4 (Hunger (1981: 37))

[ma'θon ðe ton du isaŋ'geli 'θanato(n), o vasi'lefs 'ɣrafi pros
Having-learned and the of-the St Gilles death, the emperor writes to

to 'ðuka tis 'kipru 'in ek'pempsi to ni'kita(n) to xa'lidzi(n) me'ta
the duke of-the Cyprus so-that he-may-send the Nikétas the Khalítzis with

xri'maton pros to jel'ielmo(n), os-an ikono'misi (a)ton ke o'mosi
money to the Guillaume, so-that he-may-fund him and he-may-swear

'ina fi'lati tim bros to vasi'lea 'pistin a'tu ame'taθeto(n), ka'θos ke
that he-keep the to the emperor pledge of-him untransferred, just-as also

o 'θios a'tu e'filaksen.
the uncle of-him kept.

oz ðe 'emaθen o vasi'lefs 'oti ke o taŋ'gre ti lao'ðikjan
When and learned the emperor that also the Tancred the Laodicea

e'kratise, 'ɣrafi pros to vai'mundo(n) 'tafta: 'ji'noskis tus 'orkus
seized, he-writes to the Bohemond these-things: 'You-know the oaths

ke tas epaŋge'lias as u 'si 'monos, a'la ke 'pandes i 'komites
and the promises which not you alone, but also all the counts

pros tin vasi'lian e'piisan. si ðe 'proton 'arti e'piorkos jeɣo'nos,
to the empire made. You but first just-now perjurer having-become.

e'kratisas tin andi'oçja(n) kj 'etera 'kastra   ke af'tin ti
took   the Antioch   and other   fortified-towns and itself   the

lao'ðikja(n). 'ekselθe 'tinin a'po tis 'poleos tis andio'çias ke a'po ton
Laodicea.   Go-out   then   from the city   the Antioch   and from the

'alon a'pandon ðj af'to to 'ðikeo(n), ke mi'ðen   θe'lisis   ka'ta su
others all   for itself the justice,   and in-no-way wish(subjunc.) against you

po'lemus ke 'maxas ðje'jire.']
wars   and battles   to-arouse.'

'Having learned of St Gilles's death, the emperor wrote to the duke of Cyprus
to tell him to send Nikétas Khalítzes to Guillaume with money to "meet his
expenses", so that he would swear to keep unchanged his pledge of allegiance to
the emperor, just as his uncle had.

But when the emperor learned that Tancred had also seized Laodicea, he wrote
the following to Bohemond: "You are aware of the oaths and the promises which
not only you but all the counts made to the empire. But now you have perjured
yourself first by taking Antioch, as well as other fortified towns including Laodicea
itself. So for the sake of justice, leave the city of Antioch and all the other places,
and do not seek to stir up wars and battles against yourself."'

It is, of course, precisely the more 'literary' features of the original that have been
removed in the metaphrase, which in general is more explicit in style, and inter-
polates clarificatory phraseology quite freely. Though certain originally perfect
forms had become integrated into the paradigms of the relevant forms as substitute
aorists in even the spoken language (see 11.8.4), the free use of ancient perfects
as aorists, so typical of high-style writing, is now avoided. Note, for example, the
aorist participle $\mu\alpha\theta\dot{\omega}\nu$ [ma'θon] in place of perfect $\mu\epsilon\mu\alpha\theta\eta\kappa\dot{\omega}\varsigma$ [memaθi'kos] at
the beginning of the extract. Indeed, the range of participial usage is much more
restricted, with all the surviving forms serving as subject-orientated adjuncts (nominative) or in absolute constructions (genitive), as expected. Taking the first sentence of the second paragraph as an illustration, the initial participle of the original
has been replaced by a finite clause, and the neuter accusative plural $\pi\epsilon\rho\iota\dot{\epsilon}\chi o\nu\tau\alpha$
[peri'exonda] modifying a direct object has been quietly dropped.

In similar modernizing vein, the prohibition in the last sentence is expressed
by $\mu\eta\delta\dot{\epsilon}\nu$ [mi'ðen] + subjunctive, the classical split between the use of a negated
imperative in the imperfective aspect and a negated subjunctive in the perfective
having been levelled in favour of the latter, as in modern Greek. There is also some
reduction in infinitival usage; note in particular the 'modern' use of a subjunctive
clause introduced by $\ddot{\iota}\nu\alpha$ ['ina] after the control verb $\dot{o}\mu\dot{o}\sigma\eta$ [o'mosi] 'swear' (i.e.
I swear [that I keep] in place of *[I swear [to keep]]*). In general, however, the use
of infinitives after verbs of this type is maintained intact, as probably still in the
spoken language at this time.

Other long-abandoned categories and formations are also avoided, along with
much of the self-consciously literary/recherché vocabulary of the original. Non-
lexicalized middle verb forms are therefore replaced by active equivalents or sim-
ply dropped, so that $\gamma\rho\dot{\alpha}\mu\mu\alpha\tau\alpha$ $\dot{\epsilon}\kappa\tau\dot{\iota}\theta\epsilon\tau\alpha\iota$ $o\dot{\upsilon}\tau\omega\sigma\dot{\iota}$ $\pi\epsilon\rho\iota\dot{\epsilon}\chi o\nu\tau\alpha$ ['ɣramata ek'tiθetai

uto'si peri'exonda] 'letter sets-forth thus containing', for example, is replaced by the prosaic γράφει ταῦτα ['ɣrafi 'tafta] 'writes these-things'. Note also γινώσκω [ji'nosko] for οἶδα ['iða] 'I know', ἐξέρχομαι/ἐξῆλθον [eks'erxome/eks'ilθon] for ἀφίσταμαι/ἀπέστην [a'fistame/a'pestin] 'I withdraw', διεγείρω [ðje'jiro] for ἐρεθίζω [ere'θizo] 'I provoke/arouse', ὅρκος ['orkos] for ὅρκιον ['orkion] 'oath', etc.

Nonetheless, the 'educated' quality of this middle register is revealed in the persistently classical morphology of the categories and paradigms still in use: only the genitive Ἰσαγγέλ-η [isaŋgel-i], with -η [-i] for -ου [-u], has a distinctively modern look (cf. 11.7.3), and even this has ancient precedent in the case of proper names. The favourite Byzantine final conjunction ὡς ἄν [os an] is also in evidence, verb-final order is still a freely available option, especially in subordinate clauses, and αὐτός [af'tos] retains its classical use as an emphatic pronominal (i.e. = 'self' rather than modern 'this'). We should be in no doubt, therefore, that this 'simplified' style still belongs very firmly within the range of the written norms of its period.

10.6 Academic Greek in the late period: Máximos Planoúdes (c. 1255–1305)

Manouél Planoúdes (*c.* 1255–*c.* 1305) took the name Máximos when he became a monk. He ran a school in the capital, and served as secretary to the emperor Andrónikos II Palaiológos (reigned 1282–1328), for whom he went on an embassy to Venice. He is best known, however, as a scholar of prodigious range and learning, and as one of the first Byzantine academics to master Latin (see Wilson (1983: 230–41)). The following extract is taken from a pamphlet on Arabic numerals (which he writes in their Persian rather than western form):

(12) Οἱ τῶν ἀστρονόμων φιλοσοφώτεροι, ἐπεὶ ὁ μὲν ἀριθμὸς ἔχει τὸ ἄπειρον, τοῦ δὲ ἀπείρου γνῶσις οὐκ ἔστιν, ἐφεῦρον σχήματά τινα καὶ μέθοδον δι' αὐτῶν, ὡς ἂν τὰ τῶν ἐν χρήσει ἀριθμῶν εὐσυνοπτότερόν τε κατανόηται καὶ ἀκριβέστερον. εἰσὶ δὲ τὰ σχήματα ἐννέα μόνα, ἃ καὶ εἰσὶ ταῦτα: 1, 2, 3, 4, 5, 6, 7, 8, 9. τιθέασι δὲ καὶ ἕτερόν τι σχῆμα ὃ καλοῦσι τζίφραν, κατ' Ἰνδοὺς σημαῖνον οὐδέν· καὶ τὰ ἐννέα δὲ σχήματα καὶ αὐτὰ Ἰνδικά ἐστιν· ἡ δὲ τζίφρα γράφεται οὕτως 0.

Τούτων τῶν θ' σχημάτων ἕκαστον καθ' αὐτὸ μόνον κείμενον εἴτ' οὖν κατὰ τὴν πρώτην χώραν ἀπὸ τῆς δεξιᾶς χειρὸς ἡμῶν ἀρχομένων τὸ μὲν 1 σημαίνει ἕν, τὸ δὲ 2 δύο, ... κατὰ δὲ τὴν δευτέραν χώραν τὸ μὲν 1 δέκα, τὸ δὲ 2 εἴκοσι, ... κατὰ δὲ τὴν τρίτην χώραν τὸ μὲν 1 ἑκατόν, τὸ δὲ 2 διακόσια, ... καὶ κατὰ τὰς λοιπὰς χώρας ὡσαύτως γίνεται.

Edition: Gerhardt (1865) (extract in Wilson (1971: 126–7)).

[i ton astro'nomon filoso'foteri, e'pi o men   ariθ'mos 'eçi to
The of-the astronomers   wiser,   since the on-the-one-hand number   has the

'apiron, tu ðe   a'piru 'ɣnosis uk 'estin, e'fevron   'sçima'ta
infinity, of-the on-the-other-hand infinity knowledge not there-is, they-invented symbols

tina ke 'meθoðon dj af'ton, os-an ta   ton en 'xrisi ariθ'mon
some and method   for them,   so-that the(things) of-the in use   numbers

efsinop'tote'ron   te   katano'ite   ke akri'vesteron. i'si   ðe ta
more-easily-at-a-glance both may-be-understood and more-accurately. They-are and the

'sçimata e'nea 'mona, a   ke   i'si 'tafta: 1, 2, 3, 4, 5, 6, 7, 8, 9. ti'θeasi
symbols nine only,   which in-fact are these: 1, 2, 3, 4, 5, 6, 7, 8, 9. They-put

ðe ke 'ete'ron ti   'sçima o   ka'lusi 'tsifran, kat   in'ðus si'menon
and also other   some symbol which they-call 'cipher', among Indians meaning

u'ðen;   ke ta e'nea ta 'sçimata ke af'ta inði'ka estin; i ðe 'tsifra
'nothing'; and the nine the symbols also these Indian are; the and cipher

'ɣrafete 0.
is-written 0.

'tuton ton e'nea sçi'maton 'ekaston kaθ af'to 'monon 'kimenon,
Of-these the nine   symbols   each(nom.) by itself alone   being-placed(nom.),

it-un ka'ta tim 'brotin 'xoran a'po tiz ðeksi'as çi'ros i'mon arxo'menon,
then in   the first space from the right   hand us(gen.) beginning(gen.),

to men   1 si'meni en,   to ðe 2 'ðio, ... ka'ta ðe ti(n) ðef'teran
the on-the-one-hand 1 means   'one', the and 2 'two', ... In   and the   second

'xoran to men   1 'ðeka, to de 2 'ikosi, ... ka'ta ðe tin 'dritin 'xoran
space the on-the-one-hand 1 'ten', the and 2 'twenty', ... In and the third   space

to men   1 eka'ton, to ðe 2 dja'kosja, ... ke ka'ta tas li'pas   ðe
the on-the-one-hand 1 'hundred', the and 2 'two hundred', ... Also in   the remaining and

'xoras os'aftos   'jinete.]
spaces in-the-same-way it-is-done.

'Since the set of numbers is infinite and there can be no knowledge of infinity, the wisest of the astronomers invented some symbols and a framework of interpretation for them so that the properties of the numbers in actual use might be understood at a glance more readily and more accurately. The symbols are only nine in number, as follows: 1, 2, 3, 4, 5, 6, 7, 8, 9. They also use another symbol which they call "cipher", meaning "nothing" among the Indians; as for the nine symbols, these too are Indian; the cipher is written 0.

When each of these nine symbols is used by itself, then, if we begin with the first column on the right, 1 means "one", 2 means "two", ... In the second column 1 means "ten", 2 means "twenty", ... In the third column 1 means "a hundred", 2 means "two hundred", ... And the same conventions apply in the remaining columns.'

It is nice to see an educated Byzantine of the later period writing so naturally about something which obviously interested him. The language here is again less classicized than that of literary composition, though the treatment of academic issues did require an extensive technical vocabulary which was usually taken over, along with certain stylistic preferences, from the relevant scholarship of antiquity. Superficially, then, the language is more archaizing than that of the last extract, especially in the range of its morphology and lexicon, though even in syntax there is still the possibility of using verb-final order neutrally in subordinate clauses, especially those involving more learned uses of participles and infinitives. Ancient government and/ or agreement requirements are also strictly maintained, as, for example, the use of 3sg. κατανόηται [kata'noite] with a neuter plural subject.

But in main clauses the regular preverbal constituents are now either subjects, preposed elements functioning as sentence topics or emphatic/contrastive foci, rather as in modern Greek. There are other contemporary details too, including the (apparent) use of a comparative adjective with the article in superlative sense at the beginning of the piece; the use of διά [ðja] to mean 'for' (albeit with 'classical' genitive rather than the accusative); the topicalization structure in the penultimate clause of the first paragraph, where αὐτά [af'ta] seems to be used as a resumptive pronoun meaning 'these' rather than emphatic 'themselves'; and the nominative absolute at the beginning of the second paragraph, where the sense, but not strictly the grammar, links the adjunct to the set of subjects that follow. Participles are also chiefly subject-orientated and function as circumstantial adjuncts, and this too probably reflects the syntactic practice of contemporary educated speech.

10.7   Official Greek of the later empire

It remains to complete this chapter with a brief examination of the written Greek of the imperial and ecclesiastical bureaucracy. The extract below comes from a decree of December 1326 issued by the emperor Andrónikos III Palaiológos (co-emperor with his grandfather from 1325, sole ruler 1328–41), and confirms that the monastery of St John the Evangelist on Patmos has sole ownership of various properties on Lemnos, Leros and Kos against the claims of the archbishop of the last-named island:

(13) Ἐπεὶ οἱ μοναχοὶ τῆς κατὰ τὴν νῆσον τὴν Πάτμον διακειμένης σεβασμίας
μονῆς τῆς βασιλείας μου τῆς εἰς ὄνομα τιμωμένης τοῦ ἁγίου ἐνδόξου
πανευφήμου ἀποστόλου καὶ εὐαγγελιστοῦ Ἰωάννου τοῦ Θεολόγου ἐζήτησαν
καὶ παρεκλήτευσαν τὴν βασιλείαν μου, ἵνα ἐπὶ τοῖς προσοῦσιν αὐτοῖς
κτήμασί τε καὶ μετοχίοις καὶ λοιποῖς ἀναστήμασιν, ἃ κατέχουσι διά τε
χρυσοβούλλων διαφόρων καὶ προσταγμάτων ἀλλὰ δὴ καὶ ἀπογραφικῶν
καταστάσεων καὶ ἑτέρων δικαιωμάτων, πορίσωνται καὶ χρυσόβουλλον
τῆς βασιλείας μου, ὡς ἂν κατέχωσι ταῦτα καὶ εἰς τὸ ἑξῆς ἀβαρῶς πάντη
καὶ ἀτελῶς, καθὼς ταῦτα κατέχουσι μέχρι τοῦ νῦν, ἤγουν τὸ ἐν τῇ νήσῳ
Λήμνῳ μετόχιον, τὸ ἐπικεκλημένον ὁ ἅγιος Γεώργιος ὁ Μυροβλύτης, καὶ
διακείμενον ἐν τῇ τοποθεσίᾳ τῆς Ἁγίας Εἰρήνης μετὰ τῶν προσόντων
αὐτῷ πάντων ἀμπελίων καὶ χωραφίων.

Miklosich and Müller (1860–90: Vol. VI, p. 248)

[e'pi	i	mona'çi tis	ka'ta ti	'nison tim	'batmon diaki'menis sevaz'miaz
Whereas	the monks	of-the on	the island	the Patmos	located venerable

mo'nis	tiz	vasi'liaz	mu tis	is 'onoma timo'menis tu	a'jiu
monastery	the(one)	of-the majesty	of-me the(one)	in name honoured	of-the holy

en'ðoksu pane'fimu   apo'stolu ke evaŋgeli'stu jo'anu tu θeo'loɣu
illustrious   all-praiseworthy apostle   and evangelist   John   the Theologian

e'zitisan ke pare'klitefsan ti vasil'ia mu i'na e'pi   tis pro'susin
have-sought and implored   the majesty of-me that in-the-matter-of the belonging

a'tis   'ktima'si te   ke meto'çiis ke li'pis   ana'stimasin, a   ka'texusi
to-them possessions both and communes and remaining buildings,   which they-occupy

'ðja te   xriso'vulon ðja'foron ke prostaɣ'maton, a'la ði   ke
through both chrysobulls   various   and ordinances,   but indeed also

apoɣrafi'kon apokata'staseon ke e'teron ðikeo'maton, po'risonde   ke
registered   restitutions   and other   judgements,   they-may-obtain also

xri'sovulon tiz   vasi'liaz mu, os-an ka'texosi   'tafta   ke is to
chrysobull   of-the majesty   of-me, so-that they-may-occupy these(places) also into the

e'ksis ava'ros   'pandi ke ate'los,   ka'θos 'tafta   ka'texosi
thereafter without-burden altogether and without-taxation, just-as these(places) they-hold

'mexri tu nin, 'iɣun   to en di 'niso 'limno me'toçion, to
until   the now, that-is-to-say the on the island Lemnos commune,   the(one)

epikekli'menon o 'ajos 'jorjos o miro'vlitis, ke ðja'kimenon en di
called   the Saint George the Myroblytes, and situated   in the

topoθe'sia tis   a'jias i'rinis me'ta tom bro'sondon a'to 'pandon ambe'lion
locality   of-the Saint Irene with   the   belonging   to-it all   vineyards

ke xora'fion.]
and fields.

'Whereas the monks of my majesty's venerable monastery located on the island of
Patmos, honoured in the name of the holy, illustrious, all-praiseworthy apostle and
evangelist John the Divine, have asked and implored my majesty in the matter of
the possessions, communes, and remaining buildings belonging to them, which they
occupy by virtue both of divers chrysobulls and ordinances, but also of duly registered
restitutions and other judgements, that they may obtain a further chrysobull of my
majesty to the effect that, just as they have occupied these until now, so too they may
occupy them in the future wholly free of public burdens and taxation, specifically the
commune on the island of Lemnos, called St George Myroblytes and situated in the
locality of St Irene, together with all the vineyards and fields belonging to it . . .'

Anyone who has signed a contract will instantly recognize the archaizing verbosity
of the legal profession, though the elaborate appellations and technical vocabulary
here are taken from both the world of land law and the equally obscurantist ecclesiastical tradition. It is interesting to note, however, that though both styles were
heavily archaizing, most of the technical vocabulary in the extract above is not in
fact attested in classical Greek, and that the items which are now have different
meanings. Such writing belongs to the living tradition of high officialdom.

Thus beneath the over-elaborated surface, the official Koine of late antiquity has
been significantly updated. Although the complexity of nominal structures involving the 'classical' insertion of modifiers between article and noun has been taken
to extremes, all specifically possessive genitives follow the nouns that govern them,

and regularly do so without a repeated article, just as in modern Greek (i.e. we have *the X of-Y* rather than the classical structures *the of-Y X* or *the X the of-Y*). Note too the avoidance of possessive adjectives in favour of genitive clitic pronouns, the invariant positioning of direct objects after the verbs that govern them (i.e. there are no neutral verb-final clauses), and the 'modern' use of a ἵνα ['ina]-clause after the control verbs of 'asking/imploring' in place of the classical infinitive, even though the same subject is involved in both clauses. In some respects, therefore, this is structurally more 'modern' than the academic style of the previous section, and we should be in no doubt that it is simply one more 'antiqued' version of the late-medieval Koine rather than a half-hearted imitation of its late-antique predecessor.

10.8   Conclusion

It is hoped that sufficient evidence has now been presented to show that the range of middle-register writing in Byzantium was not the product of more or less incompetent archaizing, but rather reflected a continuously evolving tradition that was subject to conventions controlling the mix of ancient and modern according to period, register, and style. Though educated Byzantines did not write in the educated vernacular of their time, they did write in varieties that reflected both the conventions of the relevant written traditions and the 'natural' rules of contemporary spoken Greek in an on-going process of evolution and compromise.

Looking in a general way at the patterns of usage revealed above, it would seem fair to say that, by the later Byzantine period, the fundamental principles of sentence structure for middle-style compositions were fairly constant, being essentially those of educated speech, while the principal archaizing deviations were comparatively superficial (and so readily taught and learned), involving genre-conditioned lexical and phraseological substitutions, the strict deployment of classical morphology in the paradigms still in use, and adherence to ancient rules governing the realization of the relationship between heads and their local dependants (involving, for example, case government and agreement patterns, parochial word-order requirements, or the choice of infinitival complements). There was, in other words, an emerging common written style with an essentially modern syntax that was archaized in various ways in accordance with the conventions of different genres.

It was, broadly speaking, this variably 'archaized' but fundamentally unitary middle style that eventually developed, under various external pressures, into the standard written language of the Greek intelligentsia of the seventeenth and eighteenth centuries (see Section III, Chapter 15), with only the most ambitious forms of composition, aiming for a truly classical style, still requiring a detailed mastery of the rules and stylistic conventions of ancient Greek at a more profound level.

Chapter 11

Spoken Greek in the Byzantine empire: the principal developments

11.1 Introduction

Because so little vernacular material has been preserved from the period before the twelfth century, there are many phenomena which cannot be dated with any precision. Some developments carried through in the early and middle Byzantine periods had already begun in late antiquity. Others, attested for the first time in the latter part of the Byzantine period, almost certainly began some centuries earlier, when the political and military circumstances of the seventh and eighth centuries and the prevailing cultural attitudes of the middle period worked decisively against the production and preservation of the kind of texts that might otherwise have given us a clearer picture of change in progress.

What follows, however, is an attempt not only to summarize the evidence for the later period, but also to reconstruct, in the light of the available materials, the contents of the 500-year 'gap' between the latest colloquial texts from antiquity and the earliest medieval vernacular literature. The work of Gignac (1976, 1981) is an indispensable guide in discriminating between those developments which began in the spoken Greek of the ancient world and innovations which belong to the medieval period proper.

11.2 The completion of sound changes beginning in antiquity

(1) The shift of /y/ > /i/, already apparent in some substandard varieties in the ancient world, was probably completed for all speakers of mainstream dialects by the tenth/eleventh century (see Macharadze (1980) for the evidence of Georgian loans, and cf. Browning (1983: 56–7)).

The major exception is provided by Tsakonian, the speech of the Mani in the south of the Peloponnese, and the Old Athenian group of modern dialects, comprising the traditional speech of Athens (i.e. before it became the capital of modern Greece in the nineteenth century), together with Megarian (which survives among the oldest inhabitants), Euboean (still spoken by the older generation in and around Kymi), and Old Aeginetan (which survived until perhaps the middle of the twentieth century). This group perhaps represents the remnants of a once quite homogeneous dialect type spoken across much of south-eastern Greece away from the major political centres. Here the 'marked' /y/ of the Koine shifted back to /u/ rather than to standard /i/; in the absence of strong structural support from the phonological system (e.g. with lip-rounding functioning contrastively along the whole of the front axis: /i/~/y/, /e/~/ø/, /ɛ/~/œ/), such vowels are prone to change towards one or other 'norm', i.e. [+front +spread] or [+back +rounded].

(2) The simplification of double consonants (degemination), again sporadically attested in popular papyri, spread widely and eventually became quite general, though again with important dialectal exceptions, including South Italian (cut off from the Byzantine mainstream after 1071), the contemporary south-eastern group (i.e. Cypriot, Dodecanesian and Khian), and perhaps the neighbouring dialects of western and southern Asia Minor in earlier times.

(3) The loss of final -ν [-n] was a sporadic and apparently random feature of many popular varieties of Greek from ancient times (Gignac 1976: 111–6), though Cypriot is a major exception, with some evidence of early analogical spread of -ν [-n] (cf. Consani (1986, 1990), Brixhe (1988b: 177–8). This loss now became more widespread, though the south-eastern dialects are excluded, as expected, together with (in part) South Italian, Pontic and Cappadocian (the latter pair cut off by the Seljuk invasions after 1071).

The process was apparently inhibited in higher registers by the influence of literacy, but it ceased to be random where it did occur, and specifically manifested itself first in assimilation to a following fricative or continuant (as still attested in Cypriot), followed by degemination in those dialects that underwent this change.

Subsequently, the retention of final -ν [-n] before vowels and plosives became restricted, mainly for reasons of grammatical disambiguation, to a small set of word-forms, especially when these were closely linked syntactically to an adjacent item, e.g. clitic pronouns within verb phrases, or articles and certain forms of adjectives (the latter only prevocalically) within noun phrases. In standard modern Greek, final nasals are now preserved before vowels and plosives in the accusative singular forms of articles and clitic pronouns, genitive plurals, negative particles and adverbial conjunctions, and 3pl. verb forms.

(4) The deletion of nasals before fricatives, a process already in place in classical Greek before [s] and [z] (cf. σύ-στημα [sý-stɛːma] 'system', < *σύν-στημα [sýn-stɛːma]), was given greater scope with the shift of the voiceless aspirated plosives to fricatives. Voiced plosives, however, which in general also became fricatives, were retained after nasals in popular Greek (cf. 6.4 number (19)), as sometimes reflected subsequently in the orthography, e.g. ἄντρας ['andras] for original ἄνδρας 'man'. Thus the renewed onset of nasal deletion was effect- ively restricted to the context of a following voiceless fricative: e.g. νύφη ['nifi] 'bride', < νύμφη ['nimfi], etc.

But among educated speakers the rule requiring the retention of voiced plosives after nasals was undermined, just as that deleting nasals before voiceless fricatives was inhibited, by interference from the orthography of the written language, which spawned a great many spelling pronunciations that contravened the rules of popular spoken Greek in its 'pure' form. Thus 'popular' words like δέντρο(ν) ['ðendro(n)] 'tree' (traditionally spelled δένδρον), and πλύθηκα ['pliθika] (< ancient ἐπλύνθην [e'plinθin], aorist passive of πλύνω ['plino] 'I wash', now sit side by side with 'learned' forms like σύνδεσμος ['sinðezmos] 'conjunction', and πένθος ['penθos] 'mourning'.

(5) Other than in 'learned' words with a spelling pronunciation of the ancient form, a voiceless plosive followed by a voiced plosive was subject to voicing assimilation; and since voiced plosives were ultimately permitted only after nasals, any voiced plosives in such clusters became fricatives (cf. 6.4).

This principally affected the preposition ἐκ [ek] in composition, where the voicing assimilation began in ancient times and the shift to obligatory sequences of voiced fricatives was completed by the early Byzantine period at the latest. Thus classical [ekdýnoː] 'I undress', for example, first became [egdýnoː], then [(e)'yðino] ((ἐ)γδύνω); cf. βγαίνω ['vjeno] 'I go out', < classical ἐκβαίνω [ekbaínoː], but with metathesis of [yv]. The process, however, was again inhibited by interference from written Greek, so that, for example, γδύνω ['yðino] and ἐκδρομή [ekðro'mi] 'excursion' are both standard in the modern language.

(6) Synizesis ([-iV]/[-eV-] > [-jV-]) was standardized in much non-learned vocabulary, with a shift of the accent to the following vowel if [i/e] was originally accented: παιδία [pe'ðia] > παιδιά [pe'ðja] 'children', etc. The influence of written Greek again inhibited the process in educated speech, and in modern Greek many learned forms have been reintroduced (e.g. ἐλευθερία [elefθe'ria] for λευτεριά [lefter'ja] 'freedom', etc.). There is some evidence for random synizesis from Hellenistic times onwards in many popular varieties, but its relative absence in the conservative dialects of Southern Italy, Pontus, and the Old Athenian group (cf. Newton (1972: 14–17)) shows that its eventual standardization was not a general phenomenon.

(7) Many forms affected by aphaeresis (i.e. the loss of unstressed initial vowels in hiatus, the inverse of the elision of final vowels) were standardized in this period. This is rare in classical Greek, but moderately frequent in the Ptolemaic papyri and very frequent in Roman/early Byzantine documents (Gignac (1976: 319 ff.). Once again Pontic is a major exception to the trend.

In the early medieval period aphaeresis seems to have been particularly common when like vowels were involved, e.g. τὸ (ὁ)σπίτιν [to 'spitin] 'the house', ἡ (ἡ)μέρα [i 'mera] 'the day', τότε (ἐ)γράψαμε(ν) ['tote 'yrapsame] 'then we-wrote', ἔγραψά (ἀ)το ['eyra‚psa to] 'I wrote it' (with the pronoun derived from the familiar reduced form of αὐτό [af'to]), etc.

From cases such as these, many forms lacking their original initial vowel eventually became the norm in popular speech, though again with much uncertainty deriving from the influence of the written language and the co-existence of related forms with an accented initial vowel (e.g. in the case of the syllabic augment, ἔγραψα ['eɣrapsa] 'I wrote', beside (ἐ)γράψαμε(ν) [(e)'ɣrapsame] 'we wrote', etc.).

11.3 Grammatical consequences of aphaeresis

Apart from the vast number of individual words affected by aphaeresis, the following general phenomena should be noted (cf. Browning (1983: 58)):

(8) (a) The weak (clitic) 3rd-person pronouns increasingly take the form τόν/τήν/ τό [ton/tin/to] 'him, her, it'.
   (b) The syllabic augment, after a long period of uncertainty, eventually disappeared unless accented, with exceptions in western Asia Minor (formerly), the Dodecanese, Khios, many of the Cyclades, and (in part) Crete.
   (c) The preposition εἰς [is] combines with a following definite article: (εἰ)ς τό(ν)/τή(ν)/τό [ston/stin/sto], a pronunciation later recognized orthographically in forms such as στόν [ston], etc.

Uncertainties about word-division arising from the spread of aphaeresis also led to misanalyses within closely-knit syntactic phrases, so that ἂν τὸν ἐλύσαμε(ν) [an don e'lisame(n)] 'if him we-had-freed', for example, was thought of as representing ἂν τόνε λύσαμε(ν) [an done 'lisame(n)], etc. From examples such as this came the widespread practice of adding a 'protective' final -ε [-e] to pronouns and other forms ending in -ν [-n] if the loss of this consonant threatened to create an ambiguity.

11.4 Old and new patterns of subordination: clitic pronouns and VSO order

Aphaeresis also affected an important class of particles and conjunctions, including the negative particle (οὐ)δέν [(u)ðen] (originally = 'nothing', 'not at all', but from the sixth century onwards increasingly used in place of the ancient οὐ(κ) [u(k)] 'not'), the conditional conjunction (ἐ)άν [an] (in so far as this did not simply continue the ancient contracted form ἄν [an]), the subjunctive marker (ἵ)να [na] (formerly a fully-fledged subordinating conjunction in final, consecutive, and control clauses), and the complementizers (ὅ)πως [pos] 'that' (neutral as to the factual status of the following clause), and (ὅ)που [pu] 'that' (factive, and also used in relative clauses). Of these, the former originally meant 'how', the latter 'where', in which sense it has retained its full form in modern Greek.

   In the case of the last three conjunctions, the loss of the initial vowel was apparently preceded by a shift of the accent to the final syllable (or more accurately, the loss of their true lexical accent and the acquisition of a secondary 'phrasal' accent, as explained below). In the case of ἵνα ['ina], there is clear evidence for this in the accentual metres of the hymns of Romanós the Melode, the greatest Byzantine hymnographer, dating from the first half of the sixth century (see Trypánis (1960), Maas and Trypánis (1963, 1970)). The change seems to have involved the generalization of a rhythmical readjustment initially associated with the role of the conjunction as 'host' for a following enclitic pronoun, i.e. ἵνα 'το μάθω ['ina to 'maθo] 'that it I-may-learn' > ἰνά 'το μάθω [i̩na to 'maθo], in which form it then succumbed to aphaeresis.

It may be that the other 'modern' complementizers (ὁ)πώς [(o)'pos] and (ὁ)ποῦ [(o)'pu] underwent the same accent shift, for similar reasons, though in these cases confusion with the corresponding interrogatives πῶς [pos] 'how?', and ποῦ [pu] 'where?', is also likely, in that relatives and interrogatives overlap in the complement structures of verbs such as 'know'; compare *I know what you know*, where the subordinate clause can be taken either as an indirect question or as a free (i.e. indefinite) relative clause. Indefinite relatives (e.g. ὅστις ['ostis] 'who(ever)') were therefore used in indirect questions alongside true interrogatives (e.g. τίς [tis] 'who?') even in classical Greek, but in the case of manner and locative expressions the relative/interrogative element slipped easily into the role of complementizer because the 'know'-class takes both interrogative and non-interrogative complements (cf. *know how/know that*, and the dialectal use of *how* as a non-interrogative complementizer in English: *I know (as) how he's a fool, but . . .*).

The word order associated with these modern complementizers and conjunctions was different from that used with their traditional counterparts, and both orders are reflected in medieval vernacular texts which, in typical fashion, continued to use both systems side-by-side. In classical Greek, there was a large set of enclitic sentence connectives and particles which appeared in second position in the clause (the so-called Wackernagel position). Enclitic pronouns were originally attracted to this slot, away from their governing verbs, though later there was a counter-tendency for them to appear to the right of verbs, away from the clitic group (as often in classical Attic prose). The verb could, however, also be drawn optionally to a clitic in second position, and appear initially if there was no complementizer (giving the order verb+clitic(s)+subject), or immediately to the right of the clitic if there was (giving the order conjunction+clitic(s)+verb+subject). This solution was eventually standardized in the spoken forms of post-classical and medieval Greek (4.8, 6.5.1). The modern conjunctions were naturally associated with this living syntactic framework, and in medieval Greek the movement of the verb was generalized, even in the absence of motivating clitics, thus enforcing the order conjunction+V+S in virtually all subordinate clauses. This eventually led to VS becoming routine in main clauses too, always provided that neither the subject nor any other constituent had been preposed for discourse reasons (see Mackridge (1993a), Horrocks (1994)).

By contrast, the use of the 'traditional' complementizers and conjunctions ὅτι ['oti] 'that', διότι [ði'oti] 'because', and εἰ [i] 'if', continued to be associated with the rules of later classical Greek, not only in learned writing but even in vernacular productions, wherever these elements survived alongside their modern counterparts. Thus clitics regularly followed the verb, and in subordinate clauses the verb itself could stand either after the subject within the verb phrase (conjunction +subject+[verb(+clitic(s))]) or in second position before the subject (conjunction+ [verb+(clitic(s))]+subject).

There was, however, considerable interference between the two systems, and the uncertainty still persists in modern Greek, where complementizer–subject–verb order frequently occurs in written styles, cf. Mackridge (1985: 237). The situation is summarized diagrammatically in (9), where CP = the phrase headed by the complementizer or conjunction, ConP = the position for enclitic connectives (to which clitic pronouns were optionally attracted), ClP = clitic phrase (the post-classical development of ConP where clitic pronouns stood obligatorily), S = sentence, NP = noun phrase (subject), and VP = verb phrase. (9)(a) represents the case of traditional conjunctions, (9)(b) that of their modern replacements:

(9) (a)

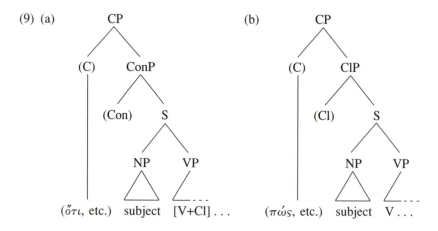

In (9)(a), the verb and its clitics could be fronted to C (if this was empty, as in main clauses) or to Con (otherwise), though neither movement was required, and both SV and VS remained available in both main and subordinate clauses. In (9)(b), however, the verb was obligatorily shifted if there were clitics in ClP, either to C (if empty) or to Cl (otherwise, in the order Cl+V), and such movements later became the preferred option even when there were no clitic pronouns present. Subjects then necessarily followed the verb, unless preposed to function as topics or foci.

The presence of a preposed interrogative or focal phrase within CP had the same effect as the presence of an overt complementizer in C, i.e. to force the verb to appear after the clitic pronouns in ClP. Preposed topics, however, were clearly placed outside the clause structure proper (being adjoined, say, to CP), so that the true clause-initial position remained free to accept V, thereby effecting the normal main-clause order (i.e. V+clitic) in these cases. (See Mackridge (1993a) for a ground-breaking analysis of clitic pronoun placement in vernacular medieval Greek).

The complementizer *vá* [na], however, ultimately came to function as a subjunctive marker, and in this reduced role formed (along with negative particles and clitic pronouns) part of a word-like 'complex' with the verb. Thus ὅτι [νά + verb] (['oti na-V], lit. 'that will-V'), for example, became a regular combination in the subordinate clauses of popular medieval Greek. This more complex clausal structure can be represented as in (10), where MP = modality phrase and NegP = negative phrase. (Cf. Philippaki-Warburton (1990) for a detailed exposition of the structure of the verb complex in modern Greek):

(10)

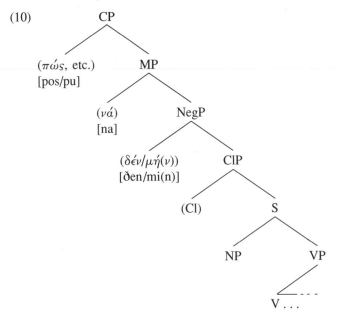

Here the verb raises obligatorily to Cl, as before (giving clitic+V). But the option of raising further to C (if empty) is excluded if either, or both, of MP and NegP are present, since the particles heading these phrases, as proclitic modifiers of the verb, must appear before it, and any verb movement to a higher position would leave them ungrammatically 'stranded'.

Clitic–verb order was now obligatory both in negative and subjunctive clauses (main and subordinate) and, even in the absence of νά [na] or negation, in any 'modern' syntactic structure in which CP was filled. Though the pronouns in all these structures were originally enclitic on the material to their left, it was natural that the emergence of the verb-complex as a structural unit should lead to a reinterpretation of all the elements involved in it as verb-dependent and proclitic. Only 'simple', i.e. non-interrogative, non-modal, and non-negative, main clauses therefore retained the option of verb-raising to C, giving verb–clitic order and traditional pronominal enclisis.

This 'mixed' treatment of clitic pronouns remained the norm in medieval Greek, and it has been retained in a number of modern dialects, most notably, Cretan, many Cycladic varieties, Cypriot, and the south-eastern group in general. In Pontic, however, the post-verbal (enclitic) position was generalized, pointing to an early divergence, while in standard modern Greek the pre-verbal (proclitic) position of clitic pronouns has now been adopted for all finite verb-forms, even in the absence of elements preceding the verb-complex; weak pronouns are therefore enclitic on the verb only in the case of imperatives and gerunds, and these remain the only verb forms still subject to the rule of verb-preposing to C in standard speech (cf. Rivero and Terzi (1995)).

11.5 Dialect diversity in medieval Greek: the northern dialects

Many of the most characteristic dialectal distinctions of spoken modern Greek began to develop strongly in the Middle Ages, in line with the progressive loss of Byzantine control over large parts of the former empire. But, as we have seen, the process of dialect differentiation in the spoken Koine had begun on a regional basis even in late antiquity, and it is therefore particularly unfortunate that the absence of relevant 'dialect texts' for most of the Byzantine period makes the dating of many of the crucial medieval innovations extremely difficult.

The early development of Cretan and Cypriot is discussed in 12.4, and both these and a number of other dialects are considered further in Section III (Chapter 14). Here we shall consider the rather fundamental distinction between the contemporary 'northern' and 'southern' dialects, whereby the former but not the latter exhibit (rather variably instantiated) high-vowel deletion and mid-vowel raising: i.e. unstressed 'standard' /i/ and /u/ > ø, and unstressed 'standard' /e/ and /o/ > /i/ and /u/. Such varieties are still spoken, subject to the growing impact of the standard, throughout the mainland north of Attica, as well as on Thasos, Lesbos, Lemnos, Imbros (formerly, since it now belongs to Turkey), and Samos (in the southern area, but repopulated from the north in the fifteenth century). Cf. Newton (1972: ch. 7) for a recent survey.

A key issue is the dating of the onset of these changes (see Andriótis (1933), Sympósio (1977)). Possible linkage to similar developments in Thessalian dialect inscriptions from the third century BC onwards is difficult to substantiate while so much of the interpretation of particular forms remains uncertain, though it remains a possibility that relevant articulatory habits were carried over to variants of the Koine that became established in the north, and that the beginnings of the modern split between north and south go back to ancient times.

Against this interpretation, however, we may note that consonants palatalized before original /i/ are retained as such after high-vowel deletion, but that there is no corresponding palatalization before the secondary /i/ (< /e/) in dialects that did not also palatalize consonants before /e/. This points to a considerable delay in the onset of high-vowel raising *vis-à-vis* palatalization, since otherwise the latter would have applied equally to the relevant consonants before the new /i/.

The argument for the lateness of high-vowel raising is confirmed when we examine a number of other interacting phenomena. Thus the regular manner dissimilation of voiceless obstruents (i.e. [stop+stop] or [fricative+fricative] > [fricative+stop], cf. (12) below for the details) is almost unknown in the secondary consonant clusters arising from high-vowel deletion. Similarly, although the originally voiceless plosives that find themselves adjacent to voiced fricatives are voiced, they do not themselves normally become fricatives (contrast (5) above). Thus κουτί [ku'ti] 'box', typically becomes [kti] rather than [xti], and πηγάδι [pi'ɣaði] 'well', becomes [bɣað] rather than [vɣað]. These differences clearly distinguish the treatment of the products of high-vowel deletion from that of original clusters, and show that such deletions must have post-dated the application of the relevant rules of manner assimilation/dissimilation. And since we already know that high-vowel deletion preceded mid-vowel raising (otherwise secondary /i/ and /u/ would also have disappeared), it follows that the manner dissimilation of voiceless obstruents and the manner assimilation of voiced obstruents preceded both of these processes.

There are, of course, examples of various consonant assimilations and dissimilations in the late antique papyri (cf. Gignac (1976: 86–98, 165–77), and in particular we know that the obligatory manner assimilation of voiced plosives to voiced fricatives belongs, at the latest, to the early Byzantine period (cf. (5) above). But, crucially, there are no examples of true manner dissimilation in voiceless obstruent clusters, inevitably so in the case of the fricatives [f, θ, x], given their late development from aspirated plosives (cf. 6.4).

The modern treatment of voiceless clusters is therefore a product of the medieval period, and since the developments in the South Italian dialects are aberrant *vis-à-vis* the standard pattern ([pt], [fθ], [kt], [xθ], and [sθ] all > [st] in Bova, for example, with other patterns attested elsewhere), it seems that the completion of the relevant changes took place after this part of the Greek-speaking world had become detached from the Byzantine mainstream by the Norman conquests. They are therefore conventionally placed in the later Middle Ages (cf. Browning (1983: 76)).

Putting these various observations together, we obtain the chronology in (11):

(11)   manner assimilation of voiced obstruents   (early Byzantine)
       manner dissimilation of voiceless obstruents (post-11th century)
       high-vowel deletion
    ▼ mid-vowel raising
   time

with the diagnostic features of the northern dialects of modern Greek placed firmly in the period after *c*. AD 1100. This ties in well with the evidence of the body of 'unaffected' loan words in the language of Vlach migrants, who settled in Epirus and Pindus between the eighth and tenth centuries (Andriótis (1933)).

Similar changes in the realization of vowels also characterized the dialects of Silli, Cappadocia, and, at least in part, Pontus. But in the first there was only raising, and this chiefly in inflectional endings, while in Cappadocia raising and deletion occurred mainly in final syllables; in Pontic, on the other hand, these processes are restricted to the immediately post-tonic syllable. These important and rather varied restrictions on the range of the phenomena suggest very strongly that we are dealing with similar, but independent, developments of relatively recent origin in the Asia Minor Koine rather than with a single process directly linked to the northern Greek developments (cf. Dawkins (1916: 192–3)).

11.6 Later phonetic and phonological developments

The most important of these are summarized in (12)–(15) below (the first of which, the rule of manner dissimilation in voiceless obstruent clusters, has already been mentioned above):

(12) Other than in 'learned' words, voiceless obstruent clusters consisting of [stop+ stop] or [fricative+fricative] all took the form [fricative+stop].

There are, however, two exceptions:

(i)   if the second member is /s/, we get stop + /s/
(ii) the cluster /sf/ remained unchanged

The first began during the early/middle Byzantine period (giving e.g. ἔπαψα ['epapsa] for ἔπαυσα ['epafsa] as the aorist of παύω ['pavo] 'I stop', cf. 12.1.2), and is therefore a distinct phenomenon not only in its effects but also in its chronology. Examples involving [s] followed by φ, θ, χ [f, θ, x] are also in origin distinct, in that the Egyptian papyri provide good evidence for a colloquial development to [sp, st, sk] at the stage when the latter still represented the aspirated plosives [pʰ, tʰ, kʰ]. Indeed, in the specific case of σθ, the development to [st] was a particular characteristic of North West Greek from the earliest times, and many ancient dialects show at least sporadic στ spellings in their 'later' periods.

It seems, then, that the pairs [sp]/[sf], [st]/[sθ], [sk]/[sx] began as alternative (i.e. popular vs. formal) descendants of earlier [spʰ], [stʰ], [skʰ], and that [st] progressively superseded its rival in popular spoken Greek during the course of the early Byzantine period, with [sk] eventually following in its wake (but [sf], rather mysteriously, being preferred to [sp]). The more or less contemporaneous shift of [au/eu] to [af/ef] added greatly to the frequency of clusters involving a voiceless fricative followed by a voiceless plosive (cf. αὐτός [af'tos], etc.), and it was presumably the increasing dominance of this pattern that led to the assimilation of other voiceless fricative combinations (involving two of [f, θ, x] < [pʰ, tʰ, kʰ], always assuming the second element underwent this shift rather than being deaspirated) and then of plosive + plosive clusters to what had by then become the phonotactic 'norm'. Note, however, that only the last two steps of this series of developments strictly involve the change of a voiceless fricative to a voiceless plosive or that of a voiceless plosive to a voiceless fricative, and it is these changes alone which fall properly under (12) above.

(13) Other than in learned words, voiced fricatives were deleted before a nasal (except that /z/ before /m/ was retained).

Taking (12) and (13) together, words such as κτίζω ['ktizo] 'I build, and ἐτρίφθην [e'trifθin] (the aorist passive of τρίβω ['trivo] 'I rub'), became χτίζω ['xtizo], and (ἐ)τρίφτη-κα [(e)'trifti-ka], respectively, while ῥεῦμα ['revma] 'torrent/river bed', became ῥέμα [rema], as πρᾶγμα ['praɣma] 'thing', became πράμα ['prama]. But just as with some of the earlier changes, there was significant interference from written Greek, leading to uncertainty and inconsistency, and to a feeling among the educated that the innovative forms were 'vulgar'. Consequently, those who had learned to write 'correctly' continued in general to spell (and presumably in part to pronounce) words in the traditional way long after the changes in (12) and (13) had set in; 'adapted' spellings of other than the most everyday items are therefore quite rare even in vernacular written texts until the modern period.

There is clearly no prospect now that these partial changes will ever be completed, and in modern Greek many doublets survive, some clearly distinguished, e.g. λεπτά [le'pta] 'minutes', beside λεφτά [le'fta] 'money', ρεύμα ['revma] 'current' (including electrical), beside ρέμα ['rema] 'torrent/river bed'), others partially so, e.g. πρά(γ)μα ['pra(ɣ)ma] 'thing', beside πράμα ['prama] 'pussy/cock'. Furthermore, many 'learned' variants have now been fully assimilated, so that ἐλευθερία [elefθe'ria], for example, is standard in place of earlier, and popular, λευτεριά [lefter'ja], while σχολεῖο [sxo'lio] 'school', seems never to have been seriously challenged in the standard by the now-defunct σκολειό [sko'ʎo].

From the seventeenth century onwards, a great deal of innovative terminology was either created directly from ancient Greek source material or, as often, calqued on the neologisms of other European languages using ancient Greek lexical and derivational formants. Indeed, since a great deal of lexical innovation in modern European languages involved the creative use of ancient Greek roots in the first place, many such words were simply absorbed into modern Greek without significant change (see 15.2 and 17.4).

(14) In popular speech a sequence of two like vowels was simplified (though once again many exceptions persisted under the influence of the written language). This was frequently associated with a regression of the accent if the first of the two vowels was stressed: e.g. ἐποίηκα [e'piika] 'I made/did' (a new aorist built on the old perfect stem, see 11.8.4) > (ἐ)ποῖκα [(e)'pika] or ἔποικα ['epika] (alongside ποιητής [pii'tis] 'poet').

(15) Palatalization of velars before high front vowels and [j] became more marked, especially in the insular dialects and the Old Athenian group, where ultimately [ḱ]/[c] (/k/) > [tʃ] or [ts], and [ç] (/x/) > [ʃ] or [s]; in Cretan, [j] (/ɣ/) also > [ʒ]. Dental palatalization also took place quite widely (involving [n, l, s, z] > [ɲ, ʎ, ʃ, ʒ]), and this was especially important in the northern dialects, where the loss of unstressed [i] led to minimal pairs involving new phonemic contrasts between /s/ and /ʃ/, /z/ and /ʒ/.

Certain popular diminutive formations, including names and appellatives, were particularly subject to velar palatalization. Thus -άκι(ο)ν ['-aki(o)n] and -άκι(ο)ς ['-aki(o)s] > both [-'aki(n)]/[-'akis] (without palatalization) and [-'atsi(n)]/[-'atsis] (with palatalization). This type is the source of surnames such as Βασιλάκης [vasi'lakis] and Χορτάτσης [xor'tatˢis]. Similar developments affected -ίκι(ο)ν [-'iki(o)n]/-ίκι(ο)ς [-'iki(o)s], and -ούκι(ο)ν ['uki(o)n]/-ούκι(ο)ς ['uki(o)s], to give [-'iki(n)]/[-'ikis] alongside [-'itsi(n)]/[-'itsis], and [-'uki(n)]/[-'ukis] alongside [-'utsi(n)]/[-'utsis]. This last often acquired an adjectival termination to give -ούτσικος [-'utsikos].

In the light of what has been said about the phonological developments of the medieval period as a whole, it should by now be clear that any attempt to explain the emergence of standard modern Greek exclusively in terms of the development of the popular spoken Greek of the Middle Ages is doomed to failure. The educated spoken usage of the late Byzantine and Turkish periods, and much 'vernacular' writing based on it, consistently involved a blend of learned/written and popular/spoken variants. Indeed, contemporary modern Greek remains very much a mixed language, with a strongly vernacular base but with elements clearly derived from the learned tradition (a process that seems, ironically, to be accelerating with the final abandonment of the learned *katharévousa* and the progressive loss of the traditionally polarized/politicized perception of the language 'question'). These observations are strongly reinforced when we turn to examine the major morphological and syntactic developments of the Middle Ages.

11.7 Nominal morphology and syntax

11.7.1 The dative case; prepositional phrases

(16) (a) The dative case came to occupy an ever more tenuous position in the nominal morphology of the vernacular. Though it remained a fixture of the written Koine throughout the Byzantine period and beyond, the continued use of this case in spoken Greek had become restricted, during the course of the middle period, to the most formal speech of the educated population in the major urban centres, and its functions, both adverbial and grammatical, were therefore steadily transferred to the accusative or genitive (indirect objects, the former sometimes supported by εἰς [is] 'to'), and to various prepositional constructions (adverbial uses), cf. Trapp (1965). In the later Middle Ages there was still much fluctuation of usage, even within a single text. In the case of indirect objects, the final choice between genitive and accusative belongs to a later period, with northern dialects, along with Pontic and Cappadocian, eventually favouring the accusative, and other varieties opting for the genitive.

(b) The accusative had eventually emerged as the sole prepositional case in popular spoken varieties by the beginning of the later Byzantine period at the latest, and the array of prepositions in common use was reduced to:

εἰς [is] 'at/in/on/to/into/onto'; subsequently σέ [se] was regularized, with epenthetic final vowel added after aphaeresis to aid pronunciation, though regularly reduced to [s] before the definite article (now written στό [sto], etc.), and frequently also before words beginning with a vowel (now written σ' [s]).

ἀπό [apo] 'from/since (time)/by (agent)'; with frequent deletion of the final vowel before the definite article and words beginning with [o] or [a]; in vernacular texts we also find ἀπέ [ape] with epenthesis, especially before the article.

διά [ðja] 'for/about'; later simplified to γιά [ja]

μέ [me] 'with'; perhaps the product of 'simplification' in phrases like με(τὰ) τὰ παιδία [me(ta) ta pe'ðja] 'with the children', etc.

χωρίς [xo'ris] 'without'

ὥς [os] 'up to/until'

Some of these, however, were optionally specified by an adverbial element to give further precision, e.g. μέσα σε ['mesa se], lit. 'within at', i.e. 'inside'; (ἐ)πάνω ἀπό [(e)'pano a'po], lit. 'above from', i.e. 'over'; etc.

Other prepositions, though belonging properly to the written tradition, were sometimes exploited even in more popular forms of writing by educated authors: e.g. ἀντί [an'di] 'instead of', now often followed by γιά [ja]; κατά [ka'ta] 'according to/about (time)/during'; μετά [me'ta] 'after'; μεταξύ [meta'ksi] 'among/between'; μέχρι ['mexri] 'until'; παρά [pa'ra] 'against/despite'; πρός [pros] 'towards/in respect of/for the purpose of', etc. Many of these are still widely used in standard modern Greek, though others, such as ἐν [en] 'in', and ἐκ [ek] 'out of', ultimately survived only in fixed expressions: e.g. ἐντάξει [en'daksi] 'in order/all right'; ἐν μέρει [em 'meri] 'in part'; ἐν ἀνάγκῃ [en a'nangi] 'in need/if need be'; ἐκ τῶν προτέρων [ek tom bro'teron], lit. 'from the former', i.e. 'in advance/a priori'; ἐκ νέου [ek 'neu], lit. 'from new', i.e. 'afresh', etc.

11.7.2 Feminine nouns of the 1st declension: paradigm standardization

(17) In classical Greek, 1st declension (a-stem) feminine nouns followed one of four declensional sub-patterns:

   (i)   nom. -ᾱ [-aː] + gen. -ᾱς [-aːs] (e.g. χώρα [kʰóːraː])

   (ii) nom. -ă [-a] + gen. -ης [-ɛːs] (e.g. θάλασσα [tʰálassa])

   (iii) nom. -ă [-a] + gen. -ᾱς [-aːs] (e.g. πεῖρα [peîra])

   (iv) nom. -η [-ɛː] + gen. -ης [-ɛːs] (e.g. τιμή [tiːmɛ́ː])

After the loss of vowel-length distinctions, analogical levelling produced a simplified system, in which genitives consistently followed their nominatives in choice of vowel:

(i)–(iii) nom. -α [-a] + gen. -ας [-as]

(iv)   nom. -η [-i] + gen. -ης [-is]

Interference between types (ii) and (iii), and to a lesser extent between types (i) and (ii), had begun to affect more popular varieties in late antiquity (Gignac 1981: 3–11, 213), but the more radical simplification belongs to the Middle Ages.

11.7.3 Masculine nouns of the 1st declension: paradigm standardization

(18) Masculine nouns of the 1st declension in -ας [-as] and -ης [-is], both originally with gen. -ου [-u], replaced their classical genitives with -α [-a] and -η [-i] respectively.

Such 'regularized' declensional patterns, i.e. with the vowel of the genitive follow-ing that of the nominative, were already used for personal names in classical Greek (especially in Ionic inscriptions and in Great Attic texts from Ionic-speaking territ-ories), but from the first century AD onwards examples involving common nouns start to appear in the papyri.

11.7.4 Interplay between the 1st and 3rd declensions; imparisyllabic paradigms

(19) The elimination of the class of masculine and feminine consonant-stem nouns of the 3rd declension proceeded quite quickly in popular speech. Some were replaced early by neuter diminutives in -ιν [-in]. Otherwise, the development proceeded from the addition of an analogical -ν [-n] to the original acc. sg. in -α [-a], beginning in Roman times (Gignac (1981: 45–6), cf. 4.11.3). The consequential parallelism with 1st declension accusatives in -α(ν) [-a(n)] led to interference between the two paradigms and ultimately to their merger. Thus new nominatives in -α (fem.) and -ας (masc.) were built to the accus-ative in -α(ν) [-a(n)], and genitives in -ας [-as] (fem.) and -α [-a] (masc.) quickly followed.

With the final elimination of -ν [-n] in the accusative singular, we therefore move to the modern system of a-stem nouns (i.e. comprising both original a-stems and original consonant-stems), in which feminine nouns have a common nom./acc. sg. in -α/-η [-a/-i], genitive -ας/-ης [-as/-is], and masculine nouns have nom. sg. in -ας/-ης [-as/-is], with a common acc./gen. sg. in -α/-η [-a/-i].

In the plural, however, it was the consonant-stem pattern of nom. -ες [-es], acc. -ας [-as] that influenced the corresponding 1st declension forms -αι [-e] and -ας [-as]: thus χῶραι ['xore] 'countries', for example, became ['xore-s], eventually spelled χῶρες. The partial falling together of nom. and acc. forms in the consonant stems, already noted in the Roman period (4.11.1), then gradually became the norm for the new 'mixed' paradigm, with nom. -ες [-es], acc. -ες [-es] increasingly replac-ing nom. -ες [-es], acc. -ας [-as] (though with exceptions in Pontic, and sometimes in Khian and Rhodian). Only in the gen. pl. did the paradigms remain partially dis-tinct, since all original 1st declension nouns have retained their accented suffix -ῶν [-'on], while former consonant-stem nouns which originally carried the accent on the penultimate syllable have kept it there, e.g. ἐλπίδων [el'piðon] 'of-hopes', etc.

It should be noted, however, that there was a marked reduction in the use of the genitive plural in spoken Greek up until the modern era and the advent of universal education (cf. for example Thumb (1912: 31) on the vernacular of the late nineteenth century). Subsequently, however, the case has enjoyed a revival, and it is now once again routinely employed in the full range of modern genitive functions (though with some competition from ἀπό [a'po] 'from', + acc. in partitive constructions).

This set of developments brought with them the major advantage of eliminat-ing allomorphy between the nom. sg. and the rest of the consonant-stem para-digm (compare ἐλπίδα [el'piða]/ἐλπίδας [el'piðas] beside ἐλπίς [el'pis]/ἐλπίδος [el'piðos]); but the process was again greatly inhibited by knowledge of the written language (including passive knowledge, through the liturgy), and the original forms are still used in the 'learned' written forms of particular vocabulary items (cf. *Τράπεζα της Ελλάδος* ['trapeza tis e'laðos] 'Bank of-the Greece', etc.). Genitives in accented *-ός* [-'os] still persist in some local varieties, especially in the Ionian islands (where there has even been some extension to the original a-stem paradigm, giving not only *τοῦ πατρός* [tu pa'tros] 'of-the father', but also *τῆς πορτός* [tis por'tos] 'of-the door', from *πόρτα* ['porta]).

(20) This partial conflation of 1st and 3rd (consonant-stem) declensions led to further remodellings. Thus the consonant-stem type nom. sg. *φυγάς* [fi'ɣas] (later *φυγάδας* [fi'ɣaðas]) 'fugitive', with nom. pl. *φυγάδες* [fi'ɣaðes], led to the modification of the ancient 'contracted' 1st declension type, with accented nom. sg. in *-âs* [-'as] (<-*έας* [-'eas]), gen. sg. in *-â* [-'a], and nom. pl. in *-aî* [-'e]. These forms were originally mainly pet-names, but subsequently the type was widely extended in popular speech to denote professions and bodily peculiarities ('big-head', 'thick-lip', etc.). The partial transfer of these to the consonant-stem paradigm is already apparent in texts of the Hellenistic and Roman periods, but in the medieval period the consonant-stem forms were standardly adopted in the plural: thus *ἀββᾶς* [a'vas] 'abbot', with old gen. sg. *ἀββᾶ* [a'va], but nom. pl. *ἀββάδες* [a'vaðes], etc.

From this type the pattern was then extended to most nouns ending in accented vowel + *-s* [-s], e.g. *παπποὺς* [pa'pus] 'grandfather', plural *παππούδες* [pa'puðes], and subsequently to a great many loanwords from Turkish. All these types have retained the imparisyllabic paradigm in modern Greek.

The pattern also attracted the modified forms of the old 3rd declension type in *-εύς* [-'efs], e.g. *βασιλεύς* [vasi'lefs] 'king/emperor'. Here the accusative *βασιλέα* [vasi'lea] spawned a new nominative *βασιλέας* [vasi'leas], which in everyday speech developed to *βασιλιᾶς* [vasi'ljas] by synizesis. From this base we then get a new 'popular' paradigm with plural *βασιλιάδες* [vasi'ljaðes] (also retained in modern Greek).

The suffix *-άδες* [-'aðes] was also sometimes extended to ordinary 1st declension masculines and feminines: thus *μαθητής* [maθi'tis] 'pupil', for example, may have plural *μαθητές* [maθi'tes] or *μαθητάδες* [maθi'taðes], while *ἀδερφή* [aðer'fi] 'sister', may have plural *ἀδερφές* [aðer'fes] or *ἀδερφάδες* [aðer'faðes], etc. In the case of masculines, if the accent fell originally on the root, there is also often a by-form in *-ηδες* [-iðes], e.g. *ράφτης* ['raftis] 'tailor', with plurals *ραφτάδες* [raf'taðes] and *ράφτηδες* ['raftiðes] alongside the regular *ράφτες* ['raftes]. The longer forms of this type sometimes still occur dialectally, but are not used in standard modern Greek.

(21) This period also saw the beginnings of the assimilation of the 3rd declension type in *-ις* [-is], e.g. *πόλις* ['polis] 'city', to the 1st declension. Some early examples involve transfer to the type in *-ίς* [-'is]/*-ίδος* [-'idos], whence a new accusative in *-ίδα(ν)* [-'iða(n)] and the rebuilding of the paradigm in the familiar way. But in general the process was based on the existing phonetic overlap in the acc. sg., e.g. 3rd declension *πόλιν* ['pol-i(n)]: 1st declension

νίκην ['nik-i(n)] 'victory'. This led to a nom. sg. πόλι ['poli] (or πόλη: such forms were not, of course, written until later), and gen. sg. πόλις ['polis] (or πόλης), and even nom./acc. pl. πόλες ['poles].

Again, however, the process was slow and partial, with the ancient gen. sg. πόλεως ['poleos] and the old plural paradigm in general showing particular resistance to assimilation in all but the most popular/local varieties because of the influence of written/liturgical Greek. In the modern standard, the new nom./acc. sg. has now been adopted (spelled with -η), but both gen. sg. forms are acceptable, and in the plural it is the ancient paradigm that has been standardized: nom./acc. πόλεις ['polis], gen. πόλεων ['poleon].

11.7.5 *Neuters*

(22) Since neuters generally ended in vowel + ν [n] (cf. the two principal 2nd declension paradigms illustrated by ξύλον ['ksilo(n)] 'wood', and παιδίν [pe'ði(n)] 'child' (where -ί(ν) [-'i(n)] < -ίον [-'ion], cf. 6.5.2)), it was natural that the 3rd declension type in -μα [-ma], gen. sg. -ματος [-matos] should fall into line. Forms such as πρά(γ)μαν ['pra(ɣ)ma(n)] 'thing, deed', are therefore quite standard by the time vernacular literature starts to appear in the twelfth century.

There is also a tendency to substitute the 2nd declension genitive ending, to give πρα(γ)μάτου [pra(ɣ)'matu] besides πρά(γ)ματος ['pra(ɣ)matos], on the assumption that forms such as nom./acc. plural πράγματα ['pra(ɣ)mata], etc. were of 2nd declension type. In standard modern Greek it is again the ancient form of the gen. sg. which has been adopted.

The 3rd declension s-stem type in -ος [-os] (e.g. δάσος ['ðasos] 'forest'), with gen. -ους [-us] and nom./acc. pl. -η [i], also survived, and even attracted some 2nd declension neuters in -ο(ν) [-o(n)], so that we find plurals such as κάστρη ['kastri] 'forts', δέντρη ['ðendri] 'trees', beside the expected κάστρα ['kastra], δέντρα ['ðendra].

(23) From the fifth/sixth century onwards the new deverbative suffix -σιμον [-simo(n)], used to denote actions and associated meanings of a more concrete nature, begins to make an appearance, in part to replace the old feminine abstracts in -σις [-sis] (disfavoured because of their declensional irregularity and homophony with 1st declension masculines in -ης [-is]), in part to replace the nominalized infinitive which, in popular speech, was increasingly restricted to use as a temporal adverbial adjunct: thus τὸ ἰδεῖν [to i'ðin], lit. 'the to-see', could be used to mean 'when/after s/he had seen . . .', in vernacular texts of the later Middle Ages.

11.7.6 *The definite article*

(24) On the basis of the feminine singular forms of the article, ἡ [i], τή(ν) [ti(n)], τῆς [tis], there was a natural tendency for the plural also to acquire an i-vowel

in the nom. and acc., giving first [i] for αἱ [e] and, in the modern period, [tis] for τάς [tas] (the latter having first been subject to levelling under the influence of nominal and pronominal fem. acc. pls in -ες [-es], giving standard medieval [tes]).

Such innovative forms were not, of course, written for a long time, and when they did begin to appear in texts, there was much uncertainty about how they should be spelled. The modern orthography uses οἱ [i] and τις [tis]. Note, however, that nom. pl. αἱ [e] survived in the South Italian dialects (with generalization to the masculine paradigm, at least in some areas), while acc. pl. τάς [tas] was apparently still used until recently in some island dialects (e.g. on Khios and Rhodes); τές [tes] is still in use on Cyprus.

11.7.7 *Adjectives*

(25) (a) In the adjectival paradigms, there was a strong tendency to provide all surviving types with three distinct terminations (masc., fem., and neut.) according to the model of the most common type with 2nd declension masc. and neut. in -ος [-os] and -ο(ν) [-o(n)], and 1st declension fem. in -α [-a]/-η [-i]. Thus compound adjectives of the 2nd declension type, which had lacked a distinct feminine in classical Greek (i.e. with masc./fem. in -ος [-os]), were supplied with a 1st declension feminine in -α [-a] or -η [-i] to bring them into line with the regular paradigm.

(b) Adjectives with forms belonging to 3rd declension paradigms, just like nouns and participles, were increasingly disfavoured, and frequently subject to reformation or loss. The major survivor was the class of u-stem adjectives, which had always had a distinct 1st declension feminine form (cf. βαρύς [va'ris] (masc.), βαρεῖα [va'ria] (fem.), βαρύ [va'ri] (neut.) 'heavy'), though this too was subject to considerable reformation. By contrast, the consonant-stem types had only two terminations, and were very largely abandoned in favour of more regular replacements. The s-stems, however (e.g. εὐγενής [evje'nis] (masc./fem.), εὐγενές [evje'nes] (neut.) 'noble'), though also subject to replacement, were sometimes retained in an adapted form.

The principal changes, most of which belong to the later Middle Ages, are summarized in (26)–(28).

(26) The u-stem masc./neut. paradigm (sg. -ύς [-'is]/-ύ [-'i], pl. -εῖς [-'is]/-έα [-'ea]) was partially incorporated into the 1st and 2nd declensions through the homophony of its masc. sg. with that of masc. 1st declension nouns in -ής [-'is] and that of its neut. sg. with that of 2nd declension neuter nouns in -ί(ν) [-'i].

These forms were, of course, originally exclusive to spoken Greek, and there was much uncertainty about orthography when they were finally written. Forms without a learned history were in general written as if they belonged to the 1st and 2nd declension: e.g. masc. σταχτής [stax'tis] (gen. σταχτή [stax'ti] or σταχτιού [stax'tju], pl. σταχτιοί [stax'tji]); feminine σταχτιά [stax'tja]; neuter σταχτί [stax'ti] 'ashen'. In other cases, however, there was interference from the written language. Thus in the case of βαρύς [va'ris]/βαρύ [var'i] 'heavy', the modern orthography has kept the -υ- in the singular, but retained the 2nd declension paradigm and the spellings with -ι- in the plural (βαριοί [var'ji]/βαριά [var'ja]). As a result, the masc. and neut. singular forms ceased to belong to a 'living' paradigm, and now lack an accepted genitive inflection. Earlier, however, forms in (-ύ)/-ή [-'i] and -ιού [-'ju] were used quite freely, and the paradigm as a whole was sufficiently productive to attract some regular adjectives in -ός [-'os] (some of which then became 'standard', most notably μακρύς [ma'kris] 'long' for ancient μακρός [ma'kros]).

Occasionally, however, the levelling process seems to have been carried through systematically for accidental phonetic reasons. Thus masc. and fem. nom. plurals γλυκιοί [ɣli'kji] (replacing ancient γλυκείς [ɣli'kis]) and γλυκιές [ɣli'kjes] 'sweet' (< ancient γλυκείαι [ɣli'kie]) seem to have been re-interpreted as γλυκοί [ɣli'ki] and γλυκές [ɣli'kes], i.e. with 'normal' palatalization of the velar before [i/e]. On this basis, a 2nd declension neut. plural γλυκά [ɣli'ka] was also constructed without the [j]-element, and the masc. and neut. pl. forms then led to corresponding 2nd declension singulars, γλυκός [ɣli'kos] and γλυκό [ɣli'ko], in place of ancient γλυκύς [ɣli'kis] and γλυκύ [ɣli'ki]. Ironically, however, the fem. sg. remains γλυκιά [ɣli'kja] (< ancient γλυκεία [ɣli'kia]), thus blocking the full regularization of the paradigm. Examples of this type also led to -ιά [-'ja] feminines in regular 2nd/1st declension adjectives when the stem ended in a velar.

Alongside these partial, and rather confused, attempts to integrate members of a dying paradigm into living alternatives in the popular language, there are also words taken directly from the written language which have now been incorporated into standard modern Greek with their ancient paradigm intact. A good example is εὐρύς [ev'ris] 'broad' (with genitive εὐρέος [ev'reos], pl. εὐρεῖς [ev'ris]).

(27) The ancient n-stem type in masc./fem. -ων [-on], neut. -ον [-on], was almost completely lost apart from rare imports from the learned written language. There are also a few ancient participles of the -ων [-on]/gen. -οντος [-ondos] type in common use as adjectives, again with a complete ancient paradigm; e.g. ἐνδιαφέρων [enðia'feron], fem. ἐνδιαφέρουσα [enðia'ferusa], neut. ἐνδιαφέρον [enðia'feron] 'interesting'.

(28) Adjectives of the s-stem type in masc./fem. -ής [-'is], neut. -ές [-'es], were variously replaced by existing alternatives or remodelled using more regular suffixes (not all of which have survived into modern Greek): e.g. ἀκριβής [akri'vis] 'accurate' > ἀκριβός [akri'vos]; ἀληθής [ali'θis] 'true' > ἀληθινός [aliθi'nos]; ἀμαθής [ama'θis] 'ignorant' > ἄμαθος ['amaθos] and ἀμάθητος [a'maθitos]; εὐγενής [evje'nis] 'noble' > εὐγενός [evje'nos] and εὐγενικός [evjeni'kos]; ὑγιής [i'jis] 'healthy' > ὑγιηρός [iji'ros] and ὑγιεινός [iji'nos]; etc. In many cases, however, the ancient form survived in the written language and has now been re-incorporated into standard modern Greek with its ancient paradigm intact. In cases where both forms have been retained,

there is often some semantic differentiation (e.g. ἀκριβής [akri'vis] 'accurate', ἀκριβός [akri'vos] 'expensive'; ὑγιής [i'jis] 'healthy', ὑγιεινός [iji'nos] 'hygienic').

Others, however, were taken to belong to the type of 1st declension substantives, such as συγγενής [suŋge'nis] 'related' > 'a relative', with gen. συγγενή [siŋge'ni] and pl. συγγενήδες [siŋge'niðes]. These were then given parallel feminines in -ισσα [-isa] (e.g. συγγένισσα [siŋ'genisa]) and neuters in -ικό [-i'ko] (e.g. συγγενικό [siŋgeni'ko]). All three forms were properly nouns, though if the sense was appropriate, they could also be used in apposition to other nouns and so acquire something like true adjectival status. The neuter suffix then often spread to the masculine and feminine to produce a regular adjectival paradigm in -ικός [-i'kos]/-ική [-i'ki]/-ικό [-i'ko] (cf. εὐγενικός [evjeni'kos] 'noble/polite', above). Thus the modern adjective is συγγενικός [siŋgeni'kos], while the ancient συγγενής [siŋge'nis], together with its classical paradigm, has now been re-incorporated into the language as a noun meaning '(a) relative'.

Many neologisms ending in -άτης [-'atis], -ίτης [-'itis], and -ώτης [-'otis] were later added to this declensional type, despite the difference in accent, to give '-ης [-is]/-ισσα [-isa]/-ικο [-iko]. From this arose a set of popular adjectives in '-ικος ['-ikos], e.g. χωριάτης [xo'rjatis] 'peasant/villager', χωριάτικος [xor'jatikos] 'of the country'. The masculine nouns of this type have now very largely been assimilated into the regular 1st declension paradigm with plural in -ες [-es].

11.7.8 *Pronouns*

(29) This very complex area is summarized below under the following subheadings:

    (a) Indefinite pronouns
    (b) Interrogative pronouns
    (c) Relative pronouns
    (d) Demonstrative pronouns
    (e) Personal pronouns

(a) Indefinite pronouns

The indefinite pronoun/adjective τις [tis] 'someone/some' was increasingly replaced in its use as an indefinite article by the numeral εἷς [is], later ἕνας ['enas], lit. 'one' (as already sporadically from Hellenistic times). In its strictly pronominal uses ('someone/anyone') it was remodelled as τινάς [ti'nas], though this in turn was eventually replaced, as explained immediately below.

The particle κἄν [ka(n)], originally a combination of καί [ke] 'even' with the modal ἄν [an] used in potential clauses with an optative verb, was already used as a free-standing intensifier even in classical Greek. In combination with εἷς [is] this gradually passed from the sense 'even/at least one' to become a new indefinite pronoun meaning 'anyone'. The κἄν [ka(n)] element (with -ν [-n] retained only prevocalically and in the form κάμ-ποσος ['kambosos] lit. 'some-many', i.e. '(quite) a few') was then compounded with other ancient indefinite pronouns and adverbs to form the set of modern indefinites. But unlike the ancient forms, which were used to mean both 'any-X' and 'some-X', the replacement forms were divided into negative-polarity ('any/no') and affirmative ('some') subtypes. See 12.3.2 for discussion of the development of this important contrast.

Thus κανείς [ka'nis] and the more 'modern' κανένας [ka'nenas] (the latter used both pronominally and adjectivally) appear in negative, interrogative and generic contexts with the sense 'anyone', and are also used absolutely with the emphatic negative sense of 'no one'. A number of other (emphatic) indefinites were assimilated to this model: τίποτε ['tipote] 'anything/nothing' (i.e. τι [ti] 'something/ anything' + intensifying ποτέ [po'te] 'ever', later τίποτα ['tipota]); ποτέ [po'te] 'ever/never' (felt to be inherently emphatic because of its accented final); πουθενά [puθe'na] 'anywhere/nowhere' (i.e. ποθέν [po'θen] '(from) anywhere/somewhere', remodelled to πού [pu] 'anywhere/somewhere', and given the intensive suffix -ά [-'a] also used colloquially in demonstratives).

A different set of indefinite forms was used in affirmative contexts with the sense 'some-X': e.g. κάτι ['kati] 'something' (< κά(ν) + τι [ka + ti]), κάποιος ['kapjos] 'someone' (< κά(ν) + ποιός [ka + pjos], where the second element, originally adjectival = 'some kind of', assumed an additional pronominal function to replace τις [tis] in all its positive functions), κάπου ['kapu] 'somewhere' (< κά(ν) + που [ka + pu]), etc. Modern orthography has now dispensed with the mark of crasis, giving κάτι ['kati] etc. For the medieval variants with prefixed ό- [o-] (e.g. όκάτι [o'kati], όκάποιος [o'kapjos]), see 12.3.3.

(b) Interrogative pronouns

Just as the animate indefinite τις [tis] 'some(one)' was replaced by κά-ποιος ['kapjos], so interrogative τίς; [tis] 'who?' was replaced by ποίος; ['pios], originally = 'which?/what kind of?', with the same extension from adjectival to pronominal function. The substitution was promoted by the general demise of 3rd declension masc./fem. forms, and the fact that most other interrogative elements already began with π- [p-], cf. πού; [pu] 'where?', πότε; ['pote] 'when?', etc. The accent was subsequently shifted to the final syllable, through synizesis, to give ποιός; [pjos] 'who?'

However, the neuter τί; [ti] 'what?', just like the second element of indefinite κά-τι ['kati] 'something', was retained, and in some dialects (e.g. the Old Athenian and south-eastern groups, Cretan, and many Cycladic varieties) it was used so habitually in the phrase τί (έ)ν(ι) τό/τά; ['ti n do/da], lit. 'what is-it/are-they that?' (cf. French *qu'est-ce que?*), that this eventually developed, by dissimilation, into the fused pronominal interrogative είντα/ίντα; ['inda] 'what?'

(c) Relative pronouns

The 'weak' ancient forms ὅς [os]/ἥ [i]/ὅ [o], invariably beginning, and often also ending, in a vowel, were prone to contraction and loss, and so, beginning in classical times, were frequently replaced by stronger forms in popular speech.

The regular substitutes in the early-to-middle period are forms of the article beginning with τ- [t-] (as already in classical Ionic, where the once protective initial /h/ of the true relative was lost prehistorically), and (especially in cases where the article also began with a vowel) the formerly indefinite relative ὅστις ['ostis] or the emphatic relative ὅσπερ ['osper]. The interrogative τίς; [tis] is also sometimes used as a relative. This originated in overlap with ὅστις ['ostis] in indirect questions/free relatives (cf. *I know what(ever) she knows*), whence it acquired first a free-relative and then a simple-relative use, in line with the extended post-classical use of ὅστις ['ostis].

During the latter part of the period under review, however, all of these forms came to be widely replaced by ὅπου ['opu] and its more developed (de-accented) forms ὁπού [opu] and πού [pu], again with some interference from the corresponding interrogative ποῦ; [pu] 'where?'. Originally a purely locative relative (or indirect interrogative) meaning 'where', this gradually acquired the wider range of functions carried by the 'locative' prepositions ἐν [en]/εἰς [is], i.e. not only 'where-at', but also 'where-to' (goal) and 'where-with' (instrumental/comitative). It could then naturally be used, by a simple extension, as an indirect object relative (cf. '(anyone) where-with/where-to I spoke', etc.). Re-interpreted in this role as a substitute not only for an adverbial prepositional phrase but also for a 'bare' genitive or accusative pronoun fulfilling the grammatical function of indirect object, it soon became available to express the grammatical function of direct object (again as an accusative substitute), and was finally extended to subject function. Since it now functioned as little more than a relative complementizer (cf. English *that*), and since relative clauses, as identifying modifiers, are inherently 'factive', it was eventually extended to use after factive verbs like 'regret'.

We also start to find examples of the simple relative use of classical ὁποῖος [o'pios] (originally = 'of such a kind as', or 'what kind of?' in indirect questions) in place of ὅστις ['ostis]. This conformed with both the general preference for π-forms over τ-forms, and the general pattern of redeploying indirect-interrogative/free-relative adjectivals as simple relative pronouns. There was again a tendency for this to be confused with the corresponding direct interrogative ποῖος; ['pios] 'who?', and in consequence for further confusion to arise with regard to the status of ὁ- [o-] in the longer form: i.e. was this really ὁποῖος [o'pios], ὁ ποῖος [o 'pios] (the article + the interrogative used as a relative) or ὁ 'ποῖος [o 'pios] (the article followed by the longer form reduced by aphaeresis)? We therefore also start to find the 'corrected' form of the last of these options, namely ὁ ὁποῖος [o o'pios], the use of which was reinforced under the influence of Romance after the capture of Constantinople by the fourth crusade in 1204 and the subsequent division of the empire amongst the conquering Latin powers (cf. French *le quel*, Italian *il quale*, etc.). In the non-classicizing literature of late Byzantium we therefore find ὁποῖος/ὅποιος [o'pios/'opjos] (for the accent of the second, cf. ὅστις ['ostis]), ὁ ὁποῖος [o o'pios], and (with aphaeresis and/or conflation of interrogative and relative) ὁ ποιός/ὁ ποιός [o 'pios/o pjos], all in use alongside indeclinable ὅπου [('o)pu].

Ὁποῖος [o'pios], like its predecessor ὅστις ['ostis], was also employed as an indefinite relative, but in this case, the accent was standardized on the first syllable to give ὅποιος ['opjos], reflecting the continuing influence of the classical neuter ὅ,τι ['oti] 'whatever', which was retained alongside κά-τι ['kati] 'something'. This duality naturally led to ὅπου ['opu] and its variants also being used, at least for a time, in free relatives.

In modern Greek, however, πού [pu] and ὁ ὁποῖος [o o'pios] are used only as simple relatives (the latter with a slightly learned feel), ὅποιος ['opjos] only as an indefinite/generic pronoun in free relatives, though there was much uncertainty in the later Middle Ages before this stable pattern finally emerged.

(d) Demonstrative pronouns

As already noted, αὐτός [af'tos] became a true demonstrative (= 'this') in late antiquity or the early Byzantine period, replacing ancient ὅδε ['oðe]. A local variant, which still survives in some contemporary spoken dialects, was ἐ(ὐ)τός [e(f)'tos], with ἐ- [e-] by analogy with ἐκεῖνος [e'kinos] 'that'.

Ancient οὗτος ['utos]/αὕτη ['afti]/τοῦτο ['tuto] 'this', also survived, but with regularization of the paradigm through generalization of the stem τουτ- [tut-], to give τοῦτος ['tutos]/τούτη ['tuti]/τοῦτο ['tuto] (sometimes with initial ἐ- [e-], again on the analogy of ἐκεῖνος [e'kinos] 'that', ἐ-γώ [e'ɣo] 'I', ἐ-σύ [e'si] 'you').

There was also some interference between αὐτός [af'tos] and οὗτος ['utos] based on their respective feminine forms, αὐτή [af'ti] and αὕτη ['afti]. The latter spawned a rival paradigm with masculine αὖτος (or αὗτος) ['aftos] and neuter αὖτο (or αὗτο) ['afto], forms which provide useful metrical variants to αὐτός [af'tos], etc., and occur quite frequently in the vernacular poetry of the twelfth century and beyond as true demonstratives and strong (i.e. non-clitic) 3rd person pronouns. This development also led to the formation of εὖτος/ἔτος ['eftos/'etos] beside ἐ(ὐ)τός [e(f)'tos].

This last form may provide the explanation for the modern manner adverbial ἔτσι ['etsi] 'thus'. The phrase τί λογῆς; [ti lo'jis], lit. 'what of-kind/manner?' (i.e. 'what sort (of)?'), consisting of the now indeclinable neuter interrogative plus the fossilized genitive of the feminine noun λογή [lo'ji], is used today only with a following noun. But in medieval Greek it could apparently also be used absolutely to mean '(in) what manner/how?', to which a possible answer was the elliptical use of the feminine genitive singular ἔτης ['etis] '(in) this (manner)', agreeing with λογῆς [lo'jis]. From this, the general adverbial use (= 'so/thus') developed directly. But at this stage, the termination was re-interpreted as an adverbial suffix (cf. the ending of τόντις ['tondis] 'really', < τῷ ὄντι [t(o) 'ondi], lit. 'in-the existing', with addition of 'adverbial' -ς [-s] as in τότε+ς ['totes] 'then', etc.). This gave rise to attested forms such as ἐδ-έτις [e'ðetis] (see the following paragraph for the prefix) and (ἐ)ίτις ['itis] (with assimilation of the initial vowel). The form ἔτσι ['etsi] involves syncope of the unaccented vowel of ἔτις ['etis] followed by anaptyxis, while early Cypriot ἤτζου ['itsu] is perhaps a related derivative of (ἐ)ίτις ['itis] (in which the final vowel, however, remains unexplained).

Ἐκεῖνος [e'kinos] and (ἐ)τοῦτος [(e)'tutos] ἐ- [e-], could be augmented by an intensifying suffix -ά [-'a] (sometimes -έ [-'e]), or prefixed by ἐδε- [eðe-] < ἰδέ [i'ðe] 'look'. The strengthened form αὐτόνος [af'tonos] has a double inflection outside the nom. sg. masc. (e.g. gen. sg. αὐτούνου/αὐτουνοῦ [af'tunu/aftu'nu], fem. sg. αὐτήνη [af'tini], etc.), and appears to have been built to ἐκεῖνος [e'kinos], but with the continuing influence of the simplex αὐτός [af'tos] leading to the more complex declensional pattern.

(e) Personal pronouns

The development of a set of reduced clitic forms for the 3rd person pronouns has already been dealt with. The beginnings of the reconstruction of the system of 1st/2nd person pronouns were already apparent in some of the later papyri (cf. 6.5.4, example (37)(c)). In this period the changes were completed.

The form of the nom. sg. of the 1st person pronoun (ἐγώ [e'ɣo]), together with the existence of parallel strong and weak oblique forms (e.g. acc. ἐμέ [e'me]/μέ [me]), led to analogous 2nd person formations: ἐσύ [e'si] (replacing classical σύ [si]), with strong acc. ἐσέ [e'se] alongside weak σέ [se], etc.

Since the 1st/2nd plural forms had become homophonous (ἡμεῖς/ὑμεῖς [i'mis]), new pl. paradigms were built in the early/middle Byzantine period to the stem forms of the sg.: nom. ἐμεῖς [e'mis]/ἐσεῖς [e'sis], acc. ἐμᾶς [e'mas]/ἐσᾶς [e'sas], beside weak μᾶς [mas]/σᾶς [sas], etc.

For the use of the acc. pl. forms of 1st/2nd/3rd person pronouns in genitive as well as normal accusative functions, see 12.3.3.

From the early second century, the acc. sg. forms acquired a characteristic final -ν [-n] (ἐμέν [e'me(n)]/ἐσέν [e'se(n)]), and by the fourth century the 1st person pronoun had been formally adapted to the 3rd declension (perhaps on the analogy of ἕνα ['ena] 'one/a(n)', and τινά [tina] 'some(one)/a(n)'), through the addition of final -α [a]. This form naturally received its own analogical -ν [-n] along with other 3rd declension nominals, with ἐμέναν [e'mena(n)] already attested in papyri of the late fourth century. The parallel evolution of the 2nd person form (ἐσέναν [e'sena(n)]), however, belongs to the early/middle Byzantine period.

Since these types were then re-interpreted as belonging to the 1st declension, they were given the appropriate genitives (following the masculine declensional pattern), i.e. ἐμένα [e'mena]/ἐσένα [e'sena]. With the loss of final -ν [-n], these then served also as accusative–genitives in the usual way. (See Dressler (1966), Gignac (1981: 161–5)).

11.8 Verb morphology and syntax

11.8.1 The infinitive

(30) The aorist infinitive was reformed in the later Middle Ages to the model of the present (imperfective) infinitive, i.e. -(σ)αι [-(s)e] > -(σ)ει(ν) [-(s)i(n)] on the basis of -ειν [-i(n)].

In popular spoken usage infinitives were progressively confined to the complements of control verbs (i.e. 'want', 'try', etc., with an understood subject in the infinitival clause: *I want to go* = 'I want [that I go]'), and of auxiliaries expressing modal and aspectual notions (i.e. 'will', 'can', 'have', 'start', 'stop', etc.).

In the later Middle Ages νά [na] + subjunctive largely replaced the infinitive in the former category, while the infinitive when used with appropriate verbs of the second type was sometimes strengthened with the article to form a nominalized direct object (e.g. *I start [to talk]* → *I start [the talking]*). A number of modern Greek neuter nouns originated as infinitives used in this way, e.g. φιλί [fi'li] 'kiss', < φιλεῖ(ν) [fi'li(n)] 'to love/kiss'; τὸ φαΐ [to fa'i] < φαγεῖ(ν) [fa'ji(n)] 'to eat', etc.

Eventually, even infinitivals after modal/aspectual verbs were replaced by νά [na]-clauses, with the sole exception of those following εἶχα ['ixa] 'I would (have)' (always aorist because of the incompatibility of the original meaning of this periphrasis, i.e. 'to be able (to)', with durative aspect). This, through its use in the protases of counterfactual conditionals, passed in the later part of this period from the sense of 'would (have)' to hypothetical 'had', and then to that of a true pluperfect (*if X would have Y-ed* → *if X had Y-ed* → *X had Y-ed*). Ultimately, a new perfect with ἔχω ['exo] 'I have', was built to this pluperfect, though this development belongs to the modern period, by which time the future was consistently formed in ways other than with this auxiliary (see 11.8.3 for a full treatment of perfects/pluperfects, futures and conditionals).

The articular infinitive also survived into the late Middle Ages as a subject-orientated adjunct, functionally equivalent to a temporal or circumstantial clause. In this use it no longer appeared after prepositions, was always placed immediately after the article τό [to], and never took an independent accusative subject (i.e. its interpretation was necessarily controlled by the subject of the main verb). Since it now effectively duplicated the function of the indeclinable participle/gerund, it gradually fell out of use. (See Joseph (1983) for a comprehensive survey, in the context of the Balkan *Sprachbund*, of the issues involved in the demise of the infinitive).

11.8.2 Participles

(31) The imperfective (present) and perfect medio-passive participles in -όμενος [-'omenos] and -μένος [-'menos], which belonged to the 'regular' 2nd/1st declension paradigms, both survived strongly in the early Byzantine period.

Subsequently, the present forms, which, like their active counterparts, were used almost exclusively as subject-orientated adjuncts, began to disappear in a linguistic context in which the corresponding active forms had become indeclinable (see immediately below).

Perfect passive participles, by contrast, were used only adjectivally, both attributively and predicatively (in 'stative' perfect periphrases with 'be'), in contexts where agreement was routine. Eventually, under Romance influence after 1204, these also began again to be used with 'have' to form a perfect active periphrasis, usually agreeing with the direct object: e.g. *I have the letter (in a) written (state)*, etc. With the past tense εἶχα ['ixa], 'I had' these then formed a rival to the pluperfect formed with εἶχα ['ixa] + aorist infinitive. Different areas eventually selected one or the other as the principal exponent of this tense, with the infinitival forms emerging as the norm in standard modern Greek.

The remaining participles, with complex 3rd declension paradigms, progressively disappeared amid growing confusion of gender and number (see 6.5.3 for the early stages), eventually leaving only an indeclinable active form in *-οντα* [-onda]. Whether this represents the old neuter plural or a recharacterized singular is difficult to say in view of the general confusion, but it could be formed from both imperfective (present) and perfective (aorist) stems, the latter eventually showing -(σ)οντα [-(s)onda] in place of -(σ)αντα [-(s)anda] on the model of imperfective *-οντα* [-onda] (cf. the parallel remodelling of the aorist infinitive). Subsequent interference from the Romance gerunds in *-ante/-ant* etc., used to denote contemporaneous/durative manner or circumstance, led to the eventual demise of the punctual aorist forms. Similarly, though the Greek forms were earlier used used both circumstantially and predicatively (in the case of the aorist, as a pluperfect active substitute with the past of 'be'), their sole surviving function in modern Greek is as subject-orientated adverbials.

The addition of final *-ς* [-s], as in modern Greek, also seems to have begun in the later Byzantine period; this element may represent an attempt to mark them as nominative, but perhaps also reflected the feeling that they served a related adverbial function (cf. the addition of *-ς* [-s] to τότε-ς ['totes] 'then', πότε-ς; ['potes] 'when?', τόντι-ς ['tondis] 'really', etc.).

There is, however, no reason to think that the formal usage of the educated aristocracy was greatly affected by these developments until quite late in the Byzantine period. If we consider the usage, not always obviously parodic, of the supposedly 'vernacular' poems of Poor Pródromos (12.2.2), for example, it would seem that the urban élite continued to use a fairly full array of inflected participles, albeit in a reduced range of functions reflecting the restriction in more popular registers to subject-orientated, circumstantial meanings. (Cf. Mirambel (1961) for a full discussion of the retreat of the participle).

11.8.3 *Futures and conditionals, perfects and pluperfects*

(32) The principal exponents of futurity in the early Byzantine period were ἔχω ['exo] or μέλλω ['melo] + infinitive, the present indicative (which was now indistinguishable from the present subjunctive, and may sometimes be interpreted as such when future in function), and the aorist subjunctive (with which the future indicative had been merged in regular paradigms), cf. 11.8.6 (a); in irregular/suppletive paradigms it was the aorist subjunctive rather than the future forms that normally survived, albeit with analogically levelled 'indicative' endings, because of the centrality to the verb system of the contrast between imperfective and perfective subjunctives.

In the later Byzantine period the auxiliaries in these various periphrases began to be replaced steadily by θέλω ['θelo] 'will' (originally 'wish'), while bare subjunctives,

both present and aorist, had begun as early as late antiquity to be strengthened by
ἵνα [i'na]/νά [na], the products functioning not only modally but also as futures:

(i) ἐὰν γὰρ μάθω, ἵνα αὐτῷ συντύχω   (*Lausiac History*, 1113 b)

   [e'an ɣar 'maθo,   (i)'na to sin'dixo]
   if(ever) for I-learn(subjunc.), subjunc. him I-speak(subjunc.)

   'for if I find out, I shall talk to him.'

Correspondingly, the 'conditional' (= 'would (have)', i.e. the 'past' of the future in
inferential/hypothetical contexts) was expressed by a bare imperfect (i.e. the past
of the present-used-as-a-future), and by the past-tense forms of the infinitival periphrases, i.e. εἶχα ['ixa], ἔμελλα ['emela]/ἤμελλα ['imela], and eventually ἤθελα
['iθela], + infinitive. In the later Middle Ages, however, the 'bare' modal imperfect
was regularly strengthened, in a development modelled on the established use of νά
[na] to mark a corresponding 'present' as future/subjunctive in force:

(ii) ὡς σηκωτὴς νὰ ἐδούλευα τὴν ἄπασαν ἡμέραν
                                                       Ptokhoprodromiká III, 182

   [os siko'tis na   'duleva   tin 'apasan i'mera(n)]
   as porter   subjunc. I-was-working the whole   day

   'I would have worked as a porter the whole day long.'

In some later medieval texts, however, most notably in the principal manuscript
of the *Chronicle of the Morea* (H), but also sporadically elsewhere, we also find
the particle νά [na] combined with the ἔχω ['exo] or θέλω ['θelo] periphrases to
form a complex subjunctive νὰ ἔχω/θέλω [na 'exo/'θelo] + infinitive. This was
presumably a function of the now familiar future/subjunctive overlap, representing
an attempt to mark specifically 'modal' uses of these infinitival periphrases. Sometimes in the *Chronicle of the Morea* (though again only in H), this new subjunctive
combines with θέλω ['θelo] in volitive constructions, e.g. 6773 θέλω νὰ σᾶς ἔχω
εἰπεῖ ['θelo na sas 'exo pi], lit. 'I-want that to-you I-will/may tell', i.e. 'I want to
tell you'. Such developments presumably reflect the fluid situation in the later
Middle Ages with respect to the expression of modality and futurity, but these
particular forms had a local and/or substandard character, and none survived for
very long.

   The general replacement of ἔχω ['exo]/εἶχα ['ixa] by θέλω ['θelo]/ἤθελα ['iθela]
in the infinitival periphrasis was motivated by the beginnings of the shift of εἶχα
['ixa] + infinitive towards true pluperfect status. This exemplifies a process commonly seen in the history of counterfactual constructions whereby the two clauses,
being equally 'modal' in character, are formally equated through the generalization
of the overtly modal verb-form of the apodosis to the protasis. As one option,
therefore we find the νά [na] + imperfect construction in protases in place of ἄν [an]
+ imperfect. But the infinitival construction was also transferred, and this eventually became isolated in protases as the (νά [na] +) imperfect construction became
dominant in apodoses:

(iii) ἐκεῖνοι ἄν σε εἶχαν εὑρεῖ, Συρίαν οὐκ ἐθεώρεις

[e'kini   an se 'ixan   vri,   si'rian uk e'θjoris]
those-men if you would/had to-find, Syria   not you-were-seeing(impf.)

'If those men would have/had found you, you would not have seen Syria (again).'

In this position the infinitival periphrasis gradually came to be interpreted as a hypothetical pluperfect (= 'had X-ed') rather than a true modal (= 'would have X-ed'), through the assumption that it represented a hypothetical past-of-past, i.e. something that had to happen before the hypothetical consequence could follow; since the latter was represented by a modal past tense (imperfect), the prior condition was felt to be marked as 'more past'.

From here it was only a matter of time before the εἶχα ['ixa]-periphrasis began to be used in real-time past-of-past contexts as a true pluperfect; the earliest examples come from the *Chronicle of the Morea* (cf. Khatzidákis (1905: 585–609), Aerts (1965), Moser (1988), Horrocks (1995)). The corresponding perfect, using ἔχω ['exo] + aorist infinitive, is now standard in modern Greek. This was formed to the new pluperfect, but the earliest examples in fact belong to the modern period (*pace* Browning (1983: 80), whose examples from the *Chronicle of the Morea* are not well supported by the manuscript tradition, or by the sense required in the relevant contexts. Thus Sofianós's early-sixteenth century grammar of the vernacular, for example, makes no mention of such a perfect (see Section III, 14.2.2), while Thumb (1912: 161–2) notes that such forms were still rare in the vernacular Greek of the nineteenth century, and were at that time only beginning to acquire wider popularity through their use by literary writers.

The only 'true' perfect forms available in the medieval period, therefore, were periphrases using the perfect passive participle, in combination first with 'be' (in a stative/passive sense), and later, as noted, with 'have' (in an active sense), following the impact of Romance on the western-dominated Greek lands. A stative pluperfect passive was analogously formed with the past of 'be' throughout the Byzantine period, while the later pluperfect active formations using 'had' (whether + aorist infinitive or + perfect passive participle) steadily replaced the earlier active periphrases, formed with the past tense of 'be' + aorist participle, during the course of the late Byzantine/early Ottoman periods.

As far as futurity is concerned, the θέλω ['θelo] + infinitive periphrasis (systematically distinguished from the volitive θέλω ['θelo] + νά [na] construction) continued in use throughout the later Middle Ages into the modern period. The apparent agreement of auxiliary and infinitive in the 3rd sg., e.g. θέλει ὀμόσει ['θeli (o)'mosi] 's/he will swear', led (*c.* fifteenth century onwards) to the local and/or popular use of a fully inflected 'subjunctive' paradigm for the infinitival element.

The future use of νά [na] + subjunctive, however, was eventually strengthened by the prefixation of θέ [θe], a reduced form of 3rd sg. θέλει ['θeli] 'it will be (that)', used impersonally. The postulated full-form source is not attested until later (see below), which presumably means that in this particular use the reduced variant had become fully established in popular speech, and perhaps in oral poetry, before it was ever used in writing. This construction is again systematically distinguished from the personal volitive construction involving θέλω νά ['θelo na], and it parallels the impersonal use of other modal auxiliaries with a νά [na]-clause which are well attested in late Byzantine popular texts: cf. for example, μέλλει ['meli] 'it will be (that)' (chiefly in early Cypriot texts, e.g. Makhairás's *Chronicle* I, 1); πρέπει ['prepi] 'it is necessary (that)' (e.g. *Chronicle of the Morea* 1342).

The earliest instances of θὲ νά [θe 'na] perhaps date from the twelfth or thirteenth centuries; it is used, for example, in line 24 of the poem *Porphýris*, which survives in a relatively late copy but probably reflects an earlier oral lay dealing with events of the tenth or eleventh centuries, see Mitsákis (1983: 273–4). But even if we admit that the texts of such poems are inherently unreliable because of their semi-oral origins and the later modifications of copyists and editors, the construction is well established in literate Cretan compositions from at least the beginning of the sixteenth century.

Subsequently, this form of the future began to gain in popularity over the infinitival construction and eventually, via assimilation and elision/apocope (θὲ νά [θe na] > θὰ νά [θa na] > θά(ν) [θa(n)]), the modern future particle θά [θa] was derived. Some of the earliest examples occur in Cretan literature, chiefly in 'lower-level' genres such as comedy, from the later sixteenth and seventeenth centuries, a situation which suggests that it was at first a popular/allegro form. Significantly 'earlier' attestations are probably misleading, and due to later copyists.

In modern Greek θά [θa] combines with present and aorist subjunctives (the former identical to the present indicative) to form an imperfective and perfective future, and with the imperfect indicative to form a temporally and aspectually neutral 'conditional' (which, like English *would*, may sometimes double as a past habitual = 'used to').

Finally, we may note forms such as θέλει γράψω ['θeli 'γrapso], lit. 'it-will-be I-write', consisting of the full-form of the impersonal verb + subjunctive. These formations, beginning in perhaps the sixteenth century, were particularly characteristic of the speech of the Ionian islands (Heptanese), though there are also rare examples in Cretan literature, probably under Heptanesian influence. It seems that this was a local conflation of the personal construction θέλω γράψω ['θelo 'γrapso] (see above) with the impersonal type θὲ νὰ γράψω [θe na 'γrapso], based on the apparent redundancy of person-marking in the auxiliary verb. (See Joseph (1990: chs 5 and 9), Holton (1993) for detailed studies of the development of the future in medieval and early modern Greek).

11.8.4 *The spread of κ-aorists; the aorist passive*

(33) The functional merger of perfect and aorist forms (cf. 6.5.2) was completed early. In general, forms with reduplication were abandoned, though the model of common irregular verbs such as aor. ἔθηκα ['eθika] 'I put'/perf. τέθηκα ['teθika] 'I have put/I put', or aor. ἔδωκα ['eðoka] 'I gave'/perf. δέδωκα ['ðeðoka] 'I have given/I gave', led to the use of certain other perfects (with

augment substituted for reduplication) in preference to irregular inherited aorists: e.g. perf. ἕστηκα ['estika] 'I have stood/I stood', misunderstood as beginning with an augment, replaced aor. ἕστην ['estin]; perf. εὕρηκα ['evrika] 'I have found/I found', similarly assumed to begin with an augment, replaced aor. εὗρον ['evron]; perf. ἕβηκα ['evika] 'I have gone/I went' (for classical βέβηκα ['vevika]), replaced aor. ἕβην ['evin], especially in compounds; perf. ἕγνωκα ['eɣnoka] 'I have known/I knew', replaced aor. ἕγνων ['eɣnon], etc.

This led in turn to the pattern being partly generalized to all verbs with an aorist or perfect containing [i] or [o] before the suffix: thus perf. ἐποίηκα [e'piika] (classical πεποίηκα [pe'piika]), later reduced to ἕποικα ['epika]/(ἐ)ποίκα [(e)'pika] 'I have made/I made', came to compete with aor. ἐποίησα [e'piisa], etc. Some mainland dialects (principally the Old Athenian group, many Peloponnesian varieties and the dialect of Epirus) eventually generalized the κ-forms.

We should note, however, that there was a countervailing force at work in many irregular aorist paradigms, based on the general competition of κ- and σ-forms, which led to the construction of a new σ-aorist to original futures (now re-interpreted as aorist subjunctives) in -σω [-so], e.g. γνώσω ['ɣnoso] 'I shall know', δώσω ['ðoso] 'I shall give', and to the original 3pl. aorist forms in -σαν [-san], e.g. ἕγνωσαν ['eɣnosan] 'they knew', ἕδοσαν ['eðosan] 'they gave'. Thus ἕγνωσα ['eɣnosa]/ ἕγνωκα ['eɣnoka] 'I knew', ἕδωσα ['edosa]/ἕδωκα ['eðoka] 'I gave', came to compete fairly freely as aorists. In modern Greek the σ-forms have sometimes prevailed (as with ἕδωσα ['edosa]).

In the aorist passive, the analogical addition of final -ν [-n] to 3rd sg. forms (following the past-tense 3rd sg. active forms, which had allowed such an addition optionally since classical times and now favoured it routinely) led to the homophony of 1sg. and 3sg., with both ending in -ην [-in]. The subsequent loss of final -ν [-n] did nothing to remedy the problem, and during the middle Byzantine period 1sg. -η(ν) [-i(n)] was replaced by -ηκα [-ika], following the now familiar model of ἕβ-ην ['evin]/ἕβ-ηκα ['evika] etc. This innovation then spread gradually through the paradigm, affecting popular varieties before it was finally adopted in educated speech. In modern Greek the aorist passive paradigm with stem in -ηκ- [-ik-] is now standard in all but a handful of 'learned' verbs adopted from the written language (most notably συνελήφθην [sine'lifθin] 'I was arrested').

11.8.5 *Imperfective stem-formation*

(34) During the early and middle periods there was a great reduction in the variety of imperfective formations, a process principally involving extensive remodellings on the basis of the aorist stem and other related forms. By the later Byzantine period most of the changes discussed below are well attested in vernacular texts such as the *Chronicle of the Morea*. (See Egea (1988) for a full treatment of the phonological and grammatical structure of the Greek of this poem.)

The most important issues can be summarized under the following subheadings, each of which will be discussed in turn below:

   (a) The fate of the -μι [-mi] verbs

   (b) The spread of nasal suffixes and their relationship with other verb classes

   (c) The suffixes -άζω [-'azo] and -ίζω [-'izo]: (i) interaction of -άζω [-'azo] with nasal-formations and contract verbs; (ii) links between -άζω and -άω [-'azo/-'ao], -ίζω and -έω [-'izo/-'eo], and confusion with stems in velars; (iii) 'reduced' paradigms of certain verbs with velar and vowel stems

   (d) The suffix -εύω [-'evo] and its impact on other imperfective classes (especially verbs in -πτω [-pto])

   (e) The development of the contract verbs

(a) The fate of the -μι [-mi] verbs

During the early Middle Ages, the last traces of the old athematic inflections of the ancient verbs in -μι [-mi] (which were in any case confined to the imperfective stem) finally disappeared from popular speech.

The case of εἰμί [i'mi] 'I am', has already partly been dealt with (cf. 5.11.1, ((18)(d)). This verb alone assumed a middle paradigm, beginning with the past tense, which already had the look of an aorist middle/passive in the Koine: cf. ἦν [in], ἦς [is] (for earlier ἦσθα ['isθa]), ἦ [i], ἦμεν ['imen], ἦτε ['ite], ἦσαν ['isan], all homophonous with the regular aorist passive endings. Since its sense was imperfective, however, it was given a new imperfect middle/passive paradigm (1sg. ἤ-μην ['imin], already in Ptolemaic papyri, with the corresponding 1pl. appearing a little later, ἦσο ['iso], ἦτο ['ito], etc.), and this in turn spawned a new present (εἶ-μαι ['ime], εἶ-σαι ['ise], etc., based on the form of the root seen in the original present εἰ-μί [i'mi]).

In the 3sg. and 3pl. present, however, the form ἔνι ['eni], a reduced version of ἔνεστι/ἔνεισι ['enesti/'enisi] 'there is/there are', had already come to be used widely for ἐστί/εἰσί [e'sti/i'si], and this strongly resisted replacement. It was, however, phonologically adapted over time to the rest of the new paradigm (cf. 1/2sg. εἶμαι ['ime], εἶσαι ['ise]), first to ἔναι ['ene], and finally to εἶναι ['ine]. Similarly, the original 3pl. past ἦσαν ['isan] also survived strongly, but this was eventually subject to influence from the new 3sg. ἦτο ['ito] to give ἦταν ['itan].

In the case of ἵστημι ['istimi] 'I stand' (trans.)/ἵσταμαι ['istame] 'I stand' (intrans.), a new intransitive present στήκω ['stiko] was formed to the intransitive perfect-turned-aorist ἔστηκα ['e-stik-a], while the transitive form was replaced by ἱστῶ [i'sto] (already in Herodotus, following the -άω [-'ao] type of contract verb) and then by ἱστάνω [i'stano] and στήνω ['stino] (on which see (b) below).

Since ἔστηκα ['e-stik-a], by virtue of its suffix, was readily misunderstood as an aorist middle/passive, we also start to find a present middle/passive στήκομαι ['stikome] (a process supported by middle/passive ἵσταμαι ['istame] 'I stand', and κάθομαι ['kaθome] 'I sit'). Transitive ἱστάνω [i'stano] was also remodelled as (ἱ)σταίνω [(i)'steno] (cf. below), and though this form eventually disappeared in isolation (surviving only in compounds), its characteristic e-vowel influenced intransitive στήκω ['stiko]/στήκομαι ['stikome] to give στέκω ['steko]/στέκομαι ['stekome], as in modern Greek. The ancient middle ἴσταμαι ['istame] is, however, retained in learned compounds.

Similar developments took place for the other -μι [-mi] verbs, so that τίθημι ['tiθimi] 'I put', was partially replaced by τιθῶ [ti'θo] (following the -έω [-'eo] type of contract verb, as already in Ionic), and then by θέτω ['θeto], built to the form of the root seen in θέτης ['θetis] 'one who places, adoptive father', and θετικός [θeti'kos] 'fit for placing, disputable, positive'. When the original aorist ἔθηκα ['eθika] and the functionally equivalent perfect τέθηκα ['teθika] were re-interpreted as aorist passives (the latter is the aorist passive in modern Greek), this new present acquired an aorist active ἔθεσα ['eθesa] based on the original 3pl. ἔθεσαν ['eθesan] (which also had the [-e-] of θέτης ['θetis] etc.). Similarly, δίδωμι ['điđomi] 'I give' first became διδῶ [đi'đo] (following the -όω [-'oo] type of contract verb on the basis of a number of overlapping forms), and then δίδω ['điđo] (built to the original 1pl. δίδομεν ['điđomen] where the o-vowel, properly part of the root, was taken to be thematic), or δίνω ['đino] (for this replacement, see below).

Most of the large class of verbs in -(ν)νυμι [-nimi] had already been partly replaced by regular thematic formations in late antiquity, and this process was now completed: thus ἀνοίγνυμι [a'niɣnimi] 'I open' > ἀνοιγνύω [aniɣ'nio]/ἀνοίγω [a'niɣo]. The most regular initial development in this class was from -(ν)νυμι [-nimi] > -(ν)νύω [-'nio]. In the frequently occurring 2/3sg., however, the suffixes -(ν)νύεις/-(ν)νύει [-'niis/-'nii] became [-nis/-ni] (with a shift of the accent back one syllable, cf. (14) above)), through the regular simplification of pairs of like vowels. This led in turn to a 1sg. [-no] and eventually to a full corresponding paradigm: e.g. δείκνυμι ['điknimi] > δεικνύω [đi'knio] > δείκνω/δείχνω ['đikno/'đixno].

(b) Nasal suffixes

When the preceding vowel of forms resulting from the changes described in the last section was [-o-], as in ζώνω ['zono] < ζώννυμι ['zonimi] 'I gird', the pattern of present [-'ono], aorist [-osa] (e.g. ἔζωσα ['ezosa] 'I girded'), led to most of the old contract verbs in -ῶ [-'o] < -όω [-'oo], which also had aorists in -ωσα [-osa], acquiring parallel presents in -ώνω [-'ono]: thus δηλώνω [đi'lono] replaced δηλῶ [đi'lo] 'I reveal', etc. This therefore eliminated a 'difficult' class of verbs with a large number of anomalous forms resulting from contraction.

The parallel form of ὤμοσα ['omosa], the aorist of ὀμνύω [om'nio] 'I swear', led to a parallel replacement in the present, giving ὀμώνω [o'mono] (note that the conventional orthography here is irrelevant to developments in the spoken language), while δώνω ['đono], helped by Latin *dono*, began to compete with δίδω ['điđo] 'I give' on the basis of aorist ἔδωσα ['eđosa], the form which eventually replaced ἔδωκα ['eđoka] (cf. above). Modern δίνω ['đino] represents a compro-mise between δώνω ['đono] and δίδω ['điđo].

This new principle of substituting imperfective [-n-] for aorist [-s-] then spread, so that ['zveno] < σβεννύω [sve'nio] 'I extinguish' became σβήνω ['zvino] on the basis of aorist ἔσβησα ['ezvisa] (the latter replacing classical ἔσβεσα ['ezvesa] on the analogy of the original perfect ἔσβηκα ['ezvika]). We may also compare χύνω ['çino] for χέω ['çeo] 'I pour', on the basis of aorist ἔχυσα ['eçisa] (itself a replacement for earlier ἔχενα ['eçeva], built to the many forms with stem χυ- [çi-]); ἀφίνω/ἀφήνω [a'fino] for ἀφίημι [a'fiimi] 'I let go', on the basis of aorist ἄφισα/ ἄφησα ['afisa] (itself an alternative to ἄφηκα ['afika], cf. the model of ἔδωσα ['eðosa]/ἔδωκα ['eðoka] above); δένω ['ðeno] for δέω ['ðeo] 'I bind', on the basis of aorist ἔδεσα ['eðesa]; λύνω ['lino] for λύω ['lio] 'I free', on the basis of aorist ἔλυσα ['elisa]; στήνω ['stino] 'I stand', for ἵστημι ['istimi], on the basis of the old transitive aorist ἔστησα ['estisa], etc.

This 'intrusive' -ν- [-n-] subsequently spread to verbs with stems ending in a liquid, where the present indicative and aorist subjunctive had often become homophonous: e.g. φέρω ['fero] 'I carry'/aorist subjunctive φέρω ['fero] (replacing earlier ἐνέγκω [e'neŋgo]); βάλλω ['valo] 'I throw, I put'/aorist subjunctive βάλω ['valo]. The relevant presents were therefore recharacterized with the productive -νω [-no], either added to the existing stem, as with φέρ-νω ['ferno], or with -ν- [-n-] replacing the original consonant, as with βά-νω ['vano] (this last eventually replaced in turn by βάζω ['vazo], perhaps from (βι)βάζω [(vi)'vazo] 'I cause to go (up), I put', though there are other examples of interchange between -άνω [-'ano] and -άζω [-'azo], cf. below).

The general spread of the nasal element in the imperfective system led to a situation in which, even if the present indicative and aorist subjunctive remained distinct in verbs with stems ending in a liquid, as in the case of (ἐ)παίρω [(e)'pero] 'I lift, I take'/aorist subjunctive (ἐ)πάρω [(e)'paro], or στέλλω ['stelo] 'I send'/ aorist subjunctive στείλω ['stilo], the feeling that -ρω/-λω [-ro/-lo] were properly aorist subjunctive endings became dominant, and this quickly led to the emergence of παίρνω ['perno], στέλνω ['stelno], etc. Since the dominant stem-vowel in all these present stems was [-e-], a number of verbs were recharacterized rather more radically, so that σύρω ['siro] 'I drag along, 'I pull', for example became σέρνω ['serno], and σπείρω ['spiro] 'I sow', became σπέρνω ['sperno]. Often, however, the learned and popular forms continued to coexist, and have passed as doublets into modern Greek. Finally, we should note the eventual spread of the nasal element to contract verbs with a liquid before the termination -ῶ [-'o]. Thus περῶ [pe'ro] 'I pass (through), I cross', > περνῶ [per'no]; χαλῶ [xa'lo] 'I loosen, I spoil', > χαλνῶ [xal'no], etc.

On the analogy of the reduction of -ωννύει [-o'nii] to -ώνει [-'oni] and the development of new paradigms in -ώνω [-'ono], we might have expected the parallel emergence of forms such as *πετάνω [pe'tano] from πετάννύω [peta'nio] 'I spread out'. In general, however, this class of verbs underwent a different pattern of development (see (c)(i) for the details) because of the unsatisfactory nature of -άνω [-'ano] as a present indicative suffix (as explained immediately below). The general replacement of -ῶ [-'o] < -όω [-'oo] with -ώνω [-'ono], however, did lead to sporadic replacement of -ῶ [-'o] < -άω [-'ao] with -άνω [-'ano]. Ἰστάνω [i'stano] 'I stand', beside ἰστῶ [i'sto], is an example, but this verb, and also those which had this suffix originally (e.g. μανθάνω [man'θano] 'I learn', τυγχάνω [tiŋ'xano] 'I happen', λαμβάνω [lam'vano] 'I take'), were again felt to be problematical, and most were replaced by formations in -αίνω [-'eno].

The principal reason for the avoidance and eventual abandonment of -άνω [-'ano] was the coexistence of a large class of verbs with the suffix -αίνω [-'eno] in the imperfective stem: e.g. γλυκαίνω [ɣli'keno] 'I sweeten', κερδαίνω [ker'ðeno] 'I gain', μιαίνω [mi'eno] 'I pollute', περαίνω [pe'reno] 'I accomplish, σημαίνω [si'meno] 'I signify', ὑγιαίνω [i'jeno] 'I am healthy', all of which had aorists in -ανα [-ana] (some replacing earlier forms in -ηνα [-ina], e.g. ἐσήμηνα [e'simina]). This suffix had the advantage of containing the e-vowel characteristic of most other nasal presents, both original and innovative. Since the aorist subjunctives corresponding to -αίνω [-'eno] ended in -άνω [-'ano], this last quickly came to be felt as a proper marker of that function. Many present indicatives in -άνω [-'ano] were therefore rebuilt with the more 'regular' present ending -αίνω [-'eno]. Thus ἱστάνω [i'stano] 'I stand', > (ἱ)σταίνω [(i)'steno], etc. Nonetheless, ἱστῶ [i'sto], ἱστάνω [i'stano], σταίνω ['steno], and στήνω ['stino] (cf. above) all survive in modern Greek (the first three only residually in compounds) – a perfect illustration of the mixed character of the contemporary language.

The major exceptions to the replacement of -άνω [-'ano] with -αίνω [-'eno] were monosyllabic roots such as φτάνω ['ftano] 'I arrive' (< classical φθάνω ['fθano], originally 'I anticipate', but already shifting its sense in the popular Koine of the Roman period), and κάνω ['kano] 'I do' (< classical κάμνω ['kamno] 'I toil'). These tenacious survivors even attracted a few verbs which had originally ended in -άζω [-'azo], e.g. φτιάνω ['ftjano] 'I fix', < εὐθειάζω [(e)fti'azo], πιάνω ['pjano] 'I catch', < πιέζω/πιάζω [pi'ezo/pi'azo] (originally 'I press hard', but already with the modern sense in the Hellenistic Koine); see (c) below for other -άνω [-'ano]/-άζω [-'azo] transfers.

In the class of verbs originally ending in -άνω [-'ano], however, the regular loss of nasals before voiceless fricatives in the root (e.g. μανθάνω [man'θano] 'I learn', > [ma'θano], λαγχάνω [laŋ'xano] 'I obtain by lot', > [la'xano], τυγχάνω [tiŋ'xano] 'I happen', > [ti'xano]) gave the impression that the new presents in -αίνω [-'eno] were formed to the aorist stem: e.g. μαθ-αίνω [ma'θeno]/aorist ἔ-μαθ-α ['emaθa], λαχ-αίνω [la'çeno]/aorist ἔ-λαχ-α ['elaxa], etc. This led to -αίνω [-'eno] being used quite productively to create new presents to related aorist stems, e.g. λαβ-αίνω [la'veno], 'I take', to aorist ἔ-λάβ-α ['elava], as a replacement for λαμβάνω [lam'vano] (a learned pronunciation), even though the combination -μβ-, pronounced [-mb-], was permissible by the rules of spoken Greek.

This pattern was then extended further, as in (ὑ)π-άγ-ω [(i)'paɣo], 'I go'. Originally, the aorist of this verb was ὑπ-ήγαγ-ον [i'piɣaɣon], but the clumsy root reduplication was dropped in popular speech to give (ὑ)π-ῆγ-α [(i)piɣa] (modern πῆγα ['piɣa]), with subjunctive (ὑ)π-ά(γ)-ω [(i)'pa(ɣ)o] (modern πάω ['pao]). Since this last was homophonous with the present indicative, a new present (ὑ)π-αγ-αίνω [(i)pa'jeno] was built to the stem (ὑ)παγ- [(i)paɣ-], and subsequently this was remodelled on the basis of the aorist indicative (ἐ)πῆγ-α [(e)'piɣa], to give modern πηγαίνω [pi'jeno]. A similar remodelling was involved in παθαίνω [pa'θeno] 'I suffer' (for classical πάσχω ['pasxo]), on the basis of aorist ἔπαθα ['epaθa], and πεθαίνω [pe'θeno] 'I die' (for ἀποθνήσκω [apo'θnisko]), on the basis of aorist (ἀ)π-έ-θαν-α [(a)'peθana], while many other verbs originally ending in -ύνω [-'ino], e.g. πλύνω ['plino] 'I wash', ἀπαλύνω [apa'lino] 'I soften', and παχύνω [pa'çino] 'I fatten/get fat', were likewise remodelled with the now highly productive -αίνω (or -ένω) [-'eno], though the learned and popular forms frequently survive together in modern Greek.

(c) The suffixes -άζω [-'azo]/-ίζω [-'izo]:

(i)   interaction of -άζω [-'azo] with nasal-formations and contract verbs
(ii) links between -άζω and -άω [-'azo/-'ao], -ίζω [-'izo] and -έω [-'eo]; confusion with verbs with velar stems
(iii) the 'reduced' paradigms of certain verbs with velar and vowel-stems

    (i) As noted, the development of verbs in -αννύω [-a'nio] (earlier -άννυμι [-'animi]) took a different turn from the otherwise expected reduction to -άνω [-'ano]. Since the aorist of πετаννύω [peta'nio] was ἐπέτασα [e'petasa], the alternative model of verbs in -άζω [-'azo] (e.g. δικάζω [ði'kazo], with aorist (ἐ)δίκασα [(e)'ðikasa] 'I decide/judge') suggested itself, and πετάζω [pe'tazo] arose in the Byzantine period alongside the contracted πετῶ [pe'to]. This last was originally the (irregular) future, but began even in antiquity to serve as a present in competition with πετάννυμι [pe'tanimi], on the analogy of the subset of verbs with presents in -ῶ [-'o] < -άω [-'ao] and aorists in -ασα [-'asa], e.g. γελῶ [je'lo], aorist (ἐ)γέλασα [(e)'jelasa] 'I laugh', χαλῶ [xa'lo], aorist (ἐ)χάλασα [(e)'xalasa] 'I loosen'. The eventual result was a situation in which a number of verbs once ending in -άννυμι [-'animi] came to exhibit sets of alternative present-tense formations in -αννύω [-a'nio], -ῶ [-'o] (< -άω [-'ao]), and -άζω [-'azo] (the first disappearing quite early).
    (ii) Some verbs ending in -ζω [-zo] were derived prehistorically by palatalization from roots in voiced dentals and velars, e.g. φραδ- [fraδ-] 'understanding' → φράζω ['frazo] (< *φράδ-jω) 'I inform, I tell', and ἐλπιδ- [elpiδ-] 'hope' → ἐλπίζω [el'pizo] (< *ἐλπίδ-jω) 'I hope', beside ἁρπαγ- [arpaɣ-] 'robbery, rape' → ἁρπάζω [ar'pazo] (< *ἁρπάγ-jω) 'I seize/plunder', and στηριγ- [stiriɣ-] 'support' → στηρίζω [sti'rizo] (< *στηρίγ-jω) 'I support'. But the 'suffixes' -άζω [-'azo] and -ίζω [-'izo] were soon detached and used to form verbs from many other roots: thus ἀγορ-ά [aɣo'ra] 'market' → ἀγορ-άζω [aɣo'razo] 'I attend market/buy', and δίκ-η ['ðiki] 'justice' → δικ-άζω [ði'kazo] 'I judge', beside ἀρχ-ή [ar'çi] 'beginning' → ἀρχ-ίζω [ar'çizo] 'I begin', and νόμ-ος ['nomos] 'custom, law' → νομ-ίζω [no'mizo] 'I own by custom/law, I adopt a custom/belief, I believe/think'.
    The -άζω [-'azo] type was chiefly associated with a-stem nouns (as above), so that these verbs often occupied a place in the lexicon that might well have been filled by true a-stem denominatives in -ῶ [-'o] (formed from -ά- [a] + -ω [o]). A similar relationship held between many 2nd declension (e/o-stem) nouns and verbs in -ίζω [-'izo]: we may note, beside νόμος ['nomos]/νομίζω [no'mizo], examples like καπνός [ka'pnos] 'smoke'/καπνίζω [ka'pnizo] 'I (make) smoke', λόγος ['loɣos]

'reason, word'/λογίζομαι [lo'jizomai] 'I reckon'. Thus a significant number of verbs of this type similarly occupied slots that might well have been filled by true e/o-stem denominatives in -ῶ [-'o] (formed from -έ- [-'e-] + -ω [o]).

In late antique and early medieval Greek, there was a great deal of levelling. Many verbs in -ῶ [-'o] < -άω [-'ao] acquired innovative partners in -άζω [-'azo], and many verbs in -άζω [-'azo] acquired partners in -ῶ [-'o] (-άω [-'ao] type). At the same time, one or two a-stem nouns were supplied with a corresponding -άζω [-'azo] verb even when their classical partners did not end in the expected -άω [-'ao]: e.g. φωνάζω [fo'nazo] for φωνῶ [fo'no] (< -έω [-'eo]) 'I call, I shout' (cf. φωνή [fo'ni] 'voice, cry'). In a similar fashion, many verbs in -ῶ [-'o] < -έω [-'eo] were paired with novel forms in -ίζω [-'izo], and others in -ίζω [-'izo] were paired with new forms in -ῶ [-'o] (-έω [-'eo] type), a process supported by their 'common' aorists in [-isa] (i.e. -ησα for the -έω [-'eo] type, and -ισα for the -ίζω [-'izo] type). In addition, a number of the contract verbs in -ῶ [-'o] < -όω [-'oo], originally a distinct subclass of 2nd declension denominatives, were also attracted to this pattern, even though most were replaced by -ώνω [-'ono] formations (see (b) above): e.g. κεντρίζω [ken'drizo] 'I sting', beside κεντρώνω [ken'drono] 'I sting, I graft'.

Though only the verbs in -ζω [-zo] from velar-stems originally had aorists in -ξα [-ksa] (as opposed to -σα [-sa] for the dental-stems), the aorists of non-velar -ζω [-zo] verbs had begun to adopt -ξα [-ksa] dialectally even in classical Greek (principally in West Greek, Thessalian, Boeotian and Arcado-Cypriot). This interference became much more widespread in the early Middle Ages in the case of the verbs in -ῶ [-'o] (< -άω [-'ao])/-άζω [-'azo], so that φωνάζω [fo'nazo] 'I cry, I shout', for example, shows only the aorist (ἐ)φώναξα [(e)'fonaksa]. We may compare βαστῶ [va'sto] (innovative)/βαστάζω [va'stazo] 'I lift', with aorist (ἐ)βάσταξα [(e)'vastaksa] for earlier ἐβάστασα [e'vastasa]; πετῶ [pe'to]/πετάζω [pe'tazo] (innovative) 'I spread out' (later confused with πέτομαι ['petome]/ἵπταμαι ['iptame] 'I fly'), with aorist (ἐ)πέταξα [(e)'petaksa] for earlier ἐπέτασα [e'petasa]; and φυσῶ [fi'so]/φυσάζω [fi'sazo] (innovative) 'I blow', with aorist (ἐ)φύσηξα [(e)'fisiksa] for earlier ἐφύσησα [e'fisisa]. Though in many such cases it was the contract present which finally prevailed, it was often the -ξα [-ksa] aorist, originally associated with the longer form, that remained in use alongside it (though note σπά(ζ)ω ['spa(z)o]/ἔσπασα ['espasa] 'I break', σκά(ζ)ω ['ska(z)o]/ἔσκασα ['eskasa] 'I burst').

Still further confusion arose from the fact that, in classical Greek, verbs derived from roots ending in voiceless velars had presents in -σσω [-so] (Attic -ττω [-to]) and aorists in -ξα [-ksa], e.g. φυλακ- [filak-] 'guard' → φυλασσω [fi'la-so] 'I guard', aorist (ἐ)φύλαξα [(e)'filaksa]. Since the ending [-so] was the principal mark of the aorist subjunctive, verbs with present indicative in -σσω [-so] were widely transferred to the velar subtype of -άζω [-'azo] verbs, following the model of ἁρπάζω [ar'pazo]/ἅρπαξα ['arpaksa] 'I snatch, I seize', etc. Thus τάζω ['tazo] replaced τάσσω ['taso] 'I arrange, I fix' (though with new and old forms now semantically differentiated, τάζω ['tazo] = 'I promise'), ἀλλάζω [a'lazo] replaced ἀλλάσσω [a'laso] 'I change', and ταράζω [ta'razo] replaced ταράσσω [ta'raso] 'I disturb', etc.

A few of these new verbs in -άζω [-'azo], most notably φυλάζω [fi'lazo] 'I guard', acquired partners of the -άω ['ao] type on the model of πετῶ [pe'to]/ πετάζω [pe'tazo], etc. But by the time this happened, the more common contract verbs of the -άω ['ao] type had begun to add characteristic person/number endings to the 'opaque' contracted suffix of the 3sg. (see (e) below for a fuller account of this development and its ramifications). Thus 3sg. πετᾷ [pe'ta], for example, often became πετά-ει [pe'ta-i], with the addition of the regular 3sg. ending. Subsequently, 1sg. πετῶ [pe'to], as the sole form in the singular paradigm lacking the [-a-] element, was replaced by πετά-ω [pe'tao], and the result was a 'mixed' paradigm containing both contracted and apparently 'decontracted' forms (the latter occurring before the vocalic endings): thus πετά-ω [pe'tao], πετᾷ-ς [pe'tas], πετά-ει [pe'tai], with [-a-] then optionally generalised to 1/3pl.

It was natural that a palatal glide [-j-] began to appear in this type between [-a-] and the new 3sg. ending to give [-'a(j)i], and the corresponding velar glide [-ɣ-] was then inserted optionally between [-a-] and the 1sg. ending to give [-'a(ɣ)o]. This led to considerable interference between the -άω ['ao] contract verbs and verb forms in -άγω ['aɣo] with an original velar in the stem (see immediately below), and eventually to general confusion as to whether intervocalic [-ɣ-/-j-] was serving as an optional hiatus blocker or represented the final consonant of a verb with a velar in the root/stem.

The influence of written Greek eventually led to the elimination of the by-forms of the present tense containing epenthetic [-ɣ-/-j-], though they sometimes survive dialectally, and, quite exceptionally, the variants φυλάω/φυλάγω [fi'lao]/[fi'laɣo] 'I guard', are both still available in standard modern Greek. But the earlier presence of intervocalic [-ɣ-/-j-] in the present paradigm led, on the misunderstanding that this was a part of the root/stem, to the formation of a parallel imperfect in -αγ-α [-aɣa], though the development was also promoted by the generalization of the glides that arose in the distended (recharacterized) forms of the 3sg. imperfect, just as in the corresponding 3sg. presents: i.e. 'opaque' contracted 3sg. -α + 'regular' -ε > -α(γ)ε [-a(j)e]. This variant of the imperfect is still widely used in colloquial speech, with the velar/palatal element retained throughout the paradigm, though the grammar books routinely recommend the alternative form in -οῦσα ['usa] (on which, see (e) below). In the case of φυλά(γ)ω [fi'laɣo], however, along with σκάω ['skao] 'I burst', and σπάω ['spao] 'I break', the imperfect in -αγα [-aɣa] is in fact the only option, and in this respect these verbs pattern with those discussed in (iii).

(iii) These same developments also affected a small number of verb forms ending originally in -άγω [-'aɣo], e.g. 1sg. present/1sg. aorist subjunctive (ὑ)πάγω [(i)'paɣo] 'I go/I may go', 1sg. aorist subjunctive φάγω ['faɣo] 'I may eat', and then spread to other verbs with roots ending in vowel + -γ- [-ɣ-], such as λέγω ['leɣo] 'I say'. Since it seemed that the velar/palatal glides could be added or omitted freely in the 1/3sg. forms of the large -ά(γ)ω [-'a(ɣ)o] class, we also begin to find πάω ['pao], φάω ['fao], and λέω ['leo], as if the velar here were also merely epenthetic. The first member of each pair naturally shows 'reduced' forms of 2sg. and 1/2/3pl., as if these too were contract verbs. Thus on the model of the paradigm of:

Sg. 1 πετά(γ)-ω [pet'a(ɣ)o]   Pl. 1 πετᾶ-με   [pet'ame]
   2 πετᾶ-ς [pet'as]   2 πετᾶ-τε   [pet'ate]
   3 πετά(γ)-ει [pet'a(j)i]   3 πετᾶ-σι/πετᾶ-ν(ε) [pet'asi/pet'an(e)]

we also get:

Sg. 1 πά(γ)-ω ['pa(ɣ)o]   Pl. 1 πᾶ-με   ['pame]
   2 πᾶ-ς [pas]   2 πᾶ-τε   ['pate]
   3 πά(γ)-ει [p'a(j)i]   3 πᾶ-σι/πᾶ-ν(ε) ['pasi/'pan(e)]

Λέ(γ)-ω ['le(ɣ)o] then followed the established pattern, with the endings similarly added directly to an apparent vowel-stem:

Sg. 1 λέ(γ)-ω ['le(ɣ)o]   Pl. 1 λέ-με(ν)   ['leme(n)]
   2 λέ-ς [les]   2 λέ-τε   ['lete]
   3 λέ(γ)-ει ['le(j)i]   3 λέ-σι/λέ-ν(ε) ['lesi/'len(e)]

Exceptionally, the verb θέλω ['θelo] 'I wish' also developed some short forms, namely 2sg. θές [θes], 3sg. θέ [θe] (attested only in the future periphrasis), 1pl. θέμε ['θeme], 2pl. θέτε ['θete], 3pl. θέσι/θέν(ε) ['θesi/'θen(e)], of which only the 2nd person forms are now widely used. (See (35)(c) for the 3pl. endings.)

Eventually, this type of paradigm was further extended to a number of verbs whose root originally ended in a vowel, so that ἀκού-ω [a'kuo] 'I hear', for example, came to be conjugated: ἀκού-ς [a'kus], ἀκούει [a'kui], ἀκού-με(ν) [a'kume(n)], ἀκού-τε [a'kute], ἀκού-σι/ἀκού-ν(ε) [a'kusi/a'kun(e)], the process in this case being aided by the regular deletion of one of the like vowels in the 3pl. in popular speech (ἀκούουσι [a'kuusi] > [a'kusi]). Reduced paradigms of ἀκούω [a'kuo] 'I hear', καίω ['keo] 'I burn', κλαίω ['kleo] 'I weep', λέ(γ)ω ['le(ɣ)o] 'I say', φταίω ['fteo] 'I am to blame', and τρώ(γ)ω ['tro(ɣ)o] 'I eat', are now standard in modern Greek.

On the model of λέγ-ω ['leɣo]/λέ-ω ['leo] etc., these verbs were also subject to optional velar/palatal epenthesis in 1/3sg. of the imperfective stem, giving ἀκούγ-ω [a'kuɣo] beside ἀκού-ω [a'kuo], καίγ-ω ['keɣo] 'I burn', beside καί-ω ['keo], though the process was supported, as before, by the glides that arose spontaneously in forms such as 3sg. present κλαί(γ)ει ['kle(j)i], or 3sg. imperfect ἔκλαι(γ)ε ['ekle(j)e]. The secondary character of these glides is shown by the retention of the original aorists in -σα [-sa] (e.g. ἄκουσα ['akusa] 'I heard'), though they were generalized in the imperfect paradigm in the now familiar way (cf. ἄκουγα ['akuɣa], etc.)

(d)   The suffix -εύω [-'evo] and its influence: verbs in -πτω [-pto]

A few words also need to be said here about the highly productive class of verbs with the suffix -εύω [-'evo]. Already a growing class in ancient Greek, this continued to add new members throughout the Middle Ages. But the shift in pronunciation from classical [-eú(w)oː], aorist -ευσα [-eusa], to [-'evo], aorist -εψα [-epsa] (cf. (12)(i) above), had profound consequences in that the now very frequent pattern of present in accented vowel + [-vo] with aorist in [-psa] (earlier confined to a handful of verbs such as τρίβω ['trivo]/ἔτριψα ['etripsa], 'I rub') led quickly to the formation of analogous innovative presents to virtually all -ψα [-psa] aorists: e.g. κλέβω ['klevo] 'I steal' (for κλέπτω ['klepto] to aorist ἔκλεψα ['eklepsa]; κόβω ['kovo] 'I cut' (for κόπτω ['kopto]), to aorist ἔκοψα ['ekopsa]; κρύβω ['krivo] 'I hide' (for κρύπτω ['kripto]) to aorist ἔκρυψα ['ekripsa], etc.

We should, however, note the existence of by-forms displaying the expected phonetic outcome -φτω [-fto], which were once widespread, and in later times particularly characteristic of northern dialects and the speech of Constantinople. In some cases these have also prevailed in the standard language over the analogical -βω [-vo] type (e.g. βλάφτω ['vlafto] 'I damage'), and it is not unusual for the original form in -πτω [-pto] also to have been re-introduced as a variant from the learned tradition (sometimes superseding the alternatives, as with καλύπτω [ka'lipto] 'I cover').

In the south-eastern dialects, Cretan, and the Old Athenian group, -εύω [-'evo] regularly takes the form -εύγω [-'evɣo], and the epenthesis is sometimes extended to [-'avo]. The phenomenon is still poorly understood (cf. Krumbacher (1886), Khatzidákis (1892: 123), Kretschmer (1905: 193–204) for a variety of competing theories), though some of the earliest attested examples, if the manuscript readings can be trusted, date from around the eighth century (cf. Jannaris (1897: 220)). It is probably simplest to assume that -εύω was pronounced uniformly as [-eú(w)oː] in the classical period, and that the subsequent shift of [eu] > [ew] > [eβ/ev] produced standard late antique [-'evo], after automatic simplification of the geminate in the intermediate [-'ew(w)o]. In some areas, however, geminates were retained for longer. Thus even though the phenomenon is residual in the remnants of the Old Athenian group, it remains standard in the south-eastern area, and may once have been characteristic of early medieval Cretan too. In these dialects we may assume that [-'ewwo] > [-'eβɣʷo], the second member of the cluster resulting from assimilatory frication, and representing the still characteristically Greek pronunciation of English /w/ in words such as *woman* ['ɣʷuman]. This would then develop naturally into the attested [-'evɣo].

(e) The contract verbs

Since these classes have already been partly discussed above, it is sufficient here to list the principal points concerning the -άω [-'ao] and -έω [-'eo] types (the -όω [-'oo] class having been eliminated in the early Middle Ages, as noted).

In the vast majority of cases the aorist systems of the -άω [-'ao] and -έω [-'eo] types were already identical in classical Greek (i.e. with stem in -η- [-i-]), and only a handful of irregular verbs retained the [-a-] or [-e-] of the imperfective. The major developments in post-classical and medieval Greek therefore concern the imperfective system, where much reciprocal interference is already apparent in both the New Testament and the Egyptian papyri from the early centuries AD onwards. The vast majority of such cases involve the substitution of -οῦ- [-'u-] (< -έ+ο- [-'eo-]) for -ῶ [-'o-] (< -ά+ο- [-'ao-]) in the 1sg. imperfect, the 1/3pl. present and imperfect, and the participles of the -άω [-'ao] class, a development probably due to the greater frequency of the former, which occurred not only in the -έω [-'eo] type, but even more widely in the -όω [-'oo] class (prior to its recharacterization in -ώνω [-'ono]).

Though many common verbs eventually generalized [-a-] (giving present -ά(γ)ω [-'a(γ)o], imperfect -άγα [-'aγa], as noted), the forms of the present and imperfect most often used in the later Middle Ages were as follows:

(i) Present: Sg. 1 -ῶ   [-'o]   Pl. 1 -οῦμε(ν)   [-'ume(n)]
                    2 -ᾷς   [-'as]   2 -ᾶτε   [-'ate]
                    3 -ᾷ   [-'a]   3 -οῦσι/-οῦν(ε)   [-'usi/-'un(e)]
(ii) Imperfect: Sg. 1 -ουν   [-un]   Pl. 1 -οῦμε(ν)   [-'ume(n)]
                    2 -ας   [-as]   2 -ᾶτε   [-'ate]
                    3 -α(ν)   [-a(n)]   3 -ουν(ε)   [-un(e)]

    [For innovations in the endings, see (35)(b–c) below.]

But since verbs of the -άω [-'ao] class were by now more numerous in popular speech than those of the -έω [-'eo] type (many of which had a learned character), the mixed paradigms in (i) and (ii) gradually attracted the majority of verbs of the latter class that still remained in common use, principally on the basis of the subset of already shared forms containing -ου- [-u-]. Thus the present endings 2sg. -εῖς [-'is], 3sg. -εῖ [-'i], and 2pl. -εῖτε [-'ite], were eventually replaced by -ᾶς [-'as], -ᾶ [-'a], and -ᾶτε [-'ate] (with the a-vowel optionally generalized throughout the paradigm in the modern period). The imperfect endings 2sg. -εις [-is], 3sg. -ει [-i], and 2pl. -εῖτε [-'ite] similarly began to be replaced by -ας [-as], -α [-a], and -ᾶτε [-'ate], though here the original forms were retained in parallel use for longer, and so subject to further developments in their own right (see below).

The conflation process can be seen in progress in the vernacular texts of the fourteenth and fifteenth centuries, but its completion belongs to the early modern period. The remaining -έω [-'eo] verbs, along with their traditional paradigm, were progressively confined to the learned language and the formal speech of the educated minority (for the relatively few exceptions, see below), though many such verbs have since been re-introduced into standard modern Greek from the learned tradition.

Paradigmatic interference naturally extended also to the medio-passive paradigm, where a similar substitution of -οῦ- [-'u-] for -ῶ- [-'o-] took place in the -άω [-'ao] subtype: thus 1sg. present -οῦμαι [-'ume] replaced -ῶμαι [-'ome], and 1/3pl. present -ούμεθα [-'umeθa]/-οῦνται [-'unde] replaced -ώμεθα [-'omeθa]/-ῶνται [-'onde]. This paradigm, which retained 2/3sg. -ᾶσαι [-'ase]/-ᾶται [-'ate] and 2pl. -ᾶσθε [-'asθe], then attracted the commonly used 'deponent' (i.e. middle only) verbs of the -έω [-'eo] class, such as φοβοῦμαι [fo'vume] 'I am afraid', and λυποῦμαι [li'pume] 'I regret'. These verbs have retained their mixed paradigm in modern Greek (with the additional option of 1sg. -ᾶμαι [-'ame], and one or two more recent changes to the endings, cf. (35)(d)).

The medio-passive paradigm of the great majority of -άω [-'ao] verbs, however, began to be remodelled in the later Middle Ages on the basis of earlier developments in the -έω [-'eo] class. These began in the imperfect active, where they were eventually superseded, but also spread to the passive voice, where they predominated. While the changes in (ii) were still in progress, an alternative development began to affect the original 3sg. imperfect of -έω [-'eo]-verbs, namely -ει [-i] (< -ε+ε [-ee]). Since this was homophonous with the regular ending of the 3sg. present, it was widely recharacterized (like the corresponding -α [-a] of the -άω [-'ao] class) by the addition of the normal 3sg. imperfect termination, to give -ει-ε(ν) [-(i)je(n)], e.g. (ἐ)κράτειε(ν) [(e)'kratje(n)] 's/he used to hold'. This development also led to the change of 2sg. (ἐ)κράτεις [(e)'kratis] to (ἐ)κράτειες [(e)'kratjes] (and perhaps of 2pl. (ἐ)κρατεῖτε [(e)kra'tite] to (ἐ)κρατειέτε [(e)kra'tjete]); in some varieties the singular was then fully regularized, giving 1sg. (ἐ)κράτεια [(e)'kratja]. In the case of -έω [-'eo] verbs still in regular use, these new forms began to supersede not only those of the original paradigm but also the 'interpolated' -άω [-'ao] forms of (ii).

In the plural of the imperfect, however, a different set of innovations began to take place in the late Middle Ages. The changes involved started in the mixed paradigm of (ii) and gradually spread to the singular, the new paradigm eventually replacing all other options apart from -αγα [-aɣa] (i.e. not only (ii), but also the innovative -έω [-'eo] forms just described). Since the old 3pl. imperfect -ουν [-un] was homophonous with both the 1sg. form and the regular 3pl. present of non-contract verbs, it was widely replaced by -ουσαν [-'usan] (with the accented syllable following that of 1/2pl.) through the incorporation of aorist -σαν [-san] as a formally distinctive '3pl. past-tense' suffix. Examples already occur in the *Chronicle of the Morea*.

Subsequently, the element -ουσ- [-'us-] was extended to 1pl., where the instability of the syllabic augment had led to frequent homophony between present and imperfect: thus γελοῦμε(ν) [je'lume(n)] 'we laugh'/(ἐ)γελοῦμε(ν) [(e)je'lume(n)] 'we were laughing' → γελοῦμε(ν) [je'lume(n)]/(ἐ)γελοῦσαμε(ν) [(e)je'lusame(n)]. Then, during the early modern period, a full imperfect paradigm in -οῦσα [-'usa], -οῦσες [-'uses], -οῦσε(ν) [-'use(n)], etc., was gradually constructed to this model, the process being completed first in northern dialects, including that of Constantinople. Earlier, however, plural forms of this type were combined with elements taken from the other competing paradigms. In standard modern Greek (perhaps as a direct result of the influx of speakers from the Ottoman capital during the nineteenth century), the -οῦσα [-'usa] forms are now regarded as the norm for contract verbs, including even learned verbs of the -έω [-'eo] class, though more 'popular' verbs of the -άω [-'ao] type (e.g. κρατῶ/κρατάω [kra'to/kra'tao] 'I hold', etc.) still retain -αγα [-aɣa] in the colloquial speech of many Greeks, especially in the south.

But before these changes took place, the substitution of -ειε- [-je-] for -ει- [-i-] in the imperfect active of popular verbs of the -έω [-'eo] type (cf. 3sg. (ἐ)κράτειε [(e)'kratje], etc.), had led to a parallel substitution in the 3sg. and 2pl. of the imperfect medio-passive (i.e. -εῖτο(ν) [-'ito(n)] > -ειέτο(ν) [-'jeto(n)], and -εῖσθε [-'isθe] > -ειέσθε [-'jesθe]).

From the imperfect, the innovation spread to the present middle/passive, affecting

2/3sg. (-$\epsilon\hat{\iota}\sigma\alpha\iota$ [-'ise]/-$\epsilon\hat{\iota}\tau\alpha\iota$ [-'ite]), and 2pl. (-$\epsilon\hat{\iota}\sigma\theta\epsilon$ [-'isθe]), so as to give the paradigm in (iii):

(iii) Sg. 1 -$o\hat{v}$-$\mu\alpha\iota$ [-'umai]   Pl. 1 -$o\acute{v}$-$\mu\epsilon\sigma\tau\epsilon$ [-'umeste]
         2 -$\epsilon\iota\acute{e}$-$\sigma\alpha\iota$ [-'jesai]   2 -$\epsilon\iota\acute{e}$-$\sigma\tau\epsilon$ [-'jeste]
         3 -$\epsilon\iota\acute{e}$-$\tau\alpha\iota$ [-'jetai]   3 -$o\hat{v}$-$\nu\tau\alpha\iota$ [-'unde]

[For the changes in the endings, see (35)(d).]

Subsequently, the -ov- [-u-] element of 1sg. and 1/3pl. was adapted to the other forms, giving -$\epsilon\iota ov$- [-ju-]:

(iv) Sg. 1 -$\epsilon\iota o\hat{v}$-$\mu\alpha\iota$ [-'jumai]   Pl. 1 -$\epsilon\iota o\acute{v}$-$\mu\epsilon\sigma\tau\epsilon$ [-'jumeste]
         2 -$\epsilon\iota\acute{e}$-$\sigma\alpha\iota$ [-'jesai]   2 -$\epsilon\iota\acute{e}$-$\sigma\tau\epsilon$ [-'jeste]
         3 -$\epsilon\iota\acute{e}$-$\tau\alpha\iota$ [-'jetai]   3 -$\epsilon\iota o\hat{v}$-$\nu\tau\alpha\iota$ [-'junde]

And finally, though these changes belong properly to the modern period, the -$\epsilon\iota\acute{e}$- [-'je-] formant was generalized to 1sg., while -$\epsilon\iota\acute{o}$- [-'jo-] was substituted for -$\epsilon\iota o\acute{v}$- [-'ju-] in 1pl. on the basis of the regular -$\acute{o}\mu\alpha\sigma\tau\epsilon$ [-'omaste] of non-contract verbs (see (35)(d) for details); this formant was then sometimes extended to 2pl. (giving -$\epsilon\iota\acute{o}$-$\sigma\tau\epsilon$ [-'joste]).

This emerged as the dominant medio-passive paradigm for all contract verbs, and the forms of the -$\acute{\alpha}\omega$ [-'ao] class (other than deponents) were progressively incorporated into it from the later Middle Ages onwards. Contemporary Greek therefore uses $\alpha\gamma\alpha\pi\iota\acute{e}\mu\alpha\iota$ [aɣa'pjeme] 'I am loved', alongside $\kappa\rho\alpha\tau\iota\acute{e}\mu\alpha\iota$ [kra'tjeme] 'I am held', etc. (the spelling now standardized with -ι-). But the classical paradigms of both -$\acute{\alpha}\omega$ [-'ao] and -$\acute{e}\omega$ [-'eo-] types were retained in the learned language, and a number of verbs of learned origin still employ the classical endings.

It was noted earlier that most commonly used verbs of the -$\acute{e}\omega$ [-'eo] class were incorporated into the combined contract-verb paradigms given in (i)/(ii) and (iii)/(iv). But even in the popular spoken language, a number of such verbs survived into the later Middle Ages and beyond with their classical paradigms intact, or at least in partial use. Obvious examples include $\epsilon\dot{v}\chi\alpha\rho\iota\sigma\tau\hat{\omega}$ [efxari'sto] 'I thank', $\pi\alpha\rho\alpha\kappa\alpha\lambda\hat{\omega}$ [paraka'lo] 'I appeal to/(if you) please', $\lambda\alpha\lambda\hat{\omega}$ [la'lo] 'I speak', $\kappa\rho\alpha\tau\hat{\omega}$ [kra'to] 'I hold/keep', $\theta\epsilon\omega\rho\hat{\omega}$ [θeo'ro] 'I consider'. There was, however, some uncertainty even in these cases, and a number have now been partly or wholly absorbed into the combined paradigms (e.g. $\kappa\rho\alpha\tau\hat{\omega}$ [kra'to] in its entirety, $\lambda\alpha\lambda\hat{\omega}$ [la'lo] in the middle/passive, the active of $\pi\alpha\rho\alpha\kappa\alpha\lambda\hat{\omega}$ [paraka'lo] optionally and its passive obligatorily, etc.).

One verb which remained steadfastly in the -$\acute{e}\omega$ [-'eo] camp, however, was $\mu\pi o\rho\hat{\omega}$ [bo'ro] 'I am able', which gradually replaced classical $\delta\acute{v}\nu\alpha\mu\alpha\iota$ ['ðiname] in the spoken language. This derived from the classical compound $\epsilon\dot{v}$-$\pi o\rho\hat{\omega}$ [efpo'ro], properly 'I am well off/I have resources', but was already used colloquially in its modern sense in ancient Greek. Its aorist was $\epsilon\dot{v}\pi\acute{o}\rho\epsilon\sigma\alpha$ [ef'poresa] or later $\eta\dot{v}\pi\acute{o}\rho\epsilon\sigma\alpha$ [if'poresa] (both with post-classical replacement of -$\rho\eta\sigma\alpha$ [-'risa] on the model of -$\rho\acute{\alpha}\omega$ [-'rao] verbs where the imperfective stem-vowel was regularly preserved in the aorist).

Aphaeresis quickly led to a present [(f)po'ro] beside aorist [(f)'poresa], whose phonotactically difficult initial clusters were regularly simplified to [p-]. When such forms followed negative (οὐ)δέν [(u')ðen] or conditional ἄν [an], as happened particularly frequently with a verb of this meaning, the initial plosive was voiced in accordance with the rules of spoken Greek to give [ðem/am bo'ro]. This pronunciation then became so habitual through constant repetition in such contexts that it also came to be used independently of them. The present thus became μπορῶ, with a parallel aorist (ἐ)-μπόρεσα [(e)'boresa]. But since this new form had the appearance of a compound with ἐν- [en-], it also resulted in the formation of the 'corrected' present ἐμπορῶ [embo'ro], which sometimes appears in later medieval texts.

The alternative (originally post-classical, but still ancient) aorist ηὐπόρεσα [if'poresa] was adapted to the innovatory ἐμπόρεσα [e'boresa], to give ἠμπόρεσα [i'boresa], and the pattern of ἐμπορῶ [embo'ro]/ἐμπόρεσα [e'boresa] led to the formation of a new present ἠμπορῶ [imbo'ro] to partner ἠμπόρεσα [i'boresa]. This variant is also commonly used in vernacular texts of the later Middle Ages.

11.8.6   Personal endings

(35) The principal developments will be summarized under the following subheadings:

   (a) Indicative and subjunctive
   (b) Past-tense morphology: active, and aorist middle/passive; the augment
   (c) The active paradigm: present tense
   (d) The middle/passive paradigm: present tense
   (e) The middle/passive paradigm: the imperfect

(a)   Indicative and subjunctive

In late antiquity, as noted, the regular endings of the imperfective (without -σ- [-s-]) and aorist (with -σ- [-s-]) subjunctive:

sg. -(σ)ω [-(s)o]   -(σ)ης [-(s)is]   -(σ)η [-(s)i]
pl. -(σ)ωμεν [-(s)omen] -(σ)ητε [-(s)ite] -(σ)ωσι(ν) [-(s)osi(n)]

merged respectively with those of the present (without -σ- [-s-]) and future (with -σ- [-s-]) indicative:

sg. -(σ)ω [-(s)o]   -(σ)εις [-(s)is]   -(σ)ει [-(s)i]
pl. -(σ)ομεν [-(s)omen] -(σ)ετε [-(s)ete] -(σ)ουσι(ν) [-(s)usi(n)]

through a combination of sound change (i.e. classical ω [oː] and o [o] > [o], classical ει [eː] and η/ῃ [εː/εːi] > [i]) and analogical levelling (i.e. 2/3pl. -(σ)ητε [-(s)ite]/-(σ)ωσι(ν) [-(s)osi(n)] > -(σ)ετε [-(s)ete]/-(σ)ουσι(ν) [-(s)usi(n)]). The destabilization of the future indicative led to the widespread use of what, from a classical perspective, look like present indicatives (imperfective) and aorist subjunctives

(perfective) in future function (with the stem of the latter often surviving in preference to that of the future in suppletive paradigms). Subsequently the future was
formally renewed through the use of various infinitival periphrases and constructions with νά [na], later θὲ νά [θe na], as discussed in 11.8.3.

Similar levelling took place in the imperfective medio-passive paradigm between the present indicative (e.g. λύομαι ['liome]) and present subjunctive (e.g.
λύωμαι ['liome]). The future middle (e.g. λύσομαι ['lisome]) and aorist middle
subjunctive (e.g. λύσωμαι ['lisome]) might well have fallen together in the same
way, but the demise of the aorist middle as a separate paradigm led to the early
loss of this whole set of forms. The passive system was, however, distinctive, in
that the future in -(θ)ήσομαι [-'(θ)isome] was related to, but formally distinct
from, the aorist (soon medio-passive) in -(θ)ην [-(θ)in], with its subjunctive in
-(θ)ῶ [-'(θ)o]. Lacking independent support in a developing system where futures
were in any case threatened, the future passive was the first future paradigm to
disappear (being widely replaced by infinitival periphrases in late antiquity). The
aorist passive indicative and subjunctive, however, survived as expected, the latter
acquiring future uses like other aorist subjunctives (and subject to the same later
developments with νά [na], θὲ νά [θe na], etc.). Since, however, its active-type
terminations were accented, the forms involved were levelled to those of the partially homophonous present indicative/subjunctive active paradigm of -έω [-'eo] verbs,
to give (as still in modern Greek): -(θ)ῶ [-'(θ)o], -(θ)εῖς [-'(θ)is], -(θ)εῖ [-'(θ)i],
-(θ)οῦμεν [-'(θ)umen], -(θ)εῖτε [-'(θ)ite], -(θ)οῦσι [-'(θ)usi]/-(θ)οῦν [-'(θ)un].

The continued written use of graphically distinct subjunctive endings in the
Middle Ages was largely a feature of the learned tradition, though at least formal
educated speech probably continued to distinguish those subjunctives whose 'correct' written form justified a pronunciation distinct from that of corresponding
indicatives.

(b) Past tense morphology: active, and aorist middle/passive;
     the augment

As noted (5.8, 6.5.2), a common set of past-tense endings evolved in late antique
and early medieval Greek out of the old imperfect, aorist and perfect active paradigms. Thus the imperfect:

(i) sg. -ον [-on]   -ες [-es]   -ε(ν) [-e(n)]
    pl. -ομεν [-omen] -ετε [-ete] -ον [-on]

aorist:

(ii) sg. -(σ)α [-(s)a]   -(σ)ας [-(s)as]   -(σ)ε(ν) [-(s)e(n)]
     pl. -(σ)αμεν [-(s)amen] -(σ)ατε [-(s)ate] -(σ)αν [-(s)an]

and perfect endings:

(iii) sg. -(κ)α [-(k)a]   -(κ)ας [-(k)as]   -(κ)ε(ν) [-(k)e(n)]
      pl. -(κ)αμεν [-(k)amen] -(κ)ατε [-(k)ate] -(κ)ασι(ν) [-(k)asi(n)]

were all combined into the single system given in (iv) (with variants in 2pl. and 3pl.; forms of the imperfect of contract verbs are ignored here):

(iv) sg. -α [-a]   -ες [-es]   -ε(ν) [-e(n)]
     pl. -αμεν [-amen] -ατε [-ate] -αν(ε) [-an(e)]
                       -ετε [-ete] -ασι(ν) [-asi(n)]

The characteristic aorist/perfect markers -σ-[-s-]/-κ-[-k-] were prefixed, as appropriate.

The κ-version of the aorist/perfect paradigm was gradually adopted in the aorist middle/passive (-(θ)η-κα [-(θ)i-ka] etc.), as we have seen, a process completed in popular spoken Greek by the later Byzantine period (the true aorist middle, with a few high-frequency exceptions such as ἠρξάμην [ir'ksamin] 'I began', having been very largely abandoned in late antiquity).

In standard modern Greek 2/3pl. -ατε [-ate] and -αν [-an] are now normal, but the alternatives still occur dialectally. In medieval vernacular poetry, however, there is general fluctuation in the use of the two 3pl. forms (much of it metrically motivated). But since even early prose pieces show parallel uncertainty, and Sofianós's grammar (see Section III, 14.2.2) allows both forms in many instances, it seems that the variants were in widespread parallel use in the later Middle Ages and early modern period, and that even a single speaker might well have used them fairly indiscriminately.

In classical Greek all past tenses carried an augment, which involved either the prefixation of the syllable ἐ- [e-] (occasionally ἠ- [i-], see below) to forms beginning with a consonant, or the lengthening of the initial segment of forms beginning with a vowel or diphthong. The latter (the so-called 'temporal' augment') fell quickly out of favour because of its variable form and the destruction of the relevant notion of lengthening by sound change. In some areas the syllabic augment was used in place of the initial vowel, but in standard modern Greek past tenses now normally have the same initial vowel as the non-past forms (learned survivals excepted).

The syllabic augment survived more strongly, but its role too was partially undermined by aphaeresis. In standard modern Greek it therefore survives only when accented, though in some dialects it is retained across-the-board. It is also worth noting that, on the basis of frequently-occurring verb forms augmented at least optionally in ['i-], some inherited from antiquity (e.g. ἤθελα ['iθela] 'I wanted', ἤμελλα ['imela] 'I was about to', εἶπα ['ipa] 'I said'), a number of dialects generalized ἠ- ['i-] as the basic form of the syllabic augment. This is particularly characteristic of much of the south-eastern area, many Cycladic varieties, and the speech of eastern Crete. Where the unaccented augment is retained, some of these dialects substitute ἐ- [e-], while others keep ἠ- [i-] throughout.

From late antiquity onwards, the practice of using an 'internal' augment with compound verbs (e.g. εἰσ-έ-βαλον [is'evalon] 'they invaded') was steadily abandoned in favour of a regular 'external' augment (or no augment at all if the initial element began with a vowel). This was inevitable, given that word formation using the classical prepositions had ceased to be productive and many compound verbs survived only as lexicalized fossils.

(c) The active paradigm: the present tense

The parallel existence of past-tense 3pl. -αν(ε) [-an(e)] and -ασι(ν) [-asi(n)] very quickly generated a present-tense (and subjunctive) 3pl. -ουν(ε) [-un(e)] to partner the inherited -ουσι(ν) [-usi(n)]. The earliest examples of the innovative form date from the late antique/early Byzantine period, and the variants alternate freely, exactly like their past-tense analogues, in popular writing of the later Middle Ages. In modern Greek the -ουσι [-usi]/-ασι [-asi] variants are typical of the south-eastern dialects and some Cretan and south Italian varieties.

In the modern period -ουν(ε) [-un(e)] influenced the 1pl. ending -ομε(ν) [-ome(n)] to give -ουμε [-ume]. This is now the preferred option, though both forms remain widely in use, the traditional form being employed chiefly by older speakers.

(d) The middle/passive paradigm: the present tense

The ancient set of endings in the regular thematic paradigm (i.e. with verb stem in -e-/-o-) was as follows:

sg. -o-μαι [-ome]   -ει [-i]   -ε-ται [-ete]
pl. -ό-μεθα [-omeθa] -ε-σθε [-esθe] -o-νται [-onde]

This was partially remodelled:

(i) 2sg. -ει (earlier -η) [-i], which derived from an original *-εσαι [-esai] through prehistoric loss of intervocalic [s] and contraction, was analogically restored, beginning in the Hellenistic period, on the basis of the perfect middle/passive in -σαι [-se] and common athematic verb forms such as δύνα-σαι ['ðinase] 'you can', ἵστα-σαι ['istase] 'you stand', etc.

(ii) 2pl. -εσθε [-esθe] became -εστε [-este] by regular phonetic development (cf. (12) above). The 2pl. ending also influenced 1pl. -όμεθα [-omeθa], to give first -όμεσθα [-'omesθa]/-όμεστα [-'omesta], and then -όμεσθε [-'omesθe]/-όμεστε [-'omeste], the latter widely attested in later medieval texts. Subsequently, the imperfect 1pl. and 2pl. endings -όμαστε [-'omaste] and -όσαστε [-'osaste] (on which, see (e) below) often replaced these forms (in the case of 1pl. standardly in modern Greek), perhaps on the basis of the historic lack of distinctiveness between present and past terminations (i.e. -ομεθα [-'omeθa] and -εσθε [-esθe] in both paradigms).

(iii) In the early medieval period, 3pl. -ονται [-onde] was influenced by the new active ending -ουν [-un] to give -ουνται [-unde], and the -ου- [-u-] element then spread dialectally to the other forms with the thematic vowel [-o-] (in northern varieties often automatically, through mid-vowel raising). Both sets of variants continued in use, however, though now, apart from continued variation in 1sg., the [-o-] forms have prevailed in standard modern Greek, doubtless in part under the influence of the written language.

(e) The middle/passive paradigm: the imperfect

The classical thematic paradigm:

sg. -ό-μην [-omin]   -ου [-u]   -ε-το [-eto]
pl. -ό-μεθα [-omeθa] -ε-σθε [-esθe] -ο-ντο [-ondo]

was also widely remodelled, but its relative rarity led to a wider range of innovations:

(i) the 3pl. suffix was widely affected by the corresponding active past-tense ending -αν(ε) [-an(e)] to give -ονταν [-onda(n)]/-όντανε [-'ondane], and then a number of extended variants gradually emerged: e.g. -όντησαν [-'ondisa(n)], used in the *Chronicle of the Morea* and modelled on ἦσαν [isan], the traditional 3pl. imperfect of the verb 'to be' (cf. (34)(a)), and later -όντουσαν [-'ondusa(n)], a form now typical of Peloponnesian varieties and Athenian colloquial, in which -ουσαν [-usan] has apparently been borrowed from the 'regular' 3pl. active imperfect of contract verbs (cf. (34)(e) above, and see (iv) below for a similar development in 1sg.).

(ii) 3sg. -ετο(ν) [-eto(n)], with analogical final -ν [-n] on the basis of 3sg. active forms, was partly remodelled under the influence of the new 3pl. -ονταν [-onda(n)]/-όντανε [-'ondane], to give -οτον [-oto(n)]/-ότονε [-'otone], and then -οταν [-ota(n)]/-ότανε [-'otane]. This last development also led to the recharacterization of 3sg. ἦτο(ν) ['ito(n)], 's/he was', as ἦταν(ε) ['itan(e)], which was homophonous with the innovative version of the 3pl. of the same verb (cf. (34)(a)). On this model, the properly 3pl. endings -ονταν [-onda(n)]/-όντανε [-'ondane] were sometimes used also as 3sg. terminations, a usage now characteristic of the northern dialects, including the speech of Thessaloniki.

(iii) As in the present paradigm, 1pl. -όμεθα [-'omeθa] was remodelled to the 2pl. form. But in this case, beginning in Roman times, and in line with other developments of that period (cf. 3pl. imperfect active -ον [-on] > -ο-σαν [-osan], etc.), the 2pl. aorist-middle suffix -σασθε [-sasθe] had replaced the original termination -(ε)-σθε [-(e)-sθe] in popular speech, the substitution being motivated by the formal distinctiveness of this termination *vis-à-vis* the corresponding present. The starting point was the new 2pl. imperfect ἤ-σασθε ['isasθe] (for classical ἦτε ['ite]/ἦστε ['iste]) 'you were', built in part to 3pl. ἦ-σαν ['isan], but using the middle endings characteristic of the remainder of the remodelled paradigm of this verb (see (34)(a)). Thus, via an extension of the thematic vowel of 1pl. -ό-μεθα [-'omeθa], we first get the innovative 2pl. -ό-σασθε [-'osasθe] (later -όσαστε [-'osaste]) in place of -εσθε [-esθe], and only then was the 1pl. form itself remodelled to this termination, giving -όμασθα [-'omasθa]/-όμαστα [-'omasta], and finally -όμασθε [-'omasθe]/-όμαστε [-'omaste].

The new 1pl. endings of the present and imperfect paradigms were, however, widely interchanged, while the 2pl. imperfect was also commonly substituted for the 2pl. present. In some areas, and especially in northern dialects, the imperfect 1pl. and 2pl. endings were given the a-vowel of 3pl. -ονταν [-ondan]/-όντανε

[-'ondane], to produce -όμασταν [-'omastan]/-όσασταν [-'osastan]. In standard modern Greek, however, -όμαστε [-'omaste] is obligatorily used for both present and imperfect 1pl., while -όσαστε [-'osaste], the regular 2pl. imperfect, doubles only optionally as a present ending alongside -εστε [-este].

(iv) The 1sg. imperfect middle/passive -όμην [-'omin] had a termination that ceased to be associated with passive 1sg. past-tense forms after the replacement of the majority of 1sg. aorists in -ην [-in] by -ηκα [-ika]. The 2sg. ending -ου [-u], which derived prehistorically from *-ε-σο [-e-so] through loss of intervocalic [s] and contraction (cf. 2sg. present -ει [-i] < *-ε-σαι [-e-sai]), was even more opaque and ripe for replacement.

Since the aoristic -κα [-ka] was unsuitable as a substitute in the 1sg. imperfect, it seems that -ουν [-un], the active 1sg. imperfect ending of the contract verbs, was substituted for -ην [-in], just as their 3pl. -ουσαν [-usan] later replaced -ησαν [-isan] in the extended 3pl. middle/passive formations discussed in (i) above. This produced -ό-μουν [-'omun], which immediately provided a model for a new 2sg. -ό-σουν [-'osun], where [s] replaced [m] as in the present forms -μαι [-me]/-σαι [-se], and the thematic o-vowel paralleled the developments in the 2pl. termination.

The overall result of these various developments was a paradigm in which the thematic vowel [o] was generalized and normally bore the accent:

singular

-όμουν(α/ε) [-omun(a/e)]
-όσουν(α/ε) [-'osun(a/e)]
-όταν(ε)[-'otan(e)]/-οταν['-otan]

plural

-όμαστε [-'omaste]
-όσαστε [-'osaste]
-όνταν(ε)[-'ondan(e)]/-ονταν['-ondan]

The 1sg. and 2sg. endings naturally acquired an optional final vowel to protect the weak -ν [-n]. This was either the expected -ε [-e] in both forms, or the 1sg. 'past-tense' suffix -α [-a], apparently generalized to the formally parallel 2sg. The a-option was originally characteristic of the northern dialects, including the speech of Constantinople, and perhaps again passed into the standard through the influence of the many speakers who came from there in the early nineteenth century. The forms of 1/2/3sg. and 3pl. without a final vowel are now regarded as more formal/ correct in the contemporary standard language.

In these 'short' forms, the accent now remains fixed in 3sg. -όταν [-'otan], following the model of 1/2sg., but it may still be thrown back to the last syllable of the verb-root in the case of 3pl., to give either -όνταν [-'ondan] or -ονταν ['-ondan]. Some dialects, however, generalized the accent associated with the original short-form 3sg./3pl. endings, to give a paradigm -ομουν ['-omun], -οσουν ['-osun], -οταν ['-otan], etc.

Finally, we should note that, on the basis of 3pl. present -ουνται [-unde] (itself modelled on the innovative 3pl. active -ουν [-un]), an alternative 3pl. imperfect ending -ουντο [-undo] inevitably appeared (later -ουνταν [-unda(n)]/-ούντανε [-'undane]). The -ου- [-u-] element spread naturally in some dialects to replace thematic -o- (accented or not according to area) throughout the paradigm, though in northern or Asia Minor dialects in which the accent fell on the syllable before the thematic vowel, the regular mid-vowel raising produced -ου- [-u-] independently. This thematic -ου- [-u-] was certainly a feature of the speech of many in the capital during the later Middle Ages, and it is well reflected in the usage of the poems of Poor Pródromos (cf. 12.2.2). But, as noted above in the discussion of the present endings, it has now been eliminated from the middle/passive paradigm of standard modern Greek with two exceptions: the 1sg. present, where it remains as an option, and the imperfect passive of learned verbs of the -έω [-'eo] class (e.g. στερούμαι [ste'rume] 'I lack'), where it has been generalized, on the basis of the inherited -ού- [-'u-] of many of the forms in the classical paradigm, to give: -ούμουν [-'umun], -ούσουν [-'usun], -ούνταν [-'undan], -ούμαστε [-'umaste], -ούσαστε [-'usaste], -ούνταν [-'undan].

As with other cases of change in progress, a variety of imperfect middle/passive forms is attested in vernacular literature after the twelfth century, and it seems that a number of these developing variants were not only passively understood but also in active use in the major urban centres of the empire in the last few centuries before its final fall. Though particular forms may well originally have been characteristic of particular regions, general mobility created a situation in which dialect mixture and extensive free variation seem to have been the norm among city dwellers of all classes.

11.9   Conclusion

Though it is clear that spoken Greek changed very considerably during the Middle Ages, with a significant increase in regional heterogeneity among illiterate speakers at the lower levels of society, the continued existence of the Byzantine state and its institutions (primarily the education system, the bureaucracy, and the Orthodox Church) guaranteed that the evolution of the spoken language overall was constrained by knowledge of, or at least widespread exposure to, the learned written language in its various forms (most importantly, because of its universal impact, the language of the liturgy). Even the wholly illiterate could not escape the passive impact of ecclesiastical Greek or the levelling effects of military service in the imperial army, while the upper classes, concentrated in the major urban centres, continued not only to maintain mutual contact across the empire, but also to learn, and actively to employ, traditional forms of written Greek, a process which influenced their speech and inhibited the development of major regional differentiation in educated varieties at other than the phonological level.

Thus early medieval Greek, unlike Latin, did not fragment into regional dialects which later acquired official status and evolved as separate languages within independent states. Only with the advent of Norman rule in southern Italy and the Seljuk domination of eastern and central Asia Minor did the increasingly isolated dialects of these peripheral territories start to develop along radically independent lines.

After 1204, however, in the context of widespread western rule and the political fragmentation of the former empire, similarly independent developments began to take effect even in the spoken dialects of areas closer to the 'centre'. Crucially, these changes now affected all levels of society, since there was no longer a Byzantine state of any significance, and the educated classes eventually integrated with their Romance-speaking rulers. Some local dialects thus acquired official, and even literary, status at the expense of archaic written Greek (e.g. in Cyprus, Crete, and the Ionian islands). These and other issues will be taken up in more detail in Chapter 12.

Chapter 12

Texts in the 'vernacular'

12.1 The early and middle periods

12.1.1 Introduction

We have a unique collection of ninth-century inscriptions set up at the instigation of the Turkic Bulgars, who had established themselves during the seventh century as the rulers of the Slavic peoples in much of the territory of modern Bulgaria. Though a few of these are in Bulgar (using the Greek alphabet), most are in Greek. Whether they were composed under orders by Greek inhabitants of the conquered towns or by Slavs and/or Bulgars who had learned Greek remains unclear, but they reveal a contemporary vernacular style that shows little influence from any official variety used in the Byzantine empire.

For the early and middle periods, we also have a small collection of 'acclamations' with which the Hippodrome factions used to greet/harangue emperors and other public figures on formal occasions and in response to major incidents in the political life of the capital. The majority are preserved in the manuscript traditions of historians and chroniclers, and many have suffered 'correction'/corruption in the course of their transmission. Those composed for orchestrated chanting on official occasions naturally reveal a mixture of popular and formal characteristics, but some of the hostile pieces have a more consistently vernacular character, and provide an important, if limited, source for the spoken Greek of the urban masses in a period for which there is otherwise a serious lack of evidence.

12.1.2 The Protobulgarian inscriptions

Despite their privileged position as evidence for the vernacular of the ninth century, these documents must be interpreted with caution in so far as some at least may have been composed by non-native speakers. See Beševliev (1963, 1970, 1981) for a critical edition of the documents, and discussion of their historical and cultural significance.

The following inscription describes the destruction of a Byzantine army by the Bulgars in 813, and belongs to a period quite close to the events which it commemorates:

(1) ... [κ]ὲ ὁ ἀδελφὸς αὐ[τ]οῦ οὐκ ἐληθάρ[γ]ησεν αὐτὸν κὲ ἐξῆλ[θ]εν, κὲ ἔδοκε[ν] αὐτὸν ὁ θεὸς κὲ τόπ[ου]ς κ[ὲ] κάσστρα ἐρημῶσε{ν} [τ]άδε· {Σε} τὴν Σερδικήν, τὴν{ν} Δεβελτόν, τὴν Κονσταντήαν, τὴν [Βερσ]ηνικίαν, <τὴν>

254

Ἀδρηαν[ού]πολην. Τοῦτα τὰ κάστρα [ἔ]λαβεν. Τὰ δὲ λυπὰ κ[ά]στρα ἔδοκεν
ὁ θε[ὸ]s φόβον, κὲ ἄ[φ]ηκ[α]ν κὲ ἔφυγαν, κὲ ὁ κά[τ]ου τόπος [ἐξε]ληθάργησεν
τὸν τόπον τοῦτον, {τ}ὅπου ἐ[ξ]ῆλθε[ν μὲ] τὸν ὅλον λαὸν κὲ ἔκ[α]ψ[εν τὰ]
χωρηά ἡμὸν{ν} α[ὐ]τὸς ὁ γέρων ὁ βασιλεὺ[s] ὁ φαρακλός, [κ]ὲ ἐπῆρεν ὅλα,
κὲ τοὺς ὅρκους ἐλησμόνησεν, κὲ ἐξῆλθεν ἐπὴ [αὐτὸν] ὁ ἄρχων {ὁ ἄ} ὁ
Κρο[ύ]μος πρὸς [τ]ὸ πολ[εμῆσε] . . .   Inscription 2, ll. 5–35

[. . . ke o aðel'fos a'tu   uk eli'θarjisen a'ton kj eks'ilθen, kj 'eðoken
        and the brother   of-him not abandoned   him   and went-out,   and gave

a'ton   o θe'os ke 'topus ke 'kastra eri'mose 'taðeː ti serði'kin, ti
him(acc.) the god   both places and towns to-devastate these: the Serdike,   the

ðevel'ton,   ti ko(n)stan'dian, ti versini'kian, tin aðrja'nupolin. 'tuta ta
Debeltos,   the Constantia,   the Bersinicia,   the Adrianople.   These the

'kastra 'elaven. ta ðe ly'pa   'kastra 'eðoken o θe'os   'fovon, ke
towns   he-took. The but remaining towns(acc.) gave   the god(nom.) fear,   and

'afikan   kj 'efyɣan, ke o 'katu 'topos ekseli'θarjisen   ton
they-surrendered (them) and fled,   and the below place   completely-abandoned the

'dopon 'tuton, 'opu eks'ilθen me ton 'olon la'on kj 'ekapsen ta xor'ja
place this,   where had-gone-out with the whole army and burned   the villages

i'mon af'tos o 'jeron o vasi'lefs o fara'klos, kj e'piren 'ola,   ke tus
of-us himself the old-man the emperor the bald,   and had-taken everything, and the

'orkus eliz'monisen, ke eks'ilθen e'pi af'ton o 'arxon o 'krumos
oaths   had-forgotten, and had-gone-out against him   the leader   the Krum

pros   to pole'mise . . .]
with-a-view-to the to-fight . . .

'. . . and his brother did not desert him, but went out, and God granted it to him to destroy the following places and fortified towns: Serdike, Debeltos, Constantia, Bersinicia,
Adrianople. These were the fortified townships that he took. But God put fear into the
remaining towns, and they [*i.e. the Byzantines*] surrendered them and fled, and the land
of the south [*i.e. Byzantium*] completely abandoned this place, where the aged emperor
himself, the bald one, had gone out with his whole army and seized everything, forget-
ting his oaths, and our leader Krum had gone out against him to make war.'

This is the first time since we left the Egyptian papyri that spelling directly reflecting the sound changes of late antiquity and the early Middle Ages has been encountered. Note ι, ει, η = [i]; ε, αι = [e]; ο, ω = [o]; υ and οι, however, both still = [y],
and are together distinguished from the set of letters representing [i], as expected
(there are occasional exceptions in other documents in the collection, cf. 11.2 (1)).
The manner dissimilation of [fs] > [ps] is also apparent in ἔκαψε ['ekapse] for
ἔκαυσε ['ekafse], suggesting that the distinctive treatment of groups of voiceless
fricatives containing [s] as their second component began rather earlier than that
involving other such clusters (cf. 11. 6 (12)).

In morphology, we may note that the augment is still used routinely in past-tense
verb forms whether or not it bears the accent, and that final -ν [-n] has been

standardized in all past-tense 3sg. verb forms. The expected 'past-tense' paradigm (11.8.6 (35)(b)) is also well attested in the regular use of 3pl. forms in -αν [-an]. Note, however, that ἄφηκαν ['afikan] still displays the ancient k-form of the aorist (generalized from the singular in antiquity), and that the innovative s-form ἄφησα ['afisa] (built to future/aorist subjunctive ἀφήσω [a'fiso] and the base for modern ἀφήνω [a'fino], 11.8.5 (34)(b)) has yet to make its appearance (cf. also ἔδοκεν ['eðoken]). On the assumption that the final -ν [-n] of ἐρημῶσε{ν} [eri'mose] has been written in error, it would appear that the infinitive complementing control verbs is still alive and well, as is the articular infinitive used after prepositions.

The form τοῦτα ['tuta] for ταῦτα ['tafta] shows that the levelling of the 'anomalous' forms of this demonstrative to the majority containing -ου- [-u-] was already under way (11.7.8 (29)(d)). The general substitution of regular 2nd/1st declension ὅλος ['olos], originally meaning only 'whole/entire', for irregular 3rd/1st declension πᾶς [pas] 'all', has also taken place, in line with the general weakness of 3rd declension morphology in popular spoken Greek: cf. ἐπῆρεν ὅλα [e'piren 'ola] 'he took everything'. The bare accusative, both of enclitic 3rd person pronouns and full noun phrases, is used routinely to mark the indirect object after 'give' (perhaps already a northern characteristic, 11.7.1 (16)), and we can also see here the kind of context in which ὅπου ['opu] began the shift from purely locative relative to all-purpose relative complementizer (11.7.8 (29)(c)).

12.1.3 Acclamations; origins of the 'political' verse form

These fragments of a more everyday language are unfortunately neither common nor extensive, but they do serve to confirm, as the latest of the personal papyri from Egypt would suggest, that popular spoken Greek in the early and middle Byzantine periods was developing strongly in the direction of the modern language in terms of grammar and lexicon. (See Maas (1912), Bádenas (1985) for collections and commentary).

In (2) we have a piece directed against the emperor Mauríkios (Theophánes AM 6093, AD 602; de Boor (1963: 283)). The text as transmitted is as follows:

(2) *Εὕρηκε τὴν δαμαλίδα ἁπαλήν, καὶ ὡς τὸ καινὸν ἀλεκτόριν ταύτῃ πεπήδηκεν καὶ ἐποίησε παιδία ὡς τὰ ξυλοκούκουδα· καὶ οὐδεὶς τολμᾷ λαλῆσαι, ἀλλ' ὅλους ἐφίμωσεν· ἅγιέ μου, ἅγιε φοβερὲ καὶ δυνατέ, δὸς αὐτῷ κατὰ κρανίου, ἵνα μὴ ὑπεραίρεται· κἀγώ σοι τὸν βοῦν τὸν μέγαν προσαγάγω εἰς εὐχήν.*

We should note at this point that M. Jeffreys (1974) has argued that the origins of the fifteen-syllable 'political' verse (the adjective πολιτικός [politi'kos] here seems to mean no more than 'public/common', cf. the later use of πολιτική [politi'ki] to mean 'prostitute'), which is the standard accentual metre of oral folk songs, medieval and early modern vernacular poetry, and much learned Byzantine writing in the ceremonial and exegetical traditions (Hörandner (1974)), in fact go back to the acclamations originally employed to greet triumphant generals in Republican Rome. According to this account, the metre would then have evolved orally into its familiar Byzantine Greek form over the course of the following millennium. Others such as Polítis (1970) and Koder (1972, 1983), however, have argued equally strongly for a learned origin of some kind, and we may readily concede the similarity with the ancient iambic tetrameter and note that the final shaping of the metre in the tenth/eleventh centuries probably took place at least partly through the intervention of learned/literate poets. Nonetheless, pieces such as (2), as well as (4) below, provide evidence in support of the thesis of a popular origin (though without necessarily confirming Jeffreys's view *in toto*).

The mature form of the political verse has eight syllables in the first hemistich before a strong caesura, followed by seven syllables in the second. Typically, there are two clearly felt stresses in each half of the line, usually on the second or fourth, sixth or eighth, tenth or twelfth, and fourteenth syllables (the last obligatory), giving an iambic rhythm overall. But stresses on the first or third and ninth or eleventh syllables are not uncommon, and this introduces a trochaic counterpoint which was readily tolerated.

There is, however, evidence that oral accentual verse, involving lines of seven or eight syllables and a mixture of trochaic and iambic rhythms, was in use during the early Byzantine period, and a piece such as (2) can be readily rewritten, given minor emendation, into predominantly trochaic couplets comprising an eight-syllable line followed by a seven-syllable line. From such a basis, it is not difficult to imagine the evolution of the fully developed metre:

(3) Εὕρηκε τὴν δαμαλίδα

['evrike ti(n) ðama'liða
he-found   the   heifer

ἀπαλήν <καὶ τρυφεράν>,

apa'liŋ ge trife'ra(n),
tender   and soft

καὶ ὡς τὸ καινὸν ἀλεκτόριν

kj 'os to ke,non alek'tori(n)
and like the young   cock

ταύτῃ <ἐ>πεπήδηκεν

'tafti   epe'piðike(n)
her(dat.) he-fucked

καὶ ἐποίησε παιδία

ke e'piise pe'ðia
and he-made children

ὡς τὰ ξυλοκούκουδα·

'os ta ksilo'kukuða;
like the chips-off-the-block;

καὶ οὐδεὶς τολμᾷ λαλῆσαι,

ke u'ðis tol,ma la'lise,
and no-one dares   to-speak,

ἀλλ' ὅλους ἐφίμωσεν·

al 'olus   e'fimose(n);
but everyone he-has-muzzled;

ἅγιέ μου, ἅγιέ <μου>,

,aji'e   mu, ,aji'e   mu
holy (Lord) of-me, holy (Lord) of-me

φοβερὲ καὶ δυνατέ,

fove're ke ðina'te
fearful   and mighty,

δὸς αὐτῷ κατὰ κρανίου,

'ðos   ato   ka,ta kra'niu
give (it) to-him(dat.) on   head(gen.)

{ἵ}να μὴ ὑπεραίρεται.   'na mi yper'erete
                          that not he-may-be-puffed-with-pride
κἀγώ σοι τὸν βοῦν τὸν μέγαν   ka₁yo 'sy   to vun do(m) 'meya(n)
                          and-I   to-you the bull the   great
προσαγάγω εἰς εὐχήν.   prosay'ayo is ef'çi(n)]
                          shall-bring   in blessing

'He found his heifer tender and soft, and he fucked her like the proverbial young cock, and fathered children like chips off the block. Now no one dares speak; he's muzzled us all. My holy Lord, my holy Lord, fearful and mighty, let him have it on the head to stop his conceit, and I'll bring you the great bull in thanksgiving.'

Mauríkios (ruled 582–602) was a competent administrator and soldier, but he had inherited a bankrupt state, a situation which, in the context of continual warfare, forced him to adopt unpopular austerity measures. These were needlessly exacerbated by lack of sensitivity to what the army and the people could reasonably tolerate and, despite an impressive record overall, he was regularly faced by popular unrest. This came to a head when he ordered the army fighting along the Danube frontier to remain on station over the winter of 602–3. The army revolted, proclaiming an officer named Phokás as its leader, and marched on the capital. Though Mauríkios turned to the Blues and Greens (the popular circus factions), only the former proved loyal, and on the night of 22 November 602 a mob assembled outside the palace baying for blood. The imperial family managed to escape to Asia Minor, and Phokás was duly crowned emperor. Once installed, he sent troops to arrest Mauríkios, and the former emperor and his sons were put to death.

Earlier in the same year, however, the emperor and his eldest son had again escaped from a riotous mob. On this occasion, the crowd, frustrated in its ambition, had found someone who looked like Mauríkios and strapped him to the back of an ass, chanting the words in (2)/(3) (to understand which we need to know only that the emperor and his wife Konstantína had five sons and three daughters).

A number of linguistic features are worth noting here, in particular that the metre ordinarily requires the absence of synizesis (cf. παιδία [pe'ðia]), like-vowel simplification (cf. ἐποίησε [e'piise]), elision, and aphaeresis (the sole exceptions being the connectives κ(αί) [k(e)] and ἀλλ(ά) [a'l(a)], and perhaps the subjunctive marker (ἵ)νά [(i)'na]). Evidently, none of these had yet become 'standard' in the speech of the capital.

In verb morphology the old 'perfect' εὔρηκε ['evrike] 'he found', is used as an aorist, while <ἐ>π-επήδη-κεν [ep-e'piði-ke(n)], lit. 'on-jumped', shows a true k-aorist with internal augment rather than reduplication (cf. 11.8.4 (33)), if we accept the metrically motivated restoration. The infinitive is still used to complement control verbs like τολμῶ [tol'mo], but note that even after {ἵ}νά [na], the ending of ὑπεραίρεται [yper'erete] is already that of the indicative, as expected, while the former aorist subjunctive προσαγάγω [prosa'yayo] is used with the force of a future indicative, as often even in late antiquity (see 11.8.6 (35)(a)).

In nominal morphology, the most striking feature is perhaps the continued use of dative pronouns (ταύτῃ ['tafti] and σοι [sy]), though we should not forget that Constantinople was in origin a Dorian colony, and that it had retained a majority of Greek native speakers throughout its expansion in the later Roman and early Byzantine periods. Having then emerged as the capital of an empire in which Greek was the dominant official language, a certain conservatism is therefore to be expected, even in the speech of its urban masses.

Note, however, the transfer of δάμαλις ['ðamalis] from the i-stem to the consonant-stem declension (with accent-shift, δαμαλίς [ðama'lis], cf. 11.7.4 (21)). The neuter ἀλεκτόριν [ale'ktorin], a diminutive of the Koine form ἀλέκτωρ [a'lektor] rather than the Attic ἀλεκτρύων [alek'trion], shows the expected reduction of -ι(o)ν [-i(o)n], while ξυλο-κούκουδο [ksilo'kukuðo], the last element meaning 'fruit-stone, pip, seed, spot, hailstone', exemplifies nicely the free compounding which is a particular characteristic of the medieval vernacular.

All in all, then, we have the impression of a fairly natural continuation of the spoken Koine of late antiquity, a language more conservative than that of the most 'vulgar' documents from Egypt, but reflecting well the general direction of development in the spoken Greek of the time. This same metropolitan vernacular appears in a somewhat more 'advanced' form in the following piece, which was directed against the empress Theophanó in AD 970:

(4) Ὁ χαλκεὺς βαρεῖ τ' ἀμόνι<ν> καὶ βαρεῖ τοὺς γείτονας·
   ὁ συνάπτης καὶ ὁ πριψίδης εἰς τὴν θύραν στήκουσιν.
   ἡ Θεοφουνοῦ {ἐ}πόθειν πίτταν καὶ ἡ καλὴ τὴν ἔφαγεν.
   ὅπου φόρειν τὸ διβίκιν τώρα δέρμαν ἔβαλεν,
   καὶ ἂν τόνε φθάσει {ἐδώ} ὁ χειμών, φέρε<ι> καὶ τὴν γούναν του·
   κουκκουροβουκινάτορες φουκτοκωλοτρυπᾶτοι
   εἰσὲ σέλλαν μίας μούλας καυχόκτονο<ν> πομπεύουν.

Line 7: πομπεύουν has been substituted for πομπεύουσιν

[o xal'kefs va,ri t a'moni(n), ke va'ri   tuz 'jitonas;
The blacksmith strikes the anvil,   and he-strikes the neighbours;

o si'naptis kj o pri'psiðis is ti 'θira 'stikusi(n).
The matchmaker and the princeling at the door stand.

i   θjofu,nu 'poθin 'pita   kj i ka'li tin 'efaje(n).
The Theophanó wanted pie/cake and the beauty it ate.

'opu   'forin to ði'viki(n)   'tora 'ðerman 'evale(n),
(He)who wore the coronation-robe now   leather/hide put(on),

kj an ,done 'fθasi o çi'mon, 'feri   ke ti 'ɣunan du;
and if to-him comes the winter,   he-wears also the fur   of-him;

kukurovuki'natores fuktokolotri'pati
shrivelled-horn-players palm/hand-arse-holed

ise 'sela(m) ,mias 'mulas kaf'xoktonom   pom'bevun.]
on saddle   of-a mule   adulteress-murderess they-parade (for public ridicule).

'"The blacksmith strikes his anvil, and he strikes his neighbours too"; (for) the matchmaker and the princeling are standing at the door. Theophanó wanted her cake but it was the beauty who ate it. He who wore the coronation robe now donned a leather hide, and if wintry weather comes upon him, he will wear his fur coat too; (for) men with shrivelled cocks and hand-sized arseholes parade the murdering adulteress on the saddle of a mule.'

Unlike most 'acclamations', this piece has been preserved in its own right, but the text has been seriously corrupted in several places. Morgan (1954) is the indispensable foundation for any attempt to establish a coherent text and interpretation.

The background is as follows. Theophanó had married Romanós II, son of Konstantínos VII Porphyrogénnetos, against his father's wishes. The young man succeeded to the throne in 959, but died in 963. By this time Theophanó had given birth to two sons and a daughter, and found herself in a vulnerable position as the sole guardian of the true heirs of the Macedonian dynasty. At this time, Nikephóros Phokás had already been proclaimed emperor by his troops, and when the austere and ugly general, already well over 50 years of age, returned to the capital, the 22-year-old Theophanó persuaded him to marry her, and to act as co-emperor with her children. But she quickly took a lover, Nikephóros's flamboyant nephew Ioánnes Tzimiskés, and they together plotted to murder the emperor, who was duly killed in December 969. But the plan that they should marry and rule together was foiled by the aged Patriarch Polýeuktos, who had already objected on the basis of canon law to Theophanó's second marriage, and now refused to sanction a third, especially in the wake of a murder. The ambitious Tzimiskés therefore betrayed his accomplice, and agreed to the Patriarch's conditions for his coronation, including the banishment of Theophanó. Once Tzimiskés had become emperor the wily *parakoimómenos* ('chamberlain') Basíleios, who as the bastard son of Romanós I Lakapenós (regent for Konstantínos VII till 944) had been castrated for his own protection, quickly arranged his marriage to Konstantínos's daughter Theodóra. His motives in this matter were in part personal, since he had been dismissed from his post by Theophanó's first husband Romanós II.

The first line in (4) is clearly proverbial (i.e. 'avoid the blacksmith if you do not want a hammering'/'bad company brings bad consequences'), and in line 2 we may take the 'matchmaker' to be Basíleios the *parakoimómenos* and the 'princeling' to be Ioánnes Tzimiskés, both of whom turned out to be 'bad company' for Theophanó. The forms συνάπτης [si'naptis] and πριψίδης [pri'psiðis] (possibly < πρι(γκη)ψίδης [pri(ŋgi)'psiðis], i.e. *princeps* + diminutive suffix) may, however, conceal personifications of σινάπιν [si'napi(n)] 'mustard', and τριψίδιν [tri'psiði(n)], some other caustic herb/spice, used in the allegorical manner that appealed so strongly to the Byzantines. The 'beauty' of line 3 is clearly Theodóra, while lines 4 and 5 perhaps imply that Tzimiskés, once crowned, acquired a thick skin, and would add further layers if the going got tougher. Finally, given that elderly unmarried churchmen and eunuchs were widely assumed to play the passive role in homosexual relationships, the men in line 6 with 'shrivelled cocks and hand-sized arseholes' are presumably Polýeuktos (an ex-monk) and Basíleios the *parakoimómenos*.

Phonologically, the piece is more advanced in its development than the last, with aphaeresis of unaccented vowels (e.g. in the clitic pronouns (ἀ)τήν [(a)tin]/ (ἀ)του [(a)tu], or the imperfect (ἐ)φόρειν [(e)'fori(n)] 'she wore') and synizesis (e.g. Θεοφουνοῦ [θjofu'nu]) both now in evidence. Note too the anaptyctic vowels in τόν-ε φθάσει [tone 'fθasi] (line 5) and εἰσ-ε σέλλαν [ise 'selan] (line 7), introduced to protect an unaccented monosyllable threatened in context with phonetic erosion (cf. 11.2 (3) and (8), 11.7.1 (16)(b)).

In verb morphology, the present στήκω ['stiko] 'I stand', built to aorist (formerly perfect) ἔστηκα ['estika], is a medieval innovation (see 11.8.5 (34)(a)). Note that the old 3pl. present indicative ending -ουσιν [-usi(n)] and the new -ουν [-u(n)] are both in use (cf. 11.8.6 (35)(c), assuming the correctness of the metrically motivated emendation in line 7), but that there is as yet no evidence for erosion of the paradigm of -έω [-'eo] verbs under the influence of the -άω [-'ao] class (cf. 11.8.5 (34)(e)); thus imperfect 3sg. (ἐ)πόθειν [(e)'poθi(n)]/(ἐ)φόρειν [e'fori(n)] retain the inherited -ει [-i] < -ε + ε [-ee].

In the area of nominal morphology, we should note once again the liking for newly coined compounds in this type of 'popular' verse. Thus κουκκουρο-βουκινάτορ-ες [kukurovuki'natores] combines the colloquial/dialectal κούκκουρος ['kukuros] 'parched', with the Latin loan βουκινάτωρ [vuki'nator] (cf. Spanish *bocina* 'trumpet/car horn'), while φουκτο-κωλο-τρυπᾶτος [fuktokolotri'patos] combines φοῦκτα ['fukta 'palm/handful' (later φούχτα/χούφτα ['fuxta/ 'xufta]) with κῶλος ['kolos] + τρύπα ['tripa] 'arse' + 'hole', the whole finally being turned into an adjective by means of the now domesticated Latin perfect passive participle suffix -ᾶτος [-'atos].

Other points worth noting include: the now completely regular reduction of the neuter suffix -ιον [-ion] > -ι(ν) [-i(n)]; the retention of the acc. pl. suffix in γείτονας ['jitonas] (11.7.4 (19)); the use of εἰς/εἰσε [is/ise] + accusative in a locative sense (11.7.1 (16)); the simple relative use of ὅπου ['opu] (11.7.8 (29)(c)); the form τώρα ['tora] 'now' < τ(ῇ) ὥρᾳ [t(i) 'ora] 'at-the hour/time'; the addition of an analogical -ν [-n] to neuters of the type exemplified by δέρμα ['ðerma] (11.7.5 (22)); the preverbal positioning of clitic pronouns when clause-initial position is filled by a contrastive focus (ἡ καλὴ τὴν ἔφαγεν [i ka'li tin 'efajen]) or a 'modern' conjunction (ἄν τόνε φθάσει ['an done 'fθasi]), cf. 11.4; and the use of εἰς/ἕνας [is/'enas] 'one', as an indefinite article (μίας μούλας [ˌmias 'mulas]).

12.2 Vernacular literature of the twelfth century

12.2.1 The epic of Digenés Akrítes

Our earliest extended text in 'vernacular' Greek is the cycle of poems preserved in a fifteenth-century manuscript (E) now in the monastery of the Escorial in Madrid, which tell of the exploits of the legendary Basíleios Digenés Akrítes ('Basil Two-race Borderer'). The hero is the son of an Arab emir from Syria who married the daughter of a Roman general, but though the boy had blood from two races, he grew up to serve the Byzantine emperor as a frontier guard (ἀκρίτης [a'kritis]), protecting 'Romania' from Arab incursions and banditry.

The ultimate origins of these poems, and the relationship between the text of E and five other surviving versions, especially the fuller and less episodic, middle-register version contained in a manuscript (G) in the Grottaferrata monastery outside Rome, remain the subject of much dispute. The standard edition is Alexíou

(1985). Ricks (1990) provides a text and translation with introduction and notes, and treats the work as a collection of five separate but related poems (an analysis accepted here). The papers in Beaton and Ricks (1993) give a recent survey of the central questions, together with a literary evaluation of the poems.

Their language combines, in different proportions according to subject matter and context, a foundation from the folk tradition (supplemented by the spoken vernacular) with forms borrowed from literary compositions (cf. 8.4.3). A great many of the innovations discussed in Chapter 11 are therefore already well attested, some regularly, others more sporadically. We must, however, be careful not to exaggerate the impact of the learned overlay, since Byzantine oral poetry undoubtedly preserved archaisms alongside innovations. Such blending as did take place was the result of the first attempt to develop a 'literary' partner for contemporary spoken Greek out of linguistically limited and thematically underdeveloped oral-vernacular material, an enterprise in which the compiler/adapter was obliged willy-nilly to exploit the language and conventions of more sophisticated middle-register compositions. But the 'mixed' product provided a crucial precedent, and the makings of an appropriately stylized linguistic vehicle, for the later development of vernacular poetry.

The following extract is taken from the first of the poems in E, which tells how Digenés's father, an Arab emir, sacks a Roman province and carries off the daughter of a nobleman. Pursued by the girl's brothers, he eventually agrees to turn Christian, marry her, and live in Romanía, but when this provokes accusations of treachery from his own family, he returns to Syria, and persuades his mother to come with him, thus effecting a reconciliation between the two families. Here the emir has just agreed to apostatize, and has taken the girl's five brothers to the tent where she has been kept:

(5) *Καὶ ὡς εἴδασιν τὰ ἀδέλφια της τὴν κόρην μαραμένην,*
ἀντάμα οἱ πέντε ἐστέναξαν, τοιοῦτον λόγον εἶπαν:
'Ἐγείρου, ἡ βεργόλικος, γλυκύν μας τὸ ἀδέλφιν·
τὸ ἄνθος τοῦ προσώπου σου ἐμάρανεν ἡ θλίψις.
[Ἡμεῖς θανοῦσαν σε εἴχομεν καὶ σπαθοκοπημένην,]   5
καὶ ἐσὲν ὁ Θεὸς ἐφύλαξεν διὰ τὰ ὡραῖα σου κάλλη.
Πολέμους οὐ φοβούμεθα διὰ τὴν σὴν ἀγάπην.'
Οἱ πέντε τὴν καταφιλοῦν καὶ ἐλιγοθυμῆσαν·
οἱ μὲν φιλοῦν τὰ χείλη της, οἱ ἄλλοι τοὺς ὀφθαλμούς της.
Κάθουνται οἱ πέντε ἀδελφοὶ καὶ ὁ ἀμιρὰς ἐκεῖνος·   10
κοινὴν βουλὴν ἐδώκασιν νὰ πάρουν τον γαμπρόν τους.
{εἰς Ῥωμανίαν νὰ ἔβγουν}
Καὶ εἰς μίαν ὁρίζει ὁ ἀμιρὰς κ' ἐκράτησε μετ' αὐτον
τοὺς θαυμαστοὺς ἀγούρους του, τοὺς εἶχε εἰς τὴν βουλήν του·
τοὺς ἄλλους ἐπιλόγιασε καὶ ὑπᾶν εἰς τὴν Συρίαν.
Καὶ ὁ ἀμιρὰς ἐδιάγειρεν ἀντάμα μὲ τὴν κόρην   15
καὶ μὲ τοὺς γυναικαδελφοὺς 'ς τὴν Ῥωμανίαν ὑπᾶσιν.

Digenés Akrítes (E): 187–203 (following Ricks 1990)

[kj os ˈiðasin t aˈðelfja tis tiŋ ˈgorin maraˈmeni(n),/ anˈdama‿
And when saw the brothers(subject) of-her the girl(object) withered/ together

i ˈpende ˈstenaksan, tiˈuto(n) ˈloɣon ˈipa(n)ː/ ‘eˈjiru, i verˈɣolikos,
the five groaned, such word said:/ ‘Arise, the lissom,

ɣliˈki(m) mas to aˈðelfi(n);/ to ˈanθos tu proˈsopu su eˈmaranen i
sweet of-us the sister;/ the flower of-the face of-you has-withered the

ˈθlipsis./ 5: iˈmis θaˈnusa(n) s ˈixome(n) ke spaθokopiˈmeni(n),/
grief (subject)./ 5: We dead(acc. sg. fem.) you had and cut-by-the sword,/

kj eˈsen o ˌθjos eˈfilakse(n) (ð)ja t oˈrea su ˈkali./ poˈlemus u
and you the God has-guarded because-of the beautiful of-you looks./ Wars/battles not

foˈvumeθa ðiˌa ti ˈsin aˈɣapi(n).’/ i ˈpende tiŋ gatafiˈlun ke
we-fear because-of the your love.’/ The five her kissed-eagerly and

eliɣoθiˈmisan;/ i-ˌmen fiˈlun ta ˈçili tis, j ˈali tus ofθalˈmus tis./ 10:
swooned;/ some kissed the lips of-her, the others the eyes of-her./ 10:

ˈkaθunde i pendj aðelˈfi kj o amiˈras eˈkinos;/ kiˈni(n) vuˈlin eˈðokasi(n)
Sit the five brothers and the emir that;/ common decision they-gave

na ˈparun to(ŋ) ɣamˈbron dus./ kj iz ˈmjan oˌrizj o amiˈras kj
that they-take him (as)brother-in-law of-them./ And at once gives-orders the emir and

eˈkratise met ˈafton/ tus θavmasˈtus aˈɣurus tu, tus ˈiçe s ti(n) vuˈlin
kept with him/ the wonderful lads of-him, whom he-had at the will

du;/ tus ˈalus epiˈlojase kj iˈpan is ti siˈria(n)./ 15: kj o amiˈras
of-him;/ the others he-picked-off and they-go to the Syria/ 15: And the emir

eˈðjajiren anˈdama me tiŋ ˈgori(n),/ ke ˈme tus jinekaðelˈfus s ti romaˈnjan
returned together with the girl,/ and with the wife’s-brothers to the Romania

iˈpasi(n).]
they-go.

‘And when her brothers saw the girl withered, the five groaned together, and spoke as follows: “Arise, the lissom one, our sweet sister; grief has withered the bloom of your face. We had you for dead and cut by the sword, but you were protected by God for your beautiful looks. Through our love for you, we fear no battles.” The five kissed her fervently and collapsed; some kissed her lips, the others her eyes. The five brothers and that emir sat down; they gave a joint decision to accept him as their brother-in-law. And at once the emir gave orders, and kept with him the wonderful lads that he had at his command; the others he picked off and they went to Syria. And the emir returned together with the girl, and they went to Romania with his wife’s brothers.’

The metre is the fully formed fifteen-syllable political verse, henceforth the standard metre of Greek poetry, now with a predominantly iambic rhythm. The high incidence of elision, aphaeresis, crasis, and synizesis is metrically guaranteed (the orthography is quite conservative), and characteristic both of popular speech and poetry based on it.

Most obviously in evidence here is the parallel use of functionally equivalent morphology; e.g. 3pl. non-past -ουν [-un]/-ουσι(ν) [-usi(n)], 3pl. past -αν [-an]/

-ασι(ν) [-asi(n)], as well as analogous variants in the 'reduced' present-tense paradigm of (ὑ)πά(γ)ω [(i)'pa(ɣ)o], namely ὑπᾶν [i'pan]/ὑπᾶσι(ν) [i'pasi(n)], (see 11.8.5 (34)(c), 11.8.6 (35)(b) and (c)). The possible explanations for this are many and varied, and by no means mutually exclusive. In the case of verse with an oral background, it is tempting to think in terms of source materials in different dialects (e.g. Probonás (1985), Trapp (1971)). But since early prose texts show similar inconsistencies, it seems simplest to accept that, in a period of rapid change, widespread free variation was typical of spoken and vernacular written styles (though doubtless the options were exploited particularly freely in poetry).

As a possible example of local dialect influence, however, we may note above in line 7 the use of the negative οὐ [u] rather than the more modern δέν [ðen], the absence of synizesis in διά [ði'a], and the use of the possessive adjective σήν [si(n)] in place of the genitive pronoun σου [su] (in a passive rather than active sense). All of these are potentially 'learned' features, and they do occur elsewhere in the poem. But when they are concentrated into a single line, as here, one inevitably thinks of the Pontic dialects which typically preserve all of these characteristics, and presumably reflect a linguistic situation which was once characteristic of large parts of eastern Anatolia, where many of the akritic lays originated. Note also the postposed clitic in line 11 (if we do not take this as the definite article), where, in the context of νά [na], we would expect a preverbal pronoun; this too is/was a characteristic feature of some modern Pontic and Cappadocian dialects, and may conceivably reflect some original Anatolian source (cf. Mirambel (1963), Janse (1993)).

Common 'vernacular' features of (5) include: the abandonment of the reduplication in the perfect passive participle (μαραμένην [mara'meni(n)]), and the general absence of inflected active participles (other than in line 5 borrowed by the editor as a supplement from G); ἀντάμα [an'dama] 'together' < ἐν τ(ῷ) ἄμα [en d(o) 'ama]; the analogical -ν [-n] in the neuter adjective γλυκύν [ɣli'ki(n)]; the acc. pl. forms of clitic pronouns used not only in direct and indirect object functions but also as possessives, in this function already to the exclusion of the old genitive (cf. γαμπρόν τους [ɣam'bron dus]); 3pl. aorist subjunctive πάρουν ['parun] 'they (may) take', with aphaeresis standardized, cf. classical ὑπ-άρ-ωσι(ν) [i'parosi(n)], from ὑπ-αίρω [i'pero] 'lift'; the pronoun αὗτον ['afto(n)], built to the feminine demonstrative αὗτη ['afti] 'this' (cf. 11.7.8 (29)(d)); ἄγουρος ['aɣuros] 'lad', < ἄωρος ['aoros] 'unripe' (note the possible 'Asiatic' vowel weakening (11.5): modern ἀγόρι [a'ɣori] 'boy', < ἀώριον [a'orion] 'unripe', the neuter of an alternative form of the adjective); the continued use of the article as a relative pronoun (cf. τοὺς εἶχε [tus 'içe], probably a traditional feature of oral poetry); μέ [me], the reduced form of μετά [me'ta], used consistently with the accusative in the sense 'with', and the frequent reduction of εἰς [is] to [s], anticipating the modern form as used before words beginning with vowels and the definite article (cf. 11.7.1 (16)).

Note in particular, however, that a νά [na]-clause is used after 'give a decision' where a control infinitive might have been expected; already, in compositions based on vernacular material, complement infinitives are most commonly used after verbs expressing aspectual (e.g. l. 66: ἤρξαντο πάλιν κλαίειν ['irksando 'palin 'klein] 'they-began again to-weep') or modal notions (e.g. l. 142: ἂν σε εἶχαν εὑρεῖ [an s ‚ixan e'vri] 'if you they-had/would(have) to-find (i.e. found)'), cf. 11.8.1 (30).

Though there are no relevant contexts in (5), one of the most important features in this early vernacular literature is the almost complete absence of the dative case other than in 'literary' passages. The accusative (e.g. l. 499: τοὺς ἀγούρους του ἔλεγεν [tus a'ɣurus tu 'elejen], 'to-the lads(acc.) of-him he-spoke') and genitive (e.g. l. 390: τῶν ἀδελφῶν της ἔλεγεν [ton aðel'fon tis 'elejen] 'to-the brothers(gen.) of-her she-spoke') alternate quite freely in indirect object function, both in pronouns and full noun phrases, though the use of the genitive is normal, if far from obligatory, when a preceding direct object co-occurs (e.g. l. 53: δάκτυλον του δείχνει ['ðaktilon du 'ðiçni] 'finger to-him(gen.) he-shows' (as a gesture of peace)).

12.2.2 Ptokhopródromos

In the twelfth century, the Komnenian court provided a fresh impetus to creative writing, ushering in a new period of literary experimentation under imperial patronage against the background of attitudinal changes associated with the revival of learning in the eleventh century and societal changes connected with the return of a prosperous middle class.

Particularly significant in the present context is the small corpus of didactic and satirical verse composed in a more everyday language, including the poem addressed to the emperor Manouél I by the prominent intellectual Mikhaél Glykás from his prison cell, and the didactic/advisory poem with the mysterious title *Spanéas* (cf. 8.4.3). The most important of the surviving works in this category, however, are the four 'begging' pieces known as the *Poems of Poor Pródromos* (*Ptokhoprodromiká*), after the persona of the narrator ('Ptokhopródromos') of two of them. The standard work is that of Hesseling and Pernot (1910), though there is now a new edition by Eideneier (1991) (but see S. Alexíou (1994) for a rather critical review).

These are very similar in character to the tongue-in-cheek appeal for employment which Theódoros Pródromos, having fallen out of favour at court, addressed to the emperor Manouél I in 1149 (see Majuri (1919)). The arresting use of everyday language in the piece is explained by reference to the author's desperate plight, and the indifference of the intermediary through whom previous appeals had been made in the learned language. Scholars are now increasingly inclined to accept that Pródromos is the author of the other four poems too.

Characterized by a distinctively wry Byzantine humour, these take the form of 'autobiographical' narratives, punctuated by petitions to the emperor or members of the imperial family, in which the author complains in turn of: 1, the pain of coping with a nagging wife who regrets her marriage to an educated pauper; 2, the impossibility of keeping body and soul together on the meagre patronage he receives; 3, the arrogance and corruption of his superiors in the monastery where he lives as a young monk; and 4, the acute distress of the educated man of letters in the face of the impoverishment which his learning has brought him. (The order here follows that of Hesseling and Pernot; Eideneier reverses the order of 3 and 4.)

The 'autobiographies' of the personae involved should not, of course, be taken too literally, though we should note that the highly conservative Pródromos was not born into the aristocracy, that he did fall from grace in the early years of Manouél's reign, and that, failing to regain his position at court, he remained at the church of the Holy Apostles, ultimately in monastic retreat, until his death (*c.* 1165–70). It was for him a painful sign of the times that an interest in literature had begun to spread 'down' from its traditionally aristocratic preserve, and worse, that wealth had to a considerable extent been appropriated by the townspeople, so that merchants and craftsmen could easily become richer than those, like himself, who were dependent on the generosity of the court.

It is a matter of the greatest importance to note that nearly all of the vernacular literature of the twelfth century originated in the same court circles that simultaneously cultivated extreme linguistic archaism (cf. 9.5), and that the impetus for the use of such language came from 'above'. Any partial breakthrough of 'popular' culture into writing, as seen in *Digenés* or the proverbial folklore of Glykás's poem, was due entirely to the new-found interest which a few educated individuals now began to take in the folk tradition as an expression of contemporary Greekness.

The *Ptokhoprodromiká*, however, owe little to such considerations, and exploit 'topoi' familiar from other forms of satirical writing in a straightforward assault, rooted in a mixture of envy and contempt, on the materialism of an age in which the privileged position of court dependants was being undermined by 'new money'. At most one might say that the model provided by other forms of vernacular composition may have provided some incentive for such experimentation (there are a number of verbal parallels), but even the most cursory comparison between the E *Digenés Akrítes* and the *Ptokhoprodromiká* reveals that the density of learned language in the latter is consistently greater (and not only in the middle-register passages addressed to the emperor and composed in the rhetorical style of contemporary court poetry). If this is indeed based on the 'vernacular', it is the speech of the educated aristocracy which provided the foundation for the poet's diction, a variety which is sometimes deliberately distorted in the mouths of the would-be upwardly mobile, and supplemented for comic or satirical effect with items of everyday vocabulary and urban slang.

The following extract is taken from poem 3 in Eideneier's edition (number 4 in Hesseling and Pernot), and bemoans the failure of education to deliver the promised life of leisured ease. The range of variant readings is considerable, and for the sake of simplicity the text given here very largely follows that of Eideneier (1991: 119–20), apart from a number of minor changes of orthography and punctuation, and the substitution of one or two alternative readings more in keeping with the general style of the passages in question (see below for some discussion):

(6) Ἀπὸ μικρόθεν μ᾽ ἔλεγεν ὁ γέρων ὁ πατήρ μου,
    'Τέκνον μου, μάθε γράμματα, καὶ "ὡσανν᾽ ἐσέναν ἔχει".
    Βλέπεις τὸν δεῖνα, τέκνον μου, πεζὸς περιεπάτει,
    καὶ τώρα ἔν᾽ διπλοεντέληνος καὶ παχυμουλαρᾶτος.
    Αὐτός, ὅταν ἐμάνθανεν, ὑπόδησιν οὐκ εἶχεν,   5

καὶ τώρα, βλέπε τον, φορεῖ τὰ μακρομύτικά του.
Αὐτὸς μικρὸς οὐδὲν εἶδεν τὸ τοῦ λουτροῦ κατώφλιν,
καὶ τώρα λουτρακίζεται τρίτον τὴν ἑβδομάδα.
Ὁ κόλπος του ἐβουρβούριζεν φθείρας ἀμυγδαλάτας,
καὶ τώρα τὰ νομίσματα γέμει τὰ μανοηλάτα.   10
Τζάντζαλον εἶχεν στούπινον, καβάδιν λερωμένον,
κ' ἐφόρει το μονάλλαγος χειμῶνα καλοκαίριν.
Καὶ τώρα, βλέπεις, γέγονε λαμπρὸς καὶ λουρικᾶτος,
παραγεμιστοτράχηλος, μεταξοσφικτουρᾶτος.
Αὐτός, ὅταν ἐμάνθανε, ποτέ του οὐκ ἐκτενίσθη,   15
καὶ τώρα ἕν' καλοκτένιστος καὶ καμαροτριχάρης.
Καὶ πείσθητι γεροντικοῖς καὶ πατρικοῖς σου λόγοις
καὶ μάθε γράμματα καὶ σύ, καὶ "ὡσανν' ἐσέναν ἔχει".
Ἄν γὰρ πεισθῆς ταῖς συμβουλαῖς καὶ τοῖς διδάγμασί μου,
σὺ μὲν μεγάλως τιμηθῆς, πολλὰ νὰ εὐτυχήσῃς,   20
ἐμὲ δὲ τὸν πατέρα σου κἂν ἐν τῇ τελευτῇ μου,
νὰ θρέψῃς ὡς ταλαίπωρον καὶ νὰ γηροτροφήσῃς.'
Ὡς δ' ἤκουσα τοῦ γέροντος, δέσποτα, τοῦ πατρός μου,
(τοῖς γὰρ γονεῦσι πείθεσθαι φησὶ τὸ θεῖον γράμμα),
ἔμαθον τὰ γραμματικά, πλὴν μετὰ κόπου πόσου!   25
Ἀφοῦ δὲ γέγονα κἀγὼ γραμματικὸς τεχνίτης,
ἐπιθυμῶ καὶ τὸ ψωμὶν καὶ τοῦ ψωμιοῦ τὴν μάνναν,
καὶ διὰ τὴν πεῖναν τὴν πολλὴν καὶ τὴν στενοχωρίαν
ὑβρίζω τὰ γραμματικά, λέγω μετὰ δακρύων:
'Ἀνάθεμαν τὰ γράμματα, Χριστέ, καὶ ὁπού τὰ θέλει,   30
ἀνάθεμαν καὶ τὸν καιρὸν καὶ ἐκείνην τὴν ἡμέραν,
καθ' ἣν μ' ἐπαραδώκασιν εἰς τὸ διδασκαλεῖον,
πρὸς τὸ νὰ μάθω γράμματα, τάχα νὰ ζῶ ἀπ' ἐκεῖνα.'

Ptokhoprodromiká 4 (Eideneier 3): 56–88

[a'po mi'kroθen m   'elejen   o   'jeron o pa'tir mu,/ ''teknon mu,
From   small   me(acc.) used-to-say the   the father of-me, 'Child   of-me,

'maθe 'ɣramata, kj "osan   e'senan 'eçi"./ 'vlepis ton 'ðina,   'teknon
learn   letters,   and "Hosannah to-you   there-is". You-see the so-and-so, child

mu, pe'zos perie'pati,/   ke 'tora n   ðiplen'delinos ke
of-me, on-foot he-used-to-walk-about,/ and now   he-is double-breastplated and

paçimula'ratos./ 5 af'tos,   'otan e'manθanen, i'poðisin uk 'içen,/ ke 'tora,
fat-muled.   This-man, when he-was-a-student, footwear not had,   and now,

'vlepe ton, fo'ri   ta makro,miti'ka tu./   af'tos mi'kros u'ðen   ¡iðen to
look-at him, he-wears the long-nosed(shoes) of-him. He   small   not-at-all saw the

tu   lu'tru   ka'toflin,/ ke 'tora lutra'kizete 'triton   tin evðo'maða./ o
of-the bath-house threshold, and now he-bathes   third(time) the week.   The

'kolpos tu   vur'vurizen 'fθiras amiɣða'latas,/ 10 ke 'tora ta
lap   of-him jumped   (with)lice like-almonds,   and now (of)the

no'mizmata 'jemi ta manoi'lata./   'dzandzalon 'içen 'stupinon,
coins   it-is-full the-(ones)-with-Manouél's-head. Rags   he-had of-sackcloth,

ka'vaðin lero'menon,/ kj e'fori to mo'nalaɣos çi'mona kalo'kerin./ ke
coat   filthy,   and he-wore it without-change winter   summer.   And

'tora, 'vlepis, 'jeɣone   lam'bros ke luri'katos,/ parajemisto'traçilos,
now,   you-see, he-has-become splendid and armoured,   very-thick-necked,

metaksosfiktu'ratos./ 15 af'tos, 'otan e'manθane, po'te tu   k
silk-tight-squeezed.   He,   when   he-was-a-student, (n)ever of-him not

ekte'nisθin,/ ke 'tora n   kalo'ktenistos ke kamarotri'xaris./ ke 'pisθiti
combed-his-hair, and now he-is smartly-coiffured and arch-hairy.   Both obey

jerondi'kis   ke patri'kis   su   'lojis/ ke 'maθe 'ɣramata ke 'si, kj
old-man's(dat.) and father's(dat.) of-you words and learn letters   also you, and

"osan   e'senan 'eçi"./ an ɣar pis'θis tes simvu'les ke tiz ði,ðaɣma'si
"Hosannah to-you there-is". If for you-obey the advice   and the teachings

mu,/ 20 si men   me'ɣalos timi'θis,   po'la na efti'çisis,/ e'me
of-me,   you on-one-hand greatly   will-be-rewarded, much will you-prosper, me

ðe   tom ba'tera su   kan en di telef'ti mu,/ na 'θrepsis os
on-other-hand the father of-you even in the end(dat.) of-me, will you-nurse as

ta'leporon ke na jirotro'fisis.'/   oz ð 'ikusa tu 'jerondos, 'ðespota,
wretch   and will you-look-after-in-old-age.' As and I heard the old-man(gen.), master,

tu pa'troz   mu,/ tiz ɣar ɣo'nefsi 'piθesθe fi'si to 'θion 'ɣrama,/
the father(gen.) of-me, the for parents(dat.) to-obey says the holy writing,

25 'emaθon ta ɣramati'ka,   plin meta 'kopu 'posu!/ a'fu ðe
   I-learned the elements-of-reading/writing, except with toil how-much! Since but

'jeɣona ka'ɣo ɣramati'kos tex'nitis,/ epiθi'mo ke to pso'min ke tu
became   also-I in-letters   expert,   I-desire/miss both the bread   and of-the

pso'mju tim 'manan,/ ke ðja   tim 'binan tim bo'lin ke tin stenoxo'rian/
bread   the crumb,   and through the hunger the much and the distress

i'vrizo ta ɣramati'ka,   'leɣo meta ða'krion:/ 30 'a'naθema(n) ta
I-revile the elements-of-reading/writing, I-say with tears: 'Damn   the

'ɣramata, xris'te, kj o'pu   ta 'θeli,/ a'naθema(n) ke toŋ ge'ro(n) kj
letters,   Christ, and whoever them wants, damn   also the time   and

e'kini(n) tin i'mera(n),/ kaθ in   m epara'ðokasin is to ðiðaska'lio(n),/ pros
that   the day,   on which me they-handed-over to the school,   for

to na 'maθo   'ɣramata, ,taxa   na 'zo⌣   (a)p e'kina.']
the that I-learn(subjunc.) letters, as-though that I-live(subjunc.) from those.'

'Ever since I was small, my old father used to say to me, "My child, learn your letters, and 'it's praise be to you' [*i.e. you're all right, Jack*]. You see so-and-so, he used to go about on foot, but now he's wearing a double breast-plate and riding a fat mule. When he was a student, he didn't have shoes, but now, just look at him, he is wearing his 'long-toes'. When he was a student, he hadn't seen the threshold of the bath-house at all, but now he's taking his third bath this week. His lap used to heave with lice the size of almonds, but now it's full of coins stamped with Manouél's head. He had rags of sackcloth, a filthy overcoat that he wore without changing, winter and summer, but now, you see, he's become splendid in his armour, thick-necked, with tight silk drawers. When he was a student, he'd never combed his hair in his life, but now he's well groomed with a bouffant style. Just obey your old father's words and learn your letters too, and then 'it's praise be to you'. For if you follow my advice and my instructions, you will be greatly valued and enjoy much good fortune, while I your father, even at the end of my life, will be nursed by you in my misery and looked after in my old age." When I heard my old father, master, (for holy scripture says one should obey one's parents), I learned to read and write – but what an effort! And ever since I too became an expert in letters, I've been longing for bread and even a crumb of bread, so in my great hunger and distress I curse literacy and say with tears: "Damn letters, Christ, and all who want them, and damn the time and the day when they handed me over to the school to learn my letters, as if I could live on them." '

The immediate impression is of 'modern' syntax: cf. for example, the standard medieval-vernacular positioning of clitic pronouns; ἔχει ['eçi] in the sense 'there is' (2/18, though this is a quoted colloquialism (Eideneier (1964: 336)); the use of the modern conjunctions ἀφοῦ (i.e. ἀφ' οὗ [a'fu] (26) and ὅταν ['otan] + indicative (5, 15) in temporal clauses); the idiomatic use of ποτέ [po'te] + genitive pronoun (15); νά [na] + subjunctive in a future sense (20, 22); ἐπιθυμῶ [epiθi'mo] + accusative instead of genitive (27); the relative use of ὅπου/ὁπού ['opu/o'pu] (30); the substitution of a νά [na]-clause for the traditional infinitive in the nominalized clause after πρός [pros] (33); the modern idiomatic use of τάχα νά ['taxa na] to mean 'as though' (33); and ἀπό [a'po] + accusative (33).

By contrast, the morphology remains quite traditional, subject only to the usual variations in verb endings (e.g. 3pl. present in -ουν [-un]/-ουσι [-usi], past in -αν [-an]/-ασι [-asi], etc.) and the incorporation of modern inflections for necessarily, or deliberately selected, colloquial forms (e.g. synizesis in the genitive of ψωμίν [pso'min] (27), or the addition of final -ν [-n] to neuter ἀνάθεμα-ν [anaθe'man] in (30/31)). Thus the 3rd declension consonant-stems, for example, generally retain their classical paradigm, and the relatively few adaptations, typically involving accusative singular in -ν [-n], should perhaps be restored to their original form, except where popular expressions are pointedly employed in a particular context or quoted, as with the phrase containing ἐσέναν [e'senan] in lines 2 and 18. As already noted (cf. 10.8), this blend of ancient morphology and more contemporary syntax was highly characteristic of all educated usage in the period, even if the updating process has been taken further here than in more conventional compositions.

In general, then, the narrative parts of the poems blend an overtly contemporary approach to sentence structure with an otherwise conservative 'local' morphosyntax which continues many of the features of the basic (but not vulgar) Koine of late antiquity, including a general preference for the negative οὐ(κ) [u(k)] over (οὐ)δέν [(u)ðen] (except when the latter is emphatic, = 'not at all'), the use of γέγονα ['jegona] rather than innovations such as ἔγινα ['ejina], the preference for strong aorist forms in -ον [-on] rather than their replacements in -α [-a], the retention of some aorist middles, the widespread use of both inflected participles (all cases) and infinitival complements to control verbs, and the retention of many ancient government requirements, such as the use of the genitive, and even of the dative, after certain prepositions. There seems to be no reason to doubt that this represents a somewhat elaborated version of the 'mixed' contemporary vernacular of the upper classes in Constantinople, fashionably adapted in the direction of vernacular poetry of the period.

This style is also sometimes carried over into passages of direct speech, but here the concentration of modern forms typically increases in line with the relatively lowly social status of the speaker and/or with the passion with which s/he is speaking. Consider, for example, the last four lines of (6), where the language of the speaker's heated sentiments is deliberately contrasted with the learned written language that has been so painfully and uselessly acquired. We therefore find neuter ἀνάθεμαν [a'naθeman] with analogical -ν [-n], relative ὁπού [o'pu] with shifted accent (or de-accented), 3pl. aorist ἐπαραδώκασιν [epara'ðokasin] with external augment (at least as one variant), τό [to] plus a νά [na]-clause, the colloquial expression τάχα νά ['taxa na], and ἀπό [apo] + accusative.

In the passages addressed to the emperor, by contrast, the writing is deliberately archaizing, in line with the established 'middle' style of much of the literature of the period (e.g. Manassés's chronicle, etc.); note the genitive after ἀκούω [a'kuo] (23), the ancient verb φημί [fi'mi] (24) with its infinitival complement (24), the dative after the middle πείθομαι ['piθome] (24), and the avoidance of synizesis in στενοχωρίαν [stenoxo'rian] (28).

Occasionally, however, the more learned and more popular styles are amusingly combined, as in the father's speech, where, especially in the 'peroration', the old man attempts, not altogether successfully, to practise what he preaches. Thus the learned τέκνον ['teknon] (2/3), the internal augment of περιεπάτει [perie'pati] (3), and the 'sandwiched' genitive of line 7 introduce a deliberately incongruous note in the context of the popular syntax, phraseology and vocabulary, including the characteristically over-the-top compounds, used throughout lines 2–16. Thereafter, a more consistently 'learned' style predominates, with the appearance of an aorist passive imperative (17), an adverb in -ως [-os] rather than -α [-a] (20), the contrastive particles μέν [men] and δέ [ðe] (20/21), and dative complements after πείθομαι ['piθome] (17/19) and ἐν [en] (21). But note too the solecistic use of the 2nd person pronoun in line 17, where strictly speaking a 1st person form is required in so far as the element in question modifies the head noun λόγοις ['lojis] ('*my* words') rather than the adjective πατρικοῖς [patri'kis] ('belonging to *your* father'), and the repeated quotation of the colloquial phrase meaning 'you're all right, Jack' (18).

The language of the *Ptokhoprodromiká* is certainly 'mixed', but it is a wickedly contrived mixture (whose impact is somewhat disguised by the insensitivity of later copyists) that reflects beautifully the 'language problem' of their time, while simultaneously satirizing the changing economic circumstances that were bringing their author such distress. There is some reason to believe that it reflects specifically Constantinopolitan varieties in its marked preference for accusative indirect object pronouns, and in its tendency to favour the extension of thematic -ου- [-u-] in many innovative verb forms (e.g. 1sg. imperfect middle/passive in -ούμουν

[-'umun], cf. 11.8.6 (35), and see Section III, 17.4 for discussion of later forms of Constantinopolitan Greek).

12.3 The fourteenth and fifteenth centuries: the Palaiologan court and Frankish rule

12.3.1 The original romances of the Palaiologan period

Though the type of experimentation seen in the *Ptokhoprodromiká* ceased some time before the capture of the Byzantine capital in 1204, Constantinople was also the context for the first romances to exploit the vernacular in the Palaiologan period, and it is clear once again that these original compositions were associated with the patronage of the imperial court. Though there is clearly some generic affiliation with the contemporary romances of chivalry familiar in the west, the true roots of these works lie in the Hellenistic, Roman, and Byzantine traditions, including the learned and vernacular romantic writings of the twelfth century.

The following extract is taken from *Kallímakhos and Khrysorróe*, composed between 1310 and 1340 by Andrónikos Palaiológos, nephew of Mikhaél VIII Palaiológos. The standard edition is Pichard (1956); see also Kriarás (1955: 17–83), Apostolópoulos (1984):

(7) Ἀλλ᾽ ἦν τὸ τεῖχος ὑψηλόν, εἰσέλευσιν οὐκ εἶχεν·
  ἄνθρωπος οὐ παρέτρεχεν, οὐδὲ θηρίου φύσις,
  οὐδὲ πτηνόν, οὐδὲ στρουθός· ἄγριος ἦν ὁ τόπος.
  Ἀνέτρεχον, παρέτρεχον, τὴν εἴσοδον ἐζήτουν·
  εἶχεν γὰρ πύργους ὑψηλούς, οὐρανομήκεις τοίχους.   5
  Εὗρον τὰς πόρτας τὰς λαμπρὰς τούτου, τὰς πολυτίμους,
  εἶδον τοὺς ὄφεις, ἔφριξαν τοὺς πυλωροὺς ἐκείνους.
  Οὐκ ἔγνωσαν τὴν φοβερὰν καὶ θαυμασίαν πόλιν
  τίνος τὸ κάστρον τὸ λαμπρόν, τίνα δεσπότην ἔχει.
  Οἱ μὲν γὰρ ἐπεστράφησαν, ἐστάλησαν ὀπίσω,   10
  τάχα μὴ γένωνται τροφὴ τῶν πυλωρῶν ἐκείνων·
  εἶδαν, ἐξεθαμβήθησαν, ἐτράπησαν, ἐφύγαν.
  Kallímakhos and Khrysorróe 197–208

[al in to 'tixos ipsi'lon, is'elefsin uk 'içen;/   'anθropos ou
But was the wall   high,   entrance   not it-had/there was; man   not

pa'retreçen, u'ðe   θi'riu 'fisis,/   u'ðe   pti'non,   u'ðe   stru'θos;
ran-past,   not-even of-beast nature/species, not-even winged-creature, nor-yet bird;

'aɣrios in o 'topos./ a'netrexon, pa'retrexon, tin 'isoðon e'zitun;/ 5
wild   was the place.   They-ran-up, they-ran-down, the entrance they-sought;

'içen   ɣar 'pirɣus ipsi'lus, urano'mikis 'tixus./ 'evron   tas 'portas
it-had/there-were for   towers   high,   heaven-high   walls.   They-found the gates

tas lam'bras 'tutu, tas poli'timus,/ 'iðon   tus 'ofis,   'efriksan   tus
the bright   of-this, the inestimable,   they-saw the snakes, they-shuddered-at the

pilo'rus e'kinus./ uk 'eɣnosan   tin fove'ran ke θavma'sian 'polin/
gatekeepers those.   Not they-got-to-know the terrible   and amazing   city,

'tinos to 'kastron to lam'bron, 'tina ðes'potin 'eçi./ 10 i   men   ɣar
whose the castle   the bright,   what master   it-has.   They on-one-hand for

epe'strafisan, e'stalisan o'piso,/ 'taxa mi 'jenonde tro'fi tom bilo'ron
turned-round,   they-shrank back,   perhaps lest they-become food   of-the gatekeepers

e'kinon;/ 'iðan,   ekseθam'viθisan, e'trapisan, e'fiɣan.]
those;   they-saw, they-were-amazed,   they-turned, they-fled.

'But the wall was high, there was no entrance; no man passed by, nor any kind of beast, nor fowl, nor bird; the place was grim. They ran up and down and looked for the entrance; for there were high towers and walls rising to heaven. They found its splendid priceless gates, they saw the snakes, they shuddered at those gatekeepers. But as for this fearful and amazing township, they did not discover who owned the splendid castle, nor who its master was. For they turned and shrank back, in case they became food for those gatekeepers; they saw, they were astonished, and they fled.'

The tale is set in a folkloric land of marvels in which a king, unable to decide which of his three sons should succeed him, sends them off to prove themselves. Kallímakhos, the youngest, leads his brothers up a mountain to an ogre's castle guarded by snakes and dragons. The older brothers, after first giving Kallímakhos a magic ring, beat a hasty retreat, but he vaults the wall and wrests the beautiful Khrysorróe from the ogre who is holding her prisoner. After a series of thrilling adventures, the pair finally live happily together as lord and lady of the castle.

The learned origins of the writer are apparent here not only in the conservative morphology and lexicon, but also in his metrical practice, which permits occasional line-end enjambement (not illustrated) and over-running of the mid-line caesura (e.g. line 6), and his not-infrequent use of complex rhetorical periods, especially in elaborate descriptive passages (*ekphráseis*) and speeches made at moments of high drama, where the influence of the ancient/learned romantic tradition is greatest.

In the passage above, for example, only εἰσέλευσις [is'elefsis], πόρτα ['porta], κάστρον ['kastron], and ἐκθαμβῶ [ekθam'vo] are non-classical, though the first belongs to the higher registers of Byzantine writing and the last occurs in the Septuagint and the New Testament. Correspondingly, the small number of popular derivational formations seem often to be used for their 'affective' content in context rather than as simple variants of more learned forms. This is particularly true of 'marked' diminutives (i.e. those with suffixes other than -ιν [-in]): cf., for example, δενδρούτσικον [ðen'ðrutsikon] 'little tree' (1751), and δακτυλιδόπουλον [ðaktili'ðopulon] 'little ring' (1769), in a passage where Khrysorróe, thinking Kallímakhos to be dead, finds her hero's magic ring hanging in a tree.

Similarly in inflectional morphology, only the suffix used in εἶδαν ['iðan] and ἐφύγαν [e'fiɣan] (for classical -ον [-on], and doubtless motivated by a desire for homoeteleuton in this line) reveal vernacular influence. The restricted use of such popular variants seems often to be metrically motivated: e.g. ἦτον ['iton] for ἦν [in] 'was', or aorist passives in -ηκα [-ika] for -ην [-in], because of their extra syllable (177, 1877), etc.

Where the epic of *Digenés Akrítes* seemed to be built on a vernacular base with a learned overlay, this poem seems rather to be rooted in the middle-register tradition with concessions to the vernacular. The basis for including it among the vernacular compositions of the period lies primarily in the relative simplicity of its syntactic structure, which, elaborated passages and inflected participles notwithstanding, reflects the paratactic and coordinating conventions of popular compositions using the political verse form, and regularly builds lines using the same metrical/ rhetorical cola. Note too the regular use of the accusative to mark the indirect object (perhaps a Constantinopolitan feature), the frequent use of adverbially modified prepositional phrases headed by εἰς [is] and ἀπό [apo] (e.g. μέσον ['meson] (275), ἐπάνω [e'pano] (1765)), the regular appearance of νά [na]-clauses in place of infinitives (except after control and modal verbs, and occasionally in nominalized clauses (e.g. 286)), and the use of non-sandwiched adnominal genitives (e.g. 275, 1760) alongside their sandwiched counterparts, all of which point to a predominantly vernacular syntactic base.

We must, however, be cautious in our assessments in so far as the text of *Kallímakhos* has come down to us in a single manuscript dating from around 1520. It is likely, however, to be a fairly close copy of the original, in that the high concentration of learned language goes against the prevailing trend in manuscript 'copying' of that period towards a simpler style. On this basis, it is tempting to conclude that a morphologically conservative vernacular was used for all the original fourteenth-century romances, and that the greater frequency of more popular forms in *Vélthandros* and *Líbistros* is due largely to later adaptation on the part of copyists in western-dominated areas, including Crete and the Dodecanese.

12.3.2 Greek–Romance contact after 1204: perfects, pluperfects, negative polarity items, and clitic pronouns

The most obvious linguistic consequence of the Latin conquest of 1204 was a massive influx of Romance loan words into Greek, especially from Italian (Venetian and Genoese) and French. The overall impact of Romance, however, was less profound than might be supposed, and we may note in this connection that a number of striking syntactic parallelisms between Greek and Romance, which might be attributed to renewed contact, turn out, on closer inspection, to have independent roots. As in the Roman imperial period (5.3), the most that one can argue for in many such cases is the mutual consolidation of changes already independently under way. A number of examples may briefly be considered here.

(8) The local reintroduction, e.g. in Crete, parts of the Peloponnese, and Roumeli, of the perfect active periphrasis involving 'have' + perfect passive participle agreeing with the object.

This construction appeared sporadically in the literary register of the Koine in the Roman period, but is virtually unknown in medieval Greek before the period of Frankish domination. Nevertheless, there are a few isolated examples from the pre-Frankish period of the type seen in (9):

(9) τὸν γρόθον του εἰς τὸ μάγουλον εἶχεν ἀκουμπισμένον.

Digenés Akrítes (E), 418

[to 'ɣroθon du   sto   'maɣulo(n) 'içen akumbiz'meno(n)]
the fist   of-him at-the cheek   he-had rested (perf. pass. pple.)

'He held his fist at rest against his cheek.'

Though the near-literal sense of 'have' and the stative sense of the participle are clear here, it must be assumed that it was this rather unusual 'native' construction that lent itself to local grammaticalization as a true pluperfect/perfect active under the impact of Romance.

In other cases too, the relevant constructions are well developed in Greek before any Romance influence can plausibly be invoked. In ancient Greek, for example, there was a pronominal/adverbial system comprising strongly negative items on the one hand (meaning 'no-X', and requiring no independent verb-negation when used preverbally), and indefinite items (formally related to interrogatives) on the other. The latter meant 'some-X' in assertive contexts, but 'any-X' in negative, interrogative, and conditional ones, though the strongly negative items could also be used after a negative particle to impart a more emphatic negative force (i.e. in this order, the cumulated negatives were reinforcing). Compare (10)(a) and (b):

(10) (a) <u>οὐκ</u> ἄν <u>τινα</u> . . . φαίης ἔχειν τὴν ἀκριβεστάτην ἐπιστήμην

Plato *Parmenides*, 134c

[uk án   tina . . . pʰaíɛːs   ékʰeːn tɛ̀ːn akribestátɛːn epistéːmeːn]
not would anyone . . . you-would-say to-have the   most-accurate   knowledge

'You would not say that anyone had completely accurate knowledge.'

(b) <u>οὐκ</u> ἄρα . . . γιγνώσκεται τῶν εἰδῶν <u>οὐδέν</u>   Plato *Parmenides*, 134b

[uk ára . . . gignóːsketai toːn eːdôːn udén]
not then . . . is-known   of-the forms nothing

'Of the forms then **nothing** is known.'

During the medieval period the indefinite system was subjected to a process of formal renewal whereby the assertive ('some-X') and negative-polarity ('any-X') variants were progressively distinguished, to give, for example, κάποιος ['kapjos] 'some(one)', and κανένας [ka'nenas] 'any(one)', in place of τις [tis] 'some-/any-(one)' (see 11.7.8 (29)(a)). The negative-polarity forms could, however, also be pronounced emphatically, and used like the strong negatives in (10)(b). In this case they acquired a correspondingly 'negative' sense (though again reinforcing the negative particle rather than cancelling it), and as such could be preposed as negative foci, thus assuming the positions/functions of strong negative elements.

Over time, therefore, the classical negatives disappeared in favour of emphatically stressed negative-polarity items, but since these, unlike the original forms, presupposed a negative (or interrogative/modal) licensing context, the conditioning negative particle was retained even when they appeared before it. Compare (11)(a), where no independent sentence-negation is required, with the negative 'concord' of (11)(b):

(11) (a) <u>οὐδὲν</u> αὐτῶν ἀτιμάσεις   Plato *Parmenides*, 130e

    [udén   autô:n atimáse:s]
    <small>nothing of-them you-will-undervalue</small>

    'You will undervalue **none** of them.'

  (b) <u>τίποτε</u> <u>οὐ</u> λογίζεται   *Digenés Akrítes* (E), 706

    ['tipote   u lo'jizete]
    <small>nothing/anything not he-thinks-of</small>

    'He thinks of **nothing**.'

The dual use of negative-polarity items is very similar to that familiar from Romance (cf., for example, French *rien* = 'nothing/anything', etc.), but the usage was in fact well established in vernacular Greek by the twelfth century, e.g. in *Digenés* and the *Ptokhoprodromiká*.

Similar observations apply to the apparently related restrictions on the order and combination of object clitic pronouns: i.e. if there are two such pronouns, the first must denote the indirect object and the second the direct object, while the latter has also to be 3rd person (Mackridge (1985: 222–3). Yet once again, all the examples involving two pronouns in the E *Digenés Akrítes* (64, 130, 475, 664, 668, 951, 1729) and the lay of *Armoúres* (47, 133) already conform to this rule, in a period, and from a region, in which any Romance influence can safely be discounted.

Note too that the regular post-verbal order after gerunds and imperatives in standard modern Greek (despite some fluctuation with monosyllabic imperatives) remains IO + DO: e.g. δώστε μου το ['ðoste mu to] 'give to-me it'. This contrasts with the Romance practice (cf. French *donnez-le-moi*), and it is again significant that in the modern Asia Minor dialects and many insular varieties, which have retained more of the medieval distribution of these elements, the same verb + IO + DO order applies even in simple declarative sentences with finite verb forms (cf. Mirambel (1963)). The routine placing of IO before DO, then, seems to have been a characteristic of popular medieval Greek in general, and any partial correspondence with Romance must be seen as essentially accidental, particularly as the un-Romance positioning of clitics *after* finite verbs remained the normal practice in areas such as Crete and Cyprus, which were subject to the most prolonged western occupation.

That said, the overall effects of Latin rule were ultimately quite liberating, and a revival of vernacular writing took place, despite a fresh commitment to classicism, even in Palaiologan Constantinople. But in the vast Greek-speaking areas under western control, where the old capital was no longer the focus of political and cultural life, a knowledge of learned written Greek, even where this could still be obtained, gradually ceased to be the prerequisite for a successful career, and traditional values began to be eroded. With the return of more settled conditions after *c.* 1300, therefore, Greek 'vernacular' writing, encouraged by the already widespread use of contemporary Romance for literary and official purposes, received a significant boost in the Latin-dominated west.

12.3.3 *The* Chronicle of the Morea

The occupation of Greek lands led to the writing of a number of vernacular chronicles celebrating the exploits of western dynasties (cf. 8.4.4), including the famous *Chronicle of the Morea*, the first such composition in verse. Following a lengthy prologue (1–1338), the anonymous narrator turns specifically to the conquest of the Peloponnese by Guillaume de Champlitte and members of the de Villehardouin family, and its subsequent transformation, apart from a few Venetian strongholds, into the Principality of the Morea.

The oldest and fullest surviving version (H, in Copenhagen) comprises 9,219 lines, but unfortunately the first pages of the codex are missing. This and other, comparatively minor, lacunae may often be filled by reference to the shorter P (Paris) version, though this has omissions of its own, and seems to represent a later adaptation of the original in both language/metre and content (especially in the moderation or deletion of the more rabid expressions of anti-Greek sentiment in H).

The work is customarily dated to the beginning of the fourteenth century, and since the story is told from the conqueror's point of view, it is usually attributed to a Greek-speaking Frank, a view amply corroborated by the often poor versification, the almost wholly vernacular language, and the extensive use of Romance vocabulary and idiom. It is still a matter of dispute whether the Greek text is an original composition or a translation (there are prose versions in three Romance languages), although some scholars have argued strongly for its primacy (see, for example, M. Jeffreys (1975)). The standard editions are Schmitt (1904, repr. 1967) and Kalonáros (1940); there is now an important analysis of the language of the *Chronicle* in Egea (1988). See also Beck (1971: 157–9).

The special significance of this work derives from the fact that the 'poet' had little contact with the classicizing tradition of 'serious' Greek literature, and wrote in a style closely reflecting his natural speech, subject only to the observations that (a) literacy at any level involved contact with non-vernacular forms, and (b) the use of the political verse form, however poorly handled, presupposed familiarity with the conventions of Greek vernacular poetry (including its archaisms).

The language of the *Chronicle* therefore exhibits the usual morphological and syntactic variation, though in this case there are clear misunderstandings in the use of certain non-vernacular forms (see below), while extremely high concentrations of 'popular', even vulgar, features are strongly in evidence. These include:

(12) (a) the appearance of many innovative present-stem formations, with a large number of competing doublets (11.8.5).

(b) the use of much innovative verb morphology, including aorist passive -θηκα [-θika] (11.8.4 (33)), imperfect passive -ομουν [-omun] (11.8.6 (35)(e): e.g. 6104), etc.

(c) some confusion of -έω [-'eo] and -άω [-'ao] contract verbs (11.8.5 (34)(e)).

(d) the absolute restriction of the dative to a set of fixed phrases.

(e) the rather limited use of feminine nouns in -ις [-is]/pl. -εις [-is], and neuters in -ος [-os]/pl. -η [-i], and the frequent assimilation of other 3rd declension nouns to the 1st declension (11.7.3–4 (18–21)).

(f) regularization of nominative plural -ες [-es] in the 1st declension, as well as in consonant and i-stem 'transfers' (11.7.4 (19) and (21)).

(g) the appearance of heteroclitic declensional patterns, including imparisyllabic a-stem plurals in -άδες [-'aðes] (11.7.4 (20): e.g. 4390, 6056).

(h) a tendency to regularize the accent in proparoxytone nouns and adjectives, so as to give ἄνθρωπος ['anθropos]/genitive ἄνθρωπου ['anθropu], in place of ἀνθρώπου [an'θropu] (e.g. 6844).

(i) the regular use of many innovative pronominal forms (11.7.8).

A particular feature of the syntax of the poem, however, is the destabilization of the future periphrasis consisting of ἔχω ['exo] + infinitive occasioned by the development of the corresponding conditional into a true pluperfect (cf. 11.8.3 (32)). The standard forms of the future/conditional, as already in the *Ptokhoprodromiká*, include the substitution of θέλω ['θelo]/ἤθελα ['iθela] + infinitive 'I will/would', and the use of νά [na] + subjunctive/past indicative. But we also find a modally strengthened form of the threatened ἔχω ['exo]-periphrasis involving the prefixation of νά [na] (there are no examples yet of ἔχω ['exo] + infinitive used as a perfect). This rather clumsy transitional form is also found occasionally in other works of roughly the same period (e.g. in Crete), but it did not find favour (lines containing it are regularly rephrased or omitted in P, for example), and it quickly disappeared.

In the category of straightforward errors involving learned forms, we may note in particular the frequent use of classical 3rd declension nominative singulars denoting family relatives as accusatives (Browning (1983: 7–8)). Examples include γυνή [ji'ni] 'woman/wife' (e.g. 7424), ἀνήρ [a'nir] 'man/husband' (e.g. 2519), πατήρ [pa'tir] 'father' (e.g. 454), μήτηρ ['mitir] 'mother' (e.g. 1323), and θυγάτηρ [θi'yatir] 'daughter' (e.g. 2477), as illustrated in (13):

(13) καὶ χαιρετᾷ τοῦ βασιλέως ἐκείνου τὴν θυγάτηρ

Chronicle of the Morea, 2492

[ƙe çere'ta tu   vasi'ljos e'kinu ti θi'yatir]
and he-greets of-the king   that   the daughter

'and he greets the daughter of that king'

This usage follows the model of the corresponding feminine vernacular forms where, after the widespread loss of final -ν [-n], nominative and accusative became identical (e.g. θυγατέρα [θiya'tera]), though we have to suppose an analogical extension to the masculines (where nom. and acc. vernacular forms were distinct). The metrical usefulness of the shorter learned forms is self-evident, and it seems that the author was simply ignorant of the classical paradigm.

The following extract (based on H) describes how the brothers Louis and Guillaume de Champlitte came to an agreement that the former should stay in France to manage the family estate while the latter sought his fortune in the east:

(14) Κι ὡσὰν ἀκούσουν κ' ἔμαθαν τὸ πῶς οἱ Φράγκοι ἐκεῖνοι,
    ὅπου ὑπαγαῖναν στὴν Συρίαν μὲ θέλημα τοῦ Πάπα,
    ἀφῆκαν τὸ ταξεῖδιν τους κι ἀπῆλθαν εἰς τὴν Πόλιν
    κι ἐκέρδισαν τὴν Ρωμανίαν κ' ἐγίνησαν ἀφέντες,
    βουλὴν ἀπήρασιν ὁμοῦ ἐκεῖνοι οἱ δύο αὐταδέλφοι·   5
    νὰ μείνῃ ἕνας ἀπὸ αὐτοὺς ἐκεῖ εἰς τὸ ἰγονικόν τους,
    κι ὁ ἄλλος νὰ ἀπέλθῃ εἰς Ρωμανίαν διὰ νὰ κερδίσῃ τόπον.
    Λοιπόν, ὡς τὸ ἔχει ἐριζικὸν ἡ χάρις τῶν ἀνθρώπων,
    κι οὐδὲν ὁμοιάζουν οἱ ἀδελφοὶ εἰς πρόσοψιν καὶ χάριν,
    ἦτον ὁ ὑστερνότερος ἀπὸ τοὺς αὐταδέλφους   10
    ὀκάτι ἐπιδεξιώτερος καὶ φρονιμώτερός τους.
    Κ' ἰσιάστησαν οἱ δύο ἀδελφοί, ὁ πρῶτος ν' ἐνεμείνῃ
    ἐκεῖσε εἰς τὸ κοντᾶτο του ἐκεῖνο τῆς Τσαμπάνιας,
    κι ὁ δεύτερος ἀπὸ τοὺς δύο, μισὶρ Γουλιάμος ἄκω,
    εἶχεν καὶ ἐπίκλην ὁ λόγου του, τὸν ἐλέγαν ντὲ Σαλοῦθε,   15
    νὰ εὕρῃ φουσσᾶτα ὅσα ἠμπορεῖ νὰ ἐπάρῃ μετὰ ἐκεῖνον,
    κ' ἐκεῖνος νὰ ἔλθῃ εἰς Ρωμανίαν τοῦ νὰ ἔχῃ κουγκεστήσει
    κάστρη καὶ χώρας τίποτε νὰ τὰ ἔχῃ ἰγονικά του.
    Ὁ κόντος γὰρ τοῦ ἐξέδωκεν ὅσον λογάριν εἶχε,
    καὶ εἶπεν του· Ἀδελφούτσικε, ἀφῶν ἐγὼ ἐνεμένω   20
    ἀφέντης εἰς τὰ κάστρη μας κ' εἰς τὸ ἰγονικόν μας,
    ἔπαρε τὸ λογάριν μας καὶ τὰ κοινά μας ὅλα
    κι ἄμε μὲ τὴν εὐχίτσα μου ὁμοίως καὶ τοῦ πατρός μας,
    κ' ἐλπίζω εἰς τὸ ἔλεος τοῦ Θεοῦ ὅτι νὰ εὐτυχήσῃς.'

Chronicle of the Morea, 1366–89

[kj o'san a'kusun k 'emaθan to pos   i 'fraŋgj e'kini,/o'pu pa'jenan
And when they-hear and learned the how/that the Franks those, that were-going

sti si'rja me 'θelima tu   'papa,/ a'fikan to ta'ksiði tus   kj a'pilθan
to-the Syria with will   of-the Pope, abandoned the journey of-them and went

is tim 'boli/ ke 'kerðisan ti roma'nja ke 'jinisan a'fendes,/ 5 vu'lin
to the City and won the Romania and became lords,   counsel

a'pirasin o'mu e'kinj i ðjo‿afta'ðelfi;/ na 'mini   'enas ap af'tus e'ki
they-took together those the two full-brothers; that should-stay one from them there

sto‿ iɣoni'kon dus,/ kj o‿'alos n a'pelθi   s roma'nja (ð)ja na
on-the family-estate of-them, and the other that he-should-go to Romania for that

ker'ðisi 'topo./ li'pon, os 'to   çi rizi'kon i 'xaris ton a'θropo(n),/ kj
he-win place. So, as it(obj.) has (as)fate the talent of-the men,   and

u'ðen o'mjazun j aðel'fi is 'prosopsi(n) ke 'xari(n),/ 10 'iton o
not are-alike the brothers in looks   and talent, was the

ister'noteros a,po tuz ðjo‿afta'ðelfus/o'kati   piðe'ksjoteros ke
younger   from the two full-brothers somewhat more-skilled and

froni,mote'ros tus./ k i'sjastisan i djo‿adel'fi, o 'protos na ne'mini/
wiser   of-them. And they-agreed the two brothers, the first that he-stay-put

e'kis is to kon'dato   tu   e'kino tis   tsam'banjas,/ kj o   'ðefteros a,po
there on the count's-estate of-him that   of-the Champagne,   and the second   from

tuz 'ðjo, mi'sir   ɣu'ʎamos 'ako,/ 15 'içe(n) k   e'piklj o 'loɣu tu,   ton
the two, Monsieur Guillaume hear!,   he-had also surname the self of-him, him

'leɣan   de sa'luθe,/ na vri   fu'sata ,osa   mbo'ri na 'pari   met
they-called de Salute,   that he-find armies   as-big-as he-can that he-should-take with

e'kino,/ k e'kinos 'na lθi   s roma'nja tu   'na çi
him,   and he   that he-should go to Romania   for-the that he-will/may

kuŋges'tisi/ 'kastri ke 'xoras 'tipote na 'ta çi   ɣoni'ka   tu./
conquer   castles and lands some   that them he-may-have (as) patrimony of-him.

o 'kondos ɣar tu   'kseðoken ,oso   lo'ɣarin 'içe,/ 20 kj 'ipen du:
The count   then to-him gave   as-much-as money   he-had   and said   to-him

'aðel'futsike, a'fon e'ɣo ne'meno/ a'fendis is ta 'kastri mas k is to
'My-dear-brother, since I   stay-put   (as)lord in the castles of-us and in the

iɣoni'ko   mas,/ e'pare to lo'ɣari mas ke ta ki'na   mas 'ola,/ kj
family-estate of-us, take   the money of-us and the common-goods of-us all,   and

'ame me tin ef'çitsa mu o'mjos ke tu   pa'troz mas,/ k el'pizo s to
go   with the blessing of-me likewise also of-the father of-us, and I-hope in the

'eʎos tu   θe'u ,oti na efti'çisis.']
pity   of-the God that will you-succeed.'

'And when they heard and learned that those Franks who were on their way to Syria by the will of the Pope had abandoned their journey and gone to the City [*Constantinople*] and won Romania and become masters, the two full-brothers together adopted a plan, that one of them should stay there on the family estate, and the other should go to Romania to win a place. Now, as the talents of men are a matter of fate, and the brothers were not alike in looks or talent, it was the younger of the two full-brothers who was in some degree the more skilled and wiser of them. So the two brothers agreed that the first should stay behind there in that county of his in Champagne, and that the second of the two, Sir Guillaume mark you, and he also had a surname on his own account, he was called de Salute [*the chronographer is confused, as often, since the individual concerned is Guillaume de Champlitte*], should find as large an army as he could to take with him, and should go to Romania to conquer some castles and estates to have as his patrimony. So the count gave him all the money he had, and said to him: "My dear younger brother, since I am staying behind as lord in our castles and our family estate, take our money and all our common goods, and go with my blessing and our father's likewise, and by the mercy of God I hope that you will have good fortune."'

Perhaps the most striking feature here is the consistent mismatch between the colloquial pronunciation required to meet the demands of the metre (as reflected in the transcription) and the conservative orthography which, if taken seriously, would produce many unmetrical lines. The principal difficulties arise when hiatus is naturally resolved in speech by elision, aphaeresis or crasis, while the archaizing conventions for writing Greek (the only ones available) generally ignore such junctural phenomena as well as word-internal synizesis, and require the uniform presence of final -ν [-n]: note how line 15, for example, can be made to scan correctly only if the -ν [-n] of ἐπίκλην [e'pikli] is ignored and the exposed final vowel runs into the initial vowel of the following word.

Both morphology and syntax are also consistently popular in character, and many of the relevant features have already been listed in general terms above, but note here:

(15) (a) the spread of the productive -άζω [-'azo] suffix (11.8.5 (34)(c)), cf. (ὁ)μοι-άζω [(o)'mjazo] (9).
   (b) the verb ἠμπορῶ [imbo'ro] 'be able', (16), cf. 11.8.5 (34)(e).
   (c) the present stem (ὑ)παγ-αίν- [(i)pa'jen-] for earlier ὑπάγ- [i'paɣ-] (2), cf. 11.8.5 (34)(b), and the aorist 'passive' ἐγίν-η(ν)/-ηκα [e'jini(n)/-ika] (4), built to γίν-ομαι ['jinome].
   (d) confusion about the character and function of unstressed initial vowels, illustrated in ἀπήρασιν [a'pirasin] (5) (P has ἐπήρασιν [e'pirasin]), alongside ἐπάρη [e'pari] (16) and ἔπαρε ['epare] (22).
   (e) the frequent reduction of εἰς [is] to [s], and its conflation with a following definite article.
   (f) the use of accusative plural clitic pronouns as genitives (3, 6, etc.), perhaps because of the unsatisfactory nature of gen. pl. μω(ν)/σω(ν)/τω(ν) [mo(n)/so(n)/to(n)], which sounded like neuter singular possessive adjectives (cf. μων/(ἐ)μόν [(e)'mon] 'my', σων/(ἐ)σόν [(e)'son] 'your' (sg.)), or the masculine accusative singular of the definite article (cf. τω(ν)/τό(ν) [to(n)]).
   (g) many innovative pronominal forms (11.7.8 (29)), including: relative ὅπου, probably pronounced [o'pu] (2); ἔνας ['enas] for εἶς [is] (6); ὀκάτι [o'kati] for 'assertive' τι [ti] (11) (where the initial ὀ- [o-], apparently extended from free-relative pronouns, is a regular feature of such forms in this period and seems to be associated with the expression of indefiniteness).

In syntax, all prepositions are now used with the accusative (though the genitive may still be used with some, especially ἀπό [apo], and certain fixed expressions with the dative survive, such as ἐν τούτῳ [en'duto] 'meanwhile'). There is also a nice example of the νά [na] + ἔχω ['exo] + infinitive construction in line 17, used here in a final sense and supported by the pleonastic genitive article τοῦ [tu]. In general, however, simple νά [na] + subjunctive is used in both true modal functions (6, 7, etc.) and as a future (24), and wherever ancient Greek would have employed an infinitival complement. The infinitive in this register, unlike in the more refined Greek of the romances where it was still retained as an option after control verbs (occasionally), ἄρχομαι ['arxome] 'begin', and in indirect questions (e.g. *we don't know what to do*), is now restricted to the complements of modal auxiliaries and to nominalized adjuncts of the type τὸ ἰδεῖ [to i'ði]/τὸ ἀκούσει [to a'kusi], lit. 'the to-see/the to-hear . . .', i.e. 'on seeing, hearing . . .' (e.g. 555, 631).

The locution ὁ λόγου του [o 'loɣu tu] 'himself' (emphatic, as in *he did it himself*) in line 15 is also of interest. We should first note the fixed expressions ἀπό/διὰ τοῦ λόγου του [ap(o)/ðja tu 'loɣu tu] (e.g. 1395, 3460), lit. 'on his account', with genitive preserved. As these came to be used idiomatically with the sense of emphatic 'self', the preposition was sometimes dropped, and (τοῦ) λόγου του [(tu) 'loɣu tu] (with free choice of possessive) was used as an emphatic pronoun. Such expressions continue in colloquial use in modern Greek, now often ironically/humorously.

We also find substitution of the semantically related reflexive pronoun ἑαυτοῦ/ αὑτοῦ [eaf'tu/af'tu] for (τοῦ) λόγου [(tu) 'loɣu] to give ἀπ' (τοῦ) (ἑ)αυτοῦ του [ap (tu) (e)af'tu tu], with or without the article, lit. 'from (the) self of-him'. From the abstraction of τοῦ ἑαυτοῦ του [tu eaf'tu tu] began the replacement of the simple reflexive pronoun with the phrasal reflexive of modern Greek, τον εαυτό του [ton eaf'to tu] etc., where the 'self' (like λόγος['loɣos]) is a masculine noun. And since 'emphatic' pronouns naturally require a nominative form, we soon find ὁ ἑαυτός του [o eaf'tos tu], and by analogy ὁ λόγου του [o 'loɣu tu], as in l. 15.

Given the assumption that an 'emphatic' pronominal should agree with the item it modifies, there was also substitution of fully inflected (ἑ)αυτός [(e)af'tos] for the genitive phrase in ἀπ' (ἑ)αυτοῦ του [ap (e)af'tu tu] to form the rather odd-looking ἀπ' α(ὐ)τός του [apa(f)'tos tu], which, in view of the non-prepositional force of the preposition, is perhaps best written ἀπα(υ)τός (του) (e.g. 5827). Such expressions enjoyed a lively later history in the spoken dialects of modern Greek, but they are no longer a feature of the contemporary standard.

In early Cypriot there are also phrases like ἀπό 'ξ αὐτῆς του [apo ks af'tis tu], lit. 'from/by [[out-of self] of-him]', where ἀπό [apo] is a true preposition with a local or agentive sense, but takes as its complement a fossilized phrase (ἑ)ξ-αὐτῆς του [(e)ksaf'tis tu], where the 'self' is a feminine noun governed by the preposition ἐκ/ἐξ [ek/eks] 'out of'. In a fashion analogous to that described in the case of (τοῦ) λόγου [(tu) 'loɣu] and (ἑ)αυτοῦ [(e)af'tu], (ἑ)αυτῆς [(e)af'tis] was clearly substituted for the feminine noun of phrases such as ἐκ μερίδος του/ἐκ μεριᾶς του [ek me'riðos tu/ek mer'jas tu] 'from part/side of-him', an expression which then served as a 'pronoun' in its own right. Subsequently, we also find a modernized version in which ἀπό [apo] governs an accusative masculine 'pronoun' ξαυτόν [ksaf'ton], parallel to ἑαυτόν [eaf'ton] (cf. 12.4.2, 14.2.4).

12.3.4 The translated romances

Though the language of the romances translated or adapted from western originals is certainly less 'vulgar' than that of the *Chronicle of the Morea*, it nevertheless belongs much more solidly to the vernacular tradition than that of the original romances composed in the Byzantine capital. The translation of *Phlórios and Plátzia-Phlóre*, for example, was probably completed in the Frankish-dominated Peloponnese by a poet who knew the *Spanéas* poem and (probably) the *Chronicle of the Morea*, but was generally unfamilar with Greek literature in the learned language. The free use of innovative descriptive compounds, the verbal echoes of folk poetry, the avoidance of complex sentence structure and rhetorical periods, and the low incidence of learned forms are all familiar features of original compositions using popular forms of Greek.

The action of *Phlórios* takes place in Spain and Cairo, where Plátzia-Phlóre is sold into slavery. The heroine's father is a knight of Rome (the original), the hero a prince of Saracen Spain. After the usual adventures, the story closes with the reunion of the lovers, the conversion of the Spanish Muslims, and the election of Phlórios's father as king of Rome! In the following extract Plátzia-Phlóre laments her misfortune on being sold to slavers (see Kriarás (1955: 131–96)):

(16)　Πρῶτον ψυχὴν ἐχώριζον μόνον ἀπὲ τὸ σῶμα,
　　　　μὲ τῆς πυρᾶς τὴν συμφοράν, μὲ τῆς ἱστιᾶς τὴν καῦσιν,
　　　　καὶ νῦν ἐμὲ χωρίζουσιν ἐκ τὸν ἐμὸν τὸν πόθον,
　　　　ζωὴν νὰ ζῶ ἐπώδυνον, πάντοτε πονεμένην,
　　　　νύκτες νὰ κλαίω, νὰ θλίβωμαι, ἡμέρες νὰ λυποῦμαι,　　　　　　5
　　　　τὸ τρώγω νὰ ἔνι ὀδυνηρόν, τὸ πίνω νὰ ἔναι πόνος,
　　　　δεῖπνος νὰ ἔναι συμφορά, ὀδύνη νὰ μὲ σφάζη,
　　　　ποτὲ νὰ μὴ ἔχω ἀνάπαυσιν, ἀλλὰ πικριὲς μεγάλες.
　　　　Πόθε μου, ἀγάπη μου καλή, ψυχή μου, ἐνθύμησίς μου,
　　　　ἐπιθυμιά μου, Φλώριε, καρδιά μου, ψύχωσίς μου,　　　　　　10
　　　　παρηγοριὰ τῶν πόνων μου, γδίκη τῶν πειρασμῶν μου,
　　　　πάλιν κινδύνοι ἐφτάσασιν διὰ νὰ μὲ ξενώσουν
　　　　καθόλου ἀπὸ τὸν πόθον σου καὶ ἀπ' τὴν ἀσχόλησίν σου.
　　　　Τὴν πουλησιὰν οὐκ ἤξευρα καὶ θέλημά μου οὐκ ἦτον·
　　　　μ' ἐπιβουλιὰν τὸ ποίκασιν, ὁ θεὸς αὐτοὺς νὰ κρίνη!　　　　　15
　　　　Ἐπαίρνουν με, ξενώνουν με, καὶ πλέον οὐδὲν μὲ βλέπεις.
　　　　　　　　　　　　　　　　　　Phlórios and Plátzia-Phlóre, 1002–17

['proto(n) psi'çin e'xorizon　　　'monon a‚pe to 'soma/ me tis　　pi'ras ti
First　　　soul　　they-were-parting only　　from the body　　with of-the pyre　　the

si(m)fo'ra(n), me tis　　i'stjas tiŋ 'gapsi(n),/ ke 'nin e'me xo'rizusin　　ek
misfortune,　　with of-the fire　　the burning,　　and now me　　they-are-parting from

ton e'mon dom 'boθo(n),/ zo'i na 'zo　　e'poðino(n), 'pandote
the my　　the desire,　　life that I-may-live of-pain,　　always

pone'meni(n),/ 5 'niçtes na 'kleo,　na 'θlivome,　　i'meres na
afflicted,　　　　nights that I-may-weep, that I-may-be-distressed, days　　that

li'pume,/ to 'troɣo 'na nj　　oðini'ro(n), to 'pino 'na ne　　'ponos,/
I-may-grieve, what I-eat　　that may-be painful,　　what I-drink that may-be toil,

'ðipnos 'na ne　　si(m)fo'ra, o'ðini 'na me 'sfazi,/　　po'te na 'mi
dinner　　that may-be misfortune, pain　　that me may-butcher, never that not

xo⌣　　(a)'napapsi(n), a'la pi'krjes me'ɣales./ 'poθe mu⌣, (a)'ɣapi mu
I-may-have respite,　　but bitternesses great.　　　Desire of-me, love　　of-me

ka'li, psi'çi mu⌣, (e)n‚θimi'siz mu,/ 10 epiθi'mja　mu, 'florie, kar'ðja
fine,　　soul　of-me, source-of-passion of-me,　　object-of-desire of-me, Phlórios, heart

mu, ˌpsixoˈsiz mu,/ pariɣoˈrja tom ˈbono(m) mu, ˈɣðiki   tom
of-me, source-of-life of-me, consolation of-the pains   of-me, vengeance of-the

birazˈmo(m) mu,/ ˈpali(n) kinˈðini ˈftasasi(n) ðiˈa na ˈme kseˈnosuṇ/
trials   of-me, again   dangers   have-come for that me   they-may-deprive

kaˈθolu ap tom ˈboθo su   kj ap tin asˌxoliˈsi su./ tim buliˈsjan uk
altogether of the desire of-you and from the attention of-you. The sale   not

ˈiksevra   ke ˌθeliˈma m   uk ˈito(n);/ 15 m epivuˈʎa(n) to ˈpikasin, o
I-knew-about and will   of-me not it-was;   with treachery   it they-did, the

θjos afˈtus na ˈkrini!/   eˈpernu(m) me, kseˈnonu(m) me, ke ˈpljon
God them   that he-may-judge! They-take   me, they-deprive/exile me, and (no)more

uˌðe me ˈvlepis.]
not   me you-see.

'At first they tried only to part my soul from my body through the calamity of the pyre, by the burning of the fire, but now they part me from my beloved to live a life of pain, forever grievous, to weep by night and suffer, to grieve by day, that what I eat may be a source of sorrow, what I drink a source of pain, that food may be my misfortune, that my agony may slay me, that I may never have respite, but only great bitterness. My desire, my true love, my soul, my inspiration, object of my longing, Phlórios, my heart, source of my life, consolation of my sufferings, avenger of my torments, dangers have come once more to deprive me altogether of your desire and your attention. I did not know of the sale and it was not my wish; they did it treacherously, may God be their judge! They are taking me, they are exiling me, and you will see me no more.'

The impression is of a poem written in a stylized 'literary' vernacular, a relatively polished language assimilated to the conventions not only of folk poetry but also of literate compositions in the popular style. Thus synizesis is usually guaranteed by the metre, and the final vowel of ἀπό [apo] is usually elided before the article. Note too the 'modern' morphology of nominative plurals of a-stem nouns, e.g. ἡμέρες [iˈmeres] in line 5, see 11.7.4 ; of 3sg. forms of the verb 'be', ἔναι [ˈene], ἦτον [ˈito(n)], cf. 11.8.5 (a); and of the 3pl. aorist ποίκασιν [ˈpikasi(n)], cf. 11.6 (14), 11.8.4. We may also mention the standard use of the accusative with prepositions, and the regular use of the genitive (mainly with pronouns, e.g. 491) or the accusative (mainly with full noun phrases, e.g. 986) to mark the indirect object.

The only archaic (possibly learned) features worthy of note are the use of the possessive adjective in line 3, the rather free use of 3rd declension nouns in -σις [-sis] (in comparison, say, with the *Chronicle of the Morea*), and the retention of the old two-termination declensional system for compound adjectives of the classical type (distinguishing only masculine and neuter forms, with the former used to modify feminine nouns): e.g. ζωήν ... ἐπώδυνον [zoˈi(n) ... eˈpoðinon] 'life ... of-pain', in line 4. Such 'progressive' forms of the vernacular *Dichtersprache*, not always quite as 'basic' as that of *Phlórios* but representing an evolved and homogenised development of the style first seen in *Digenés*, constituted the norm for much of the fictional poetry of the fourteenth and fifteenth centuries, and crucially provided the foundation for much of the emerging dialectal literature of Crete, as discussed below (see also 14.2.4).

12.4   The first 'dialect' literature: Cyprus and Crete

12.4.1   Introduction

Cypriot is the first modern dialect to appear in its distinctive regional guise, our earliest example being a fourteenth-century legal text (*The Assizes*) translated into Greek from a French original. The early official and literary use of local dialect in Cyprus was undoubtedly connected with the fact that the island was partially insulated from the influence of the capital in the middle Byzantine period when, from the middle of the seventh century till the campaigns of Nikephóros Phokás in 965, it was under Arab or joint Arab–Byzantine rule. It was then reoccupied barely 200 years later by the knights of the Third Crusade, and sold first to the Order of the Templars of Jerusalem, and subsequently to the French Lusignan dynasty (1192). French government continued until 1489, when the island passed to the Venetians, who were forced to abandon it to the Turks in 1571. The long period of western rule therefore simply continued an established tradition of detached development in which the developing local vernacular had acquired a status generally denied to it in areas that remained under continuous Byzantine rule.

The situation on Crete was superficially similar, in that Crete also suffered a period of Arab occupation (from 827 to 961), and was later administered by the Venetians (from 1211 to 1669). But the language of the vernacular literature which began to appear there from the late fourteenth century onwards is not very different from that used elsewhere in the Greek-speaking world, and though Cretan dialect words and forms can certainly be found, the thoroughgoing use of what we now think of as Cretan dialect did not become established in literary composition until the second half of the sixteenth century. This difference merits careful examination.

In Cyprus, the early weakening of the Byzantine tradition is confirmed by the writings of Leóntios Makhairás, who composed his *Recital concerning the sweet land of Cyprus* in the first half of the fifteenth century. The author describes a world in which the Greek élite had long been integrated, and was subject to only residual influence from the higher forms of Byzantine culture. Thus, even though he remained an Orthodox Christian, Makhairás shows the greatest respect for the feudal government, and instinctively supports its suppression of revolt. His compositional technique, correspondingly, owes much to the practice of contemporary French writers, and his written Greek, as far as we can tell, already reflects the developed Cypriot dialect of the period. Learned language is almost entirely confined to scriptural quotation, and the fact that he sometimes misquotes the canonized text is a further indication that he lacked a conventional Greek education (e.g. in paragraph (1) he substitutes ψέματα τῶν ψεμάτων ['psemata tom pse'maton], lit. 'lies of lies', for ματαιότης τῶν ματαιοτήτων [mate'otis tom mateo'titon] 'vanity of vanities').

In Crete, by contrast, where the Arab occupation was comparatively short, Byzantine cultural traditions seem to have remained more firmly in place, a situation later reinforced by reaction to the oppression that marked the first two centuries of Venetian rule. Classical Greek, for example, could still be studied in the mid-fourteenth century, classical and Byzantine texts continued to be copied (Holton

(1991a: 3)), and even the vernacular literature which began to be composed in the latter part of the fourteenth century often looked back to Byzantine models, even if some poets were also beginning to show an interest in their own folk traditions and contemporary Italian work. This situation was reinforced by the influx of scholarly Byzantine refugees before and after 1453, and by the establishment of Venice as the most important printing centre in Europe, an industry in which Greeks, including many Cretans, played a prominent role.

Nevertheless, the fully-fledged Cretan dialect of late sixteenth- and seventeenth-century literature did not emerge overnight, and the local speech, as with other dialects in the Middle Ages, must have evolved over a considerable period, with changes starting amongst the mass of the people gradually spreading to the middle and upper classes, before a version of it eventually came to be accepted in literary compositions. In this connection, we should note that Venetian administrative documents, composed in, or relating to, Crete during the thirteenth and early-fourteenth centuries, employ Greek styles ranging from a mildly modernized standard-official in decrees of the state (e.g. Miklosich and Müller (1860–9: vol. VI, no. XC, pp. 220–2)) to near-vernacular officialese in documents of a more local character (e.g. Miklosich and Müller (1860–9: vol. VI, no. CII, pp. 238–9)). But even the worst-spelled texts of the latter type, which presumably reflect the spoken and 'civil-service' Greek learned *in situ* by minor officials, display few clearly dialectal elements. Similarly, the agreement of 1299 between the rebellious Cretan aristocrat Aléxios Kallérges and the Venetian authorities (Mértzios (1949: 264–74)), which Panayiotákis (1993) presents as one of the earliest documents in vernacular prose, looks similarly 'standard'. It seems, then, that the period in which Cretan developed most strongly in the direction of its modern form, at least for the educated/literate classes, began during the fourteenth century, perhaps a little before vernacular literature started to be produced on the island.

If this is so, it would seem that the relative rarity of dialectal features in earlier Cretan poetry reflects both the continuing influence of Byzantine written traditions and the still-developing character of Cretan among educated speakers in a period when many 'common' vernacular features remained in use, either instead of, or alongside, the originally 'popular' local variants that eventually replaced them.

The probable period of rapid linguistic development coincided with important social changes which help to explain the spread and general acceptance of dialect forms. Though the condition of the peasants remained wretched throughout the Venetian period, the Cretan and Venetian aristocracies eventually embarked on a process of symbiosis and integration (cf. Maltézou (1991)), and it was against this background that the hold of the Byzantine tradition began to wane and Cretan dialect developed as the common language of the island. Even the Venetian colonists began to abandon Italian, and by the mid-sixteenth century, the enhanced status of the local vernacular finally overcame any residual reluctance to its adoption as the basis for a literary language. This innovation was undoubtedly supported by contemporary Italian movements to elevate the more prestigious local dialects, including Venetian, into written languages (Cochrane (1988: 19–23)), and an elaborated, somewhat stylized form of Cretan soon became the vehicle for dramatic and poetic works of a quality that has since led to the period *c*. 1580–1669 becoming known as the 'Cretan Renaissance'.

Since the major early works in Cypriot dialect belong to the fourteenth and fifteenth centuries, and since there is a natural break in the Cretan vernacular tradition that corresponds roughly with the end of the period covered by this chapter, the discussion of Cypriot and Cretan literature is conveniently divided into two parts. The earlier period is discussed below, and works of the sixteenth and (for Crete) seventeenth centuries are presented and analysed in Chapter 14.

12.4.2 *Early dialect literature in Cyprus: Makhairás's chronicle*

This fifteenth-century work is one of the earliest examples of extended vernacular prose writing, and is one of the most important documents for the study of the popular Greek of its period. It has survived in two manuscripts, one in Venice (V, sixteenth century), the other in Oxford (O, also sixteenth century, but with serious lacunae and a slightly more colloquial/dialectal style overall, including a larger set of French loanwords). The two versions, of which V is usually taken to be the better guide to the original, are sometimes strikingly different, and the extent of internal linguistic variation is again noteworthy, with both non-regional vernacular and learned variants in use alongside specifically Cypriot forms. The learned forms (outside scriptural quotations) may be due to some familiarity with the tradition of chronography, but in general it seems that educated Cypriot of the period tolerated a fair measure of free variation between older (common) vernacular and local innovations. The standard edition, based on V, is that of Dawkins (1932).

Modern Cypriot is markedly different from standard Modern Greek (see e.g. Newton (1970)), and a number of its more prominent characteristics are already in evidence, directly or indirectly, in Makhairás's work.

(17) There are many instances of assimilation of a vowel to that of a following syllable (γεναίκα [je'neka] for γυναίκα [ji'neka] 'woman'; παρπατῶ [parpa'to] for περπατῶ [perpa'to] 'walk').

(18) In contemporary Cypriot, intervocalic voiced fricatives are often lost, and we already find examples in the *Chronicle* such as ὁ ρήας [o 'rias] for ὁ ρήγας [o 'riɣas] 'the king'.

(19) Palatalization of voiceless velar fricatives before [i (j)] and [e] has led to [ʃ] (as opposed to common [ç]) in modern Cypriot, and there is an identical palatal articulation of σ (originally [s]) before [j]. Spelling confusions reflecting these developments are already found: e.g. πεντακόχιες [penda'koʃ(j)es] for πεντακόσιες 'five hundred'.

(20) A particular characteristic of Cypriot is the retention of word-final [n], and its assimilation to a following word-initial continuant. This is occasionally reflected in variant spellings before words beginning with fricatives and nasals. Thus alongside -ν σ-/φ-/ν-, we also find examples where -ν is dropped (e.g. πᾶσα φοράν ['pasa(f) fo'ran] 'every time'), together with variants involving

-νς σ- (e.g. εἰς αὐτούς σου [is aftōs su] 'to self of-you') and -ς σ- (e.g. ἃς σᾶς ξηγηθῶ [ās sas ksiji'θo] 'if I to-you explain', assuming that the first word is ἂν [an] 'if', rather than ἃς [as], < ἔασε ['ease] 'let', which is often used equivalently in medieval Greek)).

(21) In contemporary Cypriot the double consonants of the ancient language are pre-served, and many other words have acquired a secondary double-consonant articulation. This is well attested in the *Chronicle*, though whether there are any precisely formulable 'rules' controlling its operation is unclear. The poten-tial 'targets' are initial and intervocalic liquids, nasals, voiceless plosives (pronounced [pp^h, tt^h, kk^h] in modern Cypriot), and fricatives, though the effect is sometimes restricted to specific grammatical morphemes (e.g. already in Makhairás the comparative in -ττερος [-tt^{h}eros], and the perfect passive participle in -μμένος [-m'menos], etc.), sometimes apparently a feature of specific words (e.g. in the text of Makhairás νναί [nne] 'yes'; ἔσσω ['esso] 'within'; ἔππεσα ['epp^{h}esa] 'I fell'; πολλύς [pol'lis] 'much'; ποττέ [pot't^{h}e] '(n)ever'; etc.).

The major issue, however, is variation, and two examples will suffice to illustrate the problem (references are to the paragraphs of Dawkins's text). First, virtually the full set of possible feminine plural variants, apart from articular nom. pl. αἱ [e], is in apparently free use (cf. 11.7.2–4 (17–21), 11.7.6 (24)); thus nominative οἱ 'μέραι [i 'mere] 'the days', with classical nominal ending, occurs beside οἱ 'μέρες [i 'meres], with vernacular nominal suffix (1); and the wholly classical accusative τὰς παλαιὰς ἱστορίας [tas pale'as isto'rias] 'the old histories', is used alongside the mixed τὰς παλαιὰς ἱστορίες [tas pale'as isto'ries] (2) and the wholly vernacu-lar τὲς γυναῖκες [tez ji'nekes] (26), 'the women'. Secondly, the classical form ἀπό [apo] 'from', appears freely alongside dialectal ἀπού [apu] without any apparent shift of register. The general vernacular ἀπ' [ap] is also used before words begin-ning with a vowel, but ἀπέ [ape] with anaptyxis is used regularly before the forms of the definite article beginning with [t-] (and often with other words with the same initial).

Some of this is probably due to the inconsistency of later scribal practice, some to Makhairás himself, who may well have used certain learned and educated ver-nacular forms (later replaced) alongside local variants. Nor should we discount the possibility that some of the orthographic variation between 'standard' spellings and representations of local speech conceals a more consistent pronunciation in an era when the only standardized orthography was that of the traditional written language.

The following brief extract, dealing with the aftermath of the Templars' sale of Cyprus to Guy de Lusignan of Jerusalem, provides a typical sample of the language (the transcription attempts to represent a specifically Cypriot pronunciation):

(22) Καὶ ὄντα τὴν ἐγόρασεν ὁ αὐτὸς ρὲ Οὔνγκε τὴν Κύπρον ἀπὲ τοὺς Τεμπλιῶτες καὶ τοὺς Λαγκοβάρδους, μανθάνοντα τὴν ἀγανάκτησιν ὅπου τοὺς ἐποῖκαν καὶ τὸν σφαμὸν εἰς τὴν χώραν, ἦτον εἰς μεγάλην ἔννοιαν καὶ

ἐννοιάζετον πῶς νὰ ποίσῃ νὰ μὲν ἔχουν κακὸν εἰς τὴν Κύπρον, ὅτι ὅλος ὁ
τόπος ἦτον γεμᾶτος Ῥωμαῖοι, καὶ ἐλάλεν εἰς τὸν ἐμαυτόν του· Ὅποτε
θελήσου νὰ ρεβελιάσουν κατὰ μένα, ἠμποροῦ νὰ τὸ ποίσουν καὶ θέλουν
ἔχειν βοήθειαν τὸν βασιλέαν τῆς Κωνσταντινόπολις, καὶ ἐμποροῦν μὲ
δύναμιν νὰ σηκώσουν τὸ ρηγάτον ἀπὲ τὰς χεῖρας μου.'

Recital concerning the sweet land of Cyprus: 22

[tʃe 'onda tin e'ɣorasen o af'tos re   'uŋge tin 'dʒipron ape tus
And when   it he-bought the same king Guy the Cyprus   from the

temb'ʎotes ke tus laŋgu'varðus, maθ'θanonda tin aɣa'naktisim pu tus
Templars   and the Lombards,   learning   the vexation   that for-them

e'pikan tʃe tos sfam'mon (i)s tix 'xoran, 'iton iz me'ɣalin 'ennjan tʃ
they-made and the slaughter in the land, he-was in great   concern and

en'njazeton pos na 'pisi   na men 'exun ka'kon (i)s tin 'dʒipron,
gave-thought-to how that he-may-make(it) that not they-have trouble in the Cyprus,

'oti   'olos o 'topos 'iton je'matos ro'mei,   tʃ e'laʎen   (i)s ton
because all the place was full(of) Byzantines/Greeks, and he-was-saying to the

emaf'ton du: ''opote θe'lisun na reve'ʎasun kata 'menan, imbo'run
self   of-him: 'Whenever they-want that they-rebel against me,   they-can

na to 'pisun tʃe 'θelun 'eʃin vo'iθjan tov vasi'ʎan tis   kostandi'nopolis,
that it they-do and they-will to-have (as)help the king   of-the Constantinople,

tʃ embo'run me 'ðinamin na ʃi'kosun to ri'ɣaton ape taʃ 'ʃiraz mu.']
and they-can with force   that they-take the kingdom from the hands of-me.'

'And when the aforementioned king Guy bought Cyprus from the Templars and the
Lombards, learning of the vexation that they [*the Greeks*] had caused them and the
slaughter in the land, he was greatly concerned and began to consider how he could
arrange for them not to have trouble in Cyprus, because the whole place was full of
Greeks, and he would say to himself: "Whenever they want to rebel against me, they
can do it, and they will have the support of the king of Constantinople, and they can
take the kingdom from my hands by force."'

Some of the forms used here have already been mentioned. Note, however, ὄντα(ν)
['ondan] 'when', a by-form of ὅταν ['otan] widely used in vernacular Greek, and
the aorist ἐ-γόρασεν [e'ɣorsen] from ἀγοράζω [aɣo'razo] 'I buy', involving the
typically south-eastern extension of the syllabic augment to verbs with an initial
vowel (11.8.6 (b)). The clitic doubling construction of the first sentence is also
highly characteristic of popular Greek (the effect being to topicalize/background
the doubled noun), though it is also important to observe here the continued influence of the old chronicle style (cf. 10.2), seen, for example, in the discourse deictic
use of ὁ αὐτός [o af'tos] 'the same', and the participial syntax of the subordinate
clause (albeit using the modern indeclinable gerund μανθάνοντα [maθ'θanonda]).

Vernacular assimilation of the voiced fricative [ɣ] before a nasal is seen in
σφαμός [sfam'mos] < σφαγμός [sfaɣ'mos] 'slaughter' (cf. forms such as πρᾶμμαν
['pramman] < πρᾶγμα ['praɣma] 'thing', for the geminate), while the form ἐλάλεν,
which superficially seems to involve the surprising transfer of the contract

verb λαλῶ [la'lo] to the non-contract paradigm (i.e. we might have expected imperfect ἐλάλει(ν) [e'lalin]), in fact conceals the 'popular' recharacterized formation ἐλάλει-ε(ν) [e'lali-en/e'laljen] (11.8.5 (e)), in which the palatalization of the lateral has proceeded to the point where it seemed more appropriate to write -λεν, representing [-ʎen].

The contrast between the νά [na] and infinitival constructions as complements to θέλω ['θelo] is nicely illustrated in Guy's speech to himself, the former meaning 'want' and the latter marking future 'will'. The construction underlying the standard modern Greek future, namely the impersonal use of the reduced 3sg. θέ [θe] + νά [na], is not attested, but the synonymous μέλλει να ['melli na] + subjunctive 'it will (be) that', is already a regular future formation (e.g. in paragraph 1, and already in the *Assizes*).

12.4.3 Early vernacular literature in Crete

The first known Cretan poet, Stéphanos Sakhlíkes (*c*. 1331–*c*. 1396), belonged to the bourgeoisie of Kástro (modern Iráklio), but dissipated most of his considerable inheritance on whoring and gambling, and ended up in jail. After a period of retirement in the country, living on his sole remaining fief, he enjoyed a characteristically flawed career as an advocate back in Kástro (cf. van Gemert (1991: 51–6)).

Making use of the techniques and language of the songs of the Cretan oral tradition, his early surviving work, much of it written (?as if) from his cell, consists of bawdy satirical poems of a highly personal kind composed in the fifteen-syllable metre and clearly designed to be recited. Later work, clearly designed to be read, is composed in rhyming couplets, an innovation which became standard in the Cretan tradition, and led to the rhyming of a number of earlier heroic and romantic classics in Venetian printed editions.

Sakhlíkes is remarkable for his early use of elements of folk song and local dialect; and his vividly realistic treatments, inspired in part by the contemporary work of Francesco di Vannozzo, mark a break with the traditions of the Greek world (despite some allusions to written sources). The contrast with Linárdos Dellapórtas (*c*. 1330–1419/20) could hardly be greater. Like Sakhlíkes, Dellapórtas was born into the bourgeoisie of Kástro, and at one point found himself in jail. But there the similarity ends, since he spent his youth abroad in the service of Venice, returning in 1389 to be appointed as an advocate, and ended his life as director of the hospital of St Lazarus (cf. van Gemert (1991: 56–8)). Though most of his work has still to be published, it is at once apparent that he rejected both dialectal language and rhyme, and persisted with the written traditions of Byzantium.

The work of Marínos Faliéros (1397–1474), however, who belonged to the Venetian family of Falier, and was one of the greatest landowners in the eastern half of the island (cf. van Gemert (1991: 58–62)), takes much of its inspiration from Italian literature, especially the work of the Venetian poet Leonardo Giustinian. Nonetheless, we should note the natural use of Greek language and metre by a Venetian nobleman, confirming that by the fifteenth century many of the colonists not only spoke and understood Greek but also used it for writing. His Greek, like that of Sakhlíkes, has a mildly dialectal feel, reflected in features such as a tendency to generalize ἤ- [i-] as the accented augment (an east Cretan characteristic, cf, 11.8.6 (b)), the appearance of the intrusive -γ- [-ɣ-] in the suffix -εύ(γ)ω [-'ev(ɣ)o] (cf. 11.8.5. (d)), and the occasional use of weak forms of the definite article ending in -ς [-s], e.g. τς [ts] for fem. gen. sg. τῆς [tis]. See 14.2.4 for discussion of Cretan innovations.

The most important work of this period, however, is undoubtedly the *Apókopos* ('Exhausted') of Bergadés (no first name is known), who was perhaps connected with the noble Bragadin/Bregadin family of Réthymno (cf. van Gemert (1991: 62–5)). The poem, now dated to the beginning of the fifteenth century, takes its title from the opening words: Μιὰν ἀπὸ κόπου ἐνύσταξα . . . [mjan apo 'kopu 'nistaksa . . .] 'once after toil I-felt-weary . . .', and, in the form of a narrated dream involving a visit to the underworld, apparently urges its readers to enjoy their life on earth because the dead are soon forgotten, a clearly anti-traditional line of argument. (Interpretation remains controversial in that the original ending has been lost through later adaptation, perhaps in an effort to give the poem a more conventional moralizing character.)

Its language is a now familiar blend of 'standard' medieval vernacular (itself 'mixed', and, in line with the subject matter, combined here with archaisms from ecclesiastical writing) and elements of the developing Cretan dialect such as -εύγω [-'evɣo], accented augment ἤ- ['i-], loss after [-s-/-r-] of the [-j-] resulting from synizesis (more accurately, thoroughgoing palatalization of [-s-/-r-], giving e.g. μερά [me'ṛa] for μεριά [mer'ja] 'side'), and many local vocabulary items.

12.5 Conclusion

It was noted at the end of Section I that most of the major phonological developments in the transition from 'ancient' to 'modern' Greek were complete by the late antique period. But though some of the major changes in morphology and syntax also have their roots in the same period, the completion of these changes, and the advent of many new ones, belongs properly to the medieval period. By the end of the fifteenth century, however, the component parts of what has now evolved into standard modern Greek were largely in place, but the language itself remained fundamentally fragmented. Archaizing written Greek had variants of its own, while attempts at writing the vernacular remained unstable, involving a variable admixture of forms from the written middle registers and educated speech into bases reflecting different oral traditions and/or regional developments. Only in the realm of romantic verse fiction had anything like a 'standard', non-regional, style developed as a model, and even this was undermined by the fragmentation of the empire as it fell first under western and then Turkish domination, the latter invariably fatal to creative writing.

The subsequent story of the Greeks' struggle for national survival, and the efforts made to forge a modern standard from the disparate elements of their medieval linguistic legacy is the theme of Section III.

Modern Greek: from the Ottoman Empire to the European Union

Chapter 13

Ottoman rule and the war of independence (1453–1833)

13.1 The early years

Since most of the Byzantine empire had already been occupied by the Ottoman Turks, the capture of Constantinople in May 1453, though shocking, was largely symbolic. The remnants of Greek-speaking territory, including some of the lands formerly under western rule, were then progressively incorporated into the Ottoman state. Some islands, however, held out for a while longer, Rhodes till 1522, Khios and Naxos till 1566, Cyprus till 1571, and Crete till 1669. Uniquely, the Ionian islands (Heptanese) remained under Venetian control, after a brief interlude of Ottoman rule, until 1797, when they were first ceded to France, and then became a British 'protectorate'.

Many Greeks, recalling the treachery of 1204, initially claimed to prefer Ottoman to Venetian rule, but the Venetian connection at least had the merit of promoting cultural life. In the first centuries of Ottoman rule the University of Padua began to draw large numbers of Greek students from both Venetian and Ottoman lands, and Venice itself became a major centre of Greek publishing. Even after the fall of Crete, the Ionian islands continued to provide an important channel for western influence.

After the fall of Constantinople, the Turks consolidated their grip on the Balkans and brought Moldavia and Wallachia (the component parts of modern Romania), together with much of Hungary, under their control. The subject peoples were organized into *milletler* ('nations') on the basis not of language but of religious faith, and in return for guaranteeing the loyalty of the Orthodox population, the patriarch of Constantinople was granted wide-ranging powers, including the administration of justice, the organization of education, and the raising of taxes. But despite these concessions, the Christians of the empire remained seriously disadvantaged. Inevitably, many converted to Islam, and the Greek population of the empire was thus depleted through apostasy, a situation exacerbated by the progressive adoption of the dominant language.

In these difficult years the Patriarchate provided a vital focal point. Thanks to Turkish willingness to devolve authority (a policy prompted by indifference rather than generosity), the church was able to sustain Byzantine values. Though in time these began to seem unenlightened, and though the church itself eventually fell victim to Ottoman venality, the Patriarchate's policies were instrumental in the preservation of a sense of Greek identity in an era when the chief preoccupation of the Greek population was the struggle for survival. As a result, most ordinary

Greeks were able to keep their faith and their language, drawing inspiration for the present from their traditions, while looking forward to their liberation by a foreign power, as foretold in popular legend and folk song.

The role of the church was particularly important in the field of language, since it was the conservatism of the ecclesiastical intelligentsia that dominated the education system, and provided a written 'standard' which not only sustained an educated spoken norm, but also helped to constrain the regional development of popular Greek in circumstances that would otherwise have promoted wider fragmentation of the kind that had begun in the most peripheral regions. The cultural and linguistic foundations for a Greek national movement were therefore in place when the Ottoman empire began its long decline.

13.2 Ottoman decline and the Greek revival

In Europe, decay began quite quickly. Growing military weakness spawned internal corruption, and in a context of failing central authority, provincial governments began to operate semi-autonomously. Though revolutionaries sought periodically to exploit Turkish difficulties by risking insurrection, the most persistent resistance came from *kléftes*, bandits who had fled to the mountains to avoid taxation and/or Turkish jurisdiction. Though they cheerfully robbed anyone with money, their assaults on Ottoman officials earned them a Robin Hood reputation and spawned a magnificent collection of 'kleftic' ballads (see 14.3). In response, the authorities recruited irregulars called *armatolí*, though in practice the distinction between these and the klefts was a fine one, with frequent defections in both directions, determined largely by the rate and regularity of government pay. Such bands became increasingly powerful as central authority waned, and provided much of the military muscle in the struggle for independence that began in the 1820s.

The Turks also began to encounter serious external difficulties, as Russia's territorial ambitions combined, in the reign of Peter the Great (1682–1725), with a growing political interest in the fate of their fellow Orthodox Christians under Ottoman rule. Russian propaganda began to be distributed, fresh uprisings were encouraged, and faith in the Russians as the liberators of popular legend thrived as never before.

These changes coincided with shifts in the higher levels of Greek society. As the empire declined, it was obliged to negotiate with the European powers, and here the Turks relied on Greek 'interpreters', who thereby acquired great influence over foreign policy. The members of this new élite, which had grown up around the Patriarchate, were known as the *Phanariótes* (Phanariots), after the Phanári ('beacon/lighthouse') district along the Golden Horn to which the Patriarchate had moved in 1601. Individuals from these families soon came to be appointed as governors of the Aegean islands and eventually became hereditary princes (*hospodars*) of the Danubian principalities of Moldavia and Wallachia, where their courts, directly accessible to western influence from Vienna via the Danube, advanced Greek culture and provided vital political experience for a future Greek ruling class.

The ambition of the Phanariots was reflected *inter alia* in an expansion of the education system, which, by the end of the seventeenth century, was staffed largely by western-educated graduates and included not only the long-established patriarchal academy in Constantinople but newly founded academies in the cities of Jassy (the capital of Moldavia) and Bucharest (the capital of Wallachia). During the eighteenth century, other 'advanced' schools were founded in Khios, Smyrna, and Ayvalik, and the emphasis in the curriculum began to shift to the ancient classics, mathematics, and the natural sciences under the influence of the French Enlightenment.

Just as important for the growth of a Greek national movement was the rise of a business class during the eighteenth century. The Greek population of Constantinople, Smyrna (Izmir), and Thessaloniki grew rapidly, commercial colonies were established in Italy, the South of France, central Europe, and Russia's Black Sea ports, and the Greek merchant navy became a major force. It has sometimes been argued that this new bourgeoisie, intolerant of Ottoman incompetence, threw its influence behind the struggle for independence in the hope of establishing a more profitable business climate. But the merchants' overall reluctance to rock the boat is well documented, though many contributed financially to the educational and consciousness-raising programmes that took place in the period before independence, partly for patriotic motives, but chiefly in response to the need for educated Greeks to help run their companies.

One consequence of these developments was the secularization of educated Greek society, in combination with a growing awareness that ancient Greek culture was greatly admired in the West. This bred a new confidence among the intelligentsia, who increasingly saw themselves as the 'heirs' of the ancients. Unfortunately, it also led to a depressingly predictable debate about the future development of a national language, which proved to be both ferocious and protracted (see Chapters 15 and 17).

As yet, however, such considerations remained the concern of intellectuals, many of whom lived outside the empire. The vast majority of Greeks were illiterate, and their ignorance was reinforced by the clergy, who opposed the western ideas seen to be undermining their authority. With the example of the French Revolution before them, many intellectuals came to despise the church, and sought to promote secular education among their less fortunate compatriots. Their efforts were not without success, and many ordinary Greeks, while retaining their faith, came also to blame the clergy for their stifling of national aspirations.

Against a background of increasing frustration with Ottoman brutality and incompetence, the scene was now set for an assertion of Greek independence. The chief obstacle was that many of the most enterprising, who might have provided leadership, lived outside the empire, while the élite within had a vested interest in preserving the *status quo*, from which they were currently deriving considerable advantage. At this juncture, the aftermath of the French Revolution proved to be catalytic.

Alarmed by the ceding of the Ionian islands to France in 1797 and Bonaparte's invasion of Egypt in 1798, the Turks concluded a hasty alliance with Russia and sought to repel the French. After a turbulent period, the Ionian islands became a British protectorate in 1814, and this independence, however notional, provided an important example to Greeks elsewhere, and offered a safe haven for mainland klefts who used the opportunity to learn how warfare was conducted by a professional army.

Another important development was the foundation of the Friendly Society (η Φιλική Εταιρεία [i fili'ki ete'ria]) in Odessa in 1814. While other organizations had promoted educational and cultural projects, this one sought national liberation by armed insurrection. Its initiators and chief supporters were mainly members of the lower middle class, and an important factor in its success was the fiction, never denied, that it had the support of the Russians, still seen by many as their future liberators. This fiction was sustained through the society's attempts to forge connections with important expatriate Greeks such as Count Ioánnis Kapodístrias, joint foreign minister of Tsar Alexander I, and the Tsar's *aide-de-camp* Prince Aléxandros Ypsilándis, who eventually became the society's leader in 1820.

13.3 Revolution and independence

In the summer of that year, as the Turkish government was attempting to restrain Ali Pasha, the maverick ruler of mainland Greece, Ypsilándis saw his opportunity. While large numbers of Ottoman troops were engaged in Greece, an invasion of the Danubian principalities was planned for the spring of 1821 in the hope that Russia might be drawn into the struggle. Though this assault proved disastrous, it provided a distraction from the simultaneous uprisings which took place in the Peloponnese, perhaps as part of a coordinated strategy. The revolt spread quickly to parts of mainland Greece north of the isthmus, and to the islands of Hydra, Spetses, and Psará, the home of the now powerful Greek navy. This guaranteed Greek control of the seas and proved to be a major factor in their eventual success.

In the short term, however, the Greeks had little hope of final victory without western support, and although the execution of the Patriarch Gregórios V for his failure to guarantee the loyalty of the sultan's Orthodox subjects provoked widespread outrage, the powers maintained a neutral position until 1823. Nevertheless, the news of the Greek revolt won support from enlightened opinion throughout Europe, and led to the establishment of philhellenic societies dedicated to fundraising and the recruitment of volunteers, including Lord Byron, whose death from fever at Mesolongi in 1824 promoted international awareness of the struggle.

In 1824 and 1825 the war began to turn in favour of the Ottoman forces, but the Greek effort in sustaining the fight brought about a change of attitude among the western powers, and Britain now joined with Russia in proposing an autonomous Greek state, undertaking, with France, to impose mediation. Though the Greeks endorsed the proposal, the Ottoman government refused to suspend hostilities, whereupon its fleet was destroyed at the battle of Navarino (Pylos) by combined British, Russian, and French forces on 20 October 1827.

Some form of Greek independence was now assured, and Kapodístrias, elected president *in absentia*, arrived in Greece in January 1828. He immediately alienated all shades of opinion with his autocratic style, and was eventually assassinated in October 1831, but, in the meantime, the conference convened to consider the frontier question recommended a boundary running from Arta to Volos as a basis for negotiation with the Ottoman government. Thereupon the search began for a king (the great powers having decided in their wisdom that Greece should be a monarchy), and some reforms were attempted, including the setting up of a national army, an administrative bureaucracy, and an education system.

Unfortunately, the war had led to internal confrontation between fighting men like the former kleftic leader Theódoros Kolokotrónis, and elements of the traditional élite. The former thought in terms of a religious struggle against Turkish oppression, and hoped to impose their own oligarchy in the event of a successful outcome, with the church retaining its traditional role; the latter conceived of the revolution in overtly nationalist terms, and planned for a modern, secular state on western lines. Though the westernizers were a minority, their education and external connections, combined with the need to retain European backing, allowed them to force through their vision of the future. But their superimposition of western-style government on a conservative and still rather oriental rural society created tensions which had a profound effect on Greek politics for much of the country's subsequent history.

Despite these problems, and the temporary anarchy following the murder of Kapodístrias, the hereditary sovereignty of Greece was finally offered in 1832 to Prince Frederick Otto, second son of King Ludwig of Bavaria. Greece, against all earlier expectation, had achieved its formal independence, with a provisional capital at Náfplion. The young king arrived there on a British warship in February 1833, to be greeted by an ecstatic crowd, though this early enthusiasm proved to be short-lived (see Chapter 16).

Before considering subsequent developments, however, we must first examine the impact on the Greek language of nearly 400 years of Ottoman rule.

Chapter 14

Spoken Greek in the Ottoman empire

14.1 The impact of Turkish

The Greek of the areas under Ottoman control, including eventually the dialects of Cyprus and Crete, naturally began to adopt Turkish vocabulary. In general, words were adapted to Greek phonology in predictable ways. The chief correspondences are as follows:

(1) (a) ç [tʃ] and c [dʒ] > τσ [ts] and τζ [dz]
   (b) ş [ʃ] > σ/s [s]
   (c) ğ > γ [ɣ/j] (this was originally a voiced velar/palatal fricative, but in modern Turkish merely marks a preceding vowel as long)
   (d) ö [œ] > ε/ο [e/o]
   (e) ü [y] > ου [u]
   (f) ı [ɯ] > ι [i]

Nouns and adjectives were also morphologically assimilated to established paradigms:

[Since we are now dealing indisputably with modern Greek, the monotonic system of accentuation (actually adopted in 1982) will be employed henceforth.]

(2) (a) In the case of nouns ending in a vowel denoting inanimate objects, some of those in -a, such as boya [bo'ja] 'paint', were taken over directly as feminines, μπογιά [bo'ja]; others, such as yaka [ja'ka] 'collar', acquired a final -ς [-s] and appear as masculines, γιακάς [ja'kas] (cf. (2)(b)).
   (b) Nouns ending in a vowel denoting males, like baba [ba'ba] 'dad', also added a final -ς [-s], μπαμπάς [ba'bas].
   (c) Nouns in -i or -ı that denote objects, such as cami [dʒa'mi] 'mosque', naturally appeared as neuters in -ί [-'i], τζαμί [dza'mi].
   (d) In the case of nouns ending in a consonant, those denoting objects, like sokak [so'kak] 'street', typically added -ι [-i] and appear as neuters, σοκάκι [so'kaki]; those denoting people, such as bakkal [bak'kal] 'grocer', added -ης [-is] to give μπακάλης [ba'kalis], etc.
   (e) Turkish agent nouns in -ci [-dʒi], or, given that Turkish suffixes are subject to vowel harmony, -cı, -cu, and -cü [-dʒɯ, -dʒu, -dʒy], were standardized with the suffix -τζής [-'dzis]. Examples include μπογιατζής [boja'dzis] 'painter' < boya-cı [boja'dʒɯ], τενεκετζής [teneke'dzis] 'tinsmith' < teneke-ci [teneke'dʒi].

(f) Adjectives ending in a consonant acquired the suffix -ης [-is], e.g. tembel [tem'bel] 'lazy' > τεμπέλης [tem'belis]. The neuter of this type ended in -ικο [-iko], from which -ικος [-ikos] was sometimes generalized, e.g. bol [bol] 'abundant' > μπόλικος ['bolikos] (cf. 11.7.7).

(g) Adjectives ending in -i (or its vowel-harmonic equivalents) usually appeared in Greek with the suffix -ής [-'is], e.g. ατζαμής [adza'mis] 'unskilled' < acemi [adʒe'mi], with feminine in -ιά ['ja], neuter in -ί ['i], phonetically analogous to γλυκ-ύς [ɣli'k̩-is]/-ιά ['ja]/ (< -εία) -ύ ['i] 'sweet'.

Particularly interesting are the set phrases which Greek and Turkish came to share through loan translation. To mention just a few of the more obvious examples, the standard greetings καλώς ήρθατε/ορίσατε [ka'los 'irθate/o'risate] and *hoş geldiniz* [hoʃ geldi'niz], lit. 'well you-came', and the standard replies καλώς σας βρήκαμε [ka'los sas 'vrikame] and *hoş bulduk* [hoʃ bul'duk], lit. 'well (you) we-found', correspond almost exactly morph for morph. Similarly, the varied uses of ορίστε [o'riste] and buyurun ['buirun] (used to ask someone what they want, or to repeat or accept something, etc.) are very largely parallel, and both forms are originally imperatives of verbs meaning 'command'. Though some of these seem to be the product of Turkish influence on Greek, we must be wary of assuming that the process was entirely one way. The phrase καλώς ήλθες [ka'los 'ilθes], for example, is a routine greeting in vernacular texts like the *Chronicle of the Morea* (e.g. l. 4101).

Though a large number of words and phrases of Turkish origin remain in common use today, equally large numbers have disappeared, either because the circumstances conditioning their use have themselves passed into history or as a result of language planning in the years following independence (see Chapter 17), so that one of the difficulties involved in reading material from this period (e.g. folk songs or the *Memoirs* of General Makriyánis) is the large number of Turkish loans that have since fallen out of use (or become restricted to the most colloquial registers).

In most areas where Greek survived, the influence of Turkish was confined to such lexical borrowings. But in eastern and central Anatolia, where Turkish influence had begun earlier and apostasy and bilingualism became routine, the dialects of beleaguered Greek villages eventually began to show considerable phonological and grammatical convergence with the dominant language (see 14.2.5).

14.2 The spoken dialects of modern Greek

14.2.1 *Introduction: diversification, and the basis for a modern spoken standard*

As communications became more difficult, most people in the provinces of the empire came to lead increasingly circumscribed lives, and though the 'standard' speech of the educated aristocracy continued (in conjunction with written Greek) to form a relatively stable conservative 'core', the more popular regional dialects began to diverge quite rapidly, especially at the periphery.

The remote varieties of Pontus and Cappadocia had already started to develop idiosyncratically when they were cut off from Byzantium by the Seljuk invasions of the eleventh century. Similar observations apply to the south Italian dialects, which were permanently detached from the Byzantine mainstream by the Norman conquests in the same period; and we have already seen that the southern dialects of Cyprus and Crete had begun to take on their characteristically local forms as a result of disrupted Byzantine administration and the subsequent advent of Latin government (12.4). Even rural parts of Greece itself had acquired many local idiosyncrasies, partly through the dislocating effects of Slavic and then Albanian immigration, partly through the impact of Latin rule.

The continuation of such regional developments during the Ottoman period, in conjunction with population movements (some major), led to the creation and consolidation of the principal dialect divisions of modern Greek, as summarized in (3) (cf. Newton (1972: 13–18), Kondosópoulos (1981), Browning (1983: 119–37) for general surveys):

(3) (a) Pontic, with offshoots in Georgia, Abkhazia and areas of the Caucasus south of Rostov (see Oikonomídis (1958), Drettas (1995)); and Cappadocian, together with the dialects of Phárasa and Sílli (see Dawkins (1916)). Pontic is now residual, Cappadocian extinct.

   (b) South-eastern, spoken on Khios, in the Dodecanese, and in Cyprus. (See Pernot (1907b), Newton (1970)).

   (c) Cretan–Cycladic. (See Anagnostópoulos (1926), Pángalos (1955), Kondosópoulos (1970), Thumb (1893, 1897), Iméllos (1963)).

   (d) Peloponnesian–Heptanesian, including other offshore islands; this region provided the principal vernacular input to the formation of standard modern Greek, on which see below.

   (e) Tsakonian, surviving residually in remote villages on the eastern slopes of Mt Parnon in the Peloponnese, but also once spoken by colonists on the southern shore of the Sea of Marmara (cf. 4.4.3). See Pernot (1934), Kostákis (1951, 1980), Kharalambópoulos (1980)).

   (f) Old Athenian, surviving residually in Megara, central Euboea, and, if this is properly to be included here, the Mani. (See Khatzidákis (1915–16), Alexandrís (1958), Fávis (1911), Karatzás (1944), Mirambel (1929)).

   (g) Northern, spoken widely in the mainland north of Attica and in the northern Aegean, though see below on the impact of the standard. (cf. 11.5, and see Papadópoulos (1927), Andriótis (1933, 1943–4), Sympósio (1977)).

   (h) South Italian, perhaps surviving residually in isolated villages of Apulia and Calabria. (See Rohlfs (1924, 1930, 1933, 1950, 1962), Karatzás (1958).)

In the later Byzantine and Turkish periods, the Peloponnesian area was unique in a number of respects. Once recovered after the Slavic invasions of the early Middle Ages, it remained a Byzantine possession until the arrival of the Franks in the thirteenth century. But large areas were later restored to Byzantine rule, and even under Ottoman occupation, it managed to retain a large class of Greek landowners, who began to engage in trade in line with the general upsurge of commercial activity in the eighteenth century. The resulting development of the Peloponnesian towns and ports then revived contacts with the great centres of Greek population, both inside and outside the empire.

Much of this region had therefore remained closely linked with the Greek 'mainstream', and in the years before independence, the educated speech of Constantinople and major expatriate communities was widely used in its commercial and cultural centres. Such links had their effect even on popular varieties, which neither developed the radical innovations nor retained the archaisms of more peripheral regions.

The fact that the war of independence was carried to a successful conclusion in this same area led to its dialects becoming the principal 'vernacular' component in the formation of a modern spoken standard in the independent kingdom, and these were relatively easily subsumed beneath the educated varieties of the more privileged classes, whose impact was reinforced by the arrival of influential immigrants to take up positions of power. The creation of state institutions, and the building of a new capital in Athens, quickly provided the cultural and political focus necessary for the forging of a new spoken standard from these two components.

With minor differences, an evolved version of this standard has now replaced the former local varieties in most of southern and central Greece, including Athens and many neighbouring areas once dominated by Albanians, in Thessaloniki and areas of the north previously occupied by Slavs, Vlachs, Albanians, and Turks, and in many of the smaller islands. Indeed, with the partial exception of Cyprus, dialect speech everywhere is succumbing to the standardizing effects of universal education, access to the mass media, the flight of the young to the cities, and the advent of easy mobility.

14.2.2 Local vernaculars in the central region; Sofianós's grammar and the educated standard

Within the central Greek-speaking area comprising mainland Greece, Constantinople, and the western coasts of Asia Minor, the Ottoman period probably saw the completion of the final stages of the northern sound changes discussed in 11.5, producing forms such as [put'kos] (Thasos) < ποντικός [po(n)di'kos] 'mouse', and [ʒba'θo] (Ayássos on Lesbos) < συμπαθῶ [si(m)ba'θo] 'feel sympathy for'.

The regularization of either the genitive or the accusative of clitic pronouns to mark the indirect object also belongs to the later Turkish period, with the genitive favoured in the south, and the accusative in the north, including in this case the dialects of Constantinople and most of Asia Minor. Indeed, most of the variation inherited from the Middle Ages now tended to be settled one way or the other in each region. The choice between -σα [sa] and -κα [ka] as the regular aorist of vowel-stem verbs, for example, was standardly resolved in favour of the former, with the latter prevailing only in Epirus and a geographically more or less coherent area comprising parts of the Peloponnese and the region of Old Athenian speech (excluding the Mani).

Though certain northern characteristics still persist as variants in standard modern Greek (e.g. the use of accusative indirect object pronouns), it was, as noted above, the more important Peloponnesian–Heptanesian vernaculars which predominated, as shaped by the common educated speech of the central region. We must therefore turn now to the evidence provided by the first grammar of the 'vernacular' of the Greek intelligentsia in the Ottoman period, written during the first half of the sixteenth century by the Corfiot Nikólaos Sofianós (cf. Legrand (1874)).

The motivation for this work was undoubtedly connected with contemporary Italian movements to elevate the spoken language to written status. Though its immediate impact in a Greek context still dominated by traditional thinking was minimal, the long-term significance of the demonstration that a systematic account could be given of 'common/vulgar' Greek, and that the production of such a grammar was in itself a worthwhile exercise, cannot be overestimated.

Sofianós himself was educated in Rome, where he worked for a time copying Greek manuscripts and publishing drawings of ancient sites in Greece. He then moved to Venice where he resolved to address the problem of the lack of modern teaching materials by planning a series of introductory works in and about the contemporary language.

In the dedication to Book One of his Grammar he informs the reader (in Latin) of his motives:

(4) 'When I saw that most nations . . . in our time honour their (spoken) languages with enthusiasm not only by writing things worthy of note in them . . . but by diligently reducing them to the rules of Grammar, I myself began to wonder whether it would be worth my while if I brought our language, which we Greeks use for everyday purposes, back to order and rule, and I thought it would not be a waste of effort that those engaged in the study of Greek should be able to understand not only the ancient language of the Greeks but also the more recent, and further that those who wanted to travel in Greece and the adjacent territories subject to the Turkish empire might readily communicate. So while I was comparing this language of ours, which they call 'vulgar', with that of the ancients . . . I found that in many respects ours was very little inferior to the ancient one.'   Legrand (1874: 25)

A grammar in three parts is promised (morphology, orthography, and syntax), together with a lexicon, but the surviving manuscripts, one in the Bibliothèque Nationale in Paris and one in the Vatican, have only the first part, containing a list of the parts of speech and a set of illustrative morphological paradigms, of which he observes in his closing remarks:

(5) 'And let no one grumble if he now sees in such a common form of language that even women may almost understand it those items [*i.e. paradigms etc.*] which are learned under duress over long years and periods with great labour and good teachers [*i.e. in the traditional education system based on ancient Greek*], because . . . in this way young men will abandon their reluctance to study in Greek classes.'   Legrand (1874: 78)

Though this reveals all too clearly the position of women, we may, on this evidence, be sure that the work provides an insider's account of the state of the spoken language of the educated élite, who alone could afford the privilege of learning ancient Greek.

As expected, the morphology of this variety is considerably removed from that of standard written Greek, but it is striking that it is also quite conservative in comparison with developments on display in the vernacular literature of the fourteenth and fifteenth centuries. The following are revealing:

(6) (a) The syllabic augment is used uniformly in all past tenses.

(b) The extension of the κα-paradigm to the aorist passive is still restricted to 1sg.

(c) (i) The -έω [-'eo] class of contract verbs shows little sign of collapse with the -άω -['ao] type, and retains its ancient present paradigm. It does, however, show a mixed imperfect combining ancient forms (e.g. 1sg. ἐκράτουν [e'kratun] 'I was keeping') with different types of innovation (e.g. 2/3sg. ἐκράτεις [e'kratjes]/ἐκράτειε [e'kratje], and 3pl. ἐκρατούσαν [ekra'tusan]). Subsequently, many dialects (including the modern standard) generalized -ουσ- [-us-] throughout (in -άω [-'ao] verbs too), but in some Aegean and Heptanesian varieties a split system developed, with generalization of -ει- [-j-] in the singular and -ουσ- [-us-] in the plural. The origins of this can be seen plainly here.

(ii) The present passive is similarly mixed (retaining ancient -ού- [-'u-], but substituting -ειέ- [-'je-] for -εί- [-'i-]), while the imperfect passive has been substantially reworked (but as yet without a coherent overall pattern of innovation).

(d) The -άω [-'ao] type shows the expected substitution of -ού- [-'u-] for -ώ- [-'o-] but not in 3pl. present passive and 1/3pl. imperfect passive (which is odd in other respects). In the imperfect active the innovative -ουσ- [-'us-] formant has already been generalized from 3pl. to 1pl. though the extension of -ειέ- [-'je-] to the passive paradigm (as already in the *Chronicle of the Morea*) is not in evidence.

(e) Though 3rd declension consonant stems normally have 'modern' nom. sg. in -α [-a]/-ας [-as], and modern acc. pl. in [-es] (written -αις), the acc. sg. and gen. sg. still end in -α [-a] and -ος [os]; the latter has even been extended to a few 1st declension nouns like κοπέλα [ko'pela]/gen. κοπέλος [ko'pelos] 'girl' (on the model of θυγατέρα [θiɣa'tera]/gen. θυγατρός [θiɣa'tros] 'daughter'), a Heptanesian feature.

(f) The traditional i-stem paradigm is retained except, oddly, in nom./acc. pl. where the form -ες [-es] is given.

Apparently, this is a snapshot of a language in transition, a version of the vernacular that contains many of the features familiar from late Byzantine texts, but which also reveals retarded development *vis-à-vis* popular varieties. As a further example, we may note that Sofianós offers only θέλω ['θelo] + infinitive as the future tense, despite giving νά [na] + subjunctive as the normal realization of various modal functions. Since we know that the latter and its reinforced variants θε να [θe na]/

θα να [θa na] + subjunctive were also widely used in the sixteenth century, it seems that these have been 'censored' as too colloquial for the language level that Sofianós was seeking to describe. On the other hand, the pluperfect is given in two forms, εἶχα ['ixa] + perfect passive participle and εἶχα + aorist infinitive, while the corresponding perfect with ἔχω ['exo] is represented only by the participial construction. Clearly the infinitival perfect had yet to be formed to the model of the pluperfect; and given the total absence of this innovation in even the most 'vulgar' texts of the late Byzantine period, we may be confident that this 'gap' was not exclusive to educated varieties.

Nevertheless, a number of issues are decisively settled. The relaxed spoken language of the educated classes in the sixteenth century did not include the dative case, inflected participles, or the infinitive (other than as a fossilized complement to θέλω ['θelo] 'I will' and εἶχα ['ixa] 'I had'), even if such elements retained a place in the written language. We may note in passing that, though Sofianós continues to recognize the full set of traditional grammatical categories as abstract entities, presumably to show that modern Greek has all the resources of its predecessor, he does not hesitate to list genitive forms of nouns as instantiations of the 'dative', or to give να [na] + subjunctive as the form of the 'infinitive', etc.

There are, however, a number of oddities which defy explanation, most notably the inclusion of a so-called 'second aorist', which appears to consist of εἶχα ['ica] 'I had' + the imperfective infinitive, an otherwise unattested combination. Assuming that it is not simply an invention (which seems improbable), we can only speculate that in contemporary Heptanesian it denoted completed (hence aorist) activities in their course (hence the imperfective infinitive), i.e. 'had been doing X/used to do X'. Almost as mysteriously, 3pl. present -ουν [-un]/-ουσι [-usi] and past -αν [-an]/-ασι [-asi] are given as free variants with indicative forms, while in 'optatives' and 'infinitives' after να [na] we have only -ουν [-un], and in 'subjunctives' after εάν [e'an] only -ουσι [-usi].

14.2.3 Greek in the west: the south Italian dialects

Magna Graecia had been a major centre of Hellenism in the ancient world. The whole of Sicily, for example, was effectively Greek-speaking by the first century BC, while a reading of Petronius' novel *The Satyricon* (first century AD) still reveals a southern Italian world in which Greeks and Greek remained prominent.

We should not be surprised, therefore, that Greek was spoken widely as a native language in north-western Sicily, Calabria and Apulia at the beginning of the second millennium AD. Though the koineization process of the Hellenistic and Roman periods proceeded much as in other areas where West Greek was long-established, producing popular spoken varieties with a considerable dialect residue, the prolonged Byzantine presence consistently reinforced the use of written Greek and the spoken standard, both of which served to keep the local vernaculars in touch with the mainstream of medieval Greek development.

But the severing of the political connection with the empire after 1071, combined with a steady influx of Italians and the spread of Catholicism, led to a gradual decline of Greek language and culture, and to more autonomous dialectal development in the later Middle Ages. We should be careful not to exaggerate the rapidity of the process, however. Petrarch in the fourteenth century, for example, could still advise someone who wished to learn Greek to go to Calabria, while the Orthodox Church retained adherents well into the late sixteenth/early seventeenth centuries. The really sharp decline set in during the eighteenth and nineteenth centuries, though Greek remains a native language in the mountainous Aspromonte region at the tip of Calabria (*Bovézika*), *c*. 3,000 speakers, and the Otranto peninsula south of Lecce in Apulia (*Otrandínika*), *c*. 20,000 speakers.

As peripheral dialects detached from the core at the end of the eleventh century, these varieties have preserved a great many archaic features, some of which go back to the Koine spoken in ancient Magna Graecia. But there are also elements which were once more widespread in medieval Greek before falling out of mainstream use. Similar remarks apply to the Asia Minor dialects, and points of agreement between the western and eastern peripheries are clearly of importance for the reconstruction of the medieval vernacular.

Of particular interest in this connection is the partial retention of infinitives in both South Italian and the Pontic dialects of the Muslim communities in the region of Trebizond (see Mackridge (1993b), from which the data below are taken: Tombaídis's (1977) arguments that the Pontic infinitive is a fiction appear not to apply at least to the speech of this area). In the Italian dialects, control verbs can still optionally be complemented by an infinitive (perfective only) (cf. Rohlfs (1950)):

(7) (a) Bova: *e   θθéli   míni*   (μείνει(ν)   ['mini(n)])
                not s/he-wants to-stay
    (b) Otranto: *áfiston dzísi*   (ζήσ-ει(ν)   ['zisi(n)])
                let-him to-live

Deffner (1877) lists parallel uses for Pontic, though these have not been confirmed by Mackridge (1993b). It seems likely, however, that we are dealing with a fairly recent loss rather than erroneous observation, since the dialects east of Trebizond residually retain infinitival complementation with 'want' when this is aorist and negative.

In addition, the South Italian dialects use infinitives in indirect questions, a retention doubtless supported by the corresponding Italian construction (cf. *non ho dove andare/cosa fare*):

(8) Bova: *ðen éxo pu   pái*   (πά-ει(ν)   ['pai(n)])
          not I-have where to-go

These have no surviving correlates in Pontic, though the constructon is common in medieval vernacular literature (e.g. *Digenés Akrítes* (E) 869: οὐκ ἔχω τί ποιήσει [uk 'exo ti pi'isi] 'not I-have what to-do'), and is still in use in Cretan Renaissance literature (cf. 14.2.4).

The progressive abandonment of the infinitival complementation of control verbs,

and the gradual restriction of the occurrence of the infinitive to embedded interrogatives and the complementation of future/conditional or potential auxiliaries
(the former often generic, the latter almost always negative) can be seen clearly in
medieval vernacular texts. For example, with only one exception (109), the infinitives in the poem *Spanéas* are used exclusively in prospective/generic clauses after
θέλω ['θelo] 'will' (e.g. '*if anyone does X, s/he will Y*'), and in potential contexts
with negative/interrogative δύναμαι ['ðiname]/εὐπορῶ [efpo'ro] 'can' (e.g. '*should
anyone do X, s/he cannot Y/how can s/he Y?*'). Similarly, in the romances of the
fourteenth/fifteenth centuries, both future θέλω ['θelo] and negated verbs of 'capability' may still take an infinitive, though this construction is extremely rare
with true control verbs and aspectual verbs like 'begin'. Given that this process
of reduction has barely begun in the west, and was severely retarded in the east,
we may be confident that the restricted infinitival usage of medieval vernacular
literature is not a learned/archaic feature but offers a fair picture of the spoken
norm of the period in the more central regions (cf. Joseph (1983: 77)).

14.2.4 Greek in the south and south-east: the Dodecanese, Cyprus and Crete

While still free of Ottoman control, literature continued to be produced in these
areas. From the Dodecanese, for example, we have a collection of love songs and
a number of poems by Emmanouíl Yeoryillás (early sixteenth century, though the
cultural life of the islands declined quickly after the Turkish conquest of 1522), and
something has already been said about the dialect of Cyprus and the extent to which
its modern characteristics can be traced in the earliest documents (cf. 12.4.2). From
the sixteenth century, we have a collection of love poems (sonnets), composed in
the Petrarchan manner, the style and quality of which can be seen in the following
extract:

(9) *Κοντεύγ' η ώρα κι ο καιρός, κυρά μου,*
    που μέλλει νά μισέψω από ξαυτό(s) σου·
    όμως αφήννω 'δά στον ορισμόν σου
    όλον τον εμαυτόν μου, αγγέλισσά μου.

    Μηδέ απορής, αν εμπορώ, θεά μου,
    μισεύγοντα ν' αφήσω εμέν σ' αυτόν σου·
    μισεύγω αμμ' όπου πάγω, γοιόν δικό(s) σου,
    μένουσιν μετά σεν τα πνεύματά μου.

                              Siapkarás-Pitsillídes (1952: 118)

[kon'devj i 'ora tʃ o tʃe'ros, tʃi'ra-mu,
Approaches the hour and the time,   lady of-me,

pu 'melli   na mi'sepso-a'po ksaf'tos su;
that it-will(be) that I-leave   from self   of-you;

'omos a'finno ða ston oriz'mos su
but   I- leave now at-the command of-you

'olon don emaf'tom mu,   aŋ'gelis'sa mu.
all   the self   of-me, angel   of-me.

mi'ðe ⏌apo'ris,   an embo'ro, θe'a   mu,
and-not you-be-at-a-loss, if I-can,   goddess of-me,

mi'sevɣonda n   a'fiso⏌ e'men s af'tos su.
in-leaving   that I-entrust me   to self   of-you.

mi'sevɣo amm 'opu 'pao, joð ði'kos-su,
I-leave   but   when I-go, as yours,

'menusim me'ta sen ta 'pnevma'ta mu]
remain   with   you the spirits   of-me

'The hour and the time approach, my lady, when I shall leave you, but now I leave my
whole self at your command, my angel. And do not be perplexed, my goddess, if, in
leaving, I am able to leave myself to you; I am leaving, but when I go, as yours, my
spirit stays with you.'

The phonetic transcription assumes that certain characteristically Cypriot changes,
not noted in the orthography, had already gone through, e.g. palatalization of [k, x]
before [i] and [e] (typical of many 'southern' dialects, including that of Crete).
Another south-eastern/Cretan phenomenon is the appearance of -γ- [-ɣ/j-] between
original root-final [a/ev] and a verb ending, as in κοντεύ-γ-ει [kon'dev-j-i] 'approaches' (cf. 11.8.5 (d)). The retention of final -ν [-n] (with assimilation to a following continuant, sometimes noted, sometimes not) is a specifically south-eastern
characteristic, while the selection of 3pl. present endings in -ουσι [-usi] is again
typical not only of Cyprus and the Dodecanese but also (in part) of Khios and
Crete.

In the second line, the aorist subjunctive μισέψω [mi'sepso] (from Latin *miss-
us* 'sent', + -εύ(γ)ω [-'ev(ɣ)o]) forms part of a future periphrasis with the impersonal μέλλει να ['melli na] 'it-will-be that', a medieval Cypriot variant of the later
and more usual θε να [θe na] (cf. modern Cypriot εννά [en'na] < θέλ'να [θen'na]).
The tendency for modal verbs with epistemic force to assume an impersonal form
(cf. μπορεί να [bo'ri na] 'it is possible that', and πρέπει νά ['prepi na] 'it is necessary that'), points strongly to the hypothesis that θέ [θe] too reflects an impersonal
construction based on a reduction of θέλει ['θeli] (cf. Joseph (1990: 114–15)).

After the Turkish conquest of Cyprus in 1571, the most important cultural centre
in the Greek world was the island of Crete, where a more integrated urban society
had emerged with the decline of the feudal system, and intellectual life was stimu-
lated not only by its western connections but also by the arrival of scholars and
artists from the capital after 1453.

In contrast with the earliest Cretan literature (see 12.4.3), the magnificent collection of dramatic and narrative texts dating from the later sixteenth century onwards is composed in a refined, and more or less consistent, form of Cretan dialect.
The Cretan Renaissance, and in particular the revival of drama (which had withered
in Byzantium), owed much to the influence of Italian models. One of its leading
figures was Yeóryios Khortátsis, a contemporary of Shakespeare and El Greco (the

Cretan Domínikos Theotokópoulos), who wrote the tragedy *Erofíli*, the comedy *Katzoúrbos*, and the pastoral drama *Panória*, a play from each of the genres of contemporary Italian theatre. The other surviving plays of this period are the tragedies *King Rodolínos* by Ioánnis Andréas Tróilos, and *Zínon* (possibly composed in the Ionian islands by a refugee after the fall of Crete), together with the comedies *Státhis*, (possibly by Khortátsis and surviving only in a late abridgement), and *Fortounátos* by Márkos Andónios Fóskolos. We also have the important biblical drama, *The Sacrifice of Abraham*, which is often attributed on stylistic grounds to Vitséntzos Kornáros, the author of the romantic epic *Erotókritos*, which represeats the pinnacle of Cretan Renaissance literature (see Holton (1991a)).

This long romantic poem, written in the late sixteenth or early seventeenth century, follows in the tradition of the Hellenistic romances and their medieval successors, and tells in five books (comprising some 10,000 lines) the story of Aretoúsa, daughter of the king of Athens, and her lover Rotókritos (as his name appears in the text itself), son of the king's counsellor.

It was once routine to compare its language and versification with those of popular song, but more recent scholarship has revised this view in a number of important respects (cf. Holton (1991b, 1991c)). We should recall that the decapentesyllable was the metre not only of oral poetry but also of literate personal, narrative, and (after Khortátsis) dramatic poetry, a major characteristic of which, from the fourteenth century onwards, was the use (as in *Erotókritos*) of rhyming couplets taken over from western models. By contrast, traditional folk poetry was always unrhymed, and those branches which adopted rhyme did so under the influence of written compositions.

Other characteristics of folk poetry also distinguish it sharply from the more sophisticated techniques of *Erotókritos*:

(10) (a) Apart from occasional stresses on the first syllable, departure from an iambic rhythm is quite rare.
   (b) Lines of verse invariably coincide with syntactic boundaries.
   (c) Within the line, there are formulaic 'building blocks', of the type which have formed the basis of the oral poet's compositional technique from the earliest times.
   (d) The 'popular' line falls into two balancing halves, though the first half may be divided in turn, and there is considerable verbal redundancy and repetition typical of an oral style.

While the very familiarity of such 'folksy' patterns is sometimes exploited in *Erotókritos*, Kornáros regularly employs complex subordination, extensive enjambement, and a much greater variety of rhythm and phrasing (including trochaic rhythms with stresses on odd-numbered syllables).

The language of the poem is clearly based on the dialect of eastern Crete (Kornáros was from Sitía). Note in particular the following:

(11) (a) the characteristic loss of [j] after [s] and sometimes [r] in words such as άξος ['akços] for άξιος ['aksios] 'worthy'.

(b) the use of 3pl. verb forms in -ου(νε) [-u(ne)] rather than west Cretan -ουσι [-usi].

(c) the stressed syllabic augment ή- ['i-] instead of west Cretan έ- [e-], in e.g. ή-φερα ['ifera] 'I was bringing'.

(d) the use of 3pl. clitic possessive τως [tos] (or ντως [dos], with the initial consonant deriving from misanalysis after words ending in -ν [-n]), rather than west Cretan τωνε/ντωνε ['tone/'done] 'their'.

(e) the use of the east Cretan aorist passive singular in -θηκα [-θika], -θηκες [-θikes], -θηκε [-θike], rather than the west Cretan -θη [-θi], -θης [-θis], -θη(ν) [-θi(n)] (the extended forms are regular in the plural).

West Cretan variants are also admitted, however, when these are metrically different and offer the poet some advantage in composition (i.e. by having a different number of syllables). Other features are general Cretan, and include both 'invisible' developments like the palatalization of /k/ to [tʃ] or the softening of [ç]/[j] to [ʃ]/ [ʒ] before [i/e] (the use of the Latin alphabet in a number of manuscripts of literary works is particularly helpful here), as well as many other characteristics represented orthographically, including:

(12) (a) the standard loss of final -ν [-n] (even in gen. pl. -ω(ν) [-o(n)] and 3pl. verb forms in -ουν [-u(n)]) except where the word forms part of an intonational phrase with the next word, and that word begins with a vowel or voiceless plosive.

(b) the partial generalization of clitic possessives with initial ντ- [d-] (e.g. ντου [du] 'his/its') from contexts after a word ending in -ν [-n].

(c) the loss of medial -ν- [-n-] before a fricative: e.g. άθρωπος ['aθropos] 'man', for άνθρωπος ['anθropos].

(d) the genitive singular feminine of the article and the clitic pronoun is not only της [tis] but also τση [tsi] or τς [ts], and the masculine and feminine accusative plural, beside their standard forms, also appear as τσι [tsi] and τσ' [ts]. The spellings of these variants are largely conventional, and all derive from syncope and the addition of a final [-i] to aid pronunciation when the next word began with a consonant.

(e) αυτόνος [af'tonos] (genitive αυτουνού [aftu'nu]) and αυτείνος [af'tinos] are sometimes used for αυτός [af'tos] 'this', with suffixes modelled on that of εκείνος [e'kinos/e'tʃinos] 'that'. Genitive -νού [-'nu] is also used with ετούτος [e'tutos], giving ετουνού [etu'nu], and sometimes with other pronouns.

(f) forms of the article beginning with τ- [t-], το(ν)/τη(ν)/το [to(n)/ti(n)/to], etc., are used as relative pronouns (alongside οπού [o'pu]/απού [a'pu] 'that').

(g) (ε)ίντα ['inda] 'what?', < τί είναι τα ['ti n da], 'what is-it which?', is used for τί [ti].

(h) perfects and pluperfects are formed on the Romance model, with perfect passive participles and the verb έχω ['eco] 'have'. The participle usually agrees with a pronominal or lexical direct object, though it may also have an invariant neuter plural form if the sense is generic (e.g. with direct object ὅ,τι ['oti] 'whatever', as in a free relative clause).

(i) the future is formed with θέλω ['θelo] + aorist infinitive, or with θε να [θe na] + subjunctive (the innovative/colloquial θα [θa] also appears, but chiefly in the more natural language of comedy, cf. Holton (1993)); the conditional uses either ἤθελα ['iθela] or εἴχα ['ixa] + aorist infinitive. The latter also express past habituality in temporal clauses (but are never used as a true (real-time) pluperfect).

(j) object pronouns are regularly placed after the verb that governs them unless there is a subordinating conjunction or sentential operator in initial position (i.e. the normal pattern of medieval Greek is preserved (cf. 11.4)).

We must be careful, however, not to fall into the trap of supposing that the language of the poem is a straightforward representation of any dialect then spoken on the island. It is, for example, immediately apparent from a comparison with the language of comedy or the usage of prose documents of the period (such as wills) that the Italian vocabulary which played a significant part in the island vernacular has been systematically excluded. At the same time, Kornáros employs words of learned origin which never appear in the folk-songs, and would probably never have been used in ordinary conversation. Examples include βρέφος ['vrefos] 'infant', εὐλάβεια ['ev'lavja] 'awe', ἤγουν ['iɣun] 'namely', κάλλος ['kalos] 'beauty', λίθος ['liθos] 'stone', ὀδύνη [o'ðini] 'pain', συμβουλεύγω [simvu'levɣo] 'confer', τέκνο ['tekno] 'child'.

We are therefore dealing with a consciously and artfully 'refined' vernacular, and if we still have the impression of a 'popular' style, it is because the folk tradition has preserved characteristics which were once also widely used in literate poetry but which have now come to seem rustic/archaic from the point of view of standard modern Greek. In this connection, we must remember that the modern standard developed from a different dialect base, and that it has since been greatly influenced by the learned tradition, absorbing in the course of the intervening 200 years a large vocabulary unknown to the seventeenth century (see Chapter 17).

The following extract (taken from the authoritative edition of Alexíou (1980)) illustrates many of the phenomena mentioned above, as well as providing a further example of 'literary sophistication' in the form of an authorial appeal to the hero. Here Rotókritos, in disguise, is about to test Aretoúsa's fidelity by telling her that he is dead, and the narrator pleads with him to reconsider:

(13)   Ἄδικον εἴν', Ρωτόκριτε, ἐτούτα να τα κάνης,
       βλέπε μ' αὐτάνα ἔτσ' ἄδικα να μην την ἀποθάνης.
       Θωρεῖς τη πώς εὑρίσκεται, μ' ἀκόμη δεν πιστεύγεις·
       ἰντ' ἄλλα μεγαλύτερα σημάδια τση γυρεύγεις;
       Τα πλούτη και την ἀφεντιάν ἀρνήθηκε για σένα,
       πάντα 'ν' τα χείλη της πρικιά, τα μάτια της κλαημένα·
       ζει με τσι κακοριζικιές, θρέφεται με τους πόνους
       και μες στη βρωμερή φλακήν ἐδά 'χει πέντε χρόνους.

                                                    (V. 723–30)

['aðikon 'in, ro'tokrite, e'tuta   na ta   'kaṇis,
Wrong   is,   Rotókritos,   these-things that them you-do

'vlepe m   af'tanaˬ   'ets 'aðika na min din apo'θaṇis.
beware with these-things so   wrong   that not   her you-kill.

θo'ris ti pos ev'riskete, m a'komi dem bis'tevʒis;
you-see her how she-is found, but still   not   you-believe;

'ind 'ala meɣa'litera si'maðja tsi   ʒi'revʒis?
What other greater   signs   of-her you-seek?

ta   'pluti tʃe tin afen'djan ar'niθitʃe ʒa 'sena,
The wealth and the nobility   she-refused for you,

'panda n da 'ʃili tis   pri'tʃa, ta 'matja tis   klai'mena;
always are the lips of-her bitter,   the eyes   of-her tearful;

zi   me tsi kakorizi'tʃes, 'θrefete me tus 'ponus
she-lives with the misfortunes,   she-is-fed by   the pains

tʃe mes sti   vrome'ri fla'tʃin e'ða ʃi   'pende 'xronus]
and inside at-the filthy   prison   now she-has five   years

'It is wrong to do this, Rotókritos, beware in case you kill her with these wrongs. You
see the state she is in, but still you do not believe; what other, greater tokens do you
seek from her? She has refused wealth and nobility for you, her lips are always bitter,
her eyes full of tears; she lives with misfortunes, she is nourished on pain, and has now
been inside her vile prison for five years.'

14.2.5 Greek in the east: Pontus and Cappadocia

The dialects of the eastern 'frontier' districts were subject to foreign influence even
in Byzantine times, and had become detached from the rest of the Greek world after
the Byzantine defeat at Manzikert in 1071. Cappadocia fell under immediate Seljuk
control and, with the steady growth of bilingualism and conversion to Islam, its
dialects began to show early signs of Turkish influence and later to converge with
the dominant language, sometimes in quite remarkable ways. After the disaster of
1922–3 and the deportation of the Christian population (see 16.1), the dialects of
central and eastern Anatolia fell into terminal decline.

By contrast, Pontus, never properly occupied by the Seljuks, was finally incorporated into the Ottoman empire only after the fall of Trebizond in 1461. Thereafter,
the large and stable Greek-speaking population of this important region managed
to preserve its distinctive identity and its language with considerable success. Even
after the deportations of 1923, the authorities in Trebizond were obliged to employ
interpreters to work with the remaining Muslim Pontic speakers in the law courts,
and the language is still spoken as a mother tongue in many places in that region
(see Mackridge (1987)). Though the dialects of refugees and their descendants now
spoken in Greece have been subject to steady convergence with the standard language, and were already affected prior to 1923 by church attendance and the language policies of the Greek state implemented through local schools, the varieties

still *in situ*, with their Muslim speakers cut off from standardizing influences, have remained very much in their 'natural' state despite growing Turkish influence.

Quite apart from the large stock of antique vocabulary unknown elsewhere (including the standard Pontic negative *ki* < (οὐ)κί [(u)'ki]), there are many phonological and grammatical archaisms which continue the late-antique and medieval speech of this region:

(14) (a) the retention of many unstressed initial vowels, including the syllabic augment, where standard dialects have undergone aphaeresis; note too the absence of synizesis in *-ía* [-'ia], etc.

   (b) the survival of some ancient pronominal forms: e.g. possessive clitic *emón* < ancient gen. pl. ἡμῶν [(h)ɛːmôːn] 'of us', in place of the standard μας [mas], and ancient possessive adjectives, e.g. *temón* < τὸ ἐμόν [tò emón], lit. 'the my' (also in Cappadocian).

   (c) many ancient/medieval verb-forms, including:
      (i)   2sg. imperatives in *-son* continuing ancient aorist forms, where standard dialects have -σε [-se].
      (ii) the absence of the /k-/ element in aorist passives (also in Cappadocian), thus 3sg. *efovéthe* < ancient ἐφοβήθη [epʰobɛ́ːtʰɛː] for standard φοβήθηκε [fo'viθike] 's/he was afraid'.
      (iii) the retention of some archaic suppletions such as *féro : énga* continuing ancient φέρω : ἤνεγκα [pʰéroː/ɛ́neŋka] 'I bring/I brought', instead of standard φέρνω : ἔφερα ['ferno/'efera]).
      (iv) the loss of the ancient perfect system has not been made good, thus supporting the conclusion that spoken Greek of the early/middle Byzantine periods, prior to contact with Romance, lacked a formal expression of this category.
      (v)   the use of the ancient passive in *-oúmai* [-'ume] of verbs originally in *-óo* [-óɔː]; these have been replaced by formations in *-óno* [-'ono] in all modern dialects, but only Pontic (and Cappadocian) have failed to generalize the new stem-form to the passive.
      (vi) the residual retention of the infinitive (perfective only), though apparently now only in dialects still spoken in Pontus, and sometimes in modified forms (e.g. with the addition of personal endings, cf. 14.2.3).

One further feature of Pontic which is often presented as an archaism is the pronunciation in certain contexts of etymological -η- as [e] rather than standard [i] (as, for example, in 3sg. aorist passive *efovéthe* < ancient ἐφοβήθη [epʰobɛ́ːtʰɛː], above). But closer inspection gives pause for thought. The most obvious difficulty, apart from the inherent implausibility of a theory which supposes that this important part of the Roman empire was unaffected by a sound change that went through everywhere else, is that the [i]-vowel of standard speech is often represented by Pontic [e] even where the source of [i] is spelled ι, ει, οι, and υ, i.e. never represented the sound [ɛː] even in ancient Greek. Thus alongside πεγάδ' [pe'ɣað] 'well' (standard πηγάδι [pi'ɣaði]), κλέφτες ['kleftes] 'robber' (standard κλέφτης ['kleftis]), etc., we also find ἐμορφεσσα ['emorfesa] 'beautiful (fem.)' (these formations are not directly paralleled in the standard, but the usual form of this suffix is -ισσα [-issa]), όνερον ['oneron] 'dream' (standard όνειρο ['oniro]), 'κοδέσπενα [ko'despena] 'mistress of the house' (standard οικοδέσποινα [iko'ðespina]), λεχνάρι [lex'nari] 'oil lamp' (standard λυχνάρι [lix'nari]), etc. (data from Oikonomídis (1958)).

It therefore seems more likely that this is a manifestation of the vowel-weakening processes which sometimes also result (especially in immediately post-tonic syllables) in the loss of unstressed [i] and [u]. Similar developments also seem to have affected [o] in άλεγον ['aleɣon] 'horse' (standard άλογο ['aloɣo]), and όνεμα ['onema] 'name' (standard όνομα ['onoma]). It is characteristic of such weakenings that they do not conform to fixed rules and seem to be subject both to variable local phonetic conditioning and to extensive analogical levellings. One obvious consequence of the latter is the secondary appearance of 'weakened' vowels in stressed syllables, e.g. fem. ψηλέσσα [psi'lesa] to masc. ψηλός [psi'los] 'high'/tall', on the basis of fem. έμορφεσσα ['emorfessa] to masc. έμορφος ['emorfos] 'beautiful/ handsome', and the large numbers of adjectives where the suffix was unaccented.

Long separation from the mainstream also encouraged independent development, however, and there are many striking innovations:

(15) (a) the changes of unstressed [ia/ea] > [æ] and unstressed [io/eo] > [œ], vowels unknown in the standard.

(b) (as already noted) the weakening and/or deletion of many unstressed vowels, in some ways reminiscent of the northern dialects, except that in Pontic the effects of weakening are more variable, and loss is predominantly confined to post-tonic syllables (in Cappadocian to final syllables).

(c) 'columnar' stress in adjectives and verbs, even where this breaks the standard rule that the accent must fall on one of the last three syllables; thus eɣápisa/eɣápisame 'I loved'/'we loved', beside standard αγάπησα/ αγαπήσαμε [a'ɣapisa/aɣa'pisame].

(d) loss of the imperfective/perfective opposition outside the indicative in most varieties, with imperfective forms used exclusively in 'subjunctive' clauses.

(e) the uniform post-verbal positioning of clitic pronouns, even where the verb complex involves negatives, mood markers, and other sentential operators; the accusative also replaces the ancient dative to mark the indirect object, as in the northern dialects.

(f) the beginnings of the breakdown of the gender system, involving a distinction into έμψυχα ['embzixa] and άψυχα ['apsixa], things with and without 'personality'. Modifiers of the former in the plural tend to adopt universally masculine forms, while modifiers of the latter (with the partial exception of immediately preceding definite articles) take neuter forms across the board. Feminine έμψυχα ['embzixa] themselves sometimes have masculine forms in the plural (at least as variants), while plural άψυχα ['apsixa], if not already neuter, show parallel signs of assimilating to neuter declensional patterns (i.e. with accusative forms serving also as nominative, and sometimes with substitution of actual neuter endings). Consider the examples below:

(i)   *i*   *kalí*   *i*   *jinékes*

the(masc.nom.pl.) good (masc.nom.pl.) the(masc.nom.pl.) women (fem.nom.pl.)

(ii) *to*   *kókinon*   *i*   *kosára*

the(neut.nom./acc.sg.) red(neut.nom./acc.sg.) the(fem.nom.sg.) hen (fem.nom.sg.)

(iii) *ta*   *palǽ*   *ta*

the(neut.nom./acc.pl.) old(neut.nom./acc.pl.) the(neut.nom./acc.pl.)

kerús

times (masc.nom./acc.pl.)

This declensional system, shared by Cappadocian, was perhaps initiated by the local transfer in antiquity of unusually large numbers of masculine and feminine inanimates of the 3rd declension to the neuter paradigm in -*ίν* [-in] (cf. 11.7.4 (19)), and subsequently accelerated by expanded use of neuter possessive adjectives, first with other inanimates regardless of gender, then more generally, a development perhaps prompted by the gender-invariant form of the corresponding genitive pronominal possessives: e.g. *temón*/*teméteron i nífe* 'the-my/our the daughter-in-law'. This might then have provided a model for other adjectival usage (at least for *άψυχα* ['apsixa]). The correspondence with Cappadocian, despite differences due to later Turkish influence on the latter, points to a period of common development prior to the advent of Turkish, which has no grammatical distinctions based on animacy.

Another oddity of Pontic is that masculine nouns of the 2nd declension (the type in [-os]) show the 'accusative' ending [-o(n)] (some dialects retain final [-n], others do not) in subject as well as object function when the noun in question is definite, and employ the 'standard' nominative form in [-os] only when a subject is indefinite: thus *(o) fílo(n)*/*(ínas) fílos* 'the friend'/'(a) friend'. In Cappadocian, the use of the accusative ending was latterly confined to definite direct objects, with an associated generalization of the nominative form to indefinite objects (a clear case of Turkish influence, since this language has only a definite object-marker). But there were also residual examples of the use of the accusative to mark definite subjects, which once again points to an early common origin (Dawkins (1916: 94)).

The basis for this development seems to have been the need to re-mark the definiteness of subjects involving nouns 'of personality' in a dialect area where the definite article with nominative forms of this class was increasingly dropped (with some spread to masculine and feminine *άψυχα* ['apsixa] too, if they retained their masculine/feminine articles). This was presumably connected with the inherent phonological weakness of *o/η/οι* [o/i/i] (recall that *άψυχα* ['apsixa] tended to acquire neuter determiners and modifiers), which we must suppose were locally so prone to crasis and/or loss when in contact with words beginning or ending in a vowel that they eventually all but disappeared. Since Turkish, as noted, marks only definite objects, it cannot be the source of the Pontic phenomenon, which is clearly ancient. Indeed, if Thumb's attempts to link the change with the parallel use of the accusative for the nominative in 2nd declension nouns in a number of third-century inscriptions from Cyprus is well founded (Thumb (1906: 258)), as seems likely, it may well once have characterized much of the eastern Koine.

Though the specific model for the change remains unclear, it engendered paradigm interference with 3rd declension masculines in -ων [-on]/gen. -ονος [-onos] and neuters in -ον [-on], which often followed the declensional model of neuters in -ίν [-'in], where the original genitive -ίου [-'iu] (without synizesis) had developed to -ί' [-'i] through the loss of unstressed final [u]. Thus (ο) λύκον [(o) 'likon] 'wolf'/gen. λύκονος ['likonos], (ο) άρθωπον [(o) 'arθopon] 'man'/gen. αρθωπί [arθo'pi], etc.

The tenacity of Greek in Pontus, based on its status as a majority language in much of the region for more than 2,000 years, limited the impact of Turkish to the lexicon and phraseology, but the scale of such borrowing far exceeds that seen elsewhere (other than in Cappadocia). Thus not only nouns and adjectives but also verbs have been widely borrowed (the last involving the addition of -εύω [-'evo] to the Turkish present stem: e.g. konuʃmak [konuʃ-'mak] 'to speak', present stem konuʃ-, giving *konuʃévo* 'I speak'). The erosion of the Greek lexicon is, of course, particularly marked in the varieties still spoken in Turkey, where Turkish phraseology is now beginning to introduce Turkish syntactic structures (Mackridge (1987: 135)).

This latter-day assimilation of the dialects still spoken in Pontus must be very similar to what had long been happening to those spoken in central Anatolia before 1922/3. Indeed, the early decline of Greek there is clearly revealed in a Latin document dated 1437:

(16) '... in many parts of Turkey [*meaning Asia Minor*] clerics are to be found ... who wear the dress of infidels and speak their language and know how to pronounce nothing in Greek beyond singing the mass and reciting the gospel and the letters.'

Néos Ellinomnímon VII (1910: 366)

Nonetheless, at the turn of the twentieth century, Greek still had a strong presence in Silli north-west of Konya (ancient Ikónion), in Phárasa and other villages in the region drained by the Yenice river south of Kayseri (ancient Caesarea), and in Cappadocia proper, at Arabisón (Arapsu/Gülşehir) north-west of Nevşehir (ancient Nyssa), and in the large region south of Nevşehir as far down as Niğde and Bor (close to ancient Tyana). This whole area was of great importance in the early history of Christianity, but is perhaps most famous today for the extraordinary landscape of eroded volcanic tufa in the valleys of Göreme, Ihlara and Soğanlı, and for the churches and houses carved into the 'fairy chimneys' to serve the Christian population in the Middle Ages.

Unfortunately, by the time of Dawkins's monumental study (1916), the speech of the major villages of Cappadocia (e.g. Sinasós (Mustafapaşa)) had been greatly influenced by the teaching of 'standard' Greek in local schools, while that of many others showed considerable, in some areas extreme, Turkish influence, including vowel harmony and agglutination. Thus only the speech of the remoter areas (where schools were few and Turks rarely ventured) proved to be relatively well preserved.

Features such as the loss of the article with the nominative of nouns 'of personality' (unless formally neuter), and the use of the 2nd declension masculine accusative ending -o(ν) [-o(n)] exclusively with definite objects (with -ος [-os] extended to mark not only subjects but also indefinite objects), have already been mentioned. These later developments of a declensional system apparently once shared with Pontic follow the Turkish pattern, and the treatment of adjectives reveals a similar history. Thus neuter forms became fully generalized in Cappadocian, whereas in Pontic adjectives qualifying nouns 'of personality' still retain much of their masculine/feminine paradigm, and this further step can be due only to the pressure of genderless Turkish on an already destabilized system.

Abstracting away from the obvious Turkisms, Dawkins concluded (1916, 205–6) that northern and eastern Anatolia must once have formed a single linguistic area, united by innovations such as the development of a gender/declensional system based on the distinction between ἔμψυχα ['embzixa] and ἄψυχα ['apsixa], and by the shared retention of archaisms such as the post-verbal positioning of clitic pronouns, ancient possessive adjectives, an aorist passive paradigm without -κα [-ka], and the old contracted passive in -οῦμαι [-'ume] of verbs originally in -όω [-óoː].

14.3   Popular culture in the Turkish period: the folk-songs

The earliest accounts of Greek folk-songs in the west came from eighteenth- and nineteenth-century travellers, who reported the existence of a thriving oral tradition. In Greece itself, however, the conditions prevailing in the period of the war of independence inhibited serious study, and in any case many intellectuals, preoccupied with the 'language question' (see Chapter 17), saw little merit in this manifestation of popular culture. Nevertheless, there were some who believed a national language could be built upon the foundations of the spoken language of the people, and for them the folk-songs were an important source for the study and development of 'demotic' Greek. The Heptanese in particular had remained a major centre of artistic and intellectual endeavour, and Greece's 'national poet' Dionysios Solomós, who was born in Zákynthos but later resided in Kérkyra (Corfu), was among the advocates of this solution to the language question.

The search for a 'modern' Greek identity provided fresh impetus to the study of folklore, and led eventually to the collection of large quantities of oral poetry. N. G. Polítis was the dominant figure in this movement, and his work was eventually published in 1914 (with many subsequent reprintings). This remains the principal source, though the rapid urbanization of Greece and the consequential disappearance of many rural traditions in the period after the Greek civil war (see Chapter 15) prompted a further revival of interest, and the publication of new collections (e.g. Ioánnou (1986), A. Polítis (1981), Saunier (1983), Papadópoulos (1975)).

Although twentieth-century advocates of demotic made much of the linguistic 'unity' of these poems in an effort to defend their position against accusations from linguistic purists that there was no single spoken language to provide the foundation for a written standard, their assertion of the pre-existence of a common 'popular' style was actually based on citations from work such as that of Polítis which had standardized the orthography and in part the grammar of the collected material. Much detailed evidence about dialect diversity in the late medieval and early modern periods was therefore lost in the interests of the demotic cause, though the songs still provide a useful supplementary source of information about developmental trends in popular spoken Greek.

There can be no doubt that elements of the folk-song tradition go far back into the Byzantine era, and the existence of an 'akritic cycle', thematically related to, and presumably the inspiration for, the epic of *Digenés Akrítes*, has already been discussed (cf. 8.4.3, 12.2.1). These and a number of other short lays of the Byzantine period (e.g. *The Son(s) of Andrónikos*) have survived, albeit in modified form, into the modern folk tradition. One such poem, however, the lay of *Armoúres*, has come down to us in manuscript form (two copies, the earlier dating from 1461), while, as already noted, the Escorial version of *Digenés Akrítes* itself may represent an adapted compilation of five such lays (Ricks (1990)). Clearly we must be wary of supposing, despite views to the contrary (e.g. Kakridís (1979)), that the folk tradition represents an independent channel of transmission (see Beaton (1980)). Some songs at least were written down and/or reworked by literate poets in the Middle Ages, and these versions then provided fresh inspiration for oral poets. The Cypriot song of *Azgoúres*, for example, (which preserves much of the plot and style of the written *Armoúres*), and Cretan songs based on Khortátsis's tragedy *Erofíli*, show clearly that oral poems did spring from written ones, and that there was a complex interaction between the two forms of composition. It is not, then, impossible that some of the akritic songs represent oral developments of poems that once existed in manuscript form, even if many of these in turn represented literary refinements of earlier oral material.

The tradition also includes songs dealing with historical events (e.g. the fall of Adrianople in 1361, and the last mass in Ayía Sophía in 1453), or with particular periods (e.g. the kleftic ballads of the eighteenth and early nineteenth centuries, songs of low-life in the towns of Asia Minor brought to Greece by refugees after 1923 (*rebétika*), songs of the Greek resistance during the Second World War (*andártika*), and Cypriot EOKA songs of the period 1955–60). The majority, however, are 'timeless' accompaniments to the central events of human life, dealing *inter alia* with work, feasts, customs, emigration, love, marriage, birth, childhood, and death. Some longer works, however, are better described as ballads (*paraloyés*). These have a more elaborate narrative form that presupposes a poetic tradition of some maturity, and tell stories of human, especially family, relationships. Rhyme is not ordinarily employed, despite its obvious potential usefulness for the oral poet as an *aide-mémoire*, though there are branches of the tradition that did use it, most notably those of the Cretan *rimadóri* and Cypriot *pyitárides*, under the impact of written poetry exposed to western influence.

Typically 'oral' features include formulaic diction, recurrent themes/motifs, and an 'action-orientated' style which eschews descriptive elaboration. Enjambement is systematically avoided, and lines are typically divided into two (8 syllables + 7 syllables) or three parts (4 syllables + 4 syllables + 7 syllables), which often display repetition and rhythmic parallelism. The lullaby in (17) illustrates these features very clearly:

(17) *Κοιμήσου αστρί, κοιμήσου αυγή, κοιμήσου νιο φεγγάρι,*
κοιμήσου που να σε χαρή ο νιός που θα σε πάρη.

[ḳi'misu‿as'tri, ‖ ḳi'misu‿av'ji, ‖ ḳi'misu njo feŋ'gari, ‖
sleep   little-star, sleep   dawn,   sleep   new moon,

ḳi'misu pu na se   xa'ri ‖ o 'njos   pu θa se   'pari.]
sleep   that may you(acc.) enjoy   the young-man that will you(acc.) take

'Sleep little star, sleep dawn, sleep new moon,
sleep so that the young man who will marry you may delight in you.'

Musically, the songs are monophonic, and many types are traditionally danced to, with the leader 'dragging' the other performers in a line (in the fashion familiar from films and folklore exhibitions, and occasionally still seen in 'real' contexts). The rhythms (5/8, 7/8, and 9/8) and scales (making use of intervals greater and smaller than a semitone) give a rather 'oriental' feel to the music, though we should beware of attributing this directly to Turkish influence; many elements from ancient Greek and early Byzantine secular music were adapted by the Arabs, taken up by the Turks, and then reintroduced into Greek-speaking lands during the Ottoman period.

Despite the often 'homely' themes, the treatment of the subject matter, particularly in the longer ballads, may be decidedly 'other-worldly'. Birds talk and serve as messengers, the dead go not to the Christian heaven or hell but to the grim underworld of antiquity ruled by Kháros (the ancient Kháron who ferried souls across the Styx), supernatural intervention is commonplace, and many apparently ordinary objects are endowed with mystic or symbolic significance. All of this has a distancing effect *vis-à-vis* the 'real' world, and invests the stories with something of the character of the ancient Greek myths by creating a framework which makes possible the treatment of otherwise taboo subjects.

The song in (18) comes from Arákhova near Delphi and is entitled *Kharos and the Shepherd* (['xaros ḳ o tso'panis]). Though first published in 1860, its origins clearly go back into the Ottoman period:

(18)   *Ο Χάρος και ο τσοπάνης.*

Το βλέπεις κείνο το βουνό που 'ναι ψηλό και μέγα,
πόχ' ανταρούλα στην κορφή καὶ καταχνιά στη ρίζα;
Απέκεινα κατέβαινε ένας ντελή λεβέντης,
φέρνει το φέσι του στραβά και τον γαμπά στριμμένο.
Κι ο Χάρος τον εβίγλισεν από ψηλή ραχούλα,   5
βγήκε και τον απάντησε σ' ένα στενό σοκάκι.
'Καλημέρα σου, Χάρο μου.' – 'Καλώς τον τον λεβέντη.
Λεβέντη, πούθεν έρχεσαι, λεβέντη, πού παγαίνεις;'
''γώ 'πό τα πρόβατ' έρχομαι, στο σπίτι μου παγαίνω,
πάγω να πάρω το ψωμί και πίσω να γυρίσω.'   10

'Λεβέντη, μ' έστειλε ο Θιός να πάρω την ψυχή σου.'
'Δίχως αρρώστια κι αφορμή ψυχή δεν παραδίδω.
Για έβγα να παλέψουμε σε μαρμαρέν' αλώνι,
κι αν με νικήσεις, Χάρο μου, να πάρεις την ψυχή μου,
κι αν σε νικήσω, Χάρο μου, να πάρω την ψυχή σου.'   15
Πιαστήκαν καὶ παλέψανε δυό νύχτες και τρεις μέρες,
κι αυτού την τρίτη την αυγή κοντά στό γιόμα γιόμα
φέρν' ο λεβέντης μια βολά, τού Χάρου κακοφάνη,
απ' τα μαλλιά τον άδραξε, στη γην τον αβροντάει,
ακούν το νιον και βόγγιζε και βαρυαναστενάζει·   20
'Άσε με, Χάρο μ', άσε με τρεις μέρες και τρεις νύχτες·
τες δυό να φάγω και να πιω, τη μιά να σεργιανίσω,
να πάω να διω τους φίλους μου, να διω και τους δικούς μου,
πόχω γυναίκα παρανιά, και χήρα δεν της πρέπει,
πόχω και δυό μικρούτσικα, κι ορφάνια δεν τους πρέπει,   25
πόχω τα πρόβατ' άκουρα και το τυρί στο κάδι.'
Κι αὐτού κοντά στό δειλινό τον καταβάν' ο Χάρος.

Passow (1860: no. 426)

[to 'vlepis 'ķino to vu'no pu ne psi'lo ķe 'meɣa,/ pox   anda'rula stiŋ
It you-see that   the mountain that is high and big,   that-has storm/mist at-the

gor'fi ķe katax'nja sti   'riza./ a'peķina ka'tevene 'enas de'li le'vendis,/
summit and mist/haze at-the root?   From-there descended a   bold young-man,

'ferni to 'fesi tu   stra'va ķe toŋ ɣam'ba stri'meno./ 5 kj o 'xaros ton
he-wears the fez of-him crooked and the cloak   twisted.   And the Kháros him

e'viɣlisen a'po psi'li ra'xula,/ 'vjike ķe ton ap'andise s 'ena ste'no
kept-watch-for from high ridge,   came-out and him met   at a   narrow

so'kaki./ kali'mera su,   'xaro mu. ka'los   ton ton le'vendi./ le'vendi,
lane.   'Good-day to-you, Kháros of-me.' 'Welcome him the young-man. Young-man,

'puθen 'erçese, le'vendi pu   pa'jenis./ ɣo po ta 'provat 'erxome, sto
'whence you-come, young-man where you-go?' 'I from the sheep I-come,   to-the

'spiti mu pa'jeno,/ 10 'paɣo na 'paro to pso'mi ķe 'piso na ji'riso./
house of-me I-go,   I-go   that I-take the bread and back that I-return.'

le'vendi, 'mestile o θjos na 'paro tim bziçi su./   'ðixos a'rostja kj
'Young-man, me-sent the God that I-take the soul of-you.' 'Without illness and

afor'mi psi'çi ðem bara'ðiðo./ ja ᴗ'evɣa na pa'lepsume se marma'renj
reason   soul not I-surrender. Just come-out that we-wrestle   on marble

a'loni,/   kj am me ni'ķisis, 'xaro mu, na 'paris tim bzi'çi mu,/
threshing-floor, and if me you-beat, Kháros of-me, will you-take the soul   of-me,

15 kj an se ni'ķiso, 'xaro mu, na 'paro tim bxi'çi su./
  and if you I-beat,   Kháros of-me, will I-take the soul   of-you.'

pjas'tikan   ķe pa'lepsane ðjo 'niçtes ķe tris 'meres,/ kj af'tu tin
They-came-to-blows and wrestled   two nights and three days,   and then the

'driti tin av'ji kon'da sto   'joma 'joma / fern o le'vendis mnja vo'la,
third the dawn near   to-the noon   noon   brings the young-man a   blow,

tu   'xaru kako'fani,/ ap ta ma'ʎa ton 'aðrakse, sti jin   don
to-the Kháros it-seemed-bad, by the hair   him he-grasped, to-the ground him

avron'dai,/ 20 a'kun   do njon ķe 'voŋgize ķe varjanaste'nazi./ 'ase me,
he-slams,   they-hear the youth and he-groans and sighs-heavily.   'Grant me,

'xaro m,   'ase me triz 'meres ķe triz 'niçtes./ tez ðjo na 'faɣo ķe na
Kharos of-me, grant me three days   and three nights. The two that I-eat and that

pjo, ti mnja na serja'niso,/   na 'pao na ðjo tus 'filuz mu, na ðjo ķe
I-drink, the one that I-go-for-a-walk, that I-go that I-see the friends of-me, that I-see and

tuz ði'kuz   mu,/ 'poxo   ji'neka para'nja, ķe 'çira   ðen dis
the own(people) of-me, (I-)who-have wife   very-young, and widow(hood) not her

'prepi,/ 25 'poxo   ķe djo mi'krutsika, kj or'fanja ðen dus 'prepi,/
suits,   who-have and two little-children, and orphanhood not them suits,

'poxo ta 'provat 'akura ķe to ti'ri sto 'kaði./ kj af'tu kon'da sto
who-have the sheep   unsheared and the cheese in-the tub.'   And then near   to-the

ðili'no toŋ gata'van o 'xaros]
afternoon him struck-down the Kháros.

'Do you see that great high mountain, with a storm-cloud at its summit and heat-haze at its base? From there a bold young man came down; he wore his fez at an angle and his cloak twisted back. But Kháros kept watch for him and met him in a narrow lane. "Good day, Kháros." "Welcome, young man. Young man, where are you coming from; young man, where are you going?" "I am coming from my sheep, I am going home; I am going to eat my bread and then return." "Young man, God sent me to take your soul." "I will not surrender my soul without illness or good cause. Just come out to wrestle on the marble threshing-floor, and if you beat me, Kháros, you may take my soul, and if I beat you, Kháros, I will take your soul." They came to blows and wrestled for two nights and three days, and then on the third day, quite close to midday, the young man landed a blow; Kháros grew angry, grabbed him by the hair and slammed him to the ground; and they heard the young man groan and sigh aloud: "Grant me, Kháros, grant me three days and three nights; the two that I may eat and drink, the one that I may make a journey, that I may go to see my friends, to see my family. I have a young wife who does not deserve widowhood, I have young children who do not deserve an orphan's lot, I have sheep unshorn and cheese in the tub." And then close to evening Kháros cast him down.'

This is a fully-fledged 'modern' Greek text, though certain elements, quite apart from the conventions of the genre, again convey an unintended 'old-world charm' because of the impact of *katharévousa* on the contemporary standard. We might draw here to the regular use of coordination and parataxis (e.g. in line 20 ακούν [a'kun] 'they hear', is followed by και [ķe] 'and', and not by a 'true' subordinating conjunction), much seemingly 'folksy/colloquial' vocabulary (including diminutives like ανταρ-ούλα [anda'rula] (2) 'little storm', and μικρ-ούτσικα [mi'krutsika] (25) 'little ones'), and 'dialect' characteristics like columnar stress in plural verb paradigms (3pl. πιαστήκαν [pja'stikan] (16) for 'standard' πιάστηκαν ['pjastikan]), παγαίνω [pa'jeno] (8, 9) for 'standard' πηγαίνω [pi'jeno], and διω [ðjo] (23) for 'standard' δω [ðo].

Note too such apparent 'archaisms' as neuter sg. μέγα ['meɣa] (1) 'great', instead of μεγάλο [me'ɣalo] (formed by regularization of the ancient paradigm which lacked the extended root in -λο- [-lo-] in the nom. and acc. sg. of the masculine and neuter); the former in fact survived as a regional variant into the early twentieth century (Thumb (1912: 69)). Similarly, the 3sg. aorist passive κακοφάνη [kako'fani] (18) lacks the expected -κε [-ke] formant, but we should note that Makriyánis (see 14.1) also avoids this extension in 3sg. forms, confirming that the short forms remained in use locally (cf. (15)(e) above for Cretan), and that the final standardization of the long forms, despite their first appearance in vernacular medieval texts, belongs to the late nineteenth/twentieth centuries.

Though there are no discernible Turkish elements in early classics like *The Last Mass in Ayía Sophía* or *The Bridge of Arta*, no oral tradition can remain creative without absorbing elements from contemporary speech. A striking feature of this song, therefore, is the number of Turkish loans, which remain typical (where they survive) of less formal registers: τσοπάνης [tso'panis] 'shepherd' < çoban [tʃo'ban]; ντελή(ς) [de'li(s)] 'brave' (to the point of foolhardiness) < deli [de'li] (an early borrowing, since the modern sense in both languages is 'insane'); λεβέντης [le'vendis] 'fine young man' < levend [le̞'vend] (now obsolete in Turkish, again pointing to an early loan); φέσι ['fesi] 'fez' < fes [fes]; and σοκάκι [so'kaki] '(back-)street' < sokak [so'kak].

In general, however, the major characteristics of the 'demotic' foundation of standard modern Greek are well represented. The orthography, for example, reflects normal pronunciation in its treatment of elision/crasis, final -ν [n], and synizesis, clitic pronouns are fixed in position before finite verb forms even in main clauses (1, 6, 11, etc.), and νά [na] + subjunctive has replaced any lingering complement infinitives (10); this construction also retains its final function (11, 22, 23), and its subjunctive and future uses in main clauses (14, 15) (the latter now superseded by θα [θa], though this is again a recent standardization).

The existence of a 'literary' tradition closely reflecting the development of 'demotic' Greek was an important source of inspiration for those who sought, during the eighteenth and nineteenth centuries, to develop a modern written standard out of contemporary spoken varieties of Greek. The fact that the standard language of today, both spoken and written, has become rather distanced from this demotic tradition is due to the continuing influence of traditional written forms of Greek and above all of *katharévousa* (see 17.3). The background to the 'language question' in the later years of the Turkish period is therefore considered in Chapter 15, and its subsequent development and final resolution are presented in Chapter 17, following a brief historical introduction to modern Greece (Chapter 16).

Written Greek in the Turkish period

15.1 Continuity

Within the devastated Greek communities of the Ottoman empire there was little room for the kind of vernacular literature produced in the Komnenian and Palaiologan periods, and most of the surviving forms of writing continued to employ archaizing styles as before, a situation reinforced by the perception of the intelligentsia and the clergy that fate had cast them in the role of guardians of the national heritage.

Nonetheless, the more privileged Greeks both inside and outside the empire continued to travel, at first mainly for educational purposes (to the west to study and to Ottoman lands to teach) but later also on business, as the empire began to trade with the expanding economies of Russia and western Europe. As noted in Chapter 14, more or less 'standard' varieties of educated spoken and written Greek continued to be used, and the tendency towards greater regional differentiation did not greatly affect the higher forms of the language in the core Greek-speaking regions.

Most day-to-day administration employed a 'middle' style which continued the Byzantine practice of blending a restricted set of ancient morphological paradigms into a fairly basic syntactic structure that reflected contemporary syntactic norms. This practical written language continued to serve as a standard, and it was convenient even for the Ottoman Sultan, as for the Venetians, to exploit it as a diplomatic language. The following early example is an extract from a treaty of 1450 between Mehmet II (the Conqueror-to-be) and the Grand Master of the Knights of St John on Rhodes:

(1) *Εγώ ο μέγας αυθέντης και μέγας αμηράς σουλτάνος ο Μεχεμέτ-πεις ...*
ομνύω εις τον θεόν του ουρανού και της γης και εις τον μέγαν ημών προφήτην
τον Μουάμεθ και εις τα επτά μουσάφια, τα έχομεν και ομολογούμεν ημείς
οι μουσουλμάνοι, και εις τους εκατόν ηκοσυτέσσαρεις χιλιάδας προφήτας
του θεού και εις την ζωήν μου και εις την ζωήν των παιδίων μου ... καὶ
ομνύω εις τους άνωθεν γεγραμμένους όρκους, ότι να έχω αγάπην μετά του
πατρός της αφεντείας μου, του μεγάλου μαΐστορος Ρόδου, και ποτέ κανμίαν
ζημίαν να μηδέν τον ποιήσω ...

Miklosich-Müller (1860–90: Vol. III, p. 286)

e'ɣo o   'meɣas af'θendis ḳe 'meɣas ami'ras sul'tanos o mehe'met-beis ...
I   the great   lord   and great   emir   Sultan   the Mehmet   Bey ...

om'nio is ton θe'on tu   ura'nu ḳe tiz jis ḳe is tom 'meɣan i'mon
I-swear by the god   of-the heaven and the earth and by the   great   of-us

pro'fitin ton mu'ameθ ķe is ta ep'ta mu'safja, ta   'exomen ķe
prophet   the Mohammed and by the seven *musafia*,   which we-have   and

omolo'ɣumen i'mis i   musul'mani, ķe is tus eka'ton ikosi'tesaris çil'jaðas
confess   we   the Muslims,   and by the hundred twenty-four   thousands

pro'fitas tu   θe'u ķe is tin zo'in mu   ķe is tin zo'in tom be'ðiom mu . . .
prophets of-the god and by the life of-me and by the life   of-the children of-me . . .

ķe om'nio is tus 'anoθen jeɣgra'menus 'orkus, 'oti na 'exo a'ɣapin me'ta
and I-swear by the above   written   oaths   that will I-have affection with

tu pa'tros tis   afen'diaz mu, tu me'ɣalu ma'istoros 'roðu,   ķe po'te
the father of-the honour   of-me, the Grand   Master   of-Rhodes, and never

ka(m)'mian zi'mian na mi'ðen dom bi'iso . . .
no   harm   will not(hing) him I-do . . .

'I the great lord and great emir Sultan Mehmet Bey . . . swear by the God of heaven and earth, and by our great prophet Mohammed, and by the seven musafia [*copies of the Koran*] that we Muslims hold and on which we profess our faith, and by the hundred and twenty four thousand prophets of God, and by my life, and by the life of my children, . . . and I swear by the oaths written above that I shall have affectionate relations with my (majesty's) father, the Grand Master of Rhodes, and that I shall never do him any harm . . .'

The underlying structure and the word order are already fundamentally those of modern Greek. Note in particular the *να* [na]-futures, the negative polarity items, and the fully developed verb complex (modality+negation+clitic+verb), alongside the free use of contemporary vocabulary, including Romance and Turkish loans.

Nonetheless, the orthography and morphology still reflect the conventions of the written Koine: final *-ν* [-n] is consistently noted and synizesis is not represented (though conservative pronunciations might still have been current), while the genitive of 1st declension masculines is in *-ου* [-u] not *-η* [-i] (*αυθέντου* [af'θendu]), and 3rd declension consonant-stems have genitives in *-ος* [-os] (*πατρός* [pat'ros], though see below). Note too the formulaic/learned expression *τους ἄνωθεν γεγραμμένους ὄρκους* [tus 'anoθen jeɣgra'menus 'orkus] with its archaic adverb and reduplicated perfect participle.

The bilingual writer is, however, prone to occasional 'lapses'; e.g. *ηκοσυτέσσαρεις* for *εικοσιτέσσαρεις* [ikosi'tesaris], a form which also shows modern *-(ε)ις* [is] for classical *-ες* [es] under the influence of *τρεῖς* [tris] 'three'. The appearance in a later part of the text of innovative 1st declension nominatives (*πατέρας* [pa'teras] 'father', *μαΐστορας* [ma'istoras] 'master') is a similar concession to the spoken language, and this may well indicate that the genitive in *-ος* [-os] (locally preserved in some modern dialects) was still a feature of the dialect of the writer; it is significant that such forms are the only ones given in Sofianós's grammar (see 14.2.2).

From examples of this kind we can see how the written Koine evolved through compromise with the spoken language; once a given innovation entered educated speech, it also began to infiltrate the more basic written styles, and so might eventually compete with, and then replace, its conservative equivalent in all but the highest styles.

A related middle style continued to be used for official purposes throughout the Ottoman period. Consider, for example, the following legislation from Moldavia, dated 1788, in which the dative is avoided and inflected participles are used only adjectivally, while established and familiar loan words (from Turkish, Italian and Romanian) appear freely:

(2) Περί του αυθεντικού Διβανίου (divan). Το Αυθεντικόν Διβάνι να γίνεται τρεις φορές την εβδομάδα, δευτέραν δηλ. τετράδην καὶ σάββατον· καὶ εις μεν την δευτέραν και τετράδην να θεωρούνται αι διαφοραί εκείνων, οπού εκρίθησαν εις τα δεπαρταμέντα (dipartimento) ή εις τους Βελιτζήδες (veli(ci)), και δεν ευχαριστήθησαν εις την απόφασιν εκείνων και εζήτησαν με απελατζιόνε (appelazione) να έβγουν εις το Διβάνι, ή αι διαφοραί οπού ηθέλαμεν προστάξει να θεωρηθώσιν επί Διβανίου μας χωρίς να προσδιορισθώσιν εις άλλο κριτήριον, το δε σάββατον να θεωρώνται αι εγκληματικαί υποθέσεις και καταδίκαι και αποφάσεις τούτων.

Article 1 of the City Code (text in Triandafyllídis (1938: 359–60))

[pe'ri   tu afθendi'ku ðiva'niu. to afθendi'kon ði'vani na 'jinete   tris
Concerning the Ruling   Council.   The Ruling   Council shall take-place three

fo'res tin evðo'maða, ðef'teran ðil(a'ði), te'traðin ķe 'savaton; ķe is
times   the week,   Monday   that-is,   Wednesday and Saturday;   and on

men   tin ðef'teran ķe te'traðin na θeo'runde e ðiafo're e'kinon,
on-the-one-hand the Monday   and Wednesday shall be-considered the differences of-those,

o'pu e'kriθisan is ta ðeparta'menda i is tus veli'dziðes, ķe ðen
who were-judged in the departments   or at the Guardians,   and not

efxaris'tiθisan is tin a'pofasin e'kinon ķe e'zitisan me apelatsi'one na
were-satisfied   at the decision   of-them and sought   with appeal   that

'evɣun   is to ði'vani, i e ðiafo're o'pu i'θelamen pros'taksi na
they-appear at the Council, or the differences which we-would   order   that

θeori'θosin e'pi   ðiva'niu mas xo'ris na prozðioris'θosin is 'alo kri'tirion,
be-considered before Council of-us without that they-be-settled   in other court,

to ðe   'savaton na θeo'runde e eŋglimati'ķe ipo'θesis ķe
the on-the-other-hand Saturday shall be-considered the criminal   cases   and

kata'ðiķe ķe apo'fasis 'tuton.]
sentences   and decisions of-these.

'Concerning the Ruling Council (lit. Bench). The Ruling Council shall take place three times per week, that is on Mondays, Wednesdays, and Saturdays; on Mondays and Wednesdays the disputes will be considered of those who were judged in their regional courts or before the Guardians, and were not satisfied with the decisions of these bodies and sought by means of appeal to appear before the Council, or the disputes which we would order to be considered before our Council without their being settled in another court, while on Saturdays criminal cases will be considered, together with the sentences and decisions concerning these.'

Traditional endings are generally retained, however, though 3pl. -ουν [-un] is now preferred except in contract verbs and the aorist passive subjunctive (a tendency also apparent in Byzantine middle-style writing at the more vernacular end of the spectrum). But where lexical items have a 'modern' meaning, modern endings are also used, as with φορά [fo'ra], plural φορές [fo'res], in the sense of 'time/occasion' rather than 'motion/impulse', a development from κατά φοράν [ka'ta fo'ran] 'in a movement/in one go').

On the other hand, more classical forms of Greek continued to be used for higher scholarship and learned correspondence, particularly by the political and ecclesiastical élite of Constantinople. The extract below comes from a letter of Aléxandros Mavrokordátos (1636–1708), the progenitor of the greatest of the Phanariot families, to his son Nikólaos. It provides a good example of the 'high' style of the establishment, though the views expressed show a refreshingly realistic grasp of the problems involved in using such a language 'naturally':

(3) Ἔστω δέ σοι κατά νουν ἀεί τα ἐμά παραγγέλματα, ὅσα μοι τῇ προειρημένῃ
   ἐπιστολῇ διεσαφήθη. Τας δε ποιητικάς και τας ἀήθεις λέξεις ἴσθι μέν,
   ἀλλά μη χρῶ παντελῶς αυταίς, μηδέ μοι τους πάλαι λογογράφους μάρτυρας
   προΐστασο· οις γαρ εκείνοι, πάμπολλα συγγράψαντες, ἅπαξ ἡ δις εχρήσαντο,
   ταύτα πώς ημάς εκμιμείσθαι δει, τους πολύ κατόπιν υστερίζοντας;

                                                    Text in Triandafyllídis (1938: 319)

['esto ðe si   ka'ta nun a'i   ta e'ma paraŋ'gelmata, 'osa   mi   ti
Let-be and for-you in   mind always the my   instructions,   as-many-as by-me in-the

proiri'meni episto'li ðiesa'fiθi.   taz ðe piiti'kas ke tas a'iθis 'leksis 'isθi
forementioned letter   were-made clear. The and poetic   and the unusual words, know

men,   a'la mi xro pande'los af'tes, mi'ðe mi   tus 'pale loɣo'ɣrafus
on-the one-hand, but   not use at-all   them,   nor   for-me the of-old writers

'martiras   pro'istaso; iz   ɣar e'kini, 'pambola siŋ'grapsandes, 'apaks
(as) witnesses put-before;   which-things for   they,   very-much having-written,   once

i ðis e'xrisando, 'tafta   'pos i'mas ekmi'misθe ði,   tus   po'li
or twice used,   these-things how   for-us   to-imitate   is-it-necessary, the-ones much

ka'topin iste'rizondas?]
after   coming-later?

'And be sure that all the instructions of mine that were explained in the letter mentioned earlier are always in your mind. As for poetic and unusual words, by all means know them, but avoid their use completely, and do not present me with the testimony of the writers of old; for how should we, who come so long after them, imitate what they, who wrote so very much, used only once or twice?'

This 'living' use of the learned language continues the high Byzantine tradition, and its artificiality is best demonstrated by comparing the word order of the original with that of the English translation; whereas modern Greek and English generally follow the same sequence of phrases and clauses, the considerable differences here, natural enough in the classical language, present the translator with something of a challenge.

Nevertheless, in his *Memoirs* of 1682, Mavrokordátos also felt free to use a relaxed, semi-vernacular style, directly reflecting the Ottoman institutional context in which he worked. This rather curious blend of demotic and conservative forms (the latter including inflected active participles, full-form pronouns for clitics, datives, and perfect passive participles with reduplication) is clearly not the result of any lack of knowledge, and must reflect a deliberate choice ultimately based upon the formal spoken style of the aristocracy:

(4) Μετά το τραπέζι και τον καϊφέ επῆρεν ο κεχαγιάς (kâhya) τον Νουραδίνον και επῆγεν εις την τζέργαν (çerge), όπου εκουρδίσθηκε πλησίον του οτακίου (otağ) του επιτρόπου δια τον χάνην (han), και καθίσαντες μόνοι, ο επίτροπος και ο χάνης, εσυνωμίλησαν πάλιν ικανῶς. Εἶτα απῆλθεν ο χάνης εις την προητοιμασμένην τζέργαν και ἔμεινεν ο επίτροπος· επῆρεν απτέσι (aptes), εκίλδισε (kılmak) ναμάζι (namaz) του μεσημερίου. Επῆγεν ο κεχαγιάς και ο ρεΐζ-εφέντης (reis-efendi) και ἔφεραν τον χάνην πάλιν εις τον επίτροπον, ος προϋπήντησεν αυτῷ εφ' ικανῷ διαστήματι.

Text in Khatzidákis (1915: 143)

[meta to tra'pezi ke toŋ gai'fe e'piren o kexa'jas ton nura'ðinon ke e'pijen
After the table   and the coffee took   the steward   the Nouradinos, and went

is tin 'dzeryan, 'opu ekur'ðisθike pli'sion tu ota'kiu tu   epi'tropu ðja toŋ
to the tent,   which had-been-pitched beside the pavilion of-the ambassador for the

'xanin, ke ka'θisandes 'moni, o e'pitropos ke o 'xanis, esino'milisan
sovereign, and sitting   alone,   the ambassador and the sovereign, they-talked-together

'palin ika'nos. 'ita a'pilθen o 'xanis   is tin proitimaz'menin 'dzeryan ke
again sufficiently. Then went-away the sovereign to the previously-prepared tent   and

'eminen o e'pitropos; e'piren ap'tesi, e'kilðise   na'mazi tu   mesime'riu.
stayed   the ambassador; he-took ablution, he-performed prayer   of-the mid-day.

e'pijen o kexa'jas ke o re'iz-e'fendis ke 'eferan   ton 'xanin 'palin is
Went   the steward and the chief-master and they-brought the sovereign back   to

ton e'pitropon, os proi'pindisen af'to ef ika'no   ðia'stimati.]
the ambassador, who came-to-meet him at sufficient distance.

'After the meal and the coffee the steward took Nouradinos [*the foreign minister*] and went to the tent which had been pitched beside the pavilion of the ambassador for the sovereign, and the ambassador and the sovereign, sitting alone, spoke together again at some length. Then the sovereign went to the previously prepared tent and the ambassador remained behind; he undertook his ablutions and performed the mid-day prayer. Then the steward and the foreign minister went and brought the sovereign back to the ambassador, who came to meet him at an appropriate distance.'

The word order and syntactic structure of this piece are again natural to the modern idiom, and (with the exceptions mentioned above) the morphology too is broadly 'demotic' if we ignore the systematic use of final -ν [-n] and the absence of synizesis (also perhaps reflecting the actual usage of the élite). In so far as a 'vernacular' prose style was already in use in even the highest society, the objections that were soon to be raised against spoken Greek as the basis for a national language were clearly more ideological than practical (cf. Chapter 17).

15.2 The impact of the Enlightenment

A great many writers came to use a similarly 'demoticising' style during the seventeenth and eighteenth centuries, in recognition of the growing readership and increasingly diverse needs of a more enlightened and prosperous era. Typical text types now include bible anthologies and religious tracts (including a 'translation' of the New Testament in 1638, quickly suppressed in the face of ecclesiastical opposition), histories, chronicles, and technical treatises on a wide variety of 'modern' subjects. It seems that the growing body of western-educated intellectuals had at last begun to appreciate the importance of a 'modernized' language for educational purposes, and the publication in Venice and elsewhere of such texts bears witness to a more 'progressive' outlook based on the conviction, first adumbrated in the work of Sofianós, that an extension of education was the key to the revival of the nation.

Many of these works make explicit reference to 'the common dialect' in their titles or prefaces. For example, the 'Salvation of Sinners' (published in Venice in 1664) by the Cretan monk Agápios, contains the following preface:

(5) 'An excellent book called "the Salvation of Sinners", composed with the greatest care in the common dialect of the Greeks by the Cretan monk Agapios (who practised the ascetic life on the Holy Mountain of Athos) and now recently corrected with care.'

Agápios (1664: 1)

Though this is composed, according to tradition, in ancient Greek, the language of the text itself is clearly distanced from that of 'learned' literature. We should note, however, that it is not written in the Cretan vernacular either, despite its author's origins. The 'common language' referred to is the basic written style familiar even to the moderately educated throughout the Greek-speaking areas, a variety that reflected many of the changes in spoken Greek in a neutral way by avoiding regionalisms, and retaining a conservative orthographic aspect:

(6) Δεν ζημιώνεσαι καιρόν τον πολύτιμον οπού σου εχάρισεν ο Θεός να τον εξοδιάσης εις αγαθά έργα, διά να λάβης την ουράνιαν βασιλείαν. Η οποία ζημία είναι τρανύτερη (του καιρού λέγω) παρά του πράγματος, διατί πράγμα όσον θέλεις ευρίσκεις αμή καιρόν όχι.   Agápios (1664: 21)

[ðe(n) zimi'onese ķero(n) tom bo'litimo(n) o'pu su   e'xarisen o θe'os na
Not   waste   time   the   precious   that   to-you has-granted the God   that

ton eksoði'asis is aɣa'θa 'erɣa, ðia na 'lavis   tin u'rania(n) vasi'lia(n). i
it   you-spend   on good   deeds, for   that you-obtain the heavenly   kingdom.   The

o'pia zi'mia 'ine tra'niteri (tu   ķe'ru 'leɣo) para tu   'praɣmatos, ðia'ti
which waste   is   greater   (of-the time   I-mean) than of-the matter,   because

'praɣma 'oso(n)   'θelis   e'vriskis a'mi ķe'ron 'oçi]
matter   as-much-as you-want you-find   but   time   not

'Do not waste the precious time that God has given you to spend on good deeds in order for you to gain the kingdom of heaven. Such a waste (of time, I mean) is more serious than that of material things, because you will find all the material things you want, but not the time.'

The publication of such work reveals a growing appreciation within the otherwise conservative Orthodox church of the need for an accessible religious literature, not only to edify but also to 'protect' the faithful against conversion, whether to Islam, Catholicism, or even Protestantism. Once again, it is clear that the foundations for a modern written language, reflecting the norms of educated speech quite closely, were already in place long before the 'language question' assumed an acute form in the period after independence. Indeed, writers such as Ilías Miniátis (1669–1714), who came from Kefaloniá, but worked at different times in the Ionian islands, Venice, Constantinople, and the Peloponnese, developed a highly sophisticated religious-educational programme in just such a 'popularized' Greek, by skilfully deploying the rhetorical techniques adopted from Italian models by the Catholic Frangískos Skoúfos (1644–97, a refugee from Khaniá in Crete, who studied in Rome, and then worked in Italy and the Ionian islands).

The advance of intellectual curiosity and economic development during the eighteenth century also led to the appearance of secular writings in fields as diverse as geography, politics, and science, subjects which necessitated a considerable expansion of the lexicon. This was achieved principally through calques and loan translations from French and English, which themselves had often used classical Greek elements for the same purpose. Many such works were written in a 'demoticizing' language related to the spoken standard of the upper classes, and published not only in western Europe, but also in the Ottoman principalities of Wallachia and Moldavia, where a number of linguistically progressive figures had begun to speak out (see Henderson (1971), Kondosópoulos (1978)). Prominent among these were Iosípos Moisiódax (*c.* 1730–90), sometime principal of both the Jassy and Bucharest academies, and Dimítrios Katartzís (*c.* 1720–1807), a high court judge in Bucharest of Constantinopolitan birth, who urged the general use of a 'modern' written language for education, and composed a grammar to provide a basis for his programme (unpublished until 1970). Katartzís also advocated a written standard based upon 'the domestic style of Constantinople' (i.e. the domestic style of his class), and on this platform entered into a vigorous and polemical correspondence with Lámbros Photiádis, the arch-archaist headmaster of the Bucharest academy (see Triandafyllídis (1938: 435–8) for extracts). He was followed by Daniíl Philippídis and Dimítrios Konstandás, whose *Geography* of 1791 is often taken to provide the best indication of contemporary educated speech (cf. Beaton (1994: 331)); this apparently still employed, *inter alia*, 3rd declension genitives in -oς [-os], accusative plurals in -aς [-as], and present passive participles. Moisiódax, however, though approving the view that the simple style was adequate for the expression of all scientific subject matter, conceived of this as requiring the 'correction' of common usage through the introduction of appropriate elements from the ancient language, a programme which anticipated the later development of *katharévousa* (cf. (7) below, and see Chapter 17).

It is important to note, however, that almost all contributors to the language debate at this time, whatever the thrust of their proposals, instinctively employed the currently standard 'academic' form of the written language for putting forward and defending their views, and even those who sought to establish a more popular medium in the long term felt obliged to engage with the opposition within the framework of the established conventions. Consider, for example, the following extract from the preface of Moisiódax's *Theory of Geography* (1781). The writer has justified his use of the 'simple style' in the main body of the work, and now explains the basis on which he has 'improved' it:

(7) *Εγώ διά λόγους, τους οποίους επιφέρω, έκρινα να εξυφάνω την παρούσαν συγγραφήν εν τω απλώ ύφει, σώζων όμως αεί τους ωρισμένους όρους των πραγμάτων, οίτινες ήσαν εν χρήσει παρά τοις αρχαίοις, και μεθαρμόζων αεί το απλούν ύφος επί το σεμνότερον, ή το ελάχιστον επί το πρεπωδέστερον τη ανά χείρας πραγματευομένη ύλη.*   Text in Sáthas (1870: 150)

[e'ɣo ði'a 'loɣus, tus o'pius epi'fero, 'ekrina na eksi'fano tim ba'rusan
I   for reasons, the which I-adduce, I-judged that I-weave the present

siŋgra'fin en do a'plo 'ifi, 'sozon 'omos a'i tus oriz'menus 'orus tom
work   in the simple style, keeping however always the settled   terms of-the

braɣ'maton, 'itines 'isan eŋ 'xrisi pa'ra tis ar'çeis, ķe meθar'mozon a'i
things, (terms) which were in use   among the ancients, and adapting   always

to a'plun 'ifos e'pi   to sem'noteron, i to e'laçiston e'pi   to
the simple style towards the more-dignified, or the least   towards the

prepo'ðesteron ti   a'na 'çiras praɣmatevo'meni 'ili.]
more-fitting   for-the in   hands being-worked   material.]

'For the reasons which I adduce, I judged it right to compose the present work in the simple style, while always retaining the established terminology that was in use among the ancients and always adapting the simple style in a more dignified direction or at least in a direction more fitting for the subject matter in hand.'

A number of archaisms are typical of this elaborated rhetorical style used by the eighteenth-century intelligentsia:

(8) (a) The systematic retention of ancient nominal and verbal morphology, including here:
 (i) 'contracted' 2nd declension and traditional 3rd declension forms (cf.
  απλούν [a'plun] < *απλό-ον* [a'ploon] for modern *απλό* [a'plo], and the
  ancient 3rd declension accusative plural *χείρ-ας* ['çiras]).
 (ii) monolectic comparatives rather than *πιο* [pjo] 'more' + the simple
  adjective (e.g. *πρεπωδέστερον* [prepo'ðesteron]).
 (iii) the dative case (e.g. *τη ... πραγματευομένη ύλη* [ti ...
  praɣmatevo'meni 'ili]
 (iv) the use of inflected participles, both active and present/aorist passive
  (e.g. *σώζων* ['sozon], *πραγματευομένη* [praɣmatevo'meni].
 (v) reduplication (cf. *ωρισμένους* [oriz'menus]).
 (vi) retention of the syllabic augment, including 'internal' augments in

compounds (no example in the extract, but cf. μετ-ερρύθμισα [mete'riθmisa] 'I reformed', used subsequently in the preface).

(b) Ancient prepositions (e.g. ανά [a'na], εν [en], επί [e'pi], παρά [pa'ra] + their ancient case requirements, including the dative (e.g. εν τω απλώ ύφει [en do a'plo 'ifi]).

(c) Vocabulary items (and paradigms) alien to popular spoken registers (e.g. feminine χειρ [çir]) for neuter χέρι ['çeri], αεί [a'i] for πάντα ['panda], οίτινες ['itines] and τους οποίους [tus o'pius] instead of (ο)πού [(o)'pu], etc.

Most of the actual constructions, however, correspond closely to those of the contemporary language: e.g. νά [na]-clauses replace ancient infinitives, and genitives directly follow the items on which they depend rather than being inserted between article and noun, or requiring a repeated article ([article + noun] + [article + [genitive phrase]]). This fundamentally contemporary syntax is particularly apparent in the word order; heads precede their complements, and the sequence of phrases within clauses, and of clauses with respect to one another, presents the content of propositions in a straightforwardly cumulative way quite alien to the classically inspired 'high style'. In other words, the 'archaic' elements have chiefly been inserted into structural slots determined by modern rules of syntax in the time-honoured fashion (always allowing for minor knock-on effects in terms of complement selection and case assignment; for example, archaizing πρεπωδέστερον [prepo'ðesteron] 'more fitting' + dative in place of πιο κατάλληλο [pjo ka'talilo] + prepositional phrase, etc.)

15.3 Contemporary 'demotic'

All of these written styles contrast sharply with the 'true' demotic of the period, as written in ignorance by those who had received only a rudimentary education. A typical example is provided by the passage in (9), taken from the will of Dimítrios Kharítis, dated 1708. Kharítis's family originally lived in Roúmeli but had fled to Zákynthos when a Turkish force arrived in the region to drive out a Venetian raiding party:

(9) Αφίνω το τίποτές μου εις το αδέρφι μου το Γηώργη και θέλω να με θάψη χωρίς καμμία εξόδευσι και κοσμοπομπή. Να μου αφήση μονάχα το βρακί και το μαύρο ποκάμισο και τίποτας άλλο, και να με ρίξη 's ένα ταφί. Και αν δώση ο πανάγαθος και πανοικτίρμονας Θεός και καπιτάρη να ελευθερωθή το δυστυχισμένο Γένος μας από τον τρομερό και αντίχριστο και ανελεήμονα Αγαρηνόν, να ξεθάψη τα κόκκαλά μου, και τα κόκκαλα του μακαρίτου αδερφού μου Φιλόθεου, που τα έχω κρυμμένα σε μιάν σακκούλα στην σπηλήάν που εγνωρίζει, και να το θάψη μαζί και κοντά 's τα κόκκαλα των γονηών μας εις την εκκλησιά της πατρίδος μας.

Text in Valaorítis (1907: 278)

[a'fino to 'tipo'tez mu is to a'ðerfi mu to 'jorji ķe 'θelo na me 'θapsi
I leave the nothing of-me to the brother of-me the Yóryis and I-wish that me he-bury

xo'ris ka'mia e'ksoðepsi ķe kozmopom'bi. na mu a'fisi mo'naxa to
without any expense and grand-procession Let to-me he-leave only the

'vraki ķe to 'mavro po'kamiso ķe 'tipotas 'alo, ķe na me 'riksi s 'ena
trousers and the black shirt and nothing else, and may me he-throw into a

ta'fi. ķj an 'ðosi o pan'aγaθos ķe panik'tirmonas θe'os ķe kapi'tari na
grave. And if grants the all-good and all-pitying God and it-happens that

elefθero'θi to ðistiçiz'meno 'jenoz mas ap ton drome'ro ķe an'dixristo ķe
be-freed the unhappy race of-us from the terrible and anti-Christ and

anele'imona aγari'non, na kse'θapsi ta 'koka'la-mu, ķe ta 'kokala tu
pitiless Muslim, may he-dig-up the bones of-me, and the bones of-the

maka'ritu aðer'fu mu fi'loθeu, pu ta 'exo kri'mena se m(n)ja(n) sa'kula
late brother of-me Filótheos, that them I-have hidden in a bag

sti(n) spi'ʎa(n) pu eγno'rizi, ķe na ta 'θapsi ma'zi ķe kon'da s ta
in-the cave that he-knows, and let them he-bury together and near to the

'kokala ton γon'jon mas is tin eklis'ja tis pa'triðoz mas]
bones of-the parents of-us in the church of-the country of-us

'I leave the little I have to my brother Yóryis, and I want him to bury me without expense or a funeral procession. Let him leave me only my trousers and my black shirt and nothing else, and let him throw me in a grave. And if all-merciful and all-pitying God grants this, and it turns out that our unhappy race is freed from the terrible and merciless anti-Christ the Muslim, let him disinter my bones and the bones of my late brother Philótheos, which I have hidden in a sack in the cave which he knows, and let him bury them together next to the bones of our parents in the church of our homeland.'

Features of demotic phonology represented here include:

(10) (a) Final -ν [n] of accusative singulars is regularly found only in the article and in pronouns, and in contexts where the contemporary language would also retain it (cf. 11.2 (3)).

 (b) Synizesis is routinely represented graphically (e.g. σπηλιάν [spi'ʎa(n)], γονηών [γon'jon]).

 (c) The accent is retained on the antepenultimate syllable of 2nd declension genitives such as Φιλόθεου [fi'loθeu] (cf. nominative Φιλόθεος [fi'loθeos]), where learned styles would require a shift to the penultimate.

The morphological picture is also consistently demotic. Note, for example:

(11) (a) 3rd declension i-stem forms have lost their original final -ς [-s] in the nominative, suggesting that this paradigm has been at least partly merged with the 1st declension type in -η [-i].

 (b) 3rd declension consonant stems seem to have been assimilated to the 1st declension types in -α [a] (feminine) or -ας [as] (masculine) in the nominative and accusative. The genitive, however, still ends in -ος [os] (της πατρίδ-ος [tis pa'triðos]), with the old termination intact. Such forms are given in Sofianós's grammar, and remained in use in the Ionian islands.

(c) Large numbers of neuters in -ί ['i] are used where the learned language would employ 3rd declension masculines and feminines.

(d) The verbal prefix ξε- [kse] appears regularly in the sense of 'undo X'; this arose though misanalysis of augmented compounds (e.g. (ε)ξ-έφυγα [(e)ks-'efiɣa] > ξέ-φυγα ['kse-fiɣa], spawning present ξε-φεύγω [kse-'fevɣo]).

(e) Only indeclinable active participles are employed.

(f) Although subjunctive endings homophonous with their indicative counterparts are spelled with the traditional 'long' vowels (e.g. 3sg. aorist subjunctive δώσ-η ['ðosi]), those where the classical ending differs phonetically from the corresponding indicative are always spelled with the indicative endings (cf. 3pl. aorist subjunctive πάρ-ουνε ['parune]).

(g) Aorist passives with the -κ- [k] suffix appear alongside forms without it, reflecting the still-developing character of the paradigm.

(h) The perfect active is formed with έχω ['exo] 'have' + perfect passive participle (τα έχω κρυμμένα [ta 'exo kri'mena]); the 'regular' modern periphrasis with έχω ['exo] plus (fossilized) aorist infinitive is still a thing of the future.

Though Kharítis expresses himself effectively, the content of this, and similar texts, is of an everyday character well suited to its everyday language. Conservative intellectuals, studiously ignoring the increasingly rich educational literature written in a more polished demoticizing Greek, chose to focus on popular speech, and all too readily dismissed the idea that this could ever, without incongruity, incorporate the lexical, structural, and rhetorical resources that a future standard would need. For them, only the established forms of written Greek had the necessary wherewithal.

15.4   The roots of the 'language question'

If we ignore both virtuoso 'high-style' compositions and the concessions made to the vernacular in private memoirs or in the interests of wider access to education, it was still the middle styles of administration and learned debate that defined the range of 'normal' prose writing in the decades before independence. But though actual practice remained largely constant in the short term, the advent of the belief in progressive circles that a 'demoticized' written language would be essential in the modern world marked the beginnings of the breakdown of the consensus, which had originated in Roman imperial times, that it was both natural and acceptable to have radically distinct spoken and written languages.

Diglossia was a consequence of the persistence of political and cultural circumstances that had consistently inhibited the evolution of a modern written language along western European lines. Initially, the coherence of the Roman empire in the east prevented diversification of the kind that had led to the emergence of the

Romance languages in the Latin-speaking provinces; and the continuing proximity of written Greek to its (educated) spoken partner meant that there was little pressure for change in a society where literacy was restricted and cultural perceptions were dominated by the past. Eventually, the potential of the vernacular began to be reassessed, but before such experiments could bear fruit, the Turkish conquests, and the renewed centrality of the Orthodox church, produced a fresh conservative reaction.

When Greek intellectuals again began to be exposed to modern ideas, and sought to revitalize Greek education and science, they were therefore faced with a dilemma. Should the Greek revival attempt to follow the model of other European states, with a national language based on a contemporary variety that had been elaborated, codified, and promoted as 'standard'? Or should the national standard be based on the old written language, with its continuous tradition and in-built prestige? Opinion among the Greeks of the diaspora was generally 'progressive', while the majority of 'conservatives', some of whom were sufficiently encouraged by the revival of classical learning in Europe to plan the reintroduction of ancient Greek, were concentrated in the Ottoman capital and its Danubian satellites (though these were not exclusively bastions of reaction, as noted).

In the event, however, since there were no acknowledged vernacular 'classics' that might provide a model, and educational writing based on educated speech was in its infancy, the political class, though divided on the issue of future language planning, instinctively fell back on the established written standard as it had developed during the seventeenth and eighteenth centuries (cf. (7) and (8) above), and it was this which became, *faute de mieux*, the official language of independent Greece (see Chapter 17).

Chapter 16

The history of the modern Greek state

16.1 Irredentism: triumph and disaster

The seat of government was quickly moved to Athens, and a new city was constructed in neo-classical style as part of a programme for giving the infant nation a distinctive identity through reconnection with its classical past. At the same time, great emphasis was placed on the teaching of classical Greek in schools and universities.

But economic measures imposed by the great powers in their efforts to restore financial order caused widespread hardship, and king Otto, following the classic strategy of leaders in difficulty, embraced the 'Great Idea', a vision of an extended Greece incorporating all the lands associated with Greek history and culture. The first manifestation of this policy was an educational programme designed to re-Hellenize the Orthodox peasant populations under Ottoman rule, many of whom spoke Turkish and had little awareness of their 'Greek' nationality. Though the Ottoman authorities, with typical indifference, did little to oppose this initiative, the emphasis placed on the archaizing written language seriously undermined its impact.

Such efforts were scarcely needed in the great cities, however, where national consciousness was running high. But many Ottoman Greeks felt the empire could be successfully Hellenized from within, and pointed to the extent to which the Greek upper and middle classes had by then come to dominate its political and economic life. The conflict between those who hoped for an aggressive policy from the kingdom and those who felt that such a strategy could only do damage was never resolved. But in Greece itself, the irredentists triumphed over those who, conscious of Greece's parlous economic and military situation, advocated a more cautious policy. Thus despite the acquisition of the Ionian islands in 1864, handed over by Britain in the hope that Greece might moderate its demands, the government resolved to take advantage of Russia's declaration of war on the Ottoman empire in 1877, and moved troops to the northern frontier. Subsequent pressure from the great powers led to the Turks' ceding of Thessaly and the Arta region of southern Epirus to Greece in 1881, in an apparent endorsement of the irredentists' ambition.

Over the next few years the Greek economy began to improve, but the reforms again entailed unpopular taxes, and great damage was done when a government came to power on a populist platform of reducing taxation and resuming the pursuit of 'occupied' territory. A force was therefore sent to help Cretan insurgents in

1897, but when hostilities also broke out in Thessaly, the Greek army was roundly defeated. Though a lenient peace settlement was secured, Greece had to agree to the external supervision of interest payments on its debt, and the resultant economic difficulties led to the first round of large-scale migration, especially to the USA.

By this time the political situation in Macedonia had deteriorated. The Greek National Society had for some time been working to Hellenize Macedonia and Epirus in the face of Bulgarian, Serbian, and Romanian rivalry, and now a guerrilla war broke out between Greek and Slavic groups. Faced with territorial and economic crisis, the government, under threat of military intervention, instigated the so-called 'bourgeois revolution' by turning in 1910 to the Liberal Cretan statesman Elefthérios Venizélos. When revolt broke out among the Albanians, and the Slavic states of the Balkans sought to exploit Turkish weakness, Venizélos determined to protect Greek interests in the north despite the risk of reprisals against the Asia Minor Greeks, who still numbered nearly a million and a half. Greece, Serbia, and Bulgaria together declared war on the Ottoman empire on 18 October 1912. Thessaloniki was taken by the Greek army on 9 November, just ahead of a Bulgarian force, while the Greek navy seized the islands of Khios, Lesbos, and Samos. Early in 1913 the Greeks also moved in the north-west, taking Ioannina and advancing into northern Epirus.

Though the Turks agreed to these gains, a fresh dispute over Macedonia broke out among the victors, and the Greek army now advanced further east, taking the towns of Drama, Serres, and Kavalla. The Bulgarians were obliged to agree to the division of most of Macedonia between Greece and Serbia, and there were population exchanges between the three countries. (The contemporary independence of Slavic Macedonia, following the break-up of Yugoslavia, is therefore seen as a major destabilization of the region.) At the same time, Greek sovereignty over Crete and the Aegean islands was recognized, and the government's ambitions were thwarted only in northern Epirus by the creation of an independent Albania (the harsh treatment of the Greek minority, together with the influx of illegal Albanian immigrants into Greece, remains a major source of friction at the present time).

Greek territory had now been increased by nearly 70 per cent since independence, and the prevailing euphoria even prompted talk of recovering Constantinople, but such hopes were quickly shattered by the First World War and its catastrophic aftermath. The king at this time, Konstandínos I, aimed for a policy of neutrality, but Venizélos supported Greece's traditional allies (Britain, France, and Russia), and when Turkey entered the war on the side of the Central Powers (Germany and Austria-Hungary), troops were at once committed to the Dardanelles campaign in the hope that Greece might obtain a share of the spoils. But the king quickly reconsidered his cautious conversion to the allied cause in the light of warnings from his chief-of-staff about the difficulties of retaining territory in Asia Minor, and Venizélos was forced to resign. This initiated the National Schism, which dominated Greek politics until the Second World War.

A pro-Venizélos coup was staged in Thessaloniki on 30 August 1916, and a provisional government set up. When British and French troops dispatched to Athens to pressurize the royalist government were forced to retreat, the allied powers recognized the provisional government and blockaded areas loyal to the king, forcing Konstandínos into exile. Venizélos then returned as Prime Minister and counter-reprisals against royalists followed, thereby establishing the disastrous practice of tit-for-tat purges at each change of administration.

Venizélos immediately committed the army to the Macedonian front to support the allied campaign in the Balkans, and, following the armistice of November 1918, attended the peace conference in Paris in the expectation that Greek loyalty would be rewarded. His immediate objective was the annexation of Smyrna (Izmir) and its hinterland, where the military situation was becoming critical. The Italians, in their belated search for a colonial empire, had already taken advantage of Ottoman weakness by seizing the Dodecanese in 1912. Now they had landed troops at Antalya, having been promised the region in return for supporting the allies, and it was reported that this force was moving westward. In the absence of any agreement about the dismemberment of the Ottoman empire, the allies agreed to the landing of Greek troops for 'the protection of the local population'. Fighting between Greek and Turkish irregulars immediately followed, while in Ankara the circle around Mustafa Kemal (Atatürk), the victor in the fighting at Gallipoli, declared independence from the government in Constantinople, making it clear they would not tolerate occupation of the Turkish heartland.

It was eventually agreed that Smyrna should be administered by Greece for five years, followed by a plebiscite on the issue of union. But Venizélos had underestimated domestic resentment caused by the over-zealousness of his supporters and the persistence of Anglo-French interference. He lost the elections of 1920, and the incoming royalist government arranged for Konstandínos's return amid fresh purges of leading Venizelists and the tacit withdrawal of British support. Though the French and Italians now came to terms with Mustafa Kemal, the Greeks, under the impression that they retained British backing, launched an offensive in Asia Minor in March 1921. Though their advance was halted only some 50 kilometres from Ankara, the Turks, believing the Greek military position had become untenable, insisted on unconditional evacuation. When this was refused, a crushing counter-offensive was launched on 26 August 1922. The Greek army retreated in disarray, pursuing a scorched earth strategy, and in the ensuing chaos, while western warships stood by, the Christian population of Smyrna was massacred, and large areas of the city devastated by fire.

The king immediately abdicated, to be succeeded by his son Yeóryios, and a revolutionary committee formed from the survivors of the Asia Minor army took charge. By the terms of the treaty of Lausanne (July 1923) Greece forfeited the Smyrna enclave, eastern Thrace, and the islands of Imvros and Tenedos (strategically placed at the entrance to the Dardanelles); and though already under pressure as a result of repatriation from Russia in the aftermath of the revolution, the government was further obliged to agree to an exchange of populations with Turkey (excluding the Turks of western Thrace and the Greeks of Constantinople), with religion, not language, applied as the criterion of nationality. Nearly 400,000 Muslims and well over a million Christians were affected. Although land reform and the departure of Turkish communities allowed some of the refugees to be resettled in country areas, many of those with an urban background set up shanty towns around Athens and Thessaloniki.

16.2   Dictatorship and war

The arrival of a sophisticated bourgeoisie and the expansion of the urban working class had immediate political consequences, including in 1924 a vote for the abolition of the monarchy. A series of weak republican governments soon gave way, however, to military dictatorship under General Pángalos in 1925, and though the return of Venizélos in 1928 ushered in a period of relative stability, including foreign policy successes in repairing relations with Bulgaria and Turkey, his position was quickly undermined by the great depression. At this juncture, the election of a new royalist government and the king's return produced only fresh instability, and bungled attempts at a military takeover by republican sympathizers led to renewed purges of Venizelists. Venizélos himself died in exile in 1936.

In the elections of that year the vote was split between the Liberals (Venizélos's old party) and the Populists (most of whom supported the monarchy), and both parties began secret negotiations with the communists, who held the balance of power. This provoked a warning from the army, and finally, amid massive unrest at the continued hardships of the depression and growing disillusionment with the antics of the politicians, General Ioánnis Metaxás, having secured the king's agreement to a 'temporary' suspension of parliament, took control and set about creating a 'strong Greece' in conscious imitation of Nazi Germany and Fascist Italy.

With the partial exception of the communists, Metaxás suppressed political opposition, and established his 'third Hellenic civilization', which was supposed to herald a modern state that incorporated the best of ancient Greece and Byzantium. Though temperamentally attracted to fascism, Metaxás maintained strict neutrality until Mussolini delivered an ultimatum on 28 October 1940 which directly challenged Greek sovereignty. This was immediately rejected, and the Italians launched their threatened invasion. Within days, however, the reorganized army under General Papágos had not only pushed the invaders back to the Albanian border but counterattacked across it, capturing the principal towns of the region, many with large Greek populations, by the end of December.

Metaxás died in January 1941, amid growing evidence that Hitler intended to secure his Balkan flank before attacking the Soviet Union. British troops were now dispatched to Greece, but owing to a disastrous misunderstanding, the defensive action against the German invasion was uncoordinated, and resistance crumbled. The Greek and British armies were evacuated first to Crete, and then, following a successful German airborne attack, to Egypt, while the king and the Greek government established themselves in London.

Though the government in exile discouraged acts of resistance out of a justified fear of reprisals (many villages were destroyed and their inhabitants killed), resistance organizations emerged, with the communist party (the KKE [ku ku 'ɛ]) playing a major role out of all proportion to its pre-war influence. The National Liberation

Front (EAM), dominated by the KKE, was formed in September 1941, and began to organize strikes and relief work, most notably during the catastrophic famine of 1941–2 caused by German food requisitioning. EAM then founded a military wing, the National Popular Liberation Army (ELAS, an acronym non-coincidentally homophonous with the name of Greece), and other, non-communist, resistance organizations emerged, most importantly the National Republican Greek League (EDES).

Throughout this period, Britain remained involved through the activities of the Special Operations Executive (SOE), which infiltrated sabotage teams and liaised with the resistance. Such contacts quickly revealed that, despite official British support for the king, the feelings of the Greek people were overwhelmingly republican. By mid-1943 ELAS/EAM controlled large areas of the mainland, bringing much-needed educational and health facilities and attracting widespread support from a population exhausted by the occupation, and convinced of the inability of the old political class to address its needs. The failure of a conference in Cairo called to resolve the question of the country's post-war future only reinforced EAM's claims that the British were determined to re-establish the discredited pre-war constitutional arrangements, and fighting soon broke out between ELAS and EDES, with EAM announcing the formation of the Political Committee of National Liberation (PEEA), a direct challenge to the government in exile.

The immediate crisis was partly defused by the appointment of the anti-communist, but also anti-royalist, Yeóryios Papandréou as Prime Minister, who called a conference in the Lebanon at which the communist representatives agreed to the placing of all guerrilla forces under a future government of national unity. EAM/ ELAS initially repudiated the agreement and was ready to take over in the wake of the German withdrawal, but eventually accepted its terms, almost certainly under orders from Stalin, who had agreed to give the British a free hand.

When the Papandréou government arrived in Greece in October 1944, ELAS and EDES were supposed to disband, but relations between the communists and Papandréou collapsed after the suppression of an EAM demonstration, and ELAS responded by attacking the capital's police stations. The archbishop of Athens was then appointed regent pending a plebiscite on the monarchy, and the replacement of Papandréou, accompanied by the arrival of British reinforcements, led to a ceasefire in January 1945. ELAS again agreed to disband, and the government committed itself both to an amnesty for 'political crimes' and to the purging of collaborators. But the government was unable to prevent a right-wing backlash after the discovery that a number of hostages taken by ELAS had been killed, and the left abstained in protest from the elections of March 1946. Subsequently, the restoration of the monarchy was approved in the plebiscite through a combination of ballot-rigging and the defection of former anti-monarchists who now saw the king as a bulwark against communism. Leftists were again persecuted, and attacks by communist forces, soon to form the Democratic Army, led on to full-scale civil war in the winter of 1946. Britain, no longer able to finance the maintenance of government, passed the responsibility on to the Americans.

The aid supplied through Greece's communist neighbours to the Democratic Army was soon surpassed by American support for the government so that, despite early successes, the odds gradually turned against the communists. By the summer of 1949 the National Army had achieved military superiority and, after a series of fiercely fought battles, the Democratic Army, together with the communist leadership, retreated into Albania and exile. During the civil war 700,000 Greeks had been made homeless and 80,000 had been killed, with dreadful atrocities on both sides. In its aftermath, 20,000 more were convicted of offences against the state, many being sentenced to death. Unsurprisingly, the resulting hatred and bitterness dominated the post-war political scene for decades to come.

16.3 Recovery, the colonels, and the restoration of democracy

Martial law ended in February 1950, but subsequent elections produced a political stalemate and a climate dominated by legislation which banned the communist party and harassed the left. The Americans, increasingly concerned, reduced their financial contribution pending changes in the electoral system, but the elections of 1952 at last produced a period of stability, under a right-wing government, that lasted until 1963. Despite the arrival of fresh refugees from Nasser's revolution in Egypt, much desperately needed reconstruction work was now undertaken, and a return to financial orthodoxy helped to curb inflation just as tourism and migrants' remittances, especially from Germany, began to redress the chronic balance of payments problem.

Greece now became a member of NATO, though relations with its new 'ally' Turkey were quickly soured by problems in British-ruled Cyprus, where violence had broken out in 1955 at the instigation of the National Organization of Cypriot Fighters (EOKA) who sought to exploit the growing desire of the Greek majority on the island (80 per cent of the total) to achieve union with Greece. With the tacit acquiescence of the British government, angered by developments in its colony, tit-for-tat riots were organized in Istanbul (the official name of Constantinople after 1930) against the 100,000 Greeks who remained in the city. Many who survived now cut their losses in the face of growing persecution, and emigrated to Greece. In the short term, however, Greece withdrew from NATO headquarters in Izmir in protest. Disenchantment with NATO and support for the left grew hand-in-hand, so that the new Prime Minister, Konstandínos Karamanlís, became increasingly anxious for a settlement, not only to secure his vote but to appease the Americans who were dismayed by the disarray on NATO's southern flank. The deal that emerged, however, involving Cypriot independence, was widely seen as a betrayal of Greek interests in favour of NATO and the Americans. To bind Greece further to her allies, Karamanlís therefore began negotiations for associate status within the European Economic Community (EEC), as a result of which an agreement came into force in 1962, with full membership anticipated in 1984.

The corrupt conduct of the elections held in the previous year, however, had led to growing resentment of the repression of the left. Matters came to a head with the murder of the left-wing deputy Grigóris Lambrákis in Thessaloniki in 1963. Karamanlís resigned and departed for self-imposed exile in Paris, while new elections were called in which the centre parties, led by Papandréou, were victorious. Important educational reforms were now introduced, including for the first time the establishment of equal rights for 'demotic' Greek, while reconciliation was sought through the relaxation of fiscal policy, the release of political prisoners, and increased trade with the Eastern Bloc.

These moves, however, provoked alarm in business and military circles, and the new king, Konstandínos II, secured Papandréou's resignation by refusing to accede to the dismissal of army and intelligence officers manifestly working against the government. Papandréou's supporters now demanded new elections, while the army drew up contingency plans for intervention should Papandréou be successful. But to everyone's surprise a triumvirate of junior army officers struck first. On 21 April 1967 a successful coup d'état was mounted. Martial law was declared, political parties dissolved, and civil rights suspended. Left-wingers were then rounded up into camps, and a puppet civilian government established.

Despite claims that a communist takeover was imminent, it is clear that the coup was primarily motivated by fear of a purge of the far right in the event of a Papandréou victory. The king acquiesced in the dictatorship, and even accepted the 'retirement' of royalist officers, but when surviving loyalists attempted an unsuccessful counter-coup, he went into exile in Rome and all pretence of civilian government was abandoned. Yeóryios Papadópoulos, the regime's strong man, now became Prime Minister, gradually assuming control of all areas of policy, and dismissing anyone whose loyalty was in doubt. Papandréou's educational reforms were also reversed, and the regime re-established the teaching and use of *katharévousa*. Glaring inequalities of income soon opened up, and in order to keep Greece's foreign investors and over-mighty shipowners sweet, the Colonels agreed to a series of economically disastrous arrangements.

Resentment grew rapidly in response to the Colonels' manifest incompetence, though the secret police ruthlessly suppressed efforts at organized resistance. But despite mounting allegations of torture and Greece's enforced withdrawal from the Council of Europe, the regime's commitment to NATO ensured continued American support. The Colonels' prestige, however, suffered a mortal blow when some 10,000 troops, secretly infiltrated into Cyprus, had to be withdrawn under American pressure after a series of guerrilla raids against Turkish villages. By 1973 the price was also being paid for the junta's economic failings, with inflation running at 30 per cent and rising. Student protests, naval mutinies and other manifestations of discontent followed, to which Papadópoulos responded by blaming the exiled king for rabble-rousing and appointing himself the president of a 'parliamentary republic'. Despite the promise of fair elections in the future, there were increasingly violent clashes between students and the police, and university buildings were occupied in Athens and other major cities. Papadópoulos replied by sending in the tanks, only to find himself deposed almost at once by a fresh coup mounted by officers fearful of his planned 'electoral adventure'. Power now passed into the hands of Dimítrios Ioannídis, the sinister commander of the military police.

The new regime proved to be even more incompetent than its predecessor, and its demise was assured after a further Cyprus fiasco. The Cypriot President,

Archbishop Makários, had accused the Greek government of seeking to destroy the state by supporting the activities of the recently revived EOKA. The Cyprus National Guard, led by officers from the mainland and operating under orders from Athens, immediately launched a coup, abetted by the Greek army contingent on the island. Makários escaped, and an EOKA thug was installed as president. Turkey responded by unilaterally exercising its right of intervention as one of the guarantors of the Cypriot state, and landed troops at Kyrenia. Ioannídis ordered a Greek mobilization, but the army refused to obey, and the dictatorship collapsed when a powerful section of the army issued an ultimatum demanding a return to civilian government. Karamanlís was then invited to supervise the return to democracy.

He was at once plunged into a fresh crisis in Cyprus, where the breakdown of peace talks led to a Turkish advance and the seizing of some 40 per cent of the island. Many thousands of Greeks were forced to flee south and anti-NATO feelings ran high, since the Americans, already seen as the prime backers of the junta, were now suspected of favouring Turkey. Karamanlís responded by withdrawing from the NATO command structure and threatening the future of the American bases in Greece. Though the resulting tension made it impossible to purge the army or deal decisively with those responsible for the coup, the ringleaders were at least banished and their appointees sacked, while growing demands for 'dejuntification' led to the release of political prisoners and the reinstatement of those unfairly dismissed from their jobs.

Karamanlís now argued that the country's economic, political, and foreign-policy problems could only be tackled by a properly elected government, though his haste in calling elections was widely criticized, not least because it gave no time for opposition parties to reorganize and allowed him to capitalize on his own prestige as the restorer of democracy. At this time, the left favoured a non-aligned foreign policy and opposed the restoration of the monarchy, while the centre and right wanted stronger ties with Europe within the EEC and NATO; only the far right espoused the king's return. The result was a massive victory for Karamanlís, and in a subsequent referendum, a decisive 69 per cent of the electorate opposed the king's return.

Despite his achievements, no fewer than four attempted coups were foiled within the first six months of Karamanlís's return, though he eventually succeeded in establishing his authority. Trials of the leaders of the 1967 coup and of their army of torturers now began in earnest. Papadópoulos and his co-conspirators were sentenced to death, though the sentences were commuted to life imprisonment, while Ioannídis and others also received life sentences.

Constitutional changes also followed, designed to produce a stronger decision-making process that would reduce the likelihood of any recurrence of the circumstances that had led to the 1967 coup. Fiscal orthodoxy also did something to restore the country's financial position, though the world-wide energy crisis of the early 1970s and rising unemployment in Germany led to falls both in gross domestic product and overseas remittances. Greece's shipowners were nonetheless constrained to make a more realistic contribution to the treasury, and some of the Colonels' more disastrous foreign investment schemes were renegotiated.

Though significant welfare reforms were also introduced, especially in education, the country's massive commitment to defence remained a major brake on government spending. This was justified not only by the festering Cyprus problem but also by other periodic manifestations of Turkish hostility.

Karamanlís's initial response to these difficulties was to seek better relations with his Balkan neighbours, partly to build up support against Turkey but also (prophetically) out of concern about the future of Yugoslavia. Still more importantly, he sought to accelerate Greece's accession to full membership of the European Community (EC). In the long term, this offered the prospect of a significant improvement in Greece's economic fortunes, but in the shorter term it was hoped that membership would help to compensate for poor relations with the USA and difficulties within NATO, while simultaneously cementing democracy in place by offering protection against fresh military intervention and the threat of Turkish attack.

Arguing once more that the issues facing the country required a fresh mandate, Karamanlís called elections for November 1977. His conservative New Democracy party reiterated its commitment to the EC and NATO, and pointed to the success of its free enterprise policies and educational reforms, in particular the raising of the school leaving age and the final abandonment of *katharévousa* as the official language, a move that terminated the institutionalization of diglossia and opened the way for a final resolution of the language question that had bedevilled the cultural, political, and educational development of the nation. By contrast Andréas Papandréou's socialist PASOK party advocated the decentralization of power, withdrawal from NATO, and rejection of the government's drive for membership of the EC, organizations which it saw as forcing Greece into the role of capitalist pawn. In the event, Karamanlís retained a majority despite an impressive PASOK performance.

In 1980 Karamanlís resigned as Prime Minister to become President, and the following year Greece became a full member of the EC (subsequently the EU), an event ironically coinciding with the election of Papandréou as Greece's first socialist Prime Minister. Happily, the army stayed in its bases, and Papandréou's aggressive election rhetoric was tempered by the realities of office. In 1983 a five-year defence and economic cooperation agreement was signed with the United States, and EC membership brought significant benefits for Greek agriculture and investment in the country's infrastructure, both of which did much to allay earlier fears. Papandréou was accordingly re-elected in 1985, and steps were then taken to improve relations with Turkey, though these remained, and still remain, delicate.

But the initial optimism of the left that a PASOK government would bring integrity and reform was eventually superseded by a weary recognition that the power of governments is limited (especially in a country where state institutions remain weak and a 'black' economy flourishes), and that the behaviour of even socialist ministers is subject to the frailties of human nature. The abandonment of tight financial policies had already led to renewed economic difficulties, and accusations of bribery, corruption, and illegal wiretapping proliferated. Growing disappointment led to Papandréou's defeat in the elections of 1989, and various criminal charges followed. After a series of indecisive elections, New Democracy was then returned to power under the veteran Konstandínos Mitsotákis, with a mandate to restore financial order and curb inflation. But the hardship created by New Democracy's economic measures, together with disillusionment at the handling of the crisis following the break-up of Yugoslavia, led to the fall of Mitsotákis's administration and the election in 1993 of a new PASOK government under the ageing Papandréou. PASOK remains in power at the time of writing (September 1996), under the leadership of Kóstas Simítis after Papandréou's reluctant retirement and subsequent death. The Cyprus question remains unresolved, the political situation along the northern frontier remains tense, and there have been renewed problems with Turkey in the Aegean. (See Clogg (1986, 1992) for a full account of the central issues of modern Greek history.)

Chapter 17

The 'language question' and its resolution

17.1 Koraís

A key issue in the early nineteenth century was whether spoken Greek could provide the basis for a written language of law, administration, and education if and
when power passed into Greek hands. As noted earlier, many from the Ionian
islands and the diaspora were optimistic; a demoticizing style was already in limited use, and this could be extended, while the spoken dialects would gradually be
assimilated to the developing standard as education took its course. But for the
traditionally minded, who emphasized what they perceived as the expressive limitations and fundamental disunity of the spoken dialects, it was unthinkable that a
national language should fail to continue the tradition inherited from ancient Greece
and Byzantium.

Both parties were satirized by D. K. Vyzándios in his play *Babel*, published in
1836. The cast comprises an archaizing pedant, an Albanian with a limited command of Greek, and speakers of five different local dialects. This group, having met
in Nafplio on the day when news arrives of the Turkish defeat at Navarino (1827),
attempts to celebrate the success of the Greek revolution, but mutual misunderstanding leads to a fight, incarceration, and still further mishaps. It is, of course,
significant that the dialect speakers are barely literate, and come with only one
exception from outside the kingdom, while the pedant is wholly uncompromising.
Though funny, the play, rather like the archaizers, exaggerates the difficulties; the
local dialects of the Peloponnese were not radically different from educated speech
in phonology and morphology, and 'normal' written Greek was still far from being
an attempt to replicate the ancient language.

The central figure in the development of the language debate in the early nineteenth century, however, was the expatriate doctor-cum-classicist Adamándios Koraís
(1748–1833), who was born in Smyrna, but spent much of his life in Paris. Beaton
(1994: 301 ff.) has identified three key principles underlying his thinking on the
language issue:

(1) (a) That national self-determination depended on re-accessing the treasures of
the ancient language.

    (b) That a modern written language must comply with the grammar of the con-
temporary spoken language, which he regarded as an inalienable possession.

    (c) That these two proposals could be reconciled through a pragmatic pro-
gramme of 'correcting' elements in the spoken language which separated
it most conspicuously from its ancient source.

A major part of this process was to involve the 'restoration' of the orthography and the replacement of foreign loans with Greek equivalents, but Koraís also saw the need for enrichment of the lexicon, and advocated the reintroduction of ancient words, either by direct borrowing or through calquing, usually (given Koraís's base in Paris) on the model of French.

Thus, unlike certain members of the élite in the Ottoman territories, such as Neófytos Doúkas (*c.* 1760–1845) and Konstandínos Oikonómos (1780–1857), Koraís was not an out-and-out archaizer. He had no doubt that their ultra-conservative programme for a return to ancient Greek, based on a view of the modern language as a symbol of national servitude, was hopelessly out of touch with reality. It is therefore deeply ironic that his pragmatic proposals should have been overtaken by the zeal of later generations of archaizers, and that he himself came to be thought of as the founding father of *katharévousa*. His ideas had much in common with those of the 'progressive' Moisiódax (15.2), and his insistence on the identity of language and nation reveals an outlook shared by many demoticists.

The following extract from the beginning of his *Autobiography* gives an impression of the kind of 'corrected' style which he had in mind:

(2) *Η μήτηρ μου έλαβεν ελευθερωτέραν ανατροφήν, διότι ευτύχησε να έχη*
πατέρα Αδαμάντιον τον Ρύσιον, τον σοφώτατον εκείνου του καιρού εις
την ελληνικήν φιλολογίαν άνδρα, όστις απέθανεν εν έτος (1747) προ της
γεννήσεως μου. Αυτός εχρημάτισεν, έτι νέος ων, διδάσκαλος της ελληνικής
φιλολογίας εις Χίον· μετά ταύτα ήλθεν εις Σμύρνην, όπου ενυμφεύθη χήραν
τινά Αγκυρανήν. Ούτος μη γεννήσας αρσενικόν, επαρηγόρησε την αποτυχίαν
του, σπουδάσας να αναθρέψη ως υιούς τας τέσσαρας θυγατέρας του ...

Koraís (1964), ed. Valétas

[i 'mitir mu 'elaven elefθero'teran anatro'fin, ði'oti ef'tiçise
The mother of-me took   free-er   upbringing, because she-had-the-good-fortune

na 'eçi   pa'tera aða'mandion ton 'rision, ton so'fotaton e'ķinu tu ķe'ru is
that she-have father Adamándios the Rysios, the wisest   of-that the time in

tin elini'ķin filolo'jian 'andra, 'ostis a'peθanen en 'etos (1747) pro tiz
the Greek   'philology' man, who died   one year (1747) before the

je'niseoz mu. af'tos exri'matisen, 'eti 'neos on, ði'ðaskalos tis   elini'kis
birth   of-me. He served,   still young being, (as a)teacher of-the Greek

filolo'jias is 'çion; me'ta 'tafta 'ilθen iz 'zmirnin, 'opu enim'fefθi 'çiran
'philology' in Khíos; after this   he-came to Smyrna, where he-married   widow

di'na aŋgira'nin. 'utos mi je'nisas   arseni'kon, epari'ɣorise tin apoti'çian
a   from-Ankara. He   not having-fathered male (child), consoled   the failure

du,   spu'ðasas   na ana'θrepsi os i'jus tas 'tesaras θiɣa'teras tu.]
of-him, having-become-eager that he-bring-up as sons the four   daughters of-him.

'My mother received a more liberal upbringing because she was lucky enough to have as her father Adamándios Rysios, the most learned man of that era in Greek literature, who died (1747) one year before I was born. While still a young man he served as a teacher of Greek literature on Khíos; after that he came to Smyrna where he married a

widow from Ankara. But when he did not father a male child he consoled himself in
his failure by his eager resolve to bring up his four daughters as sons . . .'

With the exceptions of the lengthy hyperbaton (τον . . . άνδρα [ton . . . 'andra]) and
the inflected participles (γεννήσας [je'nisas] and σπουδάσας [spu'ðasas]), most of
the syntactic structure corresponds to that of the (educated) spoken Greek of its
time, while the remaining discrepancies involve little more than item-for-item substitutions (e.g. διότι [ði'oti] for γιατί [ja'ti], όστις ['ostis] for που [pu], προ [pro]
for πριν από [prin a'po], έτι ['eti] for ακόμα [a'koma], etc.). Thus Koraís avoids
the reintroduction of archaisms like infinitives and datives, which had no place in
the normal spoken language, and confined his 'corrections' to the reintroduction of
ancient lexical items and the reinstatement of ancient orthography and morphosyntax
in forms and structures that were actually in use. Thus noun and verb morphology
is mostly ancient, but compound verbs display their augment externally, because the relevant compositional process was not a part of the living language (cf.
ε-παρηγόρησε [epari'yorise]). Similarly, learned prepositions are substituted for
the popular counterparts, and these are used with their ancient cases (e.g. προ
[pro] + genitive) except where this would involve an 'artificial' revival (thus εις [is]
+ accusative is preferred to ancient εν [en] + dative, and με [me] + accusative is
retained in preference to the bare dative to mark the instrumental).

Koraís's 'middle way' provoked opposition from traditionalists and advocates of
the spoken language, each of whom, for different reasons, found his proposals
'artificial'. Among the former, the name of Neófytos Doúkas has already been mentioned as one who objected in principle to any elements of spoken Greek that
Koraís wished to retain. A less extreme case was made by the talented civil servant
Panayótis Kodrikás (1762–1827) who, like Koraís himself, spent much of his life
in Paris. Though he tacitly agreed with many of Koraís's objectives, he felt unable to support what he saw as arbitrary prescription, arguing that a better middle
way already existed in the form of 'the style of the Great Church' (Daskalákis
(1966: 503)), i.e. a 'higher' administrative style that continued, in updated form,
its Byzantine predecessor (see 10.7). As an example of the often trivial differences involved, Browning (1983: 102) notes that where Koraís opted merely to
'correct' ψάρι ['psari] 'fish', to οψάριον [o'psarion], Kodrikás advocated the substitution of ancient ιχθύς [ix'θis]).

Obviously, this variety shared the 'artificiality' of being neither ancient nor
modern Greek, though Kodrikás could at least point in his defence to a body of
existing writing. But it is again striking that, although Koraís and Kodrikás presented themselves as rivals, their 'natural' written styles, used when defending
rather than exemplifying their positions, are all but indistinguishable. In reality,
it seems that much of the hostility derived from the clash of perspectives between
the Orthodox/Ottoman establishment on the one hand and the liberal/republican
diaspora on the other; see Beaton (1994: 330–1), from whom the extracts in (3)
are taken, the first published in 1804, the second in 1818:

(3) (a) *Η γλώσσα είναι το εργαλείον, με το οποίον η ψυχή πλάττει πρώτον
        ενδιαθέτως, έπειτα προφέρει τους λογισμούς της. Όταν το εργαλείον*

εἶναι ἀνακόνητον, ιωμένον, ἡ κακά κατασκευασμένον, ατελές εξ ανάγκης
μένει και το έργον του τεχνίτου.   Koraís (1964: A850), ed. Valétas

[i 'ɣlosa 'ine to erɣa'lion, me to o'pion i   psi'çi 'plati 'proton
The language is   the tool,   with the which the soul   shapes first

enðia'θetos, 'epita pro'feri tus lojiz'mus tis. 'otan to erɣa'lion 'ine
mentally   then   utters   the thoughts of-it. When the tool   is

ana'koniton, io'menon, i ka'ka katasķevaz'menon, ate'les eks a'naŋgis
blunt,   rusty,   or badly made,   imperfect from necessity

'meni ķe to 'erɣon tu   tex'nitu.]
remains also the work   of-the craftsman.

'Language is the tool with which the soul first shapes in the mind, and then utters
its thoughts. When the tool is blunt, rusty, or badly made, the work of the craftsman
also necessarily remains imperfect.'

(b) *Η διάλεκτος προς τον άνθρωπον είναι το υλικόν όργανον, δι' ου η άϋλος
δύναμις του ενδιαθέτου λόγου υπόστασιν, ως ειπείν, προσλαμβάνουσα
υλικήν, και σχήμα, και μορφήν οργανικήν, συνθέτει τον προφορικόν
λόγον, δι' ου ο άνθρωπος ... ενδιαθέτως εξηγεί τας εννοίας του ...*
Kodrikás: text in Daskalákis (1966: 485–6)

[i ði'alektos pros ton 'anθropon 'ine to ili'kon 'orɣanon, ði   u   i
The language   to   the man   is   the material instrument through which the

'ailos   'ðinamis tu   enðia'θetu 'loɣu i'postasin, os i'pin,
insubstantial force   of-the in-the-mind utterance [existence,   so to-speak,

prozlam'vanusa ili'ķin, ķe 'sçima, ķe mor'fin orɣani'kin, sin'θeti tom
assuming   material, and shape, and form   organic,]   composes the

brofori'kon 'loɣon, ði   u   o 'anθropos ... enðia'θetos
spoken   utterance, through which [i.e. *language*] the man ...   internally

eksi'ji tas e'nias tu ...]
explains the ideas   of-him ...

'Language is to man the material instrument through which the insubstantial force
of an utterance conceived in the mind composes a spoken utterance by assuming,
as it were, a material existence, a shape and organic form; through this, man ...
internally elucidates his ideas ...'

The most one can say is that the second is a little more conservative in its archaizing
substitutions than the first (note, for example, the modern adverb κακά [ka'ka], or
the relative το οποίον [to o'pion] in (3)(a), versus the traditional adverb ενδιαθέτως
[enðia'θetos] and the ancient relative in δι' ου [ði u] 'through which' in (3)(b)).

It was unfortunate for Kodrikás that by the time of the revolution 'the style of
the Great Church' was firmly identified with the reactionary political attitudes of
the Constantinopolitan élite. In the context of the rampant nationalism and classical
revivalism of the independent kingdom, his conservative compromise, reflecting
the official language used in the early nineteenth century, was soon overwhelmed

by the upsurge of patriotic archaism that also engulfed the more progressive compromise proposed by Koraís (see 17.3).

17.2   The roots of demoticism: Solomós and the Ionian islands

Koraís was also attacked from the other direction, and brief mention may be made here of the comedy *Korakístika*, published in Vienna in 1813 by Iákovos Rízos Neroulós (1778–1849). The title (literally 'ravens' language') originally denoted a children's argot, but has now come to mean simply 'jargon' or 'gibberish'. In this particular context, however, it also puns on the name Koraís, and the work seeks to expose, via fanciful extensions, the supposedly preposterous results of applying his prescriptions. Accordingly, we find amongst the *dramatis personae* an enthusiastic 'correctionist' who is made to choke when he attempts to order a plate of coleslaw by uttering the absurd ελαδιοξιδιολατολαχανοκαρύκευμα [elaðioksiðiolatolaxanoka'rikevma].

The principal 'popularizing' opposition to Koraís, however, came from poets working outside the Phanariot sphere of influence, who felt that artistic integrity and linguistic artificiality were incompatible. Given that education rather than fiction was still seen as the central task of prose writers, it was this poetic revival which first sought to give Greece an identity in terms of its contemporary history and culture; and the emphasis now began to shift away from the idea of a written language based on educated speech towards that of a literary/poetic language based directly on popular speech. This development, in the context of conservative determination to develop ever 'purer' varieties, marks the beginning of the polarization that quickly came to dominate the language debate.

An important pioneer in the demotic movement was the poet and writer Ioánnis Vilarás (1771–1823), whose grammar, entitled *The Romaic Tongue*, was based on the dialect of his native Epirus and published in 1814 in Kérkira (Corfu). The outstanding contribution, however, came from Dionýsios Solomós, now regarded as Greece's 'national poet'. Solomós was born in Zákynthos, the child of an affair between his aristocratic father and a servant girl whom he married on his deathbed. The family came originally from Crete and spoke Italian, the language in which Solomós himself was educated, but he also spoke the local dialect of Greek with his mother, and later, when he had settled in Kérkira, he was inspired by the Greek independence movement and became, with his compatriot Andréas Kálvos (1792–1869), one of the founding fathers of modern Greek poetry.

But where Kálvos used a form of Greek loosely based on Koraís's prescriptions, Solomós was a thoroughgoing demoticist. He later familiarized himself with literature composed in more popular styles (including the Byzantine verse romances, the poetry of the Cretan renaissance, and the work of Vilarás), and he was influenced by the tradition of folk-song, in which he found much inspiration for his efforts to forge a modern perspective on the Greek world.

For the most part, Solomós avoided local dialect forms and Italian loans in his more serious poetry, since he wished to be read by the Greek people as a whole, but the few 'local' features which remain present few problems (see Mackridge (1989: 57–9)). The following stanza from *O Lámbros* (worked on between 1824 and 1826, but never finished) describes a beautiful Easter Day (η ημέρα της Λαμπρής [i 'mera tis lam'bris]) in terms that contrast sharply with the predicament of the brave but selfish Lámbros, who, in his determination to be 'free', has steadfastly refused to marry María, the mother of his children. When Ali Pasha of Ioánnina executes María's brother, Lámbros sets off to take his revenge, but on his way meets and seduces a girl who turns out to be his own daughter, placed long ago in an orphanage. The girl commits suicide, and when Lámbros returns to confess to María, he finds himself excluded from the Easter celebrations. The metre is ottava rima, eight eleven-syllable iambic lines rhymed ABABABCC:

(4) *XXI: Η ΗΜΕΡΑ ΤΗΣ ΛΑΜΠΡΗΣ*

1

Καθαρώτατον ήλιο επρομηνούσε
της αυγής το δροσάτο ύστερο αστέρι,
σύγνεφο, καταχνιά, δεν απερνούσε
τ' ουρανού σε κανένα από τα μέρη·
και από 'κεί κινημένο αργοφυσούσε
τόσο γλυκά στο πρόσωπο τ' αέρι,
που λες και λέει μες της καρδιάς τα φύλλα·
γλυκειά η ζωή και ο θάνατος μαυρίλα.

Text in Polítis (1948/1986[5])

[kaθa'rotaton 'iʎoᴗ epromi'nuse /tis   av'jis to ðro'satoᴗ'isteroᴗ a'steri,/
Clearest   sun   was-heralding of-the dawn   the cool   last   star,

'siɣnefo, kata'xnja, den aper'nuse/ t   ura'nu se ka'nen a'po ta 'meri;/ kj
cloud,   mist   not was-crossing of-the heaven in any   from the parts;   and

apo 'ḳi ḳini'menoᴗ arɣofi'suse /   'toso ɣli'ka sto 'prosopo t a'eri,/ pu
from there moved   was-slowly-blowing so   sweetly in-the face   the breeze, that

les   ḳe lei   mes tis   karð'jas ta 'fila;/ ɣli'kjaᴗ i zo'i kj o
you-say and it-speaks within of-the heart   the leaves; sweet   the life and the

'θanatos mav'rila.]
death   blackness.

'The last cool star of dawn was heralding purest sun; in no quarter of the sky did cloud or mist pass over; and rising there, the gentle breeze began to blow so sweetly in their faces that you would say it was speaking into the leaves of the heart: "life is sweet, and death is darkness".'

This is sophisticated writing of a high order, but almost wholly demotic in its language if we abstract away from the marked word order (note particularly the pre-head genitives and 'delayed' subjects).

In the present context, however, the most important of Solomós's works is his unfinished *Dialogue*, written in 1824–5 but not published till 1859 when the author had already been dead for two years. It constitutes one of the earliest defences of the use of the ordinary spoken language for writing, and stands in sharp contrast to the views of both traditionalists and Koraís. The dialogue in question (there is a short draft as well as a full-length version) is between 'a poet', 'a friend', and 'a pedant'. The poet argues that 'the common dialect' of the Phanariots is the language of those who served the Turks, and has no place in an independent Greece. Koraís's proposals are also dismissed because the language they attempt to define is no one's native tongue, and the poet instead appeals to the prestige of written vernaculars in the west, and though he fully accepts the need for lexical development, it is suggested that new terminology will have to evolve by natural processes rather than by arbitrary selection from a dead language.

17.3   The rise of *katharévousa*

In the short term, however, Solomós and his followers, based in the Ionian islands, remained 'outsiders'. In the capital, the 'Old Athenian School', whose principal figures were Aléxandros (1803–63) and Panayótis (1806–68) Soútsos, and Aléxandros Rízos Rangavís (1809–92), sought to boost the prestige of 'standard' written Greek by trying to adapt it to the needs of verse composition. The earliest fictional prose was also widely composed in this style, though the Ionian islands were again the exception.

Despite these successes, however, the principal disputes of the period were between different groups of archaizers. In 1853, Panayótis Soútsos published a book condemning 'solecisms' in the work of other writers, and argued that the problem of correct usage could be resolved only by making the written language conform more closely to ancient Greek. In his view, the poor quality of much contemporary writing derived directly from the arbitrary mixture of ancient and modern grammar embodied in Koraís's 'inadequate compromise'.

This marked the beginning of what soon developed into an accelerating flight from the living language. Dissatisfaction with Koraís's proposals peaked, first in the 1850s with Soútsos's proposals, and again in the 1880s, by which time the terms *demotic* and *katharévousa* were becoming established as the names for the 'uncorrected' spoken language (including its use in writing) and the 'corrected' written language respectively. Throughout this period 'progress' was almost universally equated with greater archaism, and by the early 1880s there were once again people prepared to argue for the 'ideal' of ancient Greek perfection.

The core problem was clear enough: for as long as the product of correction remained a compromise between ancient and modern Greek, the objections levelled against Koraís's proposals could just as easily be levelled against any others. There could be no 'standard' to which appeal might be made when the 'rules' conformed neither to the intuitions of Greeks as native speakers nor to the practice of writers in any earlier period. Fresh criticism therefore served only to exacerbate the very linguistic uncertainty it sought to eliminate.

17.4   Reaction: Psykháris and the demoticist programme

In 1884, Dimítrios Vernardákis, professor of History and Philology at the University of Athens, proposed a return to the more realistic framework of Koraís (only to be forced to resign). Still more radically, the prose writer and satirist Emanouíl Roídis (1836–1904), an accomplished stylist in *katharévousa*, now used his skills in the archaizing language to press the cause of spoken Greek (*The Idols* (1893)). In this context of incipient doubt about the viability of *katharévousa*, the publication in 1888 of *My Journey* by Jean Psykháris (1824–1929) proved to be of critical importance. (Though born in Odessa and educated in Constantinople, Psykháris settled in Paris to pursue an academic career, and claimed to feel comfortable only with the French version of his Christian name.)

The book is a novel-cum-travelogue recounting a journey made in 1886 from Paris to Constantinople, Khíos, and Athens, which exploits the author's horrified reaction to the prevailing linguistic climate of the Greek capital as a pretext for the inclusion of a passionate defence of the spoken language as a medium for writing Greek. Its language is a 'regularized demotic' devised by Psykháris himself, and the text introduces a new political dimension to the language question by adapting conservative rhetoric to the demoticist cause, and explicitly linking the issue to the survival and future prosperity of Greece. Just as the army was fighting to free the Greeks still living under Ottoman domination, so demotic was to be the means of liberating them from linguistic oppression.

Particularly offensive to Psykháris were many of the French-based calques (not only individual words like πραγματοποιώ [praɣmatopi'o] 'réaliser', and ψυχραιμία [psixre'mia] 'sang-froid', but also clichéd phraseology like εξασκώ επιρροήν [eksas'ko epiro'in] 'exercer une influence') and new but ancient-looking words created by analogy with existing formations that had flooded into the purist language. His objection was not, of course, to neologism *per se*, since he followed much the same practice when words were lacking in demotic, and many useful creations have survived in standard modern Greek: commonplace examples include εγκυκλοπαιδεία [eŋgiklope'ðia] 'encyclopaedia', οξύγονο [o'ksiɣono] 'oxygen', the names of new sciences and their practitioners (e.g. γλωσσολογία [ɣlosolo'jia]/γλωσσολόγος [ɣloso'loɣos] 'linguistics/linguist'), πανεπιστήμιο(ν) [panepi'stimio(n)] 'university', ενδιαφέρον [enðia'feron] 'interest', etc. His real target was the systematic replacement of established vocabulary with pompous compounds whenever the words in question, many of which were loans from Turkish, displayed formal properties incompatible with the structure of *katharévousa*. The more ludicrous of such items, satirized in Vyzándios's *Babel* by the example of νηφοκοκκόζυμον [nifo+ko'ko+zimon] 'sober+berry+brew', for καφές [ka'fes] 'coffee', have died a well-deserved death. Others, however, have also passed successfully into the standard modern language, sometimes with formal adaptation, and often as alternatives to the 'popular' terms. Examples include αδιέξοδον [a+ði'eks+oðon], lit. 'not+through-and-out+road', i.e. 'cul-de-sac/blind alley', for τυφλοσόκακο [tiflo+'sokako], lit. 'blind alley' (a compound of Greek and Turkish elements, now obsolete), and χρηματοκιβώτιον [xrimato+ki̧'votion], lit.

'money+chest', i.e. 'safe', alongside κάσ(σ)α ['kasa], an Italian loanword. Where both terms survive, the element taken from *katharévousa* often belongs to a more formal register, though in some cases it has acquired the status of the neutral term, with the 'popular' equivalent being thought old-fashioned or sub-standard (e.g. διαβατήριο(ν) [ðja+va+'tirio(n)], lit. 'through+go+instrument', i.e. 'passport', versus πασαπόρτι [pasa'porti]).

But Psykháris was first and foremost a linguist, and a novel perspective was brought to bear on the language question through the application of the theoretical framework developed by the *Junggrammatiker* in Germany and taught in Paris, prior to his move to Geneva, by Ferdinand de Saussure (see Philippáki-Warburton (1988)). While the Neogrammarians are best known for formulating the principle that sound change is exceptionless, their work also led to a growing understanding of synchronic structure and to an emphasis on the internal coherence of languages. By these criteria, *katharévousa* was not a 'real' language; its failure to change other than by arbitrary say-so was proof of its artificial status, and its lack of internal coherence precluded scientific analysis. Psykháris instead argued that demotic was the 'real' descendant of classical Greek, the product of rule-governed change rather than 'decay', and the living embodiment of its ancient predecessor.

But the new emphasis on consistency also led Psykháris to 'systematize' demotic, and to adapt elements from ancient Greek to his own 'rules'. Thus where the archaizers antiqued the modern, he modernized the antique, and many of his proposals were as arbitrarily prescriptive and 'artificial' as those of his opponents. It could therefore be fairly argued that his written demotic employed forms which no one used, and this opening quickly spawned a mythology of alleged hyperdemoticisms among the apologists of archaism.

The central plank of Psykháris's demoticism was that the written language had to be based on the educated speech of Athens and Constantinople, the principal centres of Greek culture, and he had no doubt that it was for the Ionian islands, despite the contribution of their writers to the demoticist cause, to compromise with the practice of the kingdom. It is important to note, however, that significant changes were made between the first edition of *My Journey* in 1888 and the second in 1905. Psykháris took great pride in his Constantinopolitan connections, and the language of his youth at first took precedence, but by the time of the second edition, his conception of demotic had changed in the light of criticism and his growing awareness of the importance of the developing standard in the new capital (see Mackridge (1988), on which the following discussion largely depends).

Syntactic Constantinopolitanisms of the first edition, largely eliminated from the second, include:

(5) (a) The use of the accusative rather than the genitive for the indirect object.
    (b) The use of που [pu] as a complementizer (= 'that') in contexts where the standard language would employ πως [pos] or ότι ['oti]; in standard modern Greek που [pu] is used only for 'factive' complements (cf. Khristídis (1985), Roússou (1994)).

Many features of Constantinopolitan verb morphology were similarly revised, including:

(6) (a) Durative stems in -φτ- [-ft-] of verbs which in ancient Greek had -ππ-
        [-pt-] but in standard modern Greek have the remodelled -β- [-v-]:
        κόφτ-ω ['kofto] 'cut', κρύφτ-ω ['krifto] 'hide'.

    (b) Durative stems in -χτ- [-xt-] of verbs which in standard modern Greek
        have -χν- [-xn-]: δείχτ-ω ['ðixto] 'show', σπρώχτ-ω ['sproxto] 'push'.

    (c) Aorist stems of contract verbs in -αω ['ao] in -ηξ- [iks] rather than standard
        -ησ- [is]: ρωτήξ-ω [ro'tikso] 'ask', ζητήξ-ω [zi'tikso] 'seek'.

Many changes in terminations, however, were motivated by Psykháris's new commitment to the avoidance of final -ν [n] except in genitive plurals and masculine/feminine accusative singular articles and clitic pronouns. The following are worth noting:

(7) (a) In the first edition 3pl. presents end in -ουνε [-une] if the next word begins
        with a continuant (which would require elision of final -ν [-n]), otherwise
        in -ουν [-un]. In the second edition -ουνε [-une] is used without exception;
        similarly 3pl. past tenses in -αν [-an] > -ανε [-ane]. The more natural usage
        of the first edition was therefore sacrificed in the interests of consistency.

    (b) In the middle/passive paradigm, Psykháris's 'natural' usage, reflecting Constantinopolitan thematic -ου- [-u-] in 1sg. and 1/3pl. forms, was partly
        remodelled in favour of Athenian forms with -ο- [-o-], especially in the
        imperfect, where final -ν [-n] is again avoided by systematic addition of
        final -ε [-e].

But though Psykháris shifted his original bias considerably towards developing Athenian practice, his ultimate aim was still for regularity of formation, and he undoubtedly employed forms and paradigms that reflected the usage of more than one speech community. He also adapted loans from ancient Greek/*katharévousa* to conform to his own 'consistent' phonotactic and morphological rules, and it is perhaps in this area above all that charges of artificiality carry weight, since the standard modern language has proved to be extremely tolerant of 'archaic' characteristics in elements drawn from the learned tradition. 'Corrected' words like συθήκες [si'θikes] 'conditions', σκετικός [sçeti'kos] 'relevant', αρφάβητο [ar'favito] 'alphabet', πομονή [pomo'ni] 'patience', and έχταση ['extasi] 'extension', (adapted from συνθήκαι [sin'θike], σχετικός [sçeti'kos], αλφάβητον [al'faviton], υπομονή [ipomo'ni], and έκτασις ['ektasis]), therefore seem very odd today.

   The failure of many of his proposals reflects the fact that many otherwise sympathetic Greeks felt compelled to rebel at what constituted an affront to a well-developed *Sprachgefühl* shaped in part by an education system committed to *katharévousa*. The ideal of a common language created by an act of individual will was clearly as unattainable for Psykháris as it was for the theorists of archaism, and what has finally emerged in the late twentieth century has come about through more natural processes of compromise between the two traditions (see below).

The following extract from the second edition of *My Journey* gives something of the flavour of Psykháris's later style, which, apart from minor morphological and orthographic ideosyncrasies, is not greatly different from the modern standard:

(8) *Κάποτες μου έρχεται να φωνάξω δυνατά, που όλος ο κόσμος να μ' ακούσῃ*
– 'Μη, μη, μη, μη χαλνάτε τη γλώσσα! Καταστρέφετε την αρχαία και τη
νέα μαζί. Θέλετε γλώσσα που να μοιάζῃ τόντις με την αρχαία, που να είναι
η ίδια γλώσσα; Πάρτε τη γλώσσα του λαού. Θέλετε ξένη γλώσσα; Πάρτε
την καθαρέβουσα· θα δείξῃ σ' όλο τον κόσμο, πως τόντις χάθηκε η αρχαία.
Θέλετε να παίξετε; Θέλετε νοστιμάδες, χωρατάδες και κωμωδίες; Τότες
να γράφετε την καθαρέβουσα. Θέλετε επιστήμη, κόπο και μάθηση; Θέλετε
να πιάσετε σοβαρή δουλειά; Να γράφετε την εθνική μας γλώσσα. Από την
απόφασή σας, θα φανή αν είστε η άντρες η παιδιά.

Psikháris My Journey (1905: 212)

['kapotes mu 'erçete na fo'nakso ðina'ta, pu 'olos o 'kozmos na m
Sometimes to-me it-comes that I-shout aloud, that all the world that me

a'kusi- mi, mi, mi, mi xal'nate ti 'ɣlosa! kata'strefete tin ar'çea ḱe ti
hear – Not, not, not, not ruin(imp.) the language! You-destroy the ancient and the

'nea ma'zi. 'θelete 'ɣlosa pu na 'mjazi 'tondis me tin ar'çea, pu na
modern together. You-want language that may resemble truly with the ancient, that may

'ine i 'iðja 'ɣlosa? 'parte ti 'ɣlosa tu la'u. 'θelete 'kseni 'ɣlosa?
be the same language? Take(imp.) the language of-the people. You-want foreign language?

'parte tiŋ gaθa'revusa; θa 'ðiksi s 'olo toŋ 'gozmo, pos 'tondis
Take(imp.) the *katharévousa*; will it-show to all the world, that truly

'xaθiḱe i ar'çea. 'θelete na 'peksete? 'θelete nosti'maðes, xora'taðes
has-been-lost the ancient. You-want that you-play? You-want funninesses, jokings

ḱe komo'ðies? 'totes na 'ɣrafete tiŋ gaθa'revusa! 'θelete epi'stimi,
and comedies? Then should you-write the *katharévousa*! You-want science,

'kopo ḱe 'maθisi? 'θelete na 'pjasete sova'ri ðu'lja? na 'ɣrafete tin
hard-work and learning? You-want that you-take-on serious work? Should you-write the

eθni'ki maz 'ɣlosa. a'po tin a'pofa'si sas, θa fa'ni an 'iste i
national of-us language. From the decision of-you, will it-appear if you-are either

'andres i pe'ðja.]
men or children.

'Sometimes I have the urge to shout out loud for everyone to hear – do not, do not, do not, do not ruin the language! You are destroying the ancient and the modern tongue alike. Do you want a language to resemble the ancient one in reality, to be the same language? Take the language of the people. Do you want a foreign language? Take *katharévousa*; it will show everyone that the ancient tongue has been truly lost. Do you want to play games? Do you want some fun, a joke, a good laugh? Then write *katharévousa*. Do you want science, hard graft and learning? Do you want to take on some serious work? Then write our national language. Your decision will show whether you are men or children.'

To show how far written practice had become polarized in the latter part of the nineteenth century, however, it will be useful at this point to compare contemporary *katharévousa*. The extract in (9) is taken from the introduction to K. Rangavís's *Julian the Transgressor*, a 'dramatic poem' published in 1877:

(9) *Επείσθημεν ότι, της δοτικής ήδη γενικώς παραδεκτής γενομένης, ακολουθήσει αυτήν ο μέλλων, ο νυν παρά τοις κρείττοσιν εν χρήσει, τούτον το απαρέμφατον, το πολλαχού ανατέλλον, και τα αρνητικά μόρια, ότι δ' αφ' ετέρου ουδέποτε αναβιώσουσιν η ευκτική μετά του αποφωλίου αν, και ο παρακείμενος, πλην αυτού της μετοχής, και υπερσυντελικός ... Το εισαγαγείν πρώτον ήδη εν τη νέα ελληνική ποιήσει το απαρέμφατον, και τόσα έτερα νεωτερίσαι, εστί τόλμημα, και τόλμημα μέγα, αλλ' εις το κοινόν ανατίθεμεν την κρίσιν εάν όλως επετύχομεν.*   K. Rangavís (1877: 28 ff.)

[e'pisθimen   'oti, tiz ðoti'kis 'iði   jeni'kos paraðek'tis
We-have been-persuaded that, the dative   already generally accepted

jeno'menis, akolu'θisi af'tin o 'melon, o ke nin pa'ra tis 'kritosin en
having-become, will-follow it   the future, the even now among the better   in

'xrisi, 'tuton   to apa'remfaton, to pola'xu   ana'telon, ke ta
use,   this (will follow) the infinitive,   the in-many-places rising-up,   and the

arniti'ka 'moria, 'oti ð af e'teru   u'ðepote anavi'osusin i   efkti'ki me'ta
negative particles, that but from other(hand) never   will-revive   the optative with

tu apofo'liu an, ke o para'kimenos, plin af'tu tis meto'çis, ke
the empty   'an', and the perfect,   except of-it the participle, and

ipersindeli'kos ... to isaɣa'jin   'proton 'iði en di nea   ellini'ki 'piisi
pluperfect ...   The introduction (of) first   now in the modern Greek   poetry

to apa'remfaton, ke 'tosa   'etera   neote'rise,   es'ti 'tolmima, ke
the infinitive,   and so-many other-things to-have-innovated, is   bold-act,   and

'tolmima 'meɣa, al is to ki'non ana'tiθemen tiŋ 'grisin   e'an 'olos
bold-act   big,   but to the public we-assign   the judgement if   altogether

epe'tixomen.]
we-have-succeeded.

'We are convinced, now that the dative has become generally accepted, that the future, which is already in use among the better writers, will follow it, and that the infinitive, on the increase in many quarters, will follow this in turn, together with the negative particles, but that the optative on the other hand, with its meaningless (particle) *an*, will never be revived, and that the same applies to the perfect, apart from its participle, and the pluperfect ... The introduction now for the first time in modern Greek poetry of the infinitive alongside so many other innovations is a bold stroke, and a bold stroke of some magnitude, but we leave it to the public to decide whether we have been altogether successful.'

The sentiments speak for themselves; all contact with the real world seems to have been lost. The author, of course, places himself among 'the best writers' by his own use of the dative (e.g. *κρείττοσιν* ['kritosin], which also revives an obsolete comparative), the monolectic classical future (e.g. ακολουθήσει [akolu'θisi], unfortunately homophonous with the aorist subjunctive, a major reason for its demise), and the full array of infinitives (e.g. εισαγαγείν [isaɣa'jin], an ancient 'strong' aorist), together with a host of other long-departed forms and structures, among which the participial genitive absolute (της δοτικής ... γενομένης [tiz ðoti'kis ... jeno'menis]) and the revival of the ancient class of 'athematic' verbs in -μι [mi] (e.g. 'classical' ανα-τίθε-μεν [ana'tiθemen]) stand out.

It should be emphasized, however, that while the literary vanguard was marching backwards into the ancient world, less extreme versions of *katharévousa* continued to be taught in schools and to be used for more practical purposes. Nonetheless, the general drift of the age had its impact even here, with the result that what was taught in school became increasingly remote from what was spoken at home, and received little reinforcement from the majority of parents, themselves often poorly educated. What had once been natural to the old élite, and acceptable to the growing middle class, was much harder to sell to the population as a whole.

17.5 The progress of demoticism

Psykháris's challenge therefore seemed to many, especially in literary and educational circles, to be the harbinger of an inevitable shift in favour of demotic. But it was not at first the exclusiveness of the official language programme which provoked opposition. Indeed, for many, *katharévousa* was a hard-won badge of upward mobility. Furthermore, the earliest advocates of demoticism, long before it became identified with the causes of the political left (see below), came from backgrounds just as privileged as those of their rivals, and objected to *katharévousa* principally on the grounds of its pretentiousness and vulgarity (Mackridge (1990: 41)). Their primary objective was to construct a modern language to express a modern identity based on a vision of Greece as a liberal, European nation, speaking and writing the language which 'expressed its soul' (Tzióvas (1985: 272–5)).

Change did not set in overnight, however, and Psykháris's advocacy of demotic met with vociferous opposition. One of the more reasoned responses came from Yeóryios Khatzidákis (1848–1941), Professor of Linguistics at the university of Athens. Applying what he saw as the dispassionate perspective of the linguist, Khatzidákis insisted that, since different forms of the Greek language had traditionally been felt to be appropriate for speaking and for writing, the demoticists' efforts were fundamentally misguided. If in later times the written language came to resemble the spoken, he would accept it, but it was not for expatriates like Psykháris to meddle with the status quo (Khatzidákis (1901: 296)).

The central problem was that no form of Greek existed to fulfil all the functions of a written language in a modern state, but all theorists behaved as if this were a desirable objective. Ideally, the richness and diversity of the Greek tradition should have led to the emergence of an array of written registers, each stylistically adapted to its purpose, but all bound together by the developing spoken standard and a basic written norm linked to it. This, by and large, is what finally happened, but the artificial terms of the academic debate in the late nineteenth century demanded exclusive choices and internal consistency, attributes as unattainable as they were undesirable.

But against this increasingly acrimonious background, practical steps towards a solution were already being taken by literary writers. As the ideology of archaism became more and more of a barrier to creativity, demotic was adopted even in Athenian circles by the new generation of poets represented by Kostís Palamás (1859–1943). In this same period serious research at last began into the popular literature of the Middle Ages and the tradition of Greek folk-song; and these developments contributed further to the growth of an alternative, but equally patriotic, conception of the roots of the modern Greek nation. By the 1870s, even writers of prose fiction were turning their backs on the archaizing ideal, just as the rhetorical posturing of the movement was approaching its climax. For the first time, the establishment began to feel threatened by the progress of demoticism.

The obvious reason for the shift was that writers could not ignore the fundamental principle that communication is more important than outward form. The idea that use of the ancient language would somehow bring about a rebirth of classical values was therefore rejected by the only groups who could, even in principle, have attempted to deliver such a programme. Thus in reality Psykháris only controversialized an issue that was already being addressed. But with the advent of demoticism as a coherent movement, and the increasingly violent reactions of the establishment, diglossia in its modern sense soon set in, involving not merely the old split between spoken and written Greek, but the use of two distinct written varieties for different purposes in the same community. Thereafter, writers like Palamás and the Nobel laureate Yórgos Seféris (real name Seferiádis, 1900–71), who combined literary activity with a professional career in the first half of the twentieth century, were obliged to operate in two quite distinct linguistic 'worlds'.

17.6 The twentieth century: crisis and resolution

In 1901, the businessman Aléxandros Pállis published in the Athens newspaper *Akrópolis* the first instalments of his translation of the Gospels into a demoticizing style. The capital's university was a major institutional backer of linguistic archaism, and the academic community was outraged by this perceived assault on the sanctity of the divine text and the position of the church. Several days of violent protest by students and professors followed, including attacks on newspaper offices.

Similar troubles attended the demotic production of Aeschylus's *Oresteia* in 1903, and demoticists now began to be accused not only of atheism but also of treason; translations of ancient masterpieces, it was alleged, drove a wedge between ancient and modern Greek, thereby achieving in language what the Bulgarians at that time were trying to accomplish in Macedonia, namely the separation of Greece from its heritage. The campaign of denigration even descended to the level of name-calling, with demoticists referred to as *malliarí* ('hairies') because of their supposedly bohemian appearance and allegedly 'subversive' political views as supporters of a Slavic plot. Such charges gained ground with the later success of the Bolshevik revolution, which served further to identify the cause of demoticism in its opponents' eyes with treachery and the far left.

All of this ignored the fact that the *Oresteia* was incomprehensible to most Greeks in its original form, that demoticism had traditionally identified nation and language (cf. Psykháris's dictum 'language and country are the same' (1905: 23)), and that the attempts then being made to teach *katharévousa* to the Slavophone children of Macedonia were proving hugely unsuccessful.

This increasing antagonism provided the background to the appearance of the periodical *Noumás* (first published in 1903), which was dedicated to the promotion of demotic and soon became the leading literary journal of its era. Shortly after, the 'National Language Society' was founded (1905), which demanded the introduction of demotic into the primary school curriculum in Greece and Macedonia, and had as its ultimate objective the institution of the living language as the official language of the nation.

It was in the pages of *Noumás* that cautious reformers, under the leadership of Palamás, first began to distance themselves from the over-schematic proposals of Psykháris, and to seek to defend themselves against charges of 'hairyism' (with all that that entailed). *Noumás* was also the locus of the debate which followed the appearance of G. Sklirós's book *Our Social Question* (1907), in which it was explicitly argued for the first time that language reform and social reform should go hand-in-hand, and that the demoticist movement should be appealing directly to the people rather than engaging in futile debate with the establishment.

The overt linking of demoticism with socialism by one of its own supporters shifted the ground on which the language question had hitherto been debated. Despite the sometimes extreme rhetoric, both purists and demoticists had previously shared the same objective of developing a national language for a resurgent Greece. Now the demotic camp began to split into those who saw the cause as part of a wider political programme of social reform on the one hand, and more traditional nationalists on the other. As time went on, the latter took an increasingly narrow view of the language question, and eventually came to identify it with the establishing of control over the primary school curriculum.

As a reflection of the progress of demoticism, the first public secondary school for girls was founded in 1908 in the town of Vólos by Aléxandros Delmoúzos, who opted for demotic as the sole medium of instruction. The bishop of Vólos immediately accused him of corrupting the children of the town, and in 1911 he was obliged to close his school and defend himself in court. Though Delmoúzos was acquitted, the fact that this preposterous trial took place at all was an ominous sign of the growing ferocity of establishment reaction.

Despite this initial setback, the 'Educational Society' was founded in 1910, with Delmoúzos as a leading member. Its central objective, as the organ of 'liberal' demoticism, was the reform of primary education, but it also sought to distance itself from Psykháris by lobbying for a 'practical' demotic which made concessions to normal educated usage as influenced by *katharévousa*. But though the Society was careful to avoid overt association with left-wing politics, the links, once introduced, proved hard to shake off, and conservative opponents were not slow to exploit the situation.

Meanwhile, the so-called 'bourgeois revolution' of 1909 had brought Venizélos to power for the first time and led to the framing of a new constitution in 1911, which made explicit mention of an 'official' language:

(10) 'The official language of the State is that in which the polity and the statutes of Greek legislation are drawn up; any interference directed towards the corruption of this language is forbidden.'   Article 107; text in Dimarás (1974: ii. 307)

The language in which the constitution was written was, of course, *katharévousa*, and by implication this was the language referred to in Article 107. The institutionalization of *diglossia* represented a solid victory for the forces of reaction since, despite Venizélos's efforts to take credit for the 'sophistic' language which allegedly opened the way for demotic to become the 'official' language as soon as it was first used in legislation, an amplified version of Article 107 remained in force as late as the Colonels' constitution of 1968, and no attempt was made to draft legislation in demotic until 1977.

Nevertheless, the attitude of the Venizélos government in practice was rather more liberal. Members of the Educational Society were invited to write textbooks in demotic for use in primary schools, presumably on the basis that this concession was not felt to constitute a threat to the dominant position of *katharévousa* elsewhere. At the same time leading members of the Society were appointed to key posts; Dimítris Glínos became General Secretary of the Ministry of Education, and Aléxandros Delmoúzos and Manólis Triandafyllídis, later Professor of Linguistics at the University of Thessaloniki and author of the 'standard' grammar of demotic (yet to be fully superseded), became Chief Supervisors of Primary Education, with the result that demotic finally became the language of instruction in the first four grades (ages 7–12). Despite opposition from supporters of *katharévousa* and Psykháris, who denounced the compromises that had secured this success, the Educational Society's achievement in securing a place for demotic in the curriculum was never to be seriously threatened.

Having been introduced under Venizélos, however, it was inevitable that the reform should come under pressure when he was voted out of power in 1920. And when, in the chaotic aftermath of the disaster of 1922, a fascist dictatorship was established (1925–6), and a national conference of conservative pressure groups called for action against the corrupters of 'religion, language, family, property, morals, national consciousness and the fatherland' (Dimarás (1974: ii. 143–4); Mackridge (1990: 34)), it was all too clear who was going to be blamed for the nation's misfortune.

Triandafyllídis and Delmoúzos were therefore hard-pressed to show that demoticism and communism were not to be identified in principle or in practice, and their difficulties were greatly exacerbated by Glínos's adoption of Marxism and the formal adoption of demotic by the Communist Party of Greece in 1927. Although it might seem natural for the 'party of the people' to address its constituency in the 'popular' language, demoticism in the first quarter of the twentieth century was regarded on the left as a bourgeois/liberal movement, and between its foundation in 1918 and the reform of 1927, the Communist Party followed the general practice of using *katharévousa* as the only serious medium for political discourse.

The shift at this time was in part a response to the intensified politicization of the language issue by the right. But in an age when mass education was becoming a reality, it was also the social divisiveness of diglossia that prompted a new attitude on the part of the left towards the language question. Henceforth, until the final abolition of the official status of *katharévousa* in 1974, the written use of demotic was interpreted as a signal of left-wing sympathies, while the use of more archaic styles was seen as a mark of conservatism, and even of support for the hard right. This unfortunate development was accelerated after the appointment of Triandafyllídis and Delmoúzos to chairs at the University of Thessaloniki (opened in 1926, with demotic as the medium of instruction), when the liberal wing of the Educational Society, believing its objectives to have been achieved, stopped campaigning.

An indication of the growing strength of the links between demoticism and the left is provided by the efforts of the Metaxás dictatorship to break them, as reflected in the commissioning of Triandafyllídis, who was anxious for quite different reasons to distance demotic from communism, to produce a 'state' grammar of demotic as part of a programme of educational reform designed to 'instil discipline', including linguistic discipline, into the Greek people. This could best be achieved, it was believed, through the codification of spoken Greek, which was at last to be invested with the status of a 'real' language, with its own official rule-book. Unfortunately the work was not completed until 1941, when the population was otherwise preoccupied with the business of survival under the harsh conditions of the German occupation.

It should be noted, however, that even this work was as much a normalization as a description of usage, involving the reduction of morphological variety and a minimization of the learned features which had infiltrated educated speech. Where it appealed to precedent, it was to the usage of the folk-songs (themselves dialectally homogenized in standard editions such as that of Polítis) and of earlier demotic literature which preserved an already rustic-seeming 'purity' that was fast becoming a thing of the past in the speech of ordinary urban Greeks. Nevertheless, as the work of the finest Greek linguist of his generation, it represented a landmark achievement and played a vital role in promoting the demoticist cause.

In the short term, however, the traditionalists of the University of Athens seized their opportunity to reassert their authority in matters of language. In the spring of 1942, when large numbers of Athenians were dying daily of starvation, Professor Ioánnis Kakridís was suspended from his duties for republishing in demotic a lecture which he had originally delivered in Thessaloníki in 1936. This apparently extraordinary move becomes comprehensible when one recalls that attempts to undermine *katharévousa* had always been seen in establishment circles as a threat to national sovereignty. The use of demotic under the occupation was therefore interpreted as treachery by those who now linked demoticism not only with the internationalism of the left but also with fascist dictatorship (cf. Metaxás's reforms) and Nazi oppression.

Even though both resistance organizations, the liberal EDES and the communist EAM/ELAS, had declared their support for demotic, it was therefore almost inevitable that the civil war should usher in a reversion to the entrenched positions of the previous generation. But adherence to these positions was already a largely ideological issue, with the old dichotomy looking increasingly anachronistic in the context of the actual linguistic situation that had begun to emerge in the pre-war years and now became established in the period of post-war reconstruction and economic revival.

In 1963 the Liberal Prime Minister Yeóryios Papandréou declared a policy of equal rights for the two written varieties in the education system, while retaining 'official' status for *katharévousa* as the language of the state. This reform led at last to the introduction of Triandafyllídis's grammar into schools. But since this work failed to take into account the cumulative impact of *katharévousa* on the ordinary speech and writing of the educated classes, it prompted a critical response from the educationalist A. G. Tsopanákis, who proposed his own 'compromise' instead (yet another framework based neither on practice nor on precedent).

But in the context of the revived debate, the view at last began to be advanced that the language question was resolving itself (cf. L. Polítis (1966), Vlákhos (1967), and the grammar of 'Common Modern Greek' by Babiniótis and Kóndos (1967)): given time, it was argued, the developing standardization manifest in the speech of the educated classes would come to maturity in its own natural way. This obvious 'solution' had already been adopted by a number of writers in the inter-war years, whose practice had begun to break down the boundaries of officially sanctioned diglossia by moving away from 'rural realism' and country idioms (favoured by earlier demoticists in their pursuit of the 'honest simplicity' that 'urban artifice' was felt to have destroyed), in favour of a style which better reflected the evolving urban standard, with elements taken from educated spoken usage and non-demotic literature. Thus the 'pure' demotic de/prescribed in Triandafyllídis's grammar and later in Tzártzanos's complementary *Syntax* (1946, 1963) already had a dated feel by the time these works appeared (though Triandafyllídis himself was well aware that normal usage was often distinct from the literary practice on which his work was primarily based, cf. Triandafyllídis (1938: 155–8, 607)).

Unfortunately, official recognition of linguistic reality was delayed for a decade by the military dictatorship of 1967–74. In this unpleasant interlude, even the language of primary school textbooks was given a *katharévousa* gloss, and a pamphlet entitled *National Language*, published in 1973 by the Armed Forces Headquarters, revived all the old arguments against demotic, linking it with communism, and reasserting the view that it was a debased and anarchic version of the true national language which alone enjoyed the backing of ancient Greek precedent. The poverty of the argument was as apparent as the bankruptcy of the regime, and after its fall in 1974 Karamanlís's conservative government began to use 'demotic' from the start. At the same time, the political dimension of the language question was finally defused by the legalization of the communist party, while the education act of 1976 determined that the language of instruction in all classes should be 'Modern Greek', the latter being defined as 'the Demotic language shaped by the Greek people and classic national writers as a Panhellenic instrument of expression, codified, without local peculiarities and extremes' (cf. Landsman (1989: 171), Beaton (1994: 326)).

The trends of the post-war period were epitomized in Kóstas Takhtsís's comic novel *The Third Wedding* (1974), in which the speech of the principal characters, two middle-class women, is peppered with the clichés of written officialdom in recognition of the extent to which these had passed into everyday usage (cf. Beaton (1994: 346–7)). The final acceptance of 'Demotic' as the language of education and official business, therefore, was in reality not much more than a belated acceptance of the status quo; but the form of language involved was rather different from both Psykháris's concept of demotic and the language of Triandafyllídis's grammar.

Contemporary writers now exploit the potential of the language quite widely, with styles ranging from a traditional 'rural' demotic to something not far removed from late-nineteenth century *katharévousa* (e.g. in Andréas Embiríkos's posthumous *The Great Eastern* (1990–2)). But the language spoken by the averagely well-educated population of the major cities is accepted as 'standard', and written versions of this are employed for virtually all official and practical purposes. It is the product in part of natural developments in a social and educational context where elements of *katharévousa* had long found an automatic place, in part of the efforts of writers deliberately to circumvent the constraints of diglossia. (For detailed treatments of the history of the language question, see Mackridge (1990), and Beaton (1994: Chapter 6, on which the above is largely based).)

17.7 Standard modern Greek

The term 'standard modern Greek' (SMG) has now largely replaced the earlier 'common modern Greek' as the name of this variety (cf. Mackridge (1985), Holton, Mackridge and Philippaki-Warburton (forthcoming) for clear and comprehensive descriptions). Unlike 'pure' demotic, SMG readily allows the use of features previously thought of as 'learned'. In nominal morphology, for example, we may note:

(11) (a) The use of 2nd declension feminines in -ος [-os]: e.g. η οδ-ός [i o'ðos] 'the road'.

(b) The use of the ancient paradigm of 3rd declension s-stem and u-stem adjectives in -ής ['is] and -ύς [-'is], e.g. συνεχής [sine'çis] 'continuous', ευρύς [ev'ris] 'broad'.

(c) The use of the gen. sg., and especially the plural paradigm, of i-stems e.g. δυνάμ-εως/-εις/-εων [ði'nameos/-is/-eon] 'powers'.

(d) The use of 3rd declension neuters in -ον/gen. -οντος [-on/-ondos], -εν/ gen. -εντος [-en/-endos], and -ός/-ότος (or -ώς/-ώτος) [-'os/-'otos] from ancient participles: e.g. προϊόν [proi'on] 'product'; ενδιαφέρον [enðia'feron] 'interest'; φωνήεν [fo'nien] 'vowel'; γεγονός [jeɣo'nos] 'fact'; καθεστώς [kaθe'stos] 'regime, status quo'.

(e) The use of 3rd declension neuters in -αν/-αντος [-an/-andos]: e.g. σύμπαν ['simban] 'universe'.

(f) The virtually free use of the genitive plural, in contrast to its previously more marginal status in earlier demotic (see, for example, the observations in Thumb (1912: 31, 33).

In the verb-system, the following should be mentioned:

(12) (a) The use of many contract verbs of the -έω [-'eo] type, together with large parts of their ancient paradigm; e.g. ἐπιχειρώ [epiçiro] 'I undertake', προηγούμαι [proi'γume] 'I precede', etc.

(b) The use of learned verbs of the -άω [-'ao] type, sometimes with partial restoration of the ancient paradigm; e.g αντιδρώ [andi'ðro] 'I react', ἐξαρτώμαι [eksar'tome] 'I depend'.

(c) The use of the middle/passive of certain verbs belonging to the ancient athematic paradigm; e.g. ἐπιτίθεμαι [epi'tiθeme] 'I attack', συνίσταμαι [sin'istame] 'I consist (in/of)'.

(d) The use in compound verbs of more ancient stem-forms than in the corresponding simple verbs: e.g. μιλώ [mi'lo] 'I talk' (2sg. μιλάς [mi'las]), beside συν-ομιλώ [sinomi'lo] 'discuss' (2sg. συνομιλείς [sinomi'lis]); διώχνω [ðj'oxno] 'kick out', beside ἐπι-διώκω [epiði'oko] 'aim to get', etc.

(e) The use of much learned morphology: e.g. aorist -ευσα [-efsa] rather than -εψα [-epsa], as in συσσώρευσα [si'sorefsa] 'I accumulated'; internal augments, as in aorist εισ-έ-πραξα [i'sepraksa] from εισπράττω [is'prato] 'I collect, levy'; aorist passives in -θην/-θης/-θη [-θin/-θis/-θi] in place of -θηκα [-θika], etc., as in συν-ε-λήφ-θην [sine'lifθin] 'I was arrested' from συλλαμβάνω [silam'vano]; reduplicated perfect passive participles, as in ἐκ-τε-ταμένος [ekteta'menos] 'extended', from ἐκτείνω [ek'tino]; and so on.

(f) The use of inflected active (-ων/-ουσα/-ον [-on/-usa/-on]) and present passive participles (-όμενος/-η/-ον ['-omenos/-i/-on]), mainly in adjectival functions: e.g. ο προκύπτων τόκος [o pro'ķipton 'tokos] 'the resulting interest', οι εργαζόμενες γυναίκες [i erγa'zomenes ji'nekes] 'working women'.

There is also a large number of phrases, often involving genitive absolutes, datives, and ancient prepositions, that express an idea neatly and have no 'true' demotic equivalent: e.g. Θεού θέλοντος [θe'u 'θelondos] 'God willing'; προκειμένου (να/για) [proķi'menou (na/ja)] 'if it's a question of'; τοις εκατόν [tis eka'ton] 'per cent'; υπόψη [i'popsi] 'in mind/view'; κατευθείαν [katef'θian] 'straight (on)'; εν αντιθέσει προς [en andi'θesi pros] 'as opposed to'; and so on. A few may well represent fossilized survivals in the spoken tradition, but the great majority are clearly taken from *katharévousa*.

Widespread borrowing from the learned language has also introduced elements of learned phonology into SMG, and many of the phonotactic constraints of traditional demotic no longer apply systematically, producing some uncertainty in the pronunciation of particular words. All the following, quite regular in SMG, violate demotic rules in one way or another: ποιητής [pii'tis] 'poet'; εκδρομή [ekðro'mi] 'excursion'; στοιχείο [sti'çio] 'element'; έκταση ['ektasi] 'extension'; εχθρός [ex'θros] 'enemy'; παύση ['pafsi] 'cessation'; συμφωνώ [simfo'no] 'I agree'; ρεύμα ['revma] 'current'. Cf. 11.2 and 11.6, and see Mackridge (1985: 28–31)).

Just before the Second World War, the French linguist André Mirambel analysed the language situation then obtaining in Greece (Mirambel (1937), cf. Browning (1983: 111 ff.)). Although at that time there was in theory a state of diglossia, he found that actual practice, as noted, was more subtly graded. At one extreme stood *katharévousa*, and at the other, the artificial standardizations of demotic ('hairy' language). Between these poles stood:

(13) (a) The normal language of scientific discourse, political debate, and serious news reporting, the so-called 'mixed' variety (μικτή [mi'kti]), which retained much of the basic structure of *katharévousa* but borrowed key modern terms from demotic in unmodified form and avoided the extreme archaism, formulaic phraseology, and more complex grammatical structures of 'pure' *katharévousa*.

(b) The everyday language of the urban middle class (καθομιλουμένη [kaθomilu'meni] 'colloquial (language)'), used also for journalism and much non-fictional writing; it was based on demotic structures supplemented with elements from the learned language, and retained popular and learned forms side by side according to context (e.g. συκώτι [si'koti] = 'liver' in a recipe, but ήπαρ ['ipar] = 'liver' in a medical context, etc.).

(c) The language of the mass of the population (δημοτική [ðimoti'ki]), still little influenced by *katharévousa*, and differentiated by region; this, with varying degrees of normalization, was also the language of most creative literature, though many authors were already moving towards (b) and beyond.

Today's SMG in essence represents a continuation of (b), with the spoken varieties of (c) becoming increasingly assimilated to it. In its written form, it is the natural product of the extension of (b) into areas previously dominated by (a) and *katharévousa* proper, and the resulting incorporation of elements from those sources has had its impact on speech as well. A homogeneous demotic, based on forms of the traditional spoken language unaffected by *katharévousa*, has become more of an 'ideal' construct than ever, and it survives today chiefly among creative writers with a traditional cast of mind. As such, it may perhaps best be seen as a specialized register of SMG.

By contrast, *katharévousa* is virtually extinct, though until very recently it retained a toe-hold in the most conservative quarters, particularly the law, the church, and the armed forces. A passive ability to read it is still widespread among those exposed to it at school, but there is now a real barrier between younger readers and worthwhile older texts (e.g. the work of Aléxandros Papadiamándis (1851–1911)). Its spirit, nonetheless, survives in the continued calquing of words and expressions for new inventions and ideas, while those who know enough of its stylistic traits can still exploit its resources to deflate pomposity or silence a bore. For as long as there are people with the background necessary to comprehend such nuances, it remains a source of stylistic variation within SMG.

This is not to say, however, that debate about the state of the language is over, or that all the problems created by diglossia have yet been overcome. Generations of training are not forgotten overnight, and the clichéd corpulence of *katharévousa* often resurfaces in official forms of SMG. There are, furthermore, those who still lament the absence of a fully stable and standardized written form of Greek, and criticize writers for 'demoticizing' learned forms or creating 'neo-purist' varieties by using elements alien to the spirit of demotic (see, for example, Kriarás (1985/1987)); the old impatience for immediate, definitive, and consistent solutions lives on, hand in hand with a reluctance to accept any solution that presents itself. Most recently, there has been renewed concern about the detrimental effects of foreign loans (chiefly now from English), and a revival of the debate about the integrity of the language which has led on to fresh consideration of the relationship between ancient and modern Greek, and the place of the ancient language in the school curriculum.

All of this notwithstanding, the crucial fact remains that there is for the first time since the Hellenistic period a universal acceptance of one superordinate form of Greek, a variety that is coherent within well-defined parameters, and which offers a choice of registers appropriate to all spoken and written purposes (see Mackridge (1985: ch. 11). People can use this language without political implications or personal risk, and the old embarrassment stemming from uncertainty about 'correct' written usage is largely a thing of the past.

Freed from the old ideologies, writers too can enjoy the freedom and pleasure of experimenting with their uniquely rich and diverse traditions. Any dissatisfaction in literary circles with the blander forms of the new Koine is as natural as that of the creative writers of Ptolemaic Alexandria with its ancient equivalent, and one hopes that there will soon be an equally universal acceptance of the fact that the only fully standardized languages are dead ones, and that experimentation, diversity and change are a cause for celebration rather than concern.

Bibliography

AERTS, W. J. (1965) *Periphrastica: an investigation into the use of* εἰμί *and* ἔχειν *as auxiliaries or pseudo-auxiliaries in Greek from Homer up to the present day*, Amsterdam.

AGÁPIOS (1664) Βιβλίον ωραιότατον καλούμενον Αρματωλών σωτηρία, Venice.

ALEXANDRÍS, A. (1894) Περί του γλωσσικού ιδιώματος της Κύμης, Athens.

ALEXÍOU, M. (1982/3) 'Literary subversion and the aristocracy in 12th-century Byzantium: a stylistic analysis of the *Timaríon* (ch. 6–10)', *Byzantine and Modern Greek Studies* 8, 29–45.

ALEXÍOU, S. (1980) Βιτσέντζος Κορνάρος, Ερωτόκριτος: κριτική έκδοση, εισαγωγή, σημειώσεις, γλωσσάριο, Athens (repr. 1986).

ALEXÍOU, S. (1985) Βασίλειος Διγενής Ακρίτης (κατά το χειρόγραφο του Εσκοριάλ) και το άσμα του Αρμούρη, Athens.

ALEXÍOU, S. (1994) Review of H. Eideneier (1991) *Ptochoprodromos* (Cologne), in Ελληνικά 42, 396–402.

ALLEN, W. S. (1957) 'Some problems of palatalization in Greek', *Lingua* 7 (1957–8), 113–33.

ALLEN, W. S. (1973) *Accent and rhythm*, Cambridge.

ALLEN, W. S. (1987a)[3] *Vox graeca*, Cambridge.

ALLEN, W. S. (1987b) 'The development of the Attic vowel system' in J. T. Killen, J. L. Melena, and J.-P. Olivier (eds) (1987) *Studies in Mycenaean and Classical Greek presented to John Chadwick*, Salamanca, 21–32.

ANAGNOSTÓPOULOS, G. P. (1926) 'Περί της εν Κρήτη ομιλουμένης και ιδίως του ιδιώματος της Αγίας Βαρβάρας και περιχώρων', in Αθηνά 38, 139–93.

ANDERSON, G. (1993) *The Second Sophistic*, London.

ANDRIÓTIS, N. P. (1933) 'Περί της αρχής των βορείων γλωσσικών ιδιωμάτων της νέας ελληνικής.' Επετηρίς Εταιρείας Βυζαντινών Σπουδών 10, 340–52.

ANDRIÓTIS, N. P. (1943–4) 'Τα όρια των βορείων, ημιβορείων και νοτίων ελληνικών ιδιωμάτων της Θράκης', in Αρχείον Θρακικού Λαογραφικού και Γλωσσολογικού Θησαυρού 10, 131–85.

ANGOLD, M. (1984) *The Byzantine empire 1025–1204*, London.

APOSTOLÓPOULOS, P. (1984) *La langue du roman byzantin*, Callimaque et Chrysorrhoé, Athens.

BABINIÓTIS, G. and P. KÓNDOS (1967) Συγχρονική γραμματική της κοινής νέας ελληνικής: Θεωρία, ασκήσεις, Athens.

BÁDENAS, P. (1985) 'Primeros textos altomedievales en griego vulgar', *Erytheia* 6.2, 163–83.

BAKKER, W. (1987) 'The transition from unrhymed to rhymed: the case of the Βελισαριάδα' in H. Eideneier (ed.) (1987) *Neograeca medii aevi: Text und Ausgabe. Akten zum Symposion Köln 1986*, Cologne, 25–51.

BAKKER, W. and A. van GEMERT (1988) Ιστορία του Βελισαρίου.: κριτική έκδοση των τεσσάρων διασκευών με εισαγωγή, σχόλια και γλωσσάριο, Thessaloniki.

BARTONEK, A. (1972) *Classification of the West Greek dialects at the time about 350 BC*, Prague.

BAÜML, F. H. (1984) 'Medieval texts and the two theories of oral-formulaic composition: a proposal for a third theory', *New Literary History* 16/1: 31–49.

BAYNES, N. H. (1955) 'The *Pratum Spirituale*' in N. H. Baynes (ed.) (1955) *Byzantine studies and other essays*, London.

BEATON, R. (1980) *Folk poetry of modern Greece*, Cambridge.

BEATON, R. (1989) *The medieval Greek romance*, Cambridge.

BEATON, R. (1994) *An introduction to modern Greek literature*, Oxford.

BEATON, R. and D. RICKS (eds) (1993) *Digenes Akrites: new approaches to Byzantine heroic poetry*, London.

BECK, H.-G. (1959) *Kirche und theologische literatur im byzantinischen Reich*, Munich.

BECK, H.-G. (1965) 'Zur byzantinischen "Mönchskronik"' *Speculum Historiale*, 188–97.

BECK, H.-G. (1971) *Geschichte der byzantinischen Volksliteratur* (Byzantinisches Handbuch), Munich.

BENNET JR., E. L. and J.-P. OLIVIER (eds) (1973, 1976) *The Pylos tablets transliterated* (2 vols), Rome.

BEŠEVLIEV, V. (1963) *Die protobulgarischen Inschriften*, Berlin.

BEŠEVLIEV, V. (1970) 'Les inscriptions protobulgares et leur portée culturelle et historique', *Byzantinoslavica* 32, 35–57.

BEŠEVLIEV, V. (1981) *Die protobulgarische Periode der bulgarischen Geschichte*, Amsterdam.

BGU = W. SCHUBART *et al.* (eds) (1895–) Ägyptische Urkunden aus den Königlichen (Staatlichen) Museen zu Berlin, Griechische Urkunden, Berlin.

BIVILLE, F. (1993) 'Grec des romains ou latin des grecs? Ambiguïté de quelques processus néologiques dans la koiné' in C. Brixhe (ed.) (1993a) *La koiné grecque antique*, Nancy, 129–40.

BJÖRCK, G. (1950) *Das Alpha impurum und die tragische Kunstsprache*, Uppsala.

BLASS, F., A. DEBRUNNER, and F. REHKOPF (1984)[16] *Grammatik des neutestamentlichen Griechisch*, Göttingen (see also Funk (1961)).

BLÜMEL, W. (1982) *Die aiolischen Dialekte*, Göttingen.

BOOR, C. DE (1963 (1883)) *Theophanis chronographia* (2 vols), Hildesheim.

BORGIA, N. (1912) *Il commentario liturgico di S. Germano patriarca Constantinopolitano e versione latina di Anastasio bibliotecario*, Grottaferrata.

BOUBOULÍDIS, P. (1955) Συμφορά της Κρήτης του Μανόλη Σκλάβου, Athens.

BOURGUET, E. (1927) *Le dialecte laconien*, Paris.

BRIXHE, C. (1985) 'Bulletin de dialectologie grecque', *Revue des études grecques* 98, 260–314.

BRIXHE, C. (1987)[2] *Essai sur le grec anatolien au début de notre ère*, Nancy.

BRIXHE, C. (1988a) 'Bulletin de dialectologie grecque', *Revue des études grecques* 101, 74–112.

BRIXHE, C. (1988b) 'Dialects et koiné à Kafizin', *The history of the Greek language in Cyprus*, Nicosia, 167–78.

BRIXHE, C. (1990) 'Bulletin de dialectologie grecque', *Revue des études grecques* 103, 201–30.

BRIXHE, C. (ed.) (1993a) *La koiné grecque antique*, Nancy.

BRIXHE, C. (1993b) 'Le grec en Carie et Lycie au IVe siècle' in C. Brixhe (ed.) (1993a) *La koiné grecque antique*, Nancy, 59–82.

BRIXHE, C. (ed.) (1996) *La koiné grecque antique II: la concurrence*, Nancy and Paris.

BRIXHE, C. and R. HODOT (1993) 'A chacun sa koiné' in C. Brixhe (ed.) (1993a) *La koiné grecque antique*, Nancy, 7–21.

BROWN, P. (1971) *The world of late antiquity*, London.

BROWNING, R. (1978) 'The language of Byzantine literature' in S. Vryónis (ed.) (1978) Βυζαντινά και Μεταβυζαντινά I, Malibu, 103–33.

BROWNING, R. (1983)² *Medieval and modern Greek*, Cambridge.

BRYER, A. (1981) 'The first encounter with the west, AD 1050–1204' in P. Whiting (ed.), *Byzantium: an introduction*, Oxford, 83–110.

BUBENIK, V. (1989) *Hellenistic and Roman Greece as a sociolinguistic area* (Current Issues in Linguistic Theory 57), Amsterdam.

BUCK, C. D. (1928 (1955)²) *The Greek dialects*, Chicago.

BUCKLER, G. (1929) *Anna Comnene: a study*, Oxford.

CAMERON, A. (1985) *Procopius and the sixth century*, Berkeley and Los Angeles.

CAMERON, A. (1993) *The later Roman empire*, London.

CASSIO, A. (1981) 'Attico "volgare" e Ioni in Atene alla fine del 5. secolo a.C.', *AIΩN* 3, 79ff.

CASSIO, A. (1986) 'Continuità e riprese arcaizzanti nell' uso epigrafico dei dialetti greci: il caso dell' eolico d' Asia', *AIΩN* 8, 131–46.

CHADWICK, J. (1956) 'The Greek dialects and Greek prehistory', *Greece and Rome* NS 3, 38–50.

CHADWICK, J. (1963) 'The prehistory of the Greek language', *Cambridge Ancient History*², Vol. II, ch. 39, Cambridge.

CHADWICK, J. (1967)² *The decipherment of Linear B*, Cambridge.

CHADWICK, J. (1976a) *The Mycenaean world*, Cambridge.

CHADWICK, J. (1976b) Der Beitrag der Sprachwissenschaft zur Rekonstruktion des grie-chischen Frühgeschichte' in *Anzeiger der phil.-hist. Klasse der Österreichischen Akademie der Wissenschaften* 113:6, 183–204.

CHADWICK, J. (1976c) 'Who were the Dorians?', *Parola del Passato* 31, fasc. 166, 103–117.

CHADWICK, J. (1993) 'The Thessalian accent', *Glotta* 70, 2–14.

CLOGG, R. (1986)² *A short history of modern Greece*, Cambridge.

CLOGG, R. (1992) *A concise history of Greece*, Cambridge.

COCHRANE, E. (1988) *Italy 1530–1630* (ed. J. Kirshner), London and New York.

COLEMAN, R. G. G. (1977) 'Greek influence on Latin syntax', *Transactions of the Philo-logical Society (1975)*, 101–56.

CONSANI, C. (1986) *Persistenza dialettale e diffusione della κοινή a Cipro – il caso di Kafizin* (Testi Linguistici 10), Pisa.

CONSANI, C. (1990) 'Bilinguismo, diglossia e digrafia nella Grecia antica III: Le iscrizione digrafe cipriote', *Studi in memoria di E. Giammarco*, Pisa, 63–79.

CONSANI, C. (1991) Διάλεκτος: *contributo alla storia del concetto de 'dialetto'* (Testi Linguistici 18), Pisa.

CONSANI, C. (1993) 'La koiné et les dialectes grecs dans la documentation linguistique et la réflexion métalinguistique des premiers siècles de notre ère' in C. Brixhe (1993a) (ed.) *La koiné grecque antique*, Nancy, 23–39.

COWGILL, W. (1966) 'Ancient Greek dialectology in the light of Mycenaean' in H. Birnbaum and J. Puhvel (eds) *Ancient Indo-European dialects*, Berkeley and Los Angeles, 77–95.

CROKE, B. (1990) 'Byzantine chronicle writing I: the early development of Byzantine chronicles' in E. Jeffreys, B. Croke and R. Scott (eds) (1990) *Studies in John Malalas*, Sydney, 27–38.

CROSSLAND, R. A. (1982) 'Linguistic problems of the Balkan area in the late prehistoric and early classical periods', *Cambridge Ancient History*², Vol. III part I, ch. 20c, Cambridge.

CRUSIUS, M. (1584) *Turcograeciae libri octo*, Basel.

DASKALÁKIS, A. (1966) Κοραῆς καὶ Κοδρικάς: ἡ μεγάλη φιλολογική διαμάχη τῶν Ἑλλήνων 1815–1821, Athens.

DAWKINS, R. M. (1916) *Modern Greek in Asia Minor*, Cambridge.

DAWKINS, R. M. (1932) *Leontios Makhairas: recital concerning the sweet land of Cyprus entitled Chronicle* (2 vols), Oxford.

DAWKINS, R. M. (1953) 'The Greek language in the Byzantine period' in N. H. Baynes and H. Moss (eds) (1953) *Byzantium: an introduction to east Roman civilization*, Oxford, 252–67.

DEFFNER, M. (1877) 'Die Infinitive in den Pontischen Dialekten', *Monatsberichte der königlich-preussischen Akademie der Wissenschaften zu Berlin* (1877), 191 ff.

DENNISTON, J. D. (1952) *Greek prose style*, Oxford.

DIENSTBACH, A. (1910) *De titulorum Prienensium sonis*, Marburg.

DIETEN, J. L. VAN (1979) 'Bemerkungen zur Sprache der sog. vulgärgriechichen Niketasparaphrase', *Byzantinische Forschungen* Band VI, Amsterdam, 37–77.

DIMARÁS, A. (1974) *Η μεταρρύθμιση που δεν έγινε* (2 vols), Athens.

DINDORF, L. (1831) *Ioannis Malalae chronographia*, Bonn.

DITTENBERGER, W. (1903) *Orientis graeci inscriptiones selectae*, Berlin.

DOVER, K. J. (1960) *Greek word order*, Cambridge.

DRESSLER, W. (1966) 'Von altgriechischen zum neugriechischen System der Personalpronomina', *Indogermanische Forschungen* 71, 39–63.

DRETTAS, G. (1995) *Aspects pontiques*, Paris.

EGEA, J. M. (1988) *Gramática de la Crónica de Morea: un estudio sobre el griego medieval* (Veleia anejo 4), Vitoria/Gasteiz.

EGEA, J. M. (1990) *Documenta selecta ad historiam linguae graecae inlustrandam II (medioaevi)*, Universidád del País Vasco.

EIDENEIER, H. (1982) 'Zum Stil der byzantinischen Tierdichtung', *Jahrbuch der Österreichischen Byzantinistik* 32/3, 301–6.

EIDENEIER, H. (1982–3) 'Leser- oder Hörerkreis? Zur byzantinischen Dichtung in der Volkssprache', Ἑλληνικά 34, 119–50.

EIDENEIER, H. (1987) 'Der *Ptochoprodromos* in schriftlicher und mündlicher Überlieferung' in H. Eideneier (ed.) (1987) *Neograeca medii aevi: Text und Ausgabe. Akten zum Symposion Köln 1986*, Cologne, 101–119.

EIDENEIER, H. (1991) *Ptochoprodromos: Einführung, kritische Ausgabe, deutsche Übersetzung, Glossar* (Neograeca medii aevi V), Cologne.

FABRICIUS, C. (1962) *Zu den Jugendschriften des Johannes Chrysostomos; Untersuchungen zum Klassizismus des vierten Jahrhunderts*, Lund.

FÁVIS, V. (1911) Γλωσσικαί ἐπισκέψεις ἀναφερόμεναι εἰς τὸ ἰδίωμα Αὐλωναρίου καὶ Κονιτρῶν Εὐβοίας, Athens.

FERGUSON, C. A. (1959) 'Diglossia', *Word* 15, 325–40.

FESTUGIÈRE, A.-J. (1978) 'Notabilia dans Malalas I', *Revue de Philologie* 52, 221–41.

FRÖSÉN, J. (1974) *Prolegomena to a study of the Greek language in the first centuries AD: the problem of Koiné and Atticism*, (diss.) Helsinki.

FUNK, R. W. (1961) *A Greek grammar of the New Testament and other early Christian literature* (trans. of Blass-Debrunner), Chicago and London.

GARCÍA-DOMINGO, E. (1979) *Latinismos en la Koiné (en los documentos epigráficos desde el 212 a. J.C. hasta el 14 d. J.C.)*, Burgos.

GARCÍA-RAMÓN, J. L. (1975) *Les origines postmycéniennes du group dialectal éolien: étude linguistique* (suppl. *Minos* 6), Salamanca.

GEMERT, A. VAN (1991) 'Literary antecedents' in D. W. Holton (ed.) (1991a) *Literature and society in Renaissance Crete*, Cambridge, 49–78.

GIGNAC, F. T. (1976, 1981) *A grammar of the Greek papyri of the Roman and Byzantine periods* (Vol. I Phonology, Vol. II Morphology), Milan.

GOODWIN, W. W. (1889) *Syntax of the moods and tenses of the Greek verb*, London.

GRENFELL, B. P. and A. S. HUNT (eds) (1903) *The Oxyrhynchus papyri* Vol. III, No. 413, 41.

GRENFELL, B. P., A. S. HUNT, *et al.* (eds) (1898–) *The Oxyrhynchus papyri* (60 vols), London.

HAINSWORTH, B. (1968) *The flexibility of the Homeric formula*, Oxford.

HAURY, J. (1905–13) *Procopii Caesariensis opera omnia*, Leipzig.

HELMS, P. (1971–2) 'Syntaktische Untersuchungen zu Ioannes Malalas und Georgios Sphrantzes', *Helikon* 11–12, 309–88.

HENDERSON, G. P. (1971) *The revival of Greek thought 1620–1830*, Edinburgh.

HESSELING, D. C. (1931) *Jean Moschos*, Paris.

HESSELING, D. C. and H. PERNOT (1910) *Poèmes prodromiques en grec vulgaire*, Amsterdam.

HILLER VON GÄRTRINGEN, F. (1906) *Inschriften von Priene*, Berlin.

HODOT, R. (1990) *Le dialecte éolien d'Asie: la langue des inscriptions VII s. a. C. – IV s. p. C.*, Paris.

HOLTON, D. W. (1983) Review of H. Hunger (1981) *Anonyme Metaphrase zu Anna Komnene, Alexias XI–XIII: ein Beitrag zur Erschliessung der byzantinischen Umgangssprache* (Vienna), in *Journal of Hellenic Studies* 103, 232–3.

HOLTON, D. W. (1991a) *Literature and society in Renaissance Crete*, Cambridge.

HOLTON, D. W. (1991b) 'Romance' in D. W. Holton (ed.) (1991a) *Literature and society in Renaissance Crete*, Cambridge, 205–37.

HOLTON, D. W. (1991c) *Erotokritos*, Bristol.

HOLTON, D. W. (1993) 'The formation of the future in modern Greek literary texts up to the 17th century' in N. M. Panyiotákis (ed.) (1993) *Αρχές της νεοελληνικής λογοτεχνίας/ Origini della letteratura neogreca*, Venice, 118–28.

HOOKER, J. T. (1980) *Linear B: an introduction*, Bristol.

HÖRANDNER, W. (1974) *Theodoros Prodromos: historische Gedichte* (Wiener Byzantinische Studien 11), Vienna.

HORROCKS, G. C. (1980) 'The antiquity of the Greek epic tradition: some new evidence', *Proceedings of the Cambridge Philological Society* 206 (NS 26), 1–11.

HORROCKS, G. C. (1987) 'The Ionian epic tradition: was there an Aeolic phase in its development?' in J. T. Killen, J. L. Melena, and J.-P. Olivier (eds) (1987) *Studies in Mycenaean and Classical Greek presented to John Chadwick*, Salamanca, 269–94.

HORROCKS, G. C. (1990) 'Clitics in Greek: a diachronic review' in M. Roussou and S. Panteli (eds) (1990) *Greek outside Greece II*, Athens, 35–52.

HORROCKS, G. C. (1994) 'Subjects and configurationality: modern Greek clause structure', *Journal of Linguistics* 30.1, 81–109.

HORROCKS, G. C. (1995) 'On condition: aspect and modality in the history of Greek', *Proceedings of the Cambridge Philological Society* 41, 153–73.

HORROCKS, G. C. (forthcoming) 'Homer's dialect' in I. Morris and B. Powell (eds) (in press) *A new companion to Homer*, Leiden.

HULT, K. (1990) *Syntactic variation in Greek of the 5th century AD* (Studia Graeca et Latina Gothoburgensia LII), Göteborg.

HUNGER, H. (1978) *Die hochsprachliche Literatur der Byzantiner* (2 vols), Munich.

HUNGER, H. (1981) *Anonyme Metaphrase zu Anna Komnene, Alexias XI–XIII: ein Beitrag zur Erschliessung der Byzantinischen Umgangssprache*, Vienna.

HUNT, A. S. and C. C. EDGAR (1932) *Select papyri I: non-literary (private affairs)* (Loeb edn), Cambridge Mass. and London.

HUNT, A. S. and C. C. EDGAR (1934) *Select papyri II: non-literary (public documents)* (Loeb edn), Cambridge Mass. and London.

IG = *Inscriptiones Graecae* (1873–), Berlin.

IMÉLLOS, S. (1908) 'Γλωσσογεωγραφικά τινα εκ Νάξου', in *Αθηνά* 67, 33–46.

IOÁNNOU, P. (1986) *Το έπος της ΕΟΚΑ*, Nicosia.

JANNARIS, A. N. (1897) *An historical Greek grammar, chiefly of the Attic dialect*, London, (repr. 1987, Georg Olms: Hildesheim, Zurich, and New York.)

JANSE, M. (1993) 'La position des pronoms personnels enclitiques en grec néo-testamentaire à la lumière des dialectes néo-helléniques' in C. Brixhe (ed.) (1993) *La koiné grecque antique*, Nancy, 83–121.

JEFFREYS, E. (1979) 'The popular Byzantine verse romances of chivalry; work since 1971', *Μαντατοφόρος* 14, 20–34.

JEFFREYS, E. (1981) 'The later Greek romances; a survey' in E. Jeffreys, M. Jeffreys, and A. Moffatt (eds) (1981) *Byzantine papers* (Byzantina Australiensia 1), Canberra, 116–27.

JEFFREYS, M. (1973) 'Formulas in the *Chronicle of the Morea*', *Dumbarton Oaks papers* 27, 165–95.

JEFFREYS, M. (1974) 'The nature and origins of the political verse', *Dumbarton Oaks papers* 28, 141–95.

JEFFREYS, M. (1975) 'The *Chronicle of the Morea*: the primacy of the Greek version', *Byzantinische Zeitschrift* 68, 304–50.

JEFFREYS, M. (1987) 'Η γλώσσα του Χρονικού του Μορέως – γλώσσα μιας προφορικής παράδοσης' in H. Eideneier (ed.) (1987) *Neograeca medii aevi: Text und Ausgabe. Akten zum Symposion Köln 1986*, Cologne, 139–63.

JEFFREYS, E. and M. JEFFREYS (1979) 'The traditional style of early demotic Greek verse', *Byzantine and Modern Greek studies* 5, 115–39.

JEFFREYS, E. and M. JEFFREYS (1983) 'The style of Byzantine popular poetry: recent work', *Okeanos: essays presented to I. Ševčenko* (Harvard Ukrainian Studies 7), 309–43.

JEFFREYS, E. and M. JEFFREYS (1986) 'The oral background of Byzantine popular poetry', *Oral tradition* 1/3, 504–47.

JEFFREYS, M. and E. JEFFREYS (1971) '*Imberios and Margarona*: the manuscripts, sources and edition of a Byzantine verse romance', *Byzantion* 41, 122–60.

JEFFREYS, E., M. JEFFREYS and R. SCOTT (eds) (1990) *Studies in John Malalas*, Sydney.

JEFFREYS, E., M. JEFFREYS, R. SCOTT et al. (eds) (1986) *The chronicle of John Malalas; a translation*, Melbourne.

JENKINS, R. J. H. and GY. MORAVCSIK (1967)[2] *Constantine Porphyrogenitus: de administrando imperio*, Washington D.C.

JOSEPH, B. D. (1983) *The synchrony and diachrony of the Balkan infinitive: a study in areal, general and historical linguistics*, Cambridge.

JOSEPH, B. D. (1990) *Morphology and universals in syntactic change: evidence from medieval and modern Greek*, New York and London.

KAIMIO, J. (1979) *The Romans and the Greek language* (Commentationes Humanarum Litterarum 64), Helsinki.

KAKRIDÍS, I. T. (1979) *Homer revisited*, Lund.

KALLÉRIS, J. N. (1954, 1976) *Les anciens macédoniens: étude linguistique et historique* (2 vols), Athens.

KALONÁROS, P. P. (ed.) (1940) *Το Χρονικόν του Μορέως*, Athens.

KAPSOMÉNOS, S. G. (1958) 'Die griechische Sprache zwischen Koine und Neugriechisch', *Berichte zum XI. Internationalen Byzantinisten-Kongress*, Munich.

KARATZÁS, S. (1944) '*Παλαιοαθηναϊκά γλωσσικά*', *Byzantinisch-neugriechische Jahrbücher* 17, 125–34.

KARATZÁS, S. (1958) *L'origine des dialectes néo-grecs de l'Italie méridionale* (Collection de l'Institut d'Etudes Byzantines et Néo-helléniques de l'Université de Paris), Paris.

KATIČIČ, R. (1976) *Ancient languages of the Balkans*, The Hague.

KAZHDAN, A. and S. FRANKLIN (1984) *Studies in Byzantine literature of the 11th and 12th centuries*, Cambridge and Paris.

KERN, O. (1900) *Die Inschriften von Magnesia am Mäander*, Berlin.

KHARALAMBÓPOULOS, A. (1980) *Φωνολογική ανάλυση της τσακωνικής διαλέκτου*, Athens.

KHATZIDÁKIS, G. N. (1892) *Einleitung in die neugriechische Grammatik*, Leipzig.

KHATZIDÁKIS, G. N. (1901) *Γλωσσολογικαί μελέται Α*, Athens.

KHATZIDÁKIS, G. N. (1905) *Μεσαιωνικά και νέα ελληνικά* (2 vols), Athens.

KHATZIDÁKIS, G. N. (1915) *Σύντομος ιστορία της νεοελληνικής γλώσσης*, Athens.

KHATZIDÁKIS, G. N. (1915/16) '*Περί της μεγαρικής διαλέκτου και των συγγενών αυτής ιδιωμάτων*', in *Επιστημονική επετηρίς Εθνικού Πανεπιστημίου*, 12, 1–27.

KHRÉSTOU, P. K. (1962, 1966, 1970) *The Works of Gregory Palamás* (3 vols), Thessaloniki.

KHRISTÍDIS, A.-Ph. (1985) 'Further remarks on modern Greek complementation', *Μελέτες για την Ελληνική Γλώσσα* 3 (1982), 47–72.

KILLEN, J. T. and J.-P. OLIVIER (eds.) (1989) *The Knossos tablets; a transliteration* (Suppl. a Minos 11), Salamanca.

KODER, J. (1972) 'Der Fünfzehnsilber am kaiserlichen Hof um das Jahr 900', *Byzantinoslavica* 33, 214–9.

KODER, J. (1983) 'Kontakion und politischer Vers', *Jahrbuch der Österreichischen Byzantinistik* 33, 45–56.

KÓNDOS, K. (1882) *Γλωσσικαί παρατηρήσεις αναφερόμεναι εις την νέαν ελληνικήν γλώσσαν*, Athens.

KONDOSÓPOULOS, N. G. (1970) '*Η σημερινή γλωσσική κατάστασις εν Κρήτη και η γλώσσα των εν Αθήναις Κρητών*', in *Κρητικά Χρονικά* 22, 144–278.

KONDOSÓPOULOS, N. G. (1981) *Διάλεκτοι και ιδιώματα της Νέας Ελληνικής*, Athens.

KONEMÉNOS, N. (1873) *Το ζήτημα της γλώσσας*, Corfu.

KORAÍS, A. (1964) *Άπαντα τα πρωτότυπα έργα* (4 vols [A1, A2, B1, B2] ed. G. Valétas), Athens.

KÖRTING, G. (1879) *De vocibus latinis quae apud Ioannem Malalam chronographum Byzantinum inveniuntur*, Münster.

KOSTÁKIS, A. (1951) *Σύντομη γραμματική τσακωνικής διαλέκτου*, Athens.

KOSTÁKIS, A. (1980) *Δείγματα τσακωνικής διαλέκτου*, Athens.

KRETSCHMER, P. (1896) *Einleitung in die Geschichte der griechischen Sprache*, Göttingen (repr. 1970).

KRETSCHMER, P. (1905) *Der heutige lesbische Dialekt, verglichen mit den übrigen nordgriechischen Mundarten*, Vienna.

KRETSCHMER, P. (1909) 'Zur Geschichte der griechischen Dialekte: I. Jonier und Achäer', *Glotta* 1, 9–34.

KRIARÁS, E. (1955) *Βυζαντινά ιπποτικά μυθιστορήματα (Βασική Βιβλιοθήκη* 2), Athens.

KRIARÁS, E. (1969–) *Λεξικό της μεσαιωνικής δημώδους γραμματείας*, Thessaloniki.

KRIARÁS, E. (1985 (1987)) '*Το θέμα της γλώσσας μας σήμερα και τα ιστορικά αίτια που οδήγησαν στη σημερινή γλωσσολογική κακοδαιμονία*', in *Λόγιοι και δημοτικισμός*, Athens, 9–26.

KRUMBACHER, K. (1886) 'Ein irrationaler Spirant im Neugriechischen', *Sitzungsberichte der königlichen bayerischen Akademie der Wissenschaften*, 359–44.

LÁMBROS, S. P. (1879–80) *Mikhaél Akominátos Khoniátes: the surviving works* (2 vols), Athens.

LÁMBROS, S. P. (1908) '*Τρεις επιστολές του Καρδιναλίου Βησσαρίωνος εν τη δημώδει γλώσση*', in *Νέος Ελληνομνήμων* 5, 20–8.

LANDSMAN, D. (1989) 'The Greeks' sense of language and the 1976 linguistic reforms: illusions and disappointments', *Byzantine and Modern Greek Studies* 13, 159–82.

LEGRAND, E. (ed.) (1874) *Collection des monuments pour servir à l'étude de la langue néoellénique* (nouvelle série 2), Paris.

LEGRAND, E. (ed.) (1880–90) *Bibliothèque grecque vulgaire* (5 vols), Paris.

LEGRAND, E. (ed.) (1885–1906) *Bibliographie hellénique ou description raisonnée des ouvrages publiés en grec par des grecs aux XVe et XVIe siècles* (4 vols), Paris.

LEGRAND, E. (1891) 'Poésies inédites de Théodore Prodrome', *Revue des Etudes Grecques* 4, 70–3.

LEGRAND, E. (1894–1903) *Bibliographie hellénique ou description raisonnée des ouvrages publiés en grec par des grecs au XVIIe siècle*, Paris.

LEGRAND, E., L. PETIT, and H. PERNOT (eds) (1918–28) *Bibliographie hellénique ou description raisonnée des ouvrages publiés en grec par des grecs au XVIIIe siècle* (2 vols), Paris.

LEIB, B. (1937–45) *Anne Comnène: Alexiade* (3 vols), Paris.

LÓPEZ-EIRE, A. (1986) 'Fundamentos sociolingüisticos del origen de la Koiné', *Estudios de lingüistica, dialectología e historia de la lengua griega*, Salamanca, 401–31.

LÓPEZ-EIRE, A. (1993) 'De l'Attique à la Koiné' in C. Brixhe (ed.) (1993) *La Koiné grecque antique*, Nancy, 41–57.

LÜDDECKENS, E. (1980) 'Ägypten' in G. Neumann and J. Untermann (eds) (1980) *Die Sprachen im römischen Reich der Kaiserzeit*, Cologne, 241–66.

MAAS, P. (1912) 'Metrische Akklamationen der Byzantiner', *Byzantinische Zeitschrift* 21, 28–51.

MAAS, P. and C. A. TRYPÁNIS (1963) *Sancti Romani Melodi cantica I: cantica genuina*, Oxford.

MAAS, P. and C. A. TRYPÁNIS (1970) *Sancti Romani Melodi cantica II: cantica dubia*, Berlin.

MACHARADZE, N. A. (1980) 'Zur Lautung der griechischen Sprache in der byzantinischen Zeit', *Jahrbuch der Österreichischen Byzantinistik* 29, 144–58.

MACKRIDGE, P. (1985) *The modern Greek language*, Oxford.

MACKRIDGE, P. (1987) 'Greek-speaking Moslems of north-east Turkey: prolegomena to a study of the Ophitic sub-dialect of Pontus', *Byzantine and Modern Greek Studies* 11, 115–37.

MACKRIDGE, P. (1988) '*Ο πρακτικός δημοτικισμός του Ψυχάρη*', in *Μαντατοφόρος* 28, 40–5.

MACKRIDGE, P. (1989) *Dionysios Solomos*, Bristol.

MACKRIDGE, P. (1990) 'Katharevousa (*c*. 1800–1974): an obituary for an official language' in M. Saráfis and M. Eve (eds) *Background to contemporary Greece I*, London.

MACKRIDGE, P. (1993a) 'An editorial problem in medieval Greek texts: the position of the object clitic pronoun in the Escorial Digenes Akrites' in N. M. Panayiotákis (ed.) (1993) *Ἀρχές της νεοελληνικής λογοτεχνίας/Origini della letteratura neogreca*, Venice, 325–42.

MACKRIDGE, P. (1993b) 'The medieval Greek infinitive (12th–15th centuries) in the light of modern dialectal evidence', unpublished ms., University of Oxford.

MACLER, F. (1904) *Histoire d'Héraclius par l'évêque Sèbeos*, Paris.

MAJURI, A (1919) 'Una nuova poesia de Teodoro Prodromo', *Byzantinische Zeitschrift* 23, 397–407.

MALONEY, E. C. (1981) *Semitic interference in Marcan syntax*, Chico, California.

MALTÉZOU, K. (1991) 'The historical and social context' in D. W. Holton (ed.) (1991a) *Literature and society in Renaissance Crete*, Cambridge, 17–47.

MANGO, C. (1980) *Byzantium: the empire of the New Rome*, London.

MARTINET, A. (1955) *Economie des changements phonétiques*, Berne.

MATTHEWS, P. H. (1994) 'Greek and Latin linguistics' in G. Lepschy (ed.) (1994) *History of Linguistics: classical and medieval linguistics*, London, 1–133.

MAYSER, E. (1934) *Grammatik der griechischen Papyri aus der ptolemäer Zeit*, Vol. II, Berlin.

MAYSER, E. and H. SCHMOLL (1970) *Grammatik der griechischen Papyri aus der ptolemäer Zeit*, Vol. I, Berlin.

MÉGAS, G. (1956) '*Καλλιμάχου και Χρυσορρόης υπόθεσις*', *Mélanges Merlier* 2, Athens, 147–72.

MEILLET, A. (1965)[7] *Aperçu d'une histoire de la langue grecque*, Paris.

MELVILLE-JONES, J. R. (1988) *Eustathios of Thessaloniki; the capture of Thessaloniki*, Canberra.

MÉNDEZ-DOSUNA, J. (1985) *Los dialectos dorios del noroeste*, Salamanca.

MÉRTZIOS, K. D. (1949) '*Η συνθήκη Ενετών–Καλλέργη και οι συνοδεύοντες αυτήν κατάλογοι*', in *Κρητικά Χρονικά* 3, 264–74.

MEYENDORFF, P. (ed.) (1984) *St Germanus of Constantinople on the divine liturgy*, New York.

MEYER-LÜBKE, W. (1889) *Grammatica linguae graecae vulgaris (reproduction de l'édition de 1638 suivie d'un commentaire grammatical et historique)*, Paris.

MIGNE = J. P. MIGNE (ed.) *Patrologiae cursus completus; series graeca*.

MIKLOSICH, F. and J. MÜLLER (eds) (1860–90) *Acta et diplomata graeca medii aevi sacra et profana* (6 vols), Vienna.

MINIÁTIS, I (1727 (1870²)) *Διδαχαί*, Venice.

MIRAMBEL, A. (1929) *Etude descriptive du parler maniote méridionale*, Paris.

MIRAMBEL, A. (1937) 'Les états de langue dans la Grèce actuelle', *Conférences de l'Institut de Linguistique de l'Université de Paris 5*, Paris.

MIRAMBEL, A. (1961) 'Participe et gérondif en grec médiéval et moderne', *Bulletin de la Société de Linguistique* 56, 46–79.

MIRAMBEL, A. (1963) 'Dialectes néohelléniques et syntaxe', *Bulletin de la Société de Linguistique* 58/1, 85–134.

MIRAMBEL, A. (1964) 'Les aspects psychologiques du purisme dans la Grèce moderne', *Journal de Psychologie* 57, 405–36.

MÍSSIOS, K. (1985) . . . *καλά, εσύ σκοτώθηκες νωρίς*, Athens.

MITSÁKIS, K. (1983) *Εισαγωγή στην νέα ελληνική λογοτεχνία*, Athens.

MOHLER, L. (1942) *Kardinal Bessarion als Theologe, Humanist und Staatsman III*, Paderborn, 439–49.

MORAVCSIK, GY. (1983)² *Byzantinoturcica I: die Byzantinischen Quellen der Geschichte der Türkvölker*, Berlin.

MORGAN, G. (1954) 'A Byzantine satirical song?', *Byzantinische Zeitschrift* 47, 292–7.

MORPURGO DAVIES, A. (1987) 'The Greek notion of dialect', *Verbum* 10, 7–28.

MORPURGO DAVIES, A. (1993) 'Geography, history and dialect: the case of Oropos', *Dialectologica Graeca Miraflores* (Proceedings of the 2nd international colloquium of Greek dialectology), Madrid, 261–79.

MORPURGO DAVIES, A. and Y. DUHOUX (eds) (1985) *Linear B: a 1984 survey*, Louvain-la-Neuve.

MOSER, A. (1988) *The history of the perfect periphrases in Greek*, Ph.D. diss., University of Cambridge.

MOULTON, J. H. *et al.* (1906, 1929, 1963, 1976) *Grammar of New Testament Greek* (4 vols), Edinburgh.

NACHMANSON (HGI) = E. NACHMANSON (ed.) (1913) *Historische griechische Inschriften*, Bonn.

NACHMANSON, E. (1903) *Laute und Formen der magnetische Inschriften*, Uppsala.

NAGY, G. (1968) 'On dialectal anomalies in Pylian texts', *Atti e memorie del primo congresso internazionale di Micenologia* (1967) II, Rome, 663–9.

NEUMANN, G. (1980) 'Kleinasien' in G. Neumann and J. Untermann (eds) (1980) *Die Sprachen im römischen Reich der Kaiserzeit*, Cologne, 167–86.

NEWTON, B. (1970) *Cypriot Greek: its phonology and inflections*, The Hague.

NEWTON, B. (1972) *The generative interpretation of dialect*, Cambridge.

NICOL, D. M. (1991) *A biographical dictionary of the Byzantine empire*, London.

NICOL, D. M. (1992) *The immortal emperor*, Cambridge.

ΟΙΚΟΝΟΜΙΔΙΣ, D. E. (1958) *Γραμματική της ελληνικής διαλέκτου του Πόντου*, Athens.

OLIVIER, J.-P. (1993) 'Un même scribe à Knossos et à la Canée au MR III B: du soupçon à la certitude', *Bulletin de Correspondance Hellénique* 117, 19–33.

OSTROGORSKY, G. (1928–9) 'Die Chronologie des Theophanes im 7. und 8. Jahrhundert', *Byzantinisch-neugriechische Jahrbücher* 7, 1–56.

P. ELEPH. = O. RUBENSOHN (ed.) (1907) *Elephantine-Papyri* (Ägyptische Urkunden aus den kgl. Museen in Berlin), Berlin.

P. FAY. = B. P. GRENFELL *et al.* (eds) (1900) *Fayûm towns and their papyri*, London.

P. FLOR = D. COMPARETTI *et al.* (eds) (1906–15) *Papiri Fiorentini: documenti pubblici e privati dell' età romana e byzantina (Papiri Greco-Egizii)* (3 vols), Milan.

P. MERTON = H. I. BELL *et al.* (eds) (1948), B. R. REES *et al.* (eds) (1959), J. D. THOMAS (ed.) (1967) *A descriptive catalogue of the Greek papyri in the collection of Wilfred Merton*, London and Dublin.

P. MICH. = A. E. R. BOAK *et al.* (eds) (1933–51) *Michigan papyri*, Ann Arbor; E. M. HUSSELMAN (ed.) (1971) *Papyri from Karanis*, APA monograph 29; G. M. Browne (ed.) (1970) *Documentary papyri from the Michigan collection* (American studies in papyrology 6), Toronto; J. C. Shelton (ed.) (1971) *Papyri from the Michigan collection*, Toronto.

P. OXY. = B. P. GRENFELL, A. S. HUNT *et al.* (eds) (1898–) *Oxyrhynchus papyri* (60 vols), London.

P. PAR. = A. J. LATRONNE *et al.* (eds) (1866) *Notices et textes des papyrus grecs du Musée du Louvre et de la Bibliothèque Impériale.* Notices et extraits de manuscrits de la Bibliothèque Impériale et autres bibliothèques 18, IIe partie, Paris.

PAGE, D. L. (1950) *Greek literary papyri*, Cambridge Mass. and London (Loeb edn).

PAGE, D. L. (1951) *Alcman: the Partheneion*, Cambridge.

PALMER, L. R. (1962) 'The language of Homer' in A. B. Wace and F. Stubbings (eds) (1962) *A companion to Homer*, London, 75–178.

PALMER, L. R. (1980) *The Greek language*, London.

PANAYIOTÁKIS, N. M. (1993) 'Οι πρώτες αρχές της δημώδους Νεοελληνικής πεζογραφίας', *Παλίμψηστον* 13, 247–57.

PÁNGALOS, G. E. (1955) *Περί του γλωσσικού ιδιώματος της Κρήτης* I, Athens.

PAPADÓPOULOS, A. A. (1927) *Γραμματική των βορείων ιδιωμάτων της νέας ελληνικής γλώσσης*, Athens.

PAPADÓPOULOS, T. (1975) *Δημώδη κυπριακά άσματα εξ ανεκδότων συλλογών του ΙΘ' αιώνος*, Nicosia.

PARRY, M. (1928a) *L'épithète traditionelle dans Homère*, Paris.

PARRY, M. (1928b) *Les formules et la métrique d'Homère*, Paris.

PARRY, M. (1930) 'Studies in the epic technique of oral verse making I: Homer and the Homeric style', *Harvard Studies in Classical Philology* 41, 73–147.

PARRY, M. (1932) 'Studies in the epic technique of oral verse making II: the Homeric language as the language of an oral poetry', *Harvard Studies in Classical Philology* 43, 1–50.

PASSOW, A. (1860) *Popularia carmina Graeciae recentioris*, Leipzig.

PERNOT, H. (1907a) *Collection des monuments pour servir à l'étude de la langue néo-hellénique* (3e série, I), Paris.

PERNOT, H. (1907b) *Phonétique des parlers de Chio*, Paris.

PERNOT, H. (1934) *Introduction à l'étude du dialecte tsakonien*, Paris.

PERTUSI, A. (ed.) (1952) *Constantine Porphyrogenitus: de thematibus*, Vatican.

PHILIPPÁKI-WARBURTON, I. (1988) 'Ο Ψυχάρης ως γλωσσολόγος', in *Μαντατοφόρος* 28, 34–9.

PHILIPPÁKI-WARBURTON, I. (1990) 'The analysis of the verb group in modern Greek', *Μελέτες για την Ελληνική Γλώσσα* 11, 119–38.

PICHARD, M. (1956) *Le roman de Callimaque et de Chrysorrhoé: texte établi et traduit*, Paris.

POLÍTIS, A. (1981) *Το δημοτικό τραγούδι – κλέφτικα*, Athens.

POLÍTIS, L. (ed.) (1948 (1986)⁵) *Δ. Σολωμού Άπαντα: Ι ποιήματα*, Athens.

POLÍTIS, L. (1966) 'Τρίτη ή ενιαία δημοτική', *Εποχές* 44, 528–31.

POLÍTIS, L. (1970) 'L'épopée byzantine de Digénis Akritas: problèmes de la tradition du texte et des rapports avec les chansons akritiques', *Atti del Convegno Internazionale sul Tema: la Poesia Epica e la sua formazione* (Accademia Nazionale dei Lincei, Quaderno 139), Rome, 551–81.

POLÍTIS, N. G. (1914 (many repr.)) *Εκλογαί από τα τραγούδια του ελληνικού λαού*, Athens.

PORZIG, W. (1954) 'Sprachgeographische Untersuchungen zu den altgriechischen Dialekten', *Indogermanische Forschungen* 61, 147–69.

POWELL, B. (1991) *Homer and the origin of the Greek alphabet*, Cambridge.

POWELL, J. U. (1933) *New chapters in the history of Greek literature: third series*, Oxford.

PROBONÁS, I. K. (1985) *Ακριτικά Α'*, Athens.

PSYKHÁRIS, J. (1888 (1905)²) *Το ταξίδι μου*, Athens. (See now A. Angelou (ed.) (1971) *Ψυχάρης: Το ταξίδι μου*, Athens).

RANGAVÍS, K. (1877) *Ιουλιανός ο παραβάτης: ποίημα δραματικόν*, Athens.

REINL, W. (1994) '*Dialect variation in Mycenaean Greek: reality or myth?*', unpublished diss., University of Cambridge.

REINSCH, D. R. (ed.) (1983) *Critobuli Imbriotae historiae*, Berlin and New York.

REISKE, I. I. (1829–30) *Constantini Porphyrogeniti imperatoris de caeremoniis aulae byzantinae* (2 vols), Bonn.

RENAULD, E. (1920) *Etude de la langue et du style de Michel Psellos*, Paris.

RENAULD, E. (1926–8) *Michel Psellos: chronographie*, Paris.

RENFREW, C. (1987) *Archaeology and language*, London.

RICKS, D. (1990) *Byzantine heroic poetry*, Bristol.

RIGGS, G. (1954) *History of Mehmed the conqueror by Kritovoulos*, Princeton.

RISCH, E. (1954) 'Die Sprache Alkmans', *Museum Helveticum* 11, 20–37.

RISCH, E. (1955) 'Die Gliederung der griechischen Dialekte in neuer Sicht', *Museum Helveticum* 12, 61–76.

RISCH, E. (1966) 'Les différences dialectales dans le mycénien', *Proceedings of the 1965 Cambridge colloquium on Mycenaean studies*, Cambridge, 150–7.

RISCH, E. (1979) 'Die griechischen Dialekte im 2. vorchristlichen Jahrtausend', *Studi Micenei ed Egeo-Anatolici* 20, 91–111.

RISCH, E. (1986) 'La posizione del dialetto Dorico', in D. Musti (ed.) (1986) *Dori e mondo egeo* (Colloquio Roma 1983), Laterza.

RIVERO, M.-L., and A. TERZI (1995) 'Imperatives, V-movement and logical mood', *Journal of Linguistics* 31, 301–32.

ROBERTSON, A. T. (1919)[3] *A grammar of the Greek New Testament in the light of historical research*, New York.

ROHLFS, G. (1924) *Griechen und Romanen in Unteritalien*, Munich.

ROHLFS, G. (1930) *Etymologisches Wörterbuch der unteritalienischen Gräzität*, Halle.

ROHLFS, G. (1933) *Scavi linguistici nella Magna Grecia*, Rome.

ROHLFS, G. (1950) *Historische Grammatik der unteritalienischen Gräzität*, Munich.

ROHLFS, G. (1962) *Neue Beiträge zur Kenntnis der unteritalienischen Gräzität*, Munich.

ROSÉN, H. B. (1980) 'Die Sprachsituation in römischen Palestina', in G. Neumann, and J. Untermann (eds) (1980) *Die Sprachen in römischen Reich der Kaiserzeit*, Cologne, 215–40.

ROÚSSOU, A. (1994) *The syntax of complementisers*, Ph.D. diss., University of London.

RUIJGH, C. J. (1961) 'Le traitement des sonantes voyelles dans les dialectes grecs et la position du mycénien', *Mnemosyne* 14, 193–216.

RUIJGH, C. J. (1967) *Etudes sur la grammaire et le vocabulaire du grec mycénien*, Amsterdam.

RUIJGH, C. J. (1978a) Review of J. L. García-Ramón (1975) *Les origines postmycéniennes du group dialectal éolien* (Salamanca), *Bibliotheca Orientalis* 30, 5/6, 418–23.

RUIJGH, C. J. (1978b) Review of S.-T. Teodorsson (1974) *The phonemic system of the Attic dialect 400–340 BC* (Göteborg), *Mnemosyne* 31, 79–89.

RUIJGH, C. J. (1984) 'Le dorien de Théocrite: dialecte cyrénien d'Alexandrie et d'Egypte', in *Mnemosyne* 37, 56–88.

RUIJGH, C. J. (1991) *Scripta minora: mycenologica, homerica, morphophonologica, syntactico-semantica* (J. M. Bremer, A. Rijksbaron, F. M. J. Waanders (eds.)), Amsterdam.

RUIPÉREZ, M. (1956) 'Esquisse d'une histoire du vocalisme grec', *Word* 12, 67–81.

RUNCIMAN, S. (1965) *The fall of Constantinople 1453*, Cambridge.

SAKELLARÍOU, M. B. (ed.) (1983) *Macedonia: 4,000 years of Greek history and civilization*, Athens.

SANDFELD, K. (1930) *Linguistique balkanique: problèmes et résultats*, Paris.

SÁTHAS, K. (1870) Νεοελληνικῆς φιλολογίας παράρτημα, Athens.

SÁTHAS, K. (1872–94) Μεσαιωνικὴ βιβλιοθήκη (6 vols), Venice and Paris.

SAUNIER, G. (1983) Τὸ δημοτικὸ τραγούδι τῆς ξενιτιᾶς, Athens.

SB = F. PREISIGKE *et al.* (eds) (1913–) *Sammelbuch griechischer Urkunden aus Ägypten*, Strassburg/Wiesbaden.

SCHALLER, H. (1975) *Die Balkansprachen: eine Einführung in die Balkanphilologie*, Heidelberg.

SCHARTAU, B. (1974, 1976) 'Nathanaelis Berti monachi sermones quattordecim', *Cahiers de l'Institut du Moyen Age Grec et Latin (Copenhagen)* 12, 11–85, and 17, 70–5.

SCHERE, A. (1934) *Zur Laut- und Formenlehre der milesischen Inschriften*, Munich.

SCHMID, W. (1887–97) *Der Atticismus in seinen Hauptvertretern: von Dionysios von Halikarnassos bis auf den zweiten Philostratos* (5 vols), Stuttgart.

SCHMITT, J. (1904) *The Chronicle of the Morea*, London (repr. Groningen (1967)).

SCHWEIZER, E. (1898) *Grammatik der pergamesischen Inschriften*, Berlin.

SCHWYZER, E. (ed.) (1923) *Dialectorum graecarum exempla epigraphica potiora*, Leipzig.

SCOTT, R. (1990) 'Byzantine chronicle writing II: the Byzantine chronicle after Malalas' in E. Jeffreys, B. Croke and R. Scott (eds) (1990) *Studies in John Malalas*, Sydney, 38–54.

SEG = *Supplementum Epigraphicum Graecum*.

ŠEVČENKO, I. (1981) 'Levels of style in Byzantine prose', *Jahrbuch der Österreichischen Byzantistik* 31/1, 289–312.

SEWTER, E. R. A. (1966) *Fourteen Byzantine rulers: the* Chronographia *of Michael Psellus*, Harmondsworth.

SEWTER, E. R. A. (1969) *The Alexiad of Anna Comnena*, Harmondsworth.

SIAPKARÁS-PITSILLÍDIS, T. (1952) *Le Pétrarquisme en Chypre: poèmes d'amour en dialecte chypriote d'après un manuscrit du XVIe siècle*, Paris. (Greek tr. (1976), *Ο Πετραρχισμός στην Κύπρο: ρίμες αγάπης από χειρόγραφο του 16ου αιώνα με μεταφορά στην κοινή μας γλώσσα*, Athens).

SIG = W. DITTENBERGER (ed.) (1915–24) *Sylloge Inscriptionum Graecarum*, Leipzig.

SMITH, O. (1987) 'Versions and manucripts of the *Achilleid*' in E. Eideneier (ed.) (1987) *Neograeca medii aevi: Text und Ausgabe. Akten zum Symposion Köln 1986*, Cologne, 315–25.

SOLTA, G. R. (1980) *Einführung in die Balkanlinguistik mit besonderen Rücksichtung des Substrats und des Balkanlateinischen*, Darmstadt.

SOMAVERA, ALESSIO DE (1709) *Tesoro della lingua greca volgare ed italiana*, Paris.

SPADARO, G. (1966) *Contributi sulle fonti del romanzo greco-medievale* Florio e Platziaflora, *Κείμενα και Μελέται Νεοελληνικής Φιλολογίας* 26, Athens.

SPADARO, G. (1975) 'Problemi relativi ai romanzi greci dell'età dei Paleologi I: rapporti tra *Ιμπέριος και Μαργαρώνα* e *Φλώριος και Πλατζιαφλώρη*', in *Ελληνικά* 28, 302–27.

SPADARO, G. (1976a) 'Problemi relativi ai romanzi greci dell'età dei Paleologi II: rapporti tra la *Διήγησις του Αχιλλέως* e l' *Ιμπέριος και Μαργαρώνα*', in *Ελληνικά* 29, 287–310.

SPADARO, G. (1976b) '*Imberio e Margarona e Florio e Plaziaflore*', in *Miscellanea Neograeca: atti del I convegno nazionale di studi neogreci (Palermo 1976)*, Palermo, 181–6.

SPADARO, G. (1977) 'Sul *Teseide* neogreco', *Folia Neohellenica* 2, 157–60.

SPADARO, G. (1978a) 'Problemi relativi ai romanzi greci dell'età dei Paleologi III: *Achilleide*, Georgillàs, *Callimaco, Beltandro, Libistro, Florio, Imperio*, e *Διήγησις γεναμένη εν Τροία*', in *Ελληνικά* 30, 223–79.

SPADARO, G. (1978b) 'L'inedito *Polemos tis Troados* e l'*Achilleide*', *Byzantinische Zeitschrift* 71, 1–9.

SPADARO, G. (1981) 'L'*Achilleide* e la *Ιστορική Εξήγησις περί Βελισαρίου* di Gheorghillàs', in *Δίπτυχα Εταιρείας Βυζαντινών και Μεταβυζαντινών Μελετών* 2, 23–41.

SPADARO, G. (1982–3) 'Il *Προς Διαμονικόν* pseudoisocrateo e Spaneas', in *Δίπτυχα Εταιρείας Βυζαντινών και Μεταβυζαντινών Μελετών* 3, 143–59.

SPADARO, G. (1987) 'Edizioni critiche di testi greci medievali in lingua demotica: difficoltà e prospettive' in H. Eideneier (ed.) (1987) *Neograeca medii aevi: Text und Ausgabe. Akten zum Symposion Köln 1986*, Cologne, 327–56.

SPIRIDINOV, D. (1913) 'Methodius: vita Theophanis Confessoris', *Ekklesiastikos Pharos* 12, 88–96, 113–163.

STEIN, T. (1915) 'Zur Formenlehre der Prienischen Inschriften', *Glotta* 6, 97–145.

STERYÉLIS, A. (1967) '*Το δημοτικό τραγούδι εις το ιπποτικόν μυθιστόρημα Φλώριος και Πλατζια Φλώρα*', in *Παρνασσός* 9, 413–23.

SYMEONÍDIS, KH. P. (1987) '*Μια τελευταία θεώρηση των επιθημάτων -ιτσιν, -ίτσα, -ιτσος, -ούτσικος κλπ. Δεύτερη συμβολή: -ίτσα*', in *Μελέτες για την Ελληνική Γλώσσα* 8, 251–74.

SYMPÓSIO (1977) = *Α' Συμπόσιο γλωσσολογίας του βορειοελλαδικού χώρου* 1976 (*Ήπειρος, Μακεδονία, Θράκη*), Thessaloniki.

TAFEL, T. L. F. (1832) *Eustathii metropolitae Thessalonicensis opusculae*, Tübingen.

TEODORSSON, S.-T. (1974) *The phonemic system of the Attic dialect 400–340 BC*, Göteborg.

TEODORSSON, S.-T. (1977) *The phonology of Ptolemaic Koine*, Göteborg.

TEODORSSON, S.-T. (1978) *The phonology of Attic in the Hellenistic period*, Göteborg.

THACKERAY, H. ST J. (1909) *A grammar of the Old Testament in Greek according to the Septuagint*, Cambridge.

THIEME, G. (1906) *Die Inschriften von Magnesia am Mäander und das N.T.*, Göttingen.

THOMPSON, R. (1995) 'Dialect diversity within Mycenaean?', unpubl. ms, University of Cambridge.

THREATTE, L. (1980) *The grammar of Attic inscriptions*, Berlin.

THUMB, A. (1893, 1897) 'Der Dialekt von Amorgos', *Indogermanische Forschungen* 2, 64–125, and 7, 1–37.

THUMB, A. (1901) *Die griechische Sprache im Zeitalter des Hellenismus: Beiträge zur Geschichte und Beurteilung der Κοινή*, Strassburg.

THUMB, A. (1906) 'Prinzipienfrage der *Κοινή*–forschung', in *Neue Jahrbücher für das klassische Altertum* 17, 246–63.

THUMB, A. (1912) *Handbook of the modern Greek vernacular* (tr. of the 2nd German edn, Strassburg (1910)), Edinburgh (repr. Chicago (1964)).

TILL, W. C. (1928) *Achmimisch-koptische Grammatik*, Leipzig.

TILL, W. C. (1961)² *Koptische Grammatik (saïdischer Dialekt)*, Leipzig.

TOMBAÏDIS, D. E. (1977) 'L'infinitif dans le dialecte grec du Pont Euxin', *Balkan Studies* 8, 155–74.

TONNET, H. (1993) *Histoire du grec moderne*, Paris (tr. as *Ιστορία της Νεοελληνικής γλώσσας*, Athens (1995)).

TOYNBEE, A. (1973) *Constantine Porphyrogenitus and his world*, Oxford.

TRAPP, E. (1965) 'Der Dativ und der Ersatz seiner Funktion in der byzantinischen Vulgärdichtung bis zur Mitte des 15, Jahrhundert', *Jahrbuch der Österreichischen Byzantinistik* 14, 21–34.

TRAPP, E. (1971) 'Pontische Elemente im Wortschatz des Digenes-Epos', *Revue des Etudes Sud-Est Européennes* 9, 601–5.

TRIANDAFYLLÍDIS, M. (1938) *Νεοελληνική γραμματική: πρώτος τόμος – ιστορική εισαγωγή*, Athens.

TRIANDAFYLLÍDIS, M. (ed.) (1941) *Νεοελληνική γραμματική*, Athens.

TRYPÁNIS, C. A. (1960) 'Early medieval Greek *ίνα*', *Glotta* 38, 312–3.

TRYPÁNIS, C. A. (1981) *Greek poetry from Homer to Seféris*, London.

TSOPANÁKIS, A. G. (1963) 'Βυζαντιακά διαλεκτικά στοιχεία στην Κωνσταντινούπολη', in *Επιστημονική Επετηρίς του Αριστοτελείου Πανεπιστημίου Θεσσαλονίκης* 8 (1960– 3), 3–15.

TURTLEDOVE, H. (1982) *The* Chronicle *of Theophanes: an English translation of* AM 6095–6305 (AD 602–813), Philadelphia.

TZÁRTZANOS, A. (1946, 1963) Νεοελληνική σύνταξις (της κοινής δημοτικής) (2 vols), Athens.

TZIÓVAS, D. (1985) 'The organic discourse of nationalistic demoticism: a tropological approach', in M. Alexíou and V. Lambrópoulos (eds) (1985) *The text and its margins: poststructuralist approaches to 20th-century Greek literature*, New York, 253–77.

UPZ = U. WILCKEN (ed.) (1927) *Urkunden der Ptolemäerzeit (Ältere Funde), Band I: Papyri aus Unterägypten*, Berlin and Leipzig; (1935–57) *Urkunden der Ptolemäerzeit (Ältere Funde), Band II: Papyri aus Oberägypten*, Berlin.

VALAORÍTIS, A. (1907) Βίος και έργα Γ′, Athens.

VASILIKÓS, K. (1908) Κανέλλου Σπανού: Γραμματική της κοινής των Ελλήνων γλώσσης/Παχωμίου Ρουσάνου: Κατά χυδαϊζόντων και αιρετικών και άλλα του αυτού, Trieste.

VENTRIS, M. and J. CHADWICK (1973)² *Documents in Mycenaean Greek*, Cambridge.

VERGOTE, J. (1973) *Grammaire copte*, Louvain.

VISCIDI, F. (1944) *I prestiti latini nel greco antico e bizantino*, Padua.

VLÁKHOS, A. (1967) Νεοελληνικά, in Εποχές 46, 126–8.

VOGT, A. (1935–40) *Constantin VII Porphyrogénète: le livre des cérémonies*, Paris.

VOTTERO, G. (1996) 'Koinès et koinas en Béotie à l'époque dialectale (VIIe-IIe s. av. JC)', in C. Brixhe (ed.) (1996) *La koiné grecque antique II: la concurrence*, Nancy and Paris.

WACKERNAGEL, J. (1892) 'Über ein Gesetz der indogermanischen Wortstellung', *Indogermanische Forschungen* 1, 333 ff.

WASSILIEWSKY, B. and V. JERNSTEDT (eds) (1896 (repr. 1965)) *Cecaumeni* Strategicon *et incerti scriptoris de officiis regis libellus*, St Petersburg.

WATKINS, C. (1964) 'Preliminaries to the reconstructon of Indo-European sentence structure', *Proceedings of the 9th International Congress of Linguists (1962)*, 1035–42.

WEIRHOLT, K. (1963) *Studien in Sprachgebrauch des Malalas* (Symbolae Osloenses, suppl. 18), Oslo.

WHITING, P. (ed.) *Byzantium: an introduction*, Oxford.

WILL, C. (ed.) (1861) *Acta et scripta*, Leipzig and Marburg.

WILSON, N. G. (1971) *An anthology of Byzantine prose* (Kleine Texte für Vorlesungen und Übungen 189), Berlin and New York.

WILSON, N. G. (1983) *Scholars of Byzantium*, London.

WOODARD, R. D. (1986) 'Dialect differences at Knossos', *Kadmos* 25, 49–74.

WOOLF, G. (1994) 'Becoming Roman, staying Greek: culture, identity and the civilizing process', *Proceedings of the Cambridge Philological Society* 40, 116–43.

WORRELL, W. H. (1934) *Coptic sounds*, Ann Arbor, Michigan.

WYATT JR., W. F. (1970) 'The prehistory of the Greek dialects', *Transactions and Proceedings of the American Philological Association* 101, 557–632.

YEORGAKÁS (GEORGAKÁS), D. S. (1982) *A Graeco-Slavic controversial problem reexamined: the -ιτσ- suffixes in Byzantine medieval and modern Greek, their origin and ethnological implications*, Athens.

ZILLIACUS, H. (1935) *Zum Kampf der Weltsprachen im spätrömischen Reich*, Helsinki.

ZÓRAS, G. T. (1956) Βυζαντινή ποίησις, Athens.

Index

Ancient Greek personal names are given in their familiar (Anglo-)Latin forms, Byzantine names as transliterations of their Greek spellings, modern Greek names in a (largely) phonetic spelling. No system is entirely adequate, and none will ever satisfy all bodies of opinion; any attempt at justification is therefore otiose.

DATE DUE